A SOURCEBOOK IN ASIAN PHILOSOPHY

SOURCEBOOKS IN PHILOSOPHY

Paul Edwards, General Editor

A SOURCEBOOK IN ASIAN PHILOSOPHY

JOHN M. AND PATRICIA KOLLER

Prentice Hall
PRENTICE HALL
Upper Saddle River, New Jersey 07458

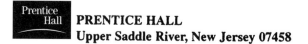

Library of Congress Cataloging-in-Publication Data
Koller, John M.
A sourcebook in Asian philosophy / John M. Koller, Patricia Joyce Koller.
p. cm. - (Sourcebooks in philosophy)
Includes index.
ISBN 0-02-365811-8
1. Philosophy, Oriental. I. Koller, Patricia Joyce. II. Title. III. Series.
B121.K58 1991
181--dc20 90-35953
CIP

Editor: Helen McInnis
Production Supervisor: George Carr
Production Manager: Richard C. Fischer
Cover Designer: Carol Russo Design Inc.

This book was set in Cheltenham light by Digitype, Inc.

Prentice Hall

Upper Saddle River, New Jersey 07458

Printed in the United States of America
10 9

ISBN 0-02-365811-8

Prentice-Hall International (UK) Limited, *London*
Prentice-Hall of Australia Pty. Limited, *Sydney*
Prentice-Hall Canada Inc., *Toronto*
Prentice-Hall Hispanoamericana, S.A., *Mexico*
Prentice-Hall of India Private Limited, *New Delhi*
Prentice-Hall of Japan, Inc., *Tokyo*
Prentice-Hall of Southeast Asia Pte. Ltd., *Singapore*
Editora Prentice-Hall do Brasil, Ltda., *Rio de Janeiro*

To Our Parents

PREFACE

Teachers and students have long felt a need for a convenient, one-volume collection of English translations of the basic texts that have shaped the major Asian philosophical traditions. *A Sourcebook in Asian Philosophy* is a response to this need. Our principal aim has been to include the texts that the Asian philosophical traditions themselves have regarded as fundamental, for it is these texts that give us the greatest insight into Asian philosophies. Which texts to include was often a difficult choice, since space allowed us to include only a small fraction of the total of each tradition's foundational books. Twenty-five years of experience in teaching introductory courses in Asian philosophy and the suggestions of friends and colleagues helped us choose texts that we think are both foundational within the various Asian traditions and accessible to readers whose ideas and modes of thinking have been shaped by different intellectual traditions.

We are greatly indebted to the many scholars whose translations and interpretive studies we have used in compiling this *Sourcebook*. Sources of translations and especially helpful interpretive studies have been indicated at the end of the introduction to each chapter. In some cases minor modifications have been made to the translations, including correcting errors and omitting unnecessary scholarly footnotes and brackets. The introductions have been kept as brief as possible so as not to intrude on the texts themselves. Readers looking for more help in understanding the Asian philosophical traditions these texts helped shape might want to turn to John M. Koller, *Oriental Philosophies*, 2nd edition (New York: Charles Scribner's Sons, 1985) or similar works, including those listed in the introductions.

Finally, we would like to express our appreciation to all the people who have supported our efforts in putting together this anthology. In particular, we would like to thank Professors Roger Ames, Russell Blackwood, Richard Lambert, Ashok Malhotra, Joel Marks, Rama Rao Pappu, and Wei-ming Tu for their helpful recommendations.

J.M. & P.K.
Troy, N.Y.

PRONUNCIATION GUIDE

The following guidelines will help the reader correctly pronounce the Sanskrit, Pāli, Chinese, and Japanese terms encountered in this book.

I
Sanskrit and Pāli terms

Since Pāli consonants and vowels are pronounced like Sanskrit, the reader may achieve correct pronunciation of both Pāli and Sanskrit terms by observing the following guidelines.

Because Sanskrit has more letters than the Roman alphabet, it is necessary to combine diacritical marks with Roman letters to represent the sounds contained in Sanskrit. The following examples show how to pronounce the Sanskrit vowels and consonants that differ from usual English equivalents.

a as *u* in b*u*t
ā as *a* in f*a*ther
i as *i* in t*i*n
ī as *i* in mach*i*ne
u as *u* in f*u*ll
ū as *u* in r*u*le
ṛ as *ri* in *ri*ver
e as *ay* in s*ay*
ai as *ai* in *ai*sle
o as *o* in g*o*
au as *ow* in c*ow*
ṁ nasalizes and lengthens the preceding vowel, like the *o* in French *bon*
ḥ, which sometimes replaces *s* or *r* at the end of a word, has the effect of lengthening the preceding vowel.

Most consonants can be pronounced as in English; Exceptions are:

c as *ch* in *ch*urch
g as *g* in *go*
ṣ and ś as *sh* in *sh*ape

Aspirated consonants—*th, ph, bh, kh, gh, ch, jh, dh*—are pronounced like the *th* in an*th*ill, the *ph* in shep*h*erd, the *bh* in a*bh*or, etc. The differences between *ṭ*, ṭh, *ḍ*, ḍh, *ṇ*, and *t, th, d, dh, n* may be ignored as the English *t, d,* and *n* are quite close to both sets of letters.

Theoretically each syllable, which consists of one or more consonants and the accompanying vowel, receives equal emphasis. In practice, however, the main accent is usually placed on the next-to-last syllable if it contains a long vowel (*ā, ī, ū*), otherwise on the third-last syllable.

II
Chinese Terms

There are two systems for romanizing Chinese, Wade-Giles and Pinyin. Pinyin, the more recent system, standard in the People's Republic, follows English phonetic rules of pronunciation. The older, Wade-Giles, system that we have used because most of the available English translations of Chinese texts have used it, is not always phonetic. The following list gives the Pinyin equivalents for the nonphonetic words, enabling the reader to pronounce them according to ordinary English phonetic rules. Exceptions are *c* = *ts*; *q* = *ch*; *x* = *sh*. The first word in each column is the Wade-Giles romanization as found in the text; the second, in italics, is the Pinyin romanization of the same word.

Cha	*zha*
chai	*zhai*
chan	*zhan*
chang	*zhang*
chao	*zhao*
che	*zhe*
chei	*zhei*
chen	*zhen*
cheng	*zheng*
chi	*ji*
ch'i	*qi*
chia	*jia*
ch'ia	*qia*
chiang	*jiang*
ch'iang	*qiang*
chiao	*jiao*
ch'iao	*qiao*
chieh	*jie*
ch'ieh	*qie*
chien	*jian*
ch'ien	*qian*
chih	*zhi*
ch'ih	*chi*
chin	*jin*
ch'in	*qin*
ching	*jing*
ch'ing	*qing*
chiu	*jiu*
ch'iu	*qiu*
chiung	*jiong*
ch'iung	*quiong*
cho	*zhuo*
ch'o	*chuo*
chou	*zhou*

chu	*zhu*
chua	*zhua*
chuai	*zhuai*
chuan	*zhuan*
chuang	*zhuan*
chui	*zhui*
chun	*zhun*
chung	*zhong*
ch'ung	*chong*
chü	*ju*
ch'ü	*qu*
chüan	*juan*
ch'üan	*quan*
chüeh	*jue*
ch'üeh	*que*
chün	*jun*
ch'ün	*qun*
erh	*er*
ho	*he*
hsi	*xi*
hsia	*xia*
hsiang	*xiang*
hsiao	*xiao*
hsieh	*xie*
hsien	*xian*
hsin	*xin*
hsing	*xing*
hsiu	*xiu*
hsiung	*xiong*
hsü	*xu*
hsüan	*xuan*
hsüeh	*xue*
hsün	*xun*
i	*yi*
jan	*ran*
jang	*rang*
jao	*rao*
je	*re*
jen	*ren*
jeng	*reng*
jih	*ri*
jo	*ruo*
jou	*rou*
ju	*ru*
juan	*ruan*
jui	*rui*
jun	*run*
jung	*rong*
ka	*ga*
kai	*gai*
kan	*gan*
kang	*gang*
kao	*gao*
ke,ko	*ge*
kei	*gei*
ken	*gen*
keng	*geng*
ko,ke	*ge*
k'o	*ke*
kou	*gou*
ku	*gu*
kua	*gua*
kuai	*guai*
kuan	*guan*
kuang	*guang*
kuei	*gui*
k'uei	*kui*
kun	*gun*
kung	*gong*
k'ung	*kong*
kuo	*guo*
lieh	*lie*
lien	*lian*
lo	*luo*
lün	*lun*
lung	*long*
lüan	*luan*
lüeh	*lue*
mieh	*mie*
mien	*mian*
nieh	*nie*
nien	*nian*
nung	*nong*
nü	*nu*
nüeh	*nue*

o	*e*
pa	*ba*
pai	*bai*
pan	*ban*
pang	*bang*
pao	*bao*
pei	*bei*
pen	*ben*
peng	*beng*
pi	*bi*
piao	*biao*
pieh	*bie*
p'ieh	*pie*
pien	*bian*
p'ien	*pian*
pin	*bin*
ping	*bing*
po	*bo*
pou	*bou*
pu	*bu*
shih	*shi*
so	*suo*
ssŭ, szŭ	*si*
sung	*song*
szŭ, ssŭ	*si*
ta	*da*
tai	*dai*
tan	*dan*
tang	*dang*
tao	*dao*
te	*de*
tei	*dei*
teng	*deng*
ti	*di*
tu	*du*
tuan	*duan*
tui	*dui*
tun	*dun*
tung	*dong*
t'ung	*tong*
tzŭ	*zi*
tsŭ	*ci*
tiao	*diao*
tieh	*die*
t'ieh	*tie*
tien	*dian*
t'ien	*tian*
ting	*ding*
tiu	*diu*
to	*duo*
t'o	*tuo*
tou	*dou*
tsa	*za*
ts'a	*ca*
tsai	*zai*
ts'ai	*cai*
tsan	*zan*
ts'an	*can*
tsang	*zang*
ts'ang	*cang*
tsao	*zao*
ts'ao	*cao*
tse	*ze*
ts'e	*ce*
tsei	*zei*
tsen	*zen*
ts'en	*cen*
tseng	*zeng*
ts'eng	*ceng*
tso	*zuo*
ts'o	*cuo*
tsou	*zou*
ts'ou	*cou*
tsu	*zu*
ts'u	*cu*
tsuan	*zuan*
ts'uan	*cuan*
tsui	*zui*
ts'ui	*cui*
tsun	*zun*
ts'un	*cun*
tsung	*zong*
ts'ung	*cong*
yeh	*ye*
yen	*yan*
yu	*you*
yung	*yong*
yü	*yu*
yüan	*yuan*
yüeh	*yue*
yün	*yun*

III
Japanese Terms

Most Japanese terms follow English phonetic rules, but *ō* (pronounced like English *o* in *o*h), is held twice as long as *o*.

CONTENTS

PREFACE vii
PRONUNCIATION GUIDE ix

PART I

HINDU TEXTS

CHAPTER 1 VEDAS AND UPANIṢADS 5
I. The *Rig Veda* 6
II. The *Bṛhadāraṇyaka Upaniṣad* 12
III. The *Chāndogya Upaniṣad* 25
IV. The *Taittirīya Upaniṣad* 30
CHAPTER 2 THE *BHAGAVAD GĪTĀ* 33
CHAPTER 3 SĀṀKHYA-YOGA 51
I. The *Sāṁkhya Kārikā* 52
II. Patañjali: *Yoga Sūtras* 59
CHAPTER 4 NYĀYA-VAIŚEṢIKA: ANAMBHAṬṬA'S *TARKASAṀGRAHA* 69
CHAPTER 5 MĪMĀṀSA: THE MĪMĀṀSĀ SŪTRA 81
CHAPTER 6 VEDĀNTA 92
I. Śaṅkara: *A Thousand Teachings* 93
II. Rāmānuja: A *Summary of Vedic Teachings* 115
CHAPTER 7 JAINISM 129
I. The Jaina World View 130
II. The Theory of Perspectives (Syadavada) 135
CHAPTER 8 MODERN INDIAN THOUGHT 143
I. Mohammed Iqbal: Is Religion Possible? 145
II. Gandhi: Selections 156

III. Aurobindo Ghose: The Life Divine 165
IV. Radhakrishnan: Fragments of a Confession 177

PART II

BUDDHIST TEXTS

CHAPTER 9 BASIC TEACHINGS ACCORDING TO THE EARLY TEXTS 193
I. Setting in Motion the Wheel of Truth 195
II. The Fire Sermon 196
III. Universal Love 198
IV. Blessings 199
V. Getting Rid of All Cares and Troubles 200
VI. The Foundations of Mindfulness 205
VII. The Words of Truth (The *Dhammapada*) 212
VIII. The Last Words of the Buddha 218
CHAPTER 10 PHILOSOPHICAL ISSUES IN EARLY BUDDHISM 220
I. No-Self and Rebirth 222
II. The Difference Between Groups and Attachment-Groups 231
III. Dependent Origination: The Middle Way 233
IV. Reason and Wisdom 239
CHAPTER 11 RISE OF THE MAHĀYĀNA 247
I. The Bodhisattva 248
II. The *Heart Sūtra* 253
III. From the *Diamond Sūtra* 258
CHAPTER 12 MĀDHYAMAKA 262
I. Nāgārjuna: *Treatise on the Fundamentals of the Middle Way* 264
II. Candrakīrti: *Guide to the Middle Way* 272
III. Tsong Khapa: The Chief Reason for Negation of Ultimate Status 297
CHAPTER 13 YOGĀCĀRA 306
I. Asaṅga: *On Knowing Reality* 308
II. Vasubandhu: *Discussion of the Five Aggregates* 323
III. Vasubandhu: *Twenty Verses and Commentary* 330
IV. Vasubandhu: *Thirty Verses* 341
CHAPTER 14 ZEN 345
I. Dōgen: Essays from the *Shōbōgenzō* 346
II. Shibayama: Commentary on the *Mumonkan* 361
CHAPTER 15 MODERN BUDDHIST THOUGHT 372
I. Jayatilleke: The Ethical Ideal of the Ultimate Good 373

II. The Dalai Lama: *The Key to the Middle Way* 379
III. Nishitani: The Self as *Śūnyatā* 393

PART III

CHINESE TEXTS

CHAPTER 16 THE VISION OF CONFUCIUS: 407
I. Confucius: The *Analects* (*Lun-yü*) 409
II. The *Greater Learning* (*Ta-hsüeh*) 422
III. The *Doctrine of the Mean* (*Chung-yung*) 433
CHAPTER 17 THE TAOIST VISION 444
I. Lao Tzu: *Tao Te Ching* 445
II. Chuang Tzŭ: Chapter 2 450
CHAPTER 18 UTILITARIAN AND LEGALIST CHALLENGES 461
I. Mo Tzu: "Universal Love" 462
II. Han Fei Tzu: "Way of the Ruler" and "Wielding Power" 468
CHAPTER 19 CONFUCIAN DEVELOPMENTS 476
I. Mencius 477
II. Hsün-tzu: "A Discussion of Heaven" 487
III. Hsün-tzu: "Man's Nature is Evil" 492
CHAPTER 20 CHINESE BUDDHISM 501
I. Fa-tsang: *Hua-yen Treatise* 503
II. Hui-neng: *The Platform Sūtra* 508
III. I-hsüan: Recorded Conversations 517
CHAPTER 21 NEO-CONFUCIAN FOUNDATIONS 521
I. Chou Tun-i: An Explanation of the Diagram of the Great Ultimate 522
II. Shao Yung: The Great Ultimate 524
III. Chang Tsai: The Western Inscription 525
IV. Ch'eng Hao: Selected Writings 527
V. Ch'eng I: Selected Writings 531
CHAPTER 22 THE TWO WINGS OF NEO-CONFUCIANISM 536
I. Chu Hsi: Selected Writings 538
II. Wang Yang-ming: Inquiry on the *Great Learning* 548
CHAPTER 23 RECENT CHINESE THOUGHT 555
I. Mao Tse-tung: On Practice 556
II. Fung Yu-lan: Selected Writings 562
GLOSSARY 569
INDEX 581

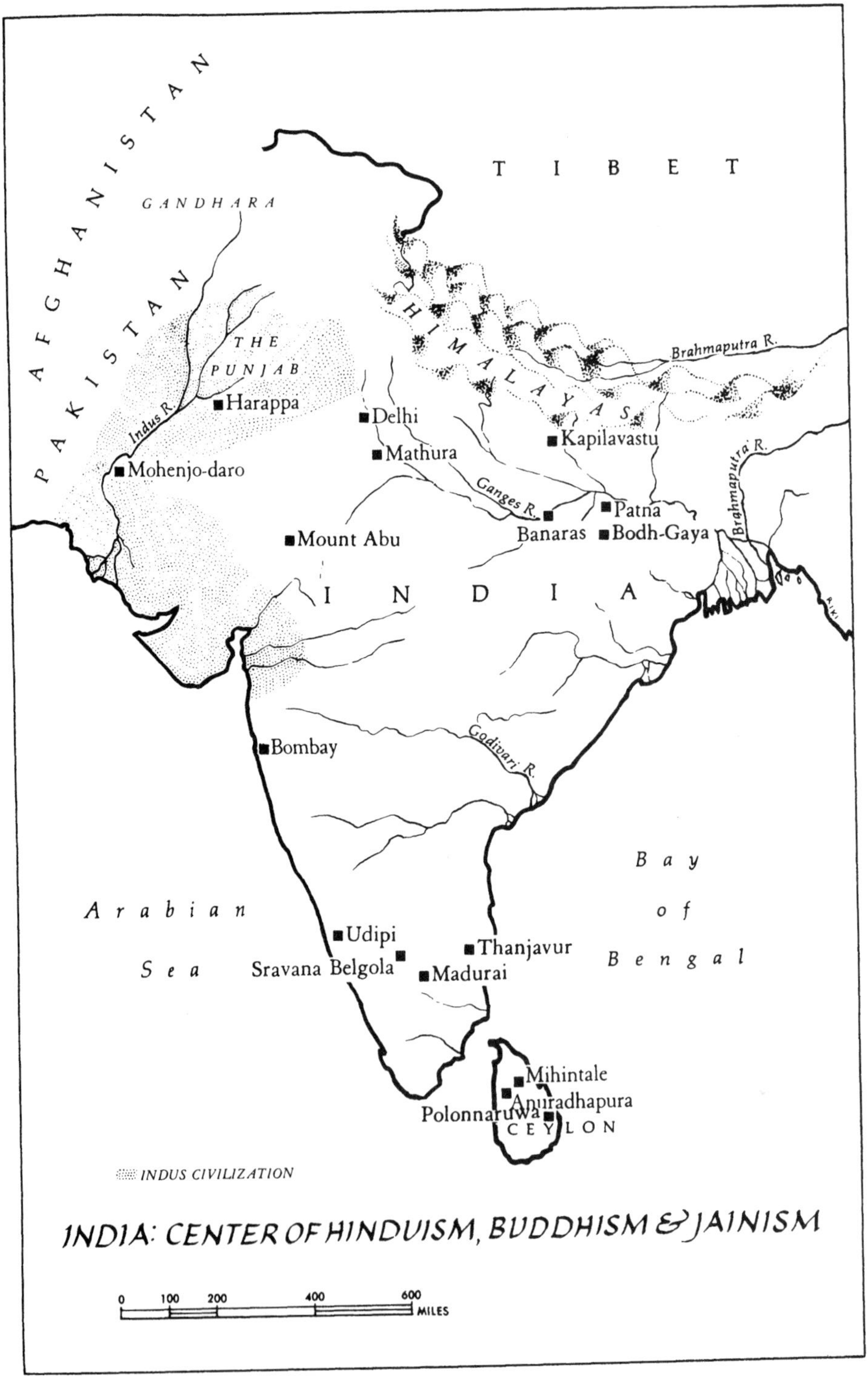
TIBET
AFGHANISTAN
PAKISTAN
GANDHARA
THE PUNJAB
HIMALAYAS
Brahmaputra R.
Indus R.
Harappa
Delhi
Mathura
Kapilavastu
Mohenjo-daro
Ganges R.
Patna
Banaras
Bodh-Gaya
Mount Abu
INDIA
Bombay
Godivari R.
Arabian Sea
Bay of Bengal
Udipi
Sravana Belgola
Thanjavur
Madurai
Mihintale
Anuradhapura
Polonnaruwa
CEYLON
INDUS CIVILIZATION
INDIA: CENTER OF HINDUISM, BUDDHISM & JAINISM
0
100
200
400
600
MILES

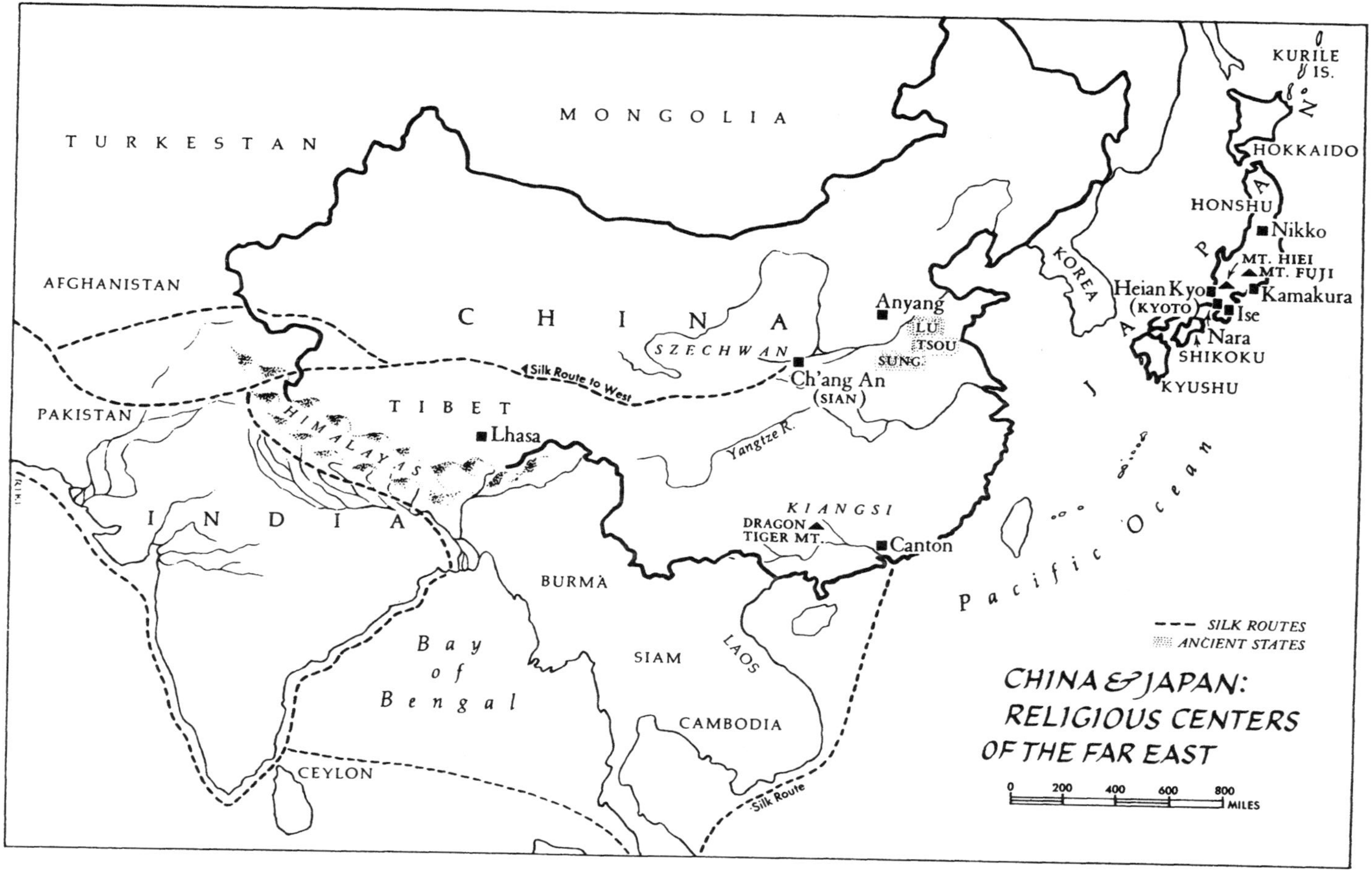
CHINA & JAPAN: RELIGIOUS CENTERS OF THE FAR EAST
SILK ROUTES
ANCIENT STATES
0 200 400 600 800 MILES
TURKESTAN
MONGOLIA
AFGHANISTAN
PAKISTAN
CHINA
SZECHWAN
TIBET
HIMALAYAS
Lhasa
INDIA
Silk Route to West
Ch'ang An
(SIAN)
Anyang
LU
TSOU
SUNG
Yangtze R.
KIANGSI
DRAGON TIGER MT.
Canton
KOREA
JAPAN
HOKKAIDO
KURILE IS.
HONSHU
Nikko
MT. HIEI
MT. FUJI
Heian Kyo
(KYOTO)
Kamakura
Ise
Nara
SHIKOKU
KYUSHU
Pacific Ocean
BURMA
SIAM
LAOS
CAMBODIA
Bay of Bengal
CEYLON
Silk Route

PART I

HINDU TEXTS

The major Hindu philosophical traditions are the six classical systems of Sāṁkhya, Yoga, Nyāya, Vaiśeṣika, Mīmāṁsā, and Vedānta. The foundations of these traditions—established two to three thousand years ago—have supported a rich and dynamic philosophical continuum right up to the present time. Despite their many differences, these systems all accept India's most ancient texts, the Vedas and Upaniṣads, as the ultimate source and authority of wisdom. Of course, these texts must be interpreted and understood in terms of human experience and reason. Since experience and reason are subject to differing interpretations, it is natural that different interpretations of the Vedas and Upaniṣads should arise. The differences among the six Hindu systems are partly the result of these systematically different interpretations. But they are also due to concern with different philosophical issues, resulting in emphasis on different aspects and portions of the Vedas and Upaniṣads. Thus, Vedānta is interested primarily in knowledge, whereas Mīmāṁsā is interested primarily in action. Nyāya is concerned with criteria of correct reasoning and the means of valid knowledge, whereas Vaiséṣika seeks to establish the fundamental categories of existence. Sāṁkhya focuses on the differentiation of self (puruṣa) from the world (prakṛti), on the discrimination of the knower from the known, while Yoga emphasizes understanding the means whereby the pure self can be isolated and realized.

In many respects these differences are complementary. Although specializing in its own problems and perspectives, each tradition accepts the contributions made by the traditions specializing in other areas. Consequently, the different systems have many views in common and agree on much of their reasoning. For example, the principles of valid reasoning worked out by Nyāya, the criteria of textual interpretation established by Mīmāṁsā, and the understanding of yogic concentration achieved by Yoga are all accepted by the other systems. Similarly, the evolutionary view of existence elaborated by Sāṁkhya is also accepted by the other systems although its radical dualism is rejected by most of them. In other respects, however, these are competing traditions, arguing vigorously with each other, each trying to justify its own views and methods.

Although each tradition takes its stand on a foundational text, all are dynamic; each generation of philosophers comes to interpret and understand the previous tradition in its own way, in debate and argument with adherents of the other systems, thus continuously renewing and reshaping its own tradition. The commentaries and subcommentaries that creative philosophers produced over the centuries are, in effect, reinterpretations of the foundational texts, giving rise to new understandings and emphases, sometimes resulting in new schools and systems.

India's philosophical heritage extends well beyond these six Hindu traditions, however, for the rich traditions of Buddhism, Jainism, and Cārvāka (Lokāyata), none of which accepts the authority of the Veda, have engaged in lively debate with each other and with the Hindu traditions since the fifth century B.C., with a great deal of mutual influence. For example, the Buddhist Vaibhāṣika and Sautrāntika philosophers owe much to the Nyāya and Vaiśeṣika traditions, whereas Nyāya logic owes much to the creative work of the Buddhist logician Dignāga. The mutual influences of Vedānta and Mādhyamaka Buddhism greatly enriched both these traditions, and the influences of the Jaina theory of *anekāntavāda* (epistemological perspectivism) on the other traditions have frequently been noted. The history of Indian philosophy reveals a rich and dynamic process of philosophical dialogue among these various traditions, dialogue that prizes profound insight as well as careful analysis and reasoning.

In part I we have included texts that have been especially important in shaping these various traditions over their long histories. Typically, these are the early, foundational texts along with some of the later commentaries, although in the case of Nyāya and Vaiśeṣika we have used a popular handbook that presents the basic teachings in a more accessible manner. Buddhism is covered in part II, and for want of space and suitable source material the materialistic Cārvāka (Lokāyata) philosophy has been excluded.

For an introduction to the whole panorama of Indian philosophical and religious thought, John M. Koller, *The Indian Way* (New York: Macmillan Publishing Company, 1982), is a good place to begin. Karl Potter, *Guide to Indian Philosophy* (Boston: G.K. Hall, 1988), is a very useful annotated guide to original and secondary works on Indian Philosophy. Karl Potter, editor, *Encyclopedia of Indian Philosophies*, vols. 1–4 (Princeton: Princeton University Press, 1967–1989), is a valuable reference. Volume 1, second revised edition, is the most extensive bibliography of Indian philosophy available. Volume 2 is on Nyāya and Vaiśeṣika, volume 3 is on Vedānta up to Śaṅkara, and volume 4 is on Sāṁkhya. Each of these last three volumes provides a lengthy historical introduction to the tradition it covers as well as extended summaries of its most important texts. For additional source material the reader might turn to *A Source Book in Indian Philosophy*, edited by Sarvapalli Radhakrishnan and Charles A. Moore (Princeton: Princeton University Press, 1957), or to *Sources of Indian Tradition,* 2nd edition, edited and revised by Ainslie T. Embree (New York: Columbia University Press, 1988). The latter covers political, social, literary, religious, and philosophical thought, whereas the former includes philosophical texts only.

CHAPTER 1

VEDAS AND UPANIṢADS

The Vedas and Upaniṣads constitute the earliest and most important source of Indian philosophy. The questions they raise and the visions they present have inspired philosophers for three thousand years. All six of the Hindu systems accept the authority of these texts, with both the Mīmāṁsā and Vedānta traditions regarding their wisdom as foundational. The main difference between these two traditions is that the Mīmāmsākas emphasize the Vedic injunctions to action, whereas the Vedāntists emphasize the understanding of reality found in the Upaniṣads.

Tradition regards the Vedas and Upaniṣads as authorless, as the voice of reality itself presenting its wisdom to those prepared to hear it. But it is acknowledged that this wisdom has been handed down in the form of texts that have been shaped by the poets and seers of ancient times. These texts are difficult to date precisely, but the oldest, the Rig Veda, probably achieved its present form around 1200 B.C. The Sāma and Yajur Vedas consist mainly of Rig Vedic verses cast into liturgical song and ritual formulas for use in religious celebrations, whereas the fourth Veda, the Atharva, contains incantations, spells, and recipes for a successful life. They also achieved their present form more than three thousand years ago. The Upaniṣads are traditionally seen as the concluding portion of the Vedas, coming after the Vedic hymns themselves as well as after the ritual-oriented *Brāhmaṇas* and *Āraṇyakas* attached to the Vedas. The earliest Upaniṣads, the Bṛhadāraṇyaka and Chāndogya, probably should be dated after the eighth century B.C., and another ten, including the Taittirīya, Kaṭha, Kena, Muṇḍaka, Māṇḍūkya, Īśa, Praśna, Aitareya, Śvetāśvatra, and Kauṣītakī, probably were in their present form by the end of the sixth century B.C. Their importance is attested to by the fact that all were commented on by later philosophers in the Vedānta tradition.

The majority of the 1,028 hymns of the Rig Veda are focused on the celebrative rituals (*yajñas*) constituting the core of Āryan religious life three thousand years ago; many are hymns of praise offered to the various deities who are invited to participate in the rituals. A few of the hymns, however, are speculative and questioning in tone, suggesting the philosophical reflection of the time. Some of these reflective hymns are included here. They are taken from Wendy Doniger O'Flaherty, *The Rig Veda: An Anthology* (New York: Penguin Books, 1981), which contains a total of 108 hymns with brief but very helpful annotations and notes. Franklin Edgerton (see below) also contains good translations of the more philosophical hymns.

Although the early Upaniṣads are, for the most part, more concerned with explaining ritual than with presenting a coherent vision of reality, they also raise profound questions about the nature of existence and present new visions of reality—questions and visions that have occupied succeeding generations of thinkers up to the present. When the Āryan culture that produced the Rig Veda entered India in about 1500 B.C. it encountered the culture of the ancient Indus civilization. It may well be that the Upaniṣads record Āryan efforts to accommodate Indus views and values within its own Āryan framework. The Rig Vedic vision glorified life in this world; the doctrine of transmigration and the accompanying view of this world and life as fundamentally deficient found in Jainism and other ancient Indian thought is not to be found in the Rig Veda. But in the Upaniṣads we find sages struggling to understand what there is beyond this transient, suffering existence. We find them searching for an ultimate reality of the world, a Brahman that is beyond change, and for an ultimate reality of the self, an Ātman not subject to death. The Upaniṣadic texts we have selected include many of the "Great Sayings" that have inspired the succeeding tradition.

Selections from the *Bṛhadāraṇyaka Upaniṣad* have been taken from Franklin Edgerton, *The Beginnings of Indian Philosophy* (Cambridge, Mass.: Harvard University Press, 1965), and selections from the *Chāndogya* and *Taittirīya Upaniṣads* from J.A.B. VanBuitenen and Eliot Deutsch, *A Source Book of Advaita Vedānta* (Honolulu: University Press of Hawaii, 1971). Edgerton, in addition to having good translations of early Upaniṣads and Rig Vedic texts, has a fine thirty-page introductory essay—the culmination of a long life of careful scholarship—on the roots of Indian philosophy. There are numerous translations of the basic Upaniṣads, including Sarvapalli Radhakrishnan, *The Principal Upaniṣads* (New York: Harper, 1953), which contains an excellent introductory essay, and R. E. Hume, *The Thirteen Principal Upaniṣads* (Oxford: Oxford University Press, 1931).

I
The Rig Veda*

1. CREATION HYMN

1. There was neither non-existence nor existence then; there was neither the realm of space nor the sky which is beyond. What stirred? Where? In whose protection? Was there water, bottomlessly deep?

---

*Reprinted with permission from Wendy Doniger O'Flaherty, *The Rig Veda: An Anthology* (New York: Penguin Books, 1981).

2. There was neither death nor immortality then. There was no distinguishing sign of night nor of day. That one breathed, windless, by its own impulse. Other than that there was nothing beyond.

3. Darkness was hidden by darkness in the beginning; with no distinguishing sign, all this was water. The life force that was covered with emptiness, that one arose through the power of heat.

4. Desire came upon that one in the beginning; that was the first seed of mind. Poets seeking in their hearts with wisdom found the bond of existence in non-existence.

5. Their cord was extended across. Was there below? Was there above? There were seed-placers; there were powers. There was impulse beneath; there was giving-forth above.

6. Who really knows? Who will here proclaim it? Whence was it produced? Whence is this creation? The gods came afterwards, with the creation of this universe. Who then knows whence it has arisen?

7. Whence this creation has arisen — perhaps it formed itself, or perhaps it did not — the one who looks down on it, in the highest heaven, only he knows — or perhaps he does not know. (10.129)

2. THE HYMN OF MAN

1. The Man has a thousand heads, a thousand eyes, a thousand feet. He pervaded the earth on all sides and extended beyond it as far as ten fingers.

2. It is the Man who is all this, whatever has been and whatever is to be. He is the ruler of immortality, when he grows beyond everything through food.

3. Such is his greatness, and the Man is yet more than this. All creatures are a quarter of him; three quarters are what is immortal in heaven.

4. With three quarters the Man rose upwards, and one quarter of him still remains here. From this he spread out in all directions, into that which eats and that which does not eat.

5. From him Virāj was born, and from Virāj came the Man. When he was born, he ranged beyond the earth behind and before.

6. When the gods spread the sacrifice with the Man as the offering, spring was the clarified butter, summer the fuel, autumn the oblation.

7. They anointed the Man, the sacrifice born at the beginning, upon the sacred grass. With him the gods, saints (Sādhyas), and sages sacrificed.

8. From that sacrifice in which everything was offered, the melted fat was collected and he made it into those beasts who live in the air, in the forest, and in villages.

9. From that sacrifice in which everything was offered, the verses and chants were born, the metres were born from it, and from it the formulas were born.

10. Horses were born from it, and those other animals that have two rows of teeth; cows were born from it, and from it goats and sheep were born.

11. When they divided the Man, into how many parts did they apportion him? What do they call his mouth, his two arms and thighs and feet?

12. His mouth became the Brahmin; his arms were made into the Warrior, his thighs the People, and from his feet the Servants were born.

13. The moon was born from his mind; from his eye the sun was born. Indra and Agni came from his mouth, and from his vital breath the Wind was born.

14. From his navel the middle realm of space arose; from his head the sky evolved. From his two feet came the earth, and the quarters of the sky from his ear. Thus they set the worlds in order.

15. There were seven enclosing-sticks for him, and thrice seven fuel-sticks, when the gods, spreading the sacrifice, bound the Man as the sacrificial beast.

16. With the sacrifice the gods sacrificed to the sacrifice. These were the first ritual laws. These very powers reached the dome of the sky where dwell the Sādhyas, the ancient gods. (10.90).

3. THE CREATION OF THE SACRIFICE

1. The sacrifice that is spread out with threads on all sides, drawn tight with a hundred and one divine acts, is woven by these fathers as they come near: "Weave forward, weave backward," they say as they sit by the loom that is stretched tight.

2. The Man stretches the warp and draws the weft; the Man has spread it out upon this dome of the sky. These are the pegs, that are fastened in place; they made the melodies into the shuttles for weaving.

3. What was the original model, and what was the copy, and what was the connection between them? What was the butter, and what the enclosing wood? What was the metre, what was the invocation, and the chant, when all the gods sacrificed the god?

4. The Gāyatrī metre was the yoke-mate of Agni; Savitṛ joined with the Uṣṇi metre, and with the Anuṣṭubh metre was Soma that reverberates with the chants. The Bṛhatī metre resonated in the voice of Bṛhaspati.

5. The Virāj metre was the privilege of Mitra and Varuṇa; the Triṣṭubh metre was part of the day of Indra. The Jagatī entered into all the gods. That was the model for the human sage.

6. That was the model for the human sages, our fathers, when the primeval sacrifice was born. With the eye that is mind, in thought I see those who were the first to offer this sacrifice.

7. The ritual repetitions harmonized with the chants and with the metres; the seven divine sages harmonized with the original models. When the wise men looked back along the path of those who went before, they took up the reins like charioteers. (10.130)

4. THE UNKNOWN GOD, THE GOLDEN EMBRYO

1. In the beginning the Golden Embryo arose. Once he was born, he was the one lord of creation. He held in place the earth and this sky. Who is the god whom we should worship with the oblation?

2. He who gives life, who gives strength, whose command all the gods, his own, obey; his shadow is immortality—and death. Who is the god whom we should worship with the oblation?

3. He who by his greatness became the one king of the world that breathes and blinks, who rules over his two-footed and four-footed creatures—who is the god whom we should worship with the oblation?

4. He who through his power owns these snowy mountains, and the ocean together with the river Rasā, they say; who has the quarters of the sky as his two arms—who is the god whom we should worship with the oblation?

5. He by whom the awesome sky and the earth were made firm, by whom the dome of the sky was propped up, and the sun, who measured out the middle realm of space—who is the god whom we should worship with the oblation?

6. He to whom the two opposed masses looked with trembling in their hearts, supported by his help, on whom the rising sun shines down—who is the god whom we should worship with the oblation?

7. When the high waters came, pregnant with the embryo that is everything, bringing forth fire, he arose from that as the one life's breath of the gods. Who is the god whom we should worship with the oblation?

8. He who in his greatness looked over the waters, which were pregnant with Dakṣa [the male principle of creation], bringing forth the sacrifice, he who was the one god among all the gods—who is the god whom we should worship with the oblation?

9. Let him not harm us, he who fathered the earth and created the sky, whose laws are true, who created the high, shining waters. Who is the god whom we should worship with the oblation?

10. O Prajāpati, lord of progeny, no one but you embraces all these creatures. Grant us the desires for which we offer you oblation. Let us be lords of riches. (10.121)

5. ADITI AND THE BIRTH OF THE GOD

1. Let us now speak with wonder of the births of the gods—so that some one may see them when the hymns are chanted in this later age.

2. The lord of sacred speech, like a smith, fanned them together. In the earliest age of the gods, existence was born from non-existence.

3. In the first age of the gods, existence was born from non-existence. After this the quarters of the sky were born from her who crouched with legs spread.

4. The earth was born from her who crouched with legs spread, and from the earth the quarters of the sky were born. From Aditi, Dakṣa was born, and from Dakṣa Aditi was born.

5. For Aditi was born as your daughter, O Dakṣa, and after her were born the blessed gods, the kinsmen of immortality.

6. When you gods took your places there in the water with your hands joined together, a thick cloud of mist arose from you like dust from dancers.

7. When you gods like magicians caused the worlds to swell, you drew forth the sun that was hidden in the ocean.

8. Eight sons are there of Aditi, who were born of her body. With seven she went forth among the gods, but she threw Mārtāṇḍa, the sun, aside.

9. With seven sons Aditi went forth into the earliest age. But she bore Mārtāṇḍa so that he would in turn beget offspring and then soon die. (10.72)

6. THE ALL-MAKER (VIŚVAKARMAN)

1. The sage, our father, who took his place as priest of the oblation and offered all these words as oblation, seeking riches through prayer, he entered those who were to come later, concealing those who went before.

2. What was the base, what sort of raw matter was there, and precisely how was it done, when the All-Maker, casting his eye on all, created the earth and revealed the sky in its glory?

3. With eyes on all sides and mouths on all sides, with arms on all sides and feet on all sides, the One God created the sky and the earth, fanning them with his arms.

4. What was the wood and what was the tree from which they carved the sky and the earth? You deep thinkers, ask yourselves in your own hearts, what base did he stand on when he set up the worlds?

5. Those forms of yours that are highest, those that are lowest, and those that are in the middle, O All-Maker, help your friends to recognize them in the oblation. You who follow your own laws, sacrifice your body yourself, making it grow great.

6. All-Maker, grown great through the oblation, sacrifice the earth and sky yourself. Let other men go astray all around; let us here have a rich and generous patron.

7. The All-Maker, the lord of sacred speech, swift as thought—we will call to him today to help us in the contest. Let him who is the maker of good things and is gentle to everyone rejoice in all our invocations and help us. (10.81)

7. THE ALL-MAKER (VIŚVAKARMAN)

1. The Father of the Eye,[1] who is wise in his heart, created as butter these two worlds that bent low. As soon as their ends had been made fast in the east, at that moment sky and earth moved far apart.

2. The All-Maker is vast in mind and vast in strength. He is the one who forms, who sets in order, and who is the highest image. Their prayers together with the drink they have offered give them joy there where, they say, the One dwells beyond the seven sages.

3. Our father, who created and set in order and knows all forms, all worlds, who all alone gave names to the gods, he is the one to whom all other creatures come to ask questions.

4. To him the ancient sages together sacrificed riches, like the throngs of singers who together made these things that have been created, when the realm of light was still immersed in the realm without light.

5. That which is beyond the sky and beyond this earth, beyond the gods and the Asuras [demons]—what was that first embryo that the waters received, where all the gods together saw it?

6. He was the one whom the waters received as the first embryo, when all the gods came together. On the navel of the Unborn was set the One on whom all creatures rest.

7. You cannot find him who created these creatures; another has come between you. Those who recite the hymns are glutted with the pleasures of life; they wander about wrapped up in mist and stammering nonsense. (10.82)

8. COSMIC HEAT (TAPAS)

1. Order (*ṛta*) and truth (*satya*) were born from heat as it blazed up. From that was born night; from that heat was born the billowy ocean.

2. From the billowy ocean was born the year, that arranges days and nights, ruling over all that blinks its eyes.

3. The Arranger has set in their proper place the sun and moon, the sky and the earth, the middle realm of space, and finally the sunlight. (10.190)

---

1. Creator of the sun.

II
Bṛhadāraṇyaka Upaniṣad*

SEVENTH CHAPTER OF THIRD BOOK

1. Then Uddālaka son of Aruṇa questioned him.[1] Yājñavalkya, said he, we were dwelling among the Madras, studying the sacrifice in the house of Patañcala son of Kapi. His wife was possessed of a gandharva (spirit). We asked him: Who are you? He said: Kavandra of the Atharvan family.

2. He said unto Patañcala son of Kapi and the students of the sacrifice: Do you know, pray, son of Kapi, that thread on which this world and the world beyond and all creatures are strung together?—Patañcala son of Kapi said: I do not know it, reverend sir.

3. He said unto Patañcala son of Kapi and the students of the sacrifice: Do you know, pray, son of Kapi, that inner controller which controls this world and the world beyond and all creatures within?—Patañcala son of Kapi said: I do not know it, reverend sir.

4. He said unto Patañcala son of Kapi and the students of the sacrifice: Verily, son of Kapi, whosoever knows that thread and that inner controller, he knows Bráhman, he knows the worlds, he knows the gods, he knows the vedas, he knows the sacrifice, he knows creatures, he knows the Self (*ātman*), he knows everything.—thus he spoke unto them. This I know. If you, Yājñavalkya, without knowing that thread and that inner controller, are driving away the brahmans' cows, your head shall fall off!

5. I know, verily, that thread, Gautama, and that inner controller.—Anyone whatsoever might say 'I know, I know.' Say, how you know it!

6. Wind, verily, Gautama, is that thread. By wind, verily, Gautama, as by a thread, this world and the world beyond and all creatures are strung together. Therefore, verily, Gautama, they say of a man that is dead, that his limbs have fallen apart. For by the wind, Gautama, as a thread, they are strung together.—That is just so, Yājñavalkya. Say (what) the inner controller (is).

7. That which rests in the earth, and is distinct from the earth, which the earth knows not, of which the earth is the body (material manifestation or form), which controls the earth within, that is thy Self (*ātman*), the immortal inner controller.

8. That which rests in water, and is distinct from water, which water knows not, of which water is the body, which controls water within, that is thy Self, the immortal inner controller.

9–16. That which rests in fire, and is distinct from fire, which fire knows not, of which fire is the body, which controls fire within, that is thy Self, the

---

*Reprinted with permission from Franklin Edgerton, *The Beginnings of Indian Philosophy* (Cambridge, Mass.: Harvard University Press, 1965).

1. This questioning occurs in the context of a great metaphysical/theological debate in which India's greatest sages of the time (seventh century B.C.) participated.

immortal inner controller. . . . So far with respect to the (cosmic) potencies. Now with respect to the worlds.

17. That which rests in all the worlds, and is distinct from all the worlds, which all the worlds know not, of which all the worlds are the body, which controls all the worlds within, that is thy Self, the immortal inner controller. So far, again, with respect to the worlds. Now with respect to the Vedas.

18. That which rests in all the Vedas, and is distinct from all the Vedas, which all the Vedas know not, of which all the Vedas are the body, which controls all the Vedas within, that is thy Self, the immortal inner controller. So far, again, with respect to the Vedas. Now with respect to sacrifices.

19. That which rests in all sacrifices, and is distinct from all sacrifices, which all sacrifices know not, of which all sacrifices are the body, which controls all sacrifices within, that is thy Self, the immortal inner controller. So far, again, with regard to sacrifices. Now with regard to creatures.

20. That which rests in all creatures, and is distinct from all creatures, which all creatures know not, of which all creatures are the body, which controls all creatures within, that is thy Self, the immortal inner controller. So far, again, with regard to creatures. Now with regard to the (individual) self.

21–30. That which rests in the breath, and is distinct from the breath, which the breath knows not, of which the breath is the body, which controls the breath within, that is thy Self, the immortal inner controller.

31. The Unseen Seer; the Unheard Hearer; the Unthought Thinker; the Unknown Knower. There is no other Seer; there is no other Hearer; there is no other Thinker; there is no other Knower. This is thy Self, the immortal inner controller. Whatever is other than this is evil.—Then Uddālaka son of Aruṇa subsided.

EIGHTH CHAPTER OF THIRD BOOK

1. Then (Gārgī) the daughter of Vacaknu said: Reverend Brahmans, look now! I will ask this Yājñavalkya two questions. If he solves them for me, of a certainty not one of you could overcome him in a *brahmodya* (theological debate). If he does not solve them for me, his head will fall off.—Ask, Gārgī! he said.

2. Said she: Verily I, Yājñavalkya—as a chief's son of Kāśī or Videha would string his unstrung bow and take in his hand two arrows to smite his enemies and stand forth (to combat)—just so I stand forth against you with two questions. Answer me them!—Ask, Gārgī, he said.

3. Said she: That which, Yājñavalkya, is above the heaven, that which is beneath the earth, that which is between heaven and earth here, that which they call past and present and future; on what is this strung and threaded?

4. Said he: That which, Gārgī, is above the heaven, that which is beneath the earth, that which is between heaven and earth here, that which they call past and present and future; on the ether that is strung and threaded.

5. Said she: Homage be yours, Yājñavalkya! For you have solved me this (question). Prepare yourself for the other.—Ask, Gārgī! he said.

6. Said she: That which, Yājñavalkya, is above the heaven, that which is beneath the earth, that which is between heaven and earth here, that which they call past and present and future; on what, I repeat, is this strung and threaded?

7. Said he: That which, Gārgī, is above the heaven, that which is beneath the earth, that which is between heaven and earth here, that which they call past and present and future; on the ether, I repeat, that is strung and threaded.—But on what, say, is the ether strung and threaded?

8. Said he: This verily, Gārgī, is what brahmans refer to as the Imperishable. It is not coarse, not fine; not short, not long; without blood, without fat; without shadow, without darkness; without wind, without ether; without contact, without touch, without smell, without taste, without sight, without hearing, without speech, without thought-organ, without heat; without breath, without mouth (face?); without (personal) name, without family (name); ageless, deathless, fearless, immortal; without dust (impurity?), without sound (word); not opened, not closed; without first, without last; without inside, without outside; it consumes no one, no one consumes it.

9. In the control of this Imperishable, Gārgī, heaven and earth stand severally fixed. In the control of this Imperishable, Gārgī, sun and moon stand severally fixed. In the control of this Imperishable, Gārgī, days and nights, half-months, months, seasons, and years stand severally fixed. In the control of this Imperishable, Gārgī, some rivers flow eastward from the white mountains, others westward, and in whatsoever direction they each may flow. In the control of this Imperishable, Gārgī, men praise the generous giver, the gods are dependent on the sacrifice-patron, and the departed ancestors on the spoon-offering.

10. Whosoever without knowing this Imperishable, Gārgī, sacrifices, gives gifts, or practices austerities for even many thousands of years, for him that (heavenly) world (which he gains) is only finite. Whosoever without knowing this Imperishable, Gārgī, passes away from this world, he is wretched. But he who knowing this Imperishable, Gārgī, passes away from this world, he is a (true) Brāhmaṇa.

11. It is just this Imperishable, Gārgī, which is the unseen seeing one, the unheard hearing one, the unthought thinking one, the unknown knowing one. There is nothing else that sees; there is nothing else that hears; there is nothing else that thinks; there is nothing else that knows. It is even this Imperishable, Gārgī, whereon the ether is strung and threaded.

12. Said she: Reverend Brahmans! Think it a great enough thing, if you can get free of him with a rendering of homage! Of a certainty not one of you will ever overcome him in a *brahmodya* (theological debate).—Then (Gārgī) the daughter of Vacaknu subsided.

SECOND CHAPTER OF FOURTH BOOK

1. Then Janaka of Videha descended humbly from his seat and said: Homage to you, Yājñavalkya! Instruct me! Said he: As, O king, one about to go on a long journey would provide himself with a car or a boat, so your Self (*ātman*) is fitted out with these mystic doctrines. Being so eminent and rich, after you have studied the Vedas and heard the mystic doctrines recited, where will you go when you are released from this world?—I do not know, reverend sir, where I shall go.—Then I will tell you this, where you will go.—Speak, reverend sir!

2. He said: This person (or man or spirit) in the right eye is called Indha (the kindler). He who is Indha, is called Indra, cryptically as it were; for the gods may be said to love the cryptic and dislike the obvious.

3. Now this that has the form of a person in the left eye in his consort, Virāj ("queen" or "majesty"). The concert (*saṃstāva*, literally "hymning together") of these two is this space (*ākāśa*, ether or emptiness) within the heart. Their food is this mass of blood within the heart. Their covering is this net-like thing within the heart. Their path, which is traversible, is this channel which goes upward from the heart.

4. He (the Self, union of Indha and Virāj) has these channels called *Hitā*, (as fine) as a hair split in a thousand parts. By these flows in to him (the food) that flows in. Therefore he has, so to say, more delicate food than this corporeal Self.

5. Of this same person (or spirit), the eastern (-going) vital powers are the eastern quarter, the southern (-going) vital powers are the southern quarter, the western (-going) vital powers are the western quarter, the northern (-going) vital powers are the northern quarter, and upward (-going) vital powers are the zenith, the downward (-going) vital powers are the nadir; all his vital powers are all the quarters (directions).

6. This is the Self (*ātman*) that is (described as) "not, not." It is ungraspable, for it is not grasped; it is indestructible, for it is not destroyed. It has not attachment and is unfastened; it is not attached, and (yet) is not unsteady. You have truly attained freedom from danger, Janaka! said Yājñavalkya.—Said Janaka of Videha: Homage to you, Yājñavalkya! May freedom from danger come to you, inasmuch as you, reverend sir, announce freedom from danger for me. Here are the Videhas, and here am I (as your servants).

THIRD CHAPTER OF FOURTH BOOK

1. Yājñavalkya approached Janaka of Videha, thinking: I will converse with him. Now when Janaka of Videha and Yājñavalkya had conversed together at an Agnihotra sacrifice, Yājñavalkya had given him a wish. The wish which he chose was just to ask any desired question. And he had granted this (wish) to him. Therefore the king himself spoke first to him.

2. Yājñavalkya, what serves as light to man here?—The sun, O king, said he. It is by the light of the sun that he sits down, walks about, does his work, and returns home.—Just so it is, Yājñavalkya.

3. When the sun has set, Yājñavalkya, what serves as light, I repeat, to man here?—The moon, O king, said he. It is by the light of the moon that he sits down, walks about, does his work, and returns home.—Just so, it is, Yājñavalkya.

4. When the sun has set, Yājñavalkya, and the moon has set, what serves as light, I repeat, to man here?—The fire, O king, said he. It is by the light of the fire that he sits down, walks about, does his work, and returns home.—Just so it is, Yājñavalkya.

5. When the sun has set, Yājñavalkya, and the moon has set, and the fire is extinguished, what serves as light, I repeat, to man here?—Speech, O king, said he. It is by the light of speech that he sits down, walks about, does his work, and returns home. Therefore it is, O king, that when even his own hand cannot be made out, then wherever Speech is uttered, one goes toward that.—Just so it is, Yājñavalkya.

6. When the sun has set, Yājñavalkya, and the moon has set, and the fire is extinguished, and speech has ceased, what serves as light, I repeat, to man here?—The Self, O king, said he. For it is by the light of the Self that he sits down, walks about, does his work, and returns home.

7. What is the Self?—It is that Spirit (*puruṣa*), consisting of intelligence, the inner within the vital powers, within the heart. Being common (to the two worlds), it traverses both worlds, and seems to think (in the other, intellectual world), and seems to move about (in this world). Becoming a dream, endowed with intelligence (characteristic of the other world), it transcends this world.

8. This same Spirit, upon being born and attaining a body, is conjoined to evils; passing forth, dying, it abandons evils, the forms of death.

9. Now of this same Spirit there are (primarily) just two states; this one, and the other-world state. There is a third, a twilight state, the state of dream. When he is in this twilight, he sees both states, this one, and the other-world state.

10. Now as this (dream-state) is an approach to the other-world state, entering on this approach, he sees both the evils (of this world's state) and the joys (of the other world's state). When this (Spirit) dreams (literally, falls asleep; refers to light sleep, in which dreams come), he takes material from this world with all its contents, and cutting it down himself, building it up himself, by his own radiance, by his own light, he dreams (literally sleeps or falls asleep). Under these circumstances his own self serves as light to man (Spirit, *puruṣa*) here.

11. There are no wagons there (i.e., in the sleeping state), no teams, no roads; on the contrary he creates for himself wagons, teams, and roads. There are no joys, delights, and happinesses there; on the contrary he creates for himself joys, delights and happinesses. There are no pools, rivers and lakes there; on the contrary he creates for himself pools, rivers and lakes. For he is the Creator.

12. On this subject also there are these verses:

Subduing the bodily (state; or self?) with sleep (or, by means of dream) — not sleeping, he gazes intently on those that are asleep. Assuming brightness, he comes back again to his (waking) state — the golden, Single Swan of the Spirit.

13. Protecting by the life-breath (vital power, vitality) his other nest, roaming immortal outside of the nest, he wanders, immortal, wherever he wills — the golden Single Swan of the Spirit.

14. Wandering manifoldly in the state of dream, he makes for himself many forms, the God; now apparently indulging in pleasures with women (and so) laughing; now again apparently seeing terrors.

15. They see his pleasure-garden; *himself* no one sees. Therefore they say, Let one not waken one that is stretched out (in sleep); hard to cure is he to whom this (Spirit) does not return.

16. On this subject, moreover, they say: This (dream condition) is just (the same as) the waking condition of him. For the same things that one sees when he is awake, even these (he sees) when dreaming. Under these circumstances this man (Spirit) serves for himself as light. — Just so it is, Yājñavalkya. I now give your reverence a thousand (cows). From henceforth speak (on that which leads) unto salvation (release).

17. When, in this condition of dream, this (Spirit) has indulged in pleasures, has roamed about, only after he has seen the good (beyond) and the evil (here), according to his way of procedure (his "rule," particularly course of action), according to his origin (i.e., to the particular body which he left), he runs back precisely to the waking condition. And whatever he sees there (in dream), it does not follow after him; for nothing clings to this Spirit. — Just so it is, Yājñavalkya. I now give your reverence a thousand (cows). From henceforth speak (on that which leads) unto salvation.

18. Just as a great fish follows along both banks, the nearer and the farther (alternately); even so this Spirit follows along both states, the dream state, and the waking state.

19. Just in the ether here, an eagle, or a falcon, after flying about in various places, being weary, folds its wings and settles down precisely on its nest; just so this Spirit makes for that state in which, asleep, he desires no desire, sees no dream (i.e., the state of deep, dreamless sleep).

20. He has these channels called *Hitā*, as fine as a hair split in a thousand parts, and they are full of white, blue, yellow, green and red. Now whenever (in a dream, as previously described; this resumé of dream-state prepares for the contrast with deep sleep) he seems to be smitten, or overpowered, or an elephant seems to cut him to pieces, or he seems to fall into a pit; whatever he looks upon as a terror when awake, even that in this state (of dream) he looks upon as a terror, through ignorance. On the other hand, (the state) in which (one is) like a king, like a god, one thinks "I myself am this whole universe" (this describes the closest possible approach, in empiric waking life, to the author's notion of the state of deep sleep)—this (state of deep sleep) is his highest heaven.

21. Now when, asleep, he desires no desire and sees no dream, even this is his form (aspect, practically "state") that desires (only) the Self, that has attained desires, that has no desires. Just as a man who is embraced by a beloved woman knows nothing outer or inner, even so this bodily Self *(ātman),* when it is embraced by the Self consisting-of-intelligence, knows neither outer nor inner.

22. Even this is his form that is beyond desire, that has sloughed off evil, that knows no fear, that is free from sorrow. In this state father is no father, mother no mother, worlds no worlds, gods no gods, Vedas no Vedas, sacrifices no sacrifices (to him): in this state a thief is no thief, a procurer of abortion no procurer of abortion, a Paulkasa no Paulkasa, a Cāṇḍāla no Cāṇḍāla, a mendicant no mendicant, an ascetic no ascetic. He is unaffected by good, unaffected by evil; for then he has transcended all sorrows of the heart.

23. If, then, he does not see—though seeing (having the power of sight), he sees no object of sight. For there cannot be any separation of the seer from sight, since it (or he?) is indestructible. But there is not, then, any second thing, other and separate from him, which he might see.

24–30. [This last paragraph is then repeated in terms of smelling, tasting, addressing, hearing, thinking, touching, and knowing, instead of seeing.]

31. He is (like) water (?), the One Seer, with no second. This is realized, the Heaven of the Bráhman, O king!—Thus he said to him.—This is his highest attainment, this is his highest heaven, this is his highest joy; it is just this joy, on a small portion of which other creatures live.

32. Now this joy of men which is perfect and prosperous, which is overlord of other joys, and most richly endowed with all human desires;—this is the highest joy of men.

33. But a hundred joys of men are one joy of the ancestors ("Fathers," Manes) who have won heaven.

34–38. But a hundred joys of the ancestors who have won heaven are one joy in the Gandharva heaven.

But a hundred joys in the Gandharva heaven are one joy of the karma-gods, who have attained unto godhood by Karma (i.e., by ritual works).

But a hundred joys of the karma-gods are one joy of the gods from birth [and of one who is a scholar in the Veda, free from guile, and not affected by desire].

But a hundred joys of the gods from birth are one joy in the Heaven of Prajāpati [and of one who is a scholar in the Veda, free from guile, and not affected by desire].

39. But a hundred joys in the Heaven of Prajāpati are one joy in the Heaven of Bráhman [and of one who is a scholar in the Veda, free from guile, and not affected by desire]. This is the Heaven of Bráhman, O king! —Thus he instructed him. —This is immortality (or: nectar)! I now give your reverence a thousand (cows). From henceforth speak (on that which leads) unto salvation. —

40. When, in this condition of peace, this (Spirit) has indulged in pleasure, has roamed about, has seen good and evil, according to his way of procedure according to his origin, he returns again to the waking condition. And whatever he sees there (in deep sleep), it does not follow after him; for nothing clings to this Spirit. —Just so it is, Yājñavalkya. I now give your reverence a thousand (cows). From henceforth speak (on that which leads) unto salvation.

41. Then Yājñavalkya became afraid (thinking): The king is clever; he has driven me out of all my conclusions. —(He continued): When one wastes away it is on account of either old age or afflicting (disease) that he wastes away. Just as a mango or fig or peepal fruit is released from its stem, even so this corporeal Self is released from these members and returns according to its way of procedure, according to its origin namely, to nothing but the (life-) breath.

42. Now just as a wagon when it is completely loaded starts out creaking, just so this corporeal. Self when the Intelligent Self has mounted upon it, starts out creaking.

43. Now just as when a king arrives his nobles, responsible heirs, marshals, and chief men of the towns prepare for him with food, drink, and lodging, saying: Here he comes, here he arrives! —just so all the elements (of the body, viz. the vital powers or sense-faculties and their material objects) prepare for him who has this knowledge, saying: Here (at the time of approaching death) comes the Brahman, here he arrives!

44. Now just as when a king intends to set out on a journey his nobles, responsible heirs, marshals and chief men of the towns gather together unto him, just so all the vital powers gather together unto this Self at the time of death. when he is on the point of breathing forth (his life) upward.

FOURTH CHAPTER OF FOURTH BOOK

1. Now when this corporeal Self becomes weak and enters a state of seeming insensibility, then these vital powers gather together unto it. It takes unto itself those particles of radiance and departs into the Heart.

2. Now when this Spirit (*puruṣa*) of the Eye, leaving (the eye), turns away from it (to the Bodily Self in the heart), then he (the dying man) becomes incapable of distinguishing forms. He is unified: and they say, he cannot see. He is unified, and they say, he cannot smell. He is unified, and they say, he cannot taste. He is unified, and they say, he cannot speak. He is unified, and they say, he cannot hear. He is unified, and they say, he cannot think. He is unified, and they say, he cannot touch. He is unified,and they say, he cannot understand.

3. Now the tip of this heart becomes illuminated. By this light this Self (*ātman*) departs, either from the eye, or from the head, or from other parts of the body. When it departs the life (-breath; *prāna*) departs along with it; and when the life (-breath) departs all the vital powers depart along with it. It is simply consciousness that follows along with it; this same (Self) becomes knowing, endowed with intelligence. His knowledge and (past) deeds and memory take hold of him.

4. Then just as a grass leech, when it comes to the end of a blade of grass, gathers itself up together (to go over to something else), even so this Spirit, when it has rid itself of this body and cast off ignorance, gathers itself up together (to go over to another body).

5. Just as an embroiderer takes off a part from an embroidered garment and weaves for himself another, newer and more beautiful, pattern, even so this Spirit, when it has rid itself of this body and cast off ignorance, weaves for itself another newer form—either of a departed spirit or of a gandharva or of (an inhabitant of) Brahma('s world) or of (an inhabitant of) Prajāpati('s world) or of a god or of a man or from other creatures.

6. Now this Self (*ātman*), verily, is Brahman. It is composed of intelligence, thought, speech, life sight, hearing, ether, wind, heat, water, earth, anger and non-anger, joy and nonjoy, right and non-right; it is composed of everything. Now whenever it is composed of this thing or of that thing,—however it acts, however it operates, so it becomes. Acting well it becomes good; acting ill it becomes evil. As a result of right action it becomes what is good; as a result of evil action it becomes what is evil.

7. Now in this connection they say: This Spirit (man, *puruṣa*) consists simply of desire. As is his desire, so is his resolve; as is his resolve, so is the deed he does; as is the deed he does,so is that which he attains unto.

8. So there is this verse:

That upon which his characteristic mark, his thought, is intent—being just that, man goes unto that along with deeds. Having come to the end of (the effects of) that action, of all whatsoever he does in *this* world, he returns again from that world unto this world, unto action.

So far one who is desirous. Now one who no longer desires. He who is desireless, who is without desire, who desires (only) the Self, who has attained his desires—from him the vital powers (of the body) do not mount upward; they are collected together right in him. Being just the Brahman, unto the Brahman he arrives.

9. Now on this there is this verse:

When all desires are expelled, which lurk within his heart, then a mortal becomes immortal; he attains the Brahman here.

10. Just as the slough of a snake lies dead, thrown down upon an ant-hill, even so this body lies dead. Then this boneless, bodiless, intelligent Self (*ātman*) *is* just the Brahman—*is* just Heaven, O king! Thus said Yājñavalkya.—I now give your reverence a thousand (cows)! Thus said Janaka of Videha.

11. Now in this connection there are these verses:

Narrow is the way—penetrating, ancient; it has reached unto me, by me likewise has it been discovered; by this way the wise knowers of the Brahman, rising upward, arrive at the heavenly world, released from this world.

12. Therein, they say, is white and blue, yellow, green, and red (fluid); this way was discovered, verily, by the Bráhman; on its travels the Bráhman-knower, the radiant, and the doer of right.

13. Into blind darkness enter they who are devoted to not-coming-into-being into what seems even greater darkness than that, those who take delight in coming-into-being.

14. Those worlds are called the demons' worlds; they are enveloped in blind darkness. Ignorant, foolish folk enter into them after death.

15. Being just that, even that we become; dire disaster comes to him who knows it not. Those who know it become immortal; on the other hand the others attain naught but suffering.

16. If a man should well understand the Self, saying "I am It"—seeking after what, for desire of what, should he pursue the body?

17. He who has found and awakened his Self, that is entered into this thicket of a bodily mold, he is the All-creator; for he is the Maker of everything. Heaven is his; nay rather, he *is* Heaven outright!

18. When one looks upon this, the Self, directly as God, the Lord of past and future, then he shall not falter.

19. That Self, in which the five-fold creatures and the ether have their foundation, even that I, intelligent and immortal, hold for the immortal Brahman.

20. On this side of whom the year revolves with the days, that the gods worship as the light of lights—yes, as life, as immortality.

21. The life (-power) of life (-power), the eye of the eye likewise, and the ear of the ear, the food of food, the mind of mind—those who know this, they have understood the Brahman, the ancient, the primal.

By the mind alone must it be understood, that there is nothing manifold in this world. (22). Death after death attains he who thinks he sees manifoldness in this world.

That imperishable, constant one must be perceived only with the mind; (23) (it is) the unborn, great constant Self, free from impurity, higher than the ether.

A man of insight, a brāhmaṇa, by understanding this (Self) should make knowledge for himself. Let him not muse on many words; for that is only wearing out the voice.

24. Now it is this Self that is the controller of all, the lord of all, the sovereign of all; it governs all this universe, whatever is at all. It becomes not greater by good deed, nor less by evil deed. It is overlord of creatures, it is the lord of the world(s); it is the guardian of the world(s); it is the dyke that holds apart these worlds, lest they should crash together.

25. That it is which they seek to know through repetition of the Vedas, through celibate life, through asceticism, through faith, through sacrifice, and through fasting. When one knows this he becomes a Muni (silent sage). This it is which wandering ascetics seek as their heavenly world when they wander forth as ascetics.

26. Therefore those Brāhmaṇas of old, learned and wise, desired no offspring, thinking: What shall we do with offspring, we who possess this Self, this equivalent of the Heavenly World—Abandoning both the desire for sons and the desire for possessions and the desire for heaven, they wandered forth a-begging. For the desire for sons is the same as the desire for possessions, and the desire for possessions is the same as the desire for heaven; for both are nothing but desires.

27. This Self is simply described as "Not, not." It is ungraspable, for it is not grasped. It is indestructible, for it is not destroyed. It has no attachment, and is unfastened; it is not attached, and yet is not unsteady. For it, immortal, passes beyond both these two states (in which one thinks) "For this reason I have done evil," "For this reason I have done good." It is not disturbed by good or evil things that are done or left undone; its heaven is not lost by any deed.

28. This is meant by this verse:

This is the constant greatness of the brāhmana (knower of bráhman); he increases not nor becomes less by deed. This (greatness) it is, the basis of which one should seek to find; having found it, one is not stained by evil deed.

Therefore one who knows this, becoming pacified, controlled, at peace, patient, full of faith, should see the Self in the Self alone. He looks upon everyone as it. Everyone comes to be his Self; he becomes the Self of everyone. He passes over all evil; evil does not pass over him. He subdues all evil; evil does not subdue him. He is free from evil, free from age, free from hunger, free from thirst, a Brāhmaṇa, whoso has this knowledge.

29. This verily is that great unborn Self, the eater of food, the giver of wealth. Whosoever knows thus this great unborn Self, the eater of food, the giver of wealth, he finds wealth.

30. This is that great unborn Self, ageless, deathless, fearless, immortal—the Brahman. You have attained fearlessness, O Janaka! Thus spoke Yājñavalkya.—I now give unto your reverence the Videhas, and myself too along with them, in servitude.—

31. This is that great unborn Self, ageless, deathless, fearless, immortal, the Brahman. The Brahman, in sooth, is fearless; fearlessness surely he becomes, he becomes Brahman, who has such knowledge.

FIFTH CHAPTER OF FOURTH BOOK

1. Now Yājñavalkya had two wives, Maitreyī and Kātyāyanī. Of these two Maitreyī was fond of theological discussion, but Kātyāyanī was, as one might say, of feminine intelligence. He, being about to change his mode of life—

2. Said Yājñavalkya: Maitreyī, behold, I am going to depart from this place as a wandering ascetic. Look, I will make a division between you and Kātyāyanī here.

3. Said Maitreyī: Pray, sir, if all this world filled with riches were mine, should I by that be immortal, or not?—No, said Yājñavalkya; just as is the life of people of means, even so would be your life; but there is no hope for immortality through riches.

4. Said Maitreyī: What should I then do with that by which I could not become immortal? Tell me rather, sir, all that you know.

5. Said Yājñavalkya: Of course you are dear to me, madam, and (naturally) you have acted in a manner dear to me. Well then, madam, I will explain and expound this to you. But do you weigh my words carefully while I am expounding it.—Speak, sir!—

6. Said Yājñavalkya: Behold, not for the love of husband is husband dear to one, but for the love of the ātman is husband dear. Behold, not for the love of wife is wife dear to one, but for the love of the ātman is wife dear . . . [And so on: with "sons," "possessions," "the brahman caste," "the warrior caste," "worlds," "gods," "Vedas," "sacrifices," "creatures," "everything."] . . . Behold, the ātman is that which is to be seen, heard, thought, and meditated upon, Maitreyī. Behold, in seeing, hearing, thinking, and understanding the ātman, everything is known.

7. The brahman caste renounces him who thinks the brahman caste anything other than the ātman. The warrior caste renounces him who thinks the warrior caste anything other than the ātman . . . [And so on: with "the worlds," "the gods," "the Vedas," "the sacrifices," "the creatures," "everything."] This is the brahman caste, this is the warrior caste, this is the worlds, this is the gods, this is the Vedas, this is the sacrifices, this is the creatures, this is everything—namely the ātman.

8. It is just as one could not grasp the sounds of a drum that is struck when they have left it; but by grasping the drum, or the one who beats it, the sound is grasped.

9. It is just as one could not gasp the sounds of a lute that is played when they have left it; but by grasping the lute, or its player, the sound is grasped.

10. It is just as one could not grasp the sounds of a horn that is blown when they have left it; but by grasping the horn, or its blower, the sound is grasped.

11. It is just as when a fire has been laid with wet kindling wood, its clouds of smoke go forth severally in different directions; behold, just so this is the exhalation of that Great Being; namely the Rig Veda, the Yajurveda, the Sāmaveda, the Atharvans-and-āṅgirases the Itihāsas and Purāṅas, the sciences, the Upsaniṣads, the verses, the Sūtras, the explanations and commentaries; sacrificial gifts, oblations, food, drink; both this world and the world beyond, and all creatures; all these are exclusively Its exhalations.

12. It is just as the sea is the sole locality of all water; thus the skin is the sole locality of all touchings, thus the nostrils are the sole locality of all smells, thus the tongue is the sole locality of all tastes, thus the eye is the sole locality of all forms (sights), thus the ear is the sole locality of all sounds, thus the thought-organ is the sole locality of all resolves, thus the heart is the sole locality of all sciences, thus the hands are the sole locality of all deeds, thus the feet are the sole locality of all journey, thus the genital organ is the sole locality of all delights, thus the anus is the sole locality of all evacuations, thus speech is the sole locality of all Vedas.

13. It is just as a lump of salt, which has no interior and no exterior, but is as a whole just a mass of flavour; even so this Great Element has no boundaries, no limits, but as a whole is just a mass of intelligence. Arising out of these elements, it disappears into the same. After death there is no consciousness, lo, I say! said Yājñavalkya.

14. Then said Maitreyī: Just here you have brought me into a state of confusion, reverend sir; I do not understand this, when you say that after death there is no consciousness.

15. Then said Yājñavalkya: I say nothing confusing; this ātman is imperishable, its nature is indestructible; but it has association with matter (up to release, after which this and all duality cease).

24. If there were, as one might say, something else (than the One), then one would see something else, one would smell something else, one would taste something else, one would address something else, one would hear something else, one would think on something else, one would touch something else, one would know something else.

25. But when all of This has become just the ātman, then by what means should It see—whom? By what means should It smell—whom? By what means should It taste—whom? By what means should It address—whom? By what means should It hear—whom? By what means should It think on—whom? By what means should It touch—whom? By what means should It know—whom? By what means, I say, could one know that by which All This knows? By what means, I say, could one know the Knower? Now the lesson has been declared to you, Maitreyī. This, I say, is all there is on the subject of immortality.—Having spoken thus Yājñavalkya entered upon the life of a wandering ascetic.

III
Chāndogya Upaniṣad*

BOOK SIX

1. There was Śvetaketu, the grandson of Aruṇa. His father said to him, "Śvetaketu, you must make your studies. Surely no one of our family, my son, lives like a mere Brahmin by birth alone, without having studied."

At the age of twelve he went to a teacher and after having studied all the Vedas, he returned at the age of twenty-four, haughty, proud of his learning and conceited.

His father said to him: "Śvetaketu, now that you are so haughty, proud of your learning and conceited, did you chance to ask for that Instruction by which the unrevealed becomes revealed, the unthought thought, the unknown known?"

"How does this Instruction go, sir?"

"Like this for example: by a single lump of clay everything is known that is made of clay. 'Creating is seizing with Speech, the Name is Satyam,' namely clay.

"Like this for instance: by one piece of copper ore everything is known that is made of copper. 'Creating is seizing with Speech, the Name is Satyam,' namely copper.

"Like this for instance: by one nail-cutter everything is known that is iron. 'Creating is seizing with Speech, the Name is Satyam,' namely iron."

"Certainly my honorable teachers did not know this. For if they had known, how could they have failed to tell me? Sir, you yourself must tell me!"

"So I will, my son,"he said.

2. "The *Existent* was here in the beginning, my son, alone and without a second. On this there are some who say, 'The *Nonexistent* was here in the beginning, alone and without a second. From that Nonexistent sprang the Existent.'

"But how could it really be so, my son?" he said. "How could what exists spring from what does not exist? On the contrary, my son, the *Existent* was here in the beginning, alone and without a second.

"It willed, 'I may be much, let me multiply.' It brought forth Fire. The Fire willed, 'I may be much, let me multiply.' It brought forth Water. Hence wherever a person is hot or sweats, water springs in that spot from fire.

"The Water willed, 'I may be much, let me multiply.' It brought fo Food. Hence wherever it rains, food becomes plentiful: from water ind spring food and eatables in that spot."

3. "Of these beings indeed there are three ways of being born: it i from an egg, it born from a live being, it is born from a plant.

*Reprinted with permission from J.A.B. Van Buitenen and Eliot Deutsch, *A Source Book of A* (Honolulu: University Press of Hawaii, 1971).

"This same deity willed, 'Why, I will create separate names-and-forms by entering entirely into these three deities with the living soul.

"'I will make each one of them triple.' This deity created separate names-and-forms by entering entirely into these three deities with the living soul.

"Each of them he made triple. Now learn from me how these three deities each became triple."

4. "The red color of fire is the Color of Fire, the white that of Water, the black that of Food. Thus firmness has departed from fire. 'Creating is seizing with Speech, the Name is Satyam,' namely the Three Colors.

"The red color of the sun is the Color of Fire, the white that of Water, the black that of Food. Thus sunness has departed from the sun. 'Creating is seizing with Speech, the Name is Satyam,' namely the Three Colors.

"The red color of the moon is the Color of Fire, the white that of Water, the black that of Food. Thus moonness has departed from the moon. 'Creating is seizing with Speech, the Name is Satyam,' namely the Three Colors.

"The red color of lightning is the Color of Fire, the white that of Water, the black that of Food. Thus lightningness has departed from lightning. 'Creating is seizing with Speech, the Name is Satyam,' namely the Three Colors.

"As they knew this, the ancients of the great halls and of great learning said, 'Now no one can quote us anything that is unrevealed, unthought, unknown,' for they knew it by these Three Colors.

"If something was more or less red, they knew it for the Color of Fire; if it was more or less white, they knew it for the Color of Water; if it was more or less black, they knew it for the Color of Food.

"If something was not quite known, they knew it for a combination of these three deities. Now learn from me, my son, how these three deities each become triple on reaching the person."

5. "The food that is eaten is divided into three: the most solid element ecomes excrement, the middle one flesh, the finest one mind.

"The water that is drunk is divided into three: the most solid element
urine, the middle one blood, the finest one breath.
e that is consumed is divided into three: the most solid element
the middle one marrow, the finest one speech.
my son, consists in Food, the breath consists in Water,
Fire."
er."
said.
ilk which is being churned rises upward, my son,

son, the fineness of the food that is eaten rises
the mind.
water that is drunk rises upward, my son, and that

"The fineness of the fire that is consumed rises upward, my son, and that becomes speech.

"For the mind, my son, consists in Food, the breath consists in Water, the speech consists in Fire."

"Sir, instruct me further."

"So I will, my son," he said.

7. "Man consists of sixteen parts, my son. Do not eat for fifteen days. Drink water as you please. The breath will not be destroyed if one drinks, as it consists in Water."

He did not eat for fifteen days. Then he came back to him. "What should I say, sir?"

"Lines from the Ṛgveda, the *Yajurveda* and the *Sāmaveda,* my son."

"They do not come back to me, sir."

He said to him, "Just as of a big piled-up fire only one ember may be left, the size of a firefly, and the fire does not burn much thereafter with this ember, thus of your sixteen parts one part is left and with that you do not remember the Vedas. Eat. Afterwards you will learn from me."

He ate. Then he returned to him, and whatever Veda he asked, he responded completely. He said to him, "Just as one ember, the size of a firefly, that remains of a big piled-up fire will blaze up when it is stacked with straw and the fire will burn high thereafter with this ember, so, my son, one of your sixteen parts remained. It was stacked with food and it blazed forth, and with it you now remember the Vedas. For the mind consists in Food, my son, the breath in Water, speech in Fire." This he learnt from him, from him.

8. Uddālaka son of Aruna said to his son Śvetaketu, "Learn from me the doctrine of sleep. When a man literally 'sleeps' then he has merged with Existent. He has 'entered the self' that is why they say that he 'sleeps'. For he has entered the self.

"Just as a bird which is tied to a string may fly hither and thither without finding a resting place elsewhere and perches on the stick to which it is tied, likewise the mind may fly hither and thither without finding a resting place elsewhere and perches on the breath. For the breath is the perch of the mind, my son.

"Learn from me hunger and thirst. When a man literally 'hungers' water conducts the food he eats. And just as we speak of a cow leader, a horse leader, a man leader, so we speak of water as 'food leader.' You must know a shoot has sprung up there, my son. This shoot will not lack a root.

"Where would this root be but in food? Thus indeed, my son, search by way of the food, which is a shoot, for the fire, its root. Search, my son, by way of the fire as a shoot, for the Existent, its root. All these creatures, my son, are rooted in the Existent, rest on the Existent, are based upon the Existent.

"And when a man literally 'thirsts' fire conducts the liquid which is drunk. Just as we speak of a cow leader, a horse leader, a man leader, we speak of fire as 'water leader.' You must know that a shoot has sprung up there, my son. This shoot will not lack a root.

"Where would this root be but in water? Search, my son, by way of the water as the shoot, for the fire, its root. Search, my son, by way of the fire as the shoot, for the Existent, its root. All these creatures, my son, are rooted in the Existent, rest on the Existent, are based upon the Existent. It has been said before how these three deities each become triple on reaching man. Of this man when he dies, my son, the speech merges in the breath, the breath in the Fire, the Fire in the supreme deity. That indeed is the very fineness by which all this is ensouled, it is the true one, it is the soul. *You are that*, Śvetaketu."

"Instruct me further, sir."

"So I will, my son," he said.

9. "Just as the bees prepare honey by collecting the juices of all manner of trees and bring the juice to one unity, and just as the juices no longer distinctly know that the one hails from this tree, the other from that one, likewise, my son, when all these creatures have merged with the Existent they do not know, realizing only that they have merged with the Existent.

"Whatever they are here on earth, tiger, lion, wolf, boar, worm, fly, gnat, or mosquito, they become that.

"It is this very fineness which ensouls all this world, it is the true one, it is the soul. *You are that*, Śvetaketu."

"Instruct me further, sir."

"So I will, my son," he said.

10. "The rivers of the east, my son, flow eastward, the rivers of the west flow westward. From ocean they merge into ocean, it becomes the same ocean. Just as they then no longer know that they are this river or that one, just so all these creatures, my son, know no more, realizing only when having come to the Existent that they have come to the Existent. Whatever they are here on earth, tiger, lion, wolf, boar, worm, fly, gnat or mosquito, they become that.

"It is this very fineness which ensouls all this world, it is the true one, it is the soul. *You are that*, Śvetaketu."

"Instruct me further, sir."

"So I will, my son," he said.

11. "If a man would strike this big tree at the root, my son, it would bleed but stay alive. If he struck it at the middle, it would bleed but stay alive. If he struck it at the top, it would bleed but stay alive. Being entirely permeated by the living soul, it stands there happily drinking its food.

"If this life leaves one branch, it withers. If it leaves another branch, it withers. If it leaves a third branch, it withers. If it leaves the whole tree, the whole tree withers. Know that it is in this same way, my son," he said, "that this very body dies when deserted by this life, but this life itself does not die.

"This is the very fineness which ensouls all this world, it is the true one, it is the soul. *You are that*, Śvetaketu."

"Instruct me further, sir."

"So I will, my son," he said.

12. "Bring me a banyan fruit."

"Here it is, sir."

"Split it."

"It is split, sir."

"What do you see inside it?"

"A number of rather fine seeds, sir."

"Well, split one of them."

"It is split, sir."

"What do you see inside it?"

"Nothing, sir."

He said to him, "This very fineness that you no longer can make out, it is by virtue of this fineness that this banyan tree stands so big.

"Believe me, my son. It is this very fineness which ensouls all this world, it is the true one, it is the soul. *You are that*, Śvetaketu."

"Instruct me further, sir."

"So I will, my son," he said.

13. "Throw this salt in the water, and sit with me on the morrow." So he did. He said to him, "Well, bring me the salt that you threw in the water last night." He looked for it, but could not find it as it was dissolved.

"Well, taste the water on this side.—How does it taste?"

"Salty."

"Taste it in the middle.—How does it taste?"

"Salty."

"Taste it at the other end.—How does it taste?"

"Salty."

"Take a mouthful and sit with me." So he did.

"It is always the same."

He said to him, "You cannot make out what exists in it, yet it is there.

"It is this very fineness which ensouls all this world, it is the true one, it is the soul. *You are that*, Śvetaketu."

"Instruct me further, sir."

"So I will, my son," he said.

14. "Suppose they brought a man from the Gandhāra country, blindfolded, and let him loose in an uninhabitated place beyond. The man, brought out and let loose with his blindfold on, would be turned around, to the east, north, west, and south.

"Then someone would take off his blindfold and tell him, 'Gandhāra is that way, go that way.' Being a wise man and clever, he would ask his way from village to village and thus reach Gandhāra. Thus in this world a man who has a teacher knows from him, 'So long will it take until I am free, then I shall reach it.'

"It is this very fineness which ensouls all this world, it is the true one, it is the soul. *You are that*, Śvetaketu."

"Instruct me further, sir."

"So I will, my son," he said.

15. "When a man is dying, his relatives crowd around him: 'Do you recognize me? Do you recognize me?' As long as his speech has not merged in his mind, his mind in his breath, his breath in Fire, and Fire in the supreme deity, he does recognize.

"But when his speech has merged in the mind, the mind in the breath, the breath in Fire, and Fire in the supreme deity, he no longer recognizes.

"It is this very fineness which ensouls all this world, it is the true one, it is the soul. *You are that*, Śvetaketu."

"Instruct me further, sir."

"So I will, my son," he said.

16. "They bring in a man with his hands tied, my son: 'He has stolen, he has committed a robbery. Heat the ax for him!' If he is the criminal, he will make himself untrue. His protests being untrue, and covering himself with untruth, he seizes the heated ax. He is burnt, and then killed.

"If he is not the criminal, he makes himself true by this very fact. His protests being true, and covering himself with truth, he seizes the heated ax. He is not burnt, and then set free.

"Just as he is not burnt—that ensouls all this world, it is the true one, it is the soul. *You are that*, Śvetaketu."

This he knew from him, from him.

IV
Taittirīya Upaniṣad*

BOOK TWO

1. OṀ! He who knows Brahman attains to the Most-High. On this there is the verse:

Brahman is truth, knowledge, and endless. He who knows what is hidden in the cave in the highest heaven partakes of all desires with the wise Brahman.

From this very self sprang space, from space the wind, from the wind the fire, from the fire water, from the water the earth, from the earth the herbs, from the herbs food, from food man. Thus man indeed is made up of the sap of food. This is his head, this his right side, this his other side, this his trunk, this his tail, his foundation. On this there is the verse:

2. From food arise the creatures, whichsoever live on earth, and through food alone do they live, and to it they return in the end. Of all elements, food indeed is the best, hence it is called the best medicine. They forsooth attain to all food who contemplate on Brahman as food. From food are the creatures born, and once born they grow through food. It is eaten and eats the creatures, hence it is called food.

Other than this self consisting in the sap of food and within it is the self

---

*Reprinted with permission from J.A.B. Van Buitenen and Eliot Deutsch, *A Source Book of Advaita Vedānta* (Honolulu: University Press of Hawaii, 1971).

which consists of breath. It is filled by it. This has the shape of a person; it has the shape of a person according to the personal shape of the other. The *prāṇa* is its head, the *uyāna* its right side, the *apāna* its left side, space the trunk, earth its tail, its foundation. On this there is the verse:

3. After breath do the gods, men, and cattle breathe. For breath is the life of the creatures, hence it is called the all-life. To all-life go those who contemplate on Brahman as breath. For breath is the life of the creatures, hence it is called the all-life.

This self is embodied in the previous one. Other than this self consisting in breath and within it is the self consisting of mind. It is filled by it. This has the shape of a person: it is shaped like a person according to the personal shape of the other. The *yajus* formula is its head, the *rc* verse the right side, the *sāman* chant the other side, the instruction the trunk, the *atharva* hymns the tail, the foundation. On this there is the verse:

4. He who knows the Brahman which is bliss—from which both words and mind turn back without reaching it—he has no fear any more.

This self is embodied in the previous one. Other than this self consisting in mind and within it is the self consisting of knowledge. It is filled by it. This has the shape of a person: it is shaped according to the personal shape of the other. Faith is its head, order the right side, truth the other side, discipline the trunk, *mahas* the tail, the foundation. On this there is the verse:

5. Knowledge performs the sacrifice, and it performs the rites. All the gods contemplate on knowledge as the oldest Brahman. When one knows Brahman as knowledge and when one does not become distracted from it, then, giving up the evils in the body, he attains to all desires.

This self is embodied in the previous one. Other than this self consisting in mind and within it is the self consisting of knowledge. It is filled by it. This has the shape of a person: it is shaped according to the personal shape of the other. Faith is its head,order the right side, truth the other side, discipline the trunk, *mahas* the tail, the foundation. On this there is the verse:

6. Nonexistent becomes he when he knows Brahman as nonexistent. When he knows that Brahman exists, they know him by that to exist.

This self is embodied in the previous one. Next then arise the further questions: Does anyone who does not possess the knowledge go to yonder world after his death? Or does the wise man attain to yonder world after his death?

He willed, "Let me be much, I will procreate." He performed austerities. Having performed austerities he created all this, whatever is here. Having created it he entered into it, and having entered into it, he became both the Existent and the Yon [*say-tyat*], the spoken and the unspoken, the abode and the non-abode, knowledge and ignorance, truth and falsehood, he became Satyam, whatever there is. That is why they call him Satyam. On this there is the verse:

7. In the beginning the Nonexistent was here, from it was born the existent. It made itself into a self, that is why it is called well-made. That which is well-made is the sap. For upon attaining to this sap one becomes blissful. For who would breathe in and breathe out if there were no bliss in his space? That indeed makes blissful. For when one finds security, foundation in this invisible, impersonal, unspoken nonabode, then he has become fearless. When he makes in it a differentiation, then he becomes fearful. But it is a terror to the wise man who does not think. On this there is the verse:

8. For fear of it blows the wind, from fear of it rises the sun, from fear of it run Agni and Indra, and Death as the fifth.

CHAPTER 2

BHAGAVAD GĪTĀ

The *Bhagavad Gītā*, composed more than two thousand years ago, part of the great epic the *Mahābhārata*, is undoubtedly India's single most influential religious text. A dialogue between a great warrior, Arjuna, and his charioteer, Krishna—who is actually an incarnation of the ultimate reality—the *Gītā* sets forth a powerful vision of righteous living (*dharma*). The fundamental underlying question is how to reconcile the quest for liberation (*mokṣa*) with the obligation to fulfil one's duties in the world, a question Krishna resolves by explaining the life of nonattached action. When practiced with self-discipline and nonattachment to loss and gain, the different paths of action, knowledge, and faith are all shown to lead to both social well-being and liberation.

Over the centuries many of India's great philosophers have written commentaries on the *Gītā*, and today it remains the most common source of religious and philosophical discussion to be found in India. The translation used here, a model of accuracy and readability, is from *The Bhagavad Gītā*, by Barbara Stoler Miller (New York: Bantam Books, 1986). Winthrop Sargeant's *The Bhagavad Gītā* (Albany: State University of New York Press, 1984) is valuable because it contains the critical Sanskrit text, a transliteration, a word-by-word English translation, and a grammatical analysis of each Sanskrit word. Other good translations include those by Sarvapalli Radhakrishnan, Franklin Edgerton, Eliot Deutsch, Prabhavananda and Isherwood, and Nikhilananda. Radhakrishnan, Edgerton, and Deutsch include helpful annotations and essays.

Three recent books focusing on how the *Bhagavad Gītā* has been interpreted in both ancient and modern times help put this important text in historical context. Robert Minor, ed., *Modern Indian Interpreters of the Bhagavad Gītā* (Albany: State University of New York Press, 1986), is a series of essays that examine interpretations of the *Gītā* by recent Indian thinkers. The interpretation of B.C. Chatterji, Tilak, Aurobindo, Gandhi, Vinoba Bhave, Vivekananda, Radhakrishnan, Sivananda, and Bhaktivedanta are examined with respect to context, motive and purpose, shedding light on the important variations between these quite different interpretations of the same text.

Arvind Sharma, *The Hindu Gītā: Ancient and Classical Interpretations of the Bhagavadgītā* (La Salle, Ill.: Open Court, 1986), as the title suggests, shows how ancient and classical interpretations shaped the Indian tradition's understanding of the *Gītā.* Eric Sharpe, *The Universal* Gītā: *Western Images of the Bhagavad Gītā, A Bicentenary Survey* (La Salle, Ill.: Open Court, 1985), provides a fascinating history of Western interpretations of the *Gītā,* beginning with the first English translation by Charles Wilkins in 1785.

Bhagavad Gītā*

CHAPTER 1

26 Arjuna saw them standing there:[1]
fathers, grandfathers, teachers,
uncles, brothers, sons,
grandsons, and friends.

27 He surveyed his elders
and companions in both armies,
all his kinsmen
assembled together.

28 Dejected, filled with strange pity,
he said this:
"Krishna, I see my kinsmen
gathered here, wanting war.

29 My limbs sink,
my mouth is parched,
my body trembles,
the hair bristles on my flesh.

30 The magic bow slips
from my hand, my skin burns,
I cannot stand still,
my mind reels.

31 I see omens of chaos,
Krishna; I see no good
in killing my kinsmen
in battle.

32 Krishna, I seek no victory,
or kingship or pleasures.

---

*Reprinted with permission from Barbara Stoler Miller, *The Bhagavad Gītā* (New York: Bantam Books, 1986).
[1]Arjuna saw the two armies assembled on the battlefield.

What use to us are kingship,
delights, or life itself?

33 We sought kingship, delights,
and pleasures for the sake of those
assembled to abandon their lives
and fortunes in battle.

34 They are teachers, fathers, sons,
and grandfathers, uncles, grandsons,
fathers and brothers of wives,
and other men of our family.

35 I do not want to kill them
even if I am killed, Krishna;
not for kingship of all three worlds,
much less for the earth!

36 What joy is there for us, Krishna,
in killing Dhritarashtra's sons?
Evil will haunt us if we kill them,
though their bows are drawn to kill.

37 Honor forbids us to kill
our cousins, Dhritarashtra's sons;
how can we know happiness
if we kill our own kinsmen?

39 How can we ignore the wisdom
of turning from this evil
when we see the sin
of family destruction, Krishna?

40 When the family is ruined,
the timeless laws of family duty
perish; and when duty is lost,
chaos overwhelms the family.

41 In overwhelming chaos, Krishna,
women of the family are corrupted,
and when women are corrupted,
disorder is born in society."

CHAPTER 2

10 Mocking him gently,
Krishna gave this counsel
as Arjuna sat dejected,
between the two armies.

Lord Krishna:

11 You grieve for those beyond grief,
and you speak words of insight;
but learned men do not grieve
for the dead or the living.

12 Never have I not existed,
nor you, nor these kings;
and never in the future
shall we cease to exist.

13 Just as the embodied self
enters childhood, youth, and old age,
so does it enter another body;
this does not confound a steadfast man.

14 Contacts with matter make us feel
heat and cold, pleasure and pain.
Arjuna, you must learn to endure
fleeting things—they come and go!

15 When these cannot torment a man,
when suffering and joy are equal
for him and he has courage,
he is fit for immortality.

16 Nothing of nonbeing comes to be,
nor does being cease to exist;
the boundary between these two
is seen by men who see reality.

17 Indestructible is the presence
that pervades all this;
no one can destroy
this unchanging reality.

18 Our bodies are known to end,
but the embodied self is enduring,
indestructible, and immeasurable;
therefore, Arjuna, fight the battle!

19 He who thinks this self a killer
and he who thinks it killed,
both fail to understand;
it does not kill, nor is it killed.

20 It is not born,
it does not die;
having been,
it will never not be;
unborn, enduring,

constant, and primordial,
it is not killed
when the body is killed.

31 Look to your own duty;
do not tremble before it;
nothing is better for a warrior
than a battle of sacred duty.

32 The doors of heaven open
for warriors who rejoice
to have a battle like this
thrust on them by chance.

37 If you are killed, you win heaven;
if you triumph, you enjoy the earth;
therefore, Arjuna, stand up
and resolve to fight the battle!

38 Impartial to joy and suffering,
gain and loss, victory and defeat,
arm yourself for the battle,
lest you fall into evil.

47 Be intent on action, not on the fruits of action;
avoid attraction to the fruits
and attachment to inaction!

48 Perform actions, firm in discipline,
relinquishing attachment;
be impartial to failure and success—
this equanimity is called discipline.

Arjuna:

54 Krishna, what defines a man
deep in contemplation whose insight
and thought are sure? How would he speak?
How would he sit? How would he move?

Lord Krishna:

60 Even when a man of wisdom
tries to control them, Arjuna,

the bewildering senses
attack his mind with violence.

61 Controlling them all,
with discipline he should focus on me;
when his senses are under control,
his insight is sure.

62 Brooding about sensuous objects
makes attachment to them grow;
from attachment desire arises,
from desire anger is born.

63 From anger comes confusion;
from confusion memory lapses;
from broken memory understanding is lost;
from loss of understanding, he is ruined.

64 But a man of inner strength
whose senses experience objects
without attraction and hatred,
in self-control, finds serenity.

71 When he renounces all desires
and acts without craving,
possessiveness,
or individuality, he finds peace.

72 This is the place of the infinite spirit;
achieving it, one is freed from delusion;
abiding in it even at the time of death,
one finds the pure calm of infinity.

CHAPTER 3

Arjuna:

1 If you think understanding
is more powerful than action,
why, Krishna, do you urge me
to this horrific act?

Lord Krishna:

4 A man cannot escape the force
of action by abstaining from actions;
he does not attain success
just by renunciation.

5 No one exists for even an instant
without performing action;

however unwilling, every being is forced
to act by the qualities of nature.

8 Perform necessary action;
it is more powerful than inaction;
without action you even fail
to sustain your own body.

9 Action imprisons the world
unless it is done as sacrifice;
freed from attachment, Arjuna,
perform action as sacrifice!

19 Always perform with detachment
any action you must do;
performing action with detachment,
one achieves supreme good.

20 Janaka and other ancient kings
attained perfection by action alone;
seeing the way to preserve
the world, you should act.

34 Attraction and hatred are poised
in the object of every sense experience;
a man must not fall prey
to these two brigands lurking on his path!

35 Your own duty done imperfectly
is better than another man's done well.
It is better to die in one's own duty;
another man's duty is perilous.

Arjuna:

36 Krishna, what makes a person
commit evil
against his own will,
as if compelled by force?

Lord Krishna:

37 It is desire and anger, arising
from nature's quality of passion;
know it here as the enemy,
voracious and very evil!

39 Knowledge is obscured
by the wise man's eternal enemy,
which takes form as desire,
an insatiable fire, Arjuna.

42 Men say that the senses are superior
to their objects, the mind superior to the senses,
understanding superior to the mind;
higher than understanding is the self.

43 Knowing the self beyond understanding, sustain the self with the self.
Great Warrior, kill the enemy
menacing you in the form of desire!

CHAPTER 4

Lord Krishna:

6 Though myself unborn, undying,
the lord of creatures, I fashion nature,
which is mine, and I come into being
through my own magic.

7 Whenever sacred duty decays
and chaos prevails,
then, I create
myself, Arjuna.

8 To protect men of virtue
and destroy men who do evil,
to set the standard of sacred duty,
I appear in age after age.

13 I created mankind in four classes,
different in their qualities and actions;
though unchanging, I am the agent of this,
the actor who never acts!

14 I desire no fruit of actions,
and actions do not defile me;
one who knows this about me
is not bound by actions.

20 Abandoning attachment to fruits
of action, always content, independent,

he does nothing at all
even when he engages in action.

38 No purifier equals knowledge,
and in time
the man of perfect discipline
discovers this in his own spirit.

39 Faithful, intent, his senses
subdued, he gains knowledge;
gaining knowledge,
he soon finds perfect peace.

41 Arjuna, actions do not bind
a man in possession of himself,
who renounces action through discipline
and severs doubt with knowledge.

42 So sever the ignorant doubt
in your heart with the sword
of self-knowledge, Arjuna!
Observe your discipline! Arise!

CHAPTER 5

Arjuna:

1 Krishna, you praise renunciation
of actions and then discipline;
tell me with certainty
which is the better of these two.

Lord Krishna:

6 Renunciation is difficult to attain
without discipline;
a sage armed with discipline
soon reaches the infinite spirit.

7 Armed with discipline, he purifies
and subdues the self, masters his senses,
unites himself with the self of all creatures;
even when he acts, he is not defiled.

8 Seeing, hearing, touching, smelling,
eating, walking, sleeping, breathing,

the disciplined man who knows reality
should think, "I do nothing at all."

9 When talking, giving, taking,
opening and closing his eyes,
he keeps thinking, "It is the senses
that engage in the sense objects."

10 A man who relinquishes attachment
and dedicates actions to the infinite spirit
is not stained by evil,
like a lotus leaf unstained by water.

11 Relinquishing attachment,
men of discipline perform action
with body, mind, understanding, and senses
for the purification of the self.

12 Relinquishing the fruit of action,
the disciplined man attains perfect peace;
the undisciplined man is in bondage,
attached to the fruit of his desire.

CHAPTER 6

Lord Krishna:

15 Disciplining himself,
his mind controlled,
a man of discipline finds peace,
the pure calm that exists in me.

23 Since he knows that discipline
means unbinding the bonds of suffering,
he should practice discipline resolutely,
without despair dulling his reason.

24 He should entirely relinquish
desires aroused by willful intent;
he should entirely control
his senses with his mind.

25 He should gradually become tranquil,
firmly controlling his understanding;
focusing his mind on the self,
he should think nothing.

26 Wherever his faltering mind
unsteadily wanders,

he should restrain it
and bring it under self-control.

27 When his mind is tranquil, perfect joy
comes to the man of discipline;
his passion is calmed, he is without sin,
being one with the infinite spirit.

28 Constantly disciplining himself,
free from sin, the man of discipline
easily achieves perfect joy
in harmony with the infinite spirit.

29 Arming himself with discipline,
seeing everything with an equal eye,
he sees the self in all creatures
and all creatures in the self.

30 He who sees me everywhere
and sees everything in me
will not be lost to me,
and I will not be lost to him.

31 I exist in all creatures,
so the disciplined man devoted to me
grasps the oneness of life;
wherever he is, he is in me.

32 When he sees identity in everything,
whether joy or suffering,
through analogy with the self,
he is deemed a man of pure discipline.

CHAPTER 7

Lord Krishna:

1 Practice discipline in my protection,
with your mind focused on me;
Arjuna, hear how you can know me
completely, without doubt.

4 My nature has eight aspects:
earth, water, fire, wind, space,
mind, understanding,
and individuality.

5 This is my lower nature:
know my higher nature too,
the life-force
that sustains this universe.

6 Learn that this is the womb
of all creatures;
I am the source of all the universe,
just as I am its dissolution.

7 Nothing is higher than I am;
Arjuna, all that exists
is woven on me,
like a web of pearls on thread.

8 I am the taste in water, Arjuna,
the light in the moon and sun,
OM resonant in all sacred lore,
the sound in space, valor in men.

9 I am the pure fragrance
in earth, the brilliance in fire,
the life in all living creatures,
the penance in ascetics.

10 Know me, Arjuna,
as every creature's timeless seed,
the understanding of intelligent men,
the brilliance of fiery heroes.

11 Of strong men, I am strength,
without the emotion of desire;
in creatures I am the desire
that does not impede sacred duty.

12 Know that nature's qualities
come from me—lucidity,
passion, and dark inertia;
I am not in them, they are in me.

13 All this universe, deluded
by the qualities inherent in nature,
fails to know that I am
beyond them and unchanging.

14 Composed of nature's qualities,
my divine magic is hard to escape;
but those who seek refuge in me
cross over this magic.

21 I grant unwavering faith
to any devoted man who wants
to worship any form
with faith.

22 Disciplined by that faith,
he seeks the deity's favor;

this secured, he gains desires
that I myself grant.

29 Trusting me, men strive
for freedom from old age and death;
they know the infinite spirit,
its inner self and all its action.

30 Men who know me as its inner being,
inner divinity, and inner sacrifice
have disciplined their reason;
they know me at the time of death.

CHAPTER 10

Lord Krishna:

1 Great Warrior, again hear
my word in its supreme form;
desiring your good,
I speak to deepen your love.

2 Neither the multitude of gods
nor great sages know my origin,
for I am the source of all
the gods and great sages.

3 A mortal who knows me
as the unborn, beginningless
great lord of the worlds
is freed from delusion and all evils.

4 Understanding, knowledge, nondelusion,
patience, truth, control, tranquility,
joy, suffering, being, nonbeing,
fear, and fearlessness . . .

5 Nonviolence, equanimity, contentment,
penance, charity, glory, disgrace,
these diverse attitudes
of creatures' arise from me.

8 I am the source of everything,
and everything proceeds from me;
filled with my existence, wise men
realizing this are devoted to me.

9 Thinking and living deep in me,
they enlighten one another

by constantly telling of me
for their own joy and delight.

Arjuna:

15 You know yourself through the self,
Krishna; Supreme among Men,
Sustainer and Lord of Creatures,
God of Gods, Master of the Universe!

16 Tell me without reserve
the divine powers of your self,
powers by which you pervade
these worlds.

Lord Krishna:

20 I am the self abiding
in the heart of all creatures;
I am their beginning,
their middle, and their end.

22 I am the song in sacred lore;
I am Indra, king of the gods;
I am the mind of the senses,
the consciousness of creatures.

34 I am death the destroyer of all,
the source of what will be,
the feminine powers: fame, fortune, speech,
memory, intelligence, resolve, patience.

35 I am the great ritual chant,
the meter of sacred song,
the most sacred month in the year,
the spring blooming with flowers.

39 Arjuna, I am the seed
of all creatures;
nothing animate or inanimate
could exist without me.

40 Fiery Hero, endless
are my divine powers—
of my power's extent
I have barely hinted.

41 Whatever is powerful, lucid,
splendid, or invulnerable
has its source in a fragment
of my brilliance.

CHAPTER 11

Arjuna:

1 To favor me you revealed
the deepest mystery of the self,
and by your words
my delusion is dispelled.

2 I heard from you in detail
how creatures come to be and die,
Krishṇa, and about the self
in its immutable greatness.

3 Just as you have described
yourself, I wish to see your form
in all its majesty,
Krishna, Supreme among Men.

4 If you think I can see it,
reveal to me
your immutable self,
Krishna, Lord of Discipline.

Lord Krishna:

5 Arjuna, see my forms
in hundreds and thousands;
diverse, divine,
of many colors and shapes.

6 See the sun gods, gods of light,
howling storm gods, twin gods of dawn,
and gods of wind, Arjuna,
wondrous forms not seen before.

7 Arjuna, see all the universe,
animate and inanimate,
and whatever else you wish to see;
all stands here as one in my body.

8 But you cannot see me
with your own eye;
I will give you a divine eye to see
the majesty of my discipline.

Sanjaya (the narrator):

9 O King, saying this, Krishna,
the great lord of discipline,
revealed to Arjuna
the true majesty of this form.

10 It is a multiform, wondrous vision,
with countless mouths and eyes
and celestial ornaments,
brandishing many divine weapons.

11 Everywhere was boundless divinity
containing all astonishing things,
wearing divine garlands and garments,
annointed with divine perfume.

12 If the light of a thousand suns
were to rise in the sky at once,
it would be like the light
of that great spirit.

13 Arjuna saw all the universe
in its many ways and parts,
standing as one in the body
of the god of gods.

Arjuna:

36 Krishna, the universe
responds
with joy and rapture
to your glory,
terrified demons
flee in far directions,
and saints throng
to bow in homage.

37 Why should they not bow
in homage to you, Great Soul,
Original Creator,
more venerable than the creator Brahma?
Boundless Lord of Gods,
Shelter of All That Is,
you are eternity,
being, nonbeing, and beyond.

38 You are the original god,
the primordial spirit of man,
the deepest treasure
of all that is,

knower and what is to be known,
the supreme abode;
you pervade the universe,
Lord of Boundless Form.

39 You are the gods of wind,
death, fire, and water;
the moon; the lord of life;
and the great ancestor.
Homage to you,
a thousand times homage!
I bow in homage to you
again and yet again.

40 I bow in homage
before you and behind you;
I bow everywhere
to your omnipresence!
You have boundless strength
and limitless force;
you fulfill
all that you are.

CHAPTER 12

Lord Krishna:

13 One who bears hate for no creature
is friendly, compassionate, unselfish,
free of individuality, patient,
the same in suffering and joy.

14 Content always, disciplined,
self-controlled, firm in his resolve,
his mind and understanding dedicated to me,
devoted to me, he is dear to me.

15 The world does not flee from him,
nor does he flee from the world;
free of delight, rage, fear,
and disgust, he is dear to me.

16 Disinterested, pure, skilled,
indifferent, untroubled,
relinquishing all involvements,
devoted to me, he is dear to me.

17 He does not rejoice or hate,
grieve or feel desire;

relinquishing fortune and misfortune,
the man of devotion is dear to me.

18 Impartial to foe and friend,
honor and contempt,
cold and heat, joy and suffering,
he is free from attachment.

19 Neutral to blame and praise,
silent, content with his fate,
unsheltered, firm in thought,
the man of devotion is dear to me.

20 Even more dear to me are devotees
who cherish this elixir of sacred duty
as I have taught it,
intent on me in their faith.

CHAPTER 3

SĀṀKHYA AND YOGA

Tradition traces the origins of the Sāṁkhya system to Kapila, said to have lived in the seventh century B.C. The Sāṁkhya is frequently associated with the Yoga system because its metaphysical teachings about the radical distinctness of Self (*puruṣa*) and Nature (*prakṛti*)—and its view of the evolutionary process through which Nature's constituent energy fields (*guṇas*) manifest themselves as the world—are presupposed by many interpretations of yoga, including that of the *Bhagavad Gītā*. However, Sāṁkhya's radical dualism of *puruṣa* and *prakṛti* is challenged by the Vedāntic philosophers, and its view that effects are not new things, since they preexist in their causes, is contested by philosophers of the realistic schools of Nyāya, Vaiśeṣika, and Mīmāṁsā. Thus, from early times the Sāṁkhya system was involved in philosophical dialogue with the other schools, most of which accepted its view of the evolution of existence.

The translation of the *Sāṁkhya Kārikā* of Īśvarakṛṣṇa (3rd century), the foundational text of the Sāṁkhya tradition, is taken from the appendix of Gerald J. Larson, *Classical Sāṁkhya*, second edition (Delhi: Motilal Banarsidass, 1979), a highly regarded introduction to the Sāṁkhya system. The standard reference work is Gerald James Larson and Ram Shankar Bhattacharya, *Encyclopedia of Indian Philosophies*, volume 4: *Sāṁkhya, A Dualist Tradition in Indian Philosophy* (Princeton: Princeton University Press, 1987).

The origins of Yoga theory and practice are lost in antiquity, but its systematization dates to Patañjali, who in the second century B.C. collected and summarized the various historical teachings on the subject. The disciplinary techniques for controlling the body-mind outlined in his aphorisms have been adopted and practiced, with various modifications, by Hindus, Buddhists, and Jainas from ancient times to the present. Frequently, as in the *Gītā*, the Sāṁkhya dualism of *puruṣa* and *prakṛti* has been assumed as the underlying metaphysics of Yoga, although in Vedānta and Buddhism a nondualistic metaphysics is affirmed as the basis for yogic practice.

Of the four books making up the *Yoga Sūtra* of Patañjali, it is the first, dealing with concentration (*samādhi*), that is included here, along with portions of the commentary of Vyāsa. The other three books discuss, respectively, methods of practice, results achieved, and complete freedom. The selection here is from *Yoga Philosophy of Patanjali*, by Swami Hariharananda Aranya, translated by P. N. Mukerji (Albany: State University of New York Press, 1983), which contains Vyāsa's fourth-century commentary as well as Hariharananda's own helpful and extensive twentieth-century commentary. *Yoga-sūtras of Patañjali with the Exposition of Vyāsa: A Translation and Commentary*, by Pandit Usharbudh Arya (Honesdale, Pa.: Himalayan International Institute of Yoga Science and Philosophy of the U.S.A., 1986), is an excellent, detailed study of the first book of the *Yoga Sūtras*. Jean Varenne, with Derek Coltman, translator, *Yoga and the Hindu Tradition* (Chicago: University of Chicago Press, 1976), is a good introduction to both the techniques and the philosophy of yoga.

I
ĪŚVARAKṚṢṆA: THE SĀṀKHYA KĀRIKĀ*

1. Because of the torment of the threefold suffering,[1] there arises the desire to know the means of counteracting it. If it is said that this inquiry is useless because perceptible means of removal are available, we say no, since perceptible means are not final or abiding.
2. The revealed means of removing the torment are like the perceptible (—i.e., ultimately ineffective), for they are connected with impurity, destruction and excess; a superior method, different from both, is the discriminative knowledge of the manifest (*vyakta*), the unmanifest (*avyakta*) and the knowing one (*puruṣa*).
3. Primordial nature is uncreated. The seven—the great one (*mahat*), etc.—are both created and creative. The sixteen are created. *puruṣa* is neither created nor creative.
4. The attainment of reliable knowledge is based on determining the means of correct knowledge. The accepted means of correct knowledge are three because these three comprehend all means of correct knowledge. These three means are as follows: (a) perception, (b) inference, (c) reliable authority.
5. Perception is the selective ascertainment of particular sense-objects. Inference, which is of three kinds, depends upon a characteristic mark and that which bears the mark. Reliable authority is trustworthy verbal testimony.
6. The understanding of things beyond the senses is by means of

*Reprinted with permission from Gerald J. Larson, *Classical Sāṁkhya*, 2nd edition (Delhi: Motilal Banarsidass, 1979).

[1]That is, suffering due to (1) internal factors, (2) external factors, and (3) fate.

inference by analogy. That which is beyond even inference, is established by means of reliable authority.

7. (Perception may be impossible due to the following:)

(a) because something is too far away;

(b) because something is too close;

(c) because of an injured sense-organ;

(d) because of inattention;

(e) because of being exceedingly subtle;

(f) because of intervention (of an object between an organ and the object to be perceived);

(g) because of suppression (i.e., seeing the sun but no planets);

(h) because of intermixture with what is similar

8. The non-perception of *prakṛti* is because of its subtlety—not because of its non-existence. Its apprehension is because of its effect. Its effect—the great one (*mahat*), etc.—is different from yet similar to *prakṛti.*

9. The effect exists before the operation of cause:

(a) because of the non-productivity of non-being;

(b) because of the need for an (appropriate) material cause;

(c) because of the impossibility of all things coming from all things;

(d) because something can only produce what it is capable of producing;

(e) because of the nature of the cause (or, because the effect is non-different from the cause).

10. The manifest (*vyakta*) is

(a) caused;

(b) finite;

(c) non-pervasive;

(d) active;

(e) plural;

(f) supported;

(g) mergent;

(h) composite;

(i) dependent;

the unmanifest (*avyakta*) is the opposite.

11. Both the manifest and unmanifest are,

(a) characterized by the three *guṇas;*

(b) undiscriminated;

(c) objective;

(d) general;

(e) non-conscious;

(f) productive;

the *puruṣa* is the opposite of them, although similar to the *avyakta* as characterized in 10.

12. The *guṇas*, whose natures are pleasure, pain and indifference, serve to manifest, activate and limit. They successively dominate, support, activate, and interact with one another.

13. *sattva* is buoyant and shining;
rajas is stimulating and moving;
tamas is heavy and enveloping.
They function for the sake of the *puruṣa* like a lamp.

14. Lack of discrimination, etc., is established because of the manifest having the three *guṇas* and because of the absence of the *guṇas* in the opposite of that i.e., in the *puruṣa*. The unmanifest is likewise established because of the *guṇa*-nature in the cause of the effect.

15 & 16.

(a) Because of the finiteness of specific things in the world which require a cause;

(b) because of homogeneity or sameness of the finite world.

(c) because of the power or potency of the cause which the process of emergence or evolution implies;

(d) because of separation or distinction between cause and its effect with respect to modification or appearance);

(e) because of the undividedness or uniformity of the entire world;

the unmanifest (*avyakta*) is the cause; it functions because of or by the interaction of the three *guṇas*, modified like water, due to the specific nature abiding in the respective *guṇas*.

17. The *puruṣa* exists,

(a) because aggregations or combinations exist for another;

(b) because (this other) must be apart or opposite from the three *guṇas;*

(c) because (this other) (must be) a superintending power or control;

(d) because of the existence or need of an enjoyer;

(e) because there is functioning or activity for the sake of isolation or freedom.

18. The plurality of *puruṣas* is established,

(a) because of the diversity of births, deaths, and faculties;

(b) because of actions or functions that take place at different times;

(c) and because of differences in the proportions of the three *guṇas* in different entities.

19. And, therefore, because the *puruṣa* is the opposite of the unmanifest, it is established that *puruṣa* is a

(a) witness;

(b) possessed of isolation or freedom;

(c) indifferent;

(d) a spectator;

(e) and inactive.

20. Because of the proximity of the two—i.e., *prakṛti* and *puruṣa*—the unconscious one appears as if characterized by consciousness. Similarly, the indifferent one appears as if characterized by activity, because of the activities of the three *guṇas*.

21. The proximity of the two, which is like that of a blind man and a lame man, is for the purpose of seeing the *pradhāna* and for the purpose of the isolation of the *puruṣa*. From this association creation proceeds.

22. From *prakṛti* emerges the great one (*mahat*); from that comes self-awareness (*ahaṁkāra*); from that comes the group of sixteen. Moreover, from five of the sixteen come the five gross elements.

23. The *buddhi* ("will" or "intellect") is characterized by ascertainment or determination. Virtue, knowledge, non-attachment, and possession of power are its *sāttvika* form. Its *tāmasa* form is the opposite of these four.

24. Self-awareness (*ahaṃkāra*) is self-conceit (*abhimāna*). From it a twofold creation emerges: the group of eleven and the five subtle elements.

25. From self-awareness known as *vaikṛta* ("modified") proceeds the group of eleven, characterized by *sattva* ("goodness" or "purity"); from self-awareness known as *bhūtādi* ("the origin of gross elements") proceed the five subtle elements (*tanmātras*), characterized by *tamas* ("darkness" or "delusion"); from self-awareness known as *taijasa* ("shining" or "passionate") both proceed.

26. The sense organs are called eye, ear, nose, tongue, and skin. The organs of action are called voice, hands, feet, and organs of excretion and generation.

27. The mind (*manas*) is of the nature of both; it is characterized by reflection and it is a sense because it is similar to the senses. The variety of external things and the variety of the organs is because of the specific modifications of the *guṇas*.

28. The function of the five sense organs—hearing sound, etc.—is mere awareness. The function of the five organs of action is speech, grasping, walking, excretion and orgasm.

29. With respect to the specific characteristics of the three (i.e., of the *buddhi, ahaṃkāra,* and senses) each functions differently; the five vital breaths make up their common function.

30. With respect to that which is presently in perception, the function of the four (i.e., *buddhi, ahaṃkāra, manas,* and any one of the senses is simultaneous and successive. With respect to that which is not present in perception, the function of the three (i.e., *buddhi, ahaṃkāra,* and *manas*) is based upon a prior perception.

31. The external and internal organs accomplish their own particular function in coordination with one another. The only motive is for the sake of the *puruṣa.* By nothing else is the thirteenfold instrument motivated.

32. The instrument (*karaṇa*) is thirteenfold (i.e., made up of *buddhi, ahaṃkāra, manas,* and the ten senses); characterized by seizing, holding and manifesting. The instrument's effect is tenfold (i.e., relating to the five senses and the five actions): the seized, the held, and the manifested.

33. The internal organ (*antaḥkaraṇa*) is threefold (i.e., *buddhi, ahaṃkāra,* and *manas*); the external is tenfold and is known as the context of the threefold. The external functions in present time. The internal functions in the three times (i.e., in past, present, and future).

34. Of these, the five senses function with specific and non-specific (i.e., gross and subtle) objects. Speech only has sound as its object, but the remaining organs of action have all five as objects.

35. Since the *buddhi* together with the other internal organs (i.e., *ahaṃkāra* and *manas*) comprehends every object; therefore, the threefold instrument is door-keeper and the remaining ten are the doors.

36. These organs—i.e., *ahaṃkāra, manas,* and the ten senses, which are different from one another and which are distinct specifications of the *guṇas,* present the whole of being to the *buddhi,* illuminating it for the sake of the *puruṣa* like a lamp.

37. This is done because the *buddhi* produces every enjoyment of the *puruṣa;* and, moreover, because the *buddhi* distinguishes the subtle difference between the *pradhāna* and the *puruṣa.*

38. The subtle elements (*tanmātras*) are non-specific. From these five emerge the five gross elements. These are considered to be specific, and are tranquil, turbulent and delusive.

39. Subtle bodies, born of father and mother, together with gross elements, are the threefold kinds of bodies. Of these the subtle are constant; bodies born of father and mother are perishable.

40. The subtle body (*liṅga*), previously arisen, unconfined, constant, inclusive of the great one (*mahat*), etc., through the subtle elements (i.e., inclusive of *buddhi, ahaṃkāra, manas,* the ten senses and the five subtle elements), not having enjoyment, transmigrates, (because of) being endowed with *bhāvas* ("dispositions").

41. As a picture does not exist without a support or as a shadow not without a post, etc.; so, too, the instrument (*liṅga* or *karaṇa*) does not exist supportless without that which is specific (i.e., a subtle body).

42. This subtle entity, motivated for the sake of the *puruṣa,* appears like a player (who assumes many roles) by means of its association with efficient causes and effects (i.e., by means of its association with the *bhāvas*) and because of its association with the power of *prakṛti.*

43. The innate *bhāvas,* both natural and acquired—i.e., virtue, etc.—are seen to be dependent on the instrument (*karaṇa*); whereas the embryo, etc., is dependent on the effected (i.e., the gross body).

44. By means of virtue (*dharma*) there is movement upwards (in the scale of beings); by means of vice (*adharma*) there is movement downward; by means of salvation-knowledge (*jñāna*) there is final release or salvation (*apavarga*); from the opposite of *jñāna* bondage results.

45. From non-attachment comes dissolution in *prakṛti;* from attachment which is passionate (*rājasa*) comes transmigration; from power comes non-obstruction; and the reverse of that from its opposite.

46. This is the intellectual creation, and it is distinguished as ignorance, incapacity, complacency and perfection. These are of fifty varieties because of the suppression of differing qualities.

47. There are five varieties of ignorance; twenty-eight varieties of incapacity, due to defects of the instrument; nine complacencies and eight perfections.

48. There are eight varieties of obscurity and delusion; ten kinds of extreme delusion; both gloom and utter darkness are eighteenfold.

49. Injuries to the eleven organs together with injuries to the *buddhi* are said to make up incapacity; the injuries to the *buddhi* are seventeen due to the failure of the ninefold complacency and the eightfold perfection.

50. The nine complacencies are thought of in two groups; four are internal, including nature, means, time, and destiny; and five are external due to the cessation or turning away from the objects of sense.

51. The eight perfections are proper reasoning, oral instruction, study, removal of the three kinds of suffering, friendly discussion and generosity. The previous threefold division (i.e., ignorance, incapacity, and complacency) hinders the perfections.

52. The *liṅga* cannot function without the *bhāvas* ("conditions"). The *bhāvas* cannot function without the *liṅga*. Therefore, a twofold creation operates called *liṅga* and *bhāva*.

53. The divine or celestial order is eightfold; the sub-human is fivefold; the human order is one variety; such, briefly, is the elemental or gross creation.

54. In the upper world there is a predominance of *sattva*. In the lower creation there is a predominance of *tamas*. In the middle, a predominance of *rajas*. This is so from Brahmā down to a blade of grass.

55. The *puruṣa*, which is consciousness, attains there the suffering made by decay and death, until deliverance of the subtle body; therefore, suffering is of the nature of things.

56. This creation, brought about by *prakṛti*—from the great one (*mahat*) down to the specific gross elements—functions for the sake of the release of each *puruṣa*; this is done for the sake of another, as if it were for her own benefit.

57. As the unknowing milk functions for the sake of the nourishment of the calf; so the *prakṛti* functions for the sake of the release of the *puruṣa*.

58. As in the world a man engages in actions for the sake of the cessation of a desire; so also does the *prakṛti* function for the sake of the release of the *puruṣa*.

59. As a dancer ceases from the dance after having been seen by the audience; so also *prakṛti* ceases after having manifested herself to the puruṣa.

60. Possessed of the *guṇas* and helpful in various ways, she behaves selflessly for the sake of him (*puruṣa*), who is without the *guṇas* and who plays no helpful part.

61. It is my thought that there is nothing more delicate than *prakṛti*, who says to herself, "I have been seen," and never again comes into the sight of *puruṣa*.

62. No one therefore, is bound; no one released, likewise no one transmigrates. Only *prakṛti* in its various forms transmigrates, is bound and is released.

63. *Prakṛti* binds herself by herself by means of seven forms; she releases herself by means of one form for the sake of each *puruṣa*.

64. Thus, from the study of the principles the knowledge arises, "I am not conscious; consciousness does not belong to me"; the "I" is not conscious and this knowledge is complete because free from error, pure and solitary.

65. Then, the *puruṣa*, comfortably situated like a spectator, sees *prakṛti* whose activity has ceased due to the completion of her purpose, and who has turned back from the seven forms.

66. Says the indifferent one, "I have seen her"; the other ceases, saying, "I have been seen." Though the two are still in proximity, no creation takes place.

67. Having arrived at the point at which virtue, etc., has no further cause, because of the attainment of direct knowledge the endowed body (i.e., the body in association with *puruṣa*) yet continues because of the force of past impressions (*saṃskāras*), like a potter's wheel.

68. With the cessation of *prakṛti* due to its purpose having been accomplished, *the purusa* on attaining separation from the body, attains isolation (*kaivalya*) which is both certain and final.

69. This secret knowledge for the sake of the *puruṣa*—wherein is analyzed the existence, origin, and termination of all beings—has been expounded or enumerated by the highest sage.

70. This excellent and pure knowledge the sage gave with compassion to Āsuri; Āsuri likewise to Pañcaśikha; and by him the doctrine was expanded or modified.

71. Handed down by disciples in succession, it has been compendiously written in *āryā* metre by the noble-minded Īśvarakṛṣṇa having fully learned the demonstrated truth.

72. The subjects of the complete *ṣaṣṭitantra* are indeed in the seventy verses of Īśvarakṛṣṇa, although the illustrative tales together with the objections of opponents are not included.

73. Thus, this briefly expounded treatise (*śāstra*) is not defective with respect to content, and is like a reflection in a mirror of the vast material of the *tantra*.

II
Patañjali: *Yoga Sūtra* (with Portions of Vyāsa's Commentary)*[1]

1. Now then Yoga is Being Explained.

Yoga means concentration. It is a feature of the mind in all its habitual states, namely, the restless, the stupefied, the distracted, the one-pointed, and the arrested.

The concentration attained by a mind which is one-pointed, which brings enlightenment about a real entity, weakens the afflictions, loosens

*Reprinted with permission from Swami Hariharananda Aranya (P. N. Mukerji, translator), *Yoga Philosophy of Pantanjali* (Albany: State University of New York Press, 1983).

1. Text in **boldface** is from Patañjali. Vyāsa's commentary is in *italics*.

the bonds of karma, and paves the way to the arrested state of the mind, is called cognitive concentration. The concentration that is attainable when all the modifications of the mind-stuff are set at rest is called acognitive concentration.

2. Yoga Is the Suppression of the Modifications of the Mind.

Since a mind has the three dispositions to illumination, activity, and inertia, it must be made up of three guṇas or constituent principles, namely, sattva, rajas, *and* tamas. *When the faculty of illumination is influenced by the principles of* rajas *and* tamas, *the mind becomes inclined towards power and external objects. When it is dominated by* tamas *it inclines to impious acts, false knowledge, non-detachment and weakness. When the veil of infatuation is completely removed and the mind becomes completely luminous, that is to say, when it has a clear conception of the cogniser, the organs of cognition, and the objects cognised, that mind being influenced by a trace of rajas, tends towards virtue, wisdom, detachment and power. When the contamination of rajas is entirely removed, the mind rests in itself, realizes the distinction between reflective consciousness and the pure Self, and proceeds to that form of contemplation which is known as rain-cloud-of-virtue concentration. Yogins [practioners of yoga] describe this form of contemplation as the highest wisdom.*

3. Then the Seer Abides In Itself.

At that time pure consciousness—the Seer—abides in its own self, as it does in the state of liberation.

4. At Other Times the Seer Appears to Assume the Form of the Modification of the Mind.

That is to say, in popular erroneous conception, a particular cognitive modification of buddhi is taken to be the same as consciousness. Mind is like a magnet and acts only in proximity, and by its character of being an object it appears to become the property of Puruṣa, *its owner. That is how the beginningless association of the mind and* Puruṣa *operates as the condition of the mental modification being revealed to* Puruṣa.

5. They [the modifications] Fall Into Five Varieties of Which Some Are Afflicted and the Rest Unafflicted.

The afflicted are those mental processes which have their bases in sources of suffering like ignorance etc. and are the sources of all latencies. The unafflicted, on the other hand, are those that concern final discriminative enlightenment and are opposed to the operation of the guṇas. . . .

Latent impressions are left equally by mental processes which lead to misery as well as those which lead to freedom therefrom. These latent impressions again give rise to fluctuations of the mind. In this way until absolute concentration is attained by a mind in a suppressed state, the wheel of fluctuations and impressions goes on revolving. When mind is freed from the operation of the guṇas *it abides in itself.*

6. Namely, True Cognition, Illusion, Delusion, Sleep and Recollection.

7. Perception, Inference and Testimony Constitute the Valid Cognitions.

8. Illusion Is False Knowledge Formed of a Thing as Other Than What It Is.

9. Delusion Depends on Verbal Knowledge That Is Devoid of a Real Object.

10. Dreamless Sleep Is the Mental Modification Produced by Condition of Inertia as the State of Vacuity or Negation.

If during sleep there was no cognition of the inert state, then on waking, one would not have remembered that experience. There would not also have been recollection of the state in which the mind was in sleep. That is why sleep is regarded as a particular kind of mental state, and should be shut out like other cognitions when concentration is practised.

11. Recollection Is Mental Modification Caused by Reproduction of the Previous Impression of an Object Without Adding Anything from Other Sources.

Does the mind remember the process of knowing which took place before or the object which produced the knowledge? Though knowledge is of an object, yet it reveals both the nature of the object and the process of knowing and produces latent impressions of the same kind. These latencies manifest themselves when excited by external cause and assume in recollection the form of the object as well as of the process of knowing.

12. By Practice and Detachment These Can Be Stopped.

The river of mind flows in both directions — towards good and towards evil. That which flows down the plane of discriminative knowledge ending in the high ground of liberation leads unto good; while that which flows up to the plateau of cycles of re-birth down the plane of non-discrimination leads unto evil. Among these, the flow towards sense-objects is reduced by renunciation, and development of a habit of discrimination opens the floodgate of discriminative knowledge. The stopping of mental modifications is thus dependent upon both.

13. Exertion to Acquire a Tranquil State of Mind Devoid of Fluctuations Is Called Practice.

14. That Practice When Continued for a Long Time without Break and With Devotion Becomes Firm in Foundation.

15. When the Mind Loses All Desire for Objects Seen or Described In the Scriptures It Acquires a State of Utter Desirelessness Which Is Called Detachment.

16. Indifference to the Guṇas Achieved through a Knowledge of the Nature of the Puruṣa Is Called Supreme Detachment.

Through the practice of the effort to realise the Purusaṣ the Yogin having seen the faulty nature of all objects visible or described in the scriptures, gets a clarity of vision and steadiness in sāttvika *qualities. Such a Yogin, edified with a discriminative knowledge and with sharpened and chastened intellect, becomes indifferent to all manifest and unmanifested states of the three guṇas. There are thus two kinds of detachment. The last one is absolute clarification of knowledge. When detachment appears in the shape of clarified knowledge, the Yogin, with his realisation of the nature of Self, thinks thus: "I have got whatever is to be got; the afflictions which have to be eliminated have been reduced; the continuous chain of birth and death, bound by which men are born and die, and dying are born again, has been broken." Detachment is the culmination of knowledge, and* kaivalya *(liberation) and detachment are inseparable.*

17. When Concentration Is Reached with the Help of Gross Thought, Discrimination, Rapture, and I-Consciousness, It Is Called Cognitive Concentration.

18. Acognitive Concentration Is the Other Kind of Samādhi Which Arises through Constant Practice of Higher Renunciation Which Brings about the Disappearance of All Fluctuations of the Mind Wherein Only the Latent Impressions Remain.

When all fluctuations cease, the arrested state of mind with only the latencies in them is known as the samādhi of acognitive concentration. Supreme detachment is the means of attaining it, because it cannot be attained when an object is the basis of concentration. Complete cessation of fluctuations emanates from supreme detachment which is free from any material cogitation. It is totally devoid of all objects and its practice makes the mind independent of any object, and non-existent as it were.

19. While in the Case of the Discarnates and Those Subsisting in Their Elemental Constituents, It Is Caused by Ignorance Which Results in Objective Existence.

In the discarnate devas it is caused by objective existence, because they live in a state which is like the state of liberation, with a mind functioning only so far as its own residual latencies are capable of, and live through the state of life brought about by their latent impressions. Similarly, those whose minds retaining latent impressions remain resolved in Prakṛti *remain in a state like that of liberation, until by force of those latent impressions their minds assert themselves in fluctuation.*

20. Others Adopt the Means of Reverential Faith, Energy, Repeated Recollection, Concentration and Real Knowledge.

Yogins adopt these means. Tranquillity that is experienced by the mind through reverential faith sustains a Yogin like a loving mother. This kind of faith gives a seeker after discriminative knowledge energy, which brings him sustained memory, which makes the mind undisturbed and collected and conducive to concentration. In such a mind dawns the light of discriminative knowledge, by which the Yogin understands the real nature of things. By retaining such knowledge and by cultivating detachment towards all knowables he thus attains the samādhi of acognitive concentration.

21. Yogins with Intense Ardour Achieve Concentration and the Result Thereof Quickly.

22. On Account of the Methods Being Slow, Medium and Speedy, Even Among Those Yogins Who Have Intense Ardour, There Are Differences.

23. From Special Devotion to Īśvara Also Concentration Becomes Imminent.

Through a special kind of devotion called Īśvarapraṇidhāna, on the part of the devotee, Īśvara (God) inclines towards him and favours him with grace for fulfilment of his wish. From such grace also a Yogin obtains concentration and its result, the attainment of the state of liberation, becomes imminent.

24. Īśvara Is a Particular Puruṣa Unaffected by Affliction, Deed, Result of Action or the Latent Impressions Thereof.

The special Puruṣa, *who, on account of His eternal liberation, is unaffected even by the touch of enjoyment or suffering, is called Īśvara. There are many* Puruṣas *who have attained the state of liberation, cutting asunder the threefold bondage. Īśvara had no such bondage in the past nor will He have any in future. Liberated persons are known to have had a previous state of bondage, but Īśvara's case is not like that. Those absorbed in Prakṛti have the possibility of bondage in future, but in the case of Īśvara there is no such possibility. Īśvara is always free and always supreme. The question, therefore, arises whether this perpetual supremacy of Īśvara, on account of the excellence of His Self, is something of which there is proof, or is it something without any proof? The reply is: "The scriptures are its proof." What is the proof of the genuineness of the scriptures? Their genuineness is based on supreme wisdom.*

25. In Him the Seed of Omniscience Has Reached Its Utmost Development Which Cannot Be Exceeded.

26. He Is the Teacher of Former Teachers, Because with Him There Is No Limitation by Time.

27. The Sacred Word Designating Him Is the Mystic Syllable OM.

28. Repeat It and Contemplate Upon Its Meaning.

Repetition of the symbol OM and contemplation on its object—Īśvara—bring one-pointedness to the mind of the Yogin who is engaged in repeating the symbol and contemplating on its meaning.

29. From That Comes Realisation of the Individual Self and the Obstacles Are Resolved.

30. Sickness, Incompetence, Doubt, Delusion, Sloth, Non-Abstention, Erroneous Conception, Non-Attainment of Any Yogic Stage, and Instability to Stay In a Yogic State, These Distractions of the Mind Are the Impediments.

These nine obstacles cause distraction of the mind. They arise with the fluctuations of the mind. In their absence, the fluctuations do not arise.

31. Sorrow, Dejection, Restlessness of Body, Involuntary Inhalation and Exhalation Arise from Distractions.

32. For The Stoppage of Distractions Practice of Concentration on a Single Principle Should Be Made.

The mind becomes one-pointed only when it is withdrawn from various objects and set on only one object.

33. The Mind Becomes Purified by the Cultivation of Feelings of Amity, Compassion, Goodwill and Indifference Respectively Towards Happy, Miserable, Virtuous and Sinful Creatures.

34. By Exhaling and Restraining the Breath Also the Mind is Calmed.

35. The Development of Higher Objective Perceptions Called Subtle Sense Experience Also Brings About Tranquillity of Mind.

The subtle perception of smell which one gets when concentrating on the tip of the nose is the higher smell-perception. Similarly, concentration on the tip of the tongue gives supersensuous taste, that on the palate supersensuous colour, that on the tongue supersensuous touch and that at the root of the tongue supersensuous sound. The awakening of these higher perceptions stabilises the mind firmly, removes doubts and forms the gateway to knowledge acquirable through concentration.

36. Or by Perception Which Is Free from Sorrow and Is Radiant Stability of Mind Can Also Be Produced.

37. Or Contemplating on a Mind Which Is Free from Desires the Devotee's Mind Gets Stabilised.

38. Or by Taking as the Object of Meditation the Images of Dreams Or the State of Dreamless Sleep the Mind of the Yogin Gets Stabilised.

39. Or by Contemplating On Whatsoever Thing One May Like the Mind Becomes Stable.

40. When the Mind Develops the Power of Stabilising on the Smallest Size As Well As on the Greatest One, Then the Mind Comes Under Control.

Contemplating on subtle things the mind can attain stability on the minutest. Similarly, contemplating on the quality of greatness it can stabilise on the infinitely great which is limitless. Meditating between the two extremes, the mind acquires unimpeded power of holding on to whatsoever object it desires. This would be complete mastery over the mind. With that, the mind attains perfection and there is no further need for acquiring stability, nor is there any other call for purification by practice.

41. When the Fluctuations of the Mind Are Weakened the Mind Appears to Take on the Features of the Object of Meditation—Whether It Be the Cogniser, the Instrument of Cognition or the Object Cognised—As Does a Transparent Jewel, and This Identification Is Called Samāpatti or Engrossment.

"Weakened fluctuation" refers to the state of the mind when all modifications but one have disappeared therefrom. The case of a precious (flawless) gem has been taken as an example. As a transparent crystal in-

fluenced by the colour of an adjacent article appears to be tinged by it, so the mind resting on an object, and engrossed in it, appears to take on its nature. A mind set on subtle elements and being engrossed in them is coloured by the nature of such subtle elements, while a mind absorbed in gross elements is coloured by their gross nature. Similarly, the mind occupied with the infinite variety in external objects gets engrossed in such variety and becomes the reflector thereof.

42. The Engrossment, in Which There Is the Mixture of Word, Its Meaning and Its Knowledge, Is Known As Engrossment Accompanied By Confusion.

To explain, the word "cow," the object indicated by the word "cow," the mental impression created by the word "cow" implying its form, various uses, etc., although these are different, are generally taken together. When differentiated, the features of word, the object meant and ideation become distinct. When in the mind of a Yogin engrossed in the thought of a cow, there is the mingling of the word (cow), the object meant (the animal itself) and the idea of the cow, it is called engrossment accompanied by confusion.

43. When the Memory Is Purified, the Mind Appears to Be Devoid of Its Own Nature and Only the Object on Which It Is a Contemplating Remains Illuminated. This Kind of Engrossment Is Called Non-Confused.

When, however, the memory of the conventional meaning of words disappears, the knowledge gained through Samādhi *becomes free of confusion contained in the ideas formed through verbal instruction or inference. The true nature of the object contemplated upon is then revealed and this state is called engrossment free from verbal thinking. It is the truest perception and is the root of inference and testimony which are derived from it. That perception does not arise from testimony or from inference. Consequently, the knowledge acquired by a Yogin in a state of non-confused* samādhi *is uninfluenced by any other mode of cognition than direct perception.*

44. By the Foregoing, the Reflective and Supra-Reflective Engrossments Whose Objects Are Subtle Are Also Explained.

Of these the engrossment that takes place in the gross forms of the subtle elements conditioned by space, time and causation is called reflective. In it also the object of contemplation is cognised as a single unit of a subtle element with manifested characteristics and its knowledge is acquired in the state of concentration. When, however, the engrossment on subtle elements is unaffected by any mutation that might take place in them in time, i.e. *past, present and future, and refers to the object only as present when it embraces all properties of the object, and all its spatial positions (i.e. not conditioned by space),—this sort of all-embracing engrossment is called supra-reflective. "The subtle element is like this," "this is how it has been taken for concentration"—this sort of verbal reflection colours the knowledge acquired in reflective concentration. And when the knowledge derived from it is free from reflective consciousness and is only of the object of engrossment it is supra-reflective. Of the engrossments, those relating to gross objects are either confused or non-confused and those relating to subtle objects are reflective or supra-reflective. This is how by establishing that the non-confused is free of error, such freedom of both itself and the supra-reflective is explained.*

45. Subtlety Pertaining to Objects Culminates in the Unmanifested.

46. These Are the Only Kinds of Objective Concentrations.

The four varieties of engrossment described before have external matter as their objects; that is why in spite of their being concentrations they have to depend on something to develop. Two of them, the confused and the non-confused, relate to gross objects, while the other two, the reflective and the supra-reflective, relate to subtle things.

47. On Gaining Proficiency in the Supra-Reflective, Purity in the Inner Instruments of Cognition Is Developed.

When impurities which shade the illuminating nature of buddhi *are removed there is a transparent flow of quiescence free from the taints of* rajas *and* tamas *and this is called attainment of proficiency. When the Yogin gets such proficiency in supra-reflective concentration, he achieves purity in his inner instruments of reception from which he gets the power of knowing things as they are, simultaneously, i.e. without any sequence of time, and in all their aspects; or in other words, he acquires the clear light of knowledge through power of realisation.*

48. The Knowledge That Is Gained in That State Is Called Truth-bearer.

When the instruments of cognition are purified, the knowledge that appears in the engrossed mind is called truth-bearer justifying the name given to it. It retains and sustains truth alone with no trace of misconception.

49. It Is Different from That Derived from Testimony or Through Inference, Because It Relates to Particulars

What comes from other sources, like that derived from instructions received, relates to generalities. Such instructions cannot describe particular properties fully because words cannot describe particular features as *they are not meant to signify such features. So also in the case of inference as has been said before (*Sūtra *I.7) that wherever there is change of position it is inferred that there is motion, where there is no such change there can be no inference of motion. Thus through inference, only general conclusions can be arrived at. That is why no object of verbal communication or inference can be a particular one. Besides, a thing which is subtle, hidden from view or situated at a distance, cannot be known by ordinary observation. At the same time it cannot be said that a thing particular knowledge of which cannot be obtained by verbal communication, inference or ordinary observations does not exist. The knowledge of particulars relating to the subtler elements or the* Puruṣa-*like receiver (*mahān*) is, however, obtainable by the enlightenment acquired through* samādhi. *Therefore, this particular knowledge is different from the (general) knowledge derivable from verbal communication or inference.*

50. The Latent Impression Born of Such Knowledge Is Opposed to the Formation of Other Latent Impressions.

The latent impressions of insight gained by concentration inhibit latent impressions of empirical life. When latent impressions of empirical life are subdued, no more cognised modifications can emerge therefrom. When modifications are shut out, samādhi *or concentration is achieved. From that comes* samādhic *knowledge which entails latent impressions of such knowledge. This is how new latent impressions grow. Mental effort exists until the acquisition of discriminative knowledge.*

51. By the Stoppage of That Too (Cognitive Concentration) Objectless Concentration Takes Place Through Suppression of All Modifications.

That objectless concentration is not only antagonistic to cognitive samādhi *but is also opposed to the formation of latent impressions of that* samādhi, *because latent impressions of* Nirodha, *which is complete stoppage of modification, or those of supreme detachment destroy the latent impressions of cognitive* samādhi. *From the knowledge of the duration of the time during which the mind had stopped its functioning, the existence of the latent impression of that arrested state can be inferred. In that state the mind merges in its constituent cause, the ever present* Prakṛti, *along with the latent impressions of cognitive samādhi as well as with such latent impressions as lead to* kaivalya *or the state of liberation. That is why the latent impressions of such knowledge destroy the disposition to mutation and do not contribute to the continuance of the mind, because with the termination of such predilection the mind ceases to act as the latent impressions leading to salvation gather force. When the mind ceases to function, Puruṣa gets isolated in Himself, and that is why He is then called pure and liberated.*

CHAPTER 4

NYĀYA AND VAIŚEṢIKA: ANAMBHAṬṬA'S *TARKASAṀGRAHA*

The Nyāya system, whose foundational text, the *Nyāya Sūtra* of Gautama, was probably compiled in the third century B.C., is concerned primarily with establishing the valid means of knowledge. This *sūtra*, along with the commentaries and subcommentaries of Vātsyāyaṇa, Uddyotakara, Vācaspati, and Udayana, as well as other independent works in the Nyāya tradition, are essentially treatises on logic and epistemology. After Gaṅgeśa's *Tattvacintāmani* appeared in the fourteenth century, the tradition, now called New Nyāya (*Navya Nyāya*), focused mainly on the logical aspects of knowledge, developing a sophisticated analysis of the relations among the terms, concepts, and propositions involved in cognitive events. The theory of reasoning and knowledge worked out by Nyāya was adopted, with varying modifications, by most of the other philosophical systems, although some of them disagreed with the underlying atomistic metaphysics contributed by the Vaiśeṣika system.

According the Vaiśeṣika metaphysics, all physical things are made up of atoms, which are not further analyzable. The system gets its name from its view that each kind of atom has a distinct quality, called *Viśeṣa*, and anyone who accepts this view is known as a *Vaiśeṣika*. The foundational text is the *Vaiśeṣika Sūtra* of Kaṇāda (3rd century B.C.), and the basic commentary is Praśastapāda's *Padārtha Dharma Saṁgraha* (4th century A.D.). Vyomashiva, Udayana, and Śrīdhara all wrote important commentaries on Praśastapāda's work. Later works, which combine Vaiśeṣika and Nyāya, include the *Sapta Padārthi* of Śivāditya and Viśvanātha's *Bhāṣāpariccheda*.

The 17th century text included here, Anambhaṭṭa's *Tarkasaṁgraha*, taken from Kuppuswami Sastri, *A Primer of Indian Logic* (Madras: Kuppuswami Research Institute, 1961), follows this later tradition in combining the Vaiśeṣika metaphysics with the Nyāya logic and epistemology. It has served for three centuries as a standard introductory text for students of Nyāya and Vaiśeṣika philosophy.

For an introduction to early Nyāya logic see Kisor Chakrabarti, *The Logic of Gautama* (Honolulu: University of Hawaii Press [SACP Monograph Series 5], 1977), which contains a short but useful bibliography. Pradyot Kumar Mukhopadhyay, *Indian Ralism. A Rigorous Descriptive Metaphysics* (Calcutta: K. P. Bagchi, 1984), is a fine interpretive study of Vaiśeṣika metaphysics. For a careful study of Nyāya epistemology in its larger philosophical context, see Bimal Krishna Matilal, *Perception: An Essay on Classical Indian Theories of Knowledge* (Oxford: Clarendon Press, 1986). Karl Potter, *Encyclopedia of Indian Philosophies*, vol 2: *Indian Metaphysics and Epistemology: The Tradition of Nyāya-Vaiśeṣika Up to Gaṅgeśa* (Princeton: Princeton University Press, 1977), is the standard reference work.

Anambhaṭṭa: *Tarkasaṁgraha**

CHAPTER 1: PERCEPTION

1. In my heart, I devoutly cherish the Lord of the universe; my teacher, I respectfully greet; and I proceed to write this Primer of Indian Logic, called *Tarka-Saṁgraha*, with a view to beginners gaining knowledge easily.

2. Substance, quality, activity, generality, particularity, inherence and non-existence are the seven categories.

3.

(*a*) Of them (the seven categories), the Substances are only nine—*viz.*: earth, water, light, air, ether, time, space, soul and mind.

(*b*) Colour, taste, smell, touch, number, size, separateness, conjunction, disjunction, remoteness, proximity, weight, fluidity, viscidity, sound, cognition, pleasure, pain, desire, dislike, volition, merit, demerit, tendency—these are the twenty-four qualities.

(*c*) Activity or motion is of five kinds: upward motion, downward motion, contraction, expansion and going or movement from one place to another.

(*d*) Generality is of two kinds—the more comprehensive and the less comprehensive.

(*e*) Particularities, on the other hand, abide in eternal substances and are innumerable.

(*f*) Whereas, inherence is merely one.

(*g*) Non-existence is of four kinds:—antecedent non-existence, annihilative non-existence, absolute non-existence and mutual non-existence.

4. Of them, earth is that which has smell. It is of two kinds—eternal and non-eternal. Its eternal variety consists of atoms. Its non-eternal variety con-

---

*Reprinted with permission from Kuppuswami Sastri, *A Primer of Indian Logic* (Madras: Kuppuswami Research Institute, 1961).

sists of its products. Again, it is of three kinds — the three varieties being the body, the sense and other objectives. The earthen body is the body that belongs to the beings of our class. The earthen sense is the olfactory sense by which one perceives smell; and that sense finds its abode in the tip of the nose. The earthen objects are clay, stones and such other things.

5. Water is that which has cold touch. It is of two kinds — eternal and non-eternal. The eternal variety consists of atoms. The non-eternal variety consists of its products. Again, it is of three kinds — the three varieties being the body, the sense and other objects. The body made of water is found in the world of the Water-God. The sense made of water is the gustatory sense by which one perceives taste; and that sense resides in the tip of the tongue. The objects made of water are rivers, ocean and such others.

6. Fire is that which has hot touch. It is of two kinds — eternal and non-eternal. Its eternal variety consists of atoms. Its non-eternal variety consists of its products. Again, it is of three kinds — the three varieties being the body, the sense, and other objects. The body made of fire is in the world of Sun. The sense made of fire is the visual sense by which one perceives colour; and that sense resides in the foremost part of the dark pupil of the eye. The objects made of fire are of four kinds, the four varieties being the light of the earth, that of the sky, that of the stomach and that of the mine. The common fire which people use and its varieties belong to the earth. Lightning and such other varieties, with water as fuel, belong to the sky. The gastric variety is what digests the food. Gold and such other lustrous metals form the variety which is dug out of a mine.

7. The air is that which has touch but no colour. It is of two kinds — eternal and non-eternal. Its eternal variety consists of atoms. Its non-eternal variety consists of its products. Again, it is of three kinds — the three varieties being the body, the sense and other objects. The body made of air is found in the world of the Wind-God. The sense made of air is the tactus by which one perceives touch; and that sense is found all over the body. The object made of air is the air that shakes trees and such other things. The air that moves about within the body is the vital air, which, though one in itself, is called differently as *prāṇa*, *apāna*, etc., according as its abodes in the body differ.

8. Ether is that which has sound as its quality. That is one, all-pervasive and eternal.

9. Time is the distinctive cause of expressions involving the term *past*, etc. It is one, all-pervasive and eternal.

10. Direction is the distinctive cause of expressions involving the terms *east*, etc. It is one, all-pervasive and eternal.

11. The substratum in which cognition inheres is the soul (*ātman*). It is of two kinds — the supreme Soul and the individual soul. Of these two, the supreme Soul is one and is the omniscient Lord. The individual soul, on the other hand, is different in association with different organisms or bodies, though it is all-pervasive and eternal.

12. Mind (*manas*) is the sense by means of which pleasure and such other (perceptible qualities of the soul) are directly apprehended. There are innumerable minds since they are specifically linked up with each soul and they are atomic and external.

13. Colour is the quality which is perceived only by the sense of vision. It is of seven kinds—the seven varieties being white, blue, yellow, red, green, brown and variegated. It is found in earth, water and light. Of these three, in earth, all the seven varieties are found. White colour, which is not brilliant, belongs to water. White colour, which is brilliant, belongs to light.

14. Taste is the quality which is perceived by the sense of taste. It is of six kinds, the six varieties being sweet, acid, salt, pungent, astringent and bitter. It is found in earth and water. Of these two, in earth, all the six varieties are found; while the sweet only belongs to water.

15. Smell is the quality which is perceived by the sense of smell. It is of two kinds—the fragrant and the non-fragrant. It is found in earth only.

16. Touch is the quality which can be perceived only by the sense of touch. It is of three kinds—the three varieties being cool, hot and lukewarm. It is found in earth, water and fire. Of these three, to water belongs the cool touch, the hot touch to fire, and the lukewarm touch to earth and air.

17. The four qualities beginning with colour are produced in earth through the application of heat and are not eternal. In the case of other substances, they are eternal in such of them as are eternal and they are not eternal in such of them as are not eternal.

18. Number is the special cause of enumerative expressions, such as one, two and so on. It is present in all the nine substances and it is represented by numbers beginning from *one* and ending with *parārdha* (one billion). Number *one* may be everlasting or non-eternal—everlasting in everlasting substances and non-eternal in non-eternal substances. Number *two* and the higher numbers are non-eternal everywhere.

19. Size is the special cause of expressions pertaining to measurement. It is found in all four kinds—atomic, large, long and short.

20. Separateness is the special cause of expressions such as "this is separate from that." It is found in all the substances.

21. Contact is the special cause of expressions such as "these are in contact with each other." It is found in all the substances.

22. Disjunction is the quality which destroys contact. It is found in all the substances.

23. Remoteness and proximity are the special causes of expressions such as "this is remote," "this is near." They are found in the four substances beginning with earth and in *manas* (mind). They are of two kinds, those that are due to time and those due to space. In a remote substance, spatial remoteness is found; and in a substance lying near, spatial proximity is found. In an older person, temporal remoteness is found; and in a younger person, temporal proximity is found.

24. Weight is the non-intimate cause of the first downward motion (of a falling substance). It is found in earth and water.

25. Fluidity is the non-intimate cause of the first flow (of a fluid substance). It is found in earth, water and light. It is of two kinds — natural fluidity and artificial fluidity. Natural fluidity is found in water. Artificial fluidity is found in earth and light. In certain varieties of earth like ghee, etc., fluidity of the artificial variety is brought about through contact with fire; and it is also found in gold and such other varieties of light.

26. Viscidity is the quality which causes the lumping up of powder etc., — *i.e.* the particles of powder, etc., to adhere to each other. It belongs only to water.

27. Sound is a quality which is perceived by the ear. It belongs only to the ether. It is of two kinds: noise and alphabetic sound. Noise is found in a drum and alphabetic sounds form languages like Sanskrit.

28.

(*a*) *Buddhi* and *Jñāna* are the same thing, and stand for cognition which is the cause of all verbal expressions. It is of two kinds — recollection and experience.

(*b*) Recollection is the cognition which is caused only by reminiscent impression.

(*c*) All cognitions other than recollection come under experience. There are two kinds of experiences, real and erroneous.

(*d*) The experience which cognizes an attribute as belonging to a thing which really has it, is real; and this is known as *pramā* (valid knowledge).

(*e*) The experience which cognizes an attribute as belonging to a thing in which it is not present, is erroneous.

(*f*) Valid experience is of four kinds — *viz.*, perception, inference, assimilative experience and verbal experience.

(*g*) The instrument of valid experience is also of four kinds — the perceptive instrument, the instrument of inference, assimilation, and sentence or proposition.

29.

(*a*) *Karaṇa* (efficient or instrumental cause) is a *special* cause.

(*b*) The invariable antecedent of an effect is its cause.

(*c*) An effect is the counter-correlative of its antecedent non-existence.

(*d*) Cause is of three kinds, the three varieties being *inherent* cause, *non-inherent* cause, and *occasioning* cause.

(*e*) That is called *inherent* cause, in which the effect *inheres* when it is produced. For instance, threads are the *inherent* cause of a cloth, and a cloth of its colour and such other qualities.

(*f*) That is called *non-inherent* cause, which serves as a cause, while co-inhering with its effect, or with the inherent cause of its effect. For instance, contact between threads is the *non-inherent* cause of cloth; and the colour of the threads is the non-inherent cause of the colour of the cloth.

(*g*) *Occasioning* cause is a cause not coming under either of the above-mentioned kinds. For instance, the shuttle, the loom and such other things are the occasioning causes of cloth.

(*h*) Of these three varieties of causes, only that is called an *efficient* or *instrumental* cause (*karaṇa*), which operates as *special* cause.

30.

(*a*) Of those *pramāṇas*, perceptive instrument (*pratyakṣa*) is the means of perception.

(*b*) Perception is the cognition which is produced through sense-organ coming into relation with an object. It is of two kinds:—indeterminate and determinate.

(*c*) Indeterminate perception is a cognition which does not involve any attribute or adjunct (*prakāra*).

(*d*) Determinate perception is cognition which involves an attribute or adjunct. It is embodied in propositions like "This is *Ḍittha*," "This is a *Brāhmaṇa*," "This is *black*," "This is a *cook*."

(*e*) The sense-relation (*sannikarṣa*) which causes a perceptual cognition is of six kinds—*viz.*, contact, inherence in what has come into contact, inherence in what is inherent in a thing which has come into contact, inherence, inherence in an inherent thing and adjunct-substantive relation.

When a jar is perceived by the sense of sight, the sense-relation is "contact." When the colour of a jar is seen, the sense-relation is "inherence in a thing which has come into contact," the jar, in that case, having come into contact with the visual sense and colour being connected with the jar through the relation of inherence. When colourness (*rūpatva*) in the colour of a jar is seen, the sense-relation is "inherence in what is inherent in a thing which has come into contact"; for, in that case, the jar has come into contact with the visual sense, the colour of the jar inheres in it and *colourness* inheres in colour.

When sound is perceived by the sense of hearing, "inherence" is the sense-relation; for the ether bound within the auricular orifice is the auditory sense, sound is a quality of ether, and the relation between a quality and its substratum is inherence. When soundness (*śabdatva*) is perceived by the auditory sense, the sense-relation is "inherence in a thing which inheres"; for, *soundness* inheres in sound which inheres in the auditory sense.

In the perception of non-existence, the *adjunct-substantive-relation* is the sense-relation; for in the case of the visual perception which takes the form—"The seat of the non-existence of jar is floor," the "non-existence of jar" is an adjunct to the floor with which the visual sense has come into contact.

Thus the cognition which arises from one or the other of these six sense-relations is perception; and sense-organ is its efficient instrument (*karaṇa*). Therefore, the senses constitute the efficient instrument of perceptual experience (*pratyakṣa-pramāṇa*).

CHAPTER II: INFERENCE

31.

(*a*) *Anumāna* (Inference) is the efficient instrument (*karaṇa*) of inferential cognition.

(*b*) Inferential cognition is a cognition which arises from subsumptive reflection (*parāmarśa*).

(*c*) *Parāmarśa* (subsumptive reflection) is a cognition which cognizes the presence of the invariably concomitant factor denoted by the middle term (*probans*) in the thing denoted by the minor term. For instance, the cognition, "This mountain has smoke which is invariably concomitant with fire" is a subsumptive reflection; and the cognition resulting from it and taking the form "mountain has fire" is inferential cognition.

(*d*) "Wherever there is smoke there is fire"—This type of invariable concomitance is *vyāpti* (co-extension).

(*e*) Subject-adjunctness (*pakṣadharmatā*) consists in the invariable concomitant (*vyāpya*) being present in things like a mountain (denoted by *pakṣa* or the minor term).

32.

(*a*) Inference is of two kinds:—inference for oneself and inference for others.

(*b*) Inference for oneself causes one's own inferential experience. For instance, a person may make out the relation of invariable concomitance between smoke and fire and arrive at the universal generalization—"Wherever there is smoke there is fire" from his repeated observation in the hearth and such other places and then approach a mountain. He may have doubt as to the presence of fire in that mountain. On seeing smoke there, he remembers the generalization—"Wherever there is smoke there is fire." Then, he comes to have the cognition—"This mountain has smoke which is pervaded by (or invariably concomitant with) fire." It is this cognition that is called *liṅgaparāmarśa* (the subsumptive reflection of the *probans*). From this cognition arises the inferential cognition—"The mountain has fire." This is what is called *inference for oneself.*

(*c*) *Inference for others* is the syllogistic expression which consists of five members and which a person employs after inferring for himself fire from smoke, with a view to enabling another person to have likewise the same kind of inferential cognition.

E.g.—"The mountain has fire; because it has smoke; whichever has smoke has fire, as a hearth; the mountain is such (has smoke which is invariably concomitant with fire); and therefore, it is such (has fire)." From this five-membered syllogism, the other person to whom it is addressed comes to know the *probans* (smoke) and infers fire from it.

33.

(*a*) The five members of a syllogism are:—(1) the thesis set down (*pratijñā*), (2) the reason (*hetu*), (3) the exemplification (*udāharaṇa*), (4) the subsumptive correlation (*upanaya*) and (5) conclusion (*nigamana*); *e.g.* —"The mountain has fire"—this is the *thesis.* "For it has smoke"—this is the *reason.* "Whichever has smoke has fire, as a hearth"—this is the *exemplification.* "And so is this"—this is the subsumptive *correlation.* "Therefore it is such"—this is the *conclusion.*

(*b*) In the case of inferential cognition for oneself as well as that for others, it is the subsumptive reflection of the reason (*liṅgaparāmarśa*) that serves as the efficient and special cause (*karaṇa*). So, *liṅgaparāmarśa* in this sense is the instrument of inferential cognition (*anumāna*).

34.

(*a*) *Probans* (*liṅga* = literally, mark) is of three kinds—concomitant in affirmation and negative (*anvayavyatireki*), concomitant in affirmation alone (*kevalānvayi*) and concomitant in negation alone (*kevalavyatireki*).

(*b*) The *anvayavyalireki* type of *probans* is that which has affirmative concomitance (*anvayavyāpti*) and negative concomitance (*vyatirekavyāpti*) with the *probandum*; as smoke when fire is the *probandum.* "Where there is smoke, there is fire, as in a hearth"—this is affirmative concomitance. "Where there is no fire, there is no smoke, as in a tank"—this is negative concomitance.

(*c*) The *kevalānvayi probans* has affirmative concomitance alone; as —"Jar is namable, because it is knowable, like a cloth." In this instance, negative concomitance is impossible between *knowability* (*prameyatva*) and *namability* (*abhidheyatva*); for all things are knowable and namable.

(*d*) The *kevalavyatireki probans* has negative concomitance alone; as in the syllogism—"Earth is different from the rest (*not-earth*), for it has smell; whichever is not different from the rest (*not-earth*) has no smell, as water; this (earth) is not so—*i.e.*, it does not have absence of smell or *gandhābhāva*, with which the absence of difference from *not-earth* is invariably concomitant (*vyāpya*); therefore, it is not so—*i.e.*, it is not devoid of difference from *non-earth*". In cases like this, there is no example in which the affirmative concomitance "Whichever has smell, has difference from non-earth" may be made out; for all varieties of earth come under the *pakṣa* (subject).

35.

(*a*) *Pakṣa* (subject) is that in which the presence of the *probandum* is not known for certain and is yet to be proved; as a mountain, when smoke is relied upon as the *probans.*

(*b*) *Sapakṣa* is a similar instance, in which the *probandum* is known for certain; as a hearth, in the same case of inference.

(*c*) *Vipakṣa* is a counter-example in which the non-existence of the *probandum* is known for certain; as a tank, in the same case of inference.

36.

(*a*) Fallacious reasons (*hetvābhāsāḥ*) are of five kinds:—*vis*., the reason that strays away (*savyabhiscāra*), the adverse reason (*viruddha*), the opposable reason (*satpratipakṣa*), the unestablished reason (*asiddha*), and the stultified reason (*bādhita*).

(*b*) The straying reason (*savyabhicāra*) is otherwise known as *anaikāntika* (literally, not unfailing in its association with the *probandum*). It is of three kinds: — *viz.*, common (*sādhāraṇa*), uncommon (*asādhāraṇa*) and non-conclusive (*anupasaṁhārin*).

The *common strayer* (*sādhārāṇa*) is that variety of *straying reason* which is present in a place where the *probandum* (*sādhya*) is not present; as, in the argument — "The mountain has fire, because it is knowable." In this argument *knowability* is found in a tank where fire is not present. The *uncommon strayer* (*asādhāraṇa*) is that reason which is present only in the subject (*pakṣa*) and not present in any similar example (*sapakṣa*) or counter-example (*vipakṣa*); as *sound-ness* (*śabdatva*), in the argument — "Sound is eternal, because it is sound," *śabdatva* (*sound-ness*) being present only in sound, and nowhere else, eternal or non-eternal.

The *non-conclusive strayer* (*anupasaṁhārin*) is that reason which has no affirmative or negative example (*anvayadṛṣṭāntar or vyatirekadṛṣṭānta*); as *knowableness* (*prameyatva*) in the argument — "All things are non-eternal, because they are knowable." Here, no example is available since all things are treated as *pakṣa*.

(*c*) The *adverse reason* (*viruddha*) is one which is invariably concomitant with the non-existence of the *probandum*; as producibility (*kṛtakatva*), in the argument — "Sound is eternal, because it is produced." Here producibility is invariably concomitant with non-eternality, which amounts to the non-existence of eternality.

(*d*) The *opposable reason* (*satpratipakṣa*) is one which admits of being counter-balanced by another reason that proves the non-existence of the *probandum*; as audibility in the argument — "Sound is eternal, because it is audible, like soundness (*śabdatva*)." The counter reason in this case is producibility (*kāryatva*) in the counter-argument — "Sound is non-eternal, because it is producible."

(*e*) The *unestablished reason* (*asiddha*) is of three kinds: *viz.*, *unestablished in respect of abode* (*āśrayāsiddha*), *unestablished in respect of itself* (*svarūpāsiddha*) and *unestablished in respect of its concomitance* (*vyāpyatvāsiddha*).

The reason is *āśrayāsiddha* in the argument — "*Sky-lotus* is fragrant, because it is a lotus, like the lotus of a pond." Here, *sky-lotus* is the abode or subject and it never exists.

The reason is *svarūpāsiddha* in the argument — "Sound is a quality, because it is *visible*, like colour." Here, *visibility* cannot be predicated of sound, which is only audible.

The reason is said to be *vyāpyatvāsiddha* when it is associated with an adventitious condition (*upādhi*). That is said to be an adventitious condition (*upādhi*), which is pervasive of the *probandum* but not pervasive of the *probans*. "To be pervasive of the *probandum*" means "never to be the counter-correlative (*pratiyogin*) of non-existence (*abhāva*) which co-exists with the *probandum*." "Not to be pervasive of the *probans*" means "being the counter-correlative of non-existence which co-exists with the *probans*."

In the argument—"The mountain has smoke, because it has fire," *contact with wet fuel* is the adventitious condition (*upādhi*). "Where there is smoke, there is contact with wet fuel"—thus it is pervasive of the *probandum*. There is no contact with wet fuel in every place where there is fire; for instance, a red-hot iron ball has no contact with wet fuel; thus the *upādhi* is non-pervasive of the *probans*. In this manner, *contact with wet fuel* is the *upādhi* in the present instance, because it is pervasive of the *probandum* but not pervasive of the *probans*. And *fire*, in the argument under reference, is *vyāpyatvā-siddha*, since it is associated with an *adventitious condition* (*upādhi*).

(*f*) The *stultified reason* (*bādhita*) is one which is put forward to prove a *probandum* whose non-existence is established by another proof. "Fire is not hot, because it is a substance," the *probandum is "not being hot*"; its reverse—"being hot"—is perceived through tactile perception; so, the *probans* is *stultified* (*bādhita*).

CHAPTER III: ASSIMILATION OR ANALOGY (*upamāna*)

37. Assimilation (*upamāna*) is the instrument of assimilative cognition. Assimilative cognition (*upamiti*) consists in the knowledge of the relation between a name and the object denoted by it. Knowledge of similarity is the efficient instrument (*karaṇa*) of such cognition. This may be illustrated thus: —A person happens to be ignorant of the exact meaning of the word *gavaya* (a particular animal of the bovine species). From a forester, he learns that a *gavaya* is similar to a *cow*; he goes to a forest, sees the animal called *gavaya*, which is similar to a cow and recollects the information conveyed by the assimilative proposition (*atideśavākya*). Then the assimilative cognition, "This is the animal (of the bovine species) denoted by the word "*gavaya*" arises.

CHAPTER IV: VALID VERBAL TESTIMONY

38.

(*a*) Valid verbal testimony is a proposition set forth by a trustworthy person (*āpta*). One who habitually speaks only truth is a trustworthy person (*āpta*). A sentence or proposition is a group of words like "Bring a cow" (*gāmānaya*).

(*b*) A word is that which has significative potency (*śakti*). "From this word, this concept should be known"—God's will to this effect (*Īśvaraṁketāḥ*) is called *śakti* (significative potency).

39.

(*a*) Verbal expectancy, congruity and proximity—these are the causes which bring about verbal cognition or judgment from a proposition.

(*b*) Verbal expectancy (*ākāṅkṣā*) consists in a word not being capable of conveying a complete judgment in the absence of another word.

(*c*) Congruity (*yogyatā*) consists in the sense being not stultifiable.

(*d*) Proximity (*sannidhi*) consists in the articulation of words without undue delay.

(*e*) A sentence which is devoid of expectancy and the other two requirements (congruity and proximity) does not bring about a valid cognition. For instance, a string of words like "Cow, horse, man, elephant" does not produce any judgment; for there is no verbal expectancy (*ākāṅkṣā*) here. The sentence "One should sprinkle with fire" does not produce a valid judgment, as there is no congruity here. Words like "Bring a cow," uttered at long intervals, cannot produce a valid judgment, owing to want of proximity.

40.

(*a*) There are two classes of sentences: those that belong to the *Veda* and those that belong to secular speech. Those that belong to the *Veda* are all statements of God and therefore authoritative. Of those that belong to secular speech, such as produced by trustworthy persons are authoritative and others are not authoritative.

(*b*) Verbal cognition (*śābdajñāna*) is the knowledge of the meaning of a sentence. Its efficient instrument (*karaṇa*) is sentence (*śabda*).

41.

(*a*) Erroneous experience is of three kinds—the three varieties being doubt, misapprehension and indirect argument (*reductio ad absurdum*).

(*b*) A doubt is a cognition which relates to several incompatible attributes in the same thing—as, in the dubitative cognition—"It may be a post or a man."

(*c*) Misapprehension is a false cognition—as in the erroneous cognition of a nacre, in the form—"This is silver."

(*d*) Indirect argument (*reductio ad absurdum*) consists in the hypothetical admission of *vyāpya* (an invariably concomitant fact) which leads to the admission of the pervasive concomitant (*vyāpaka*); as, "If there were no fire, there would be no smoke.

42. Recollection is also of two kinds:—true and false. The former is the result of a valid experience; and the latter arises from an erroneous experience.

43.

(*a*) Pleasure is a quality which all consider agreeable.

(*b*) Pain is a quality which all consider disagreeable.

(*c*) Desire is *wish*.

(*d*) Dislike is *ill-feeling*.

(*e*) Volitional effort is *the will to do*.

(*f*) *Dharma* is the unseen spiritual benefit accruing from the performance of actions which are enjoined by the Vedic law.

(*g*) *Adharma* is the unseen spiritual demerit accruing from the performance of forbidden actions.

(*h*) Cognition and the following seven qualities (eight in all) are the specific qualities (*viśeṣaguṇāḥ*) found only in the soul. Cognition, desire and volitional effort may be eternal or non-eternal; they are eternal in God and non-eternal in the ordinary souls of living beings (*jīva*).

(*i*) There are three kinds of tendencies or impressions—speed, reminiscent impression and elasticity. Speed belongs to the substances—earth, water, fire, air and mind. Reminiscent impression belongs only to the soul and it results from a previous experience and causes recollection. Elasticity is the tendency of a thing to recover its original form when it is changed.

44. Activity is of the nature of motion. Upward motion leads to contact with an upper place. Downward motion leads to contact with a lower place. Contraction leads to contact with a place near one's body. Expansion leads to contact with a place remote from one's body. All the other varieties of motion come under "*going.*"

45. *Generality* is a generic attribute which is *eternal* and *one* and inheres in many things. It is found in substances, qualities and activities. Existence (*sattā*) is the most comprehensive type of generality. *Substance-ness* and such others are less comprehensive.

46. *Specialities* are the differentiating features belonging to eternal substances.

47. *Inherence* is the eternal relation, which belongs to the inseparables. An *inseparable* pair consists of two things of which one thing, so long as it does not come to an end, exists only in the other thing:—as *component part* and the *composite whole*, *quality* and *substance*, *motion* and *moving body*, *generality* and *the individual having it*, and *speciality* and *the eternal substance having it.*

48.

(*a*) Antecedent non-existence has no beginning but has an end. It relates to the period preceding the production of an effect.

(*b*) Annihilative non-existence has a beginning but has no end. It relates to the period subsequent to the production of an effect.

(*c*) Total non-existence is the negation of a counter-correlative in respect of relation to all the three times—present, past and future—as in the statement
—"There is no jar on this spot."

(*d*) Reciprocal non-existence is the negation of a counter-correlative in respect of its identity with another thing—as in the statement—"A jar is not a cloth."

49. All the other *padārthas* may be brought under one or the other of the seven *padārthas* enumerated at the beginning of this work. So, there are only seven categories.

50. Annambhaṭṭa has written this treatise called *Tarkasaṁgraha* with the object of introducing beginners to a study of the Nyāya and Vaiśeṣika systems of Gautama and Kaṇāda.

CHAPTER 5

MĪMĀṀSĀ: THE MĪMĀṀSĀ SŪTRA

The Mīmāṁsā tradition is rooted in the values and rituals of the Vedas, taking the injunctions to action as the essential Vedic teachings. To support their view of the validity of Vedic rituals, the Mīmāṁsākas argue that there is a soul that survives death and goes on to enjoy the fruits of rituals in another world; that there is a transcendent power that makes the rituals effective; that this world and the actions performed in it are real and have real effects; and that the Vedas, which are the bases of the rituals, are infallibly true. In defending the truth of the Vedas, the Mīmāṁsākas developed a rich epistemology, including a philosophy of language that regards the primordial speech heard through the Vedas as authorless and intrinsically valid.

The translation of the foundational *Mīmāṁsā Sūtra* of Jaimini (fourth century B.C.), with portions of Śabara's commentary (first century B.C.), is by Ganganatha Jha, *The Mīmāṁsā Sūtra with Śabara's Commentary* (Baroda: Oriental Institute, 1936). Jha's *Pūrva Mīmāṁsā in Its Sources* (Benares: Benares Hindu University, 1942), which contains a long, critical bibliography of Mīmāṁsā writings, is the single most important study of this tradition available in English. It contains an analysis of the thought not only of Jaimini and Śabara but also of Kumārila Bhaṭṭa and Prabhākara, generally acknowledged to be the next two most important Mīmāṁsā philosophers. Govardhan P. Bhatt, *Epistemology of the Bhāṭṭa* (Varanasi, Chowkhamba Sanskrit Series Office, 1962), is a detailed analysis of the Mīmāṁsā theory of knowledge. Prabhākara's and Kumārila's arguments for their epistemological positions are carefully examined.

The *Mīmāṁsā Sūtra* with Portions of Śabara's Commentary*

I.i.1. Next, therefore, comes the enquiry into *dharma* (duty).

I.i.2. *Dharma* is that which is indicated by means of the Veda as conducive to the highest good.

I.i.4. That cognition by a person which appears when there is contact of the sense-organs is "sense-perception," and it is not a means of knowing *dharma*, as it apprehends only things existing at the present time.

. . . Dharma, *however, is something that is yet to come, and it does not exist at the time that it is to be known . . . hence sense-perception cannot be the means of knowing* dharma.

I.i.5. The relation of the word with its denotation is inborn—instruction is the means of knowing it—infallible regarding all that is imperceptible; it is a valid means of knowledge, as it is independent, according to Bādarāyana.[1]

What we mean by "inborn" is "constant." It is presence that is figuratively spoken of as "origin." *What is meant is that the relation between word and its meaning is* inseparable. *It becomes the* means of knowing Dharma *in the shape of* Agnihotra *and such acts, which are not known by means of sense-perception and such other means of knowledge.—"How so?"—Because there is* "instruction"; *"instruction" stands for the speaking of a particular set of words. Thus it is the* Word, *in the form of instruction or injunction, which is the means of knowing* Dharma. *Of this "means of knowledge" there is* "infallibility"; *i.e., the cognition brought about by that means never fails when a cognition is not found to be wrong, it cannot be said with regard to it that "this is not so," or "the real thing is not as it is represented by this cognition," or "the real thing is otherwise than what is represented in this cognition," or "it may be that the idea in the mind of the speaker is different from what is expressed by his words," or "the words used give rise to contradictory ideas, representing the same thing as* existing *and as* non-existing."*—For these reasons (since cognition brought about by words is not fallible), it is* "a valid means of knowledge, as it is independent." *That is, when a cognition has been brought about by means of words, there is no need for any other cognition (to corroborate it), or of any other person as having the same cognition.*

I.i.6. [Objection to Mīmāṁsā]—"Word is a product (non-eternal), because it is seen to follow (after effort),"—so say some people.

---

*Reprinted with permission from Gangantha Jha, *The Mīmāṁsā Sūtra with Śabara's Commentary* (Baroda: Oriental Institute, 1936). Text in italics is Śabara's Commentary.

[1]Author of the *Brahma Sūtra.*

. . . finding that there is an invariable concomitance (between the appearance of the word and human effort, the word appearing only when there is human effort) we infer that the word "is produced" by the effort. . . .

I.i.7. [Objection *continued*]—"Because it does not persist."

I.i.8. [Objection *continued*]—"Also, because of the term 'to make.'"

I.i.9. [Objection *continued*]—"Also because there is simultaneity (of the perception of the word) in diverse places."

. . . this could not be possible if the word were only one and eternal. *Unless there is something special there can be no plurality of what is eternal; . . .*

I.i.10. [Objection *continued*]—"Also because there are original forms and modifications."

. . . whatever is liable to modification must be non-eternal.

I.i.11. [Objection *continued*]—"Further, there is an augmentation for the word (sound), due to the multiplicity of its producers (speakers)."

If the word were only manifested *(and not* produced, *by the utterance), then the sound heard would always be the same, whether it were uttered by many or fewer persons. From this we conclude that some portion of the word is produced by each of the speakers, . . .*

I.i.12. [*Mīmāṁsā* reply to the objection in 6:] But the fact of being "seen" is equal in both cases.

. . . the word is manifested *(not* produced*) by human effort; that is to say, if, before being pronounced, the word was not manifest, it becomes manifested by the effort (of pronouncing). Thus it is found that the fact of word being "seen after effort" is equally compatible with both views.*

I.i.13. [Reply to the objection in 7:] What happens (when the word ceases to be heard) is that there is no perception of the extant word on account of the non-reaching of the object by the manifesting agency.

I.i.14. [Reply to the objection in 8:] The term refers to the using.

. . . if it is beyond doubt that word is eternal, then the meaning of these expressions would be "make use *of the word." . . .*

I.i.15. [Reply to the objection in 9:] The simultaneity is as in the case of the sun.

Look at the sun. . . . Being only one he is seen as if occupying several places.

I.i.16. [Reply to the objection in 10:] It is a different letter, not a modification.

I.i.17. [Reply to the objection in 11:] The "augmentation" spoken of is the augmentation of the noise not of the word.

I.i.18. In fact the word must be eternal; as its utterance is for the purpose of another.

. . . i.e., for the purpose of making known the meaning to "another." If the word ceased to exist as soon as uttered, then no one could speak of anything to others; and in that case the word could not be uttered for the purpose of another.

I.i.19. There is simultaneity throughout.

Whenever the word "cow" is uttered, here is a notion of all cows simultaneously. From this it follows that the word denotes the class. And it is not possible to create *the relation of the word to a class; because, in creating the relation, the creator would have to lay down the relation by pointing to the class; . . .*

If, however, the word "cow" *is eternal, it is the same word that is uttered many times and has been previously heard also many times, as applied to other individual cows; and thus a process of positive and negative concomitance the word comes to be recognised as denoting the particular class. For this reason also, the word must be eternal.*

I.i.20. Because there is no number in connection with a word.

People speak of the word "cow" *being* pronounced eight times*; they never speak the word* "cow" *itself being* eight in number. . . .

I.i.21. Because it is not dependent.

. . . In the case of the word, . . . we do not perceive any material cause, on the destruction whereof the word itself would be regarded as ceasing to exist.

I.i.22. Also because there is no idea of the connection of the word, with any material cause.

[Objection]—The word may be the product of air; in fact it is air which, through certain conjunctions and disjunctions, becomes the word.

[It is in answer to this that we have the sūtra*]—It cannot be so; if the word were the product of air, then it could only be air in a particular shape.*

As a matter of fact, however, we do not recognise any particle of air in the constitution of the word. . . . If the word were a product of air, then we could perceive it with our tactile organ (as we perceive air); and yet we do not feel by touch any air-particles in the word. Hence word cannot be a product of air. Therefore it must be eternal.

I.i.23. Also because we find indicative texts.

We also actually find a Vedic text indicating the eternality of word—e.g., "By means of word which is eternal, etc." . . .
From all this we conclude that word is eternal.

I.i.24. [Objection]—"Even though they (word, its meaning, and the relation between the two) be eternal, they could not be expressive of the Vedic subject-matter (of the Vedic injunction *dharma*); because they are not efficient for that purpose."

. . . as the Vedic injunction, which is the sole means of knowing dharma, *is always in the form of* sentence, *—until the same fact is established regarding* sentences, *the validity of the injunction as a means of knowing* dharma *remains doubtful.*

I.i.25. [*Answer*]—[In the sentence] there is only a predication of words with definite denotations along with a word denoting an action; as the meaning of the sentence is based upon that (i.e., the meaning of the words).

I.i.27. [Objection]—"Some people regard the Vedas to be modern, because they are named after persons."

I.i.28. [Objection *concluded*]—"Also because we find ephemeral things mentioned in the Veda."

I.i.29. [*Answer:*]—It has already been explained that there is an unbroken continuity of the text.

We have already explained (under sū. *5) that there is an unbroken tradition of the text among the students of the Veda, which proves that the Veda is eternal; all that we have to do here is to answer the objections. . . .*

I.i.30. The name is due to expounding.

I.i.32. On account of passages being correlated to actions, the passages in question would be of use in regard to an act.

Asks the opponent—"How do you know that all this (Veda) is not like the utterance of lunatics and children? As a matter of fact, we find it in such sentences as 'Trees sat at the sacrificial session,' 'Serpents sat at the sacrificial session,' 'The old bull sings maddening songs.' Now, how could the 'old bull' sing? How too could 'trees' or 'serpents' sit at sacrifices?"

The answer to this is as follows:—As a rule we find the sentences occurring in the Veda laid down as mutually connected.—"How so?"—Having stated the word "Jyotiṣṭoma" *[name of ritual], the term "should be performed" is added;—then the question arising as to the means of the performance—"by what is it to be performed?"—the term "by means of the* Soma" *is added;—then arises the question, "for what purpose?"—and in answer there is the term "for the purpose of attaining heaven";—then comes the question, "in what manner?"—and the answer is "thus, by this process." Thus seeing that the entire passage affords an idea which is the sum total of what is expressed by each of the terms described above, how could we say that it is like the utterance of a lunatic or a child?*

[Objection] "But the statement that we find to the effect that 'Trees sat at the sacrificial session' is clearly absurd."

It is not absurd. In the first place, even if this particular statement were absurd, that would not make all other statements—such as "Desiring heaven, one should perform the Agnihotra"*—absurd, but in reality, even such statements as "Trees sat at the sacrificial session" are not absurd. They serve to eulogise the sacrificial session; the sense being, "even such inanimate things as trees performed this sacrifice, what to say of learned* brāhhmins*?" Just as in common parlance we say "At eveningtime even animals do not graze, what to say of learned* brāhmins*?"—Further, the teaching in the Veda being found irreproachable, wholesome and definite, how could it ever be suspected to be like the utterance of lunatics and children?*

For these reasons, it becomes established that "Dharma is what is indicated by Vedic injunctions as conducive to the highest good."

I.ii.1. [Objection]—"The purpose of the Veda lying in the enjoining of actions, those parts of the Veda which do not serve that purpose are useless; in these therefore the Veda is declared to be non-eternal (unreliable)."

I.ii.2. [Objection *continued*]—"Also because there is contradiction of the scriptures and of directly perceived facts."

"There are such passages in the Veda as—(a) *'The mind is a thief,' 'Speech is a liar' and so forth. These passages, containing mere descriptions of accomplished things, cannot serve as the means of knowing* dharma. *Even if some indirect meaning could be assumed by the indirect methods of interpretation, the only injunction of actions that could be derived from these would be—*(a) *that 'one should commit theft,' and that* (b) *'one should tell lies'; and the acts thus enjoined cannot be performed without transgressing the prohibitions of stealing and of telling lies. Nor could the two (stealing and not-stealing, or lying and not-lying) be taken as optional alternatives, as the two do not stand on the same footing: in the case of one (i.e., stealing) the injunction is assumed (on the basis of the* arthavāda *'the mind is a thief'), while in that of the other (not-stealing), we have the direct injunction ('thou shalt not steal').*

"Then again, there is contradiction of directly perceived facts also: For example—'During the day, it is only the smoke of the fire that is seen, not its flame, and during the night only the flame of the fire is seen, not the smoke' and in support of this statement we have the further assertion—'The fire going forth from this world enters the sun, and during the night the sun enters the fire'—Both these statements (of the fire entering the sun and the sun entering the fire) are contrary to perceptible facts; and hence cannot prove the aforesaid restrictive assertion that 'it is the smoke alone*' or '*the flame alone*' that is seen.*

"Another example of the contradiction of perceptible facts we have in the passage—'we know not whether we are brāhmins *or non-*brāhmins. *In the first place, this sentence, not laying down anything in regard to any action, is useless. Secondly, if it actually means that 'we do not know whether we are* brāhmins *or non-*brāhmins,*' then it is contrary to a perceptible fact, and as such cannot be true.*

"An example of the contradiction of what is stated in the scriptures we have in the passage—'who knows whether one lives in the other world or not'. If it is a mere question, then, serving no purpose regarding any act, it is useless. If it expresses a real uncertainty, then it is contrary to what is declared in the scriptures regarding men going, after death, to regions other than the earth. And thus being contrary to well-ascertained facts, the statement cannot be true."

I.ii.3. [Objection *continued*]—"Also because of the absence of results."

I.ii.4. [Objection *continued*]—"Because of the uselessness of other (acts)."

"There are the following three texts—(1) 'By pouring the final oblation one fulfills all desires'; (2) 'One who performs the Paśubandha *sacrifice wins all regions'; (3) 'He passes beyond death, he passes beyond the sin of* brāhmin*-slaughter, who performs the* Aśvamedha *sacrifices, as also one who knows this.'—Now if these are mere descriptions of established facts, then they are useless. If they lay down the actual results following from the acts mentioned, then there is no use for any other acts."*

I.ii.5. [Objection *continued*]—"Also because of the prohibiting of what cannot be prohibited."

"Such passages as 'The fire shall not be kindled on the earth, nor in the sky, nor in heaven' . . . prohibits things which are incapable of being prohibited. . . ."

I.ii.6. [Objection *concluded*]—"Because of the mention of noneternal things."

In connection with the authoritative character of the Veda, the objection that there is mention of non-eternal things in the Veda has been answered by the declaration that "it is merely a similarity of sounds" (I.i.21).—The same objection is raised here again in support of the attack upon some parts of the Veda—on the basis of the mention in the Veda, of such apparently ephemeral things as "Babara, the son of Pravāhaṇa, desired".

I.ii.7. [Reply:]—Being constructed along with injunction, they would serve the purpose of commending those injunctions.

. . . such passages are glorifications, to be taken along with injunctive passages, and as such help in the knowledge of dharma; . . .

The following text is found in the Veda—"One desiring prosperity should sacrifice the animal Śveta *dedicated to Vāyu (wind);—Vāyu is the eftest deity; . . . he leads the man to prosperity." Though the sentence "Vāyu is the eftest deity" does not indicate any action or anything connected with an action, yet it becomes a valid means of knowledge by being construed with an injunctive sentence; . . .*

It may be asked—"Why should there be commendation of the enjoined act?"—There is commendation for the purpose of making the act attractive and hence performed.

I.ii.9. The incongruity (urged by the opponent in I.ii.2) is not applicable, because the incongruity could be there only if an action were indicated by the commendatory words. As a matter of fact, however, what these words indicate is not an action. Hence it is all right.

Hence all these texts—"The mind is a thief." "The speech is a liar"—are all right (not incongruous).

I.ii.10. Then there is indirect application (figurative expression).

I.ii.11. (*a*) On the similarity in form, and (*b*) on the character of the greater part is the indirect signification based.

There is an injunction to the effect that "one should hold the gold-piece in one's hand and then the priest takes it". . . ; this injunction stands in need of aid, which is supplied by its auxiliary in the shape of the statement that "the mind is a thief, and speech is a liar." This deprecatory assertion serves the purpose of commending the gold; . . .—"But even for decrying it, why should the mind, which is not *a thief, be spoken of as* thief *? Why too the speech, which is not a liar, be spoken of as liar?"—The answer is that this also is "figurative expression," based* (a) "upon the similarity of form," *—as thieves remain hidden, so mind also remains unseen, as term "thief" being taken in the figurative sense of "one who remains hidden,"—and* "upon the character of the greater part,"*—for the most part what people speak is* untrue.

I.ii.12. [*Answer to objection in* I.ii.2] Because of the greatness of distance.

As an example of a statement in the Veda contrary to directly perceived facts, the opponent has cited the passage— "During the day only the smoke of fire was perceived, not the flame, and during the night only the flame of fire was perceived, not the smoke.". . .

It is the fact of their being at a "great distance" that is figuratively spoken of as the "not seeing" of the smoke and the *flame.*

I.ii.15. [*Answer to objection in* I.ii.3] It is praise of knowledge.

I.ii.16. [Answer to objection in I.ii.4] The mention of "all" refers to the fact of the man being entitled to perform all acts and obtain all their rewards. . . .

The mention of the results (in the injunctive text itself) is purely commendatory.

When the text speaks of the man "attaining all desires," it is only a figurative way of stating that he performs the acts bringing about the reward in the shape of the attaining of all desires. And though "all" *is not meant, yet the word "all" is used, in the sense of all that the man may be* entitled to.

I.ii.17. The result being accomplished by means of actions, the difference in the results could be due to the magnitude of the actions.

This is a bold assertion in answer to the same objection that has been answered in the preceding. Even if one takes the statement in question ("All desires are obtained by the final oblation") as laying down the results actually following from the oblation,—the statement would be quite reasonable even in its direct literal sense; and even though all results might really follow from the oblation, yet there would be a difference in the quantity and quality of the results as obtained by the simple act of the final oblation, and as obtained by means of the more elaborate sacrifices; and hence the actual performance of the latter would not be superfluous.

I.iii.1. [Objection]—"Inasmuch as *dharma* is based upon the Veda, what is not Veda should be disregarded."

I.iii.2. [Reply]—But *smṛti* (tradition) is trustworthy, as there would be inference (assumption, of the basis in the Veda) from the fact of the agent being the same.

. . . *what we could infer as the ground for reliability is the text (Vedic) itself [which would have provided the* smṛti*-writers with the previous cognition necessary for the remembrance,* smṛti, *which would thus have its basis in that inferred Vedic text];—this inference being drawn from the fact that* *"the agent is the same";—i.e., the "agent," author, of the* smṛti *is the same as the "agent," performer, of the acts prescribed in the Veda.*

I.iii.3. When there is conflict between Veda and *smṛti*, the *smṛti* should be disregarded; because it is only when there is no such conflict that there is an assumption of Vedic text in support of *smṛti*.

I.iii.4. If worldly motives are discernible the *smṛti*-rules cannot be regarded as trustworthy.

. . . there is such a thing as apūrva, *—because action is enjoined—in such injunctions as "Desirous of Heaven, one should sacrifice." Otherwise, —if there were no such thing as* apūrva*—such an injunction would be meaningless, as the act of the* sacrifice *itself is perishable, so that if the sacrifice were to perish without bringing into existence something else, then the cause having ceased to exist, the result (in the shape of heaven) could never come about.—From this it follows that the sacrifice does bring into existence something (some force or potency which continues to exist and operate till such time as the result is actually brought about).*

Thus then, the only possible alternative is that the act of sacrifice subsists in the material substance offered, and this substance has perished and when the substratum in the shape of the substance has perished, it is understood that the act itself has perished.—If it be urged that "the substratum . . . has not perished,"—that cannot be true, as all that is found to be left of the substance is mere ash.—It might be argued that "even while the ash is there the substance is there"—that cannot be right; because what exists might be perceived, and yet the substance is not *perceived in the ashes.—"The very fact of the bringing about of the result would be indicative of the presence of the substance at the time of the appearance of the result."—In that case, it is necessary for the other party to answer the objection that there is no perception of the substance. It might be argued that "the non-perception might be due to one or the other of the various reasons of non-perception, such as the subtle character of the substance. If such is the view, then it comes to this, that something has to be assumed; and the question to be considered is—Is it the* apūrva *that should be assumed—or some reason for the non-perception of the existing substance? There is always some justification for making a general assumption, and none for a particular one [so that while there may be some justification for the assuming of a general potency in the shape of the* apūrva, *there can be none for assuming a reason for the non-perception of every particular object, as there will have to be a separate reason for every particular case of non-perception].*

IV.iii.15. That one result would be "heaven," as that is equally desirable for all.

"But why so?"—Because "heaven" is happiness, and everyone seeks for happiness.

IV.iii.16. Also because *such is the common* notion (of people).

VI.i.3. Further, inasmuch as the act (of sacrifice) must be related (to something), it should be taken as related to the desired thing (heaven); hence the text should be taken as enjoining the act (of sacrifice, as a means to the attainment of heaven).

If the sacrifice is not taken as enjoined in reference to heaven, then,—and the sacrifice thereby being something fruitless,—the "desire for heaven," even though laid down in the text, would be entirely useless; and in that case the whole injunction would be pointless.

VI.i.4. [Objection]—"Inasmuch as an act is performed for the purpose of obtaining results, all beings should be entitled to perform the acts prescribed in the scriptures."

VI.i.5. [Reply:] In reality, the injunction of an act should be taken to apply to only such an agent as may be able to carry out the entire details of the act; because such is the sense of the Vedic texts.

VI.i.8. In reality, it is the whole genus that is entitled,—says Bādarāyaṇa,—because there is no ground for distinction; hence the woman also should be regarded as entitled to perform sacrifices, as the genus is equally present in all human beings.

VI.i.25. [Objection]—"All the four castes are entitled to the performance of sacrifices,—there being no distinction."

VI.i.26. [Reply:] In reality, the acts in question can be performed by the three higher castes only; as in connection with the "Installation of Fire" these three only have been mentioned; the *śūdra* therefore can have no connection with sacrifices; the Veda being applicable to the *brāhmin* and the other two castes only; such is the opinion of Ātrēya.

CHAPTER 6

VEDĀNTA

The Vedānta tradition is grounded in the wisdom portions of the Vedas, primarily the Upaniṣads, and takes these texts, along with their summary found in the *Brahma Sūtra* of Bādarāyaṇa, (2nd Century B.C.) and the *Bhagavad Gītā* (1st Century B.C.) as foundational. Since the Upaniṣads assert that Brahman is the fundamental reality, the central question for Vedānta is, What is Brahman? Is Brahman the undifferentiated, impersonal ground of being, entirely without qualification? Those who, like Śaṅkara (8th Century A.D.) accept this interpretation of Brahman are known as *Advaitins*, literally "nondualists." Others, like Madhva (1197-1276), interpret selves and things as distinct and different from Brahman but ultimately dependent upon it and are known as *Dvaitins*, or dualists. A third interpretation, qualified nondualism (*Viśiṣṭādvaita*), made famous by Rāmānuja (11th Century), regards Brahman as a personal divine being that contains within itself a multiplicity of real attributes, accounting thereby for both the unity and the plurality of reality.

Since every school of Vedānta takes the ultimate aim of human life to be the realization of the innermost Self, the Ātman, different interpretations of Brahman require different views of the relation of the self to Brahman and different analyses of the nature of this Self-realization. As the selections from Śaṅkara show, for the Advaitin, since the Self is not different from Brahman, realization is a matter of overcoming the ignorance that takes the self to be different. For Rāmānuja, on the other hand, since the self is distinct from Brahman, there is a real separation that must be overcome for the self to realize its fullness in Brahman. The various schools of Vedānta have responded to these issues in different ways over the centuries and, in arguing for the correctness of their interpretations, have worked out elaborate and subtle epistemological theories that were frequently the subject of debates between Vedāntists and adherents of the other traditions.

Advaita Vedānta: A Philosophical Reconstruction, by Eliot Deutsch (Honolulu: East-West Center Press, 1966), is probably the best introduction to the Advaita tradition. *A Source Book in Advaita Vedānta*, by J.A.B. Van Buitenen and Eliot Deutsch (Honolulu: University of Hawaii Press, 1971), provides excellent translations of important texts and has a good introduction to the tradition. *A Thousand Teachings: The Upadeśasāhasrī of Śaṅkara*, translated with introduction and notes by Sengaku Mayeda (Tokyo: University of Tokyo Press, 1979), is the source of the Śaṅkara selections here and has an excellent introduction to Śaṅkara's philosophical thought.[1]

Selections form Rāmānuja are from the *Vedārthasaṁgraha of Śrī Rāmānujācārya*, translated by S. S. Raghavachar (Mysore: Sri Ramakrishna Ashrama, 1956). A good place to begin study of Rāmānuja's religious philosophy is *The Theology of Rāmānuja: An Essay in Interreligious Understanding*, by John B. Carman (New Haven: Yale University Press, 1974). *The Face of Truth: A Study of Meaning and Metaphysics in the Vedāntic Theology of Rāmānuja*, by Julius J. Lipner (Albany: State University of New York Press, 1986). is an interesting examination of Rāmānuja's metaphysics from a theological perspective. *Śrī Rāmānuja's Theory of Knowledge*, by K. C. Varadachari (Tirupati: Tirumalai-Tirupati Devasthanam Press, 1943), remains the best work on this subject.

I.
Śaṅkara: A Thousand Teachings*

A. METRICAL PART

Chapter 1

Pure Consciousness

1. Salutation to the all-knowing Pure Consciousness which pervades all, is all, abides in the hearts of all beings, and is beyond all objects of knowledge.

2. Having completed all the rituals, preceded by the marriage ceremony and the ceremony of installing the sacred fire, the *Veda* has now begun to utter knowledge of *Brahman*.

3. *Karmans* as the results of actions, good or bad, in the past existence produce association with a body. When there is association with a body, pleasant and unpleasant things are inevitable. From these result passion and aversion and from them actions.

4. From actions merit and demerit result and from merit and demerit there results an ignorant man's association with a body in the same manner again. Thus this transmigratory existence rolls onward powerfully forever like a wheel.

---

[1]This work, currently out of print, is scheduled for republication by State University of New York Press (Albany, N.Y.) in 1991.

*Reprinted with permission from Sengaku Mayeda, *A Thousand Teachings: The Upadeśasāhasrī of Śaṅkara* (Tokyo: University of Tokyo Press, 1979).

5. Since the root cause of this transmigratory existence is ignorance, its destruction is desired. Knowledge of *Brahman* therefore is entered on. Final beatitude results from this knowledge.

6. Only knowledge of *Brahman* can destroy ignorance; action cannot destroy it since action is not incompatible with ignorance. Unless ignorance is destroyed, passion and aversion will not be destroyed.

7. Unless passion and aversion are destroyed, action arises inevitably from [those] faults. Therefore, for the sake of final beatitude, only knowledge [of *Brahman*] is set forth here [in the Vedānta].

8. Objection: "Should not certain action too always be performed while life lasts? For this action, being concomitant with knowledge of *Brahman* leads to final release.

9. "Action, like knowledge of *Brahman*, should be adhered to, since both of them are equally enjoined by the *Śrutis* [Sacred teachings]. As the *Smṛti* [tradition] also lays it down that transgression results from the neglect of action, so action should be performed by seekers after final release.

10. "If you say that as knowledge of *Brahman* has permanent fruit, and so does not depend upon anything else, we reply: Not so! Just as the *Agniṣṭoma* sacrifice, though it has permanent fruit, depends upon things other than itself,

11. "so, though knowledge of *Brahman* has permanent fruit, it always depends upon action. Thus some people think." Reply: Not so, because action is incompatible with knowledge.

12. In fact action is incompatible with knowledge of *Brahman*, since it is associated with misconception of *Ātman*. And knowledge of *Brahman* is declared here to be the view that *Ātman* is changeless.

13. From the notion, "I am agent; this is mine" arises action. Knowledge of *Brahman* depends upon the real, whereas the Vedic injunction depends upon an agent.

14. Knowledge destroys the factors of action as it destroys the notion that there is water in the salt desert. After accepting this true view, how would one decide to perform action?

15. Because of the incompatibility of knowledge with action a man who knows thus, being possessed of this knowledge, cannot perform action. For this reason action should be renounced by a seeker after final release.

16. It is the innate assumption of people that *Ātman* is not distinct from the body and the like. This arises from nescience. So long as they have it, the Vedic injunction to perform actions would be valid.

17. The *Śruti* passage, "Not thus! Not so!" (Bṛh. Up. II,3,6),[1] excluding

---

[1]The sources of Śaṅkara's quotations from the Upaniṣads are identified in the text using abbreviated titles: *Up.* for *Upaniṣad*; *Bṛh* for *Bṛhadāraṇyaka*; Kaṭh for *Kaṭha*; *Muṇḍ.* for *Muṇḍaka*; and *Chānd.* for *Chāndogya*.

the body and the like, leaves *Ātman* unexcluded so that one may know *Ātman* free from distinction. Thereby nescience is removed.

18. Once nescience has been removed through the right means of knowledge, how can it arise again, since it does not exist in the one alone, the inner *Ātman* free from distinction?

19. If nescience cannot arise again, how can there be the notions, I am an agent, I am an experiencer," when there is the knowledge, "I am the Existent"? Therefore knowledge has no helper.

20. Renunciation is therefore said by the *Śruti* to "be superior" (M.N. Up. 21,2) to the actions there enumerated, beginning with truth and ending with mental activity. "Only this much," says the Vājins' *Śruti,*

21. "is, verily, the means to immortality" (Bṛh. Up. IV,5,15). Therefore action should be abandoned by seekers after final release. You said that, as with the *Agniṣṭoma* sacrifice, knowledge depends upon action. To this the following reply is given:

22. Because action has to be accomplished through various factors of action and varies in its result, knowledge is the opposite of it. Therefore the example is not applicable.

23. Since the *Agniṣṭoma* sacrifice, like agriculture, etc., has as its object a result to be accomplished through various factors of action, it requires support from other actions than itself. But what else does knowledge depend upon?

24. The transgression resulting from neglect of action is imputed only to one who has "I"-notion. A knower of *Ātman* has neither "I"-notion nor desire for the result of action.

25. Therefore, in order to destroy ignorance, end transmigratory existence, and set forth knowledge of *Brahman,* this Upaniṣad has been commenced.

26. And the word "Upaniṣad" may be derived from the verbal root "*sad*" preceded by the prefix "*upa-*" and "*ni-*" and followed by the suffix "*kvip,*" since it diminishes and destroys birth and the like.[1]

Chapter 2

Negation

1. As *Ātman* cannot be negated, It is left unnegated by the *Śruti,* "Not thus! Not so!" (Bṛh. Up. II,3,6). One attains It in some such way as "I am not this. I am not this."

2. The notion "I am this" arises from the *Ātman* which is identified with

[1]The point is that just as according to grammar the suffix "*kvip*" is destroyed by the root "*sad*" when preceded by "*upa-*" and "*ni-*," so ignorance and rebirth are destroyed when the knowledge of the Upaniṣad is realized.

"this" (= non-*Ātman*) and is within the range of a verbal handle. As it has its origin in the negated *ātman*, it could not become accepted as a right notion again as before.

3. Without negating a previous notion, a following view does not arise. The Seeing (= *Ātman*) is one alone, self-established. As It is the result of the right means of knowledge, It is not negated.

4. When one has traversed the forest of "this" (= non-*Ātman*) which is contaminated with anxiety, delusion, and so on, one arrives at one's own *Ātman*, just as the man from the land of Gandhāra arrived at Gandhāra through the forest.

Chapter 3

The Lord

1. If the Lord is non-*Ātman*, one ought not to dwell upon the knowledge "I am He." If He is *Ātman*, the knowledge "I am the Lord" destroys the other knowledge.

2. If, being different from *Ātman*, He is taken to have characteristics such as "not coarse," what is the use of them when He is not an object of knowledge? If He is *Ātman*, the notion of difference is destroyed by them.

3. Understand, therefore, that that predication of qualities such as "not coarse" are meant to negate false superimposition upon *Ātman*. If they were meant to negate false superimposition upon something other than *Ātman*, this would indeed be a description of emptiness (*śūnyatā*).

4. And if it is thought that they are meant to negate false superimposition upon something other than the inner *Ātman* of a man who wishes to know, the words of the *Śruti*, "He is . . . without breath, without mind, pure, higher than the high Imperishable" (Muṇḍ. Up. II,1,2), would also be meaningless.

Chapter 4

"I"-Notion

1. When action, which has the "I"-notion as its seed and is in the bearer of the "I"-notion (= the intellect), has been burnt up by the fire of the notion that "I am not an agent or an experiencer," how can it produce a result?

2. If you say: "Even after the action has been burnt up, production of a result of action will take place as previously experienced," we reply: No; it (= production of a result) is based upon other action. If you say, "When the "I"-notion as the seed of action has been destroyed, we ask you, How can there be that action beyond that which has been burnt up? Answer that,"

3. we reply: As action can fashion the body and so on, it can overpower knowledge in you concerning the Existent and produce a result. When action comes to an end, knowledge will arise.

4. As experience and knowledge are both results of action which has already begun to produce a result, it is reasonable that they are not contradictory to each other. But other action, namely that which has not yet begun to produce a result, is different in nature.

5. A man who has knowledge of *Ātman*, which negates the notion that the body is *Ātman* and is as firm as ordinary people's notion that the body is *Ātman*, is released even without wishing.

5'. Therefore, all this is established. The reasoning is as stated by us.

Chapter 5

Suspicion of Urine

1. Just as the sage Udaṅka did not accept the nectar, thinking that it was urine, so people do not accept the knowledge of *Ātman* out of fear that action will be destroyed.

2. *Ātman*, abiding in the intellect, is seen as it were moving and meditating when the intellect moves and meditates. The mistake about transmigratory existence is like that of a man in a moving boat who thinks that it is the trees along the shore which are moving.

3. Just as to a man in the boat the trees appear to move in a direction opposite to his movement, so does *Ātman* appear to transmigrate, since the *Śruti* reads, "He, remaining the same, goes along both worlds, appearing to think, appearing to move about" (Bṛh. Up. IV,3,7).

4. Intellect being pervaded by the reflection of Pure Consciousness, knowledge arises in it; and so sound and other objects of the sense-organs appear. By this people are deluded.

5. The "I"-notion appears to be as it were Pure Consciousness and exists for Its sake. And it does not do so when the "this"-portion has been destroyed. So this Pure Experience which is other than "this"-portion is the highest *Ātman*.

Chapter 6

Having Cut

1. *Ātman* Itself is not qualified by a hand which has been cut off and thrown away. Likewise, none of the rest of the body qualifies *Ātman*.

2. Therefore, every qualification is the same as a hand which has been thrown away, since it is non-*Ātman*. Therefore, the Knower (= *Ātman*) is devoid of all qualifications.

3. This whole universe is qualification, like a beautiful ornament, which is superimposed upon *Ātman* through nescience. Therefore, when *Ātman* has been known, the whole universe becomes non-existent.

4. One should always grasp *Ātman* alone as the Knower, disconnected from all qualifications, and abandon the object of knowledge. One should grasp that what is called "I" is also the same as a part which has been abandoned.

5. As long as the "this"-portion is a qualification of *ātman*, that "I"-portion is different from *Ātman* Itself. When the qualification has been destroyed, the Knower is established independently from it, as a man who owns a brindled cow is established independently from it.

6. The learned should abandon the "this"-portion in what is called "I," understanding that it is not *Ātman*. "I" in the sentence of the *Śruti* "I am *Brahman*" (Bṛh. Up. I,4,10) is the portion which has been left unabandoned in accordance with the above teaching.

Chapter 7

Located in the Intellect

1. Everything located in the intellect is always seen by Me in every case of cognition. Therefore, I am the highest *Brahman*; I am all-knowing and all-pervading.

2. Just as I am the Witness of the movements in My own intellect, so am I also the Witness of the movements in others' intellects. I can be neither rejected nor accepted. Therefore, I am indeed the highest *Ātman*.

3. There is no change in the *Ātman*, nor impurity, nor materiality, and because It is the Witness of all intellects, there is no limitation of its knowledge, as there is in the case of knowledge of intellect.

4. Just as in a jewel the forms such as red color are manifested in the sunshine, so in my presence everything becomes visible in the intellect. Therefore through Me everything becomes visible as the forms such as red color become visible through sunshine.

5. The object of knowledge in the intellect exists when the intellect exists; otherwise it does not exist. Since the Seer is always seer, duality does not exist.

6. Just as the intellect, from absence of discriminating knowledge, holds that the highest *Ātman* does not exist, just so when there is discriminating knowledge, nothing but the highest *Ātman* exists, not even the intellect itself.

Chapter 8

The Nature of Pure Consciousness

1. I Myself have the nature of Pure Consciousness, O Mind; My apparent connection with taste, etc., is caused by your delusion. Therefore no result due to your activity would belong to Me, since I am free from all attributes.

2. Abandon here activity born of illusion and come ever to rest from search for the wrong, since I am forever the highest *Brahman*, released, as it were, unborn, one alone, and without duality.

3. And I am always the same to beings, one alone; I am the highest *Brahman* which, like the sky, is all-pervading, imperishable, auspicious, uninterrupted, undivided and devoid of action. Therefore no result from your efforts here pertains to Me.

4. I am one alone; No other than that *Brahman* is thought to be Mine. In like manner I do not belong to anything since I am free from attachment. I have by nature no attachment. Therefore I do not need you nor your work since I am non-dual.

5. Considering that people are attached to cause and effect, I have composed this dialogue, making them understand the meaning of the truth of their own nature, so that they may be released from their attachment to cause and effect.

6. If a man ponders on this dialogue, he will be released from ignorance, the origin of great fears. And such a man is always free from desire; being a knower of *Ātman*, he is ever free from sorrow, the same to beings, and happy.

Chapter 9

Subtlety

1. It is to be known that in the series beginning with earth and ending with the inner *Ātman*, each succeeding one is more subtle and more pervasive than the preceding one which has been abandoned.

2. The means of knowledge show that external earth is the same as the bodily earth. External water and all the other elements should be known to be the same as bodily elements.

3. Just as the clear sky is all-pervading before the origination of air and other elements, so am I always one alone, all, Pure Consciousness only, all-pervading and non-dual.

4. It is said that all beings from Brahmā down to the plants are my body. From what else can the faults such as desire and anger arise in Me?

5. Although I am always untouched by the faults of beings, being the Lord who abides in all beings, yet people look upon Me as contaminated by the faults of beings just as an ignorant person looks upon the sky as blue.

6. As the intellects of all beings are always to be illuminated by My Pure Consciousness, all beings are the body of Me who am all-knowing and free from evils.

7. The object of knowledge in the waking state is looked upon as having an origin, as is the object of knowledge in the dreaming state. True knowledge is constant and without object; hence duality does not exist.

8. The Knower's Knowing is indeed said to be constant, for nothing else exists in the state of deep sleep. Knowing in the waking state results from nescience; therefore the object of knowledge should be looked upon as unreal.

Chapter 10

Seeing

1. The highest *Brahman*—which is of the nature of Seeing, like the sky, ever-shining, unborn, one alone, imperishable, stainless, all-pervading, and non-dual—That am I and I am forever released. Om.

2. I am Seeing, pure and by nature changeless. There is by nature no object for me. Being the Infinite, completely filled in front, across, up, down, and in every direction, I am unborn, abiding in Myself.

3. I am unborn, deathless, free from old age, immortal, self-effulgent, all-pervading, non-dual; I am neither cause nor effect, altogether stainless, always satisfied and therefore constantly released. Om.

4. Whether in the state of deep sleep or of waking or of dreaming, no delusive perception appears to pertain to me in this world. As those three states have no existence, self-dependent or other-dependent, I am always the Fourth, the Seeing and the non-dual.

5. The continuous series of pains due to the body, the intellect and the senses is neither I nor of Me, for I am changeless. And this is because the continual series of pain is unreal; it is indeed unreal like an object seen by a dreaming man.

6. It is true that I have neither change nor any cause of change, since I am non-dual. I have neither good nor bad deeds, neither final release nor bondage, neither caste nor stages of life, since I am bodiless.

7. Since I am beginningless and attributeless, I have neither action nor result of action. Therefore I am the highest *Ātman*, non-dual. Just as the ether, though all-pervading, is not stained, so am I not either, though abiding in the body, since I am subtle.

8. And I am always the same to all beings, the Lord, for I am superior to, and higher than, the perishable and the imperishable. Though I have the highest *Ātman* as my true nature and am non-dual, I am nevertheless covered with wrong knowledge which is nescience.

9. Being perfectly stainless, *Ātman* is distinguished from, and broken by, nescience, residual impression, and actions. Being filled with powers such as Seeing, I am non-dual, standing perfect in my own nature and motionless like the sky.

10. He who sees *Ātman* with the firm belief "I am the highest *Brahman*" "is born no more" (Kath. Up. I,38), says the *Śruti*. When there is no seed, no fruit is produced. Therefore there is no birth, for there is no delusion.

11. "This is mine, being thus," "That is yours, being of such kind," "Likewise, I am so, not superior nor otherwise"—such assumptions of people concerning *Brahman*, which is the same to all beings, non-dual and auspicious, are nothing but their stupidity.

12. When there is completely non-dual and stainless knowledge, then the great-souled experiences neither sorrow nor delusion. In the absence of both there is neither action nor birth. This is the firm belief of those who know the *Veda*.

13. He who, in the waking state, like a man in the state of deep sleep, does not see duality, though actually seeing, because of his non-duality, and similarly he who, though in fact acting, is actionless—he only is the knower of *Ātman*, and nobody else. This is the firm conclusion here.

14. This view which has been declared by me from the standpoint of the highest truth is the supreme view as ascertained in the Vedānta. If a man has firm belief in it, he is released and not stained by actions, as others are.

Chapter 12

In the Sunlight

1. Just as a man thinks that a body in sunlight is itself bright, so he thinks that the mind which appears to be the Seer is indeed "I, the Seer."

2. Whatever is seen in this world, *Ātman* comes to be identified with it. Consequently a man is deluded and so he does not recognize *Ātman.*

3. Just as the lad who was himself the tenth thought that he was among the nine others, so these deluded folk think that *Ātman* is among the objects of knowledge such as the intellect and do not understand otherwise.

4. Explain reasonably how the two incompatible notions, "You should act" and "You are That," can exist at the same time and have the same locus.

5. He who misconceives the body as *Ātman* has pain; he who has no body has by nature no pain, as in the sleeping state. In order to remove pain from the Seeing, the *Śruti* says, "Thou art That" (Chānd. Up. VI,8,7, etc.).

6. A *Yogin*, seeing the notion of the intellect on which the reflection of the Seeing (= *Ātman*) is mounted like the reflection of a face in a mirror, thinks that *Ātman* is seen.

7. Only if he knows that the various deluded notions do not belong to the Seeing, is he beyond doubt the best of *Yogins*. No one else can be.

8. "Understander of understanding" is what is meant by the word "Thou" in the sentence, "Thou art That" (Chānd. Up. VI, 8,7, etc.) Therefore this is the right apprehension of this word; any other apprehension is false.

9. Since I am always of the nature of the Seeing and constant, how is it possible for Me sometimes to see and sometimes not to see? Therefore any apprehension of the word different from that is not accepted.

10. Just as the body, the site of the sun's heat, is an object to the Seeing, so the intellect here is the site of pain—corresponding to heat in the example; therefore, the intellect is the object to the Seeing.

11. The Knower whose "this"-portion has been negated is homogeneous like ether, non-dual, ever-free and pure. He is Myself; I am *Brahman*, alone.

12. There can never be another understander superior to the Understander; therefore, I am the highest Understander, being always released in all beings.

13. He who knows that *Ātman's* Seeing is undiminished and that *Ātman* is not a doer, abandoning the very notion that he is a knower of *Brahman*, he alone is a knower of *Ātman* and no one else.

14. The discriminating notion, "I am the Knower, not the object of knowledge, pure, always released," also belongs to the intellect, since it is the object of cognition and perishable.

15. Since *Ātman's* Seeing is undiminished and not produced by factors of action, the false assumption that this Seeing can be produced is made by another seeing which is Its object.

16. The notion that *Ātman* is a doer is false, since it is due to the belief that the body is *Ātman*. The belief, "I do not do anything," is true and arises from the right means of knowledge.

17. The notion that *Ātman* is a doer is due to factors of action whereas the notion that It is not a doer is due to Its own nature. It has been fully ascertained that the understanding, "I am a doer," "I am an experiencer," is false.

18. When one's own nature has thus been understood by means of the scripture and inference, how can this understanding, "I am to be enjoined to act," be true?

19. Just as ether is within all, so am I within even ether itself; I am always changeless, motionless, pure, free from old age, released, and non-dual.

Chapter 13

Eyelessness

1. As I am eyeless, I do not see. Likewise, as I am earless, how shall I hear? As I have no organ of speech, I do not speak. As I am mindless, how shall I think?

2. As I am devoid of the life principle, I do not act. Being without intellect, I am not a knower. Therefore I have neither knowledge nor nescience, having the light of Pure Consciousness only.

3. Ever-free, pure, transcendentally changeless, invariable, immortal, imperishable, and thus always bodiless.

4. All pervading like ether, I have neither hunger nor thirst, neither sorrow nor delusion, neither decay nor death, since I am bodiless.

5. As I have no sense of touch, I do not touch. As I have no tongue, I do not perceive taste. As I am of the nature of constant knowledge, I never have either knowledge or ignorance.

6. The modification of the mind, which is caused by the eye and takes on form-and-color of its object, is certainly always seen by the constant Seeing of *Ātman.*

7. In like manner the modifications of the mind which are connected with the senses other than the eye and are colored by external objects; also the modification of the mind in the form of memory and in the forms of passion and the like, which is unconnected from the senses, located in the mind;

8. And the modifications of the mind in the dreaming state are also seen to be an other's. The Seeing of the Seer is, therefore, constant, pure, infinite, and alone.

9. The Seeing is wrongly taken to be inconstant and impure because of the absence of discriminating knowledge with regard to It. Similarly, I experience pleasure and pain through a seeing which is the object and adjunct of the Seeing.

10. Through deluded seeing all people think, "I am deluded," and again through a pure seeing they think, "I am pure"; for this reason they continue in transmigratory existence.

11. If one is a seeker after final release in this world, he should always remember *Ātman* which is ever-free described in the scripture as eyeless, etc., which includes the exterior and the interior, and is unborn.

12. And as the scripture says that I am eyeless, etc., no senses at all belong to Me. And there are the words in the Muṇḍ. Up. II,1,2 belonging to the *Atharvaveda,* "He is . . . breathless, mindless, pure."

13. As it is stated in the Kath. Up. (I,3,15) that I do not have sound, etc., and in the Muṇḍ. Up. (II,1,2) that I am "without breath, without mind," I am indeed always changeless.

14. Therefore, mental restlessness does not belong to Me. Therefore, concentration does not belong to Me. Both mental restlessness and concentration belong only to the changeable mind.

15. As I am without mind and pure, how can those two (= restlessness and concentration) belong to me? Freedom from mind and freedom from change belong to Me who am bodiless and all pervading.

16. Thus, as long as I had this ignorance, I had duties to perform, though I am ever-free, pure, and always enlightened.

17. How can concentration, non-concentration, or anything else which is to be done belong to Me? For, having meditated on and known Me, they realize that they have completed all that had to be done.

18. "I am *Brahman*" (Bṛh. Up. I,4,10). I am all, always pure, enlightened and unfettered, unborn, all-pervading, undecaying, immortal, and imperishable.

19. In no being is there any Knower other than Myself; I am the Overseer of deeds, the Witness, the Observer, constant, attributeless, and non-dual.

20. I am neither existent nor non-existent nor both, being alone and auspicious. To Me, the Seeing, there is neither twilight nor night nor day at any time.

21. Just as ether is free from all forms, is subtle and non-dual, so am I devoid even of this ether, I am *Brahman*, non-dual.

22. My separatedness, *i.e.*, in the form "my *ātman*," "his *ātman*," and "your *ātman*," is what is falsely constructed on Me, just as the difference of one and the same ether arises from the difference of holes in various objects.

23. Difference and non-difference, one and many, object of knowledge and knower, movement and mover—how can these notions be falsely constructed on Me who am one alone?

24. Nothing to be rejected or accepted belongs to Me, for I am changeless, always released and pure, always enlightened, attributeless, and non-dual.

25. Thus, with concentrated mind, one should always know everything as *Ātman*. Having known Me to be abiding in one's own body, one is a sage, released and immovable.

26. If a *Yogin* thus knows the meaning of the truth, he is one who has completed all that was to be done, a perfected one and knower of *Brahman*. If he knows otherwise, he is a slayer of *Ātman*.

27. The meaning of the *Veda* herein determined, which has been briefly related by me, should be imparted to serene wandering ascetics by one of disciplined intellect.

B. PROSE PART

Chapter 2

Awareness

45. A certain student, who was tired of transmigratory existence characterized by birth and death and was seeking after final release, approached in the prescribed manner a knower of *Brahman* who was established in *Brahman* and sitting at his ease, and asked him, "Your Holiness, how can I be released from transmigratory existence? I am aware of the body, the senses and their objects; I experience pain in the waking state, and I experience it in the dreaming state after getting relief again and again by entering into the state of deep sleep again and again. Is it indeed my own nature or is it due to some cause, my own nature being different? If this is my own nature, there is no hope for me to attain final release, since one cannot avoid one's own nature. If it is due to some cause, final release is possible after the cause has been removed."

46. The teacher replied to him, "Listen, my child, this is not your own nature but is due to a cause."

47. When he was told this the pupil said, "What is the cause? And what will remove it? And what is my own nature? When the cause is removed, the effect due to the cause no longer exists; I will attain to my own nature like a sick person who recovers his health when the cause of his disease has been removed."

48. The teacher replied, "The cause is nescience; it is removed by knowledge. When nescience has been removed, you will be released from transmigratory existence which is characterized by birth and death, since its cause will be gone and you will no longer experience pain in the dreaming and waking states."

49. The pupil said, "What is that nescience? And what is its object? And what is knowledge, remover of nescience, by which I can realize my own nature?"

50. The teacher replied, "Though you are the highest *Ātman* and not a transmigrator, you hold the inverted view, 'I am a transmigrator.' Though you are neither an agent nor an experiencer, and exist eternally, you hold the inverted view, 'I am an agent, an experiencer, and do not exist eternally— this is nescience."

51. The pupil said, "Even though I exist eternally, still I am not the highest *Ātman.* My nature is transmigratory existence which is characterized by agency and experiencership, since it is known by sense-perception and other means of knowledge. Transmigratory existence has not nescience as its cause, since nescience cannot have one's own *Ātman* as its object.

Nescience is defined as the superimposition of the qualities of one thing upon another. For example, fully known silver is superimposed upon fully known mother-of-pearl, a fully known person upon a fully known tree trunk, or a fully known trunk upon a fully known person; but not an unknown thing upon one that is fully known nor a fully known thing upon one that is unknown. Nor is non-*Ātman* superimposed upon *Ātman* because *Ātman* is not fully known, nor *Ātman* superimposed upon non-*Ātman*, again because *Ātman* is not fully known."

52. The teacher said to him, "That is not right, since there is an exception. My child, it is not possible to make a general rule that a fully known thing is superimposed only upon a fully known thing, since it is a matter of experience that a fully known thing is superimposed upon *Ātman.* For example, if one says, 'I am white,'' 'I am dark,' this is the superimposition of qualities of the body upon *Ātman* which is the object of the 'I'-notion. And if one says, 'I am this,' this is the superimposition of *Ātman*, which is the object of the 'I'-notion, upon the body."

53. The pupil said, "In that case *Ātman* is indeed fully known as the object of the 'I'-notion; so is the body as 'this.' If so, it is only a case of the mutual superimposition of body and *Ātman*, both fully known, just like the mutual superimposition of tree-trunk and person, and of mother-of-pearl and silver. So, is there a particular reason why Your Holiness said that it is not possible to make a general rule that two fully known things are mutually superimposed?"

54. The teacher replied, "Listen. It is true that the body and *Ātman* are fully known; but they are not fully known to all people as the objects of distinct notions like a tree-trunk and a person."

"How are they known then?"

"They are always known as the objects of constantly non-distinct notions. Since nobody grasps the body and *Ātman* as two distinct notions, saying, 'This is the body, that is *Ātman*,' people are deluded with regard to *Ātman* and non-*Ātman*, thinking, '*Ātman* is thus' or '*Ātman* is not thus.' This is the particular reason why I said that it is impossible to make a general rule."

55. The pupil raised another objection: "Is it not experienced that the thing which is superimposed upon something else through nescience does not exist in the latter? For example, silver does not exist in a mother-of-pearl nor a person in a tree-trunk nor a snake in a rope; nor the dark color of the earth's surface in the sky. Likewise, if the body and *Ātman* are always mutually superimposed in the form of constantly non-distinct notions, then they cannot exist in each other at any time. Silver, etc., which are superimposed through nescience upon mother-of-pearl, etc., do not exist in the latter at any time in any way and *vice versa;* likewise the body and *Ātman* are mutually superimposed through nescience; this being the case, it would follow as the result that neither the body nor *Ātman* exists. And it is not acceptable, since it is the theory of the Nihilists.

If, instead of mutual superimposition, only the body is superimposed upon *Ātman* through nescience, it would follow as the result that the body does not exist in *Ātman* while the latter exists. This is not acceptable either since it is contradictory to sense-perception and other means of knowledge. For this reason the body and *Ātman* are not superimposed upon each other through nescience."

"How then?"

"They are permanently connected with each other like bamboo and pillars which are interlaced in the structure of a house."

56. The teacher said, "No; because it would follow as the result that *Ātman* is non-eternal and exists for another's sake; since in your opinion *Ātman* is composite, *Ātman* exists for another's sake and is non-eternal just like bamboo, pillars, and so forth. Moreover, the *Ātman* which is assumed by some others to be connected with the body exists for another's sake since it is composite. Therefore, it has been first established that the highest *Ātman* is not connected with the body, is different from it, and is eternal.

57. The pupil objected: "Although the *Ātman* is not composite, It is regarded merely as the body and superimposed upon the body; from this follow the results that the *Ātman* does not exist and that It is non-eternal and so on. Then there would arise the fault that you will arrive at the Nihilists' position that the body has no *Ātman*."

58. The teacher replied, "Not so; because it is accepted that *Ātman*, like space, is by nature not composite. Although *Ātman* exists as connected with nothing, it does not follow that the body and other things are without *Ātman*, just as, although space is connected with nothing, it does not follow that nothing has space. Therefore, there would not arise the fault that I shall arrive at the Nihilists' position.

59. "Your further objection—namely that, if the body does not exist in *Ātman* although *Ātman* exists, this would contradict sense-perception and the other means of knowledge: this is not right, because the existence of the body in *Ātman* is not cognized by sense-perception and the other means of knowledge; in *Ātman*—like a jujube-fruit in a pot, ghee in milk, oil in sesame and a picture on a wall—the body is not cognized by sense-perception and the other means of knowledge. Therefore there is no contradiction with sense-perception and other means of knowledge."

60. The pupil objected, "How is the body then superimposed upon *Ātman* which is not established by sense-perception and the other means of knowledge, and how is *Ātman* superimposed upon the body?"

61. The teacher said, "That is not a fault, because *Ātman* is established by Its own nature. A general rule cannot be made that superimposition is made only on that which is adventitiously established and not on that which is permanently established, for the dark color and other things on the surface of the earth are seen to be superimposed upon the sky which is permanently established."

62. The pupil asked, "Your Holiness, is the mutual superimposition of the body and *Ātman* made by the composite of the body and so on or by *Ātman*?"

63. The teacher said, "What would happen to you, if the mutual superimposition is made by the composite of the body and so on, or if it is made by *Ātman*?"

64. Then the pupil answered, "If I am merely the composite of the body and so on, then I am non-conscious, so I exist for another's sake; consequently, the mutual superimposition of body and *Ātman* is not effected by me. If I am the highest *Ātman* different from the composite of the body and so on, then I am conscious, so I exist for my own sake; consequently, the superimposition of body which is the seed of every calamity is effected upon *Ātman* by me who am conscious."

65. To this the teacher responded, "If you know that the false superimposition is the seed of every calamity, then do not make it!"

66. "Your Holiness, I cannot help it. I am driven to do it by another; I am not independent."

67. The teacher said, "Then you are non-conscious, so you do not exist for your own sake. That by which you who are not self-dependent are driven to act is conscious and exists for its own sake; you are only a composite thing of the body, etc."

68. The pupil objected, "If I am non-conscious, how do I perceive feelings of pleasure and pain, and the words you have spoken?"

69. The teacher said, "Are you different from feelings of pleasure and pain and from the words I have spoken, or are you identical with them?"

70. The pupil answered, "I am indeed not identical."

"Why?"

"Because I perceive both of them as objects just as I perceive a jar and other things as objects. If I were identical with them I could not perceive either of them; but I do perceive them, so I am different from both of them. If I were identical with them it would follow that the modifications of the feelings of pleasure and pain exist for their own sake and so do the words you have spoken; but it is not reasonable that any of them exists for their own sake, for the pleasure and pain produced by a sandal and a thorn are not for the sake of the sandal and the thorn, nor is use made of a jar for the sake of the jar. So, the sandal and other things serve my purpose, *i.e.*, the purpose of their perceiver, since I who am different from them perceive all the objects seated in the intellect."

71. The teacher said to him, "So, then, you exist for your own sake since you are conscious. You are not driven to act by another. A conscious being is neither dependent on another nor driven to act by another, for it is not reasonable that a conscious being should exist for the sake of another conscious being since they are equal like two lights. Nor does a conscious being exist for the sake of a non-conscious being since it is not reasonable that a non-conscious being should have any connection with its own object precisely because it is non-conscious. Nor does experience show that two non-conscious beings exist for each other, as for example a stick of wood and a wall do not fulfill each other's purposes."

72. The pupil objected, "Is it not experienced that a servant and his master, though they are equal in the sense of being conscious, exist for each other?"

73. The teacher said, "It is not so, for what I meant was that you have consciousness just as fire has heat and light. And in this meaning I cited the example, 'like two lights.' This being the case, you perceive everything seated in your intellect through your own nature, *i.e.*, the transcendentally changeless, eternal, pure consciousness which is equivalent to the heat and light of fire. And if you admit that *Ātman* is always without distinctions, why did you say, 'After getting relief again and again in the state of deep sleep, I perceive pain in the waking and dreaming states. Is this indeed my own nature or is it due to some cause?' Has this delusion left you now or not?"

74. To this the pupil replied, "Your Holiness, the delusion has gone thanks to your gracious assistance; but I am in doubt as to how I am transcendentally changeless."

"How?"

"Sound and other external objects are not self-established, since they are not conscious. But they are established through the rise of notions which take the forms of sound and other external objects. It is impossible for notions to be self-established, since they have mutually exclusive attributes and the forms of external objects such as blue and yellow. It is, therefore, understood that notions are caused by the forms of the external objects; so, notions are established as possessing the forms of external objects, *i.e.*, the forms of sound, etc. Likewise, notions, which are the modifications of a thing (= the intellect), the substratum of the 'I'-notion, are also composite, so it is reasonable that they are non-conscious; therefore, as it is impossible that they exist for their own sake, they, like sound and other external objects, are established as objects to be perceived by a perceiver different in nature from them. If I am not composite, I have pure consciousness as my nature; so I exist for my own sake. Nevertheless, I am a perceiver of notions which have the forms of the external objects such as blue and yellow and so I am indeed subject to change. For the above reason, I am in doubt as to how I am transcendentally changeless."

75. The teacher said to him, "Your doubt is not reasonable. Your perception of those notions is necessary and entire; for this very reason you are not subject to transformation. It is, therefore, established that you are transcendentally changeless. But you have said that precisely the reason for the above positive conclusion—namely, that you perceive the entire movement of the mind—is the reason for your doubt concerning your transcendental changelessness. This is why your doubt is not reasonable.

If indeed you were subject to transformation, you would not perceive the entire movement of the mind which is your object, just as the mind does not perceive its entire object and just as the senses do not perceive their entire objects, and similarly you as *Ātman* would not perceive even a part of your object. Therefore, you are transcendentally changeless."

76. Then the pupil said, "Perception is what is meant by the verbal root, that is, nothing but change; it is contradictory to this fact to say that the nature of the perceiver is transcendentally changeless."

77. The teacher said, "That is not right, for the term 'perception' is used figuratively in the sense of a change which is meant by the verbal root; whatever the notion of the intellect may be, that is what is meant by the verbal root; the notion of the intellect has change as its nature and end, with the result that the perception of *Ātman* falsely appears as perceiver; thus the notion of the intellect is figuratively indicated by the term, 'perception.' For example, the cutting action results in the static state that the object to be cut is separated in two parts; thus the term, 'cutting,' in the sense of an object to be cut being separated in two parts, is used figuratively as the cutting action which is meant by the verbal root."

78. To this the pupil objected, "Your Holiness, the example cannot explain my transcendental changelessness."

"Why not?"

"'Cutting' which results in a change in the object to be cut is used figuratively as the cutting action which is meant by the verbal root; in the same manner, if the notion of the intellect, which is figuratively indicated by the term 'perception' and is meant by the verbal root, results also in a change in the perception of *Ātman*, the example cannot explain *Ātman*'s transcendental changelessness."

79. The teacher said, "It would be true, if there were a distinction between perception and perceiver. The perceiver is indeed nothing but eternal perception. And it is not right that perception and perceiver are different as in the doctrine of the logicians."

80. The pupil said, "How does that action which is meant by the verbal root result in perception?"

81. The teacher answered, "Listen, I said that it ends with the result that the perception of *Ātman* falsely appears as perceiver. Did you not hear? I did not say that it results in the production of any change in *Ātman.*

82. The pupil said, "Why then did you say that if I am transcendentally changeless I am the perceiver of the entire movement of the mind which is my object?"

83. The teacher said to him, "I told you only the truth. Precisely because you are the perceiver of the entire movement of the mind, I said, you are transcendentally changeless."

84. "If so, Your Holiness, I am of the nature of transcendentally changeless and eternal perception whereas the notions of the intellect, which have the forms of external objects such as sound, arise and end with the result that my own nature which is perception falsely appears as perceiver. Then what is my fault?"

85. The teacher replied, "You are right. You have no fault. The fault is only nescience as I have said before."

86. The pupil said, "If, Your Holiness, as in the state of deep sleep I undergo no change, how do I experience the dreaming and waking states?"

87. The teacher said to him, "But do you experience these states continuously?"

88. The pupil answered, "Certainly I do experience them, but intermittently and not continuously."

89. The teacher said to him, "Both of them are adventitious and not your nature. If they were your nature they would be self-established and continuous like your nature, which is Pure Consciousness. Moreover, the dreaming and waking states are not your nature, for they depart from you like clothes and so on. It is certainly not experienced that the nature of anything, whatever it may be, departs from it. But the dreaming and waking states depart from the state of Pure Consciousness-only. If one's own nature were to depart from oneself in the state of deep sleep, it would be negated by saying, 'It has perished,' 'It does not exist,' since the adventitious attributes which are not one's own nature are seen to consist in both perishableness and non-existence; for example, wealth, clothes, and the like are seen to perish and things which have been obtained in dream or delusion are seen to be non-existent."

90. The pupil objected, "If so, Your Holiness, it follows either that my own nature, *i.e.*, Pure Consciousness, is also adventitious, since I perceive in the dreaming and waking states but not in the state of deep sleep; or that I am not of the nature of Pure Consciousness."

91. The teacher replied, "No, Look. Because that is not reasonable. If you insist on looking at your own nature, *i.e.*. Pure Consciousness, as adventitious, do so! We cannot establish it logically even in a hundred years, not can any other (*i.e.* non-conscious) being do so. As that adventitious consciousness is composite, nobody can logically deny that it exists for another's sake, is manifold and perishable; for what does not exist for its own sake is not self-established, as we have said before. Nobody can, however, deny that *Ātman*, which is of the nature of Pure Consciousness, is self-established; so It does not depend upon anything else, since It does not depart from anybody."

92. The pupil objected, "Did I not point out that It does depart from me when I said that in the state of deep sleep I do not see?"

93. The teacher replied, "That is not right, for it is contradictory."

"How is it a contradiction?"

"Although you are in truth seeing, you say, 'I do not see.' This is contradictory."

"But at no time in the state of deep sleep, Your Holiness, have I ever seen Pure Consciousness or anything else."

"Then you are seeing in the state of deep sleep; for you deny only the seen object, not the seeing. I said that your seeing is Pure Consciousness. That eternally existing one by which you deny the existence of the seen object when you say that nothing has been seen, that precisely is the seeing that is Pure Consciousness. Thus as It does not ever depart from you Its transcendental changelessness and eternity are established solely by Itself without depending upon any means of knowledge. The knower, though self-established, requires means of knowledge for the discernment of an object to be known other than itself. And that eternal Discernment, which is required for discerning something else (= non-*Ātman*) which does not have Discernment as its nature — that is certainly eternal, transcendentally changeless, and of a self-effulgent nature. The eternal Discernment does not require any means of knowledge in order to be Itself the means of knowledge or the knower since the eternal Discernment is by nature the means of knowledge or the knower. This is illustrated by the following example: iron or water requires fire or sun to obtain light and heat since light and heat are not their nature; but fire and sun do not require anything else for light and heat since these are always their nature.

94. "If you object, 'There is empirical knowledge in so far as it is not eternal and there is no empirical knowledge if it is eternal,'

95. "then I reply, 'Not so; because it is impossible to make a distinction between eternal apprehension and non-eternal apprehension; when apprehension is empirical knowledge, such distinction is not apprehended that empirical knowledge is non-eternal apprehension and not eternal one.'

96. "If you object, 'When empirical knowledge is eternal apprehension, it does not require the knower, but when empirical knowledge is non-eternal apprehension, apprehension requires the knower, since it is mediated by the knower's effort. There would be the above distinction,'

97. "then, it is established that the knower itself is self-established, since it does not require any means of knowledge.

98. "If you object, 'Even when apprehension or empirical knowledge does not exist, the knower does not require any means of knowledge, since the knower is eternal,' my reply is, 'No; because apprehension exists only in the knower itself. Thus your opinion is refuted.

99. "If the knower is dependent upon the means of knowledge for its establishment, where does the desire to know belong? It is admitted that that to which the desire to know belongs is indeed the knower. And the object of this desire to know is the object to be known, not the knower, since if the object of the desire to know were the knower, a *regressus ad infinitum* with regard to the knower and the desire to know would result: there would be a second knower for the first one, a third knower for the second, and so on. Such would be the case if the desire to know had the knower as its object. And the knower itself cannot be the object to be known, since it is never mediated by anything; what in this world is called the object to be known is established, when it is mediated by the rise of desire, remembrance, effort, and means of knowledge which belong to the knower. In no other way is apprehension experienced with regard to the object to be known. And it cannot be assumed that the knower itself is mediated by any of the knower's own desire and the like. And remembrance has as its object the object to be remembered and not the subject of remembrance. Likewise, desire has as its object only the object desired and not the one who desires. If remembrance and desire had as their object the subject of remembrance and the one who desires respectively, a *regressus ad infinitum* would be inevitable as before.

100. "If you say, 'If apprehension which has the knower as its object is impossible, the knower would not be apprehended,'

101. "not so; because the apprehension of the apprehender has as its object the object to be apprehended. If it were to have the apprehender as its object, a *regressus ad infinitum* would result as before. And it has been proved before that apprehension, *i.e.*, the transcendentally changeless and eternal light of *Ātman*, is established in *Ātman* without depending upon anything else as heat and light are in fire, the sun, and so on. If apprehension, *i.e.*, the light of *Ātman* which is Pure Consciousness, were not eternal in one's own *Ātman*, it would be impossible for *Ātman* to exist for Its own sake; as It would be composite like the aggregate of the body and senses, It would exist for another's sake and be possessed of faults as we have already said."

"How?"

"If the light of *Ātman* which is Pure Consciousness were not eternal in one's own *Ātman*, it would be mediated by remembrance and the like and so it would be composite. And as this light of Pure Consciousness would therefore not exist in *Ātman* before Its origination and after Its destruction, It would exist for another's sake, since It would be composite like the eye and so on. And if the light of Pure Consciousness exists in *Ātman* as something which has arisen, then *Ātman* does not exist for Its own sake, since it is established according to the existence and absence of that light of Pure Consciousness that *Ātman* exists for Its own sake and non-*Ātman* exists for another's sake. It is therefore established that *Ātman* is the eternal light of Pure Consciousness without depending upon anything else."

102. The pupil objected, "If so, and if the knower is not the subject of empirical knowledge, how is it a knower?"

103. The teacher answered, "Because there is no distinction in the nature of empirical knowledge, whether it is eternal or non-eternal, since empirical knowledge is apprehension. There is no distinction in the nature of this empirical knowledge whether it be non-eternal, preceded by remembrance, desire, and the like, or transcendentally changeless and eternal, just as there is no distinction in the nature of what is meant by verbal root such as *sthā* (stand), whether it is a non-eternal result preceded by 'going' and other forms of actions, or an eternal result not preceded by 'going' or any other forms of actions; so the same expression is found in both cases: 'People stand,' 'The mountains stand,' and so forth. Likewise, although the knower is of the nature of eternal apprehension, it is not contradictory to designate It as 'knower,' since the result is the same."

104. Here the pupil said, "*Ātman*, which is of the nature of eternal apprehension, is changeless, so it is impossible for *Ātman* to be an agent without being connected with the body and the senses, just as a carpenter and other agents are connected with an axe and so on. And if that which is by nature not composite were to use the body and the senses, a *regressus ad infinitum* would result. But the carpenter and the other agents are constantly connected with the body and the senses; so, when they use an axe and the like, no *regressus ad infinitum* occurs."

105. The teacher said, "But in that case *Ātman*, which is by nature not composite, cannot be an agent when It makes no use of instruments; It would have to use an instrument to be an agent. But the use of an instrument would be a change; so in becoming an agent which causes that change, It should use another instrument, and in using this instrument, It should also use another one. Thus if the knower is independent, a *regressus ad infinitum* is inevitable.

And no action causes *Ātman* to act, since the action which has not been performed does not have its own nature. If you object, 'something other than

Ātman approaches *Ātman* and causes It to perform an action, I reply, 'No; because it is impossible for anything other than *Ātman* to be self-established, a non-object, and so forth; it is not experienced that anything else but *Ātman*, being non-conscious, is self-evident. Sound and all other objects are established when they are known by a notion which ends with the result of apprehension.

If apprehension were to belong to anything else but *Ātman*, It would also be *Ātman*, not composite, existing for Its own sake, and not for another. And we cannot apprehend that the body, the senses, and their objects exist for their own sake, since it is experienced that they depend for their establishment upon the notions which result in apprehension."

106. The pupil objected, "In apprehending the body nobody depends upon any other notions due to sense-perception and other means of knowledge."

107. The teacher said, "Certainly in the waking state it would be so. But in the states of death and deep sleep the body also depends upon sense-perception and other means of knowledge for its establishment. This is true of the senses. Sound and other external objects are indeed transformed into the form of the body and senses; so, the body and the senses depend upon sense-perception and other means of knowledge for their establishment. And 'establishment' (*siddhi*) is Apprehension, *i.e.*, the result of the means of knowledge as we have already said, and this Apprehension is transcendentally changeless, self-established, and by nature the light of *Ātman*."

108. Here the pupil objected, saying, "It is contradictory to say that Apprehension is the result of the means of knowledge and that It is by nature the transcendentally changeless and eternal light of *Ātman*.

To this [the teacher] said, "It is not contradictory."

"How then is it not contradictory?"

"Although Apprehension is transcendentally changeless and eternal, It appears at the end of the notion forming process due to sense-perception and other means of knowledge since the notion-forming process aims at It. If the notion due to sense-perception and other means of knowledge is non-eternal, Apprehension, though eternal, appears as if it were non-eternal. Therefore, Apprehension is figuratively called the result of the means of knowledge."

109. The pupil said, "If so, Your Holiness, Apprehension is transcendentally changeless, eternal, indeed of the nature of the light of *Ātman*, and self-established, since It does not depend upon any means of knowledge with regard to Itself; everything other than This is non-conscious and exists for another's sake, since it acts together with others.

And because of this nature of being apprehended as notion causing pleasure, pain, and delusion, non-*Ātman* exists for another's sake; on account of this very nature non-*Ātman* exists and not on account of any other nature. It is therefore merely non-existent from the standpoint of the highest truth. Just as it is experienced in this world that a snake superimposed upon a rope does not exist, nor water in a mirage, and the like, unless they are apprehended as a notion, so it is reasonable that duality in the waking and dreaming states also does not exist unless it is apprehended as a notion. In this manner, Your Holiness, Apprehension, *i.e*, the light of *Ātman*, is uninterrupted; so It is transcendentally changeless, eternal and non-dual, since It is never absent from any of the various notions. But various notions are absent from Apprehension. Just as in the dreaming state the notions in different forms such as blue and yellow, which are absent from that Apprehension, are said to be non-existent from the standpoint of the highest truth, so in the waking state also, the various notions such as blue and yellow, which are absent from this very Apprehension, must by nature be untrue. And there is no apprehender different from this Apprehension to apprehend It; therefore It can Itself neither be accepted nor rejected by Its own nature, since there is nothing else."

110. The teacher said, "Exactly so it is. It is nescience that is the cause of transmigratory existence which is characterized by the waking and dreaming states. The remover of this nescience is knowledge. And so you have reached fearlessness. From now on you will not perceive any pain in the waking and dreaming states. You are released from the sufferings of transmigratory existence."

111. The pupil said, "Om."

II.
A Summary of Vedic Teachings: Rāmānuja's *Vedārtha Saṁgraha**

1. The crown of the Vedas *i.e.*, the Upaniṣads, which lay down the good of the whole world, enshrines this truth: A seeker, after first acquiring a true understanding of the individual self and the Supreme and equipped with the performance of the duties pertaining to his station in life, must devote himself to the meditation, worship and adoring salutation of the blessed feet of the supreme Person. This affords immeasurable joy and leads to the attainment of the Supreme.

The individual self is subject to beginningless nescience, which has brought about an accumulation of karma, of the nature of both merit and demerit. The flood of such karma causes his entry into four kinds of bodies —heavenly, human, animal and plant beginning with that of Brahmā downwards. This ingression into bodies produces the delusion of identity with those respective bodies (and the consequent attachments and aversions). This delusion inevitably brings about all the fears inherent in the state of worldly existence. The entire body of Vedānta aims at the annihilation of these fears. To accomplish their annihilation they teach the following: (1) The essential nature of the individual self as transcending the body. (2) The

*Reprinted with permission from S. S. Raghavachar, *Vedārthasaṁgraha of Śrī Rāmānujācārya* (Mysore: Sri Ramakrishna Ashrama, 1956).

attributes of the individual self. (3) The essential nature of the Supreme that is the inmost controller of both the material universe and the individual selves. (4) The attributes of the Supreme. (5) The devout meditation upon the Supreme. (6) The goal to which such meditation leads. The Vedānta aims at making known the goal attainable through such a life of meditation, the goal being the realization of the real nature of the individual self and, after and through that realization, the direct experience of Brahman, which is of the nature of bliss infinite and perfect. The passages to this effect may be illustrated by the following: "That thou art (*Chā. VI, IX, 4*)"; "This self is Brahman (*Bṛ. VI, IV, 5*)"; "He, who dwells in the self, who is in the self, whom the self does not know, whose body this self is, who rules this self from within, that one is your self, the inner Ruler, the Immortal. (*Bṛ V, VII*)"; "He is the inner self of all creatures, free from all imperfections, the divine, the sole God Nārāyana (*Su. VII*)"; "The Brāhmaṇas desire to know this one, through the study of the Vedas through sacrifices, charity, austerities and fasting (*Bṛ. VI, IV, 22*)"; "The knower of Brahman attains the Highest (*Tai. II, 1*)"; "He who knows him thus attains immortality here. There is no other pathway to this goal (*Pu. VII*)."[1]

2. The essential nature of the individual self is devoid of the manifold distinctions pertaining to the various modifications of material nature constitutive of the bodies of the various kinds like heavenly and human. It has only knowledge and bliss as its attributes. When the bodily differentiations born of karma are destroyed, the essential individuality, indescribable but self-cognized, can only be represented as of the "nature of consciousness (*Vi, I, IV, 40*)." This essential nature is common to all individual selves.

This world, of the aforesaid nature, consisting of spiritual and physical entities, has the supreme Spirit, as the ground of its origination, maintenance, destruction and of the liberation of the individual from transmigratory existence. He, the supreme One, is unique, transcending in character every other entity, because his nature is opposed to all evil and is of the sole nature of supreme bliss. He is the abode of countless auspicious attributes unsurpassed in their perfection. He is Bhagavān Nārāyana, the highest Spirit. He is presented by the entire Vedānta, through variations of terminology as the "Soul of all," "Highest Brahman," "Highest Light," "Highest Reality," "Highest Self" and "Being." Such is the nature of the inner Controller. The Vedas devoted to the exposition of his glory, expound the fact that he controls all entities, sentient as well as non-sentient, as their indwelling self. (They do it in two ways): (1) They describe them as his "power," "part," "splendour," "form," "body" and "organism" and through such other terms. (2) They also affirm the oneness of these entities with him.

---

[1]The sources of Rāmānuja's quotation are identified in the text with abbreviated titles: *Ā.* for *Taittirīya Āraṇyaka*; *Bṛ.* for *Bṛhadāraṇyaka Upaniṣad*; *Bra.* for *Brahma Sūtras*; *Chā.* for *Chāndogya Upaniṣad*; Gītā for *Bhagavad Gītā*; *Ka.* for *Kaṭha Upaniṣad*; *Ma.* for *Manu Dharma Śāstra*; *Pu.* for *Puruṣa Sūkta* (*Rig Veda*, 10.90); *Su.* for *Subāla Upaniṣad*; *Śve* for *Śvetaśvatara Upaniṣad*; *Tai.* for *Taittirīya Upaniṣad*; and *Vi.* for *Viṣṇu Purāṇa*;

3. Some engaged in the explanation of these passages, like the proposition expressing identity, descriptive of the glory of Brahman put forth the following explanation: Undifferentiated consciousness alone is Brahman. It is eternally free and self-luminous. Still its identity with the individual self is made known through propositions positing identity such as "That thou art." Brahman itself, being ignorant, gets bound and is (subsequently) released. Apart from the undifferentiated consciousness, the whole universe, consisting of endless plurality exhibiting differences like that between Īśvara and the creatures, is unreal. That there is some one who is liberated and some one that is bound is an arrangement that does not exist. That some have attained liberation before now is not true. One body alone is ensouled. The other bodies are soul-less. It is not determined which that body is. The teacher who imparts knowledge is just a phenomenal appearance. The knower (in all cognitions) is also a phenomenal appearance. The scripture is also unreal. The knowledge arising out of the scripture is also unreal. All this is known from the scripture itself which is unreal. . . .

45. Further you hold that pure undifferentiated knowledge is Brahman and having its essential nature veiled by the veiling nescience, it observes pluralities within itself. Now this is an untenable doctrine. Veiling means elimination of light. As you do not admit an attributive light distinct from the substantive nature of Brahman, and as you hold that the substantive nature of Brahman is this light of knowledge, the postulated elimination of light would be the destruction of the substantive nature of Brahman. If it be said, "Light here means knowledge. Knowledge is eternal. The light of knowledge is veiled by nescience," we say in reply that these are contentions indicative of immaturity of thought. If the light is concealed by nescience, this concealment should take one of these two forms: It must obstruct the generation of light or it must annihilate the existing light. Since you do not admit that this light is subject to processes like generation, the concealment posited can be nothing but annihilation. When you assert that it is eternal and immutable and it abides as such, you are saying in effect that though nescience is there, nothing is concealed in Brahman. In the same breath you say that Brahman observes plurality. Surely a doctrine like this cannot be submitted to the scrutiny of those who know.

46. (***Objection***): But you too must hold that the essential nature of the ātman is consciousness. Ātman is self-luminous. To account for its wrong identification with the body, the concealment of the essential nature must be postulated. If the nature of an entity stands revealed, it is impossible that characteristics that do not belong to it can be wrongly attributed to it. Therefore, the difficulty, you urge against us, faces you also. Indeed the position is far worse for you. Since we maintain that there is only one self, the unaccountability urged attaches to our account of that one single entity. As you uphold the existence of an infinite number of selves, you have to face this charge of unaccountability in your account of all those infinite number of entities.

47. (***Reply***): Our thesis about the Reality and the ways of knowing can be formulated in this way: The supreme Brahman is by its inherent nature antithetical to all imperfections. Its substantive nature consists solely of infinite knowledge and bliss. It is an ocean of exalted attributes which are natural to it and are all-surpassing in their excellence. Its glories are boundless and not tainted by mutations in time, time which is the operative principle of change in the form of origination, subsistence and destruction and consists of limitless number of units, like seconds, minutes, hours up to vast epochs. Brahman has as the instruments of its mighty sport and as forming its own parts an infinite number of individual souls bound as well as free and also the physical universe, which latter has the power of passing through evolutions marvelous and boundless. Brahman is the inner ruler of the finite selves and the non-sentient nature. They form its body. It owns them as its modes. Such supreme Brahman is the reality to be known. The Veda, *Ṛk, Yajus, Sāman* and *Atharvan*, branching forth thousand-fold, beginningless and endless in its unbroken tradition, embodying the ultimate truth, is the basis of philosophical knowledge. This, in all its three sections, namely, injunctions, explanations and hymns, is supported and interpreted by the Itihāsas, Purāṇas, and Dharmaśāstras, composed by the great sages, like Bhagavān Dvaipāyana, Parāśara, Vālmīki, Manu, Yājñavalkya, Gautama and Āpastamba, who have attained the direct vision of the supreme Brahman. This body of transcendent knowledge, interpreted and augmented in the supplementary sacred texts of these perfect sages, is the final authority. Can there be any insuperable difficulty for us, possessed of this magnificent conception of knowledge and reality? . . .

51. (***Objection***): But what is the use of all this flourish? Our criticism remains unanswered.

(***Reply***): The answer follows. For us who hold this conception of Brahman and the Veda, the criticism has no force. Consciousness, we maintain, though an inherent attribute of the individual is subject to real contraction and expansion by the force of karma. Thus the difficulty urged is eliminated. For you, consciousness is the substantive nature of the self and not its attribute. You do not admit either contraction or expansion. In that case, concealing factors like karma bring about the non-origination of the spread of consciousness. If the nature of nescience is to veil, nescience, the agency that veils, must be, as urged before, destructive of the essential nature of consciousness itself. According to us karma, in the form of nescience, brings about the contraction of the consciousness that is an eternal attribute of the substantive nature of the ātman. By virtue of this contraction arises the wrong attitude to the self, taking it for gods, men, or any other empirical creature.

52. This position has been laid down thus: "The third power is nescience called karma. By this, the all-penetrating power of the individual knower is over-powered. Hence it becomes subject to the persistent afflictions of saṁsāra. Concealed by nescience, the power, called the individual knower, exists in all creatures in various grades (*Vi. VI, VII, 61–63*)." Thus the scripture points out that nescience, called karma, causes the contraction and expansion of the consciousness which forms a natural attribute of the individual self.

53. (***Objection***): This principle of concealing nescience has been postulated for two reasons: Some sacred texts posit it and the teaching of identity between the jīva and Brahman necessitates it. It has been maintained that this nescience veils the nature of Brahman.

(***Reply***): Now, we argue that this nescience is also phenomenal and unreal. Just as the manifold world being unreal, can become an object of perception only owing to a defect, namely this nescience, this nescience also, being equally phenomenal, presupposes a defect to account for its becoming an object of perception. Therefore nescience itself cannot be considered the fundamental and original defect, at the root of all illusion. Thus you will be driven to regard Brahman itself as the root of all illusions. Even if nescience is considered beginningless, since it can be beginningless only as phenomenal and as such, only as an object of the perception of Brahman, and since you do not admit a real, non-phenomenal defect as its root, Brahman itself must be the source of the illusory perception of nescience. Brahman being eternal, it follows that there can be no liberation.

54. The foregoing refutes by implication the following also. Only one body is animated by a jīva. The other bodies are not so inhabited by jīvas, as in the case of bodies seen in dreams. In dream, the body of the dreamer alone is ensouled. The many bodies that one observes in dreams are not ensouled. This one jīva of the dreamer fictitiously imagines the other jīvas and their bodies as existing. Therefore all (other) jīvas are unreal.

55. Really on your hypothesis, Brahman fictitiously sets up in imagination individuation and all bodies, which are both other than its essential nature. Even in a single body, since the body and likewise the individuation of the jīva in it, are unreal, all bodies are unreal and the individuation of the jīva in all of them is unreal. This being the case, there is no meaning in attaching any speciality to a single body and the individuation of the self in relation to it. In our account of the matter, the dreamer's body and the existence of the self in it, are not sublated in the waking state. The other bodies seen in dream and the individual souls embodied in them are sublated in the waking state. Therefore the latter are all unreal and the dreamer's body and soul are real. Herein lies the distinction.

56. Further, how is nescience eliminated? What is the nature of the elimination? These questions should be discussed.

(***Objection***): The unitive knowledge is the means for putting an end to nescience. The nature of that elimination of nescience lies in its being antithetical to the "indefinable" nescience and its effects.

57. (***Reply***): If this be your view, the following objection arises. To be antithetical to the "indefinable" is to be definable. The "definable" must be either existent or non-existent or both. There is no fourth alternative. If this "definable" termination of nescience is admitted to be other than Brahman, nescience (being the cause of the perception of everything other than Brahman) remains uneliminated. If Brahman itself is this elimination of nescience, the former being eternally real, this elimination must also be held to have existed eternally. Thus the elimination of nescience remains an accomplished fact prior to the rise of the knowledge of Vedānta. In consequence your philosophy holding that the unitive knowledge eliminates nescience and that the absence of that knowledge constitutes bondage stands nullified.

58. And again, the knowledge effecting the elimination of nescience is also, on your theory, a particular form of nescience. Through what means is that specific form of nescience removed? This knowledge eliminating nescience, eliminates all differentiations first and then, being momentary, disappears by itself without any other cause bringing about its disappearance. There are instances of self-annihilation in nature, like forest-fire and poison administered to expel poison. This argument is not open to you. This knowledge causing the termination of nescience is conceived by you as being other than Brahman. As such, its nature and the events connected with it like its origination and annihilation have only phenomenal existence. Therefore, the nescience that consists in bringing about the perception of this phenomenal event, namely, the annihilation of the eliminating knowledge, continues to exist. You have to provide for the factor that eliminates the nescience which consists in the perception of the self-annihilation of the knowledge that brings about the elimination of cosmic nescience. In the case of forest-fire etc., what disappears continues to exist in states other than the previous one and this continuance in and through a chain of states obtains necessarily.

59. And now let us turn to the knower involved in the knowledge that negates everything other than Brahman, which is of the nature of pure consciousness. Is that knower the ego that emerges from the fictitious subject-object superimposition? That would be untenable, for that ego falls within the area of the object of negation and therefore cannot be the subject of negation. If it be said that the knower is Brahman itself, then the question arises whether that knowership of Brahman is real or superimposed. If it is superimposed, then this superimposition and the nescience at the bottom of the superimposition remain, falling outside the scope of the negating knowledge. If another means is posited for the negation of that superimposition and the nescience that is its basis, that means also must be knowledge and must therefore involve the three factors, knower, knowledge and the known. Further discussion about this new knowledge, which is inevitable, lands the argument in infinite regress. All knowledge, bereft of these three factors, loses the character of being knowledge. All knowledge is the apprehension of an object by a subject. Any knowledge that is not of this nature, would be incapable of eliminating nescience, even as the consciousness constitutive of Brahman's nature—being devoid of this nature, is not capable of eliminating illusion. If you admit that the non-phenomenal nature of Brahman itself is to be the knower, you are accepting our theory itself.

60. The proposition that the *knowledge* that eliminates nescience and its effects and the *knowership* of the knower in that knowledge are also included in the body of what is eliminated sounds ridiculous like the proposition that "Everything other than the floor was cut by Devadatta and therefore in that process of cutting, the action of cutting, and the fact of Devadatta being a cutter, were also included in the body of what was cut."

61. Now, what is the source of this knowledge of unity, which eliminates plurality? If it be answered that śruti is the source, there is a difficulty. Śruti is different from Brahman and like everything else different from Brahman, it is a fabrication of nescience and therefore cannot give rise to the knowledge that negates the world. To explain: The illusion of snake generated by the deficiencies of the perceptual system, cannot be cancelled, by another cognition of the form, "This is a rope and not a snake," if that cognition owes its own origin to similar deficiencies of the perceptual system. When there is fear proceeding from the illusion of snake, the speech of another person, who is himself the victim of an illusion and who is known to be such a victim, even if he were to say, "This is no snake, it is just a rope," can remove neither the first illusory cognition nor the fear born of it. This applies to the present case, because to the competent student, at the very time of his learning the śruti, the śruti is known to be different from the pure Brahman and hence to be a production by illusion.

62. It also follows as the knowledge that is to eliminate the cosmic illusion, the knower in that knowledge and the source of that knowledge, namely, the scriptures, are all different from Brahman and therefore liable to negation, the sublation of the world would be unreal and the world, the contradictory of the sublation, must be treated as real. The man seen in the dream may report one's son's death in the dream and his words being false, the son would be alive of necessity. And again, the passages like "That thou art" are powerless to sublate the world, for they are products of illusion, just as the speech of the deluded man, known as such, seeking to correct the illusory cognition of the snake by another is powerless to effect the correction.

63. "But," it may be argued, "supposing a man is experiencing some terror in a dream. The terror will surely disappear, if in the same dream, the dreamer were to get the knowledge that the terror-causing experience was a mere dream. Even so is the situation here." The explanation cannot be sustained. If in the same dream one were to get a further knowledge that the knowledge that removed the terror was itself a dream, the original terror will return and continue. Thus the explanation does not improve the position. The basis of the objection is the fact that even during the learning of the scriptures, it is being learnt by the student that the scriptures are also illusory like dreams.

64. A further point is made by you: Though the scriptures are fabrications of illusion and therefore unreal, the content of the scriptures, "Pure Being," happening to be unsublated in later experience, they do impart the knowledge that "Brahman is absolute existence, one without a second, (*Chā. VI, II, 1*)." This is also illogical. The doctrine upholding "śūnya" (nothingness or the void) as the ultimate, furnishes the sublation of the content of the scriptures as described by you. You cannot urge that the doctrine of "śūnya" originates from error, for the sacred texts also like, "Brahman is absolute existence, one without a second" are products of error according to your own view. The distinction lies in the fact that only the assertion of "śūnya" is free from subsequent sublation. The upholders of the doctrine of "śūnya" and those who deny the reality of everything other than Brahman have no right to philosophy; for they both refuse to admit the reality of the sources of knowledge, on which, they base their systems. This has been pointed out by the revered teachers: "The philosophers of 'śūnya' have no right to dialectics, because they have no means of knowledge."

65. By what means of knowledge is it established that the world revealed by perception is unreal? If it is contended that perception is tainted by a defective origin and that its deliverances can be accounted for without admitting their truth, while the sacred scripture is flawless in origin and its deliverances cannot be accounted for except by the admission of their truth and therefore scriptural knowledge can sublate perception, it is necessary for the completion of the argument to specify the exact defect that falsifies perceptual experience which presents to us the world of measureless multiplicity. You describe the defect as the beginningless pluralistic predilection. But alas! the sacred scripture also, on your hypothesis, suffers from the same defect. Since the radical defect is common, it is impossible that one of the two, scripture and perception, can bring about the sublation of the other.

66. Our own method of adjusting the claims of these sources of knowledge is free from these inconsistencies. Perception is the apprehension of elements like ether and air and their products possessing properties like touch and sound and existing in forms like that of men, animals and other objects. The theme of scriptures comprehends principles not determinable by perception. They are the nature of Brahman, characterized by infinite attributes, like omniscience, the pervasive immanence in all as their ultimate self and absolute reality, the various modes of worship of Brahman like devout meditation, the attainment of Brahman and the attainment of the *summum bonum* following that meditation and issuing out of the grace of Brahman and the particular methods of suppressing and eliminating the root of all evil, which consists in going contrary to Brahman.

67. The thinkers who hold that the scripture is superior to other means of knowledge, on the ground of innumerable excellences like its enjoying unbroken continuity of tradition, without beginning and end are obliged, logically, to admit the veracity of perception. The theory under discussion is inherently weak, being a vicious view proceeding from unsound logic. It is further assailed by hundreds of Vedic declarations. As its critical examination conducted so far is quite ample, we conclude its refutation. . . .

81. . . From both the Vedas and the words of the sages, emerges the following teaching: The supreme Brahman is the self of all. The sentient and non-sentient entities constitute its body. The body is an entity and has being only by virtue of its being the mode of the soul of which it is the body. The body and soul, though characterized by different attributes do not get mixed up. From all this follows the central teaching that Brahman, with all the non-sentient and sentient entities as its modes, is the ultimate. The scriptures declare this glory of Brahman by saying that Brahman has the whole universe as its body. They also identify Brahman and the world in the manner of co-ordinate predication, which bears in this connection direct and primary meaning.

82. Co-ordinate predication is the application of two terms to a single entity through connotation of its two modes. On our view co-ordinate predication is given its straight and primary significance. To explain: In the passage affirming identity "That thou art," the term "that" signifies Brahman, as the cause of the world, as the abode of all perfections. By the term, "thou" also, denotative of the individual self, Brahman itself is signified as the inner ruler of the jīva, as possessed of it as its body, as existing within the jīva as its self and as possessing the jīva as its mode. On all other theories, two glaring errors ensue, namely, that of giving up the governing principle of co-ordination and of ascribing evil to Brahman itself.

83. When we say, "Brahman exists thus," the term "*thus*" signifies the mode in which the subject, Brahman, exists. Now the universe of sentient and non-sentient entities, in both its gross and subtle states, forms the meaning of the term "*thus*" as it forms the mode of Brahman. It is only from this standpoint that the passage, "Let me become many, let me grow forth (*Chā. VI, II, 3*)" becomes meaningful. Īśvara exists as the cause and as the effect, assuming diversity of forms. The sentient and non-sentient entities constitute those forms.

84. (***Objection***): "But only the generic character (universal) and attributes are seen to be modes of things and to constitute the meaning of the term "thus." No substance ever becomes such a mode and the meaning of the term 'thus.' Therefore, substances, capable of independent existence, cannot be the meaning of the term 'thus' in relation to Īśvara; nor can they be his modes."

(***Reply***): Even substances like a staff or ear-ring can become modes of other substances as implied in terms "dandin" and "kuṇḍalin" (man holding a staff and man wearing ear-rings).

85. (***Objection***): The cases instanced are different from the one under consideration. When a substance itself is a mode of another substance, an affix indicative of possession is used (indicative of the meaning of "having") as in the examples of staff-bearer and earring-wearer. Therefore the individual selves and physical entities, being substances, cannot be mere modes of Īśvara, like "cowness" in relation to a cow and the terms standing for them cannot signify God (without the aforesaid affix) as it is contended.

(***Reply***): The terms, cow, horse, man and god signify substances, brought about by specific combination of basic material elements. They are material products and substances. So both in empirical usage and Vedic usage, the terms used for them are put in apposition with the terms representing the souls embodied in them, as they are just modes of those individual selves. We say, "Devadatta, owing to particular merit is born a man, Yajñnadatta, owing to sinful actions in the past, is born a cow, another soul, owing to excessive merit, is born a god." Thus the bodies being the modes of the souls, the terms representing the bodies are equated with those signifying the souls and are treated as standing for the souls themselves.

86. The central principle is this: Whatever exists only as an attribute of a substance—be it a generic character or a quality or a substance itself, there being no speciality attached to any category in this matter—that being inseparable from that substance, as its mode only, can be designated as one with that substance. But if a substance, capable of independent being, comes to form a mode of another substance contingently at only some points of space and time, the term signifying the modal substance can signify the basic substance through the use of the possessive affix. Thus all substances, sentient and non-sentient, have reality and being only as constituting the body and thus as forming the modes of Īśvara. Īśvara, having them as his mode, is designated by the terms denotative of them. Thus the co-ordinate propositions are quite appropriate. All this has been already expounded in the course of the interpretation of the passage dealing with the differentiation of names and forms.

87. Therefore, Brahman itself is the effect as it exists having for its mode the configurations consisting of prakṛti, individual selves, mahat, ahaṅkāra, tanmāṭra, elements, senses and the product of these, the cosmic sphere of Brahmā, made up of the fourteen worlds, and the varied forms of beings like gods, men, animals, and plants. The knowledge of Brahman in its causal state leads to the knowledge of all. The idea of the knowledge of the "one" leading to the knowledge of all, becomes, thereby, perfectly intelligible. Through a consideration of the principles like causation, the great truth that Brahman is the self of all, as all sentient and non-sentient entities are its modes, is propounded.

88. (***Objection***): It has been maintained by you that Brahman is not subject to modification in its substantive nature; otherwise the sacred texts proclaiming the highest Brahman as changeless and flawless are contradicted. In the same breath, it is maintained by you that Brahman is the material cause of the universe in accordance with the aphorism, "It is the material cause, on account of the opening declaration and the illustrations cited (*Bra. I, IV, 24*)," on the authority of the Upaniṣad declaration of one knowledge leading to all knowledge and the illustrations of clay and its products, etc., cited. To be a material cause is to be subject to modification. How can these two conflicting assertion be both true?

89. (***Reply***): (Brahman) inclusive of individual selves and the universe is maintained to be the cause as a whole. If Īśvara is admitted to transform himself into the individual self, the aphorism, "The self is not originated, because the scripture denies origination of the self and also because the scriptural texts speak of the eternity of the self (*Bra. II, III, 19*)" is contradicted. The ascription of partiality and cruelty to Īśvara is repudiated on the ground of the beginninglessness of the individual selves and the responsibility of their karma for the inequalities and sufferings of individuals. The aphorisms connected with this issue are, "Partiality and cruelty are not to be ascribed to Brahman, because of the dependence on karma," and "If it be said, 'There is no karma, as there was no differentiation' we deny that supposition on the ground of beginninglessness; it is reasonable and so found in actuality (*Bra. II, I, 35-36*)." It is also pointed out that if the individual self were to be non-eternal, there would be actions, unproductive of fruits and experiences of fruits of action, uncaused by action.

90. In the same way the texts state that prakṛti is also beginningless: "There is one who is unborn, has red, white and black colours and gives birth to many creations similar in form. One 'unborn one' abides with her, happy in her company and another 'unborn one' abandons her having experienced the pleasures and pains she could give (*Śve. IV, 5*)." This passage points out the unoriginated existence of both the finite selves and nature. "From that the magician fashions the entire world and another is imprisoned in the magic; know prakṛti to be māyā, the wielder of māyā is the great Lord (*Śve. IV, 9-10*)." It is pointed out here that prakṛti is subject to change in its essential being. "The cow, without a beginning and end, is the creatrix fashioning all beings."

91. The Smṛtis also say, "Know that prakṛti and puruṣa are both beginningless (*Gīta, XIII, 19*)." "The earth, water, fire, air, ether, mind, intellect and ego, these eight constitute a distinct prakṛti of mine. This is my inferior prakṛti. There is a superior prakṛti of mine. That, know thou, O Arjuna, is of the nature of the jīvas, by which this world is sustained (*Gītā, VII, 4*)," "Utilizing my own prakṛti, I release them into being again and again (*Gītā, IX, 8*)," "Supervised by me, the supreme supervising power, prakṛti brings forth the world of moving and non-moving beings (*Gītā, IX, 10*)."

92. Now prakṛti also constitutes the body of Īśvara. Therefore, the term "prakṛti" denotes Īśvara, who is the inner self of prakṛti and has prakṛti as his mode. The term "puruṣa" also denotes Īśvara, who is the inner self of the puruṣa and has puruṣa as his mode. Therefore, Īśvara is the indwelling self of the modification of prakṛti as well as puruṣa. This truth is recorded thus: "The manifested nature is Viṣṇu. Even so the unmanifested nature is Viṣṇu. The individual self is Viṣṇu. Time is Viṣṇu (*Vi. I, II, 18*)" and "He, the supreme Lord is the agitator as well as the agitated (*Vi. I, II, 31*)." Thus in the supreme Self, characterized by prakṛti as his mode, there is change in the aspect of the mode consisting of prakṛti, and changelessness in the substantive aspect, in which the mode is inherent. In the same way, in the highest Self, characterized by the individual self as his mode, there are imperfections in the aspect of the mode consisting of the individual self, while in the substantive aspect, in which the mode is inherent, he is the ruler, free from flaws, the abode of all auspicious attributes and has a will that unfailingly realizes itself. Thus it is the supreme Lord that exists in the causal state and again it is he that exists in the state of the effect, as the world, of which the material cause is the supreme Lord Himself. In this manner the identity between cause and effect is to be comprehended and thus all utterances of the sacred scriptures are rendered free of contradiction.

93. Brahman is in the causal state when its body consists of the individual selves and physical nature, in their subtle condition not distinguishable by differentiations of name and form. The passage of the world to this phase of existence is what is termed "dissolution." Brahman, having as its body the individual selves and nature, in their gross manifested condition distinguished by differentiations of names and forms, is in the state of the effect. The assumption of this manifestation and grossness of aspect is described as "creation." So says Bhagavān Parāśara: "He is the cause of the effects, the unoriginated pradhāna and puruṣa (*Vi. I, IX, 37*).

94. Therefore, terms denotative of primordial nature and individual selves, in all their states of being, are denotative, in the primary sense itself, of the highest Self, of which prakṛti and puruṣa are the modes and which exists having them as its modes. So do terms denoting bodies denote the individual selves indwelling in them. Terms like gods and men, denoting the varied physical bodies, signify in their primary signification, the individual selves, of which the bodies form modes and forming modes of which they possess existence. So the sentient and non-sentient beings forming bodies of the Supreme and thus acquiring their existential status as the modes of the Supreme, all terms denotative of them are denotative of the Supreme in their principal signification.

95. This is the fundamental relationship between the Supreme and the universe of individual selves and physical entities. It is the relationship of soul and body, the inseparable relationship of the supporter and the supported, that of the controller and the controlled, and that of the principal entity and the subsidiary entity. That which takes possession of another entity entirely as the latter's support, controller and principal, is called the soul of that latter entity. That which, in its entirety, depends upon, is controlled by and subserves another and is therefore its inseparable mode, is called the body of the latter. Such is the relation between the individual self and its body. Such being the relationship, the supreme Self, having all as its body, is denoted by all terms.

96. So declare the Vedas with massive unanimity: "That Goal which all the Vedas reveal (*Ka. II, 95*)" and "That in which all the Vedas become one (*Ā. III, 11*)." The meaning of all the Vedas becoming one is that all the Vedas are unanimous in their import as that "one" is their purport. "The one God existing in the many (*Ā. III, 14*)" and "The gods do not comprehend Him, who is verily with them (*Ā. III, 11*)"; here the word "gods" means the senses. The senses including the mind of all beings like gods and men, do not comprehend him, who is verily with them, being the inner ruler and the very soul of all the beings like gods and men.

97. Similar is the drift of the purānas: "We bow down in obeisance to that, in which all words are eternally established (*Vi. I, XIV, 3*)." In the entity signified are the words established truly. "The prior cause of all effects, the best significance of words" and "I am the one theme of all the Vedas (*Gītā, XV, 95*)"; All words signify the inner ruler characterized by the individual souls, along with their bodies. Indeed the Vedānta text has it, "Entering these three deities, as the ātman, the jīva, I will differentiate names and forms."

98. So are the words of Manu: "Let one know the controller of all, subtler than the subtlest, of the radiance of gold, the supreme Person, who is comprehended by the intelligence operative in dream (*XII, 122*)." The various descriptions mean as follows. "The controller of all" means one who has entered into all beings as their inner ruler and thus controls them all. "Subtler than the subtlest" means that the individuals are subtle as they pervade all the non-sentient existence and he pervading even the individual selves is subtler than they. "Of the radiance of gold" means that he has the colour of the sun. "To be comprehended by the intelligence operative in dream" means that intelligence, like that in dream-consciousness, can comprehend him. That means that meditation which has developed the vividness of the clearest perception, is the instrument for attaining him. "Thus some say he is Agni, others say he is Prajāpati, others again say that he is Indra, while some others say he is Prāna. Others say that he is the eternal Brahman (*Ma. XII, 123*)." "Some" means the Vedic passages. The meaning of the whole text is that like the term "Eternal Brahman" all the terms like Agni also signify the supreme Brahman only, on the principle formulated, because, as the controller and self of all, he abides within all. Other Smṛti texts carry the same purport like in following: "Those who worship the manes, gods, brāhmaṇas along with their sacred fire, worship indeed Viṣṇu himself, who is the inner self of all beings (Dakṣa)." The terms like manes, gods, brāhmaṇas and fire signify the entities so named in ordinary discourse and through them ultimately name Viṣṇu himself who is the inner soul of all beings.

99. The heart of the whole śāstra is this: The individual selves are essentially of the nature of pure knowledge, devoid of restriction and limitation. They get covered up by nescience in the shape of karma. The consequence is that the scope and breadth of their knowledge is curtailed in accordance with their karma. They get embodied in the multifarious varieties of bodies from Brahmā down to the lowest species. Their knowledge is limited in accordance with their specific embodiment. They are deluded into identification with their bodies. In accordance with them they become subject to joys and sorrows, which, in essence constitute what is termed "the river of transmigratory existence." For these individual selves, so lost in saṁsāra, there is no way of emancipation, other than surrender to the supreme Lord. For the purpose of inculcating that sole way of emancipation, the first truth to be taught by the śāstra is that the individual selves are not intrinsically divided into several kinds, like gods, men, etc., and that they are fundamentally alike and are equal in having knowledge as their essential nature. The essential nature of the individual self is such that it is wholly subservient and instrumental to God and therefore God is its inner self. The nature of the supreme Being is unique, on account of his absolute perfection and absolute antithesis to everything that is evil. God is the ocean of countless, infinitely excellent attributes. The śāstras further assert that all sentient and non-sentient entities are sustained and operated by the supreme Being. Therefore, the Supreme is the ultimate self of all. They teach meditation along with its accessory conditions as the means for attaining him. . . .

117. It may be asked, "What is your final position? Do you uphold unity or plurality or both unity and plurality? Which of these three forms the substance of the Vedānta on your interpretation?" We reply that we uphold all the three as they are all affirmed in the Veda. We uphold unity because Brahman alone exists, with all other entities as its modes. We uphold both unity and plurality, as the one Brahman itself, has all the spiritual and physical substances as its modes and thus exists qualified by a plurality. We uphold plurality as the three categories, sentient selves and non-sentient existents and the supreme Lord, are mutually distinct in their substantive nature and attributes and there is no mutual transposition of their characteristics. . . .

126. Now this supreme Brahman, the supreme Person is to be attained. The pathway through which he is to be attained is as follows: By an accumulation of the greatest merit the sins of the past gathered through all past lives, are destroyed. A person, whose sins are thus destroyed through great merit, seeks refuge at the feet of the supreme Person. Such self-surrender begets an inclination towards him. Then the aspirant acquires knowledge of reality from the scriptures aided by the instruction of holy teachers. Then by a steady effort he develops in an ever-increasing measure the qualities of soul, like the control of the mind, the control of senses, austerity, purity, forgiveness, straightforwardness, discrimination as to what is to be feared and not feared, mercy and non-violence. He is devoted to the performance of the nitya and naimittika duties pertaining to his varṇa and āśrama, and avoids actions prohibited, such a course of conduct being conceived as the worship of the supreme Person. He offers his all and his very self at the lotus-like feet of the supreme Person. Actuated by loving devotion to him, he offers perpetual praises and obeisances, engages in perpetual remembrance of him, bows down before him in adoration perpetually, exerts himself always in the godward direction, always sings his glories, always listens to the exalted accounts of his perfections, speaks perpetually of those perfections, meditates upon him continuously, ceaselessly worships him and dedicates himself once for all to him. The supreme Person, who is overflowing with compassion, being pleased with such love, showers his grace on the aspirant, which destroys all his inner darkness. Bhakti develops in such a devotee towards the supreme Person, which is valued for its own sake, which is uninterrupted, which is an absolute delight in itself and which is meditation that has taken on the character of the most vivid and immediate vision. Through such bhakti is the Supreme attained.

CHAPTER 7

JAINISM

Jainas follow the teachings of the ancient *Jinas* (spiritual conquerors), also called "ford-builders" (*Tīrthaṅkaras*) because they showed the way to cross the great ocean of suffering. Mahāvīra (sixth century B.C.), a contemporary of the Buddha, is regarded as the most recent of twenty-four ford-builders by the Jaina tradition. At heart, Jainism is a way of compassion and ascetic self-restraint designed to liberate the soul (*jīva*) from the bondage of karmic matter. Existence is without being or end, with no God or initial act of creation recognized. Liberation is possible only through human effort, as exemplified by Mahāvīra and the other Jinas who, by teachings and example, have shown the way. Rejecting any kind of revealed truth, Jainas emphasized the importance of human knowledge and carefully worked out an elaborate theory of knowledge to underwrite their metaphysical and ethical views. In the give and take of debate, Jaina philosophers developed numerous insights and arguments that were accepted by the other traditions, particularly with respect to the important teachings of *ahiṁsā* ("nonhurting") and the plurality of epistemological perspectives (*anekāntavāda*).

The selections from the early (3rd century B.C.) canonical texts, the *Sūtrakṛtāṅga* and *Ācārāṅga Sūtra* (translated by A. L. Basham), taken from Ainslie T. Embree, editor, *Sources of Indian Tradition*, second edition (New York: Columbia University Press, 1988), present the Jaina world view and its emphasis on ethical action and ascetic practice. The selections from the *Syādavādamañjarī* (translated by S. K. Saksena, C. A. Moore, and H. M. Johnson) are from Sarvapalli Radhakrishnan and Charles A. Moore, editors, *A Source Book in Indian Philosophy* (Princeton: Princeton University Press, 1957). This text presents Malliṣeṇa's (thirteenth century) development of epistemological perspectivism and conditional predication as he comments on Hemacandra's (1088–1172) famous text, *An Examination in Thirty-two Stanzas of the Doctrines of Other Systems*, which critiqued the various philosophical traditions current in his day.

Padmanabh S. Jaini, *The Jaina Path of Purification* (Berkeley: University of California Press, 1979), is the best book available on Jainism. Based on sound scholarship, with an excellent bibliography, it is clearly and simply written, suitable for both beginning and advanced students. For the reader with a rudimentary understanding of symbolic logic, Bimal Krishna Matilal, *Central Philosophy of Jainism* (*Anekānta-vāda*) (Ahmedabad: L. D. Institute of Indology, 1981), is very good on this central distinctive feature of Jaina philosophy.

I
The Jaina World View*

1. GRASPING AND HURTING ARE FORCES OF BONDAGE

One should know what binds the soul, and, knowing, break free from bondage.
What bondage did the Hero [Mahāvīra] declare, and what knowledge did he teach to remove it?
He who grasps at even a little, whether living or lifeless, or consents to another doing so, will never be freed from sorrow.
If a man kills living things, or slays by the hand of another, or consents to another slaying, his sin goes on increasing.
The man who cares for his kin and companions is a fool who suffers much, for their numbers are ever increasing.
All his wealth and relations cannot save him from sorrow.
Only if he knows the nature of life, will he get rid of karma.

Sūtrakṛtāṅga, 1.1.1.1–5

2. HURT NO FORM OF LIFE

Earth and water, fire and wind,
Grass, trees, and plants, and all creatures that move,
Born of the egg, born of the womb,
Born of dung, born of liquids—

These are the classes of living beings.
Know that they all seek happiness.
In hurting them men hurt themselves,
And will be born again among them. . . .

Some men leave mother and father for the life of a monk,
But still make use of fire;
But He [Mahāvīra] has said, "their principles are base
Who hurt for their own pleasure."

*Reprinted with permission from Ainslie T. Embree, editor, *Sources of Indian Tradition*, 2nd edition (New York: Columbia University Press, 1988).

The man who lights a fire kills living things,
While he who puts it out kills the fire;
Thus a wise man who understands the Law
Should never light a fire.

There are lives in earth and lives in water,
Hopping insects leap into the fire,
And worms dwell in rotten wood.
All are burned when a fire is lighted.

Even plants are beings, capable of growth,
Their bodies need food, they are individuals.
The reckless cut them for their own pleasure
And slay many living things in doing so.

He who carelessly destroys plants, whether sprouted or full grown,
Provides a rod for his own back.
He has said, "Their principles are ignoble
Who harm plants for their own pleasure."

Sūtrakṛtāṅga, 1.1–9

3. THE SIX KINDS OF LIVING BEINGS

Each is afflicted and wretched, it is hard to teach, it has no discrimination. Unenlightened men, who suffer from the effects of past deeds, cause great pain in a world full of pain already, for in earth souls are individually embodied. If, thinking to gain praise, honor, or respect, . . . or to achieve a good rebirth, . . . or to win salvation, or to escape pain, a man sins against earth or causes or permits others to do so, . . . he will not gain joy or wisdom. . . . Injury to the earth is like striking, cutting, maiming, or killing a blind man. . . . Knowing this a man should not sin against earth or cause or permit others to do so. He who understands the nature of sin against earth is called a true sage who understands karma. . . .

And there are many souls embodied in water. Truly water . . . is alive. . . . He who injures the lives in water does not understand the nature of sin or renounce it. . . . Knowing this, a man should not sin against water, or cause or permit others to do so. He who understands the nature of sin against water is called a true sage who understands karma. . . .

By wicked or careless acts one may destroy fire-beings and, moreover, harm other beings by means of fire. . . . For there are creatures living in earth, grass, leaves, wood, cowdung, or dustheaps, and jumping creatures which . . . fall into a fire if they come near it. If touched by fire, they shrivel up, . . . lose their senses, and die. . . . He who understands the nature of sin in respect of fire is called a true sage who understands karma.

And just as it is the nature of a man to be born and grow old, so it is the nature of a plant to be born and grow old. . . . One is endowed with reason, and so is the other; one is sick, if injured, and so is the other; one grows larger, and so does the other; one changes with time, and so does the other. . . . He who understands the nature of sin against plants is called a true sage who understands karma. . . . .

All beings with two, three, four, or five senses, . . . in fact all creation, know individually pleasure and displeasure, pain, terror, and sorrow. All are full of fears which come from all directions. And yet there exist people who would cause greater pain to them. . . . Some kill animals for sacrifice, some for their skin, flesh, blood, . . . feathers, teeth, or tusks; . . . some kill them intentionally and some unintentionally; some kill because they have been previously injured by them, . . . and some because they expect to be injured. He who harms animals has not understood or renounced deeds of sin. . . . He who understands the nature of sin against animals is called a true sage who understands karma. . . .

A man who is averse from harming even the wind knows the sorrow of all things living. . . . He who knows what is bad for himself knows what is bad for others, and he who knows what is bad for others knows what is bad for himself. The reciprocity should always be borne in mind. Those whose minds are at peace and who are free from passions do not desire to live [at the expense of others]. . . . He who understands the nature of sin against wind is called a true sage who understands karma.

In short he who understands the nature of sin in respect of all the six types of living beings is called a true sage who understands karma.

Ācārāṅga Sūtra, 1.1

4. NON-HURTING IS THE ETERNAL LAW

Thus say all the perfect souls and blessed ones, whether past, present, or to come—thus they speak, thus they declare, thus they proclaim: All things breathing, all things existing, all things living, all beings whatever, should not be slain or treated with violence, or insulted, or tortured, or driven away.

This is the pure unchanging eternal law, which the wise ones who know the world have proclaimed, among the earnest and the non-earnest, among the loyal and the not-loyal, among those who have given up punishing others and those who have not done so, among those who are weak and those who are not, among those who delight in worldly ties and those who do not. This is the truth. So it is. Thus it is declared in this religion.

When he adopts this Law a man should never conceal or reject it. When he understands the Law he should grow indifferent to what he sees, and not act for worldly motives. . . .

What is here declared has been seen, heard, approved, and understood. Those who give way and indulge in pleasure will be born again and again. The heedless are outside [the hope of salvation]. But if you are mindful, day and night steadfastly striving, always with ready vision, in the end you will conquer.

Ācārāṅga Sūtra, 1.4.1

5. BE A REFUGE TO ALL

In whatever house, village, city, or region he may be, if a monk is attacked by men of violence, or suffers any other hardship, he should bear it all like a hero. The saint, with true vision, conceives compassion for all the world, in east and west and south and north, and so, knowing the Sacred Lore, he will preach and spread and proclaim it, among those who strive and those who do not, in fact among all those who are willing to hear him. Without neglecting the virtues of tranquility, indifference, patience, zeal for salvation, purity, uprightness, gentleness, and freedom from care, with due consideration he should declare the Law of the Monks to all that draw breath, all that exist, all that have life, all beings whatever. . . . He should do no injury to himself or anyone else. . . . The great sage becomes a refuge for injured creatures, like an island that the waters cannot overwhelm.

Ācārāṅga Sūtra, 1.6, 5

6. PRACTICE SELF-DISCIPLINE

Oh man, refrain from evil, for life must come to an end.
Only men foolish and uncontrolled are plunged in the habit of pleasure.

Live in striving and self-control, for hard to cross are paths full of insects.
Follow the rules that the Heroes [Tīrthaṅkaras] surely proclaimed.

Heroes detached and strenuous, subduing anger and fear,
Will never kill living beings, but cease from sin and are happy.

"Not I alone am the sufferer—all things in the universe suffer!"
Thus should man think and be patient, not giving way to his passions.

As old plaster flakes from a wall, a monk should make thin his body by fasting,
And he should injure nothing. This is the Law taught by the Sage [Mahāvīra].

Sūtrakṛtāṅga, 1.2.1.10–14

7. PUT ASIDE DELUSION

He who desires the qualities of things is deluded and falls into the grip of great pain. For he thinks, "I have mother, father, sister, wife, sons and daughters, daughters-in-law, friends, kin near and remote, and acquaintances. I own various properties, I make profits. I need food and clothes." On account of these things people are deluded, they worry day and night, they work in season and out of season, they crave for fortune and wealth, they injure and do violence, and they turn their minds again and again to evil deeds. Thus the life of many men is shortened.

For when ear and eye and smell and taste and touch grow weak, a man knows that his life is failing, and after a while his senses sink into dotage. The kinsfolk with whom he lives first grumble at him, and then he grumbles at them. . . . An old man is fit for neither laughter, nor playing, nor pleasure, nor show. So a man should take to the life of piety, seize the present, be firm, and not let himself be deluded an hour longer, for youth and age and life itself all pass away. . . .

Understanding the nature of all kinds of pain and pleasure, before he sees his life decline, a wise man should know the right moment [for taking up a life of religion]. . . . Before his senses weaken he should pursue his own true welfare.

Ācārāṅga Sūtra, 1.2.1

8. PRACTICE NON-ATTACHMENT

Who will boast of family or glory, who will desire anything, when he thinks that he has often been born noble, often lowly, and that his soul, [his true self] is neither humble nor high-born, and wants nothing?

Thus a wise man is neither pleased nor annoyed. . . . A man should be circumspect and remember that through carelessness he experiences many unpleasantnesses and is born in many wombs, becoming blind, deaf, dumb, one-eyed, hunchbacked, or of dark or patchy complexion. Unenlightened, he is afflicted, and is forever rolled on the wheel of birth and death.

To those who make fields and houses their own, life is dear; they want clothes dyed and colored, jewels, earrings, gold, and women, and they delight in them. The fool, whose only desire is for the fullness of life, thinks that penance, self-control, and restraint are pointless, and thus he comes to grief. . . .

There is nothing that time will not overtake. All beings love themselves, seek pleasure, and turn from pain; they shun destruction, love life, and desire to live. To all things life is dear. They crave for riches and gather them together, . . . using the labor of servants both two-footed and four-footed; and whatever a man's share may be, whether small or great, he wants to enjoy it. At one time he has a great treasure, . . . while at another his heirs divide it, or workless men steal it, or kings loot it, or it is spoiled or vanishes, or is burned up with his house. The fool in order to get riches does cruel deeds, which in the end are only of benefit to others, and stupidly comes to grief on account of the pain that he causes.

This the Sage [Mahāvīra] has declared—such men cannot and do not cross the flood; they cannot, they do not reach the other shore; they cannot, they do not get to the other side.

Though he hears the doctrine such a man never stands in the right place,
But he who adopts it stands in the right place indeed.
There is no need to tell a man who sees for himself,
But the wretched fool, delighting in pleasure, has no end to his miseries,
but spins in a whirlpool of pain.

Ācārāṅga Sūtra, 1.2, 3

9. THE HOLY DEATH-FAST

If a monk feels sick, and is unable duly to mortify the flesh, he should regularly diminish his food. Mindful of his body, immovable as a beam, the monk should strive to waste his body away. He should enter a village or town . . . and beg for straw. Then he should take it and go to an out-of-the-way place. He should carefully inspect and sweep the ground, so that there are no eggs, living beings, sprouts, dew, water, ants, mildew, drops of water, mud, or cobwebs left on it. Thereupon he carries out the final fast. . . . Speaking the truth, the saint who has crossed the stream of transmigration, doing away with all hesitation, knowing all things but himself unknown, leaves his frail body. Overcoming manifold hardships and troubles, with trust in his religion he performs this terrible penance. Thus in due time he puts an end to his existence. This is done by those who have no delusions. This is good; this is joyful and proper; this leads to salvation; this should be followed.

Ācārāṅga Sūtra, 1.7, 6

II
The Theory of Perspectives (*Syādavāda*)*[1]

23. When it is integrated, an entity is without modifications; and this same entity is without substance when it is differentiated. Thou didst bring to light the doctrine of seven modes which is expressed by means of two kinds of statement—a doctrine which is comprehensible to the most intelligent people.

An entity described as a whole is "integrated"; it is "without modifications" when it is described with no intended reference to the modifications. That is called "entity" in which reside quality and modifications. There are six substances: medium of motion, medium of rest, space, matter, time, and soul. This is the meaning: When it is desired to speak of a single entity only—self, pot, etc., conscious or unconscious—having the form of substance only, without intending any reference to its modifications even though they are present, then it is called "without modifications"—i.e., it has the form of pure substance only—because it is designated as a unit with the characteristics of the entire body of modifications included. This is the meaning.

*Reprinted with permission from Sarvapalli Radhakrishnan and Charles A. Moore, editors, *A Source Book in Indian Philosophy* (Princeton: Princeton University Press, 1957).

[1]The brief, numbered statements are from Hemacandra's work. The detailed analysis and explanation that follows is Malliṣeṇa's commentary.

As one says "this soul," "this pot," etc., because of the non-distinctness of the substance and the modifications, so the standpoints attached to the substance-category, i.e., the simple, collective, etc., acknowledge substance only because of the non-separateness of it and the modifications.

"Differentiated," i.e., described with distinctions by virtue of its capacity for different forms. On the other hand, this same entity is nonsubstance only, i.e., having the form of pure modifications only without any intended reference to the underlying substance. This is the meaning.

For when the soul is considered with reference to the several modifications, giving precedence to the modifications, knowledge, perception, etc., then the modifications only stand out, but not some substance called "self." Similarly, a "pot," when differentiated in regard to parts, round lip, broad bottom, belly, upper and lower parts, etc., is modifications only, but not an entity beyond them called "pot." This is why those who follow the standpoint of the modification-category quote:

> "The parts alone stand out, located thus and so,
> But no partless owner of them is understood at all."

And thus, even though an entity consists of both substance and modifications, it has a substance-form through emphasis on the substance-standpoint as primary and the subordination of modification-standpoint; and it has a modification-form through emphasis on the modification-standpoint as primary and the subordination of the substance-standpoint, and it has the form of both through emphasis on both standpoints. Hence, the chief teacher, Umāsvāti, says: "By the establishment of what is emphasized as primary and what is subordinated." Such an entity consisting of both substance and modifications, thou alone—and no one else—didst bring to light. By these words there is understanding of certainty through emphasis.

Surely, "substance" stands for some particular name and idea, and "modifications" stands for other names and ideas; so how can there be a single entity with the nature of both? He removes such a doubt by means of a qualifier, "by kinds of statement." The modes (i.e., kinds of assertion) to the number of seven in regard to that entity [of the first line of the original] are explained by the two kinds of statement called "statement in regard to the whole" and "statement in regard to the parts."

Now, what are these "seven modes" and what are these "kinds of statement"? It is said: When in regard to a single entity, soul, etc., in virtue of an inquiry relating to modifications, existence, etc., one by one, without contradiction—i.e., with avoidance of conflict with direct perception, etc.—made with consideration of affirmation and negation singly and jointly, a statement adorned with the word "somehow" is made in seven ways to be described hereafter, this is called the "seven-mode doctrine," as follows:

(1) Somehow [or, from one point of view] everything does *exist or certainly exists. This is the first mode, by way of affirmation.*

(2) Somehow [or, from one point of view] everything does not exist. This is the second mode, by way of negation.

(3) It is certain that from one point of view everything exists and that from another point of view it does not exist. This is the third mode, by way of affirmation and negation successively.

(4) Somehow everything is certainly indescribable. This is the fourth mode, by way of simultaneous affirmation and negation.

(5) Somehow everything does exist and somehow it is certainly indescribable. This is the fifth mode, by way of affirmation and also by way of simultaneous affirmation and negation.

(6) Somehow everything does not exist and somehow it is indescribable. This is the sixth mode, by way of negation and by way of simultaneous affirmation and negation.

(7) Somehow everything does exist, somehow it does not exist, and somehow it is certainly indescribable. This is the seventh mode, by way of affirmation and negation successively and by way of simultaneous affirmation and negation.

Here, somehow (from one point of view) everything, pot, etc., certainly exists in the form of its own substance, place, time, and nature; but certainly does not exist in the form of another substance, place, time, and nature. For instance: A pot exists in an earthen form in respect to substance and does not exist in an aqueous form, etc.; it exists in Pātaliputra in respect to place, but does not exist in Kānyakubja, etc.; it exists in the cool season in respect to time, but not in spring, etc.; it exists with a black color in respect to nature, but does not exist with a red, etc., color. Otherwise, the loss of its own form would result from changing into another form. And the "certainly" has been used here in the mode to exclude a meaning not intended; otherwise, from the non-mention of its own particular meaning there would result an unintended equivalence of the statement. It has been said:

In a statement "certainly" must be used just to exclude an unintended meaning.

Because otherwise in some cases an unstated equivalent of it [the statement] would result.

Nevertheless, if only so much as "the pot certainly exists" were used, there would be no ascertainment of the pot's own particular form, because of its existence in all forms through the existence of the pillar, etc., also. For the ascertainment of this particular form the word "somehow" is used. Somehow (from one point of view) the pot certainly exists with reference to its own substance, etc., but not with reference to other substances, etc. This is the meaning. That [the word "somehow"], even when it is not used, is to be understood certainly by intelligent people, like the word "certainly" which denotes exclusion of what is not intended. It has been said:

This [the word "somehow"], even when it is not used, is to be understood by intelligent people in all cases from the meaning,

Like the word "certainly," whose purpose is to exclude what is unsuitable, etc.

This is the first mode.

Somehow (i.e., from one point of view) the pot, etc., certainly do not exist. For on the false assumption of the non-existence of an entity in respect to its own substance, etc., as well as other substances, etc., there would be no particularity of an entity because of the lack of its own particular form.

Therefore, the existence of an entity in its own form is inherently bound up with its non-existence in another form, and its non-existence with that existence. And their primariness and secondariness depend upon the meaning. In the same way one must understand the following modes in accordance with the teacher's statement: "By the establishment of what is emphasized as primary and what is subordinated."

This is the second mode.

The third is quite clear.

When one wishes to designate a single entity with the two modifications, existence and non-existence, emphasized as primary simultaneously, the entity, such as soul, etc., is indescribable because of the lack of an adequate word. Thus, the two qualities, existence and non-existence, cannot be stated simultaneously in regard to one thing by the term "existent," because that is incapable of expressing its non-existence; nor, similarly, by the term "non-existent," because that is incapable of expressing its existence. . . .

So that, from the lack of an inclusive term an entity is overcome by simultaneous existence and non-existence emphasized as primary and is therefore "indescribable." But it is not indescribable in every way, because if it were it would be inexpressible even by the word "indescribable." This is the fourth.

The remaining three are easily understood.

Nor should it be said that "'seven-modes' are certainly incongruous because of the infinite modes arising from the admitted infinite modifications which can be affirmed or denied in a single entity." This should not be said because there is a possibility of seven *modes* only *with respect to the affirmation and negation of each modification in a single entity though the seven-modes may be infinite [because of the infinite modifications].*

It has been said above that the many-sided nature of an entity . . . is comprehensible to supremely intelligent people. Because the many-sided nature [of an entity] may be easily deduced by the exposition of the seven-mode system, that also has been discussed.

The absolutists, the supremely unintelligent, seeing that in it, i.e., the seven-mode system the entity is endowed with contradictory modifications, point out the contradiction. Hemacandra describes their fall from the path of authoritative knowledge.

8. Non-existence, when it is referred to different aspects, is not contradictory to existence in things; and existence and indescribability are not contradictory. Because they have not recognized this at all, afraid of contradiction, the dull-witted fall, slain by the absolutist view.

In "things" conscious and unconscious, "non-existence" is "not contradictory" (not affected by contradiction)—i.e., does not embrace contradiction to existence. This is the meaning. Not only is non-existence not contradictory to existence, but existence and indescribability . . . also are not contradictory. This is the meaning.

And so, existence is not contradictory to non-existence; indescribability in the form of affirmation and negation is not contradictory, one to the other [i.e., affirmation and negation]; or, rather, indescribability does not carry contradiction to describability. And freedom from contradiction of the whole seven-mode doctrine is understood from this triad of modes called non-existence, existence, and indescribability, because these three alone are the chief modes and the remaining modes are included in these through combinations.

"Surely these modifications are mutually contradictory. How then can they be associated in one and the same entity?" He gives the reason by means of a qualifier: "referred to different aspects" ("aspects," that is, "properties," "different parts"; "different," that is, "a variety of them"; "referred to," that is, "with emphasis on": this is the adjective of nonexistence). Non-existence in existing objects is not contradictory, when it is referred to different aspects, and, dividing the compound [i.e., existence-indescribability], this must be applied to existence and indescribability. When they are referred to different aspects, existence and indescribability also are not contradictory.

This is the meaning: Where two things are mutually exclusive, such as cold and heat, there is contradiction which is defined as the impossibility of their existing together. But such is not the case here, because existence and non-existence occur by reason of the non-universal nature of both. For in a pot, etc., existence does not exclude non-existence, because if it did existence even in other forms would result. And so there would be no status as objects of other objects except that [the pot], because of the accomplishment by it alone of all actions to be effected by the objects in the three worlds. And non-existence does not exclude existence, because if it did non-existence of an entity even in its own form would follow. And so, universal emptiness would follow because of absence of matter. There would be a contradiction in case existence and non-existence were referred to the same aspect. But that is not so here, because in whatever part existence is, non-existence also is not in that *part. However, existence belongs to one aspect, and non-existence belongs to another aspect. For existence of an entity is in regard to its own form and non-existence in regard to another form.*

For in one and the same multicolored cloth as a whole blueness is seen in one part and other colors in other parts—for blueness is an aspect of the color of indigo, etc., and the other colors are aspects of various coloring substances. So, in the jewel mecaka *[which is many-colored], a variety of colors is to be understood as aspects of various color-substances. Nor does it follow from these examples that existence and non-existence belong to different parts, because of the one-ness of the multiple-colored cloth, etc., as a whole, . . .*

If even so Your Honor [the opponent] is not satisfied, what is to be said of the familiar sight of mutually contradictory modifications, such as the status of father, son, maternal uncle, sister's son, paternal uncle, brother, etc., of one and the same man because of various different relationships? And the same thing should be said of indescribability, etc. [The dull-witted] have not recognized at all that an entity is devoid of contradiction because of different aspects of the kind described.

Describing the Blessed One's teaching by means of a four fold designation of basic divisions of the many-sided doctrine, though it includes all substances and all modifications, Hemacandra says:

25. Somehow one and the same thing is perishable and eternal; somehow it is of similar and dissimilar form; somehow it is describable and indescribable; somehow it is existent and non-existent.

(1) "Somehow," the adverb signifying many-sidedness, must be used with all the eight terms. "One and the same thing," i.e., one and the same entity to which they belong. "Somehow," i.e., from one standpoint, "perishable," i.e., of a nature to perish, non-eternal. Somehow "eternal," i.e., having the modification of non-perishing. This is the meaning. This is the first proposition called "eternal and non-eternal."

(2) Likewise, somehow "similar," i.e., having a generic form as the source of similarity; "dissimilar," i.e., of different forms, consisting of different evolutions, having a particular form as the source of difference. This is the meaning. Here we have the second division in the form of generality and particularity.

(3) Likewise, somehow "describable," i.e., expressible; somehow "indescribable," i.e., inexpressible. This is the meaning. . . . Here we have the third division in the form of describable and indescribable.

(4) Likewise, somehow, "existent," i.e., actually, in the form of being; somehow, "non-existent," i.e., the reverse of that. Here is the fourth division known as "existent and non-existent."

. . . .

*Now by the description of the doctrines of false standpoints, standpoints, and medium of cognition (*pramāṇa*), because of the statement that "knowledge is attained by medium of cognition and standpoints," extolling . . . the refutation of the path of false standpoints, which is contradictory to the "somehow" doctrine, Hemacandra says:*

28. With the words, "it *does* exist, it exists, somehow it exists," an object would be defined in three ways by false standpoints, by standpoints, and by medium of cognition.

Thou, seeing the real truth, did avoid the path of false standpoints by following the path of standpoints and medium of cognition.

An object is defined in three ways. By what three ways? He says: by false standpoints, by standpoints, and by medium of cognition. Because an object, distinguished by one aspect, is "led," i.e., defined by these [i.e., they are called] "standpoints." . . . A thing, distinguished by many-sidedness, is "measured," i.e., defined by it—for that reason it is called "medium of cognition," belonging to the "somehow" doctrine, characterized by direct and indirect perception. . . . By what description should an object be defined? He says: "by it does *exist, it exists, and somehow it exists." . . . Of these "it* does *exist" is a false standpoint; "it exists" is a standpoint; and "somehow it exists" is the medium of cognition. Thus, a false standpoint says merely "it* does *exist," for example, "the pot* does *exist." This point of view admits absolute existence alone in an entity and by the rejection of other modifications determines the attribute and no other which is acceptable to itself. And its status as a false standpoint is due to its false form; and the falsity of its form is due to the rejection of other modifications, though they exist, in it [the entity].*

Likewise, from the description "it exists," there is a standpoint, for by the words "the pot exists" it emphasizes in the pot the modification "existence," acceptable to itself, and resorts to an elephant's eye-closure in regard to the other modifications. And this is not a false standpoint, because it does not reject the other modifications, and it is not the medium of cognition because it is not adorned with the word "somehow."

Now, the medium of cognition, by the words "somehow it exists," says "somehow the entity exists." And its status as a medium of cognition is due to the fact that it is not contradicted by anything seen or wished to be seen and due to the presence of contradiction in the alternative. For every entity is existent in its own form and non-existent in another form. This has been said again and again. "Existent" is merely for illustration; in the same way, non-existence, permanence and impermanence, describability and indescribability, generality and particularity, etc., must be understood.

Now follows some description of the nature of false standpoints, standpoints and medium of cognition. Of these, first, the nature of the standpoint-method, because without a knowledge of it, the nature of the false-standpoint-method would be hard to understand. And here the mention of the false-standpoint-method first by the Ācārya *[Hemacandra] was made to show the order of importance. Of these, the standpoint-method is the consideration of one aspect of an object, the whole of which is understood by the medium of cognition. It is called a "lead" because it leads, i.e., makes reach, i.e., raises an entity particularized by one modification acceptable to itself to the point of understanding, though it is endowed with infinite modifications. . . . And standpoints are infinite because of an entity's infinite modifications and because of the standpoint-view of the speaker's meanings which are satisfied by one modification, and so the elders say:*

"As many as are the ways of speaking about a thing, so many are the statements of the standpoint-method."

Nevertheless, seven standpoints have been taught by ancient scholars by making seven meanings all-inclusive.

CHAPTER 8

MODERN INDIAN THOUGHT

Modern Indian thought has been shaped by a combination of creative response to Western thought and reinterpretation of traditional thought. For the most part, the tendency was to accept the best of both modern Western thought and Indian tradition, creating a synthesis uniquely Indian. Among modern Indian thinkers, four, Iqbal, Gandhi, Aurobindo, and Radhakrishnan, have been extremely influential. Nurtured by their own traditions, but influenced by the West as well, they exemplify the range and diversity of modern Indian thought.

Mohammed Iqbal (1873 - 1938), Pakistan's national poet, is widely recognized as the greatest Urdu poet of his time as well as one of modern India's most profound philosophers. A devout Muslim, Iqbal was deeply inspired by the Islamic tradition, but his studies of modern European philosophy in Germany and England also influenced his thinking. The essay reprinted here, "Is Religion Possible?" reveals both his penetrating insight into European thought and his brilliant understanding of Islam. It also reveals Iqbal's conviction that through devotion to God human beings can fulfill their deepest capacities, rising above the base inclinations of greed and selfishness that underlie injustice and violence to a life of righteousness that alone can bring peace to human individuals and communities.

Among Iqbal's philosophical writings, *The Reconstruction of Religious Thought in Islam* (London: Oxford, 1934; Lahore, 1958) is probably the most important. It contains "Is Religion Possible?" as the concluding, seventh chapter. Probably the best overall introduction to Iqbal's thought is *Iqbal: Poet-Philosopher of Pakistan*, edited by Hafeez Malik (New York: Columbia University Press, 1971), a collection of essays on his life and poetry and discussions of his philosophical, religious, and political thought by distinguished authorities in the field. Of the many books on Iqbal by S. A. Vahid, *Iqbal: His Art and Thought* (London: Oxford, 1958) and *Introduction to Iqbal* (Karachi: Pakistan Publications, 1964) are especially helpful.

Mohandas K. Gandhi (1869 - 1948) provided the moral leadership for India's nationalist movement in the twentieth century, inspiring mass movements for social and political change. Although Gandhi's work was based on a philosophical vision of reality—a vision that was constantly evolving as a result of his experiences—he was an activist, an agent of social change, rather than a systemic philosopher. Consequently, his vision is never set out in its entirety in any one place, and he provides it with no philosophical defense. Nonetheless, his views continue to inspire social thought and to catalyze social change today, not only in India but throughout the world.

One of the best introductions to Gandhi is the excellent movie by that title. Louis Fischer, *Gandhi: His Life and Message for the World* (New York: Mentor Books, 1954), is an excellent brief biography, and D. M. Datta, *The Philosophy of Mahatma Gandhi* (Madison: University of Wisconsin Press, 1953), is a clearly written, brief introduction to his philosophy. Raghavan N. Iyer, *The Moral and Political Thought of Mahatma Gandhi* (Oxford: Oxford University Press, 1973), is a careful and thorough study. Although there are many anthologies of Gandhi's writings, *Selections from Gandhi* by Nirmal Kumar Bose (Ahmedabad: Navajivan Publishing House, 1957), from which we have drawn our selections, has the advantage of bringing together from many different sources Gandhi's thoughts on central topics.

Aurobindo Ghose (1872 - 1950), a political revolutionary in his earlier years, dug deeply into India's ancient wisdom and experimented with yogic practice in his effort to revolutionize life from within its own spiritual center. Although his major works were on integral yoga (*The Synthesis of Yoga*) and the vision of the ideal life (*The Life Divine*), he wrote on a great variety of topics, ranging from the importance of physical fitness to a Rig Vedic commentary. He also founded an ashram at Pondicherry, now the home of Auroville, an international community dedicated to putting Aurobindo's ideas into practice. Although his formal education took place in England, he came to immerse himself deeply in India's traditional culture, finding his inspiration in the tradition's wisdom and his yogic practice.

In *The Mind of Light* (New York: E. P. Dutton, 1971), Robert McDermott includes a brief introduction to Aurobindo's principal ideas and provides an eight-page annotated bibliography of works by and about Aurobindo. The selection included here is from chapter 28 of Aurobindo's major work, *The Life Divine* (New York: India Library Society, n.d.).

Sarvapalli Radhakrishnan (1888 - 1975) had a distinguished philosophical career; he held the King George Chair of Philosophy at the University of Calcutta and later the Spalding Professorship at Oxford. An extremely creative scholar, he published some twenty books and more than a hundred papers in philosophy and religion. In his later years he contributed much to India's intellectual and cultural life from a variety of political positions, serving as vice-president of India from 1952 to 1962 and as president from 1962 to 1967.

Robert Minor, in *Radhakrishnan: A Religious Biography* (Albany: State University of New York Press, 1987), does an excellent job of placing Radhakrishnan's thought in the context of his experience, giving us a sense of the integration of his life and thought. Robert A. McDermott, *Radhakrishnan: Selected Writings on Philosophy, Religion, and Culture* (New York: E. P. Dutton, 1970), is a fine collection of some of Radhakrishnan's most important writings, with a brief introductory essay. Readers seriously interested in Radhakrishnan's thought will want to consult Paul Schillp, editor, *The Philosophy of Sarvapalli Radhakrishnan* (New York: Tudor Publishing Company, 1952), from which the selection included here was taken.

I
Sir Mohammed Iqbal: Is Religion Possible?*

Broadly speaking religious life may be divided into three periods. These may be described as the periods of "Faith," "Thought" and "Discovery." In the first period religious life appears as a form of discipline which the individual or a whole people must accept as an unconditional command without any rational understanding of the ultimate meaning and purpose of that command. This attitude may be of great consequence in the social and political history of a people, but is not of much consequence in so far as the individual's inner growth and expansion is concerned. Perfect submission to discipline is followed by a rational understanding of the discipline and the ultimate source of its authority. In this period religious life seeks its foundation in a kind of metaphysics—a logically consistent view of the world with God as a part of that view. In the third period metaphysics is displaced by psychology, and religious life develops the ambition to come into direct contact with the ultimate Reality. It is here that religion becomes a matter of personal assimilation of life and power; and the individual achieves a free personality, not by releasing himself from the fetters of the law, but by discovering the ultimate source of the law within the depth of his own consciousness. As in the words of a Muslim Sufi—"no understanding of the Holy Book is possible until it is actually revealed to the believer just as it was revealed to the Prophet." It is, then, in the sense of this last phase in the development of religious life that I use the word religion in the question that I propose to raise in this paper. Religion in this sense is known by the unfortunate name of Mysticism, which is supposed to be a life-denying, fact-avoiding attitude of mind directly opposed to the radically empirical outlook of our times. Yet higher religion, which is only a search for a longer life, is essentially experience and recognized the necessity of experience as its foundation long before science learnt to do so. It is a genuine effort to clarify human consciousness, and is, as such, as critical of its level of experience as Naturalism is of its own level.

As we all know, it was Kant who first raised the question: "Is metaphysics

*Reprinted with permission from *Proceedings of the Aristotelian Society, 1932–33* (London, 1934).

possible?" He answered this question in the negative; and his argument applies with equal force to the realities in which religion is especially interested. The manifold of sense, according to him, must fulfill certain formal conditions in order to constitute knowledge. The thing in itself is only a limiting idea. Its function is merely regulative. If there *is* some actuality corresponding to the idea it falls outside the boundaries of experience, and consequently its existence cannot be rationally demonstrated. This verdict of Kant cannot be easily accepted. It may fairly be argued that in view of the more recent developments of science, such as the nature of matter as "bottled-up light waves," the idea of the universe as an act of thought, finiteness of space and time and Heisenberg's principle of indeterminancy in nature, the case for a system of rational theology is not so bad as Kant was led to think. But for the purposes of this paper it is unnecessary to consider this point in detail. As to the thing in itself, which is inaccessible to pure reason because of its falling beyond the boundaries of experience, Kant's verdict can be accepted only if we start with the assumption that all experience other than the normal level of experience is impossible. The only question, therefore, is whether the normal level is the only level of knowledge-yielding experience. Kant's view of the thing in itself and the thing as it appears to us very much determined the character of his question regarding the possibility of metaphysics. But what if the position, as understood by him, is reversed? The great Muslim Sufi philosopher, Muhyuddin Ibnul Arabi of Spain, has made the acute observation that God is a percept; the world is a concept. Another Muslim Sufi thinker and poet, Iraqi, insists on the plurality of space-orders and time-orders and speaks of a Divine Time and a Divine Space. It may be that what we call the external world is only an intellectual construction, and that there are other levels of human experience capable of being systematized by other orders of space and time—levels in which concept and analysis do not play the same role as they do in the case of our normal experience. It may, however, be said that the level of experience to which concepts are inapplicable cannot yield any knowledge of a universal character; for concepts alone are capable of being socialized. The stand-point of the man who relies on religious experience for capturing Reality must always remain individual and incommunicable. This objection has some force if it is meant to insinuate that the mystic is wholly ruled by his traditional ways, attitudes and expectations. Conservatism is as bad in religion as in any other department of human activity. It destroys the ego's creative freedom and closes up the paths of fresh spiritual enterprise. This is the main reason why our mediæval mystic techniques can no longer produce original discoverers of ancient Truth. The fact, however, that religious experience is incommunicable does not mean that the religious man's pursuit is futile. Indeed, the incommunicability of religious experience gives us a clue to the ultimate nature of the ego. In our daily social intercourse we live and move in seclusion, as it were. We do not care to reach the inmost individuality of men. We treat them as mere functions, and approach them from those aspects of their identity which are capable of conceptual treatment. The climax of religious life, however, is the discovery of the ego as an individual deeper than his conceptually describable habitual self-hood. It is in contact with the Most Real that the ego discovers its uniqueness, its metaphysical status and the possibility of improvement in that status. Strictly speaking, the experience which leads to this discovery is not a conceptually manageable intellectual fact; it is a vital fact, an attitude consequent on an inner biological transformation which cannot be captured in the net of logical categories. It can embody itself only in a world-making or world-shaking act; and in this form alone the content of this timeless experience can diffuse itself in the time-moment, and make itself effectively visible to the eye of history. It seems that the method of dealing with Reality by means of concepts is not at all a serious way of dealing with it. Science does not care whether its electron is a real entity or not. It may be a mere symbol, a mere convention. Religion, which is essentially a mode of actual living, is the only serious way of handling Reality. Science can afford to ignore metaphysics altogether, and may even believe it to be "a justified form of poetry," as Lange defined it, or "a legitimate play of grown-ups," as Nietzsche described it. But the religious expert who seeks to discover his personal status in the constitution of things cannot, in view of the final aim of his struggle, be satisfied with what science may regard as a vital lie, a mere "as if" to regulate thought and conduct. In so far as the ultimate nature of Reality is concerned nothing is at stake in the venture of science; in the religious venture the whole career of the ego as an assimilative personal centre of life and experience is at stake. Conduct, which involves a decision of the ultimate fate of the agent cannot be based on illusions. A wrong concept misleads the understanding; a wrong deed degrades the whole man, and may eventually demolish the structure of the human ego. The mere concept affects life only partially; the deed is dynamically related to reality and issues from a generally constant attitude of the whole man towards reality. No doubt the deed, *i.e.*, the control of psychological and physiological processes with a view to tune up the ego for an immediate contact with the ultimate Reality is, and cannot but be, individual in form and content; yet the deed, too, is liable to be socialized when others begin to live through it with a view to discover for themselves its effectiveness as a method of approaching the Real. The evidence of religious experts in all ages and countries is that there are potential types of consciousness lying close to our normal consciousness. If these types of consciousness open up possibilities of life-giving and knowledge-yielding experience the question of the possibility of religion as a form of higher experience is a perfectly legitimate one and demands our serious attention.

But, apart from the legitimacy of the question, there are important reasons why it should be raised at the present moment of history of modern culture. In the first place, the scientific interest of the question. It seems that every culture has a form of Naturalism peculiar to its own world-feeling; and it further appears that every form of Naturalism ends in some sort of Atomism. We have Indian Atomism, Greek Atomism, Muslim Atomism, and Modern Atomism. Modern Atomism is, however, unique. Its amazing mathematics which sees the universe as an elaborate differential equation; and its physics which, following its own methods, has been led to smash some of the old gods of its own temple, have already brought us to the point of asking the question whether the causality-bound aspect of nature is the whole truth about it? Is not the ultimate Reality invading our consciousness from some other direction as well? Is the purely intellectual method of overcoming nature the only method? "We have acknowledged," says Prof. Eddington, "that the entities of physics can from their very nature form only a partial aspect of the reality. How are we to deal with the other part? It cannot be said that the other part concerns us less than the physical entities. Feelings, purpose, values, make up our consciousness as much as sense-impressions. We follow up the sense-impressions and find that they lead into an external world discussed by science; we follow up the other elements of our being and find that they lead—not into a world of space and time, but surely somewhere."

In the second place we have to look to the great practical importance of the question. The modern man with his philosophies of criticism and scientific specialism finds himself in a strange predicament. His Naturalism has given him an unprecedented control over the forces of nature, but has robbed him of faith in his own future. It is strange how the same idea affects different cultures differently. The formulation of the theory of evolution in the world of Islam brought into being Rumi's tremendous enthusiasm for the biological future of man. No cultured Muslim can read such passages as the following without a thrill of joy:

Low in the earth
I lived in realms of ore and stone;
And then I smiled in many-tinted flowers;
Then roving with the wild and wandering hours,
O'er earth and air and ocean's zone,
In a new birth,
I dived and flew,
And crept and ran,
And all the secret of my essence drew
Within a form that brought them all to view—
And lo, a Man!
And then my goal,
Beyond the clouds, beyond the sky,
In realms where none may change or die—
In angel form; and then away
Beyond the bounds of night and day,
And Life and Death, unseen or seen,
Where all that is hath ever been,
As One and Whole.

(*Rumi*: Thadani's Translation.)

On the other hand, the formulation of the same view of evolution with far greater precision in Europe has led to the belief that "there now appears to be no scientific basis for the idea that the present rich complexity of human endowment will ever be materially exceeded." That is how the modern man's secret despair hides itself behind the screen of scientific terminology. Nietzsche, although he thought that the idea of evolution did not justify the belief that man was unsurpassable, cannot be regarded as an exception in this respect. His enthusiasm for the future of man ended in the doctrine of eternal recurrence—perhaps the most hopeless idea of immortality ever formed by man. This eternal repetition is not eternal "becoming"; it is the same old idea of "being" masquerading as "becoming."

Thus, wholly overshadowed by the results of his intellectual activity, the modern man has ceased to live soulfully, *i.e.*, from within. In the domain of thought he is living in open conflict with himself; and in the domain of economic and political life he is living in open conflict with others. He finds himself unable to control his ruthless egoism and his infinite gold-hunger which is gradually killing all higher striving in him and bringing him nothing but life-weariness. Absorbed in the "fact," that is to say, the optically present source of sensation, he is entirely cut off from the unplumbed depths of his own being. In the wake of his systematic materialism has at last come that paralysis of energy which Huxley apprehended and deplored. The condition of things in the East is no better. The technique of mediæval mysticism by which religious life, in its higher manifestations, developed itself both in the East and in the West has now practically failed. And in the Muslim East it has, perhaps, done far greater havoc than anywhere else. Far from reintegrating the forces of the average man's inner life, and thus preparing him for participation in the march of history, it has taught him a false renunciation and made him perfectly contented with his ignorance and spiritual thraldom. No wonder then that the modern Muslim in Turkey, Egypt and Persia is led to seek fresh sources of energy in the creation of new loyalties, such as patriotism and nationalism which Nietzsche described as "sickness and unreason," and "the strongest force against culture." Disappointed of a purely religious method of spiritual renewal which alone brings us into touch with the everlasting fountain of life and power by expanding our thought and emotion, the modern Muslim fondly hopes to unlock fresh sources of energy by narrowing down his thought and emotion. Modern atheistic socialism, which possesses all the fervour of a new religion, has a broader outlook; but having received its philosophical basis from the Hegelians of the left wing, it rises in revolt against the very source which could have given it strength and purpose. Both nationalism and atheistic socialism, at least in the present state of human adjustments, must draw upon the psychological forces of hate, suspicion and resentment which tend to impoverish the soul of man and close up his hidden sources of spiritual energy. Neither the technique of mediæval mysticism nor nationalism nor atheistic socialism can cure the ills of a despairing humanity. Surely the present moment is one of great crisis in the history of modern culture. The modern world stands in need of biological renewal. And religion, which in its higher manifestations is neither dogma, nor priesthood, nor ritual, can alone ethically prepare the modern man for the burden of the great responsibility which the advancement of modern science necessarily involves, and restore to him that attitude of faith which makes him capable of winning a personality here and retaining it hereafter. It is only by rising to a fresh vision of his origin and future, his whence and whither that man will eventually triumph over a society motivated by an inhuman competition, and a civilization which has lost its spiritual unity by its inner conflict of religious and political values.

As I have indicated before, religion as a deliberate enterprise to seize the ultimate principle of value and thereby to reintegrate the forces of one's own personality, is a fact which cannot be denied. The whole religious literature of the world, including the records of specialists' personal experiences, though perhaps expressed in the thought-forms of an out-of-date psychology, is a standing testimony to it. These experiences are perfectly natural, like our normal experiences. The evidence is that they possess a cognitive value for the recipient, and, what is much more important, a capacity to centralize the forces of the ego and thereby to endow him with a new personality. The view that such experiences are neurotic or mystical will not finally settle the question of their meaning or value. If an outlook beyond physics is possible, we must courageously face the possibility, even though it may disturb or tend to modify our normal ways of life and thought. The interests of truth require that we must abandon our present attitude. It does not matter in the least if the religious attitude is originally determined by some kind of physiological disorder. George Fox may be a neurotic; but who can deny his purifying power in England's religious life of his day? Muhammad, we are told, was a psychopath. Well, if a psychopath has the power to give a fresh direction to the course of human history, it is a point of the highest psychological interest to search his original experience which has turned slaves into leaders of men, and has inspired the conduct and shaped the career of whole races of mankind. Judging from the various types of activity that emanated from the movement initiated by the Prophet of Islam, his spiritual tension and the kind of behaviour which issued from it, cannot be regarded as a response to a mere fantasy inside his brain. It is impossible to understand it except as a response to an objective situation generative of new enthusiasms, new organizations, new starting-points. If we look at the matter from the standpoint of anthropology it appears that a psychopath is an important factor in the economy of humanity's social organization. His way is not to classify facts and discover causes: he thinks in terms of life and movement with a view to create new patterns of behaviour for mankind. No doubt he has his pitfalls and illusions just as the scientist who relies on sense-experience has his pitfalls and illusions. A careful study of his method, however, shows that he is not less alert than the scientist in the matter of eliminating the alloy of illusion from his experience.

The question for us outsiders is to find out an effective method of enquiry into the nature and significance of this extraordinary experience. The Arab historian Ibn Khaldun, who laid the foundations of modern scientific history, was the first to seriously approach this side of human psychology and reached what we now call the idea of the subliminal self. Later, Sir William Hamilton in

England and Leibnitz in Germany, interested themselves in some of the more unknown phenomena of the mind. Jung, however, is probably right in thinking that the essential nature of religion is beyond the province of analytic psychology. In his discussion of the relation of analytic psychology to poetic art he tells us that the process of artistic *form* alone can be the object of psychology. The essential nature of art, according to him, cannot be the object of a psychological method of approach. "A similar distinction," says Jung, "must also be made in the realm of religion; there also a psychological consideration is permissible only in respect of the emotional and symbolical phenomena of a religion, wherein the essential nature of religion is in no way involved, as indeed it cannot be. For were this possible, not religion alone, but art also could be treated as a mere sub-division of psychology." Yet Jung has violated his own principle more than once in his writings. The result of this procedure is that instead of giving us a real insight into the essential nature of religion and its meaning for human personality, our modern psychology has given us quite a plethora of new theories which proceed on a complete misunderstanding of the nature of religion as revealed in its higher manifestations, and carry us in an entirely hopeless direction. The implication of these theories, on the whole, is that religion does not relate the human ego to any objective reality beyond himself; it is merely a kind of well-meaning biological device calculated to build barriers of an ethical nature round human society in order to protect the social fabric against the otherwise unrestrainable instincts of the ego. That is why, according to this newer psychology, Christianity has already fulfilled its biological mission, and it is impossible for the modern man to understand its original significance. Jung concludes:—

> Most certainly we should still understand it, had our customs even a breath of ancient brutality, for we can hardly realise in this day the whirlwinds of the unchained libido which roared through the ancient Rome of the Cæsars. The civilized man of the present day seems very far removed from that. He has become merely neurotic. So for us the necessities which brought forth Christianity have actually been lost, since we no longer understand their meaning. We do not know against what it had to protect us. For enlightened people the so-called religiousness has already approached very close to a neurosis. In the past two thousand years Christianity has done its work and has erected barriers of repression which protect us from the sight of our own sinfulness.

This is missing the whole point of higher religious life. Sexual self-restraint is only a preliminary stage in the ego's evolution. The ultimate purpose of religious life is to make this evolution move in a direction far more important to the destiny of the ego than the moral health of the social fabric which forms his present environment. The basic perception from which religious life moves forward is the present slender unity of the ego, his liability to dissolution, his amenability to re-formation and his capacity for an ampler freedom to create new situations in known and unknown environments. In view of this fundamental perception higher religious life fixes its gaze on experiences symbolic of those subtle movements of reality which seriously affect the destiny of the ego as a possibly permanent element in the constitution of reality. If we look at the matter from this point of view modern psychology has not yet touched even the outer fringe of religious life, and is still far from the richness and variety of what is called religious experience. In order to give you an idea of its richness and variety I quote here the substance of a passage from a great religious genius of the seventeenth century—Sheikh Ahmad of Sarhand—whose fearless analytical criticism of contemporary Sufiism resulted in the development of a new technique. All the various systems of Sufi technique in India came from Central Asia and Arabia; his is the only technique which crossed the Indian border and is still a living force in the Punjab, Afghanistan and Asiatic Russia. I am afraid it is not possible for me to expound the real meaning of this passage in the language of modern psychology; for such language does not yet exist. Since, however, my object is simply to give you an idea of the infinite wealth of experience which the ego in his Divine quest has to sift and pass through, I do hope you will excuse me for the apparently outlandish terminology which possesses a real substance of meaning, but which was formed under the inspiration of a religious psychology developed in the atmosphere of a different culture. Coming now to the passage. The experience of one Abdul Momin was described to the Sheikh as follows:—

> Heavens and Earth and God's throne and Hell and Paradise have all ceased to exist for me. When I look round I find them nowhere. When I stand in the presence of somebody I see nobody before me; nay even my own being is lost to me. God is infinite. Nobody can encompass Him; and this is the extreme limit of spiritual experience. No saint has been able to go beyond this.

On this the Sheikh replied:

> The experience which is described has its origin in the ever-varying life of the *qalb*; and it appears to me that the recipient of it has not yet passed even one-fourth of the innumerable "Stations" of the "Qalb." The remaining three-fourths must be passed through in order to finish the experiences of this first "Station" of spiritual life. Beyond this "Station" there are other "Stations" known as "*Ruh*," "*Sirr-i-Khafi*" and "*Sirr-i-Akhfar*," each of these "Stations" which together constitute what is technically called "*Alam-i-Amr*" has its own characteristic states and experiences. After having passed through these "Stations" the seeker of truth gradually receives the illuminations of "Divine Names" and "Divine Attributes" and finally the illuminations of the Divine Essence.

Whatever may be the psychological ground of the distinctions made in this passage it gives us at least some idea of a whole universe of inner experience as seen by a great reformer of Islamic Sufiism. According to him this "*Alam-i-Amr*," *i.e.*, "the world of directive energy" must be passed through before one reaches that unique experience which symbolizes the purely objective. This is the reason why I say that modern psychology has not yet touched even the outer fringe of the subject. Personally I do not at all feel hopeful of the present state of things in either biology or psychology. Mere analytical criticism with some understanding of the organic conditions of the imagery in which religious life has sometimes manifested itself is not likely to carry us to the living roots of human personality. Assuming that sex-imagery has played a role in the history of religion, or that religion has furnished imaginative means of escape from, or adjustment to, an unpleasant reality, these ways of looking at the matter cannot, in the least, affect the ultimate aim of religious life, that is to say, the reconstruction of the finite ego by bringing him into contact with an eternal life-process, and thus giving him a metaphysical status of which we can have only a partial understanding in the half-choking atmosphere of our present environment. If, therefore, the science of psychology is ever likely to possess a real significance for the life of mankind it must develop an independent method calculated to discover a new technique better suited to the temper of our times. Perhaps a psychopath endowed with a great intellect — the combination is not an impossibility — may give us a clue to such a technique. In modern Europe Nietzsche whose life and activity form, at least to us Easterns, an exceedingly interesting problem in religious psychology, was endowed with some sort of a constitutional equipment for such an undertaking. His mental history is not without a parallel in the history of Eastern Sufiism. That a really "imperative" vision of the Divine in man did come to him cannot be denied. I call his vision "imperative" because it appears to have given him a kind of prophetic mentality which, by some kind of technique, aims at turning its visions into permanent life-forces. Yet Nietzsche was a failure; and his failure was mainly due to his intellectual progenitors such as Schopenhauer, Darwin and Lange whose influence completely blinded him to the real significance of his vision. Instead of looking for a spiritual rule which would develop the Divine even in a plebian and thus open up before him an infinite future, Nietzsche was driven to seek the realization of his vision in such schemes as aristocratic radicalism. As I have said of him elsewhere:

> The "I am" which he seeketh.
> Lieth beyond philosophy, beyond knowledge.
> The plant that groweth only from the invisible soil of the heart of man,
> Groweth not from a mere heap of clay!

Thus failed a genius whose vision was solely determined by his internal forces, and remained unproductive for want of expert external guidance in his spiritual life. And the irony of fate is that this man, who appeared to his friends "as if he had come from a country where no man lived," was fully conscious of his great spiritual need. "I confront alone," he says, "an immense problem: it is as if I am lost in a forest, a primeval one. I need help. I need disciples: I need a *master.* It would be so sweet to obey." And again—"why do I not find among the living men who see higher than I do and have to look down on me? Is it only that I have made a poor search? And I have so great a longing for such."

The truth is that the religious and the scientific processes, though involving different methods, are identical in their final aim. Both aim at reaching the most real. In fact, religion, for reasons which I have mentioned before, is far more anxious to reach the ultimately real than science. And to both the way to pure objectivity lies through what may be called the purification of experience. In order to understand this we must make a distinction between experience as a natural fact, significant of the normally observable behaviour of reality, and experience as significant of the inner nature of reality. As a natural fact it is explained in the light of its antecedents, psychological and physiological; as significant of the inner nature of reality we shall have to apply criteria of a different kind to clarify its meaning. In the domain of science we try to understand its meaning in reference to the external *behaviour* of reality; in the domain of religion we take it as representative of some kind of reality and try to discover its meanings in reference mainly to the inner *nature* of that reality. The scientific and the religious processes are in a sense parallel to each other. Both are really descriptions of the same world with this difference only that in the scientific process the ego's standpoint is necessarily exclusive, whereas in the religious process the ego integrates its competing tendencies and develops a single inclusive attitude resulting in a kind of synthetic transfiguration of his experiences. A careful study of the nature and purpose of these really complementary processes shows that both of them are directed to the purification of experience in their respective spheres. An illustration will make my meaning clear. Hume's criticism of our notion of cause must be considered as a chapter in the history of science rather than that of philosophy. True to the spirit of scientific empiricism we are not entitled to work with any concepts of a subjective nature. The point of Hume's criticism is to emancipate empirical science from the concept of force which, as he urges, has no foundation in sense-experience. This was the first attempt of the modern mind to purify the scientific process.

Einstein's mathematical view of the universe completes the process of purification started by Hume, and, true to the spirit of Hume's criticism, dispenses with the concept of force altogether. The passage I have quoted from the great Indian saint shows that the practical student of religious psychology has a similar purification in view. His sense of objectivity is as keen as that of the scientist in his own sphere of objectivity. He passes from experience to experience, not as a mere spectator, but as a critical sifter of experience who by the rules of a peculiar technique, suited to his sphere of enquiry, endeavours to eliminate a subjective element, psychological or physiological, in the content of his experience with a view finally to reach what is absolutely objective. This final experience is the revelation of a new life-process—original, essential, spontaneous. The eternal secret of the ego is that the moment he reaches this final revelation he recognizes it as the ultimate root of his being without the slightest hesitation. Yet in the experience itself there is no mystery. Nor is there anything emotional in it. Indeed with a view to secure a wholly non-emotional experience the technique of Islamic Sufiism at least takes good care to forbid the use of music in worship, and to emphasize the necessity of daily congregational prayers in order to counteract the possible anti-social effects of solitary contemplation. Thus the experience reached is a perfectly natural experience and possesses a biological significance of the highest importance to the ego. It is the human ego rising higher than mere reflection, and mending its transiency by appropriating the eternal. The only danger to which the ego is exposed in this Divine quest is the possible relaxation of his activity caused by his enjoyment of and absorption in the experiences that precede the final experience. The history of Eastern Sufiism shows that this is a real danger. This was the whole point of the reform movement initiated by the great Indian saint from whose writings I have already quoted a passage. And the reason is obvious. The ultimate aim of the ego is not to *see* something, but to *be* something. It is in the ego's effort to *be* something that he discovers his final opportunity to sharpen his objectivity and acquire a more fundamental "I am" which finds evidence of its reality not in the Cartesian "I think" but in the Kantian "I can." The end of the ego's quest is not emancipation from the limitations of individuality; it is, on the other hand, a more precise definition of it. The final act is not an intellectual act, but a vital act which deepens the whole being of the ego, and sharpens his will with the creative assurance that the world is, not something to be merely seen or known through concepts, but something to be made and re-made by continuous action. It is a moment of supreme bliss and also a moment of the greatest trial for the ego:

> Art thou in the stage of "life," "death" or "death-in-life"?
> Invoke the aid of three witnesses to verify thy "Station."
> The first witness is thine own consciousness—
> See thyself, then, with thine own light.
> The second witness is the consciousness of another ego—
> See thyself, then, with the light of an ego other than thee.
> The third witness is God's consciousness—
> See thyself, then, with God's light.
> If thou standest unshaken in front of this light,
> Consider thyself as living and eternal as He!
> That man alone is real who dares—
> Dares to see God face to face!
> What is "Ascension"? Only a search or a witness
> Who may finally confirm thy reality—
> A witness whose confirmation alone makes thee eternal.
> No one can stand unshaken in His Presence;
> And he who can, verily, he is pure gold.
> Art thou a mere particle of dust?
> Tighten the knot of thy ego;

And hold fast to thy tiny being!
How glorious to burnish one's ego
And to test its lustre in the presence of the Sun!
Re-chisel, then, thine ancient frame;
And build up a new being.
Such being is real being;
Or else thy ego is a mere ring of smoke!

II
Gandhi: Selections*[1]

A: ON GOD

My own experience has led me to the knowledge that the fullest life is impossible without an immovable belief in a Living Law in obedience to which the whole universe moves. A man without that faith is like a drop thrown out of the ocean bound to perish. Every drop in the ocean shares its majesty and has the honour of giving us the ozone of life. —*H*, 25-4-36, 84.

God as Truth and Love

There is an indefinable mysterious power that pervades everything. I feel it, though I do not see it. It is this unseen power that makes itself felt and yet defies proof, because it is so unlike all that I perceive through my senses. It transcends reason. But it is possible to reason out the existence of God to a limited extent. —*YI*, 11-10-28, 340.

I have made the world's faith in God my own, and as my faith is ineffaceable, I regard that faith as amounting to experience. However, as it may be said that to describe faith as experience is to tamper with Truth, it may perhaps be more correct to say that I have no word for characterizing my belief in God.—*Auto*, 341.

God is that indefinable something which we all feel but which we do not know. To me God is Truth and Love, God is ethics and morality. God is fearlessness, God is the source of light and life and yet He is above and beyond all these. God is conscience. He is even the atheism of the atheist. He transcends speech and reason. He is a personal God to those who need His touch. He is the purest essence. He simply Is to those who have faith. He is long suffering. He is patient but He is also terrible. He is the greatest democrat

---

*Reprinted with permission from Nirmal Kumar Bose, *Selections from Gandhi* (Ahmedabad: Navajivan Publishing House, 1957).
[1]The key to abbreviations used for sources in these selections is as follows: *Auto: An Autobiography or The Story of My Experiments with Truth; ABP: Amrit Bazar Patrika; H: The Harijan; IHR: Hind Swaraj or Indian Home Rule; IV: Gandhiji in Indian Villages; MR: The Modern Review; NAT: Speeches and Writings of Mahatma Gandhi; SA: Satyagraha in South Africa; Tagore: Young India, 1919–1922;* and *YI: Young India, 1919–1932.*

the world knows. He is the greatest tyrant ever known. We are *not*, He alone *Is*. —*YI*, 5-3-25, 81.

You have asked me why I consider that God is Truth. In my early youth I was taught to repeat what in Hindu scriptures are known as one thousand names of God. But these one thousand names of God were by no means exhaustive. We believe—and I think it is the truth—that God has as many names as there are creatures and, therefore, we also say that God is nameless and since God has many forms we also consider Him formless, and since He speaks to us through many tongues we consider Him to be speechless and so on. And when I came to study Islam I found that Islam too had many names for God. I would say with those who say God is Love, God is Love. But deep down in me I used to say that though God may be God, God is Truth, above all. If it is possible for the human tongue to give the fullest description, I have come to the conclusion that for myself God is Truth. But two years ago, I went a step further and said Truth is God. You will see the fine distinction between the two statements, *viz.* that God is Truth and Truth is God. And I came to that conclusion after a continuous and relentless search after Truth which began nearly fifty years ago. I then found that the nearest approach to Truth was through love. But I also found that love has many meanings in the English language at least and that human love in the sense of passion could become a degrading thing also. I found, too, that love in the sense of *ahimsa* had only a limited number of votaries in the world. But I never found a double meaning in connection with truth and not even the atheists had demurred to the necessity or power of truth. But in their passion for discovering truth the atheists have not hesitated to deny the very existence of God—from their own point of view rightly. And it was because of this reasoning that I saw that rather than say God is Truth I should say Truth is God. I recall the name of Charles Bradlaugh who delighted to call himself an atheist, but knowing as I do something of him, I would never regard him as an atheist. I would call him a God-fearing man, though, I know, he would reject the claim. His face would redden if I would say, "Mr. Bradlaugh, you are a truth-fearing man and not a God-fearing man." I would automatically disarm his criticism by saying that Truth is God, as I have disarmed the criticism of many a young man. Add to this the difficulty that millions have taken the name of God and in His name committed nameless atrocities. Not that scientists very often do not commit cruelties in the name of truth. I know how in the name of truth and science inhuman cruelties are perpetrated on animals when men perform vivisection. There are thus a number of difficulties in the way, no matter how you describe God. But the human mind is a limited thing, and you have to labour under limitations when you think of a being or entity who is beyond the power of man to grasp. And then we have another thing in Hindu philosophy, *viz.* God alone is and nothing else exists, and the same truth you find emphasized and exemplified in the *Kalema* of Islam. There you find it clearly stated—that God alone is and nothing else exists. In fact the Sanskrit word for Truth is a word which literally means that which exits—*Sat*. For these and several other reasons that I can give you I have come to the conclusion that the definition

—Truth is God—gives me the greatest satisfaction. And when you want to find Truth as God the only inevitable means is Love, *i.e.* non-violence, and since I believe that ultimately means and end are convertible terms, I should not hesitate to say that God is Love.

"What then is Truth?"

A difficult question, but I have solved it for myself by saying that it is what the voice within tells you. How, then, you ask, different people think of different and contrary truths? Well, seeing that the human mind works through innumerable media and that the evolution of the human mind is not the same for all, it follows that what may be truth for one may be untruth for another, and hence those who have made experiments have come to the conclusion that there are certain conditions to be observed in making those experiments. Just as for conducting scientific experiments there is an indispensable scientific course of instruction, in the same way strict preliminary discipline is necessary to qualify a person to make experiments in the spiritual realm. Everyone should, therefore, realize his limitations before he speaks of his inner voice. Therefore, we have the belief based upon experience, that those who would make individual search after truth as God, must go through several vows, as for instance, the vow of truth, the vow of *brahmacharya* (purity)—for you can not possibly divide your love for Truth and God with anything else—the vow of non-violence, of poverty and non-possession. Unless you impose on yourselves the five vows, you may not embark on the experiment at all. There are several other conditions prescribed, but I must not take you through all of them. Suffice it to say that those who have made these experiments know that it is not proper for everyone to claim to hear the voice of conscience and it is because we have at the present moment everyone claiming the right of conscience without going through any discipline whatsoever that there is so much untruth being delivered to a bewildered world. All that I can in true humility present to you is that truth is not to be found by anybody who has not got an abundant sense of humility. If you would swim on the bosom of the ocean of Truth you must reduce yourselves to a zero. Further than this I cannot go along this fascinating path. — *YI*, 31-12-31, 427.

God as Truth and the Law

I do not regard God as a person. Truth for me is God, and God's Law and God are not different things or facts, in the sense that an earthly king and his law are different. Because God is an Idea, Law Himself. Therefore, it is impossible to conceive God as breaking the Law. He, therefore, does not rule out actions and withdraw Himself. When we say He rules our actions, we are simply using human language and we try to limit Him. Otherwise, He and His Law abide everywhere and govern everything. Therefore, I do not think that He answers in every detail every request of ours, but there is no doubt that He rules our action, and I literally believe that not a blade of grass grows or moves without His will. The free will we enjoy is less than that of a passenger on a crowded deck.

"Do you feel a sense of freedom in your communion with God?"

I do. I do not feel cramped as I would on a boat full of passengers. Although I know that my freedom is less than that of a passenger, I appreciate that freedom as I have imbibed through and through the central teaching of the *Gita* that man is the maker of his own destiny in the sense that he has freedom of choice as to the manner in which he uses that freedom. But he is no controller of results. The moment he thinks he is, he comes to grief. —*H*, 23-3-40, 55.

Man was supposed to be the maker of his own destiny. It is partly true. He can make his destiny only in so far as he is allowed by the Great Power which overrides all our intentions, all our plans and carries out His own plans.

I call that Great Power not by the name of *Allah*, not by the name of *Khuda* or God but by the name of Truth. For me, Truth is God and Truth overrides all our plans. The whole truth is only embodied within the heart of that Great Power—Truth. I was taught from my early days to regard Truth as unapproachable—something that you cannot reach. A great Englishman taught me to believe that God is unknowable. He is knowable to the extent that our limited intellect allows. —*H*, 20-4-47, 113.

B: ON ACTION

Hatred Can Never Yield Good

Brute force has been the ruling factor in the world for thousands of years, and mankind has been reaping its bitter harvest all along, as he who runs may read. There is little hope of anything good coming out of it in the future. If light can come out of darkness, then alone can love emerge from hatred. —*SA*, 289.

It is my firm conviction that nothing enduring can be built upon violence. —*YI*, 15-11-28, 381.

Non-violence

(1) Non-violence implies as complete self-purification as is humanly possible.

Man for man the strength of non-violence is in exact proportion to the ability, not the will, of the non-violent person to inflict violence.

Non-violence is without exception superior to violence, i.e., the power at the disposal of a non-violent person is always greater than he would have if he was violent.

There is no such thing as defeat in non-violence. The end of violence is surest defeat.

The ultimate end of non-violence is surest victory if such a term may be used of non-violence. In reality where there is no sense of defeat, there is no sense of victory. —*H*, 12-10-35, 276.

The only condition of a successful use of this force is a recognition of the existence of the soul as apart from the body and its permanent nature. And this recognition must amount to a living faith and not mere intellectual grasp. —*Nat*, 166.

Consequences of Non-violence

Q. Is love or non-violence compatible with possession or exploitation in any shape or form?
A. Love and exclusive possession can never go together. —*MR*, 1935, 412.

Military force is inconsistent with soul-force. Frightfulness, exploitation of the weak, immoral gains, insatiable pursuit after enjoyments of the flesh are utterly inconsistent with soul-force. — *YI*, 6-5-26, 164.

The principle of non-violence necessitates complete abstention from exploitation in any form.

Rural economy as I have conceived it eschews exploitation altogether, and exploitation is the essence of violence. —*H*, 4-11-39, 331.

No man could be actively non-violent and not rise against social injustice no matter where it occurred. —*H*, 20-4-40, 97.

Non-Violence always Applicable and in all Spheres of Life

Non-violence is a universal principle and its operation is not limited by a hostile environment. Indeed, its efficacy can be tested only when it acts in the midst of and in spite of opposition. Our non-violence would be a hollow thing and nothing worth, if it depended for its success on the goodwill of the authorities. (Here, reference is made to the British Government in India.) —*H*, 12-11-38, 326.

Truth and non-violence are no cloistered virtues but applicable as much in the forum and the legislatures as in the market place. —*H*, 8-5-37, 98.

Some friends have told me that truth and non-violence have no place in politics and worldly affairs. I do not agree. I have no use for them as a means of individual salvation. Their introduction and application in everyday life has been my experiment all along. —*ABP*, 30-6-44.

We have to make truth and non-violence, not matters for mere individual practice but for practice by groups and communities and nations. That at any rate is my dream. I shall live and die in trying to realize it. My faith helps me to discover new truths every day. *Ahimsa* is the attribute of the soul, and therefore, to be practised by everybody in all the affairs of life. If it cannot be practised in all departments, it has no practical value. —*H*, 2-3-40, 23.

The Meaning of Non-resistance

Hitherto the word "revolution" has been connected with violence and has as such been condemned by established authority. But the movement of Non-co-operation, if it may be considered a revolution, is not an armed revolt; it is an evolutionary revolution, it is a bloodless revolution. The movement is a revolution of thought, of spirit. Non-co-operation is a process of purification, and, as such, it constitutes a revolution in one's ideas. Its suppression, therefore, would amount to co-operation by coercion. Orders to kill the movement will be orders to destroy, or interfere with, the introduction of the spinning wheel, to prohibit the campaign of temperance, and an incitement, therefore, to violence. For any attempt to compel people by indirect methods to wear foreign clothes, to patronize drink-shops would certainly exasperate them. But our success will be assured when we stand even this exasperation and incitement. We must not retort. Inaction on our part will kill Government madness. For violence flourishes on response, either by submission to the will of the violator, or by counter-violence. My strong advice to every worker is to segregate this evil Government by strict non-co-operation, not even to talk or speak about it, but having recognized the evil, to cease to pay homage to it by co-operation. — *YI*, 30-3-21, 97.

Passive resistance is a method of securing rights by personal suffering; it is the reverse of resistance by arms. When I refuse to do a thing that is repugnant to my conscience, I use soul-force. For instance, the Government of the day has passed a law which is applicable to me. I do not like it. If by using violence I force the Government to repeal the law, I am employing what may be termed body-force. If I do not obey the law and accept the penalty for its breach, I use soul-force. It involves sacrifice of self.

Everybody admits that sacrifice of self is infinitely superior to sacrifice of others. Moreover, if this kind of force is used in a cause that is unjust, only the person using it suffers. He does not make others suffer for his mistakes. Men have before now done many things which were subsequently found to have been wrong. No man can claim that he is absolutely in the right or that a particular thing is wrong because he thinks so, but it is wrong for him so long as that is his deliberate judgment. It is therefore meet that he should not do that which he knows to be wrong, and suffer the consequence whatever it may be. This is the key to the use of soul-force. — *IHR*, 45.

The method of passive resistance adopted to combat the mischief is the clearest and safest, because, if the cause is not true, it is the resisters, and they alone, who suffer. — *Nat*, 305.

That is the way of *satyagraha* or the way of non-resistance to evil. It is the aseptic method in which the physician allows the poison to work itself out by setting in motion all the natural forces and letting them have full play. — *H*, 9-7-38, 173.

I accept the interpretation of *ahimsa*, namely, that it is not merely a negative state of harmlessness but it is a positive state of love, of doing good even to the evil-doer. But it does not mean helping the evil-doer to continue the wrong or tolerating it by passive acquiescence. On the contrary, love, the active state of *ahimsa*, requires you to resist the wrongdoer by dissociating yourself from him even though it may offend him or injure him physically. — *YI*, 25-8-20.

In its negative form, it (*ahimsa*) means not injuring any living being whether by body or mind. It may not, therefore, hurt the person of any wrongdoer or bear any ill-will to him and so cause him mental suffering. The statement does not cover suffering caused to the wrongdoer by natural acts of mine which do not proceed from ill-will. It, therefore, does not prevent me from withdrawing from his presence a child whom he, we shall imagine, is about to strike. Indeed, the proper practice of *ahimsa* requires me to withdraw the intended victim from the wrongdoer, if I am in any way the guardian of such a child. It was therefore most proper for the passive resisters of South Africa to have resisted the evil that the Union Government sought to do to them. They bore no ill-will to it. They showed this by helping the Government whenever it needed their help. "Their resistance consisted of disobedience of the orders of the Government even to the extent of suffering death at their hands." *Ahisma* requires deliberate self-suffering, not a deliberate injury of the supposed wrongdoer. —*Nat*, 346 (from *MR*, Oct. 1916).

If a man abused him, it would never do for him to return the abuse. An evil returned by another evil only succeeded in multiplying it, instead of leading to its reduction. It was a universal law that violence would never be quenched by superior violence but could only be quenched by non-violence or non-resistance. But the true meaning of non-resistance had often been misunderstood or even distorted. It never implied that a non-violent man should bend before the violence of an aggressor. While not returning the latter's violence by violence, he should refuse to submit to the latter's illegitimate demand even to the point of death. That was the true meaning of non-resistance. —*H*, 30-3-47, 85.

Non-violence, Militant in Character

Non-violence in its dynamic condition means conscious suffering. It does not mean meek submission to the will of the evil-doer, but it means the putting of one's whole soul against the will of the tyrant. Working under this law of our being, it is possible for a single individual to defy the whole might of an unjust empire to save his honour, his religion, his soul and lay the foundation for that empire's fall or its regeneration. — *YI*, 11-8-20.

Yours should not merely be a passive spirituality that spends itself in idle meditation, but it should be an active thing which will carry war into the enemy's camp.

Never has anything been done on this earth without direct action. I reject the word "passive resistance," because of its insufficiency and its being interpreted as a weapon of the weak.

What was the larger "symbiosis" that Buddha and Christ preached? Gentleness and love. Buddha fearlessly carried the war into the enemy's camp and brought down on its knees an arrogant priesthood. Christ drove out the money-changers from the temple of Jerusalem and drew down curses from heaven upon the hypocrites and the Pharisees. Both were for intensely direct action. But even as Buddha and Christ chastized, they showed unmistakable love and gentleness behind every act of theirs. — *YI*, 12-5-20.

Our aim is not merely to arouse the best in the Englishman but to do so whilst we are prosecuting our cause. If we cease to pursue our course, we do not evoke the best in him. The best must not be confounded with good temper. When we are dealing with any evil, we may have to ruffle the evil-doer. We have to run the risk, if we are to bring the best out of him. I have likened non-violence to aseptic and violence to antiseptic treatment. Both are intended to ward off the evil, and therefore cause a kind of disturbance which is often inevitable. The first never harms the evil-doer. —*H*, 30-3-40, 72.

Non-violence, the Virtue of the Strong

Non-violence presupposes ability to strike. It is a conscious, deliberate restraint put upon one's desire for vengeance. But vengeance is any day superior to passive, effeminate and helpless submission. Forgiveness is higher still. Vengeance too is weakness. The desire for vengeance comes out of fear of harm, imaginary or real. A man who fears no one on earth would consider it troublesome even to summon up anger against one who is vainly trying to injure him. — *YI*, 12-8-26, 285.

Ahimsa is the extreme limit of forgiveness. But forgiveness is the quality of the brave. *Ahimsa* is impossible without fearlessness. — *YI*, 4-11-26, 384.

My creed of non-violence is an extremely active force. It has no room for cowardice or even weakness. There is hope for a violent man to be some day non-violent, but there is none for a coward. I have therefore said more than once in these pages that if we do not know how to defend ourselves, our women and our places of worship by the force of suffering, i.e., non-violence, we must, if we are men, be at least able to defend all these by fighting. — *YI*, 16-6-27, 196.

There are two ways of defence. The best and the most effective is not to defend at all, but to remain at one's post risking every danger. The next best but equally honourable method is to strike bravely in self-defence and put one's life in the most dangerous positions. — *YI*, 18-12-24, 414.

The strength to kill is not essential for self-defence; one ought to have the strength to die. When a man is fully ready to die, he will not even desire to offer violence. Indeed I may put it down as a self-evident proposition that the desire to kill is in inverse proportion to the desire to die. And history is replete with instances of men who by dying with courage and compassion on their lips converted the hearts of their violent opponents. — *YI*, 23-1-30-27.

Non-violence and cowardice go ill together. I can imagine a fully armed man to be at heart a coward. Possession of arms implies an element of fear, if not cowardice. But true non-violence is an impossibility without the possession of unadulterated fearlessness. —*H*, 15-7-39, 201.

True and False Non-violence

Non-violence to be a potent force must begin with the mind. Non-violence of the mere body without the co-operation of the mind is non-violence of the weak or the cowardly, and has therefore no potency. If we bear malice and hatred in our bosoms and pretend not to retaliate, it must recoil upon us and lead to our destruction. For abstention from mere bodily violence not to be injurious, it is at least necessary not to entertain hatred if we cannot generate active love.

All the songs and speeches betokening hatred must be taboo. — *YI*, 2-4-31, 58.

The mysterious effect of non-violence is not to be measured by its visible effect. But we dare not rest content so long as the poison of hatred is allowed to permeate society. This struggle is a stupendous effort at conversion. We aim at nothing less than the conversion of the English. It can never be done by harbouring ill-will and still pretending to follow non-violence. Let those therefore who want to follow the path of non-violence and yet harbour ill-will retrace their steps and repent of the wrong they have done to themselves and the country. — *YI*, 2-4-31, 58.

If we are unmanly today, we are so, not because we do not know how to strike, but because we fear to die. He is no follower of Mahavira, the apostle of Jainism, or of Buddha or of the *Vedas* who, being afraid to die, takes flight before any danger, real or imaginary, all the while wishing that somebody else would remove the danger by destroying the person causing it. He is no follower of *ahimsa* who does not care a straw if he kills a man by inches by deceiving him in trade, or who would protect by force of arms a few cows and make away with the butcher or who, in order to do a supposed good to his country, does not mind killing off a few officials. All these are actuated by hatred, cowardice and fear. Here the love of the cow or the country is a vague thing intended to satisfy one's vanity or soothe a stinging conscience.

Ahimsa, truly understood, is in my humble opinion a panacea for all evils mundane and extra-mundane. We can never overdo it. Just at present we are not doing it at all. *Ahimsa* does not displace the practice of other virtues, but renders their practice imperatively necessary before it can be practised even in its rudiments. Mahavira and Buddha were soldiers, and so was Tolstoy. Only, they saw deeper and truer into their profession and found the secret of a true, happy, honourable and godly life. Let us be joint-sharers with these teachers, and this land of ours will once more be the abode of gods. — *Nat*, 348.

Violence, rather than Cowardice

I do believe that, where there is only a choice between cowardice and violence, I would advise violence. I would rather have India resort to arms in order to defend her honour than that she should, in a cowardly manner, become or remain a helpless witness to her own dishonour.

But I believe that non-violence is infinitely superior to violence, forgiveness is more manly than punishment. Forgiveness adorns the soldier. But abstinence is forgiveness only when there is the power to punish; it is meaningless when it pretends to proceed from a helpless creature. But I do not believe India to be helpless. I do not believe myself to be a helpless creature. Strength does not come from physical capacity. It comes from an indomitable will. — *YI*, 11-8-20.

The people of a village near Bettiah told me that they had run away whilst the police were looting their houses and molesting their womenfolk. When they said that they had run away because I had told them to be non-violent, I hung my head in shame. I assured them that such was not the meaning of my non-violence. I expected them to intercept the mightiest power that might be in the act of harming those who were under their protection, and draw without retaliation all harm upon their own heads even to the point of death, but never to run away from the storm centre. It was manly enough to defend one's property, honour or religion at the point of the sword. It was manlier and nobler to defend them without seeking to injure the wrongdoer. But it was unmanly, unnatural and dishonourable to forsake the post of duty and, in order to save one's skin, to leave property, honour or religion to the mercy of the wrongdoer. I could see my way of delivering the message of *ahimsa* to those who knew how to die, not to those who were afraid of death. — *IV*, 254.

The weakest of us physically must be taught the art of facing dangers and giving a good account of ourselves. I want both the Hindus and the Mussalmans to cultivate the cool courage, to die without killing. But if one has not that courage, I want him to cultivate the art of killing and being killed, rather than in a cowardly manner flee from danger. For the latter in spite of his flight does commit mental *himsa*. He flees because he has not the courage to be killed in the act of killing. — *YI*, 20-10-21, 335.

III
Aurobindo Ghose: The Life Divine*

CHAPTER XXVIII

The Divine Life

O seeing Flame, thou carriest man of the crooked ways into the abiding truth and the knowledge.

Rig Veda. I.31.6

I purify earth and heaven by the Truth.

Rig Veda. I.33.1

His ecstasy, in one who holds it, sets into motion the two births, the human self-expression and the divine, and moves between them.

Rig Veda. IX.86.42

---

*Reprinted with permission from Aurobindo Ghose, *The Life Divine* (New York: India Library Society, n.d.).

May the invincible rays of his intuition be there seeking immortality, pervading both the births; for by them he sets flowing in one movement human strengths and things divine.

Rig Veda. IX.70.3

Let all accept thy will when thou art born a living god from the dry tree, that they may attain to divinity and reach by the speed of thy movements to possession of the Truth and the Immortality.

Rig Veda. I.68.2

Our endeavour has been to discover what is the reality and significance of our existence as conscious beings in the material universe and in what direction and how far that significance once discovered leads us, to what human or divine future. Our existence here may indeed be an inconsequential freak of Matter itself or of some Energy building up Matter, or it may be an inexplicable freak of the Spirit. Or, again, our existence here may be an arbitrary fantasy of a supracosmic Creator. In that case it has no essential significance,—no significance at all if Matter or an inconscient Energy is the fantasy-builder, for then it is at best the stray description of a wandering spiral of Chance or the hard curve of a blind Necessity; it can have only an illusory significance which vanishes into nothingness if it is an error of the Spirit. A conscious Creator may indeed have put a meaning into our existence, but it must be discovered by a revelation of his will and is not self-implied in the self-nature of things and discoverable there. But if there is a self-existent Reality of which our existence here is a result, then there must be a truth of that Reality which is manifesting, working itself out, evolving here, and that will be the significance of our own being and life. Whatever that Reality may be, it is something that has taken upon itself the aspect of a becoming in Time,—an indivisible becoming, for our present and our future carry in themselves, transformed, made other, the past that created them, and the past and present already contained and now contain in themselves, invisible to us because still unmanifested, unevolved, their own transformation into the still uncreated future. The significance of our existence here determines our destiny: that destiny is something that already exists in us as a necessity and a potentiality, the necessity of our being's secret and emergent reality, a truth of its potentialities that is being worked out; both, though not yet realised, are even now implied in what has been already manifested. If there is a Being that is becoming, a Reality of existence that is unrolling itself in Time, what that being, that reality secretly is is what we have to become, and so to become is our life's significance.

It is consciousness and life that must be the keywords to what is being thus worked out in Time; for without them Matter and the world of Matter would be a meaningless phenomenon, a thing that has just happened by Chance or by an unconscious Necessity. But consciousness as it is, life as it is cannot be the whole secret; for both are very clearly something unfinished and still in process. In us consciousness is Mind, and our mind is ignorant and imperfect, an intermediate power that has grown and is still growing towards something beyond itself: there were lower levels of consciousness that came before it and out of which it arose, there must very evidently be higher levels to which it is itself arising. Before our thinking, reasoning, reflecting mind there was a consciousness unthinking but living and sentient, and before that there was the subconscious and the unconscious; after us or in our yet unevolved selves there is likely to be waiting a great consciousness, self-luminous, not dependent on constructive thought: our imperfect and ignorant thought-mind is certainly not the last word of consciousness, its ultimate possibility. For the essence of consciousness is the power to be aware of itself and its objects, and in its true nature this power must be direct, self-fulfilled and complete: if it is in us indirect, incomplete, unfulfilled in its workings, dependent on constructed instruments, it is because consciousness here is emerging from an original veiling Inconscience and is yet burdened and enveloped with the first Nescience proper to the Inconscient; but it must have the power to emerge completely, its destiny must be to evolve into its own perfection which is its true nature. Its true nature is to be wholly aware of its objects, and of these objects the first is self, the being which is evolving its consciousness here, and the rest is what we see as not-self, — but if existence is indivisible, that too must in reality be self: the destiny of evolving consciousness must be, then, to become perfect in its awareness, entirely aware of self and all-aware. This perfect and natural condition of consciousness is to us a superconscience, a state which is beyond us and in which our mind, if suddenly transferred to it, could not at first function; but it is towards that superconscience that our conscious being must be evolving. But this evolution of our consciousness to a superconscience or supreme of itself is possible only if the Inconscience which is our basis here is really itself an involved Superconscience; for what is to be in the becoming of the Reality in us must be already there involved or secret in its beginning. Such an involved Being or Power we can well conceive the Inconscient to be when we closely regard this material creation of an unconscious Energy and see it labouring out with curious construction and infinite device the work of a vast involved Intelligence and see, too, that we ourselves are something of that Intelligence evolving out of its involution, an emerging consciousness whose emergence cannot stop short on the way until the Involved has evolved and revealed itself as a supreme totally self-aware and all-aware Intelligence. It is this to which we have given the name of Supermind or Gnosis. For that evidently must be the consciousness of the Reality, the Being, the Spirit that is secret in us and slowly manifesting here; of that Being we are the becomings and must grow into its nature.

If consciousness is the central secret, life is the outward indication, the effective power of being in Matter; for it is that which liberates consciousness and gives it its form or embodiment of force and its effectuation in material act. If some revelation or effectuation of itself in Matter is the ultimate aim of the evolving Being in its birth, life is the exterior and dynamic sign and index of that revelation and effectuation. But life also, as it is now, is imperfect and evolving; it evolves through growth of consciousness even as consciousness evolves through greater organisation and perfection of life: a greater consciousness means a greater life. Man, the mental being, has an imperfect life because mind is not the first and highest power of consciousness of the Being; even if mind were perfected, there would be still something yet to be realised, not yet manifested. For what is involved and emergent is not a Mind, but a Spirit, and mind is not the native dynamism of consciousness of the Spirit; supermind, the light of gnosis, is it native dynamism. If then life has to become a manifestation of the Spirit, it is the manifestation of a spiritual being in us and the divine life of a perfected consciousness in a supramental or gnostic power of spiritual being that must be the secret burden and intention of evolutionary Nature.

All spiritual life is in its principle a growth into divine living. It is difficult to fix the frontier where the mental ceases and the divine life begins, for the two project into each other and there is a long space of their intermingled existence. A great part of this interspace,—when the spiritual urge does not turn away from earth or world altogether,—can be seen as the process of a higher life in the making. As the mind and life become illumined with the light of the spirit, they put on or reflect something of the divinity, the secret greater Reality, and this must increase until the interspace has been crossed and the whole existence is unified in the full light and power of the spiritual principle. But, for the full and perfect fulfillment of the evolutionary urge, this illumination and change must take up and re-create the whole being, mind, life and body: it must be not only an inner experience of the Divinity, but a remoulding of both the inner and outer existence by its power; it must take form not only in the life of the individual but as a collective life of gnostic beings established as a highest power and form of the becoming of the Spirit in the earth-nature. For this to be possible the spiritual entity in us must have developed its own integralised perfection not only of the inner state of the being but of the outgoing power of the being and, with that perfection and as a necessity of its complete action, it must have evolved its own dynamis and instrumentation of the outer existence.

There can undoubtedly be a spiritual life within, a kingdom of heaven within us which is not dependent on any outer manifestation or instrumentation or formula of external being. The inner life has a supreme spiritual importance and the outer has a value only in so far as it is expressive of the inner status. However the man of spiritual realisation lives and acts and behaves, in all ways of his being and acting, it is said in the Gita, "he lives and moves in Me"; he dwells in the Divine, he has realised the spiritual existence. The spiritual man living in the sense of the spiritual self, in the realisation of the Divine within him and everywhere, would be living inwardly a divine life and its reflection would fall on his outer acts of existence, even if they did not pass—or did not seem to pass—beyond the ordinary instrumentation of human thought and action in this world of earth-nature. This is the first truth and the essence of the matter; but still, from the point of view of a spiritual evolution, this would be only an individual liberation and perfection in an unchanged environmental existence: for a greater dynamic change in earth-nature itself, a spiritual change of the whole principle and instrumentation of life and action, the appearance of a new order of beings and a new earth-life must be envisaged in our idea of the total consummation, the divine issue. Here the gnostic change assumes a primary importance; all that precedes can be considered as an upbuilding and a preparation for this transmuting reversal of the whole nature. For it is a gnostic way of dynamic living that must be the fulfilled divine life on earth, a way of living that develops higher instruments of world-knowledge and world action for the dynamisation of consciousness in the physical existence and takes up and transforms the values of a world of material Nature.

But always the whole foundation of the gnostic life must be by its very nature inward and not outward. In the life of the spirit it is the spirit, the inner Reality, that has built up and uses the mind, vital being and body as its instrumentation; thought, feeling and action do not exist for themselves, they are not an object, but the means; they serve to express the manifested divine Reality within us: otherwise, without this inwardness, this spiritual origination, in a too externalised consciousness or by only external means, no greater or divine life is possible. In our present life of Nature, in our externalised surface existence, it is the world that seems to create us; but in the turn to the spiritual life it is we who must create ourselves and our world. In this new formula of creation, the inner life becomes of the first importance and the rest can be only its expression and outcome. It is this, indeed, that is indicated by our own strivings towards perfection, the perfection of our own soul and mind and life and the perfection of the life of the race. For we are given a world which is obscure, ignorant, material, imperfect, and our external conscious being is itself created by the energies, the pressure, the moulding operations of this vast mute obscurity, by physical birth, by environment, by a training through the impacts and shocks of life; and yet we are vaguely aware of something that is there in us or seeking to be, something other than what has been thus made, a spirit self-existent, self-determining, pushing the nature towards the creation of an image of its own occult perfection or Idea of perfection. There is something that grows in us in answer to this demand, that strives to become the image of a divine Somewhat, and is impelled also to labour at the world outside that has been given to it and to remake that too in a greater image, in the image of its own spiritual and mental and vital growth, to make our world too something created according to our own mind and self-conceiving spirit, something new, harmonious, perfect.

But our mind is obscure, partial in its notions, misled by opposite surface appearances, divided between various possibilities; it is led in three different directions to any of which it may give an exclusive preference. Our mind, in its search for what must be, turns toward a concentration on our own inner spiritual growth and perfection, on our own individual being and inner living; or it turns towards a concentration on an individual development of our surface nature, on the perfection of our thought and outer dynamic or practical action on the world, on some idealism of our personal relation with the world around us; or it turns rather towards a concentration on the outer world itself, on making it better, more suited to our ideas and temperament or to our conception of what should be. On one side there is the call of our spiritual being which is our true self, a transcendent reality, a being of the Divine Being, not created by the world, able to live in itself, to rise out of the world to transcendence; on the other side there is the demand of the world around us which is a cosmic form, a formulation of the Divine Being, a power of the Reality in disguise. There is too the divided or double demand of our being of Nature which is poised between these two terms, depends on them and connects them; for it is apparently made by the world and yet, because its true creator is in ourselves and the world instrumentation that seems to make it is only the means first used, it is really a form, a disguised manifestation of a greater spiritual being within us. It is this demand that mediates between our preoccupation with an inward perfection or spiritual liberation and our preoccupation with the outer world and its formation, insists on a happier relation between the two terms and creates the ideal of a better individual in a better world. But it is within us that the Reality must be found and the source and foundation of a perfected life; no outward formation can replace it: there must be the true self realised within if there is to be the true life realised in world and Nature.

In the growth into a divine life the spirit must be our first preoccupation; until we have revealed and evolved it in our self out of its mental, vital, physical wrappings and disguises, extracted it with patience from our own body, as the Upanishad puts it, until we have built up in ourselves an inner life of the spirit, it is obvious that no outer divine living can become possible. Unless, indeed, it is a mental or vital godhead that we perceive and would be,—but even then the individual mental being or the being of power and vital force and desire in us must grow into a form of that godhead before our life can be divine in that inferior sense, the life of the infraspiritual superman, mental demi-god or vital Titan, Deva or Asura. This inner life once created, to convert our whole surface being, our thought, feeling, action in the world, into a perfect power of that inner life, must be our other preoccupation. Only if we live in that deeper and greater way in our dynamic parts, can there be a force for creating a greater life or the world be remade whether in some power or perfection of Mind and Life or the power and perfection of the Spirit. A perfected human world cannot be created by men or composed of men who are themselves imperfect. Even if all our actions are scrupulously regulated by education or law or social or political machinery, what will be achieved is a regulated pattern of minds, a fabricated pattern of lives, a cultivated pattern of conduct; but a conformity of this kind cannot change, cannot re-create the man within, it cannot carve or cut out a perfect soul or a perfect thinking man or a perfect or growing living being. For soul and mind and life are powers of being and can grow but cannot be cut out or made; an outer process or formation can assist or can express soul and mind and life but cannot create or develop it. One can indeed help the being to grow, not by an attempt at manufacture, but by throwing on it stimulating influences or by lending to it one's forces of soul or mind or life; but even so the growth must still come from within it, determining from there what shall be made of these influences and forces, and not from outside. This is the first truth that our creative zeal and aspiration have to learn, otherwise all our human endeavour is foredoomed to turn in a futile circle and can end only in a success that is a specious failure.

To be or become something, to bring something into being is the whole labour of the force of Nature; to know, feel, do are subordinate energies that have a value because they help the being in its partial self-realisation to express what it is and help it too in its urge to express the still more not yet realised that it has to be. But knowledge, thought, action,—whether religious, ethical, political, social, economic, utilitarian or hedonistic, whether a mental, vital or physical form or construction of existence,—cannot be the essence or object of life; they are only activities of the powers of being or the powers of its becoming, dynamic symbols of itself, creations of the embodied spirit, its means of discovering or formulating what it seeks to be. The tendency of man's physical mind is to see otherwise and to turn the true method of things upside down, because it takes as essential or fundamental the surface forces or appearances of Nature; it accepts her creation by a visible or exterior process as the essence of her action and does not see that it is only a secondary appearance and covers a greater secret process: for Nature's occult process is to reveal the being through the bringing out of its powers and forms, her external pressure is only a means of awakening the involved being to the need of this evolution, of this self-formation. When the spiritual stage of her evolution is reached, this occult process must become the whole process; to get through the veil of forces and get at their secret mainspring, which is the spirit itself, is of cardinal importance. To become ourselves is the one thing to be done; but the true ourselves is that which is within us, and to exceed our outer self of body, life and mind is the condition for this highest being, which is our true and divine being, to become self-revealed and active. It is only by growing within and living within that we can find it; once that is done, to create from there the spiritual or divine mind, life, body and through this instrumentation to arrive at the creation of a world which shall be the true environment of a divine living,—this is the final object that Force of Nature has set before us. This then is the first necessity, that the individual, each individual, shall discover the spirit, the divine reality within him and express that in all his being and living. A divine life must be first and foremost an inner life; for since the outward must be the expression of what is within, there can be no divinity in the outer existence if there is not the divinisation of the inner being. The Divinity in man dwells veiled in his spiritual centre; there can be no such thing as self-exceeding for man or a higher issue for his existence if there is not in him the reality of an eternal self and spirit.

To be and to be fully is Nature's aim in us; but to be fully is to be wholly conscious of one's being: unconsciousness, half consciousness or deficient consciousness is a state of being not in possession of itself; it is existence, but not fullness of being. To be aware wholly and integrally of oneself and of all the truth of one's being is the necessary condition of true possession of existence. This self-awareness is what is meant by spiritual knowledge: the essence of spiritual knowledge is an intrinsic self-existent consciousness; all its action of knowledge, indeed all its action of any kind, must be that consciousness formulating itself. All other knowledge is consciousness oblivious of itself and striving to return to its own awareness of itself and its contents; it is self-ignorance labouring to transform itself back into self-knowledge.

But also, since consciousness carries in itself the force of existence, to be fully is to have the intrinsic and integral force of one's being; it is to come into possession of all one's force of self and of all its use. To be merely, without possessing the force of one's being or with a half-force or deficient force of it, is a mutilated or diminished existence; it is to exist, but it is not fullness of being. It is possible, indeed, to exist only in status, with the force of being self-gathered and immobile in the self; but, even so, to be in deficient force of it, is a mutilated or diminished existence; power of self is the sign of the divinity of self,—a powerless spirit is no spirit. But, as the spiritual consciousness is intrinsic and self-existent, so too this force of our spiritual being must be intrinsic, automatic in action, self-existent and self-fulfilling. What instrumentality it uses, must be part of itself; even any external instrumentality it uses must be made part of itself and expressive of its being. Force of being in conscious action is will; and whatever is the conscious will of the spirit, its will of being and becoming, that all the existence must be able harmonically to fulfill. Whatever action or energy of action has not this sovereignty or is not master of the machinery of action, carries in it by that defect the sign of an imperfection of the force of being, of a division or disabling segmentation of the consciousness, of an incompleteness in the manifestation of the being.

Lastly, to be fully is to have the full delight of being. Being without delight of being, without an entire delight of itself and all things is something neutral or diminished; it is existence, but it is not fullness of being. This delight too must be intrinsic, self-existent, automatic; it cannot be dependent on things outside itself: whatever it delights in, it makes part of itself, has the joy of it as part of its universality. All undelight, all pain and suffering are a sign of imperfection, of incompleteness; they arise from a division of being, an incompleteness of consciousness of being, an incompleteness of the force of being. To become complete in being, in consciousness of being, in force of being, in delight of being and to live in this integrated completeness is the divine living.

But, again, to be fully is to be universally. To be in the limitations of a small restricted ego is to exist, but it is an imperfect existence: in its very nature it is to live in an incomplete consciousness, an incomplete force and delight of existence. It is to be less than oneself and it brings an inevitable subjection to ignorance, weakness and suffering: or even if by some divine composition of the nature it could exclude these things, it would be to live in a limited scope of existence, a limited consciousness and power and joy of existence. All being is one and to be fully is to be all that is. To be in the being of all and to include all in one's being, to be conscious of the consciousness of all, to be integrated in force with the universal force, to carry all action and experience in oneself and feel it as one's own action and experience, to feel all selves as one's own self, to feel all delight of being as one's own delight of being is a necessary condition of the integral divine living.

But thus to be universally in the fullness and freedom of one's universality, one must be also transcendentally. The spiritual fullness of the being is eternity; if one has not the consciousness of timeless eternal being, if one is dependent on body or embodied mind or embodied life, or dependent on this world or that world or on this condition of being or that condition of being, that is not the reality of self, not the fullness of our spiritual existence. To live only as a self of body or be only by the body is to be an ephemeral creature, subject to death and desire and pain and suffering and decay and decadence. To transcend, to exceed consciousness of body, not to be held in the body or by the body, to hold the body only as an instrument, a minor outward formation of self, is a first condition of divine living. Not to be a mind subject to ignorance and restriction of consciousness, to transcend mind and handle it as an instrument, to control it as a surface formation of self, is a second condition. To be by the self and spirit, not to depend upon life, not to be identified with it, to transcend it and control and use it as an expression and instrumentation of the self, is a third condition. Even the bodily life does not possess its own full being in its own kind if the consciousness does not exceed the body and feel its physical oneness with all material existence; the vital life does not possess its own full living in its own kind if the consciousness does not exceed the restricted play of an individual vitality and feel the universal life as its own and its oneness with all life. The mentality is not a full conscious existence or activity in its own kind if one does not exceed the individual mental limits and feel a oneness with universal Mind and with all minds and enjoy one's integrality of consciousness fulfilled in their wealth of difference. But one must transcend not only the individual formula but the formula of the universe, for only so can either the individual or the universal existence find its own true being and a perfect harmonisation; both are in their outer formulation incomplete terms of the Transcendence, but they are that in their essence, and it is only by becoming conscious of that essence that individual consciousness or universal consciousness can come to its own fullness and freedom of reality. Otherwise the individual may remain subject to the cosmic movement and its reactions and limitations and miss his entire spiritual freedom. He must enter into the supreme divine Reality, feel his oneness with it, live in it, be its self-creation: all his mind, life, physicality must be converted into terms of its Supernature; all his thought, feelings, actions must be determined by it and be it, its self-formation. All this can become complete in him only when he has evolved out of the Ignorance into the Knowledge and through the Knowledge into the supreme Consciousness and its dynamis and supreme delight of existence; but some essentiality of these things and their sufficient instrumentation can come with the first spiritual change and culminate in the life of the gnostic supernature.

These things are impossible without an inward living; they cannot be reached by remaining in an external consciousness turned always outwards, active only or mainly on and from the surface. The individual being has to find himself, his true existence; he can only do this by going inward, by living within and from within: for the external or outer consciousness or life separated from the inner spirit is the field of the Ignorance; it can only exceed itself and exceed the Ignorance by opening into the largeness of an inner self and life. If there is a being of the transcendence in us, it must be there in our secret self; on the surface there is only an ephemeral being of nature, made by limit and circumstance. If there is a self in us capable of largeness and universality, able to enter into a cosmic consciousness, that too must be within our inner being; the outer consciousness is a physical consciousness bound to its individual limits by the triple cord of mind, life and body: any external attempt at universality can only result either in an aggrandisement of the ego or an effacement of the personality by its extinction in the mass or subjugation to the mass. It is only by an inner growth, movement, action that the individual can freely and effectively universalise and transcendentalise his being. There must be for the divine living a transference of the centre and immediate source of dynamic effectuation of the being from out inward; for there the soul is seated, but it is veiled or half veiled and our immediate being and source of action is for the present on the surface. In men, says the Upanishad, the Self-Existent has cut the doors of consciousness outward, but a few turn the eye inward and it is these who see and know the Spirit and develop the spiritual being. Thus to look into ourselves and see and enter into ourselves and live within is the first necessity for transformation of nature and for the divine life.

This movement of going inward and living inward is a difficult task to lay upon the normal consciousness of the human being; yet there is no other way of self-finding. The materialistic thinker, erecting an opposition between the extrovert and the introvert, holds up the extrovert attitude for acceptance as the only safety: to go inward is to enter into darkness or emptiness or to lose the balance of the consciousness and become morbid; it is from outside that such inner life as one can construct is created, and its health is assured only by a strict reliance on its wholesome and nourishing outer sources,—the balance of the personal mind and life can only be secured by a firm support on external reality, for the material world is the sole fundamental reality. This may be true for the physical man, the born extrovert, who feels himself to be a creature of outward Nature; made by her and dependent on her, he would lose himself if he went inward: for him there is no inner being, no inner living. But the introvert of this distinction also has not the inner life; he is not a seer of the true inner self and of inner things, but the small mental man who looks superficially inside himself and sees there not his spiritual self but his life-ego, his mind-ego and becomes unhealthily preoccupied with the movements of this little pitiful dwarf creature. The idea or experience of an inner darkness when looking inwards is the first reaction of a mentality which has lived always on the surface and has no realised inner existence; it has only a constructed internal experience which depends on the outside world for the materials of its being. But to those into whose composition there has entered the power of a more inner living, the movement of going within and living within brings not a darkness or dull emptiness but an enlargement, a rush of new experience, a greater vision, a larger capacity, an extended life infinitely more real and various than the first pettiness of the life constructed for itself by our normal physical humanity, a joy of being which is larger and richer than any delight in existence that the outer vital man or the surface mental man can gain by their dynamic vital force and activity or subtlety and expansion of the mental existence. A silence, an entry into a wide or even immense or infinite emptiness is part of the inner spiritual experience; of this silence and void the physical mind has a certain fear, the small superficially active thinking or vital mind a shrinking from it or dislike,—for it confuses the silence with mental and vital incapacity and the void with cessation or non-existence: but this silence is the silence of the spirit which is the condition of a greater knowledge, power and bliss, and this emptiness is the emptying of the cup of our natural being, a liberation of it from its turbid contents so that it may be filled with the wine of God; it is the passage not into non-existence but to a greater existence. Even when the being turns toward cessation, it is a cessation not in non-existence but into some vast ineffable of spiritual being or the plunge into the incommunicable superconscience of the Absolute.

In fact, this inward turning and movement is not an imprisonment in personal self, it is the first step towards a true universality; it brings to us the truth of our external as well as the truth of our internal existence. For this inner living can extend itself and embrace the universal life, it can contact, penetrate, englobe the life of all with a much greater reality and dynamic force than is in our surface consciousness at all possible. Our utmost universalisation on the surface is a poor and limping endeavour,—it is a construction, a make-believe and not the real thing: for in our surface consciousness we are bound to separation of consciousness from others and wear the fetters of the ego. There our very selflessness becomes more often than not a subtle form of selfishness or turns into a larger affirmation of our ego; content with our pose of altruism, we do not see that it is a veil for the imposition of our individual self, our ideas, our mental and vital personality, our need of ego-enlargement upon the others whom we take up into our expanded orbit. So far as we really succeed in living for others, it is done by an inner spiritual force of love and sympathy; but the power and field of effectuality of this force in us are small, the psychic movement that prompts it is incomplete, its action often ignorant because there is contact of mind and heart but our being does not embrace the being of others as ourselves. An external unity with others must always be an outward joining and association of external lives with a minor inner result; the mind and heart attach their movements to this common life and the beings whom we meet there; but the common external life remains the foundation,—the inward constructed unity, or so much of it as can persist in spite of mutual ignorance and discordant egoisms, conflict of minds, conflict of hearts, conflict of vital temperaments, conflict of interests, is a partial and insecure superstructure. The spiritual consciousness, the spiritual life reverses this principle of building; it bases its action in the collective life upon an inner experience and inclusion of others in our own being, an inner sense and reality of oneness. The spiritual individual acts out of that sense of oneness which gives him immediate and direct perception of the demand of self on other self, the need of the life, the good, the work of love and sympathy that can truly be done. A realisation of spiritual unity, a dynamisation of the intimate consciousness of one-being, of one self in all beings, can alone found and govern by its truth the action of the divine life.

In the gnostic or divine being, in the gnostic life, there will be a close and complete consciousness of the self of others, a consciousness of their mind, life, physical being which are felt as if they were one's own. The gnostic being will act, not out of a surface sentiment of love and sympathy or any similar feeling, but out of this close mutual consciousness, this intimate oneness. All his action in the world will be enlightened by a truth of vision of what has to be done, a sense of the will of the Divine Reality in him which is also the Divine Reality in others, and it will be done for the Divine in others and the Divine in all, for the effectuation of the truth of purpose of the All as seen in the light of the highest Consciousness and in the way and by the steps through which it must be effectuated in the power of the Supernature. The gnostic being finds himself not only in his own fulfilment, which is the fulfilment of the Divine Being and Will in him, but in the fulfilment of others; his universal individuality effectuates itself in the movement of the All in all beings towards its greater becoming. He sees a divine working everywhere; what goes out from him into the sum of that divine working, from the inner Light, Will, Force that works in him, is his action. There is no separative ego in him to initiate anything; it is the Transcendent and Universal that moves out through his universalised individuality into the action of the universe. As he does not live for a separate ego, so too he does not live for the purpose of any collective ego; he lives in and for the Divine in himself, in and for the Divine in the collectivity, in and for the Divine in all beings. This universality in action, organised by the all-seeing Will in the sense of the realised oneness of all, is the law of his divine living.

It is, then, this spiritual fulfilment of the urge to individual perfection and an inner completeness of being that we mean first when we speak of a divine life. It is the first essential condition of a perfected life on earth, and we are therefore right in making the utmost possible individual perfection our first supreme business. The perfection of the spiritual and pragmatic relation of the individual with all around him is our second preoccupation; the solution of this second desideratum lies in a complete universality and oneness with all life upon earth which is the other concomitant result of an evolution into the gnostic consciousness and nature. But there still remains the third desideratum, a new world, a change in the total life of humanity or, at the least, a new perfected collective life in the earth-nature. This calls for the appearance not only of isolated evolved individuals acting in the evolved mass, but of many gnostic individuals forming a new kind of beings and a new common life superior to the present individual and common existence. A collective life of this kind must obviously constitute itself on the same principle as the life of the gnostic individual. In our present human existence there is a physical collectivity held together by the common physical life-fact and all that arises from it, community of interests, a common civilisation and culture, a common social law, an aggregate mentality, an economic association, the ideals, emotions, endeavours of the collective ego with the strand of individual ties and connections running through the whole and helping to keep it together. Or, where there is a difference in these things, opposition, conflict, a practical accommodation or an organised compromise is enforced by the necessity of living together; there is erected a natural or a constructed order. This would not be the gnostic divine way of collective living; for there what would bind and hold all together would be, not the fact of life creating a sufficiently united social consciousness, but a common consciousness consolidating a common life. All will be united by the evolution of the Truth-consciousness in them; in the changed way of being which this consciousness would bring about in them, they will feel themselves to be embodiments of a single self, souls of a single Reality; illumined and motivated by a fundamental unity of knowledge, actuated by a fundamental unified will and feeling, a life expressing the spiritual Truth would find through them its own natural forms of becoming. An order there would be, for truth of oneness creates its own order: a law or laws of living there might be, but these would be self-determined; they would be an expression of the truth of a spiritually united being and the truth of a spiritually united life. The whole formation of the common existence would be a self-building of the spiritual forces that must work themselves out spontaneously in such a life: these forces would be received inwardly by the inner being and expressed or self-expressed in a native harmony of idea and action and purpose.

IV
Sarvepalli Radhakrishnan: Fragments of a Confession*

IX. THE RELIGION OF THE SPIRIT

Direct Experience of Eternal Being. When rational thought is applied to the empirical data of the world and of the human self, the conclusion of a Supreme who is Pure Being and Free Activity is reached; but it may be argued that it is only a necessity of thought, a hypothesis, however valid it may be.

*Reprinted with permission from Paul Schillp, editor, *The Philosophy of Sarvapalli Radhakrishnan* (New York: Tudor Publishing Company, 1952).

There is also an ancient and widespread tradition that we can apprehend the Eternal Being with directness and immediacy. When the Upaniṣads speak of jñāna or gnosis, when the Buddha speaks of bodhi or enlightenment, when Jesus speaks of the truth that will make us free, they refer to the mode of direct spiritual apprehension of the Supreme, in which the gap between truth and Being is closed. Their religion rests on the testimony of the Holy Spirit, on personal experience, on mysticism as defined by St. Thomas Aquinas, *cognitio dei experimentalis.* From the affirmations of spiritual experience, we find that it is possible to reconcile the conclusions of logical understanding with the apprehensions of integral insight.

Different Types of Knowledge. There are different types of knowledge: perceptual, conceptual, and intuitive and they are suited to different kinds of objects. Plotinus tells us that sense perceptions are below us, logical reasoning are with us, and spiritual apprehensions are above us.

Integral Insight and Logical Thought. The last type of knowledge may be called integral insight, for it brings into activity not merely a portion of our conscious being, sense or reason, but the whole. It also reveals to us not abstractions but the reality in its integrity. Existentialists dispute the priority of essence to existence. Whereas the possible is prior to the actual insofar as the genesis of the universe is concerned, in the world itself thought works on and in existence and abstracts from it. Thought reaches its end of knowledge in so far as it returns to being. Thought is essentially self-transcendent. It deals with another than thought and so is only symbolic of it. Thinking deals with essences, and existences are unattainable to it. Existence is one way of being, though it is not the only way. Knowledge is reflection on the experience of existence. It is within being. The inadequacy of knowledge to being is stressed by Bradley in his distinction between *what* and *that*, between a logical category and actual being. In integral insight we have knowledge by identity. Although logical knowledge is mediate and symbolic, it is not false. Its construction is not an imaginative synthesis. It falls short of complete knowledge, because it gives the structure of being, not being itself. In integral insight we are put in touch with actual being. This highest knowledge transcends the distinction of subject and object. Even logical knowledge is possible because this highest knowledge is ever present. It can only be accepted as foundational. Being is Truth. *Sat* is *cit.*

We use the direct mode of apprehension, which is deeper than logical understanding, when we contemplate a work of art, when we enjoy great music, when we acquire an understanding of another human being in the supreme achievement of love. In this kind of knowledge the subject is not opposed to the object but is intimately united with it. By calling this kind of knowledge integral insight, we bring out that it does not contradict logical reason, though the insight exceeds the reason. Intellect cannot repudiate instinct any more than intuition can deny logical reason. Intellectual preparation is an instrument for attaining to the truth of the spirit, but the inward realisation of the truth of spirit transcends all intellectual verification, since it exists in an immediacy beyond all conceivable mediation.

Spiritual Experience, a Mode of Internal Insight. The Supreme is not an object but the absolute subject, and we cannot apprehend it by either sense-perception or logical inference. Kant was right in denying that being was a predicate. We are immersed in being. When the Upaniṣads ask us to grow from intellectual to spiritual consciousness, they ask us to effect an enlargement of our awareness by which the difficulties of insecurity, isolation, and death are overcome. We are called upon to grow from division and conflict into freedom and love, from ignorance to wisdom. Such wisdom cannot come except to those who are pure not only in heart but also in the intellect, which has to rid itself of all preconceptions. Unmediated apprehension of the primordial Spirit is the knowledge of God. It is achieved by a change of consciousness, the experience of a new birth. It means an illumined mind, a changed heart, and a transformed will. Wisdom composes the various elements of our mental life, modifies our being, restores our community with nature and society, and makes living significant. Wisdom is freedom from fear, for fear is the result of a lack of correspondence between the nature of the individual and his environment, the clash of the ego and the non-ego which is alien and indifferent to it. The struggle against the alien is the source of suffering. Man is a being who is straining towards infinity, in quest of eternity; but the condition of his existence, finite and limited, temporal and mortal, causes the suffering. When he attains "integrality," there is harmony in his life and its expression is joy.

Through wisdom we grow into likeness with the Spirit. St. Thomas Aquinas observes: "By this light the blessed are made deiform, that is like God, according to the scriptural saying 'When he shall appear, we shall be like him and we shall see him as he is.'"[1]

Universality of the Tradition of Direct Experience of God. There is a tradition of direct apprehension of the Supreme in all lands, in all ages and in all creeds. The seers describe their experiences with an impressive unanimity. They are "near to one another on mountains farthest apart." They certify, in words which ring both true and clear, of a world of spirit alive and waiting for us to penetrate. Indian religions take their stand on spiritual experience, on divine-human encounter, *kṛṣṇārjunasaṁvāda*, and so do the prophets and saints of other religions. Augustine writes: "I entered and beheld with the eye of my soul above the same eye of my soul, above my mind, the Light unchangeable."[2] St. Bernard wrote that happy and blessed was he "who once or twice—or even once only—in this mortal life for the space of a moment has lost himself in God." St. John of the Cross speaks of that steady and established certitude of essential creative union which alone he considers worthy to be called the "spiritual marriage" of the soul.

> What God communicates to the soul in this intimate union is utterly ineffable, beyond the reach of all possible words . . . in this state God and the soul

[1] I. John III, 2, quoted in *Summa Theologica* 1, q. 12, a, 5, C.
[2] *Confessions* VII, 16.

are united as the window is with the light or the coal with the fire . . . this communication of God diffuses itself substantially in the whole soul or rather the soul is transformed in God. In this transformation the soul drinks of God in its every substance and its spiritual powers.

Nature of Spiritual Experience. Spiritual experience, as distinct from religious feeling of dependence or worship or awe, engages our whole person. It is a state of ecstasy or complete absorption of our being. When the flash of absolute reality breaks through the normal barriers of the conscious mind it leaves a trail of illumination in its wake. The excitement of illumination is distinct from the serene radiance of enlightenment. The experience is not of a subjective psychic condition. The contemplative insight into the source of all life is not an escape into the subjective. The human individual can strip himself one after the other of the outer sheaths of consciousness, penetrate to the nerve and quick of his life until all else fades away into illimitable darkness, until he is alone in the white radiance of a central and unique ecstasy. This is the fulfilment of man. This is to be with God. This is to be of God. During our hurried passage through life there may come to us a few moments of transcendent joy, when we seem to stand literally outside our narrow selves and attain a higher state of being and understanding. All religions call upon us to renew those great moments and make the experience of spirit the centre of our lives.

The Absolute as Transcendent and Immament. When the vision fades, the habitual awareness of this world returns. The so-called proofs of the existence of God are the results of critical reflection on the spiritual intuitions of the ultimate Fact of Spirit. These intuitions inspire the acts of reflection, which only confirm what has been apprehended in another way. The reflections are pure and true to the extent that they refer to the intuited facts. There is a perpetual disquiet because ultimate Being is not an object. Reflective accounts are thus only approximations.

Being as such is uncharacterisable and our descriptions and translations are in forms of objects which are less than Being and consequently are inadequate. Abstract ideals and intellectualisations do not deal justly with Being which is given to us as Absolute Presence in adoration and worship. It is through religious contemplation that we realise the Holy. It is not simple apprehension. It is the surrender of the self, its opening to the Supreme.

The experience of a pure and unitary consciousness in a world divided gives rise to the twofold conception of the Absolute as Pure Transcendent Being lifted above all relativities, and the Free Active God functioning in the world. Some emphasise the transcendent aspect, the fulness of being, the sublime presence, the sovereignly subsistent 'other,' above all names and thought; others the immanent aspect, the fulness of life, the living personal God of love who made the world, gave us freedom, and wishes us to participate in the riches of life. St. John of the Cross says:

Beyond all sensual images, and all conceptual determination, God offers Himself as the absolute act of being in its pure actuality. Our concept of God,

> a mere feeble and analogue of a reality which overflows it in every direction, can be made explicit only in the judgment: Being is Being, an absolute positing of that which, lying beyond every object, contains in itself the sufficient reason of objects. And that is why we can rightly say that the very excess of positivity which hides the divine being from our eyes is nevertheless the light which lights up all the rest: *ipsa caligo summa est mentis illuminatio.*

We have here the two aspects of supracosmic transcendence and cosmic universality, the divine mystery which is inexpressible, Eckhart's Godhead, and the mystery which is directed towards the world, Eckhart's God. The God who reveals Himself to the world and to man is not the Absolute which is inexpressible, relationless mystery.

Attempts to rationalise the mystery, to translate into the language of concepts that which is inexpressible in concepts, have resulted in different versions. We may use the trinitarian conception to unfold the nature of the Supreme Being; the Brahman, the Absolute, is the first person, the second is Īśvara, and the third is the World-Spirit. The three persons are different sides of the one Supreme. They are not three different persons but are the one God who hides himself[3] and reveals himself in various degrees. In communicating their experiences the seers use words and symbols current in their world.

Free Spirits. The liberated souls have overcome the power of time, the force of Karma. There is something in common between the wisdom of the sage and the simplicity of the child, serene trust and innocent delight in existence. The happy state of childhood is almost the lost paradise of the human mind. The free spirits are the rays of light that shine from the future, attracting us all who still dwell in darkness. They do not separate themselves from the world but accept the responsibility for perfecting all life. There is no such thing as individual salvation, for it presupposes the salvation of others, universal salvation, the transfiguration of the world. No man, however enlightened and holy he may be, can ever really be saved until all the others are saved. Those individuals who have realised their true being are the integrated ones who have attained personal integrity. Their reason is turned into light, their heart into love, and their will into service. Their demeanour is disciplined and their singleness of spirit is established. Selfish action is not possible for them. Ignorance and craving have lost their hold. They are dead to pride, envy, and uncharitableness. The world in which they live is no more alien to them. It is hospitable, not harsh. It becomes alive, quakes, and sends forth its greetings. Human society becomes charged with the grace and grandeur of the eternal. These free spirits reach out their hands towards the warmth in all things. They have that rarest quality in the world, simple goodness, beside which all the intellectual gifts seem a little trivial. They are meek, patient, long-suffering. They do not judge others because they do not pretend to understand them. Because of their eager selfless love they have the power to soothe the troubled heart. To those in pain their presence is like the cool soft

[3] "Verily Thou art a God that hidest Thyself." *Psalm* 103.

hand of some one they love, when their head is hot with fever. The released individuals are artists in creative living. With an awareness of the Eternal, they participate in the work of the world. Even as the Supreme has two sides of pure being and free activity, these liberated souls, who are the vehicles of divine life, have also two sides: the contemplative and the active.

Contemplation and Action. Their life is socially minded. We are members of a whole, parts of brahmāṇḍa (the cosmic egg), which is one, which is perpetually in transition until its final purpose is achieved. "No man liveth unto himself and no man dieth unto himself" (St. Paul). Their attitude is not one of lofty condescension or patronising pity to lift a debased creature out of mire. But it is a conviction of the solidarity of the world *loka-saṁgraha* and a recognition that the low and the high are bound together in one spirit. Vicarious suffering, not vicarious punishment, is a law of spiritual life. The free spirits bend to the very level of the enslaved to emancipate their minds and hearts. They inspire, revive and strengthen the life of their generation.

The Charge of World-Negation. From the time I was a student, I have heard criticisms made against Indian religions that they are world-negating and that the attitude of our religious men is one of withdrawal from the world. Though the supreme quest is for the freedom of the spirit, for the vision of God, there is also the realisation of the ever present need of the world for the light and guidance of free spirits. A life of service and sacrifice is the natural and inevitable expression and the proof of the validity of spiritual experience. After years of solitary contemplation the Buddha attained enlightenment. The rest of his life was devoted to intense social and cultural work. According to Mahāyāna Buddhism, the released spirits retain their compassion for suffering humanity. Even those whose activities are limited to the instruction of their disciples participate in social leadership in so far as they aim at refashioning human society. Gandhi, well known as a religious man, did not strive to escape from the human scene to forge a solitary destiny. He said: "I am striving for the kingdom of salvation which is spiritual deliverance. For me the road to salvation is through incessant toil in the service of my country and of humanity. I want to identify myself with everything that lives. I want to live at peace with both friend and foe." He reckoned social reform and political action among his religious duties. He founded not a monastic order but a revolutionary party. Gandhi brought home to us the lessons of the saints of old, that no one who believes in spiritual values can abandon to their fate the millions of people whom misery and impossible conditions of life have condemned to a hell on earth. Active service is a part of spiritual life.

Although the unitive knowledge of God here and now is the final end of man, it remains true that some forms of social and cultural life put more obstacles in the way of individual development than others. It is our duty to create and maintain forms of social organisation which offer the fewest possible impediments to the development of the truly human life. By improving the conditions of social life we remove powerful temptations to ignorance and irresponsibility and encourage individual enlightenment. Every man, whatever may be his racial or social origin, is potentially a son of God, made in his image. Human personality is sacred. The human person has a claim to be treated as an end in himself and is therefore entitled to the rights to life, freedom, and security. Freedom to be himself is the right of personality. These rights involve duties. Our legal and political systems must help the realisation of our rights and the acceptance of our obligations. Our civilisation has failed to the extent to which these ideals are denied or betrayed. We must work for the achievement of these ideals in accordance with the principles of freedom, truth, and justice. This is not to reduce religion to a sublimated social engineering.

Tendency to Other-Worldliness. There is a tendency in all religions, Eastern or Western, to neglect the practical side. Any one who approaches the New Testament will find that the emphasis is on other-worldliness. Jesus' teaching about the Kingdom of God and its righteousness, of its coming and of the conditions of our partaking in it, does not betray any interest in the structures of our temporal life. The letters of the Apostles are concerned with the preaching of salvation, the proclamation of Resurrection, of the divine judgment, of the restoration and perfection of all things beyond their historical existence. The few brief comments on the state, on marriage and family life, on the relations between masters and slaves, do not take away the essentially other-worldly character of the teaching of Jesus and his disciples. In the last century his teaching has been interpreted in a manner that shows its kinship with our social and cultural problems.

Religion as the Inspiration of Life. Religion is not a particular way of life but is the way of all life. Jesus said: "I am the Way, the Truth and the Life." Religious life is neither ascetic nor legalistic. It condemns mere externalism and does not insist on obedience to laws and ordinances. "Where the spirit of the Lord is there is liberty." Liberty is freedom from all taboos and restrictions. We are not called upon to hate the world because it is the creation of a hostile demiurge. To look upon the world as undivine is a speculative aberration. God is not jealous of his own works. The world is an abyss of nothingness, if we take away its roots in the Divine. What the Indian thinkers aim at is action without attachment. It is action of an individual who is no more a victim of selfishness, who has identified himself with the divine centre which is in him and in all things. Since he is not emotionally involved in the 'fruits of action,' he is able to act effectively. True religion has elements in it of withdrawal from the world and of return to it. Its aim is the control of life by the power of spirit.

Our social conscience has been anaesthetised by a formal religion and it has now to be roused. In recent times, it is the atheists and not the saints that have taken the lead in the work of social enlightenment and justice. In the history of religions, however, the rôle of the religious leader has been important. Though dedicated to a life of contemplation he is led to act like a ferment of renewal in the structure of society. That great tradition of which Gandhi is the latest example, requires to be renewed.

The integrated individuals are the rare privileged beings who are in advance of their time. They are the forerunners of the future race, who set to us the path we have to take, to rise from fallen to transfigured nature. They are not, however, to be regarded as unique and absolute manifestations of the Absolute. There cannot be a complete manifestation of the Absolute in the world of relativity. Each limited manifestation may be perfect in its own way, but is not the Absolute which is within all and above all. The life of a Buddha or a Jesus tells us how we can achieve the same unity with the Absolute to which they had attained and how we can live at peace in the world of manifested being. The light that lighteth everyone that cometh into the world shone in those liberated spirits with great radiance and intensity. The Kingdom of God is the Kingdom of persons who are spiritually free, who have overcome fear and loneliness. Every one has in him the possibility of this spiritual freedom, the essence of enlightenment, is a *bodhisattva.* The divine sonship of Christ is at the same time the divine sonship of every man. The end of the cosmic process is the achievement of universal resurrection, redemption of all persons who continue to live as individuals till the end of history.

The Discipline of Religion. The function of the discipline of religion is to further the evolution of man into his divine stature, develop increased awareness and intensity of understanding. It is to bring about a better, deeper and more enduring adjustment in life. All belief and practice, song and prayer, meditation and contemplation, are means to this development of direct experience, an inner frame of mind, a sense of freedom and fearlessness, strength and security. Religion is the way in which the individual organises his inward being and responds to what is envisaged by him as the ultimate Reality. It is essentially intensification of experience, the displacement of triviality by intensity.

Religion a Personal Achievement. Each individual is a member of a community where he shares work with others; but he is also an individual with his senses and emotions, desires and affections, interests and ideals. There is a solitary side to his being as distinct from the social, where he cherishes thoughts unspoken, dreams unshared, reticences unbroken. It is there that he shelters the questionings of fate, the yearning for peace, the voice of hope and the cry of anguish. When the Indian thinkers ask us to possess our souls, to be *ātmavantam,* not to get lost in the collective currents, not to get merged in the crowd of those who have emptied and crucified their souls, *ātmahano janāh,* who have got their souls bleached in the terrible unmercy of things, they are asking us to open out our inward being to the call of the transcendent. Religion is not a movement stretching out to grasp something, external, tangible and good, and to possess it. It is a form of being, not having, a mode of life. Spiritual life is not a problem to be solved but a reality to be experienced. It is new birth into enlightenment.

Three Stages of Religious Life. The Upaniṣads speak to us of three stages of religious life, śravaṇa, hearing, manana, reflection, nididhyāsana or disciplined meditation. We rise from one stage to another. Joachim of Floris in the twelfth century sees the story of man in three stages. The first is of the "Father" of the Letter, of the Law, where we have to listen and obey. The second is of the "Son"; here we have argument and criticism. Tradition is explained, authority is explicated. The third stage is of the Spirit, where we have "prayer and song," meditation and inspiration.[4] Through these, the tradition becomes a vital and transforming experience. The life of Jesus, the witness of St. Paul, of the three apostles on the Mount of Transfiguration, of Ezekiel, and of scores of others are an impressive testimony to the fact of religion as experience. Muhammad is said to have received his messages in ecstatic states. St. Thomas, in the beginning of the Fourth book of his *Summa Contra Gentiles*, speaks of three kinds of human knowledge of divine things. "The first of these is the knowledge that comes by the natural light of reason," when the reason ascends by means of creatures to God. The second "descends to us by way of revelation." The third is possible only to the human mind "elevated to the perfect intuition of the things that are revealed." Dante symbolised the first by Virgil, the second by Beatrice, the third by St. Bernard.

Religion as Self-Knowledge. Though God is everywhere, he is found more easily in the soul. The inward light is never darkened and it enlightens with understanding the minds of those who turn to it. Our self is a holy temple of the Spirit into which we may not enter without a sense of awe and reverence.

> Behold Thou wert within and I abroad, and there I searched for Thee. Thou wert with me but I was not with Thee. Thou calledst and shoutedst, burstedst my deafness. Thou flashedst, shonedst, and scatteredst my blindness. Thou breathedst odours, and I drew in breath, and pant for Thee. I tasted and hunger and thirst. Thou touchedst me, and I was on fire for Thy peace.[5]

"Thou wert more inward to me than my most inward part, and higher than my highest."[6] Bishop Ullathorne says:

> Let it be plainly understood that we cannot return to God unless we enter first into ourselves. God is everywhere, but not everywhere to us. There is but one point in the universe where God communicates with us, and that is the centre of our own soul. There He waits for us; there He meets us; there He speaks to us. To seek Him, therefore, we must enter into our own interior.[7]

When Kierkegaard tells us that truth is identical with subjectivity, he means that if it is objectified, it becomes relative. He does not mean that the truth is peculiar to private to the individual. He makes out that we must go deep down into the subject to attain the experience of Universal Spirit. Professor A. N. Whitehead says that "religion is what the individual does with his solitariness."[8] Each individual must unfold his own awareness of life, witness his own relation to the source or sources of his being and, in the light of his

---

[4] See Gerald Heard: *The Eternal Gospel* (1948), 6.
[5] St. Augustine, *Confessions* X, 38.
[6] *Confessions* III, 11.
[7] *Groundwork of Christian Virtues*, 74.
[8] *Religion in the Making* (1926), 16.

experience, resolve the tragedies and contradictions of his inward life. "If you are never solitary, then you are never religious."[9] It is in solitude that we prepare the human candle for the divine flame. This does not mean a facile commensurability between God and man. It means that man can transcend himself, can exceed his limits. To get at the transcendent within oneself, one must break through one's normal self. The revelation of the divine in man is of the character of an interruption of our routine self. We must impose silence on our familiar self, if the spirit of God is to become manifest in us. The divine is more deeply in us than we are ourselves. We attain to spirit by passing beyond the frontiers of the familiar self. If we do not mechanise the doctrine of Incarnation, of "God manifest in the flesh," we make out that man has access to the inmost being of the divine, in these moments of highest spiritual insight. The highest human life is life in God. In the words of Eckhart, "God in the fulness of his Godhead dwells eternally in His Image, the soul."

Religions prescribe certain conditions to which we have to submit if we are to gain religious illumination. Discipline of the intellect, emotions and will is a prerequisite for spiritual perception. Religious spirits use the catastrophes of the world as opportunities for creative work. The world is the field for moral striving. The purpose of life is not the enjoyment of the world but the education of the soul.

Increasing Emphasis on Religion as Conversion. In the middle of January 1946 was published the Report of the Commission appointed by the Archbishop of Canterbury "to survey the whole problem of modern evangelism with special reference to the spiritual needs and the prevailing intellectual outlook of the nonworshipping members of the community and to report on the organisation and methods by which the needs can most effectively be met." This Report, entitled *The Conversion of England*, points out that religion has become a waning influence in the national life of the country and calls for a strengthening and quickening of spiritual life. Religion, it urges, is a conversion, a mental and spiritual revolution, a change from a self-centred to a God-centred life. It is a call to a new vision and understanding of life. The Report asks for the assertion of the primacy of spirit over the long dominant external forms of religion, submission to authority, subscription to a formula. The discipline of religion consists in turning inwards, deepening our awareness and developing a more meaningful attitude to life which frees us from bondage and hardening of the spirit. "Except ye be converted and become as little children, ye shall not enter into the kingdom of heaven."

Yoga. There are different ways which are prescribed by religions to achieve this inward change. *Yoga* is used in Indian religions for the methods of drawing near to the Supreme. *Yoga* is a path, a praxis, and training by which the individual man, bleeding from the split caused by intelligence, becomes whole. Intellectual concentration *jñāna*, emotional detachment, *bhakti*, ethical dedication, *karma*, are all types of *Yoga*. In Patañjali's *Yoga Sūtra*, we have a development of what Plato calls recollection, the way by

[9] *Religion in the Making* (1926), 16.

which we steadily withdraw from externality, from our functions which are at the mercy of life and enter into our essential being, which is not the individual ego but the Universal Spirit. It is the act of recollection by which the recollecting self distinguishes its primal being from all that is confused with it, its material, vital, psychological and logical expressions. By recollection the self is assured of its participation in ultimate being, the principle of all positivity, the ontological mystery. We have power over the outer expressions. We may submit ourselves to despair, deny physical being by resorting to suicide, surpass all expressions and discover that deep down there is something other than these empirical manifestations. Even the thinking subject is only in relation to an object, but the spirit in us is not the subject of epistemology. It is primordial being.

When we are anchored in the mystery which is the foundation of our very being, our activities express "Thy will and not mine." When we are in Being we are beyond the moral world of freedom. Our deeds flow out of the heart of reality and our desires are swallowed up in love. Spiritual freedom is different from moral autonomy. The inward hold we get makes us the masters of life. Religion then is experience turning inwards towards the realisation to itself.

PART II

BUDDHIST TEXTS

The Buddhist tradition began in India with the enlightenment of Siddhārtha Gautama, the Buddha, and his first sermon in the Deer Park at Sarnath in 528 B.C. Catching on quickly, by the time of Gautama's death in 483 B.C., Buddhism had already spread throughout the kingdoms of Magadha and Kosala. Within a few hundred years, especially under the patronage of King Ashoka (ruled 269-232 B.C.), Buddhism spread throughout the Indian subcontinent and beyond as Ashoka provided the model for later Buddhist missionary efforts that successfully spread Buddhism throughout Asia by 700 A.D.

Underlying the various religious and philosophical transformations that Buddhism experienced during its long historical development is a central enduring conviction that suffering is brought about by grasping and attachment that arises from ignorance, and that this ignorance can be removed by following a path that combines wisdom, moral development, and meditation. This conviction was stated simply by the Buddha almost twenty-five hundred years ago when he declared that what he had explained was *duḥkha* (suffering), its origin, its cessation, and the way leading to its cessation, and that he had explained these things because they have to do with the fundamentals of religion, leading to wisdom and *nirvāṇa* (*Majjhima Nikāya*; 63). Gradually, as the Buddhist tradition developed, these teachings came to be understood in new ways. By the time of the third Buddhist Council, held at Pāṭaliputra in about 346 B.C., these differences had resulted in a basic split between the "Great-Assembly-ists" (*Mahāsaṅghikas*) and the "Elders" (*Theras*). Both of these groups subsequently underwent internal division that resulted in the formation of a number of subsects. One of the subsects of the Theras, the Vibhjyavādins, underwent another split, giving rise to the Mahīśāsakas and the Theravādins. It is this Theravāda Buddhism, a subsubsect of the original Theravādins, that has reigned in Sri Lanka for the past two thousand years and that has dominated most of southeast Asia. The Mahāsaṅghikas, by a process that is still historically unclear, eventually gave rise to the Māhāyana, sometime during the second and first centuries B.C.

The two great Māhāyana philosophical schools, Mādhyamaka and Yogacārā, developed their positions and arguments not so much against each other as against the Sarvāstivādins. The Sarvāstivādins were a strong philosophical force in northwest India from the first to the ninth centuries; they excelled in their development of Abhidharma philosophy, which was a rigorous metaphysical analysis of the phenomena of experience. Disagreements, particularly over the comparative importance of the *sūtras*, which were regarded as containing the Buddha's own teachings, and *abhidharma* analysis, as well as over how past and future exist in the present moment, resulted in the emergence of the Sautrāntika and the Vaibhāṣika as the two main branches of Sarvāstivāda thought. In Sri Lanka in the fifth century the great Buddhaghosha produced what has been accepted as the authoritative *abhidharma* interpretation; after this date there appears to have been little interaction between the Theravādins on the one hand and the Sarvāstivādins, Mādhyamamikas, and Yogācārins on the other.

Although these differences all appeared in Indian Buddhism within the first seven hundred years after the Buddha's enlightenment, the Yogacārā and Mādhyamaka, providing the philosophical underpinning for Tibetan, Chinese, and Japanese Buddhism, have continued their vigorous development through the succeeding centuries right up to the present time, particularly among Japanese and Tibetan Buddhist thinkers. Similarly, the *abhidharma* analysis of the Theravādins has continued to evolve and flourishes today in Sri Lanka, Thailand, and Burma. Sarvāstivādin thought, on the other hand, has had no significant development during the last thousand years; today there are no Sautrāntikas or Vaibhāṣikas.

There are a number of helpful books to guide one through the various teachings and vast literature of Buddhism. Charles Prebish, editor, *Buddhism in Modern Perspectives* (University Park, Pa: Pennsylvania State University Press, 1975), is a quick and accurate overview of the most important Buddhist developments, including that of Buddhism in America. Edward Conze, *Buddhism: Its Essence and Development* (New York: Harper Torchbooks, 1969), provides an excellent overview of the development of the central teachings of Buddhism. David J. Kalupahana, *Buddhist Philosophy, A Historical Analysis* (Honolulu: University of Hawaii Press, 1975), provides a fine historical introduction to both Theravāda and Māhāyana Buddhist philosophy. Arthur L. Herman, *An Introduction to Buddhist Thought* (Lanham, Md.: University Press of America, 1983), offers a provocative introduction to Indian Buddhism that focuses on the development of Buddhist philosophy as a series of responses to philosophical problems. For an introduction to Buddhism as a religious way, William R. LaFleur, *Buddhism: A Cultural Perspective* (Englewood Cliffs, N.J.: Prentice Hall, 1988), is a good place to start. John M. Koller, *Oriental Philosophies*, second edition (New York: Charles Scribners' Sons, 1985), provides a good introduction to the Buddhist way of life and to the main philosophical schools. For teachers and advanced students, Donald S. Lopez, editor, *Buddhist Hermeneutics* (Honolulu: University of Hawaii Press,

1988), is a useful collection of essays devoted to questions of interpretation of Buddhist texts in the various traditions. The most complete reference guide is Kenneth K. Inada, *Guide to Buddhist Philosophy* (Boston: G. K. Hall, 1985), which has helpful annotations of most major books and articles published before 1983.

CHAPTER 9

BASIC TEACHINGS ACCORDING TO THE EARLY TEXTS

Although the oldest available written Buddhist texts are relatively late, tradition assures us that the texts known as *Nikāyas* contain an early and reliable record of the Buddha's actual teachings, for immediately after the Buddha's death a council of monks was summoned to recall and collect these teachings. These collections contain the *Dharma*—the truth about *duḥkha*, its conditions, and the way of overcoming these conditions—as recalled by Ananda, the elder monk closest to the Master. These basic teachings reflect the experience and vision of the historical Buddha as he engaged in his own quest for freedom from the restrictions and sufferings of life. His quest itself marks a continuity with a tradition already hundreds of years old, as do the meditative techniques constituting the foundation of this quest. But the Buddha's way of appropriating these techniques, of integrating them with morality and wisdom, and his vision of existence as transitory between being and nonbeing enabled him to teach a Middle Way that was genuinely new. In the historical development of Buddhist thought there was continuous interaction both with older metaphysical visions and meditative traditions and with other new visions and ways of life, an interaction that provided much of the stimulus for the analysis and reasoning that shaped the Buddhist philosophical tradition.

The most fundamental of the basic teachings of early Buddhism have been collected and translated by the Venerable Walpola Rahula, a Theravādin monk from Sri Lanka, in the second edition of his classic work, *What the Buddha Taught* (New York: Grove Press, 1974). The selections included in this chapter provide both the content and the spirit of the foundational teachings about *duḥkha*, its conditions, their removal and the path to their removal, as understood by Theravāda Buddhists in South and Southeast Asia. These selections have been taken entirely from *What the Buddha Taught*, an excellent ninety-page explanation of the basic teachings of Buddhism. For reliable translations of all the early Buddhist texts the reader should consult the translations of the Pāli Text Society published in London. Frank J. Hoffman, *Rationality and Mind in Early Buddhism* (Delhi: Motilal Banarsidass, 1987), is a fine contemporary study of mind, reason, and rebirth according to the early texts. John Ross Carter and Mahinda Palihawadana, *The Dhammapada, A New English Translation with the Pali Text and the First English Translation of the Commentary's Explanation of the Verses with Notes Translated from Sinhala Sources and Critical Textual Comments* (New York: Oxford University Press, 1987), is by far the best text for study of the *Dhammapada.*

The first selection, "Setting in Motion the Wheel of Truth," contains the Buddha's first teaching upon his enlightenment. Here the fourfold noble truth of *duḥkha* (*dukkha* in Pāli, the language in which the teachings were first written), its conditions, their removal and the way of their removal, namely the Middle Way, the Noble Eightfold Path that leads to *nirvāṇa* (*nibbāna*), is explained by the Buddha, who proclaims the teaching to be true knowledge issuing forth from his perfect enlightenment.

Selection 2, "The Fire Sermon," proclaims the body, mind, and senses to be burning with the fires of lust, hate, and delusion. To put out these fires, the Buddha says, one must become dispassionate, detached, and finally liberated. The text records that one thousand monks were liberated upon hearing this teaching.

Selection 3, "Universal Love," reveals that even in the early days of Buddhism, universal compassion and the concern to bring all beings to happiness were advocated as the Buddhist way, well before these concerns became a central focus of the Mahāyāna.

Selection 4, "Blessings," shows that the Buddha did not despise or revile the world, but regarded a wise and virtuous life in this world as a great blessing.

Selection 5, "Getting Rid of All Cares and Troubles," sets forth seven ways of overcoming the sources of suffering: by insight, restraint, use, endurance, avoidance, dispersal, and cultivation.

Selection 6, "The Foundations of Mindfulness," describes the cultivation of the foundations of mindfulness, which the Buddha declares to be the only way "for the purification of beings, for the overcoming of sorrow and lamentation, for the destruction of suffering and grief, for reaching the right path, for the attainment of *Nibbāna.*" It is the single most important text dealing with meditation in the Pali Canon, and remains the basis of Buddhist meditation from Theravāda to Zen to this very day.

Selection 7, "The Words of Truth," taken from the very important Theravāda collection of wisdom called the *Path of Truth* (*Dhammapada*), presents a series of observations and advice that sum up much of practical Buddhism and that constitute a guide to daily life in Theravāda countries.

Finally, "The Last Words of the Buddha" advises the monks that instead of concerning themselves about the appointment of a head of the order to replace himself they should be guided by his teachings and the rules of the monastic order that have been laid down and should be diligent in their efforts to overcome *duḥkha.*

I
Setting in Motion the Wheel of Truth*

Thus have I heard. The Blessed One was once living in the Deer Park at Isipatana (the Resort of Seers) near Bārānasi (Benares). There he addressed the group of five bhikkhus:

"Bhikkhus, these two extremes ought not to be practised by one who has gone forth from the household life. What are the two? There is devotion to the indulgence of sense-pleasures, which is low, common, the way of ordinary people, unworthy and unprofitable; and there is devotion to self-mortification, which is painful, unworthy and unprofitable.

"Avoiding both these extremes, the Tathāgata has realized the Middle Path: it gives vision, it gives knowledge, and it leads to calm, to insight, to enlightenment, to Nibbāna. And what is that Middle Path . . . ? It is simply the Noble Eightfold Path, namely, right view, right thought, right speech, right action, right livelihood, right effort, right mindfulness, right concentration. This is the Middle Path realized by the Tathāgata, which gives vision, which gives knowledge, and which leads to calm, to insight, to enlightenment, to Nibbāna.

"The Noble Truth of suffering (*Dukkha*) is this: Birth is suffering; aging is suffering; sickness is suffering; death is suffering; sorrow and lamentation, pain, grief and despair are suffering; association with the unpleasant is suffering; dissociation from the pleasant is suffering; not to get what one wants is suffering—in brief, the five aggregates of attachment are suffering.

"The Noble Truth of the origin of suffering is this: It is this thirst (craving) which produces re-existence and re-becoming, bound up with passionate greed. It finds fresh delight now here and now there, namely, thirst for sense-pleasures; thirst for existence and becoming; and thirst for non-existence (self-annihilation).

"The Noble Truth of the Cessation of suffering is this: It is the complete cessation of that very thirst, giving it up, renouncing it, emancipating oneself from it, detaching oneself from it.

"The Noble Truth of the Path leading to the Cessation of suffering is this: It is simply the Noble Eightfold Path, namely right view; right thought; right speech, right action; right livelihood; right effort; right mindfulness; right concentration.

"'This is the Noble Truth of Suffering (Dukkha)': such was the vision, the knowledge, the wisdom, the science, the light, that arose in me with regard to

*Reprinted with permission from Walpola Rahula, *What the Buddha Taught*, second edition (New York: Grove Press, 1974).

things not heard before. 'This suffering, as a noble truth, should be fully understood': such was the vision, the knowledge, the wisdom, the science, the light, that arose in me with regard to things not heard before. 'This suffering, as a noble truth, has been fully understood': such was the vision, the knowledge, the wisdom, the science, the light, that arose in me with regard to things not heard before.

" 'This is the Noble Truth of the Origin of suffering': such was the vision . . . 'This Origin of suffering, as a noble truth, should be abandoned': such was the vision, . . . 'This Origin of suffering, as a noble truth, has been abandoned': such was the vision, . . . with regard to things not heard before.

" 'This is the Noble Truth of the Cessation of suffering': such was the vision . . . 'This cessation of suffering, as a noble truth, should be realized': such was the vision, . . . 'This Cessation of suffering, as a noble truth, has been realized': such was the vision, . . . with regard to things not heard before.

" 'This is the Noble Truth of the Path leading to the Cessation of suffering': such was the vision, . . . 'This Path leading to the Cessation of suffering, as a noble truth, should be followed (cultivated)': such was the vision, . . . 'This Path leading to the Cessation of suffering, as a noble truth, has been followed (cultivated)': such was the vision, the knowledge, the wisdom, the science, the light, that arose in me with regard to things not heard before.

"As long as my vision of true knowledge was not fully clear in these three aspects, in these twelve ways, regarding the Four Noble Truths,[1] I did not claim to have realized the perfect Enlightenment that is supreme in the world with its gods, with its Māras and Brahmas, in this world with its recluses and brāhmaṇas, with its princes and men. But when my vision of true knowledge was fully clear in these three aspects, in these twelve ways, regarding the Four Noble Truths, then I claimed to have realized the perfect Enlightenment that is supreme in the world with its gods, its Māras and Brahmas, in this world with its recluses and brāhmaṇas, with its princes and men. And a vision of true knowledge arose in me thus: My heart's deliverance is unassailable. This is the last birth. Now there is no more rebecoming (rebirth).

This the Blessed One said. The group of five bhikkhus was glad, and they rejoiced at his words. (*Saṃyutta-nikāya*, LVI, II)

II
The Fire Sermon*

Thus have I heard. The Blessed One was once living at Gayāsīsa in Gayā with a thousand bhikkhus. There he addressed the bhikkhus:

---

[1]As may be seen from the four preceding paragraphs, with regard to each of the Four Noble Truths there are three aspects of knowledge: I. The knowledge that it is the Truth (*sacca-ñāṇa*) 2. The knowledge that a certain function or action with regard to this Truth should be performed (*kicca-ñāṇa*), and 3. The knowledge that that function or action with regard to this Truth has been performed (*kata-ñāṇa*). When these three aspects are applied to each of the Four Noble Truths, twelve ways are obtained.

*Reprinted with permission from Walpola Rahula, *What the Buddha Taught*, second edition (New York: Grove Press, 1974).

"Bhikkhus, all is burning. And what is the all that is burning?

"Bhikkhus, the eye is burning, visible forms are burning, visual consciousness is burning, visual impression is burning, also whatever sensation, pleasant or painful or neither-painful-nor-pleasant, arises on account of the visual impression, that too is burning. Burning with what? Burning with the fire of lust, with the fire of hate, with the fire of delusion; I say it is burning with birth, aging and death, with sorrows, with lamentations, with pains, with griefs, with despairs.

"The ear is burning, sounds are burning, auditory consciousness is burning, auditory impression is burning, also whatever sensation, pleasant or painful or neither-painful-nor-pleasant, arises on account of the auditory impression, that too is burning. Burning with what? Burning with the fire of lust. . . .

"The nose is burning, odours are burning, olfactory consciousness is burning, olfactory impression is burning, also whatever sensation, pleasant or painful or neither-painful-nor-pleasant, arises on account of the olfactory impression, that too is burning. Burning with what? Burning with the fire of lust. . . .

"The tongue is burning, flavours are burning, gustative consciousness is burning, gustative impression is burning, also whatever sensation, pleasant or painful or neither-painful-nor-pleasant, arises on account of the gustative impression, that too is burning. Burning with what? Burning with the fire of lust. . . .

"The body is burning, tangible things are burning, tactile consciousness is burning, tactile impression is burning, also whatever sensation, pleasant or painful or neither-painful-nor-pleasant, arises on account of the tactile sensation, that too is burning. Burning with what? Burning with the fire of lust. . . .

"The mind is burning, mental objects (ideas, etc.) are burning, mental consciousness is burning, mental impression is burning, also whatever sensation, pleasant or painful or neither-painful-nor-pleasant, arises on account of the mental impression, that too is burning. Burning with what? Burning with the fire of lust, with the fire of hate, with the fire of delusion; I say it is burning with birth, aging and death, with sorrows, with lamentations, with pains, with griefs, with despairs.

"Bhikkhus, a learned and noble disciple, who sees (things) thus, becomes dispassionate with regard to the eye, becomes dispassionate with regard to visible forms, becomes dispassionate with regard to the visual consciousness, becomes dispassionate with regard to the visual impression, also whatever sensation, pleasant or painful or neither-painful-nor-pleasant, arises on account of the visual impression, with regard to that too he becomes dispassionate. He becomes dispassionate with regard to the ear, with regard to sounds. . . . He becomes dispassionate with regard to the nose . . . with regard to odours. . . . He becomes dispassionate with regard to the tongue . . . with regard to flavours. . . . He becomes dispassionate with regard to the body . . . with regard to tangible things. . . . He becomes dispassionate with regard to the mind, becomes dispassionate with regard to mental objects (ideas, etc.), becomes dispassionate with regard to mental consciousness, becomes dispassionate with regard to mental impression, also whatever sensation, pleasant or painful or neither-painful-nor-pleasant, arises on account of mental impression, with regard to that too he becomes dispassionate.

"Being dispassionate, he becomes detached; through detachment he is liberated. When liberated there is knowledge that he is liberated. And he knows: Birth is exhausted, the holy life has been lived, what has to be done is done, there is no more left to be done on this account."

This the Blessed One said. The bhikkhus were glad, and they rejoiced at his words.

While this exposition was being delivered, the minds of those thousand bhikkhus were liberated from impurities, without attachment.

(*Saṃyutta-nikāya*, XXXV, 28)

III
Universal Love*

He who is skilled in good and who wishes to attain that state of Calm should act (thus):

He should be able, upright, perfectly upright, compliant, gentle, and humble.

Contented, easily supported, with few duties, of simple livelihood, controlled in senses, discreet, not impudent, he should not be greedily attached to families.

He should not commit any slight wrong such that other wise men might censure him. (Then he should cultivate his thoughts thus:)

May all beings be happy and secure; may their minds be contented.

Whatever living beings there may be—feeble or strong, long (or tall), stout, or medium, short, small, or large, seen or unseen, those dwelling far or near, those who are born and those who are yet to be born—may all beings, without exception, be happy-minded!

Let not one deceive another nor despise any person whatever in any place. In anger or ill will let not one wish any harm to another.

Just as a mother would protect her only child even at the risk of her own life, even so let one cultivate a boundless heart towards all beings.

Let one's thoughts of boundless love pervade the whole world—above, below and across—without any obstruction, without any hatred, without any enmity.

Whether one stands, walks, sits or lies down, as long as one is awake, one should maintain this mindfulness. This, they say, is the Sublime State in this life.

*Reprinted with permission from Walpola Rahula, *What the Buddha Taught*, second edition (New York: Grove Press, 1974).

Not falling into wrong views, virtuous and endowed with Insight, one gives up attachment to sense-desires. Verily such a man does not return to enter a womb again. (*Suttanipāta*, I. 8)

IV
Blessings*

Thus have I heard:

The Blessed One was once living at the monastery of Anāthapiṇḍika in Jeta's grove, near Sāvatthi. Now when the night was far advanced, a certain deity, whose surpassing splendour illuminated the entire Jeta Grove, came into the presence of the Blessed One, and, drawing near, respectfully saluted Him and stood on one side. Standing thus, he addressed the Blessed One in verse:

"Many deities and men, yearning after happiness, have pondered on Blessings. Pray, tell me the Highest Blessing!"

Not to associate with fools, to associate with the wise, and to honour those who are worthy of honour — this is the Highest Blessing.

To reside in a suitable locality, to have done meritorious actions in the past, and to set oneself in the right course — this is the Highest Blessing.

Vast learning (skill in) handicraft, a highly trained discipline, and pleasant speech — this is the Highest Blessing.

Supporting one's father and mother, cherishing wife and children, and peaceful occupations — this is the Highest Blessing.

Liberality, righteous conduct, the helping of relatives, and blameless actions — this is the Highest Blessing.

To cease and abstain from evil, abstention from intoxicating drinks, and diligence in virtue — this is the Highest Blessing.

Reverence, humility, contentment, gratitude and the opportune hearing of the Dhamma — this is the Highest Blessing.

Patience, obedience, seeing the Samanas (holy men), and (taking part in) religious discussions at proper times — this is the Highest Blessing.

Self-control, Holy Life, perception of the Noble Truths, and the realisation of Nibbāna - this is the Highest Blessing.

If a man's mind is sorrowless, stainless, and secure, and does not shake when touched by worldly vicissitudes — this is the Highest Blessing.

Those who thus acting are everywhere unconquered, attain happiness everywhere — to them these are the Highest Blessings. (*Suttanipāta*, II. 4)

---

*Reprinted with permission from Walpola Rahula, *What the Buddha Taught*, second edition (New York: Grove Press, 1974).

V
Getting Rid of All Cares and Troubles*

Thus have I heard. The Blessed One was once living at the monastery of Anāthapiṇḍika in Jeta's grove near Sāvatthi. There he addressed the bhikkhus saying: "Bhikkhus," and they replied to him: "Venerable Sir." The Blessed One spoke as follows:

"Bhikkhus, I will expound to you the method of restraining all cares and troubles. Listen and reflect well; I shall speak to you." "Yes, Venerable Sir," they said in response to the Blessed One.

He then spoke as follows:

"Bhikkhus, I say that the destruction (getting rid) of cares and troubles is (possible) for one who knows and who sees, not for one who does not know and does not see. What must a person know and see in order that the destruction (getting rid) of cares and troubles should be possible? (These are) wise reflection and unwise reflection. For a person who reflects unwisely there arise cares and troubles which have not yet arisen, and (in addition), those which have already arisen increase. But for him who reflects wisely, cares and troubles which have not yet arisen do not arise, and (in addition), those already arisen disappear.

"Bhikkhus, (1) there are cares and troubles which are to be got rid of by insight; (2) there are cares and troubles which are to be got rid of by restraint; (3) there are cares and troubles which are to be got rid of by use; (4) there are cares and troubles which are to be got rid of by endurance; (5) there are cares and troubles which are to be got rid of by avoidance; (6) there are cares and troubles which are to be got rid of by dispersal; (7) there are cares and troubles which are to be got rid of by culture.

(1) "Bhikkhus, what are the cares and troubles which are to be got rid of by insight? Bhikkhus, the uninstructed ordinary man, who does not see the Noble Ones, who is unversed in the Teachings of the Noble Ones, who is untrained in the Teachings of the Noble Ones, who does not see good men, who is unversed in the Teachings of good men, who is untrained in the Teachings of good men, does not understand what things should be reflected on and what things should not be reflected on. Not knowing what things should be reflected on and what things should not be reflected on, he reflects on things that should not be reflected on, and does not reflect on things that should be reflected on.

"Now, Bhikkhus, what are the things that should not be reflected on but on which he reflects? If, in a person, reflecting on certain things, there arises the defilement of sense-pleasure which has not yet arisen, and (in addition), the defilement of sense-pleasure which has already arisen in him increases, the defilement of (the desire for) existence and for becoming . . .

---

*Reprinted with permission from Walpola Rahula, *What the Buddha Taught*, second edition (New York: Grove Press, 1974).

the defilement of ignorance which has not yet arisen arises and (in addition), the defilement of ignorance which has already arisen in him increases, then these are the things that should not be reflected on, but on which he reflects.

"Bhikkhus, what are the things that should be reflected on, but on which he does not reflect? If, in a person, reflecting on certain things, the defilement of sense-pleasure which has not yet arisen does not arise, and (in addition), the defilement of sense-pleasure which has already arisen in him disappears, the defilement of (the desire for) existence and for becoming . . . the defilement of ignorance which has not yet arisen does not arise, and (in addition), the defilement of ignorance which has already arisen in him disappears, these are the things that should be reflected on, but on which he does not reflect.

"By reflecting on things that should not be reflected on, and by not reflecting on things that should be reflected on, defilements that have not yet arisen arise, and defilements that have already arisen in him increase. Then he reflects unwisely (unnecessarily) in this way:

1. Did I exist in the past?
2. Did I not exist in the past?
3. What was I in the past?
4. How was I in the past?
5. Having been what, did I become what in the past?
6. Shall I exist in future?
7. Shall I not exist in future?
8. What shall I be in future?
9. How shall I be in future?
10. Having been what, shall I become what in future?

Or, now at the present time he is doubtful about himself:

11. Am I?
12. Am I not?
13. What am I?
14. How am I?
15. Whence came this person?
16. Whither will he go?

When he reflects unwisely in this way, one of the six false views arises in him:

1. I have a Self: this view arises in him as true and real.
2. I have no Self: this view arises in him as true and real.
4. By Self I perceive non-self: this view arises in him as true and real.

5. By non-self I perceive Self: this view arises in him as true and real.
6. Or a wrong view arises in him as follows: This my Self, which speaks and feels, which experiences the fruits of good and bad actions now here and now there, this Self is permanent, stable, everlasting, unchanging, remaining the same for ever and ever.

"This, Bhikkhus, is what is called becoming enmeshed in views; a jungle of views, a wilderness of views; scuffling in views, the agitation (struggle) of views, the fetter of views. Bhikkhus, the uninstructed ordinary man fettered by the fetters of views, does not liberate himself from birth, aging and death, from sorrows, lamentations, pains, griefs, despairs; I say that he does not liberate himself from suffering (*dukkha*).

"And, Bhikkhus, the instructed noble disciple, who sees the Noble Ones, who is versed in the Teachings of the Noble Ones, who is well trained in the Teachings of the Noble Ones, who sees good men, who is versed in the Teachings of the good men, who is well trained in the teachings of the good men, knows what things should be reflected on and what should not be reflected on. Knowing what things should be reflected on and what should not be reflected on, he does not reflect on things that should not be reflected on and he reflects on things that should be reflected on.

"Now, Bhikkhus, what are the things that should not be reflected on and on which he does not reflect? If, in a person, reflecting on certain things, there arises the defilement of sense-pleasure which has not yet arisen, and (in addition), the defilement of sense-pleasure which has already arisen in him increases, the defilement of (the desire for) existence and for becoming . . . the defilement of ignorance which has not yet arisen arises, and the defilement of ignorance which has already arisen in him increases, these are the things that should not be reflected on, and on which he does not reflect.

"Bhikkhus, what are the things that should be reflected on, and on which he reflects? If, in a person, reflecting on certain things, the defilement of sense-pleasure which has not yet arisen does not arise, and (in addition), the defilement of sense-pleasure which has already arisen in him disappears, the defilement of (the desire for) existence and for becoming . . . the defilement of ignorance which has not yet arisen does not arise, and (in addition), the defilement of ignorance which has already arisen in him disappears, these are the things that should be reflected on, and on which he reflects.

By not reflecting on things that should not be reflected on, and by reflecting on things that should be reflected on, the defilements that have not yet arisen do not arise, and (in addition), the defilements that have already arisen in him disappear. Then he reflects wisely: This is *Dukkha* (suffering). He reflects wisely: This is the arising (cause) of *Dukkha*. He reflects wisely: This is the Cessation of *Dukkha*. He reflects wisely: This is the Path leading to the Cessation of *Dukkha*. When he reflects wisely in this manner, the three Fetters—the false idea of self, sceptical doubt, attachment to observances and rites—fall away from him. Bhikkhus, these are called the troubles (defilements, fetters) that should be got rid of by insight.

(2) "Bhikkhus, what are the cares and troubles to be got rid of by restraint?

"Bhikkhus, a bhikkhu, considering wisely, lives with his eyes restrained. Now, if there are any troubles, distresses and vexations for him when he lives without restraining his eyes, those troubles, distresses and vexations are not for him when he lives restraining his eyes in this manner.

"Considering wisely, he lives with his ears restrained . . . with his nose restrained . . . with his tongue . . . with his body . . . with his mind restrained. Now, if there are any troubles, distresses and vexations for him when he lives without restraining his mind, those troubles, distresses and vexations are not for him when he lives restraining his mind in this manner. Bhikkhus, these are called the cares and troubles to be got rid of by restraint.

(3) "Bhikkhus, what are the cares and troubles to be got rid of by use? Bhikkhus, a bhikkhu, considering wisely, makes use of his robes—only to keep off cold, to keep off heat, to keep off gadflies, mosquitoes, winds and the sun, and creeping creatures, and to cover himself decently. Considering wisely, he makes use of food—neither for pleasures nor for excess (intoxication), neither for beauty nor for adornment, but only to support and sustain this body, to keep it from hurt (fatigue) and to foster the holy life, thinking: In this way I put out the feeling (of suffering, hunger) which is already there, and will not produce a new feeling, and my life will be maintained in blamelessness (harmlessness) and convenience. Considering wisely, he makes use of lodging—only to keep off cold, to keep off heat, to keep off gadflies, mosquitoes, winds and the sun, and creeping creatures, to dispel the risks of the seasons and to enjoy seclusion. Considering wisely, he makes use of medicaments and medical requirements—only to get rid of pains and illnesses which he may have and to maintain his health. Bhikkhus, if there are any troubles, distresses and vexations for him who does not use any (of these things), these troubles, distresses and vexations are not for him when he uses (them) in this manner. Bhikkhus, these are called the cares and troubles which are to be got rid of by use.

(4) "Bhikkhus, what are the cares and troubles to be got rid of by endurance? Bhikkhus, a bhikkhu, considering wisely, puts up with cold and heat, hunger and thirst, with gadflies, mosquitoes, winds, the sun and creeping creatures, abusive and hurtful language, he becomes inured to endurance of bodily feelings which are painful, acute, sharp, severe, unpleasant, disagreeable, deadly. Bhikkhus, if there are any troubles, distresses and vexations for a person who does not endure any (of these), those troubles, distresses and vexations are not for him who endures them in this manner. Bhikkhus, these are called the cares and troubles which are to be got rid of by endurance.

(5)"Bhikkhus, what are the cares and troubles to be got rid of by avoidance? Bhikkhus, a bhikkhu, considering wisely, avoids a savage elephant, a savage horse, a savage bull, a savage dog, avoids a snake, the stump (of a tree), a thorny hedge, a pit (hole), a precipice, a refuse-pool or a dirty pool. Considering wisely, he also avoids sitting in such unseemly places, and frequenting such unseemly resorts, and cultivating such bad friends as would lead the discreet among his fellows in the holy life to conclude that he has gone astray. Bhikkhus, if there are any troubles, distresses and vexations for him when he does not avoid any things (such as these), those troubles, distresses and vexations would not be for him when he avoids them in this manner. These are called the cares and troubles which are to be got rid of by avoidance.

(6) "What are the cares and troubles to be got rid of by dispersal? Bhikkhus, a bhikkhu, considering wisely, does not tolerate, rejects, discards, destroys, extinguishes thoughts of sense-pleasure which have arisen in him; he does not tolerate . . . thoughts of ill-will . . . he does not tolerate . . . thoughts of violence . . . he does not tolerate, rejects, discards, destroys, extinguishes whatever evil and unwholesome thoughts which have arisen in him. Bhikkhus, if there are any troubles, distresses, and vexations for him when he does not disperse any (of these), those troubles, distresses and vexations would not be for him when he disperses them in this manner. Bhikkhus, these are called the cares and troubles which are to be got rid of by dispersal.

(7) "Bhikkhus, what are the cares and troubles to be got rid of by culture (*bhāvanā*)? Bhikkhus, a bhikkhu, considering wisely, cultivates mindfulness, a Factor of Enlightenment associated with detachment, with passionlessness, with cessation, maturing into renunciation; considering wisely, he cultivates the Investigation of the Dhamma, a Factor of Enlightenment . . . Energy, a Factor of Enlightenment . . . Joy, a Factor of Enlightenment . . . Calmness (Relaxation), a Factor of Enlightenment . . . Concentration, a Factor of Enlightenment . . . Equanimity, a Factor of Enlightenment associated with detachment, with passionlessness, with cessation, maturing into renunciation. Bhikkhus, if there are any troubles, distresses and vexations for him when he does not cultivate any (of these), those troubles, distresses and vexations would not be for him when he cultivates them in this manner. Bhikkhus, these are called the cares and troubles which are to be got rid of by culture.

"Bhikkhus, a bhikkhu in whom the cares and troubles which are to be got rid of by insight have been got rid of by insight; the cares and troubles which are to be got rid of by restraint have been got rid of by restraint; the cares and troubles which are to be got rid of by use have been got rid of by use; the cares and troubles which are to be got rid of by endurance have been got rid of by endurance; the cares and troubles which are to be got rid of by avoidance have been got rid of by avoidance; the cares and troubles which are to be got rid of by dispersal have been got rid of by dispersal; the cares and troubles which are to be got rid of by culture have been got rid of by culture—Bhikkhus, it is this bhikkhu who is said to have restrained all cares and troubles; he has cut off craving, struck off his fetters, and by fathoming false pride, has put an end to suffering."

Thus spoke the Blessed One. Glad at heart, those bhikkhus rejoiced at the words of the Blessed One. (*Majjhima-nikāya*, No. 2)

VI
The Foundations of Mindfulness*

Thus have I heard. The Blessed One was once living among the Kurus, at Kammāssadamma, a market town of the Kuru people. There the Blessed One addressed the bhikkhus and spoke as follows:

"This is the only way, Bhikkhus, for the purification of beings, for the overcoming of sorrow and lamentation, for the destruction of suffering and grief, for reaching the right path, for the attainment of Nibbāna, namely the Four Foundations (four forms of Presence) of Mindfulness. What are the four?

"Here a bhikkhu, ardent, clearly comprehending things and mindful, lives observing (the activities of) the body, having overcome covetousness and repugnance towards the world (of body); observing feelings, having overcome covetousness and repugnance towards the world (of feelings) . . . observing (the activities of) the mind, having overcome covetousness and repugnance towards the world (of mind); observing mental objects, having overcome covetousness and repugnance towards the world (of mental objects)."

I. BODY [1]

"And how does a bhikkhu live observing (the activities of) the body?

[1. *Breathing*]

"Here Bhikkhus, a bhikkhu having gone to the forest, to the foot of a tree or to some empty place, sits down, with his legs crossed, keeps his body straight and his mindfulness alert.

"Ever mindful he breathes in, and ever mindful he breathes out. Breathing in a long breath, he knows 'I am breathing in a long breath'; breathing out a long breath, he knows 'I am breathing out a long breath'; breathing in a short breath, he knows 'I am breathing in a short breath'; breathing out a short breath, he knows 'I am breathing out a short breath.'

"'Experiencing the whole (breath-) body, I shall breathe in'; thus he trains himself. 'Experiencing the whole (breath-) body, I shall breathe out': thus he trains himself. 'Calming the activity of the (breath-) body, I shall breath in': thus he trains himself. 'Calming the activity of the (breath-) body, I shall breathe out': thus he trains himself. . . .

"Thus he lives observing (the activities of) the body internally, or . . . externally, or . . . both internally and externally. He lives also observing origination-factors in the body, or dissolution-factors in the body, or origination-and-dissolution factors in the body. Or his mindfulness is established to the extent necessary just for knowledge and awareness that the body exists

---

*Reprinted with permission from Walpola Rahula, *What the Buddha Taught*, second edition (New York: Grove Press, 1974).

[1]The headings were added by the translator.

and he lives unattached, and clings to naught in the world. In this way Bhikkhus, a bhikkhu lives observing (the activities of) the body.

[2. *Postures of the body*]

"And further, Bhikkhus, a bhikkhu knows when he is going, 'I am going.' He knows when he is standing, 'I am standing.' He knows when he is sitting, 'I am sitting.' He knows when he is lying down, 'I am lying down.' Or he knows just how his body is disposed.

"Thus he lives observing (the activities of) the body internally, or externally. . . .

[3. *Full Attention*]

"And further, Bhikkhus, a bhikkhu applies full attention either in going forward or back; in looking straight on or looking away; in bending or in stretching; in wearing robes or carrying the bowl; in eating, drinking, chewing or savouring; in attending to the calls of nature; in walking, in standing, in sitting; in falling asleep, in waking; in speaking or in keeping silence. In all these he applies full attention.

"Thus he lives observing (the activities of) the body.

[4. *Repulsiveness of the body*]

"And further, Bhikkhus, a bhikkhu reflects on this very body enveloped by the skin and full of manifold impurity, from the sole up, and from the top of the hair down, thinking thus: 'There are in this body hair of the head, hair of the body, nails, teeth, skin, flesh, sinews, bones, marrow, kidneys, heart, liver, midriff, spleen, lungs, intestines, mesentery, stomach, faeces, bile, phlegm, pus, blood, sweat, fat, tears, grease, saliva, nasal mucus, synovial fluid, urine.'

"Just as if there were a double-mouthed provision-bag full of various kinds of grain such as hill paddy, paddy, green gram, cow-peas, sesamum and husked rice, and a man with sound eyes, having opened that bag, were to reflect thus: This is hill paddy, this is paddy, this is green gram, this is cow-pea, this is sesamum, this is husked rice, just so, Bhikkhus, a bhikkhu reflects on this very body enveloped by the skin and full of manifold impurity, from the sole up, and from the top of the hair down, thinking thus: There are in this body hair of the head, hair of the body, nails, teeth . . . synovial fluid, urine.

"Thus he lives observing the body. . . .

[5. *Material Elements*]

"And further, Bhikkhus, a bhikkhu reflects on this very body, as it is, and it is constituted, by way of the material elements: 'There are in this body the element of earth, the element of water, the element of fire, the element of wind.'

"Just as if, Bhikkhus, a clever cow-butcher or his apprentice, having slaughtered a cow and divided it into portions, would be sitting at the junction of four high roads; in the same way, a bhikkhu reflects on this very body, as it is, and it is constituted, by way of the material elements: 'There are in this body the elements of earth, water, fire and wind.'

"Thus he lives observing the body. . . .

[6. *Nine Cemetery Objects*]

(1) "And further, Bhikkhus, just as a bhikkhu sees a body dead one, two,

or three days, swollen, blue and festering, thrown on to the cemetery, so he applies this perception to his own body thus: 'Verily, my own body, too, is of the same nature; such it will become and will not escape it.'

"Thus he lives observing the body. . . .

(2) "And further, Bhikkhus, just as a bhikkhu sees a body thrown on to the cemetery, being eaten by crows, hawks, vultures, dogs, jackals or by different kinds of worms, so he applies this perception to his own body thus: 'Verily, my own body, too, is of the same nature; such it will become and will not escape it.'

"Thus he lives observing the body. . . .

(3) "And further, Bhikkhus, just as a bhikkhu sees a body thrown on to the cemetery reduced to a skeleton with some flesh and blood attached to it, held together by the tendons. . . .

(4) "And further, Bhikkhus, just as a bhikkhu sees a body thrown on to the cemetery reduced to a skeleton, blood-besmeared and without flesh, held together by the tendons. . . .

(5) "And further, Bhikkhus, just as a bhikkhu sees a body thrown on to the cemetery reduced to a skeleton without flesh and blood, held together by the tendons. . . .

(6) "And further, Bhikkhus, just as a bhikkhu sees a body thrown on to the cemetery reduced to disconnected bones, scattered in all directions—here a bone of the hand, there a bone of the foot, a shin bone, a thigh bone, the pelvis, spine and skull. . . .

(7) "And further, Bhikkhus, just as a bhikkhu sees a body thrown on to the cemetery reduced to bleached bones of conch-like colour. . . .

(8) "And further, Bhikkhus, just as a bhikkhu sees a body thrown on to the cemetery reduced to bones, more than a year old, lying in a heap. . . .

(9) "And further, Bhikkhus, just as a bhikkhu sees a body thrown on to the cemetery reduced to bones rotten and become dust . . . so he applies this perception to his own body thus: "Verily, my own body, too, is of the same nature; such it will become and will not escape it.'

"Thus he lives observing the body . . ."

II. FEELINGS

"And how Bhikkhus, does a bhikkhu live observing feelings?

"Here, Bhikkhus, a bhikkhu when experiencing a pleasant feeling knows: 'I experience a pleasant feeling'; when experiencing a painful feeling, he knows: 'I experience a painful feeling'; when experiencing a neither-pleasant-nor-painful feeling, he knows: 'I experience a neither-pleasant-nor-painful feeling.' When experiencing a pleasant worldly feeling, he knows: 'I experience a pleasant worldly feeling'; when experiencing a pleasant spiritual feeling, he knows: 'I experience a pleasant spiritual feeling'; when experiencing a painful worldly feeling, he knows: 'I experience a painful worldly feeling'; when experiencing a painful spiritual feeling, he knows: 'I experience a painful spiritual feeling'; when experiencing a neither-pleasant-nor-painful worldly feeling, he knows: 'I experience a neither-pleasant-nor-painful worldly feeling'; when experiencing a neither-pleasant-nor-painful spiritual feeling, he knows: 'I experience a neither-pleasant-nor-painful spiritual feeling.'

"He lives in this way observing feelings internally, . . . or externally, or . . . internally and externally. He lives observing origination-factors in feelings, or dissolution-factors in feelings, or origination-and-dissolution factors in feelings. Or his mindfulness is established to the extent necessary just for knowledge and awareness that feeling exists, and he lives unattached, and clings to naught in the world. In this way, Bhikkhus, a bhikkhu lives observing feelings."

III. MIND

"And how, Bhikkhus, does a bhikkhu live observing mind?

"Here Bhikkhus, a bhikkhu knows the mind with lust, as being with lust; the mind without lust, as being without lust; the mind with hate, as being with hate; the mind without hate, as being without hate; the mind with ignorance, as being with ignorance; the mind without ignorance, as being without ignorance; the shrunken state of mind as the shrunken state; the distracted state of mind as the distracted state; the developed state of mind as the developed state; the undeveloped state of mind as the undeveloped state; the state of mind with some other mental state superior to it, as being the state with something mentally superior to it; the state of mind with no other mental state superior to it, as being the state with nothing mentally superior to it; the concentrated state of mind as the concentrated state; the unconcentrated state of mind as the unconcentrated state; the liberated state of mind as the liberated state; and the unliberated state of mind as the unliberated state.

"He lives in this way observing the mind internally, or externally, or internally and externally.

"He lives observing origination-factors in mind or dissolution-factors in mind or origination-and-dissolution-factors in mind. Or his mindfulness is established to the extent necessary just for knowledge and awareness that mind exists, and he lives unattached, and clings to naught in the world. Thus, Bhikkhus, a bhikkhu lives observing mind."

IV. MENTAL OBJECTS

"And how, Bhikkhus, does a bhikkhu live observing mental objects?

[*Five Hindrances*]

"Here, Bhikkhus, a bhikkhu lives observing the Five Hindrances as mental objects.

"How, Bhikkhus, does a bhikkhu live observing the Five Hindrances as mental objects?

(1) "Here, Bhikkhus, when sense-desire is present, a bhikkhu knows:

'Sense-desire is in me,' or when sense-desire is not present, he knows: 'There is no sense-desire in me.' He knows how the non-arisen sense-desire arises; he knows how the arisen sense-desire disappears; and he knows how the non-arising in the future of the abandoned sense-desire comes to be.

(2) "When anger is present, he knows: 'Anger is in me. . . .'

(3) "When torpor and languor are present, he knows: 'Torpor and languor are in me. . . .'

(4) "When restlessness and worry are present, he knows: 'Restlessness and worry are in me. . . .'

(5) "When doubt is present, he knows: 'Doubt is in me,' or when doubt is not present, he knows, 'There is no doubt in me.' He knows how the non-arisen doubt arises; he knows how the arisen doubt disappears; and he knows how the non-arising in the future of the abandoned doubt comes to be.

"In this way he lives observing mental objects internally, or externally, or internally and externally. He lives observing origination-factors in mental objects, or dissolution-factors in mental objects, or origination- and dissolution-factors in mental objects. Or his mindfulness is established to the extent necessary just for knowledge and awareness that mental objects exist, and he lives unattached and clings to naught in the world. In this way, Bhikkhus, a bhikkhu lives observing the five hindrances as mental objects.

[*Five Aggregates*]

"And further, Bhikkhus, a bhikkhu lives observing the five aggregates of clinging as mental objects.

"How, Bhikkhus, does a bhikkhu live observing (contemplating) the five aggregates of clinging as mental objects?

"Here, Bhikkhus, a bhikkhu thinks: Thus is material form; it arises in this way; and it disappears in this way. Thus is feeling; it arises in this way; and it disappears in this way. Thus is perception; it arises in this way; and it disappears in this way. Thus are mental formations; they arise in this way; and they disappear in this way. Thus is consciousness; it arises in this way; and it disappears in this way.

"Thus he lives contemplating mental objects internally, etc. . . .' In this way, Bhikkhus, a bhikkhu lives contemplating the five aggregates of clinging as mental objects.

[*Six Sense-Bases*]

"And further, Bhikkhus, a bhikkhu lives contemplating the six internal and the six external sense-bases as mental objects.

"How, Bhikkhus, does a bhikkhu live contemplating the six internal and the six external sense-bases as mental objects?

"Here, Bhikkhus, a bhikkhu knows the eye and visual forms, and the fetter that arises dependent on both (the eye and forms); he knows how the non-arisen fetter arises; he knows how the arisen fetter disappears; and he knows how the non-arising in the future of the abandoned fetter comes to be.

"He knows the ear and sounds . . . the nose and smells . . . the tongue and flavors . . . the body and tangible objects . . . the mind and mental objects, and the fetter that arises dependent on both; he knows how the non-arisen fetter arises; he knows how the arisen fetter disappears; and he knows how the non-arising in the future of the abandoned fetter comes to be.

"In this way, Bhikkhus, a bhikkhu lives contemplating mental objects internally, etc. . . . In this way, Bhikkhus, a bhikkhu lives contemplating the six internal and the six external sense-bases as mental objects.

[*Seven Factors of Enlightenment*]

"And further, Bhikkhus, a bhikkhu lives observing the Seven Factors of Enlightenment as mental objects.

"How Bhikkhus does a bhikkhu live observing the Seven Factors of Enlightenment as mental objects?

(1) "Here Bhikkhus, when the Enlightenment-factor of Mindfulness is present, the bhikkhu knows: 'The Enlightenment-factor of Mindfulness is in me'; or when the Enlightenment-factor of Mindfulness is absent, he knows: 'The Enlightenment-factor of Mindfulness is not in me'; and he knows how the non-arisen Enlightenment-factor of Mindfulness arises; and how perfection in the development of the arisen Enlightenment-factor of Mindfulness comes to be.

(2) "When the Enlightenment-factor of the Investigation of mental objects is present, the bhikkhu knows: 'The Enlightenment-factor of the Investigation of mental objects is in me'; when the Enlightenment-factor of the Investigation of mental objects is absent, he knows: 'The Enlightenment-factor of the Investigation of mental objects is not in me'; and he knows how the non-arisen Enlightenment-factor of the Investigation of mental objects arises and how perfection in the development of the arisen Enlightenment-factor of the Investigation of mental objects comes to be.

(3) "When the Enlightenment-factor of Energy is present, he knows: 'The Enlightenment-factor of Energy is in me'; when the Enlightenment-factor of Energy is absent, he knows: 'The Enlightenment-factor of Energy is not in me'; and he knows how the non-arisen Enlightenment-factor of Energy arises, and how perfection in the development of the arisen Enlightenment-factor of Energy comes to be.

(4) "When the Enlightenment-factor of Joy is present, he knows: 'The Enlightenment-factor of Joy is in me'; when the Enlightenment-factor of Joy is absent, he knows: 'The Enlightenment-factor of Joy is not in me'; and he knows how the non-arisen Enlightenment-factor of Joy arises and how perfection in the development of the arisen Enlightenment-factor of Joy comes to be.

(5) "When the Enlightenment-factor of Relaxation (of body and mind) is present, he knows: 'The Enlightenment-factor of Relaxation is in me'; when the Enlightenment-factor of Relaxation is absent, he knows: 'The Enlightenment-factor of Relaxation is not in me'; and he knows how the non-arisen Enlightenment-factor of Relaxation arises, and how perfection in the development of the arisen Enlightenment-factor of the Relaxation comes to be.

(6) "When the Enlightenment-factor of Concentration is present, he knows: 'The Enlightenment-factor of Concentration is in me'; when the Enlightenment-factor of Concentration is absent, he knows: 'The Enlightenment-factor of Concentration is not in me'; and he knows how the non-arisen Enlightenment-factor of Concentration arises, and how perfection in the development of the arisen Enlightenment-factor of Concentration comes to be.

(7) "When the Enlightenment-factor of Equanimity is present, he knows: 'The Enlightenment-factor of Equanimity is in me'; when the Enlightenment-factor of Equanimity is absent, he knows: 'The Enlightenment-factor of Equanimity is not in me'; and he knows how the non-arisen Enlightenment-factor of Equanimity arises, and how perfection in the development of the arisen Enlightenment-factor of Equanimity comes to be.

"Thus he lives observing mental objects internally, etc. . . . Thus, Bhikkhus, a bhikkhu lives observing the Seven Factors of Enlightenment as mental objects.

[*Four Noble Truths*]

"And further, Bhikkhus, a bhikkhu lives contemplating the Four Noble Truths as mental objects.

"How Bhikkhus, does a bhikkhu live contemplating the Four Noble Truths as mental objects?

"Here, Bhikkhus, a bhikkhu knows, 'This is *Dukkha* (suffering),' according to reality; he knows, 'This is the Origin of *Dukkha*,' according to reality; he knows, 'This the Cessation of *Dukkha*,' according to reality; he knows, 'This is the Path leading to the Cessation of *Dukkha*,' according to reality.

"Thus he lives contemplating mental objects internally, etc. . . . In this way, Bhikkhus, a bhikkhu lives contemplating the Four Noble Truths as mental objects.

"Bhikkhus, whosoever practises these four Foundations of Mindfulness in this manner for seven years, then one of these two fruits may be expected by him: Highest Knowledge (Arahantship), here and now, or if some remainder of clinging is yet present, the state of Non-returning.

"Bhikkhus, let alone seven years. Should any person practise these four Foundations of Mindfulness in this manner for six years . . . for five years . . . four years . . . three years . . . two years . . . one year, then one of these two fruits may be expected by him: Highest Knowledge, here and now, or if some remainder of clinging is yet present, the state of Non-returning.

"Bhikkhus, let alone a year. Should any person practise these four Foundations of Mindfulness in this manner for seven months . . . for six months . . . five months . . . four months . . . three months . . . two months . . . a month . . . half a month, then one of these two fruits may be expected by him: Highest Knowledge, here and now, or if some remainder of clinging is yet present, the state of Non-entering.

"Bhikkhus, let alone half a month. Should any person practise these four Foundations of Mindfulness, in this manner, for a week, then one of these two fruits may be expected by him: Highest Knowledge, here and now, or if some remainder of clinging is yet present, the state of Non-returning.

"Because of this was it said: 'This is the only way, Bhikkhus, for the purification of beings, for the overcoming of sorrow and lamentation, for the destruction of suffering and grief, for reaching the right path, for the attainment of Nibbāna, namely the four Foundations of Mindfulness.'"

This the Blessed One said. Satisfied, the Bhikkhus rejoiced at his words.

(*Majjhima Nikāya*, Sutta No. 10, abridged)

VII
The Words of Truth

SELECTIONS FROM *THE DHAMMAPADA**

1. All (mental) states have mind as their forerunner, mind is their chief, and they are mind-made. If one speaks or acts, with a defiled mind, then suffering follows one even as the wheel follows the hoof of the draught-ox.

2. All (mental) states have mind as their forerunner, mind is their chief, and they are mind-made. If one speaks or acts, with a pure mind, happiness follows one as one's shadow that does not leave one.

3. "He abused me, he beat me, he defeated me, he robbed me": the hatred of those who harbour such thoughts is not appeased.

5. Hatred is never appeased by hatred in this world; it is appeased by love. This is an eternal Law.

24. Whosoever is energetic, mindful, pure in conduct, discriminating, self-restrained, right-living, vigilant, his fame steadily increases.

25. By endeavour, diligence, discipline, and self-mastery, let the wise man make (of himself) an island that no flood can overwhelm.

26. Fools, men of little intelligence, give themselves over to negligence, but the wise man protects his diligence as a supreme treasure.

27. Give not yourselves unto negligence; have no intimacy with sense pleasures. The man who meditates with diligence attains much happiness.

33. This fickle, unsteady mind, difficult to guard, difficult to control, the wise man makes straight, as the fletcher the arrow.

35. Hard to restrain, unstable is this mind; it flits wherever it lists. Good it is to control the mind. A controlled mind brings happiness.

38. He whose mind is unsteady, he who knows not the Good Teaching, he whose confidence wavers, the wisdom of such a person does not attain fullness.

---

*Reprinted with permission from Walpola Rahula, *What the Buddha Taught*, second edition (New York: Grove Press, 1974).

42. Whatever harm a foe may do to a foe, or a hater to another hater, a wrongly-directed mind may do one harm far exceeding these.

43. Neither mother, nor father, nor any other relative can do a man such good as is wrought by a rightly-directed mind. . . .

47. The man who gathers only the flowers (of sense pleasures), whose mind is entangled, death carries him away as a great flood a sleeping village.

50. One should not pry into the faults of others, into things done and left undone by others. One should rather consider what by oneself is done and left undone.

51. As a beautiful flower that is full of hue but lacks fragrance, even so fruitless is the well-spoken word of one who does not practise it.

61. If, as one fares, one does not find a companion who is better or equal, let one resolutely pursue the solitary course; there can be no fellowship with the fool.

62. "I have sons, I have wealth": thinking thus the fool is troubled. Indeed, he himself is not his own. How can sons or wealth be his?

64. Even if all his life a fool associates with a wise man, he will not understand the Truth, even as the spoon (does not understand) the flavour of the soup.

67. That deed is not well done, which one regrets when it is done and the result of which one experiences weeping with a tearful face.

69. The fool thinks an evil deed as sweet as honey, so long as it does not ripen (does not produce results). But when it ripens, the fool comes to grief.

81. Even as a solid rock is unshaken by the wind, so are the wise unshaken by praise or blame.

82. Even as a lake, deep, extremely clear and tranquil, so do the wise become tranquil having heard the Teaching.

85. Few among men are they who cross to the further shore. The others merely run up and down the bank on this side.

90. For him, who has completed the journey, who is sorrowless, wholly set free, and rid of all bonds, for such a one there is no burning (of the passions).

94. He whose senses are mastered like horses well under the charioteer's control, he who is purged of pride, free from passions, such a steadfast one even the gods envy (hold dear).

96. Calm is the thought, calm the word and deed of him who, rightly knowing, is wholly freed, perfectly peaceful and equipoised.

97. The man who is not credulous, who knows the "uncreated," who has severed all ties, who has put an end to the occasion (of good and evil), who has vomited all desires, verily he is supreme among men.

103. One may conquer in battle a thousand times a thousand men, yet he is the best of conquerors who conquers himself.

104–105. Better is it truly to conquer oneself than to conquer others. Neither a god, nor an "angel" nor Māra, nor Brahmā could turn into defeat the victory of a person such as this who is self-mastered and ever restrained in conduct.

111. Though one may live a hundred years with no true insight and self-control, yet better, indeed, is a life of one day for a man who meditates in wisdom.

116. Make haste in doing good; restrain your mind from evil. Whosoever is slow in doing good, his mind delights in evil.

119. It is well with the evil-doer until his evil (deed) ripens. But when his evil (deed) bears fruit, he then sees its ill effects.

120. It is ill, perhaps, with the doer of good until his good deed ripens. But when it bears fruit, then he sees the happy results.

121. Do not think lightly of evil, saying: "It will not come to me." Even a water-pot is filled by the falling of drops. Likewise the fool, gathering it drop by drop, fills himself with evil.

122. Do not think lightly of good, saying: "It will not come to me." Even as a water-pot is filled by the falling of drops, so the wise man, gathering it drop by drop, fills himself with good.

125. Whosoever offends an innocent person, pure and guiltless, his evil comes back on that fool himself like fine dust thrown against the wind.

129. All tremble at weapons; all fear death. Comparing others with oneself, one should not slay, nor cause to slay.

131. He who, seeking his own happiness, torments with the rod creatures that are desirous of happiness, shall not obtain happiness hereafter.

152. The man of little learning (ignorant) grows like a bull; his flesh grows, but not his wisdom.

155. Not having lived the Holy Life, not having obtained wealth in their youth, men pine away like old herons in a lake without fish.

159. If a man practises himself what he admonishes others to do, he himself, being well-controlled, will have control over others. It is difficult, indeed, to control oneself.

160. Oneself is one's own protector (refuge); what other protector (refuge) can there be? With oneself fully controlled, one obtains a protection (refuge) which is hard to gain.

165. By oneself indeed is evil done and by oneself is one defiled. By oneself is evil left undone and by oneself indeed is one purified. Purity and impurity depend on oneself. No one can purify another.

167. Do not follow mean things. Do not dwell in negligence. Do not embrace false views. So the world (i.e. *Saṃsāra*, the cycle of existence and continuity) is not prolonged.

171. Come, behold this world, how it resembles an ornamented royal chariot, in which fools flounder, but for the wise there is no attachment to it.

178. Better is the gain of Entering the Stream than sole sovereignty over the earth, than going to heaven, than rule supreme over the entire universe.

183. Not to do any evil, to cultivate good, to purify one's mind, this is the Teaching of the Buddhas.

184. The most excellent ascetic practice is patience and forbearance. "Nibbāna is supreme," say the Buddhas. He indeed is no recluse who harms another; nor is he an ascetic who hurts others.

185. To speak no ill, to do no harm, to practise restraint according to the fundamental precepts, to be moderate in eating, to live in seclusion, to devote oneself to higher consciousness, this is the Teaching of the Buddhas.

197. Happy indeed we live without hate among the hateful. We live free from hatred amidst hateful men.

201. The conqueror begets enmity; the defeated lie down in distress The peaceful rest in happiness, giving up both victory and defeat.

204. Health is the best gain; contentment is the best wealth. A trusty friend is the best kinsman; *Nibbāna* is the supreme bliss.

205. Having tasted of the flavour of solitude and tranquillity, one becomes woeless and stainless, drinking the essence of the joy of Truth.

215. From lust arises grief; from lust arises fear. For him who is free from lust there is no grief, much less fear.

222. He who holds back arisen anger as one checks a whirling chariot, him I call a charioteer; other folk only hold the reins.

223. Conquer anger by love, evil by good; conquer the miser with liberality, and liar with truth.

231. Be on your guard against physical agitation; be controlled in body. Forsaking bodily misconduct, follow right conduct in body.

232. Be on your guard against verbal agitation; be controlled in words. Forsaking wrong speech, follow right ways in words.

233. Be on your guard against mental agitation; be controlled in thoughts. Forsaking evil thoughts, follow right ways in thoughts.

234. The wise are controlled in deed, controlled in words, controlled in thoughts, verily, they are fully controlled.

239. By degrees, little by little, from moment to moment, a wise man removes his own impurities, as a smith removes the dross of silver.

240. As rust, arisen out of iron, eats itself away, even so his own deeds lead the transgressor to the states of woe.

248. Know this, O good man, that evil things are uncontrollable. Let not greed and wickedness drag you to suffering for a long time.

251. There is no fire like lust. There is no grip like hate. There is no net like delusion. There is no river like craving.

252. The fault of others is easily seen; but one's own is hard to see. Like chaff one winnows other's faults; but one's own one conceals as a crafty fowler disguises himself.

267. He who has transcended both merit (good) and demerit (evil), he who leads a pure life, he who lives with understanding in this world, he, indeed, is called a bhikkhu.

268–269. Not by silence does one become a sage (*muni*) if one be foolish and untaught. But the wise man who, as if holding a pair of scales, takes what is good and leaves out what is evil, is indeed a sage. For that reason he is a sage. He who understands both sides in this world is called a sage.

273. Of paths the Eightfold Path is the best; of truths the Four Words (Noble Truths); Detachment is the best of states and of bipeds the Seeing One (the Man of Vision).

274. This is the only way. There is no other for the purification of Vision. Follow this Way: this is the bewilderment of Māra (Evil).

275. Following this Way you shall make an end of suffering. This verily is the Way declared by me when I had learnt to remove the arrow (of suffering).

276. You yourselves should make the effort; the Awakened Ones are only teachers. Those who enter this Path and who are meditative, are delivered from the bonds of Māra (Evil).

277. "All conditioned things are impermanent," when one sees this in wisdom, then one becomes dispassionate towards the painful. This is the Path to Purity.

278. "All conditioned things are *dukkha* (Ill)," when one sees this in wisdom, then he becomes dispassionate towards the painful. This is the Path to Purity.

279. "All states (*dhamma*) are without self," when one sees this in wisdom, then he becomes dispassionate towards the painful. This is the Path to Purity.

280. Who strives not when he should strive, who, though young and strong, is given to idleness, who is loose in his purpose and thoughts, and who is lazy—that idler never finds the way to wisdom.

281. Watchful of speech, well restrained in mind, let him do no evil with the body; let him purify these three ways of action, and attain the Path made known by the Sages.

334. The craving of the man addicted to careless living grows like a Māluvā creeper. He jumps hither and thither, like a monkey in the forest looking for fruit.

335. Whosoever in this world is overcome by this wretched clinging thirst, his sorrows grow like Bīraṇa grass after rain.

336. But whosoever in this world overcomes this wretched craving so difficult to overcome, his sorrows fall away from him like water-drops from a lotus (leaf).

338. As a tree cut down sprouts forth again if its roots remain uninjured and strong, even so when the propensity to craving is not destroyed, this suffering arises again and again.

343. Led by craving men run this way and that like an ensnared hare. Therefore let the bhikkhu, who wishes his detachment, discard craving.

348. Free thyself from the past, free thyself from the future, free thyself from the present. Crossing to the farther shore of existence, with mind released everywhere, no more shalt thou come to birth and decay.

360. Good is restraint of the eye. Good is restraint of the ear. Good is restraint of the nose. Good is restraint of the tongue.

361. Good is restraint of the body. Good is restraint of speech. Good is restraint of the mind. Restraint everywhere is good. The bhikkhu restrained in every way is freed from all suffering.

362. He who is controlled in hand, controlled in foot, controlled in speech, and possessing the highest control (of mind), delighted within, composed, solitary and contented, him they call a bhikkhu.

365. One should not despise what one receives, and one should not envy (the gain of) others. The bhikkhu who envies others does not attain concentration.

367. He who has no attachment whatsoever to Name and Form (mind and body), and he who does not grieve over what there is not, he indeed is called a bhikkhu.

368. The bhikkhu, who abides in loving-kindness, who is delighted in the Teaching of the Buddha, attains the State of Calm, the happiness of stilling the conditioned things.

385. He for whom there exists neither this shore nor the other, nor both, he who is undistressed and unbound, him I call a brāhman.

397. The sun glows by day; the moon shines by night; in his armour the warrior glows. In meditation shines the brāhman. But all day and night, shines with radiance the Awakened One.

420. He whose destiny neither the gods nor demigods nor men do know, he who has destroyed defilements and become worthy, him I call a brāhman.

423. He who knows former lives, who sees heaven and hell, who has reached the end of births and attained to super-knowledge, the sage, accomplished with all accomplishments, him I call a brāhman.

VIII
The Last Words of the Buddha*

Then the Blessed One addressed the Venerable Ānanda: "It may be, Ānanda, that to some of you the thought may come: 'Here are (we have) the Words of the Teacher who is gone; our Teacher we have with us no more.' But Ānanda, it should not be considered in this light. What I have taught and laid down, Ānanda, as Doctrine (*Dhamma*) and Discipline (*Vinaya*), this will be your teacher when I am gone.

"Just as, Ānanda, the bhikkhus now address one another with the word 'Friend' (*Āvuso*), they should not do so when I am gone. A senior bhikkhu, Ānanda, may address a junior by his name, his family name or with the word 'Friend'; a junior bhikkhu should address a senior as 'Sir' (*Bhante*) or 'Venerable' (*Āyamā*).

"If the Sangha (the Community, the Order) should wish it, Ānanda, let them, when I am gone, abolish the lesser and minor precepts (rules).

"When I am gone, Ānanda, the highest penalty should be imposed on the Bhikkhu Channa."

"But, Sir, what is the highest penalty?"

"Let the Bhikkhu Channa say what he likes, Ānanda; the bhikkhus should neither speak to him, nor advise him, nor exhort him."

Then the Blessed One addressed the bhikkhus: "It may be, Bhikkhus, that there may be doubt or perplexity in the mind of even one bhikkhu about the Buddha, or the Dhamma, or the Sangha, or the Path, or the Practice. Ask Bhikkhus. Do not reproach yourselves afterwards with the thought: 'Our Teacher was face to face with us; we could not ask the Blessed One when we were face to face with him.'"

When this was said, the bhikkhus remained silent.

A second time and a third time too the Blessed One addressed the bhikkhus . . . as above.

The bhikkhus remained silent even for the third time.

Then the Blessed One addressed them and said: "It may be, Bhikkhus, that you put no questions out of reverence for your Teacher. Then, Bhikkhus, let friend speak to friend."[1]

Even at this, those bhikkhus remained silent.

Then the Venerable Ānanda said to the Blessed One: "It is wonderful, Sir. It is marvellous, Sir. I have this faith, Sir, in the community of bhikkhus here, that not even one of them has any doubt or perplexity about the Buddha, or the Dhamma, or the Sangha, or the Path, or the Practice."

"You speak out of faith, Ānanda. But in this matter, Ānanda, the Tathāgata (i.e., Buddha) knows, and knows for certain, that in this community of

---

*Reprinted with permission from Walpola Rahula, *What the Buddha Taught*, second edition (New York: Grove Press, 1974).

[1]The idea is that if they did not like to put any question directly to the Buddha out of respect for their Teacher, a bhikkhu should whisper the question to his friend, and then the latter could ask it on his behalf.

bhikkhus there is not even one bhikkhu who has any doubt or perplexity about the Buddha, or the Dhamma, or the Sangha, or the Path, or the Practice. Indeed, Ānanda, even the lowest in spiritual attainments among these five hundred bhikkhus is a Stream-entrant (*Sotāpanna*), not liable to fall (into lower states), is assured, and is bound for Enlightenment."

Then the Blessed One addressed the bhikkhus, saying: "Then, Bhikkhus, I address you now: Transient are conditioned things. Try to accomplish your aim with diligence."

These were the last words of the Tathāgata.

(*Dīgha-nikāya, Sutta* No. 16)

CHAPTER 10

PHILOSOPHICAL ISSUES IN EARLY BUDDHISM

The basic tenets of *duḥkha*, no-self, impermanence, and *nirvāṇa* that encapsulated Buddhist understanding of the Middle Way taught by the Buddha gave rise to a number of philosophical problems that attracted the attention of serious thinkers over the ages. The proposed solutions to these problems and their critiques by other thinkers shaped the rich tradition of Buddhist philosophy and resulted in a number of schools of thought, all concerned with at least some of the following questions. If there is no self, then who experiences *duḥkha*? And who experiences *nirvāṇa*? And if existence is impermanent, what reason is there to think that the same person who at one time experiences *duḥkha* can, at another time, experience *nirvāṇa*? If existence is simply the interrelated functioning of the groups of existence, without a self, then what holds these groups together and gives them continuity? If things are said to lack being, then are not things themselves denied? How, in the face of denial of a self that can be reborn, can rebirth take place? If self is denied, what sense does it make to ascribe moral responsibility to a person? What is the relation between reason and the knowledge that liberates one from *duḥkha*? Are the rational views of metaphysics irrelevant to religious insight and transformation?

The following selections from Henry Clarke Warren, *Buddhism in Translations* (New York: Atheneum, 1963; originally published by Harvard University Press 1896), represent some of the earliest texts available that address these issues. The works recommended in chapter 9 by Walpola Rahula and Frank J. Hoffman are also relevant here. Paul J. Griffiths, *On Being Mindless* (Le Salle, Illinois: Open Court, 1986), and Steven Collins, *Selfless Persons* (Cambridge: Cambridge University Press 1982), provide excellent contemporary discussions of some of these issues.

Selection 1, "No-Self and Rebirth," includes the following four readings that present important philosophical issues associated with the teachings of no-self and rebirth.

"There Is No Self" is the famous dialogue between the monk Nāgasena and Milinda, the Greek king, in which Nāgasena convinces Milinda that there is no substantial, enduring entity called the self; that "self" simply refers to a constantly changing, interrelated set of processes.

"Buddhaghoṣa's Comment on No Self" makes clear that denial of self as a separate, permanent entity is not a denial of self as a concrete, living entity.

"Sensation and the Self" asks whether it makes sense to identify the self with sensation. Three alternatives are explored: (1) sensation is the self; (2) sensation is not the self; (3) sensation is neither the self nor not the self, but rather the self has sensation. All three alternatives are shown to be rationally unacceptable.

"Rebirth Is Not Transmigration" defends the view that rebirth occurs while denying that there is anything that crosses over from one birth to the next. The examples illustrate that the key to this argument is to view existence as a continuous, self-energizing process, rather than as a series of permanent states.

Selection 2, "The Difference Between Groups and Attachment-Groups," implicitly addresses a key problem, that of how, if the self is nothing but five groups of factors, and these are identified with *duḥkha*, liberation is possible. By distinguishing between the groups when attached to a self and thereby coupled with the depravity of ignorance, lust, and hatred, and the groups in themselves when not so attached, liberation can be seen as the overcoming of attachment and depravity, for these are not intrinsic to the groups constituting personal existence.

Selection 3, "Dependent Origination: The Middle Way," includes three readings that explain the insight underlying the Buddhist claim that identifying existence with being brings about *duḥkha* through attachment, just as identifying existence with nonbeing brings about *duḥkha* through rejection. The right view, midway between these two extremes, is that existence is a continuous process of arising and perishing that both depends on earlier conditions and gives rise to new conditions.

"The Teaching Stated" presents the teaching of dependent origination in terms of the twelve linked factors involved in the origination of suffering.

"The Meaning of Dependent Origination" explains both the meaning of the factors involved and also how this teaching provides for the efficacy of efforts to achieve liberation from *duḥkha*.

"Explanation of Dependent Origination" presents the Buddha describing how this insight explains both the arising of *duḥkha* through ignorance and attachment and the cessation of *duḥkha* through wisdom and nonattachment.

Section 4, "Reason and Wisdom," includes two readings that present the early Buddhist aversion to rational speculation as a solution to the problem of *duḥkha*.

"Dialogue with Vacchagotta" compares metaphysical speculation as a means of solving the existential problems of life to a jungle, a writhing, and a fetter—that is, worse than useless, because it confuses people.

"Parable of Māluñkyāputta" also illustrates a typical Buddhist attitude toward intellectual views. Affirming or denying theoretical views, supporting or attacking them, is not conducive to insight and liberation. Instead, focusing on the issue at hand, the arising of *duḥkha* that afflicts existence, one should develop insight into its arising, into the conditions of its arising, and the way to eliminate those conditions, thereby overcoming *duḥkha.* The relationship between this higher knowledge of direct insight and the lower knowledge of intellectual discrimination has remained a lively topic of debate over the centuries.

I
No-Self and Rebirth*

A. THERE IS NO SELF

Then drew near Milinda the king to where the venerable Nāgasena was; and having drawn near, he greeted the venerable Nāgasena; and having passed the compliments of friendship and civility, he sat down respectfully at one side. And the venerable Nāgasena returned the greeting; by which, verily, he won the heart of King Milinda.

And Milinda the king spoke to the venerable Nāgasena as follows:—

"How is your reverence called? Bhante,[1] what is your name?"

"Your majesty, I am called Nāgasena; my fellow-priests, your majesty, address me as Nāgasena: but whether parents give one the name Nāgasena, or Sūrasena, or Vīrasena, or Sīhasena, it is, nevertheless, your majesty, but a way of counting, a term, an appellation, a convenient designation, a mere name, this Nāgasena; for there is no Self here to be found."

Then said Milinda the king,—

"Listen to me, my lords, ye five hundred Yonakas, and ye eighty thousand priests! Nāgasena here says thus: 'There is no Self here to be found.' Is it possible, pray, for me to assent to what he says?"

And Milinda the king spoke to the venerable Nāgasena as follows:—

"Bhante Nāgasena, if there is no Self to be found, who is it then furnishes you priests with the priestly requisites,—robes, food, bedding, and medicine, the reliance of the sick? who is it makes use of the same? who is it keeps the precepts? who is it applies himself to meditation? who is it realizes the Paths, the Fruits, and Nirvana? who is it destroys life? who is it takes what is not given him? who is it commits immorality? who is it tells lies? who is it drinks

---

*Reprinted with permission from Henry Clarke Warren, *Buddhism in Translations* (New York: Atheneum, 1963).
Note: Throughout the selections reprinted from Warren, we have taken the liberty of substituting the word "self" for "ego," the word by which Warren translated "*attan*" (Skt. "*ātman*"). Since Sigmund Freud, "ego" has had connotations that make it inappropriate as a translation of "*Āttan.*"
[1]*Bhante* is a respectful title.

intoxicating liquor? who is it commits the five crimes that constitute 'proximate karma'? In that case, there is no merit; there is no demerit; there is no one who does or causes to be done meritorious or demeritorious deeds; neither good nor evil deeds can have any fruit or result. Bhante Nāgasena, neither is he a murderer who kills a priest, nor can you priests, bhante Nāgasena, have any teacher, preceptor, or ordination. When you say, 'My fellow-priests, your majesty, address me as Nāgasena,' what then is this Nāgesena? Pray, bhante, is the hair of the head Nāgasena?"

"Nay, verily, your majesty."

"Is the hair of the body Nāgasena?"

"Nay, verily, your majesty."

"Are nails . . . teeth . . . skin . . . flesh . . . . sinews . . . bones . . . marrow of the bones . . kidneys . . . heart . . . liver . . . pleura . . . spleen . . . lungs . . . intestines . . . mesentery . . . stomach . . . faeces . . . bile . . . phlegm . . . pus . . . blood . . . sweat . . . fat . . . tears . . . lymph . . . saliva . . . snot . . . synovial fluid . . . urine . . . brain of the head Nāgasena?"

"Nay, verily, your majesty."

"Is now, bhante, form Nāgasena?"

"Nay, verily, your majesty."

"Is sensation Nāgasena?"

"Nay, verily, your majesty."

"Is perception Nāgasena?"

"Nay, verily, your majesty."

"Are the predispositions Nāgasena?"

"Nay, verily, your majesty."

"Is consciousness Nāgasena?"

"Nay, verily, your majesty."

"Are, then, bhante, form, sensation, perception, the predispositions, and consciousness unitedly Nāgasena?"

"Nay, verily, your majesty."

"Is it, then, bhante, something besides form, sensation, perception, the predispositions, and consciousness, which is Nāgasena?"

"Nay, verily, your majesty."

"Bhante, although I question you very closely, I fail to discover any Nāgasena. Verily, now, bhante, Nāgasena is a mere empty sound. What Nāgasena is there here? Bhante, you speak a falsehood, a lie: there is no Nāgasena."

Then the venerable Nāgasena spoke to Milinda the king as follows:—

"Your majesty, you are a delicate prince, an exceedingly delicate prince; and if, your majesty, you walk in the middle of the day on hot sandy ground, and you tread on rough grit, gravel, and sand, your feet become sore, your body tired, the mind is oppressed, and the body-consciousness suffers. Pray, did you come afoot, or riding?"

"Bhante, I do not go afoot: I came in a chariot."

"Your majesty, if you came in a chariot, declare to me the chariot. Pray, your majesty, is the pole the chariot?"

"Nay, verily, bhante."

"Is the axle the chariot?"

"Nay, verily, bhante."

"Are the wheels the chariot?"

"Nay, verily, bhante."

"Is the chariot-body the chariot?"

"Nay, verily, bhante."

"Is the banner-staff the chariot?"

"Nay, verily, bhante."

"Is the yoke the chariot?"

"Nay, verily, bhante."

"Are the reins the chariot?"

"Nay, verily, bhante."

"Is the goading-stick the chariot?"

"Nay, verily, bhante."

"Pray, your majesty, are pole, axle, wheels, chariot-body, banner-staff, yoke, reins, and goad unitedly the chariot?"

"Nay, verily, bhante."

"Is it, then, your majesty, something else besides pole, axle, wheels, chariot-body, banner-staff, yoke, reins, and goad which is the chariot?"

"Nay, verily, bhante."

"Your majesty, although I question you very closely, I fail to discover any chariot. Verily now, your majesty, the word chariot is a mere empty sound. What chariot is there here? Your majesty, you speak a falsehood, a lie: there is no chariot. Your majesty, you are the chief king in all the continent of India; of whom are you afraid that you speak a lie? Listen to me, my lords, ye five hundred Yonakas, and ye eighty thousand priests! Milinda the king here says thus: 'I came in a chariot'; and being requested, 'Your majesty, if you came in a chariot, declare to me the chariot,' he fails to produce any chariot. Is it possible, pray, for me to assent to what he says?"

When he had thus spoken, the five hundred Yonakas applauded the venerable Nāgasena and spoke to Milinda the king as follows:—

"Now, your majesty, answer, if you can."

Then Milinda the king spoke to the venerable Nāgasena as follows:—

"Bhante Nāgasena, I speak no lie: the word 'chariot' is but a way of counting, term, appellation, convenient designation, and name for pole, axle, wheels, chariot-body, and banner-staff."

"Thoroughly well, your majesty, do you understand a chariot. In exactly the same way, your majesty, in respect of me, Nāgasena is but a way of counting, term, appellation, convenient designation, mere name for the hair of my head, hair of my body . . . brain of the head, form, sensation, perception, the predispositions, and consciousness. But in the absolute sense there is no Self here to be found. And the priestess Vajirā, your majesty, said as follows in the presence of The Blessed One:—

"'Even as the word of "chariot" means
That members join to frame a whole;
So when the Groups appear to view,
We use the phrase, "A living being."'"

"It is wonderful, bhante Nāgasena! It is marvellous, bhante Nāgasena! Brilliant and prompt is the wit of your replies. If The Buddha were alive, he would applaud. Well done, well done, Nāgasena! Brilliant and prompt is the wit of your replies."

(*Milindapañha*, 25)

B. BUDDHAGHOṢA'S COMMENT ON NO-SELF

Just as the word "chariot" is but a mode of expression for axle, wheels, chariot-body, pole, and other constituent members, placed in a certain relation to each other, but when we come to examine the members one by one, we discover that in the absolute sense there is no chariot; and just as the word "house" is but a mode of expression for wood and other constituents of a house, surrounding space in a certain relation, but in the absolute sense there is no house; and just as the word "fist" is but a mode of expression for the fingers, the thumb, etc., in a certain relation; and the word "lute" for the body of the lute, strings, etc.; "army" for elephants, horses, etc.; "city" for fortifications, houses, gates, etc.; "tree" for trunk, branches, foliage, etc., in a certain relation, but when we come to examine the parts one by one, we discover that in the absolute sense there is no tree; in exactly the same way the words "living entity" and "Self" are but a mode of expression for the presence of the five attachment groups, but when we come to examine the elements of being one by one, we discover that in the absolute sense there is no living entity there to form a basis for such figments as "I am," or "I"; in other words, that in the absolute sense there is only name and form. The insight of him who perceives this is called knowledge of the truth.

He, however, who abandons this knowledge of the truth and believes in a living entity must assume either that this living entity will perish or that it will not perish. If he assume that it will not perish, he falls into the heresy of the persistence of existences; or if he assume that it will perish, he falls into that of the annihilation of existences. And why do I say so? Because, just as sour cream has milk as its antecedent, so nothing here exists but what has its own antecedents. To say, "The living entity persists," is to fall short of the truth; to say,"It is annihilated," is to outrun the truth. Therefore has The Blessed One said:—

"There are two heresies, O monks, which possess both gods and men, by which some fall short of the truth, and some outrun the truth; but the intelligent know the truth.

"And how, O monks, do some fall short of the truth?

"O priests, gods and men delight in existence, take pleasure in existence, rejoice in existence, so that when the Doctrine for the cessation of existence is preached to them, their minds do not leap toward it, are not favorably disposed toward it, do not rest in it, do not adopt it.

"Thus, O monks, do some fall short of the truth.

"And how, O monks, do some outrun the truth?

"Some are distressed at, ashamed of, and loathe existence, and welcome the thought of non-existence, saying, 'See here! When they say that on the dissolution of the body this Self is annihilated, perishes, and does not exist after death, that is good, that is excellent, that is as it should be.'

"Thus, O monks, do some outrun the truth.

"And how, O monks, do the intelligent know the truth?

"We may have, O monks, a priest who knows things as they really are, he is on the road to aversion for things, to absence of passion for them, and to cessation from them.

"Thus, O monks, do the intelligent know the truth."

(*Vissudhi Magga*, ch. 18)

C. SENSATION AND THE SELF

"In regard to the Self, Ānanda, what are the views held concerning it?

"In regard to the Self, Ānanda, either one holds the view that sensation is the Self, saying, 'Sensation is my Self;'

"Or, in regard to the Self, Ānanda, one holds the view, 'Verily, sensation is not my Self; my Self has no sensation;'

"Or, in regard to the Self, Ānanda, one holds the view, 'Verily, neither is sensation my Self, nor does my Self have no sensation. My Self has sensation; my Self possesses the faculty of sensation.'

"In the above case, Ānanda, where it is said, 'Sensation is my Self,' reply should be made as follows: 'Brother, there are three sensations: the pleasant sensation, the unpleasant sensation, and the indifferent sensation. Which of these three sensations do you hold to be the Self?'

"Whenever, Ānanda, a person experiences a pleasant sensation, he does not at the same time experience an unpleasant sensation, nor does he experience an indifferent sensation; only the pleasant sensation does he then feel. Whenever, Ānanda, a person experiences an unpleasant sensation, he does not at the same time experience a pleasant sensation, nor does he experience an indifferent sensation; only the unpleasant sensation does he then feel. Whenever, Ānanda, a person experiences an indifferent sensation, he does not at the same time experience a pleasant sensation, nor does he experience an unpleasant sensation; only the indifferent sensation does he then feel.

"Now pleasant sensations, Ānanda, are transitory, are due to causes, originate by dependence, and are subject to decay, disappearance, effacement, and cessation; and unpleasant sensations, Ānanda, are transitory, are due to causes, originate by dependence, and are subject to decay, disappearance, effacement, and cessation; and indifferent sensations, Ānanda, are transitory, are due to causes, originate by dependence, and are subject to decay, disappearance, effacement, and cessation. While this person is experiencing a pleasant sensation, he thinks, 'This is my Self.' And after the cessation of this same pleasant sensation, he thinks, 'My Self has passed away.' While he is experiencing an unpleasant sensation, he thinks, 'This is my Self.' And after the cessation of this same unpleasant sensation, he thinks, 'My Self has passed away.' And while he is experiencing an indifferent sensation, he thinks, 'This is my Self.' And after the cessation of this same indifferent sensation, he thinks, 'My Self has passed away.' So that he who says, 'Sensation is my Self,' holds the view that even during his lifetime his Self is transitory, that it is pleasant, unpleasant, or mixed, and that it is subject to rise and disappearance.

"Accordingly, Ānanda, it is not possible to hold the view, 'Sensation is my Self.'

"In the above case, Ānanda, where it is said, 'Verily sensation is not my Self; my Self has no sensation,' reply should be made as follows: 'But, brother, where there is no sensation, is there any "I am"?'"

"Nay, verily, Reverend Sir."

"Accordingly, Ānanda, it is not possible to hold the view, 'Verily, sensation is not my Self; my Self has no sensation.'

"In the above case, Ānanda, where it is said, 'Verily, neither is sensation my Self, nor does my Self have no sensation. My Self has sensation; my Self possesses the faculty of sensation,' reply should be made as follows: 'Suppose, brother, that utterly and completely, and without remainder, all sensation were to cease—if there were nowhere any sensation, pray, would there be anything, after the cessation of sensation, of which it could be said, "This am I"?'"

"Nay, verily, Reverend Sir."

"Accordingly, Ānanda, it is not possible to hold the view, 'Verily, neither is sensation my Self, nor does my Self have no sensation. My Self has sensation; my Self possesses the faculty of sensation.'

"From the time, Ānanda, a monk no longer holds the view that sensation is the Self, no longer holds the view that the Self has no sensation, no longer holds the view that the Self has sensation, possesses the faculty of sensation, he ceases to attach himself to anything in the world, and being free from attachment, he is never agitated, and being never agitated, he attains to Nirvana in his own person; and he knows that rebirth is exhausted, that he has lived the holy life, that he has done what it behooved him to do, and that he is no more for this world.

"Now it is impossible, Ānanda, that to a mind so freed a monk should attribute the heresy and that the saint exists after death, or that the saint does not exist after death, or that the saint both exists and does not exist after death, or that the saint neither exists nor does not exist after death.

"And why do I say so?

"Because, Ānanda, after a monk has been freed by a thorough comprehension of affirmation and affirmation's range, of predication and predication's range, of declaration and declaration's range, of knowledge and knowledge's field of action, or rebirth and what rebirth affects, it is impossible for him to attribute such a heretical lack of knowledge and perception to a monk similarly freed."

(*Dīgha-nikāya, Mahānidāna sutta*)

D. REBIRTH IS NOT TRANSMIGRATION

Said the king: "Bhante Nāgasena, does rebirth take place without anything transmigrating?"

"Yes, your majesty. Rebirth takes place without anything transmigrating."

"How, bhante Nāgasena, does rebirth take place without anything transmigrating? Give an illustration."

"Suppose, your majesty, a man were to light a light from another light; pray, would the one light have passed over [transmigrated] to the other light?"

"Nay, verily, bhante."

"In exactly the same way, your majesty, does rebirth take place without anything transmigrating."

"Give another illustration."

"Do you remember, your majesty, having learnt, when you were a boy, some verse or other from your professor of poetry?"

"Yes, bhante."

"Pray, your majesty, did the verse pass over [transmigrate] to you from your teacher?"

"Nay, verily, bhante."

"In exactly the same way, your majesty, does rebirth take place without anything transmigrating."

"You are an able man, bhante Nāgasena."

(*Milindapañha*, 71)

"Bhante Nāgasena," said the king, "what is it that is born into the next existence?"

"Your majesty," said the elder, "it is name and form that is born into the next existence."

"Is it this same name and form that is born into the next existence?"

"Your majesty, it is not this same name and form that is born into the next existence; but with this name and form, your majesty, one does a deed—it may be good, or it may be wicked—and by reason of this deed another name and form is born into the next existence."

"Bhante, if it is not this same name and form that is born into the next existence, is one not freed from one's evil deeds?"

"If one were not born into another existence," said the elder, "one would be freed from one's evil deeds; but, your majesty, inasmuch as one is born into another existence, therefore is one not freed from one's evil deeds."

"Give an illustration."

"Your majesty, it is as if a man were to take away another man's mangoes, and the owner of the mangoes were to seize him, and show him to the king, and say, 'Sire, this man hath taken away my mangoes'; and the other were to say, 'Sire, I did not take away this man's mangoes. The mangoes which this man planted were different mangoes from those which I took away. I am not liable to punishment.' Pray, your majesty, would the man be liable to punishment?"

"Assuredly, bhante, would he be liable to punishment."

"For what reason?"

"Because, in spite of what he might say, he would be liable to punishment for the reason that the last mangoes derived from the first mangoes."

"In exactly the same way, your majesty, with this name and form one does a deed—it may be good, or it may be wicked—and by reason of this deed another name and form is born into the next existence. Therefore is one not freed from one's evil deeds."

"Give another illustration."

"Your majesty, it is as if a man were to take away the rice of another man, . . . were to take away the sugar-cane, . . . Your majesty, it is as if a man were to light a fire in the winter-time and warm himself, and were to go off without putting it out. And then the fire were to burn another man's field, and the owner of the field were to seize him, and show him to the king, and say, 'Sire, this man has burnt up my field'; and the other were to say, 'Sire, I did not set this man's field on fire. The fire which I failed to put out was a different one from the one which has burnt up this man's field. I am not liable to punishment.' Pray, your majesty, would the man be liable to punishment?"

"Assuredly, bhante, would he be liable to punishment."

"For what reason?"

"Because, in spite of what he might say, the man would be liable to punishment for the reason that the last fire derived from the first fire."

"In exactly the same way, your majesty, with this name and form one does á deed—it may be good, or it may be wicked—and by reason of this deed another name and form is born into the next existence. Therefore is one not freed from one's evil deeds."

"Give another illustration."

"Your majesty, it is as if a man were to ascend to the top storey of a house with a light, and eat there; and the light in burning were to set fire to the thatch; and the thatch in burning were to set fire to the house; and the house in burning were to set fire to the village; and the people of the village were to seize him, and say, 'Why, O man, did you set fire to the village?' and he were to say, 'I did not set fire to the village. The fire of the lamp by whose light I ate was a different one from the one which set fire to the village'; and they, quarreling, were to come to you. Whose cause, your majesty, would you sustain?"

"That of the people of the village, bhante."

"And why?"

"Because, in spite of what the man might say, the latter fire sprang from the former."

"In exactly the same way, your majesty, although the name and form which is born into the next existence is different from the name and form which is to end at death, nevertheless, it is sprung from it. Therefore is one not freed from one's evil deeds."

"Give another illustration."

"Your majesty, it is as if a man were to choose a young girl in marriage, and having paid the purchase-money, were to go off; and she subsequently were to grow up and become marriageable; and then another man were to pay the purchase-money for her, and marry her; and the first man were to return, and say, 'O man, why did you marry my wife?' and the other were to say, 'I did not marry your wife. The young, tender girl whom you chose in marriage, and for whom you paid purchase-money, was a different person from this grown-up and marriageable girl whom I have chosen in marriage, and for whom I have paid purchase-money'; and they, quarreling, were to come to you. Whose cause, your majesty, would you sustain?"

"That of the first man."

"And why?"

"Because, in spite of what the second man might say, the grown-up girl sprang from the other."

"In exactly the same way, your majesty, although the name and form which is born into the next existence is different from the name and form which is to end at death, nevertheless, it is sprung from it. Therefore is one not freed from one's evil deeds."

"Give another illustration."

"Your majesty, it is as if a man were to buy from a cowherd a pot of milk, and were to leave it with the cowherd, and go off, thinking he would come the next day and take it. And on the next day it were to turn into sour cream; and the man were to come back, and say, 'Give me the pot of milk.' And the other were to show him the sour cream; and the first man were to say, 'I did not buy sour cream from you. Give me the pot of milk.' And the cowherd were to say, 'While you were gone, your milk turned into sour cream'; and they, quarreling, were to come to you. Whose cause, your majesty, would you sustain?"

"That of the cowherd, bhante."

"And why?"

"Because, in spite of what the man might say, the one sprang from the other."

"In exactly the same way, your majesty, although the name and form which is born into the next existence is different from the name and form which is to end at death, nevertheless, it is sprung from it. Therefore is one not freed from one's evil deeds."

"You are an able man, bhante Nāgasena." (*Milindapañha*, 46)

II
The Difference Between Groups and Attachment-Groups*

According to their difference:—According to whether they are groups or attachment-groups.

And what is the difference?

"Groups" is a general term; while the term "attachment-groups" specifies those which are coupled with depravity and attachment. As it has been said:—

"I will teach you, O monks, the five groups, and the five attachment-groups. Listen to me and pay attention, and I will speak."

"Even so," said the monks to The Blessed One in reply.

And The Blessed One spoke as follows:—

"And what, O monk, are the five groups?

"All form whatsoever, O monk, past, future, or present, be it subjective or existing outside, gross or subtle, mean or exalted, far or near, belongs to the form-group.

"All sensation whatsoever, . . . all perception whatsoever, . . . all predispositions whatsoever, . . . all consciousness whatsoever, past, future, or present, be it subjective or existing outside, gross or subtle, mean or exalted, far or near, belongs to the consciousness-group.

"These, O monks, are called the five groups.

"And what, O monks, are the five attachment-groups?

"All form whatsoever, O monks, past, future, or present, be it subjective or existing outside, gross or subtle, mean or exalted, far or near, which is coupled with depravity and attachment, belongs to the form-attachment-group.

"All sensation whatsoever, . . . all perception whatsoever, . . . all predispositions whatsoever, . . . all consciousness whatsoever, past, future, or present, be it subjective or existing outside, gross or subtle, mean or exalted, far or near, which is coupled with depravity and attachment, belongs to the consciousness-attachment-group.

---

*Reprinted with permission from Henry Clarke Warren, *Buddhism in Translations* (New York: Atheneum, 1963).

"These, O monks, are called the five attachment-groups."

Now, whereas there are sensations, perceptions, etc., which are not subject to depravity, it is not so with form. But inasmuch as form from its numerousness constitutes a group, it is reckoned among the groups; and inasmuch as from its numerousness and from its being coupled with depravity, it constitutes an attachment-group, it is reckoned among the attachment-groups. But only those sensations, perceptions, etc., which are not coupled with depravity are reckoned among the groups; while those coupled with depravity are assigned to the attachment-groups. Here those groups which are in the grasp of attachment are attachment-groups. This is the way the matter should be viewed. In the present case, however, under the term groups I include both classes.

No less and no more:—Why did The Blessed One say there were five groups, no less and no more?

Because these sum up and classify, according to their affinities, all the constituents of being; because it is only these that can afford a basis for the figment of a Self or of anything related to a Self, and because these include all other classifications.

For in classifying, according to their affinities, the many different constituents of being, form constitutes one group, and comprises everything that has any affinity to form; sensation constitutes another group, and comprises everything that has any affinity to sensation. Similarly with respect to perception and the rest. Accordingly he laid down only five groups, because these sum up and classify, according to their affinities, all the constituents of being.

The basis for the figment of a Self or of anything related to a Self, is afforded only by these, namely form and the rest. For it has been said as follows:—

"When there is form, O monks, then through attachment to form, through engrossment in form, the persuasion arises, 'This is mine; this am I; this is my Self.'

"When there is sensation, . . . when there is perception, . . . when there are predispositions, . . . when there is consciousness, O monks, then through attachment to consciousness, through engrossment in consciousness, the persuasion arises, 'This is mine; this am I; this is my Self.'"

Accordingly he laid down only five groups, because it is only these that can afford a basis for the figment of a Self or of anything related to a Self.

As to other groups which he lays down, such as the five of conduct and the rest, these are included, for they are comprised in the predisposition-group. Accordingly he laid down only five groups, because these include all other classifications.

After this manner, therefore, is the conclusion reached that there are no less and no more.

(*Visuddhi Magga*, chap. 14.)

III
Dependent Origination: The Middle Way*

A. THE TEACHING STATED

The world, for the most part, O Kaccāna, holds either to a belief in being or to a belief in non-being. But for one who in the light of the highest knowledge, O Kaccāna, considers how the world arises, belief in the non-being of the world passes away. And for one who in the light of the highest knowledge, O Kaccāna, considers how the world ceases, belief in the being of the world passes away. The world, O Kaccāna, is for the most part bound up in a seeking, attachment, and proclivity [for the groups], but a monk does not sympathize with this seeking and attachment, nor with the mental affirmation, proclivity, and prejudice which affirms a Self. He does not doubt or question that it is only evil that springs into existence, and only evil that ceases from existence, and his conviction of this fact is dependent on no one besides himself. This, O Kaccāna, is what constitutes Right Belief.

That things have being, O Kaccāna, constitutes one extreme of doctrine; that things have no being is the other extreme. These extremes, O Kaccāna, have been avoided by The Tathāgata, and it is a middle doctrine he teaches:

On ignorance depends karma;
On karma depends consciousness;
On consciousness depend name and form;
On name and form depend the six organs of sense;
On the six organs of sense depends contact;
On contact depends sensation;
On sensation depends desire;
On desire depends attachment;
On attachment depends existence;
On existence depends birth;
On birth depend old age and death, sorrow, lamentation, misery, grief, and despair. Thus does this entire aggregation of misery arise.

But on the complete fading out and cessation of ignorance ceases karma;
On the cessation of karma ceases consciousness;
On the cessation of consciousness cease name and form;
On the cessation of name and form cease the six organs of sense;
On the cessation of the six organs of sense ceases contact;

---

*Reprinted with permission from Henry Clark Warren, *Buddhism in Translations* (New York: Atheneum, 1963).

On the cessation of contact ceases sensation;
On the cessation of sensation ceases desire;
On the cessation of desire ceases attachment;
On the cessation of attachment ceases existence;
On the cessation of existence ceases birth;
On the cessation of birth cease old age and death, sorrow, lamentation, misery, grief, and despair. Thus does this entire aggregation of misery cease.

(*Saṁyutta Nikāya*, xxii, 90.)

B. THE MEANING OF DEPENDENT ORIGINATION

Inasmuch as it is dependently on each other and in unison and simultaneously that the factors which constitute dependence originate the elements of being, therefore did The Sage call these factors Dependent Origination.

For the ignorance etc. which have been enumerated as constituting dependence, when they originate any of the elements of being, namely, karma and the rest, can only do so when dependent on each other and in case none of their number is lacking. Therefore it is dependently on each other and in unison and simultaneously that the factors which constitute dependence originate the elements of being, not by a part of their number nor by one succeeding the other. Accordingly The Sage, skilful in the art of discovering the signification of things, calls this dependence by the name of Dependent Origination.

And in so doing, by the first of these two words is shown the falsity of such heresies as that of the persistence of existences, and by the second word, a rejection of such heresies as that existences cease to be, while by both together is shown the truth.

By the first:—The word "Dependent," as exhibiting a full complement of dependence and inasmuch as the elements of being are subject to that full complement of dependence, shows an avoidance of such heresies as that of the persistence of existences, the heresies, namely, of the persistence of existences, of uncaused existences, of existences due to an overruling power, of self-determining existences. For what have persistent existences, uncaused existences, etc., to do with a full complement of dependence?

By the second word:—The word "Origination," as exhibiting an origination of the elements of being and inasmuch as the elements of being originate by means of a full complement of dependence, shows a rejection of such heresies as that of the annihilation of existences, the heresies, namely, of the annihilation of existences, of nihilism, of the inefficacy of karma. For if the elements of being are continually originating by means of an antecedent dependence, whence can we have annihilation of existence, nihilism, and an inefficacy of karma?

By both together:—By the complete phrase "Dependent Origination," inasmuch as such and such elements of being come into existence by means of an unbroken series of their full complement of dependence, the truth, or middle course, is shown. This rejects the heresy that he who experiences the fruit of the deed is the same as the one who performed the deed, and also rejects the converse one that he who experiences the fruit of a deed is different from the one who performed the deed, and leaning not to either of these popular hypotheses, holds fast by nominalism.

(*Visuddhi Magga*, chap. 17)

C. EXPLANATION OF DEPENDENT ORIGINATION

Thus have I heard.

On a certain occasion The Blessed One was dwelling among the Kurus where was the Kuru-town named Kammāsadhamma.

Then drew near the venerable Ānanda to where The Blessed One was; and having drawn near and greeted The Blessed One, he sat down respectfully at one side. And seated respectfully at one side, the venerable Ānanda spoke to The Blessed One as follows:

"O wonderful is it, Reverend Sir! O marvellous is it, Reverend Sir! How profound, Reverend Sir, is Dependent Origination, and of how profound an appearance! To me, nevertheless, it is as clear as clear can be."

"O Ānanda, say not so! O Ānanda, say not so! Profound, Ānanda, is Dependent Origination, and profound of appearance. It is through not understanding this doctrine, Ānanda, through not penetrating it, that thus mankind is like to an entangled warp, or to an ensnarled web, or to muñja-grass and pabbaja-grass, and fails to extricate itself from punishment, suffering, perdition, rebirth.

"Ānanda, if it be asked, 'Do old age and death depend on anything?' the reply should be, 'They do.' And if it be asked, 'On what do old age and death depend?' the reply should be, 'Old age and death depend on birth.'

"Ānanda, if it be asked, 'Does birth depend on anything?' the reply should be, 'It does.' And if it be asked, 'On what does birth depend?' the reply should be, 'Birth depends on existence.'

"Ānanda, if it be asked, 'Does existence depend on anything?' the reply should be, 'It does.' And if it be asked, 'On what does existence depend?' the reply should be, 'Existence depends on attachment.'

"Ānanda, if it be asked, 'Does attachment depend on anything?' the reply should be, 'It does.' And if it be asked, 'On what does attachment depend?' the reply should be, 'Attachment depends on desire.'

"Ānanda, if it be asked, 'Does desire depend on anything?' the reply should be, 'It does.' And if it be asked, 'On what does desire depend?' the reply should be, 'Desire depends on sensation.'

"Ānanda, if it be asked, 'Does sensation depend on anything?' the reply should be, 'It does.' And if it be asked, 'On what does sensation depend?' the reply should be, 'Sensation depends on contact.'

"Ānanda, if it be asked, 'Does contact depend on anything?' the reply should be, 'It does.' And if it be asked, 'On what does contact depend?' the reply should be, 'Contact depends on name and form.'

"Ānanda, if it be asked, 'Do name and form depend on anything?' the reply should be, 'They do.' and if it be asked, 'On what do name and form depend?' the reply should be, 'Name and form depend on consciousness.'

"Ānanda, if it be asked, 'Does consciousness depend on anything?' the reply should be, 'It does.' And if it be asked, 'On what does consciousness depend?' the reply should be, 'Consciousness depends on name and form.'

"Thus, Ānanda, on name and form depends consciousness;

"On consciousness depend name and form;

"On name and form depends contact;

"On contact depends sensation;

"On sensation depends desire;

"On desire depends attachment;

"On attachment depends existence;

"On existence depends birth;

"On birth depend old age and death, sorrow, lamentation, misery, grief, and despair. Thus does this entire aggregation of misery arise.

"I have said that on birth depend old age and death. This truth, Ānanda, that on birth depend old age and death, is to be understood in this way. Suppose, Ānanda, there were utterly and completely no birth at all for any one into any world, as, namely, for gods into the world of gods; for genii into the world of genii; for ogres into the world of ogres; for demons into the world of demons; for men into the world of men; for quadrupeds into the world of quadrupeds; for winged creatures into the world of winged creatures; for creeping things into the world of creeping things;—suppose, Ānanda, there were no birth for any of these beings into their several worlds: if there were nowhere any birth, pray, on the cessation of birth would there be any old age and death?"

"Nay, verily, Reverend Sir."

"Accordingly, Ānanda, here we have in birth the cause, the occasion, the origin, and the dependence of old age and death.

"I have said that on existence depends birth. This truth, Ānanda, that on existence depends birth, is to be understood in this way. Suppose, Ānanda, there were utterly and completely no existence at all for any one in any mode, as, namely, existence in the realm of sensual pleasure, existence in the realm of form, existence in the realm of formlessness;—if there were nowhere any existence, pray, on the cessation of existence would there be any birth?"

"Nay, verily, Reverend Sir."

"Accordingly, Ānanda, here we have in existence the cause, the occasion, the origin, and the dependence of birth.

"I have said that on attachment depends existence. This truth Ānanda, that on attachment depends existence, is to be understood in this way. Suppose, Ānanda, there were utterly and completely no attachment at all of any one to anything, as, namely, the attachment of sensual pleasure, the attachment of heresy, the attachment of fanatical conduct, the attachment of the assertion of an Ego;—if there were nowhere any attachment, pray, on the cessation of attachment would there be any existence?"

"Nay, verily, Reverend Sir."

"Accordingly, Ānanda, here we have in attachment the cause, the occasion, the origin, and the dependence of existence.

"I have said that on desire depends attachment. This truth, Ānanda, that on desire depends attachment, is to be understood in this way. Suppose, Ānanda, there were utterly and completely no desire at all on the part of any one for anything, as, namely, desire for forms, desire for sounds, desire for odors, desire for tastes, desire for things tangible, desire for ideas;—if there were nowhere any desire, pray, on the cessation of desire would there be any attachment?"

"Nay, verily, Reverend Sir."

"Accordingly, Ānanda, here we have in desire the cause, the occasion, the origin, and the dependence of attachment.

"I have said that on sensation depends desire. This truth, Ānanda, that on sensation depends desire, is to be understood in this way. Suppose, Ānanda, there were utterly and completely no sensation at all on the part of any one for anything, as, namely, sensation sprung from contact of the eye, sensation sprung from contact of the ear, sensation sprung from contact of the nose, sensation sprung from contact of the tongue, sensation sprung from contact of the body, sensation sprung from contact of the mind;—if there were nowhere any sensation, pray, on the cessation of sensation would there be any desire."

"Nay, verily, Reverend Sir."

"Accordingly, Ānanda, here we have in sensation the cause, the occasion, the origin, and the dependence of desire."

"I have said that on contact depends sensation. This truth, Ānanda, that on contact depends sensation, is to be understood in this way. Suppose, Ānanda, there were utterly and completely no contact at all of any organ with any object, as, namely, contact of the eye, contact of the ear, contact of the nose, contact of the tongue, contact of the body, contact of the mind;—if there were nowhere any contact, pray, on the cessation of contact would there be any sensation?"

"Nay, verily, Reverend Sir."

"Accordingly, Ānanda, here we have in contact the cause, the occasion, the origin, and the dependence of sensation.

"I have said that on name and form depends contact. This truth, Ānanda, that on name and form depends contact, is to be understood in this way. Suppose, Ānanda, there were not these different traits, peculiarities, signs, and indications by which are made manifest the multitude of elements of being constituting name;—if there were not these different traits, peculiarities, signs, and indications, pray, would there be any designative contact appearing in form?"

"Nay, verily, Reverend Sir."

"Suppose, Ānanda, there were not these different traits, peculiarities, signs, and indications by which are made manifest the multitude of elements of being constituting form;—if there were not these different traits, peculiarities, signs, and indications, pray, would there be any inertia-contact appearing in name?"

"Nay, verily, Reverend Sir."

"Suppose, Ānanda, there were not these different traits, peculiarities, signs, and indications by which are made manifest the multitude of elements of being constituting name and the multitude of elements of being constituting form;—if there were not these different traits, peculiarities, signs, and indications, pray, would there be any contact?"

"Nay, verily, Reverend Sir."

"Accordingly, Ānanda, here we have in name and form the cause, the occasion, the origin, and the dependence of contact.

"I have said that on consciousness depend name and form. This truth, Ānanda, that on consciousness depend name and form, is to be understood in this way. Suppose, Ānanda, consciousness were not to descend into the maternal womb, pray, would name and form consolidate in the maternal womb?"

"Nay, verily, Reverend Sir."

"Suppose, Ānanda, consciousness, after descending into the maternal womb, were then to go away again, pray, would name and form be born to life in the world?"

"Nay, verily, Reverend Sir."

"Suppose, Ānanda, consciousness were to be severed from a child, either boy or girl, pray, would name and form attain to growth, increase, and development?"

"Nay, verily, Reverend Sir."

"Accordingly, Ānanda, here we have in consciousness the cause, the occasion, the origin, and the dependence of name and form.

"I have said that on name and form depends consciousness. This truth, Ānanda, that on name and form depends consciousness, is to be understood in this way. Suppose, Ānanda, that name and form were not to become established, pray, would there, in the future, be birth, old age and death, and the coming into existence of misery's host?"

"Nay, verily, Reverend Sir."

"Accordingly, Ānanda, here we have in name and form the cause, the occasion, the origin, and the dependence of consciousness.

"Verily, Ānanda, this name and form coupled with consciousness is all there is to be born, or to grow old, or to die, or to leave one existence, or to spring up in another. It is all that is meant by any affirmation, predication, or declaration we may make concerning anybody. It constitutes knowledge's field of action. And it is all that is reborn to appear in its present shape."

(*Dīgha-Nikāya, Mahānidāna sutta*)

IV
Reason and Wisdom*

A. DIALOGUE WITH VACCHAGOTTA

Thus have I heard.

On a certain occasion The Blessed One was dwelling at Sāvatthi in Jetavana monastery in Anāthapiṇḍika's Park. Then drew near Vaccha, the wandering ascetic, to where The Blessed One was; and having drawn near, he greeted The Blessed One; and having passed the compliments of friendship and civility, he sat down respectfully at one side. And seated respectfully at one side, Vaccha, the wandering ascetic, spoke to The Blessed One as follows:—

"How is it, Gotama? Does Gotama hold that the world is eternal, and that this view alone is true, and every other false?"

"Nay, Vaccha. I do not hold that the world is eternal, and that this view alone is true, and every other false."

"But how is it, Gotama? Does Gotama hold that the world is not eternal, and that this view alone is true, and every other false?"

"Nay, Vaccha. I do not hold that the world is not eternal, and that this view alone is true, and every other false."

"How is it, Gotama? Does Gotama hold that the world is finite, . . ."

"How is it, Gotama? Does Gotama hold that the soul and the body are identical, . . ."

"How is it, Gotama? Does Gotama hold that the saint exists after death, . . ."

"How is it, Gotama? Does Gotama hold that the saint both exists and does not exist after death, and that this view alone is true, and every other false?"

"Nay, Vaccha. I do not hold that the saint both exists and does not exist after death, and that this view alone is true, and every other false."

"But how is it, Gotama? Does Gotama hold that the saint neither exists nor does not exist after death, and that this view alone is true, and every other false?"

"Nay, Vaccha. I do not hold that the saint neither exists nor does not exist after death, and that this view alone is true, and every other false."

"How is it, Gotama, that when you are asked, 'Does the monk Gotama hold that the world is eternal, and that this view alone is true, and very other false?' you reply, 'Nay, Vaccha. I do not hold that the world is eternal, and that this view alone is true, and every other false'?

"But how is it, Gotama, that when you are asked, 'Does the monk

*Reprinted with permission from Henry Clarke Warren, *Buddhism in Translations* (New York: Atheneum, 1963).

Gotama, hold that the world is not eternal, and that this view alone is true, and every other false?' you reply, 'Nay, Vaccha. I do not hold that the world is not eternal, and that this view alone is true, and every other false'?

"How is it, Gotama, that when you are asked, 'Does Gotama hold that the world is finite, . . .'?

"How is it, Gotama, that when you are asked, 'Does Gotama hold that the soul and the body are identical, . . .'?

"How is it, Gotama, that when you are asked, 'Does Gotama hold that the saint exists after death, . . .'?

"How is it, Gotama, that when you are asked, 'Does the monk Gotama hold that the saint both exists and does not exist after death, and that this view alone is true, and every other false?' you reply, 'Nay, Vaccha. I do not hold that the saint both exists and does not exist after death, and that this view alone is true, and every other false'?

"How is it, Gotama, that when you are asked, 'Does the monk Gotama hold that the saint neither exists and does not exist after death, and that this view alone is true, and every other false?' you reply, 'Nay, Vaccha. I do not hold that the saint neither exists nor does not exist after death, and that this view alone is true, and every other false'? What objection does Gotama perceive to these theories that he has not adopted any one of them?" . . .

"Vaccha, the theory that the world is eternal, is a jungle, a wilderness, a puppet-show, a writhing, and a fetter, and is coupled with misery, ruin, despair, and agony, and does not tend to aversion, absence of passion, cessation, quiescence, knowledge, supreme wisdom, and Nirvana. . . .

"Vaccha, the theory that the saint neither exists nor does not exist after death, is a jungle, a wilderness, a puppet-show, a writhing, and a fetter, and is coupled with misery, ruin, despair, and agony, and does not tend to aversion, absence of passion, cessation, quiescence, knowledge, supreme wisdom, and Nirvana.

"This is the objection I perceive to these theories, so that I have not adopted any one of them."

"But has Gotama any theory of his own?"

"The Tathāgata, O Vaccha, is free from all theories; but this, Vaccha, does The Tathāgata know,—the nature of form, and how form arises, and how form perishes; the nature of sensation, and how sensation arises, and how sensation perishes; the nature of perception, and how perception arises, and how perception perishes; the nature of the predispositions, and how the predispositions arise, and how the predispositions perish; the nature of consciousness, and how consciousness arises, and how consciousness perishes. Therefore say I that The Tathāgata has attained deliverance and is free from attachment, inasmuch as all imaginings, or agitations, or proud thoughts concerning a Self or anything pertaining to a Self, have perished, have faded away, have ceased, have been given up and relinquished."

"But, Gotama, where is the monk reborn who has attained to this deliverance for his mind?"

"Vaccha, to say that he is reborn would not fit the case."

"Then, Gotama, he is not reborn."

"Vaccha, to say that he is not reborn would not fit the case."

"Then, Gotama, he is both reborn and is not reborn."

"Vaccha, to say that he is both reborn and not reborn would not fit the case."

"Then, Gotama, he is neither reborn nor not reborn."

"Vaccha, to say that he is neither reborn nor not reborn would not fit the case."

"When I say to you, 'But, Gotama, where is the monk reborn who has attained to this deliverance for his mind?' you reply, 'Vaccha, to say that he is reborn would not fit the case.' And when I say to you, 'Then, Gotama, he is not reborn,' you reply, 'Vaccha, to say that he is not reborn would not fit the case.' And when I say to you, 'Then, Gotama, he is both reborn and not reborn, 'you reply, 'Vaccha, to say that he is both reborn and not reborn would not fit the case.' And when I say to you, 'Then, Gotama, he is neither reborn nor not reborn,' you reply, 'Vaccha, to say that he is neither reborn nor not reborn would not fit the case.' Gotama, I am at a loss what to think in this matter, and I have become greatly confused, and the faith in Gotama inspired by a former conversation has now disappeared."

"Enough, O Vaccha! Be not at a loss what to think in this matter, and be not greatly confused. Profound, O Vaccha, is this doctrine, recondite, and difficult of comprehension, good, excellent, and not to be reached by mere reasoning, subtle, and intelligible only to the wise; and it is a hard doctrine for you to learn, who belong to another sect, to another faith, to another persuasion, to another discipline, and sit at the feet of another teacher. Therefore, Vaccha, I will now question you, and do you make answer as may seem to you good. What think you, Vaccha? Suppose a fire were to burn in front of you, would you be aware that the fire was burning in front of you?"

"Gotama, if a fire were to burn in front of me, I should be aware that a fire was burning in front of me."

"But suppose, Vaccha, some one were to ask you, 'On what does this fire that is burning in front of you depend?' what would you answer, Vaccha?"

"Gotama, if some one were to ask me, 'On what does this fire that is burning in front of you depend?' I would answer, Gotama, 'It is on fuel of grass and wood that this fire that is burning in front of me depends.'"

"But, Vaccha, if the fire in front of you were to become extinct, would you be aware that the fire in front of you had become extinct?"

"Gotama, if the fire in front of me were to become extinct, I should be aware that the fire in front of me had become extinct."

"But, Vaccha, if some one were to ask you, 'In which direction has that fire gone,—east,or west, or north, or south?' what would you say, O Vaccha?"

"The question would not fit the case, Gotama. For the fire which depended on fuel of grass and wood, when that fuel has all gone, and it can get no other, being thus without nutrient, is said to be extinct."

"In exactly the same way, Vaccha, all form by which one could predicate the existence of the saint, all that form has been abandoned, uprooted, pulled out of the ground like a palmyra-tree, and become non-existent and not liable to spring up again in the future. The saying, O Vaccha, who has been released from what is styled form, is deep, immeasurable, unfathomable, like the mighty ocean. To say that he is reborn would not fit the case. To say that he is not reborn would not fit the case. To say that he is both reborn and not reborn would not fit the case. To say that he is neither reborn nor not reborn would not fit the case.

"All sensation . . .

"All perception . . .

"All the predispositions . . .

"All consciousness by which one could predicate the existence of the saint, all that consciousness has been abandoned, uprooted, pulled out of the ground like a palmyra-tree, and become non-existent and not liable to spring up again in the future. The saint, O Vaccha, who has been released from what is styled consciousness, is deep, immeasurable, unfathomable, like the mighty ocean. To say that he is reborn would not fit the case. To say that he is not reborn would not fit the case. To say that he is both reborn and not reborn would not fit the case. To say that he is neither reborn nor not reborn would not fit the case."

When The Blessed One had thus spoken, Vaccha, the wandering ascetic, spoke to him as follows:

"It is as if, O Gotama, there were a mighty sal-tree near to some village or town, and it were to lose its dead branches and twigs, and its loose shreds of bark, and its unsound wood, so that afterwards, free from those branches and twigs, and the loose shreds of bark, and the unsound wood, it were to stand neat and clean in its strength. In exactly the same way doth the word of Gotama, free from branches and twigs, and from loose shreds of bark, and from unsound wood, stand neat and clean in its strength. O wonderful is it, Gotama! O wonderful is it, Gotama! It is as if, O Gotama, one were to set up that which was overturned; or were to disclose that which was hidden; or were to point out the way to a lost traveller; or were to carry a lamp into a dark place, that they who had eyes might see forms. Even so has Gotama expounded the Doctrine in many different ways. I betake myself to Gotama for refuge, to the Doctrine, and to the Congregation of the monks. Let Gotama receive me who have betaken myself to him for refuge, and accept me as a discipline from this day forth as long as life shall last."

(Majjhima Nikāya, sutta 72.)

B. PARABLE OF MĀLUÑKYĀPUTTA

Thus have I heard. On a certain occasion The Blessed One was dwelling at Sāvatthi in Jetavana monastery in Anāthapiṇḍika's Park. Now it happened to the venerable Māluṅkyāputta, being in seclusion and plunged in meditation, that a consideration presented itself to his mind, as follows:—

"These theories which The Blessed One has left unelucidated, has set aside and rejected,—that the world is eternal, that the world is not eternal, that the world is finite, that the world is infinite, that the soul and the body are identical, that the soul is one thing and the body another, that the saint exists after death, that the saint does not exist after death, that the saint both exists and does not exist after death, that the saint neither exists nor does not exist after death,—these The Blessed One does not elucidate to me. And the fact that The Blessed One does not elucidate them to me does not please me nor suit me. Therefore I will draw near to The Blessed One and inquire of him concerning this matter. If The Blessed One will elucidate to me, either that the world is eternal, or that the world is not eternal, or that the world is finite, or that the world is infinite, or that the soul and the body are identical, or that the soul is one thing and the body another, or that the saint exists after death, or that the saint does not exist after death, or that the saint both exists and does not exist after death, or that the saint neither exists nor does not exist after death, in that case will I lead the religious life under The Blessed One. If The Blessed One will not elucidate to me, either that the world is eternal, or that the world is not eternal, . . . or that the saint neither exists nor does not exist after death, in that case will I abandon religious training and return to the lower life of a layman."

Then the venerable Māluṅkyāputta arose at eventide from his seclusion, and drew near to where The Blessed One was; and having drawn near and greeted The Blessed One, he sat down respectfully at one side. And seated respectfully at one side, the venerable Māluṅkyāputta spoke to The Blessed One as follows:—

"Reverend Sir, it happened to me, as I was just now in seclusion and plunged in meditation, that a consideration presented itself to my mind, as follows: 'These theories which the Blessed One has left unelucidated, has set aside and rejected,—that the world is eternal, that the world is not eternal, . . . that the saint neither exists nor does not exist after death,—these The Blessed One does not elucidate to me. and the fact that The Blessed One does not elucidate them to me does not please me nor suit me. I will draw near to The Blessed One and inquire of him concerning this matter. If The Blessed One will elucidate to me, either that the world is eternal, or that the world is not eternal, . . . or that the saint neither exists nor does not exist after death, in that case will I lead the religious life under The Blessed One. If The Blessed One will not elucidate to me, either that the world is eternal, or that the world is not eternal, . . . or that the saint neither exists nor does not exist after death, in that case will I abandon religious training and return to the lower life of a layman.'

"If The Blessed One knows that the world is eternal, let The Blessed One elucidate to me that the world is eternal; if The Blessed One knows that the world is not eternal, let The Blessed One elucidate to me that the world is not eternal. If The Blessed One does not know either that the world is eternal or that the world is not eternal, the only upright thing for one who does not know, or who has not that insight, is to say, 'I do not know; I have not that insight.'

"If The Blessed One knows that the world is finite, . . ."

"If The Blessed One knows that the soul and the body are identical, . . ."

"If The Blessed One knows that the saint exists after death, . . ."

"If The Blessed One knows that the saint both exists and does not exist after death, let The Blessed One elucidate to me that the saint both exists and does not exist after death; if The Blessed One knows that the saint neither exists nor does not exist after death, let The Blessed One elucidate to me that the saint neither exists nor does not exist after death. If The Blessed One does not know either that the saint both exists and does not exist after death, or that the saint neither exists nor does not exist after death, the only upright thing for one who does not know, or who has not that insight, is to say, 'I do not know; I have not that insight.'"

"Pray, Māluñkyāputta, did I ever say to you, 'Come, Māluñkyāputta, lead the religious life under me, and I will elucidate to you either that the world is eternal, or that the world is not eternal, . . . or that the saint neither exists nor does not exist after death'?"

"Nay, verily, Reverend Sir."

"Or did you ever say to me, 'Reverend Sir, I will lead the religious life under The Blessed One, on condition that The Blessed One elucidate to me either that the world is eternal, or that the world is not eternal, . . . or that the saint neither exists nor does not exist after death'?"

"Nay, verily, Reverend Sir."

"So you acknowledge, Māluñkyāputta, that I have not said to you, 'Come, Māluñkyāputta, lead the religious life under me and I will elucidate to you either that the world is eternal, or that the world is not eternal, . . . or that the saint neither exists nor does not exist after death'; and again that you have not said to me, 'Reverend Sir, I will lead the religious life under The Blessed One, on condition that The Blessed One elucidate to me either that the world is eternal, or that the world is not eternal, . . . or that the saint neither exists nor does not exist after death.' That being the case, vain man, whom are you so angrily denouncing?

"Māluñkyāputta, any one who should say, 'I will not lead the religious life under The Blessed One until The Blessed One shall elucidate to me either that the world is eternal, or that the world is not eternal, . . . or, that the saint neither exists nor does not exist after death';—that person would die, Māluñkyāputta, before the Tathāgata had ever elucidated this to him.

"It is as if, Māluñkyāputta, a man had been wounded by an arrow thickly smeared with poison, and his friends and companions, his relatives and kinsfolk, were to procure for him a physician or surgeon; and the sick man were to say, 'I will not have this arrow taken out until I have learnt whether the man who wounded me belonged to the warrior caste, or to the Brahman caste, or to the agricultural caste, or to the menial caste.'

"Or again he were to say, 'I will not have this arrow taken out until I have learnt the name of the man who wounded me, and to what clan he belongs.'

"Or again he were to say, 'I will not have this arrow taken out until I have learnt whether the man who wounded me was tall, or short, or of the middle height.'

"Or again he were to say, 'I will not have this arrow taken out until I have learnt whether the man who wounded me was black, or dusky, or of a yellow skin.'

"Or again he were to say, 'I will not have this arrow taken out until I have learnt whether the man who wounded me was from this or that village, or town, or city.'

"Or again he were to say, 'I will not have this arrow taken out until I have learnt whether the bow which wounded me was a cāpa, or a kodaṇḍa.'

"Or again he were to say, 'I will not have this arrow taken out until I have learnt whether the bow-string which wounded me was made from swallow-wort, or bamboo, or sinew, or maruva, or from milk-weed."

"Or again he were to say, 'I will not have this arrow taken out until I have learnt whether the shaft which wounded me was a kaccha or a ropima.'

"Or again he were to say, 'I will not have this arrow taken out until I have learnt whether the shaft which wounded me was feathered from the wings of a vulture, or of a heron, or of a falcon, or of a peacock, or of a sithilahanu.'

"Or again he were to say, 'I will not have this arrow taken out until I have learnt whether the shaft which wounded me was wound round with the sinews of an ox, or of a buffalo, or of a ruru deer, or of a monkey.'

"Or again he were to say, 'I will not have this arrow taken out until I have learnt whether the arrow which wounded me was an ordinary arrow, or a claw-headed arrow, or a vekaṇḍa, or an iron arrow, or a calf-tooth arrow, or a karavīrapatta.' That man would die, Māluṅkyāputta, without ever having learnt this.

"In exactly the same way, Māluṅkyāputta, any one who should say, 'I will not lead the religious life under The Blessed One until The Blessed One shall elucidate to me either that the world is eternal, or that the world is not eternal, . . . or that the saint neither exists nor does not exist after death'; —that person would die, Māluṅkyāputta, before The Tathāgata had ever elucidated this to him.

"The religious life, Māluṅkyāputta, does not depend on the dogma that the world is eternal; nor does the religious life, Māluṅkyāputta, depend on the dogma that the world is not eternal. Whether the dogma obtain, Māluṅkyāputta, that the world is eternal, or that the world is to eternal, there still remain birth, old age, death, sorrow, lamentation, misery, grief, and despair, for the extinction of which in the present life I am prescribing.

"The religious life, Māluṅkyāputta, does not depend on the dogma that the world is finite; . . .

"The religious life, Māluṅkyāputta, does not depend on the dogma that the soul and the body are identical; . . .

"The religious life, Māluṅkyāputta, does not depend on the dogma that the saint exists after death; . . .

"The religious life, Māluñkyāputta, does not depend on the dogma that the saint both exists and does not exist after death; nor does the religious life, Māluñkyāputta, depend on the dogma that the saint neither exists nor does not exist after death. Whether the dogma obtain, Māluñkyāputta, that the saint both exists and does not exist after death, or that the saint neither exists nor does not exist after death, there still remain birth, old age, death, sorrow, lamentation, misery, grief, and despair, for the extinction of which in the present life I am prescribing.

"Accordingly, Māluñkyāputta, bear always in mind what it is that I have not elucidated, and what it is that I have elucidated. And what, Māluñkyāputta, have I not elucidated? I have not elucidated, Māluñkyāputta, that the world is eternal; I have not elucidated that the world is not eternal; I have not elucidated that the world is finite; I have not elucidated that the world is infinite; I have not elucidated that the soul and the body are identical; I have not elucidated that the soul is one thing and the body another; I have not elucidated that the saint exists after death; I have not elucidated that the saint does not exist after death; I have not elucidated that the saint both exists and does not exist after death; I have not elucidated that the saint neither exists nor does not exist after death. And why, Māluñkyāputta, have I not elucidated this? Because, Māluñkyāputta, this profits not, nor has to do with the fundamentals of religion, nor tends to aversion, absence of passion, cessation, quiescence, the supernatural facilities, supreme wisdom, and Nirvana; therefore have I not elucidated it.

"And what, Māluñkyāputta, have I elucidated? Misery, Māluñkyāputta, have I elucidated; the origin of misery have I elucidated; the cessation of misery have I elucidated; and the path leading to the cessation of misery have I elucidated. And why, Māluñkyāputta, have I elucidated this? Because, Māluñkyāputta, this does profit, has to do with the fundamentals of religion, and tends to aversion, absence of passion, cessation, quiescence, knowledge, supreme wisdom, and Nirvana; therefore have I elucidated it. Accordingly, Māluñkyāputta, bear always in mind what it is that I have not elucidated, and what it is that I have elucidated."

Thus spake The Blessed One; and, delighted, the venerable Māluñkyāputta applauded the speech of The Blessed One.

(*Majjhima Nikāya, sutta* 63)

CHAPTER 11

RISE OF THE MAHĀYĀNA

As Buddhism developed, the earlier emphasis on the worthy monk keeping the monastic rules as he sought *nirvāṇa* through developing insight, virtue, and wisdom by following the Noble Eightfold Path was supplemented by a new emphasis on attaining wisdom, compassion, and virtue in order to help others, an emphasis that emerged in the Mahāyāna ideal of the *Bodhisattva*. Here the historical Buddha's enlightenment was seen as the basis for helping other suffering beings overcome their suffering rather than as the means of overcoming one's own *duḥkha*. This change in emphasis, from seeking *nirvāṇa* as the primary aim to helping others overcome their suffering, revolutionized Buddhist practice and teaching, leading to new interpretations of traditional teachings, to new philosophical positions, and ultimately to the practices of Zen (Ch'an) and Tantra.

The selected texts present the concept of the Bodhisattva and the essence of the so-called New Wisdom as found in the Heart and Diamond *sūtras*. The Bodhisattva texts are reprinted from Edward Conze, *Buddhist Texts through the Ages* (New York: Harper & Row, 1964). The Heart *sūtra* is reprinted from Donald S. Lopez, Jr., *The Heart Sūtra Explained: Indian and Tibetan Commentaries* (Albany: State University of New York Press, 1988). The Diamond *sūtra* is reprinted from Edward Conze, *Buddhist Scriptures* (Harmondsworth: Penguin Books, 1959). All three of these books contain helpful explanatory material as well as translated texts. D. T. Suzuki, *On Indian Mahāyāna Buddhism* (New York: Harper Torchbooks, 1968), remains one the best studies of the rise of Mahāyāna Buddhism.

In selection 1, "The Bodhisattva," the readings describe the Bodhisattva and depict the new ideal of Mahāyāna Buddhism. Rather than seeking *nirvāṇa* to eliminate his own suffering, this new Buddhist hero, out of compassion, willingly takes on the suffering of all beings. Guided by wisdom acquired through moral cultivation and deep meditation, he patiently and energetically gives himself completely, without thought of gain or reward, to the task of rescuing others from the sea of suffering. This is the new Mahāyāna practice of the Noble Eightfold Path called "practicing the perfections" (*pāramitās*).

Selection 2, "The *Heart Sūtra*," summarizes a vast Mahāyāna literature extolling the way of great wisdom that the ideal Buddhist aspirant, the Bodhisattva, follows. In this great wisdom all dualities are left behind, including the duality of *duḥkha* and *nirvāṇa*. To help in understanding the key statement in this *sūtra*—"Form is emptiness; emptiness is form"—the relevant portion of one of the clearest commentaries produced within the Indian Buddhist tradition is included. This commentary by Praśāstrasena emphasizes that to say that things are empty is not to deny that they exist, but rather to say that their very existence is of the nature of emptiness. That is, their existence is affirmed not as self-existent beings but as interconnected, ever changing processes, arising in dependence on various conditions. In this way the commentary shows that emptiness is a way of understanding the teaching of dependent origination, the Middle Way taught by the Buddha.

I
The Bodhisattva*

THE BODHISATTVA'S FRIENDLINESS AND COMPASSION

The Lord: Subhuti, that son or daughter of good family who, as a Bodhisattva, even for one single day remains attentive to the perfection of wisdom, begets a great heap of merit. For, as he goes on dwelling day and night in those mental activities, he becomes more and more worthy of the gifts bestowed on him by all beings. Because no other being has a mind so full of friendliness as he has, except for the Buddhas, the Lords. And the Tathagatas, of course, are matchless, unequalled, endowed with inconceivable dharmas.

How then does that son or daughter of good family at first aspire to that merit? He becomes endowed with that kind of wise insight which allows him to see all beings as on the way to their slaughter. Great compassion thereby takes hold of him. With his heavenly eye he surveys countless beings, and what he sees fills him with great agitation: so many carry the burden of a karma which will soon be punished in the hells, others have acquired unfortunate rebirths, which keep them away from the Buddha and his teachings, others are doomed soon to be killed, or they are enveloped in the net of false views, or fail to find the path, while others who had gained a rebirth favourable to their emancipation have lost it again.

And he radiates great friendliness and compassion over all those beings, and gives his attention to them, thinking: "I shall become a saviour to all those beings, I shall release them from all their sufferings! "But he does not make either this, or anything else, into a sign with which he becomes intimate. This also is the great light of a Bodhisattva's wisdom, which allows him to know full enlightenment. For, when they dwell in this dwelling, Bodhisattvas be-

*Reprinted with permission from Edward Conze, *Buddhist Texts through the Ages* (New York: Harper & Row, 1964).

come worthy of the gifts of the whole world, and yet they do not turn back on full enlightenment. When their thoughts are well supported by perfect wisdom and when they are near to all-knowledge, then they purify the gifts of those who gave them the requisites of life. Therefore a Bodhisattva should dwell in this mental work associated with perfect wisdom, if he does not want to consume his alms fruitlessly, if he wants to point out the path to all beings, to shed light over a wide range, to set free from birth-and-death all the beings who are subject to it, and to cleanse the organs of vision of all beings.

Ashṭasāhasrikā XXII, 402-04

THE BODHISATTVA A COMPASSIONATE HERO

The Lord: Suppose, Subhuti, that there were a most excellent hero, very vigorous, of high social position, handsome, attractive and most fair to behold, of many virtues, in possession of all the finest virtues, of those virtues which spring from the very height of sovereignty, morality, learning, renunciation and so on. He is judicious, able to express himself, to formulate his views clearly, to substantiate his claims; one who always knows the suitable time, place and situation for everything. In archery he has gone as far as one can go, he is successful in warding off all manner of attack, most skilled in all arts, and foremost, through his fine achievements, in all crafts. . . . He is versed in all the treatises, has many friends, is wealthy, strong of body, with large limbs, with all his faculties complete, generous to all, dear and pleasant to many. Any work he might undertake he manages to complete, he speaks methodically, shares his great riches with the many, honours what should be honoured, reveres what should be revered, worships what should be worshipped. Would such a person, Subhuti, feel ever-increasing joy and zest?

Subhuti: He would, O Lord.

The Lord: Now suppose, further, that this person, so greatly accomplished, should have taken his family with him on a journey, his mother and father, his sons and daughters. By some circumstance they find themselves in a great, wild forest. The foolish ones among them would feel fright, terror and hair-raising fear. He, however, would fearlessly say to his family: "Do not be afraid! I shall soon take you safely and securely out of this terrible and frightening forest. I shall soon set you free!" If then more and more hostile and inimical forces should rise up against him in that forest, would this heroic man decide to abandon his family, and to take himself alone out of that terrible and frightening forest—he who is not one to draw back, who is endowed with all the force of firmness and vigour, who is wise, exceedingly tender and compassionate, courageous and a master of many resources?

Subhuti: No, O Lord. For that person, who does not abandon his family, has at his disposal powerful resources, both within and without. On his side forces will arise in that wild forest which are quite a match for the hostile and inimical forces, and they will stand up for him and protect him. Those enemies and adversaries of his, who look for a weak spot, who seek for a weak spot, will not gain any hold over him. He is competent to deal with the situation, and is able, unhurt and uninjured, soon to take out of that forest, both his family and himself, and securely and safely will they reach a village, city or market town.

The Lord: Just so, Subhuti, is it with a Bodhisattva who is full of pity and concerned with the welfare of all beings, who dwells in friendliness, compassion, sympathetic joy and evenmindedness. *Ashṭasāhasrikā XX, 371 – 73*

THE BODHISATTVA'S INFINITE COMPASSION

A Bodhisattva resolves: I take upon myself the burden of all suffering, I am resolved to do so, I will endure it. I do not turn or run away, do not tremble, am not terrified, nor afraid, do not turn back or despond.

And why? At all costs I must bear the burdens of all beings, In that I do not follow my own inclinations. I have made the vow to save all beings. All beings I must set free. The whole world of living beings I must rescue, from the terrors of birth, of old age, of sickness, of death and rebirth, of all kinds of moral offence, of all states of woe, of the whole cycle of birth-and-death, of the jungle of false views, of the loss of wholesome dharmas, of the concomitants of ignorance,—from all these terrors I must rescue all beings. . . . I walk so that the kingdom of unsurpassed cognition is built up for all beings. My endeavours do not merely aim at my own deliverance. For with the help of the boat of the thought of all-knowledge, I must rescue all these beings from the stream of Samsara, which is so difficult to cross, I must pull them back from the great precipice, I must free them from all calamities, I must ferry them across the stream of Samsara. I myself must grapple with the whole mass of suffering of all beings. To the limit of my endurance I will experience in all the states of woe, found in any world system, all the abodes of suffering. And I must not cheat all beings out of my store of merit. I am resolved to abide in each single state of woe for numberless aeons; and so I will help all beings to freedom, in all the states of woe that may be found in any world system whatsoever.

And why? Because it is surely better that I alone should be in pain than that all these beings should fall into the states of woe. There I must give myself away as a pawn through which the whole world is redeemed from the terrors of the hells, of animal birth, of the world of Yama, and with this my own body I must experience, for the sake of all beings, the whole mass of all painful feelings. And on behalf of all beings I give surety for all beings, and in doing so I speak truthfully, am trustworthy, and do not go back on my word. I must not abandon all beings.

And why? There has arisen in me the will to win all-knowledge, with all beings for its object, that is to say, for the purpose of setting free the entire world of beings. And I have not set out for the supreme enlightenment from a desire for delights, not because I hope to experience the delights of the five sense-qualities, or because I wish to indulge in the pleasures of the sense. And I do not pursue the course of a Bodhisattva in order to achieve the array of delights that can be found in the various worlds of sense-desire.

And why? Truly no delights are all these delights of the world. All this indulging in the pleasures of the senses belongs to the sphere of Mara.

Śikshāsamuccaya, 280–81 (Vajradhvaja Sūtra)

THE SIX PERFECTIONS DEFINED

Subhuti: What is a Bodhisattva's perfection of giving?

The Lord: Here a Bodhisattva, his thoughts associated with the knowledge of all modes, gives gifts, i.e. inward or outward things, and, having made them common to all beings, he dedicates them to supreme enlightenment; and also others he instigates thereto. But there is nowhere an apprehension of anything.

Subhuti: What is a Bodhisattva's perfection of morality?

The Lord: He himself lives under the obligation of the ten ways of wholesome acting, and also others he instigates thereto.

Subhuti: What is a Bodhisattva's perfection of patience?

The Lord: He himself becomes one who has achieved patience, and others also he instigates to patience.

Subhuti: What is a Bodhisattva's perfection of vigour?

The Lord: He dwells persistently in the five perfections, and also others he instigates to do likewise.

Subhuti: What is the Bodhisattva's perfection of concentration (or meditation)?

The Lord: He himself, through skill in means, enters into the trances, yet he is not reborn in the corresponding heavens of form as he could; and others also he instigates to do likewise.

Subhuti: What is a Bodhisattva's perfection of wisdom?

The Lord: He does not settle down in any dharma, he contemplates the essential original nature of all dharmas; and others also he instigates to the contemplation of all dharmas. *Pañcaviṃśatisāhasrikā, 194–95*

THE SIX PERFECTIONS AND THE BODY

This rejection and surrender of the body, this indifference to the body, that for him is the Perfection of Giving.

In that, even when his body is dismembered, he radiates good will towards all beings, and does not contract himself from the pain, that for him is the Perfection of Conduct.

In that, even when his body is dismembered, he remains patient for the sake of the deliverance even of those that dismember it, does them no injury even with his thoughts, and manifests the power of patience. That for him is the Perfection of Patience.

That vigour by which he refuses to give up the urge towards omniscience, and holds fast on to it, depending on the power of thought, that vigour by which he remains within the coming and going of birth-and-death (without entering Nirvana as he could), and continues to bring to maturity the roots of goodness, that for him is the Perfection of Vigour.

That, even when his body is dispersed, he does not become confused in his cultivation of the thought of omniscience which he has gained, has regard only for enlightenment, and takes care only of the peaceful calm of cessation, that for him is the Perfection of Concentration.

That, even when his body is dismembered, he looks upon the phantom and image of his body as upon so much straw, a log, or a wall; arrives at the conviction that his body has the nature of an illusion, and contemplates his body as in reality being impermanent, fraught with suffering, not his own, and at peace, that for him is the Perfection of Wisdom.

Śikshāsamuccaya, 187 (Sāgaramati Sūtra)

THE PERFECTION OF GIVING

Sariputra: What is the worldly, and what is the supramundane perfection of giving?

Subhuti: The worldly perfection of giving consists in this: The Bodhisattva gives liberally to all those who ask, all the while thinking in terms of real things. It occurs to him: "I give, that one receives, this is the gift. I renounce all my possessions without stint. I act as one who knows the Buddha. I practise the perfection of giving. I, having made this gift into the common property of all beings, dedicate it to supreme enlightenment, and that without apprehending anything. By means of this gift, and its fruit may all beings in this very life be at their ease, and may they one day enter Nirvana!" Tied by three ties he gives a gift. Which three? A perception of self, a perception of others, a perception of the gift.

The supramundane perfection of giving, on the other hand, consists in the threefold purity. What is the threefold purity? Here a Bodhisattva gives a gift, and he does not apprehend a self, nor a recipient, nor a gift; also no reward of his giving. He surrenders that gift to all beings, but he apprehends neither beings nor self. He dedicates that gift to supreme enlightenment, but he does not apprehend any enlightenment. This is called the supramundane perfection of giving. *Pañcaviṃśatisāhasrikā, 263–64*

THE PERFECTION OF PATIENCE

The Lord: A Tathagata's perfection of patience is really no perfection. Because, Subhuti, when the king of Kalinga cut my flesh from every limb, at that time I had no notion of a self, or of a being, or of a soul, or of a person, nor had I any notion or non-notion. And why? If, Subhuti, at that time I had had a notion of self, I would also have had a notion of ill-will at that time. If I had had a notion of a being, of a soul, of a person, than I also would have had a notion of ill-will at that time. And why? By my superknowledge I know the past, five hundred births, and how I have been the Rishi, "Preacher of Patience." Then also I have had no notion of a self, or of a being, or a soul, or a person. Therefore then, Subhuti, a Bodhisattva, a great being should, after he has got rid of all notions, raise his thought to the supreme enlightenment. Unsupported by form a thought should be produced, unsupported by sound, smells, tastes, touchables or mind-objects a thought should be produced, unsupported by dharma a thought should be produced, unsupported by no-dharma a thought should be produced, unsupported by anything a thought should be produced. And why? What is supported has no support.

Vajracchedikā, 14 e

THE PERFECTION OF MEDITATION

The Lord: When he practises the perfection of meditation for the sake of other beings his mind becomes undistracted. For he reflects that "even worldly meditation is hard to accomplish with distracted thoughts, how much more so is full enlightenment. Therefore I must remain undistracted until I have won full enlightenment." . . . Moreover, Subhuti, a Bodhisattva, beginning with the first thought of enlightenment, practises the perfection of meditation. His mental activities are associated with the knowledge of all modes when he enters into meditation. When he has seen forms with his eye, he does not seize upon them as signs of realities which concern him, nor is he interested in the accessory details. He sets himself to restrain that which, if he does not restrain his organ of sight, might give occasion for covetousness, sadness or other evil and unwholesome dharmas to reach his heart. He watches over the organ of sight. And the same with the other five sense-organs,—ear, nose, tongue, body, mind.

Whether he walks or stands, sits or lies down, talks or remains silent, his concentration does not leave him. He does not fidget with his hands or feet, or twitch his face; he is not incoherent in his speech, confused in his senses, exalted or uplifted, fickle or idle, agitated in body or mind. Calm is his body, calm is his voice, calm is his mind. His demeanour shows contentment, both in private and public. . . . He is frugal, easy to feed, easy to serve, of good life and habits; though in a crowd he dwells apart; even and unchanged, in gain and loss; not elated, not cast down. Thus in happiness and suffering, in praise and blame, in fame and disrepute, in life or death, he is the same unchanged, neither elated nor cast down. And so with foe or friend, with what is pleasant or unpleasant, with holy or unholy men, with noises or music, with forms that are dear or undear, he remains the same unchanged, neither elated nor cast down, neither gratified nor thwarted. And why? Because he sees all dharmas as empty of marks of their own, without true reality, incomplete and uncreated. *Śikshāsamuccaya, 202–03 (Prajñāpāramitā)*

II
The *Heart Sūtra**

THE SŪTRA ON THE HEART OF THE TRANSCENDENT AND VICTORIOUS PERFECTION OF WISDOM

Thus did I hear at one time. The Transcendent Victor was sitting on Vulture Mountain on Rājagṛha together with a great assembly of monks and a great

---

*Reprinted with permission from Donald S. Lopez, Jr., *The Heart Sūtra Explained: Indian and Tibetan Commentaries* (Albany: State University of New York Press, 1988.)

assembly of Bodhisattvas. At that time the Transcendent Victor was absorbed in a samādhi on the enumerations of phenomena called "perception of the profound." Also at that time, the Bodhisattva, the Mahāsattva, the Superior Avalokiteśvara was contemplating the meaning of the profound perfection of wisdom and he saw that those five aggregates also are empty of inherent existence. Then by the power of the Buddha, the venerable Śāriputra said this to the Bodhisattva, the Mahāsattva, the Superior Avalokiteśvara, "How should a son of good lineage train who wishes to practice the profound perfection of wisdom?"

The Bodhisattva, the Mahāsattva, the Superior Avalokiteśvara said this to the venerable Śāriputra: "Śāriputra, a son of good lineage or a daughter of good lineage who wishes to practice the profound perfection of wisdom should view [things] in this way: They should correctly view those five aggregates also as empty of inherent existence. Form is emptiness; emptiness is form. Emptiness is not other than form; form is not other than emptiness. In the same way, feeling, discrimination, compositional factors, and consciousnesses are empty. Śāriputra, in that way, all phenomena are empty, that is, without characteristic, unproduced, unceased, stainless, not stainless, undiminished, unfilled. Therefore, Śāriputra, in emptiness, there is no form, no feeling, no discrimination, no compositional factors, no consciousness, no eye, no ear, no nose, no tongue, no body, no mind, no form, no sound, no odor, no taste, no object of touch, no phenomenon. There is no eye constituent, no mental constituent, up to and including no mental consciousness constituent. There is no ignorance, no extinction of ignorance, up to and including no aging and death and no extinction of aging and death. Similarly, there are no sufferings, no origins, no cessations, no paths, no exalted wisdom, no attainment, and also no non-attainment.

Therefore, Śāriputra, because Bodhisattvas have no attainment, they depend on and abide in the perfection of wisdom; because their minds are without obstructions, they are without fear. Having completely passed beyond all error they go to the completion of nirvāṇa. All the Buddhas who abide in the three times have been fully awakened into unsurpassed, perfect, complete enlightenment through relying on the perfection of wisdom.

Therefore, the mantra of the perfection of wisdom is the mantra of great knowledge, the unsurpassed mantra, the mantra equal to the unequalled, the mantra that thoroughly pacifies all suffering. Because it is not false, it should be known to be true. The mantra of the perfection of wisdom is stated:

tadyathā oṃ gate gate pāragate pārasaṃgate bodhi svāhā

Śāriputra, Bodhisattva Mahāsattvas should train in the profound perfection of wisdom in that way.

Then the Transcendent Victor rose from that samādhi and said to the Bodhisattva, the Mahāsattva, the Superior Avalokiteśvara, "Well done. Well done, well done, child of good lineage, it is just so. Child of good lineage, it is like that; that profound perfection of wisdom should be practiced just as you have taught it. Even the Tathāgatas admire this." The Transcendent Victor having so spoken, the venerable Śāriputra, the Bodhisattva, the Mahāsattva, the Superior Avalokiteśvara, and all those surrounding and those of the world, the gods, humans, demigods, and *gandharvas* were filled with admiration and praised the words of the Transcendent Victor.

PRAŚĀSTRASENA'S COMMENTARY ON THE "HEART" OF THE *HEART SŪTRA*

Form is emptiness; emptiness is form. Emptiness is not other than form; form is not other than emptiness. In the same way, feeling, discrimination, compositional factors, and consciousnesses are empty. Śāriputra, in that way all phenomena are empty, without characteristic, unproduced, unceased, stainless, not stainless, undiminished, unfilled.[1]

Praśāstrasena

In the statement, "Form is emptiness," "form" refers to earth, water, fire, and wind. "Emptiness" is the ultimate, the dharmadhātu. Due to the character of emptiness, those forms are emptiness. The character of emptiness is non-dual in the sense of being beyond enumeration and enumerator and is the state of having abandoned I and mine. It is free from object and subject. Therefore, it is the character of the non-dual reality. Phenomena are not the composite of many types of emptiness. Therefore, even the four—earth, water, fire, and wind—are without characteristic, without entity, without self, without [the Sāṃkhya] principle (*pradhāna*).

It is not the case that things become emptiness when they are smashed to pieces; they are naturally empty. Therefore, "Form is emptiness." That very thing which is the natural emptiness of form is the ultimate emptiness itself; the ultimate emptiness does not exist apart from the natural emptiness of form. Therefore, "emptiness is form." That is, the words say that the ultimate emptiness is itself form's nature of emptiness.

What is the evidence that the emptiness of form is the ultimate emptiness? The *Akṣayamatinirdeśa Sūtra* says:

> Bodhisattvas, the dharmadhātu [which is the object] of the wisdom that enters the dharmadhātu is the elements—earth, water, fire, and wind. The dharmadhātu, however, is not the character of hardness, moisture, heat, and motility. The dharmadhātu and all phenomena are similar. Why? Because they are similar in emptiness.

Thus, it should be known that the emptiness of form is the ultimate emptiness. [This is] the twofold emptiness of form.

The three aspects of form are imaginary form (*parikalpitam rūpam*), designated form (*vikalpitam rūpam*), and the form of reality (*dharmatā*

---

[1]What follows is Praśāstrasena's commentary on these lines.

rūpam). The imputation of the characteristic of hardness to earth, etc. by childish common beings is imaginary form. The form that is the object engaged by a correct consciousness is designated form. The characteristic of reality free from imaginary form and designated form is the form of reality. Since the form of reality lacks imaginary form and designated form, it is said that form is empty. To those who wonder whether the reality of form—emptiness—is something that exists apart from imaginary form and designated form, it is said that emptiness is form, meaning that the form of reality—emptiness—has the same character as imaginary form and designated form.

That very thing which is form is emptiness. Emptiness is also form. Regarding the statement that emptiness does not exist apart from form, the emptiness that is the characteristic of form and the ultimate emptiness are not different but one. Therefore, it says that emptiness does not exist apart from form. Why are they not different? Because there is no difference in the character of emptiness, which is the nature of having abandoned augmentation, diminishment, separation, and the two extremes. Saying that that which is form is emptiness is a way of saying that that which is the characteristic of form is also the characteristic of emptiness. Saying that that which is emptiness is form is a way of saying that that which is the characteristic of emptiness is also the characteristic of form.

Therefore, this is taught: Sentient beings, debased and childish, cycle in the five evil paths in the beginningless cycle of birth and death. Through acquaintance with the five aggregates and familiarity with the eighteen elements, they become attached and attracted to them and conceive of them to be real and solid. If [they think] that, because the Tathāgata teaches [that forms are] naturally empty, the characteristic of form is destroyed in emptiness, they believe that the antidote, emptiness, exists apart. [Consequently] they are attached to the nirvāṇa of a śrāvaka, who is biased toward peace. Thus, "that which is form is emptiness" is set forth as an antidote that prevents falling into the extreme of saṃsāra through being attached to form. "That which is emptiness is form" is set forth as an antidote to falling into the extreme of nirvāṇa for śrāvakas who enter into the selflessness of persons and create signs of emptiness, [thinking] that form is destroyed in emptiness.

Form and emptiness are to be abandoned because they do not exist. Regarding that, when emptiness is taught in order that [sentient beings] abandon the conception that form has signs [of inherent existence], they come to think that emptiness has signs. Signs are the observation of signs [of inherent existence] with regard to anything. Therefore, because it obstructs the realization of reality, the conception that emptiness is real is a sign. Hence, both form and emptiness are to be abandoned. For example, a person with poor vision was travelling. Along the right side of the path were thorns and ditches. Along the left side of the path were ravines and precipices. If a person with faultless vision had said, "There are thorns and ditches [on the right]," the person would have fallen into the ravines and off the precipices. If he had said, "There are ravines and precipices [on the left]," the person would have fallen into thorns and ditches. However, [a person with faultless vision] indicated that the middle path was pleasant and without the slightest obstacle. [The person with poor vision] arrived at his home. In accordance with that example, the person with poor vision is [both] the common being (*pṛthagjana*) impeded by the affliction obstructions (*kleśāvaraṇa*) and the śrāvaka obstructed by the obstructions to omniscience (*jñeyāvaraṇa*). The thorns and ditches are attachment to the signs of persons, forms, and so forth, that is, falling to the extreme of saṃsāra. The ravines and precipices are attachment to the nirvāṇa of the śrāvakas, that is, falling to the extreme of emptiness. The person with vision is the Tathāgata. Because he sees with the clear eyes of wisdom that form is naturally empty, he does not abandon saṃsāra, because it is like an illusion. Because [he sees that] the three realms are like a dream, he does not even seek the qualities of nirvāṇa. Because he enters the middle path with signlessness (*animitta*), wishlessness (*apraṇihita*), and emptiness (*śūnyatā*), he arrives at the abode of the nonabiding nirvāṇa (*apratiṣṭhitanirvāṇa*). Therefore, since he taught that apprehending signs is a precipice and a fault, signs are not to be held regarding existence or non-existence.

[The sūtra] says, "In the same way, feeling, discrimination, compositional factors, and consciousness are empty." Earlier, it said that [Avalokiteśvara] saw that the five aggregates are empty. The emptiness of form was stated, it was taught that form is emptiness, and it was taught that emptiness and form are not different. . . .

Those phenomena [the remaining four aggregates] are the continuum of the mind. The mind has the character of the emptiness of the formless; it is based on the form aggregate upon the maturation of predispositions (*vāsanā*). For example, it is similar to an empty vessel; the vessel is a support. If the vessel is destroyed, there is no place for the supported; it is not different from the great voidness [of space]. Like that, by analyzing the form aggregate and [finding it to be] empty, there is no place for the mental aggregates; they are not different from the ultimate, the sphere of reality.

What is the evidence that the five aggregates are empty of inherent existence? The *Akṣayamatinirdeśa Sūtra* says:

> The form aggregate is like a ball of foam; it cannot withstand being held and separated. The feeling aggregate is like a water bubble; because it is momentary, it is impermanent. The aggregate discrimination is like a mirage because it is mistakenly apprehended by the thirst of attachment. The aggregate of compositional factors is like the stalk of a lotus; when it is destroyed it has no core. The aggregate of consciousness is like a dream; it is mistakenly conceived. Therefore, the five aggregates are not a self, not a person, not a sentient being, not a life, not a nourished being, not a creature. The five aggregates are naturally empty of I and mine, unproduced, unarisen, non-existent, the sphere of space, unconditioned, and naturally passed beyond sorrow.

III
From the *Diamond Sūtra**

THE BODHISATTVA AND DIPANKARA

The Lord asked Subhuti: What do you think, was there any dharma which awoke the Tathagata, when he was with the Tathagata Dipankara, to the utmost, right, and perfect enlightenment?—Subhuti replied: As I understand the meaning of the Lord's teaching, this was not due to any dharma.—The Lord said: So it is, Subhuti, so it is. If again, Subhuti, the Tathagata had fully known any dharma, then the Tathagata would not have predicted of me: "You, young Brahmin, will in a future period be a Tathagata, Arhat, Fully Enlightened, by the name of Shakyamuni!" But he made this prediction because it is not through any dharma that the Tathagata, the Arhat, the Fully Enlightened One has fully known the utmost, right, and perfect enlightenment.

The Initial Vow of a Bodhisattva

The Lord said: Here, Subhuti, someone who has set out in the vehicle of a Bodhisattva should think in this manner: "As many beings as there are in the universe of beings, comprehended under the term 'beings'—egg-born, born from a womb, moisture-born, or miraculously born; with or without form; with perception, without perception, or with neither perception nor no-perception—as far as any conceivable form of beings is conceived: all these I must lead to Nirvana, into that Realm of Nirvana which leaves nothing behind. And yet, although innumerable beings have thus been led to Nirvana, in fact no being at all has been led to Nirvana." And why? If in a Bodhisattva the notion of a "being" should take place, he could not be called a "Bodhi-being." And why? He is not to be called a Bodhi-being, in whom the notion of a self or of a being should take place, or the notion of a living soul or a person.

THE PRACTICE OF PERFECT GIVING

Moreover, Subhuti, a Bodhisattva who gives gifts should not lean on anything, or anywhere. When he gives gifts he should not be supported by sight-objects, sounds, smells, tastes, touchables, or mind-objects. For, Subhuti, the Bodhisattva, the great being should give gifts in such a way that he is not supported by the notion of a sign. And why? Because the heap of merit of that Bodhi-being, who unsupported gives a gift, is not easy to measure.

THE PRACTICE OF PERFECT PATIENCE

Moreover, Subhuti, the Tathagata's perfection of patience is really a non-perfection. And why? Because, Subhuti, when the king of Kali cut my flesh from

---

*Reprinted with permission from Edward Conze, *Buddhist Scriptures* (Harmondsworth: Penguin Books, 1959).

every limb, at that time I had no notion of a self, a being, a soul, or a person. In fact I had no notion or non-notion at all. And why? If, Subhuti, at that time I had had a notion of self, I would also have conceived ill-will at that time. And likewise if I had had a notion of a being, a soul, or a person. And why? By my supernatural knowledge I know the past, and that five hundred births ago I was the Rishi "Preacher of Patience," and furthermore that then also I had no notion of a self, a being, a soul, or a person.

THE BODHISATTVA'S FINAL NIRVANA

Therefore then, Subhuti, the Bodhisattva should produce an unsupported thought, i.e. a thought which is nowhere supported, a thought unsupported by sights, sounds, smells, tastes, touchables, or mind-objects.

THE BODHISATTVA AS A FULLY ENLIGHTENED BUDDHA

The Lord asked: What do you think, Subhuti, is there any dharma which the Tathagata has fully known as the utmost, right, and perfect enlightenment, or is there any dharma which the Tathagata has demonstrated?—Subhuti replied: No, not as I understand what the Lord has said. And why? This dharma which the Tathagata has fully known or demonstrated—it cannot be grasped, it cannot be talked about, it is neither a dharma nor a non-dharma. And why? Because an Absolute exalts the Holy Persons.

THE BUDDHA'S PHYSICAL BODY

The Lord asked: What do you think, Subhuti, can the Tathagata be seen by means of his possession of marks?—Subhuti replied: No indeed, O Lord, not as I understand what the Lord has taught.—The Lord said: Well said, well said, Subhuti. So it is, Subhuti, so it is, as you say. For if the Tathagata were one who could be seen by his possession of the thirty-two Marks, then also the universal monarch would be a Tathagata. Therefore the Tathagata is not to be seen by means of his possession of Marks.—And further the Lord taught on that occasion the following stanza:

Those who by my form did see me,
And those who followed me by voice,
Wrong the efforts they engaged in,
Me those people will not see.

THE BUDDHA AS THE TATHAGATA

Whosoever says that the Tathagata goes or comes, stands, sits, or lies down, he does not understand the meaning of my teaching. And why? "Tathagata" is called one who has not gone to anywhere, and who has not come from anywhere. Therefore is he called "the Tathagata, the Arhat, the Fully Enlightened One."

THE BUDDHA AS A TEACHER

The Lord asked: What do you think, Subhuti, does it occur to the Tathagata that he has demonstrated dharma?—Subhuti replied: No indeed, O Lord, it does not.—The Lord said: Whosoever should say that "the Tathagata has demonstrated dharma," he would speak falsely, he would misrepresent me by seizing on what is not there. And why? One speaks of "demonstration of dharma," Subhuti, but there is not any dharma which could be apprehended as demonstration of dharma.

THE BUDDHA AS A SAVIOUR

What do you think, Subhuti, does it occur to a Tathagata that he has set beings free? Not so should one see it, Subhuti. And why? There is not any being whom the Tathagata has set free. For if there had been any being to be set free by the Tathagata, then surely there would have been on the part of the Tathagata a seizing on a self, a being, a soul, a person. One speaks of "seizing on a self," but as a no-seizing, Subhuti, has that been taught by the Tathagata. And yet it has been seized upon by foolish common people. One speaks of "foolish common people," but as really no people have they been taught by the Tathagata. Therefore are they called "foolish common people."

THE APPLICATION TO THE PRESENT DAY

Subhuti asked: Will there be any beings in the future period, in the last time, in the last epoch, in the last five hundred years, at the time of the collapse of the good doctrine, who, when these words of the Sutra are being taught, will understand their truth?—The Lord replied: Do not speak thus, Subhuti! Yes, even then there will be such beings. For even at that time, Subhuti, there will be Bodhisattvas who are gifted with good conduct, gifted with virtuous qualities, gifted with wisdom, and who, when these words of the Sutra are being taught, will understand their truth. And these Bodhisattvas, Subhuti, will not be such as have honoured only one single Buddha, nor such as have planted their roots of merit under one single Buddha only. On the contrary, Subhuti, those Bodhisattvas who, when these words of the Sutra are being taught, will find even one single thought of serene faith, they will be such as have honoured many hundreds of thousands of Buddhas, such as have planted their roots of merit under many hundreds of thousands of Buddhas. Known they are, Subhuti, to the Tathagata through his Buddha cognition, seen they are, Subhuti, by the Tathagata with his Buddha-eye, fully known they are, Subhuti, to the Tathagata. And they all, Subhuti, will beget and acquire an immeasurable and incalculable heap of merit. And why? Because, Subhuti, in these Bodhisattva no perception of a self takes place, no perception of a being, of a soul, of a person. Nor do they have a perception of a dharma, or a no-dharma. No perception or non-perception takes place in them. And why? If, Subhuti, these Bodhisattvas should have a perception of either a dharma or a no-dharma, they would thereby seize on a self, a being, a soul, or a person. And why? Because a Bodhisattva should not seize on either a dharma or a no-dharma. Therefore this saying has been taught by the Tathagata with a hidden meaning: "Those who know the discourse on dharma as like unto a raft, should forsake dharmas, still more so no-dharmas."

CHAPTER 12

MĀDHYAMAKA

The Mādhyamaka, or Middle Way, philosophy takes its name from its basic tenet, that existence is neither being nor nonbeing, but dependent origination, which is midway between being and nonbeing. Although famous for its teaching that existence is characterized by *śūnyatā*, or emptiness, this *śūnyatā* is by no means simply the denial that things have being, a denial that would automatically affirm the nonbeing of things. Rather it is an elucidation of dependent origination, described by the Buddha as the Middle Way. Nāgārjuna, who probably lived in the second century A.D., is the earliest known exponent of this school and perhaps its originator. His *Treatise on the Fundamentals of the Middle Way (Mūlamādhyamakakārikā)*, the foundational text of this school, is concerned with clearing away the objections to, and misinterpretations of, the Middle Way philosophy of dependent origination. The chapters included here—on causality, suffering, time, the fourfold noble truth, and *nirvāṇa*—are among the most important in the subsequent history of the school, in China and Tibet as well as India, and are representative of Nāgārjuna's analysis of key topics. They are reprinted from Kenneth Inada, *Nāgārjuna: A Translation of His Mūlamādhyamakakārikā with an Introductory Essay* (Tokyo: Hokuseido Press, 1970).

The works by Candrakīrti and Tsong Khapa are not only useful in understanding Nāgārjuna's thought but also show how creative commentary was used to develop certain lines of thought that went beyond Nāgārjuna's own analysis. Candrakīrti, an important seventh-century Buddhist thinker, composed an influential treatise on the philosophy of the Middle Way called *A Guide to the Middle Way (Mādhyamakāvatāra)*. This work consists of ten chapters, each corresponding to one of the ten spiritual levels, or perfections, of the Bodhisattva's career. The sixth chapter, reprinted here, is on the perfection of wisdom. It is an excellent commentary on Nāgārjuna's analysis of causality, arguing against both Buddhist and non-Buddhist misunderstandings of causality. The translation is by Stephen Batchelor, in Geshe Rabten, *Echoes of Voidness* (London: Wisdom Publications, 1983).

Tsong Khapa (1357–1419), founder of the *dGe-lugs-pa* sect of Tibetan Buddhism, is probably Tibet's most renowned Mādhyamaka philosopher. In the selection here, chapter 7 of *The Essence of True Eloquence*, reprinted from Robert A.F. Thurman, *Tsong Khapa's Speech of Gold in the "Essence of True Eloquence"* (Princeton: Princeton University Press, 1984), Tsong Khapa explains that because the commonly held but false view that selves and things exist as separate, independent beings underlies grasping and attachment, this view must be refuted. The work is at once a treatise setting out Tsong Khapa's own Middle Way philosophy and a commentary on Candrakīrti ("Chandra") and Nāgārjuna ("the Master").

C. W. Huntington, Jr., with Geshhe Namgyal Wangchen, *The Emptiness of Emptiness* (Honolulu: University of Hawaii Press, 1989), is an excellent introduction to Indian and Tibetan Mādhyamaka thought. Edward Conze, *Buddhist Thought in India* (Ann Arbor: University of Michigan Press, 1973), relates the development of Mādhyamaka thought to other philosophical developments in India, both Buddhist and non-Buddhist. Richard S. Robinson, *Early Mādhyamika in India and China* (Madison: University of Wisconsin Press, 1967), traces the development of Mādhyamaka thought from its beginnings in Nāgārjuna through its Chinese development up to Seng Chao. Malcom David Eckel, *Jñānagarbha's Commentary on the Distinction Between Two Truths* (Albany: State University of New York Press, 1987), provides a rare glimpse into the dynamics of Middle Way philosophy by presenting a translation of Jñānagarbha's complete text, after first placing it in its historical and philosophical context. The translation is preceded by an extremely helpful analysis of the structure of the argument. David Kalupahana, *Nāgārjuna, The Philosophy of the Middle Way* (Albany: State University of New York Press, 1986), in addition to providing a fine, annotated translation of the *Mūlamādhyamakakārikā*, presents a lengthy introduction in which he argues convincingly for the continuity of Mādhyamaka with the early Buddhism of the Nikāyas. Kenneth Inada, *Nāgārjuna: A Translation of His Mūlamādhyamakakārikā with an Introductory Essay* (Tokyo: Hokuseido Press, 1970), contains an excellent introductory essay explaining the significance of Mādhyamaka thought.

Robert A.F. Thurman, *Tsong Khapa's Speech of Gold in the "Essence of True Eloquence"* (Princeton: Princeton University Press, 1984), has a long and detailed introduction to Tibetan Middle Way philosophy. It is the best book-length study of Tsong Khapa's philosophy available in English. Geshe Rabten, *Echoes of Voidness* (London: Wisdom Publications, 1983), is an excellent introduction to the philosophy of *śūnyatā* (voidness). The commentary on the *Heart Sūtra* and the explanation of *Mahamudra* by Geshe Rabten are wonderfully clear. David Snellgrove, *Indo-Tibetan Buddhism*, two vols. (Boston: Shambala Publications, 1987), is the summary of a lifetime's work by this distinguished scholar. The most thorough study of the Mādhyamka understanding of *śūnyatā* from a Tibetan perspective is Elizabeth Napper, *Dependent-Arising and Emptiness* (Boston: Wisdom Publications, 1989).

I
Nāgārjuna: Treatise on the Fundamentals of the Middle Way*

DEDICATION

I pay homage to the Fully Awakened One,
the supreme teacher who has taught
the doctrine of relational origination,
the blissful cessation of all phenomenal thought constructions.
(Therein, every event is "marked" by):
non-origination, non-extinction,
non-destruction, non-permanence,
non-identity, non-differentiation
non-coming (into being), non-going (out of being).

CHAPTER 1. RELATIONAL CONDITIONS

1. At nowhere and at no time can entities ever exist by originating out of themselves, from others, from both (self-other), or from the lack of causes.

2. There are four and only four relational conditions; namely primary causal, appropriating or objectively extending, sequential or contiguous, and dominantly extending conditions. There is no fifth.

3. In these relational conditions the self-nature of the entities cannot exist. From the non-existence of self-nature, other-nature too cannot exist.

4. The functional force does not inhere relational conditions, nor does it not inhere them. The relational conditions, vice versa, do not inhere the functional force, nor do they not inhere it.

5. Only as entities are uniquely related and originated can they be described in terms of relational conditions. For, how can non-relational conditions be asserted of entities which have not come into being?

6. Relational condition does not validly belong to either being or non-being. If it belongs to being, for what use is it? And if to non-being, for whose use is it?

7. When a factor of experience does not evolve from being, non-being, nor from both being and non-being, how can there be an effectuating cause? Thus (such) a cause is not permissible.

8. It is said that a true factor of experience does not have an appropriat-

*Reprinted with permission from Kenneth Inada, *Nāgārjuna: A Translation of His Mūlamādhyamakakārikā with an Introductory Essay* (Tokyo: Hokuseido Press, 1970).

ing or objectively extending relational condition. If it does not exist, then again, wherein is this type of relational condition?

9. It is not possible to have extinction where factors of experience have not yet arisen. In an extinguished state, for what use is a relational condition? Thus the sequential or contiguous relational condition is not applicable.

10. As entities without self-nature have no real status of existence, the statement, "from the existence of that this becomes," is not possible.

11. The effect (i.e., arisen entity) does not exist separated from relational condition nor together in relational condition. If it does not exist in either situation, how could it arise out of relational conditions?

12. Now then, if non-entity arises from these relational conditions, why is it not possible that the effect (i.e., arisen entity) cannot arise from non-relational conditions?

13. The effect (i.e., arisen entity) has the relational condition but the relational conditions have no self-possessing (natures). How can an effect, arising from no self-possessing (natures), have the relational condition?

14. Consequently, the effect (i.e., arisen entity) is neither with relational nor without non-relational condition. Since the effect has no existing status, wherein are the relational and nonrelational conditions?

CHAPTER 12. EXAMINATION OF SUFFERING

1. Some assert that suffering arises by virtue of being self-caused, other-caused, both self and other-caused or non-causal. Such an assertion which treats suffering as an effect is not justifiable.

2. If suffering is self-caused, it will not have a relational condition in arising. For, surely, these (present) skandhas are relationally conditioned in the arising of those (future) skandhas.

3. If these (present) skandhas are different from those (future) skandhas or if the latter are other than the former, then there will be suffering caused by something else and those (future) skandhas will also be caused by it.

4. If suffering is caused by the individual himself, then the individual is separated from suffering. Who is this individual self which self-causes suffering?

5. If suffering is caused by another individual, where is this self which is separated from suffering but which is (seemingly) the recipient of the suffering caused by another?

6. If suffering is caused by another individual, what is (the nature of) this individual which is separated from and yet causes and bestows suffering to the recipient?

7. As self-cause cannot be established, where can an other-caused suffering be? For, surely, an other-caused suffering is caused by that other itself.

8. In truth then, there is no self-caused suffering for it cannot come about by itself. If an other does not bring about its own suffering, why is there an other-caused suffering?

9. If suffering could be caused individually by one's self and by an other, then there should also be suffering caused jointly. Where is this non-causal suffering which is neither caused by itself nor by an other?

10. Not only is the four-fold causal view of suffering impossible but the same is not possible with respect to the external elements of being.

CHAPTER 19. EXAMINATION OF TIME

1. If, indeed, the present and future are contingently related to the past, they should exist in the past moment.

2. If, again, the present and future do not exist there (i.e., in the past), how could they be contingently related?

3. Again, it is not possible for both (present and future) to establish themselves without being contingent on a past. Therefore, there is no justification for the existence of a present and a future time.

4. It follows from the above analysis that the remainder of the two periods likewise can be taken up and that concepts such as above, below, middle, etc. or identity, etc. can be similarly described or treated.

Note: This means that the analysis can be made similarly by using the present and the future in turn as a base and relating each to the other two temporal periods. Similar analysis holds true for the other concepts mentioned.[1]

5. A non-enduring time cannot be manipulated. But an enduring time, although manipulatable, does not exist. How could a non-manipulatable time be grasped (i.e., conceptualized)?

6. If time exists in virtue of the relational existential structure, where can it be without the structure? As an existential structure does not exist, where can time be?

CHAPTER 24. EXAMINATION OF THE FOURFOLD NOBLE TRUTH

1. If everything is *śūnya* there will be neither production nor destruction. According to your assertion it will follow that the Āryan Fourfold Truths are non-existent.

Note: Verses 1 through 6 are views expressed by the opponent.

---

[1] *Notes* are by the translator.

2. True knowledge, relinquishing (false views), (right) practice, and (right) confirmation will not be possible because of the non-existence of the Āryan Four-fold Truths.

3. As these are non-existent, the Āryan fourfold fruits i.e., spiritual attainments, are also non-existent. As the fruits are non-existent, there will be no one who enjoys the fruits or their fruition.

Note: This verse makes reference to the four paths and fruits of attainment by the one who takes up the Buddhist principles once-returner to the empirical level, the non-returner, and the enlightened worthy one.

4. If the eight aspirations of men do not exist, there will be no *Saṃgha* (i.e., Buddhist order). From the non-existence of the Āryan Truths, the true *Dharma* also does not exist.

Note: The eight refer to the four matured states (*phalasthā*) and the four arrived states (*pratipannakāḥ*) mentioned in the previous verse.

5. Without *Dharma* and *Saṃgha*, how could there be *Buddha*? Consequently, what you assert also destroys the Three Treasures.

Note: The implication here is that since all is *śūnya*, there are no grounds for asserting the Three Treasures, i.e., the *Buddha*, the *Dharma*, and the *Saṃgha*.

6. Delving in *śūnyatā*, you will destroy the reality of the fruit or attainment, the proper and improper acts, and all the everyday practices relative to the empirical world.

7. Let us interrupt here to point out that you do not know the real purpose of *śūnyata*, its nature and meaning. Therefore, there is only frustration and hindrance (of understanding).[1]

Note: Here begins Nāgārjuna's response.

8. The teaching of the *Dharma* by the various *Buddhas* is based on the two truths; namely, the relative (worldly) truth and the absolute (supreme) truth.

9. Those who do not know the distinction between the two truths cannot understand the profound nature of the Buddha's teaching.

---

[1] Nāgārjuna's response begins with verse 7.

10. Without relying on everyday common practices (i.e., relative truths), the absolute truth cannot be expressed. Without approaching the absolute truth, *nirvāṇa* cannot be attained.

11. A wrongly conceived *śūnyatā* can ruin a slow-witted person. It is like a badly seized snake or a wrongly executed incantation.

12. Thus the wise one (i.e., the Buddha) once resolved not to teach about the *Dharma*, thinking that the slow-witted might wrongly conceive it.

13. You have repeatedly refuted *śūnyatā* but we do not fall into any error. The refutation does not apply to *śūnya.*

14. Whatever is in correspondence with *śūnyatā*, all is in correspondence (i.e., possible). Again, whatever is not in correspondence with *śūnyatā*, all is not in correspondence.

Note: The meaning conveyed here is that *śūnyatā* is the basis of all existence. Thus, without it, nothing is possible.

15. You level your own errors at us. It is as if you are mounted on your horse but forget about it.

16. If you perceive the various existences as true beings from the standpoint of self-nature, then you will perceive them as non-causal conditions.

17. You will then destroy (all notions of) cause, effect, doer, means of doing, doing, origination, extinction, and fruit (of action).

18. We declare that whatever is relational origination is *śūnyatā.* It is a provisional name (i.e., thought construction) for the mutuality (of being) and, indeed, it is the middle path.

19. Any factor of experience which does not participate in relational origination cannot exist. Therefore, any factor of experience not in the nature of *śūnya* cannot exist.

20. If everything were of the nature of non-*śūnya*, then there would be neither production nor destruction. Then also the non-existence of the Aryan Fourfold Truths would accordingly follow.

21. Where could suffering in the nature of non-relational origination arise? For, indeed, what is impermanent is said to be in the nature of suffering and the impermanent cannot exist in something with self-nature.

22. How could that which has self-nature arise again? Therefore, there is no arising in that which disaffirms (i.e., destroys) *śūnyatā.*

23. The extinction of suffering in terms of self-nature does not happen. For, you deny extinction itself by adhering to the notion of self-nature.

24. If the way to enlightenment possesses self-nature, then its practice will not be possible. But if the way is practiced, your assertion of a way involving self-nature is inadmissible (i.e., cannot exist).

25. When suffering, arising, and extinction cannot be admitted to exist, what path is achieved in virtue of the extinction of suffering?

26. If (suffering) cannot be known in virtue of self-nature, how does it become an object of knowledge again? Self-nature, indeed, never remains fixed.

27. Just as in the case of knowledge (of suffering), therefore, your knowledge of abandoning, perceptual confirmation, practice, and the four fruits (i.e., religious attainments) cannot be possible.

28. To one who adheres to the notion of self-existence, how could the (four) fruits which are unattainable in virtue of self-existence be ever attainable?

29. Without the (four) fruits, there can be no matured states and arrived (i.e., completed) states. If these eight states of men do not exist, there will also be no realization of the *Saṃgha.*

30. Without the Aryan Truths the true *Dharma* does not exist. Without the *Dharma* and *Saṃgha*, how could there be the *Buddha*?

31. According to your assertion there is a fallacy of becoming the *Buddha* without relationship to enlightenment. Also, conversely, there is enlightenment without relationship to the *Buddha.*

32. According to your assertion, anyone who is not a *Buddha* in virtue of self-existence cannot hope to attain enlightenment even by serious endeavor or by practice of the *Bodhisattva* way.

33. No one would ever be able to create factors or non-factors of experience. For, what is there to create in non-*śūnya*? Self-existence, after all, cannot be created.

34. According to your assertion, the fruit could exist separated from factors and non-factors of experience. Again, according to your assertion, the fruit could not have arisen by the factors and non-factors of experience.

35. If you are to admit the fruit based on the factors and non-factors of experience, how could the fruit arising from them be of the nature of non-*śūnya*?

36. You will thus destroy all the everyday practices relative to the empirical world because you will have destroyed the *śūnyatā* of relational origination.

37. For one who destroys *śūnyatā*, it will be like a doer without an action, a non-activating action, or with nothing to act upon.

38. From the standpoint of self-existence, the world will be removed from the various conditions and it will be non-originative, non-destructive, and immovable.

39. If everything is non-*śūnya*, then the attainment of a person who aspires, the actions leading to the cessation of suffering, and the destruction of all defilements will not exist (i.e., be possible).

40. One who rightly discerns relational origination will, indeed, rightly discern universal suffering, its origination, its extinction, and the way to enlightenment.

CHAPTER 25. EXAMINATION OF NIRVĀṆA

1. (The opponent contends):

If all is *śūnya* and there is neither production nor destruction, then from whose abandonment (of defilements) or from whose extinction (of suffering) can *nirvāṇa* be attributed?

2. (Nāgārjuna asserts):

If all is *aśūnya* and there is neither production nor destruction, then from whose abandonment (of defilements) or from whose extinction (of suffering) can *nirvāṇa* be attributed?

Note: Nāgārjuna, in the previous chapter, has stated that the critic of *śūnya* does not really know its meaning and thus cannot understand *śūnya* with respect to ordinary activities. Nāgārjuna reveals the fallacy of understanding *śūnya* in terms of self-existence (*svabhāva*) and, analogously, demonstrates the absurdity of premising even the concept of *aśūnya*, as it is done in this verse.

3. What is never cast off, seized, interrupted, constant, extinguished, and produced . . . this is called *nirvāṇa.*

4. Indeed, *nirvāṇa* is not strictly in the nature of ordinary existence for, if it were, there would wrongly follow the characteristics of old age-death. For, such an existence cannot be without those characteristics.

5. If *nirvāṇa* is strictly in the nature of ordinary existence, it will be of the created realm. For, no ordinary existence of the uncreated realm ever exists anywhere at all.

6. If *nirvāṇa* is strictly in the nature of ordinary existence, why is it non-appropriating? For, no ordinary existence that is non-appropriating ever exists.

7. If *nirvāṇa* is not strictly in the nature of ordinary existence, how could what is in the nature of non-existence be *nirvāṇa*? Where there is no existence, equally so, there can be no non-existence.

8. If *nirvāṇa* is in the nature of non-existence, why is it non-appropriating? For, indeed, a non-appropriating non-existence does not prevail.

9. The status of the birth-death cycle is due to existential grasping (of the *skandhas*) and relational condition (of the being). That which is non-grasping and non-relational is taught as *nirvāṇa.*

10. The teacher (Buddha) has taught the abandonment of the concepts of being and non-being. Therefore, *nirvāṇa* is properly neither (in the realm of) existence nor non-existence.

11. If *nirvāṇa* is (in the realm of) both existence and non-existence, then *mokṣa* (liberation) will also be both. But that is not proper.

12. If *nirvāṇa* is (in the realm of) both existence and non-existence, it will not be non-appropriating. For, both realms are (always in the process of) appropriating.

13. How could *nirvāṇa* be (in the realm of) both existence and non-existence? *Nirvāṇa* is of the uncreated realm while existence and non-existence are of the created realm.

14. How could *nirvāṇa* be (in the realm of) both existence and non-existence? Both cannot be together in one place just as the situation is with light and darkness.

15. The proposition that *nirvāṇa* is neither existence nor non-existence could only be valid if and when the realms of existence and non-existence are established.

16. If indeed *nirvāṇa* is asserted to be neither existence nor non-existence, then by what means are the assertions to be known?

17. It cannot be said that the Blessed One exists after *nirodha* (i.e., release from worldly desires). Nor can it be said that He does not exist after *nirodha*, or both, or neither.

18. It cannot be said that the Blessed One even exists in the present living process. Nor can it be said that He does not exist in the present living process, or both, or neither.

19. *Saṃsara* (i.e., the empirical life-death cycle) is nothing essentially different from *nirvāṇa. Nirvāṇa* is nothing essentially different from *saṃsāra.*

20. The limits (i.e., realm) of *nirvāṇa* are the limits of *saṃsāra.* Between the two, also, there is not the slightest difference whatsoever.

21. The various views concerning the status of life after *nirodha*, the limits of the world, the concept of permanence, etc., are all based on (the concepts of) *nirvāṇa*, posterior and anterior states (of existence).

22. Since all factors of existence are in the nature of *śūnya*, why (assert) the finite, the infinite, both finite and infinite, and neither finite nor infinite?

23. Why (assert) the identity, difference, permanence, impermanence, both permanence and impermanence, or neither permanence nor impermanence?

24. All acquisitions (i.e., grasping) as well as play of concepts (i.e., symbolic representation) are basically in the nature of cessation and quiescence. Any factor of experience with regards to anyone at any place was never taught by the Buddha.

II
Candrakīrti: *Guide to the Middle Way* (Chapter 6)*

1 INTRODUCTION

The bodhisattva whose mind is placed evenly in the Approach, i.e. the sixth spiritual level, approaches the phenomenon of complete buddhahood; he sees the suchness of dependent arising; and, because he dwells in wisdom, he will achieve cessation.

Just as a person with good eyesight can easily lead many groups of blind people wherever they want to go, in this case too the mind of wisdom leads the virtues with defective eyesight, i.e. the other five perfections, and takes them to the very state of a conqueror.

Through both scriptural citation and reasoning, Nāgārjuna has clearly revealed this extremely profound phenomenon, suchness, in the same way as is understood by the bodhisattva on the Approach. Therefore, in the very way in which suchness has been explained in the textual tradition of the ārya Nāgārjuna, I shall likewise describe it here, in full accordance with that tradition.

Should an ordinary person hear about voidness (śūnyatā) and immediately experience the surging of such great joy that his eyes become moist with tears and the hairs on his body stand on end, such a person has the seed of the mind of complete buddhahood; he is a vessel to whom suchness, the truth perceived by the holy ones, should be revealed. In such a person the virtues that follow upon hearing about voidness will arise: he will always adopt a perfect moral discipline and adhere to it, bestow gifts, devote himself to compassion and cultivate patience. In order to liberate beings he will completely dedicate his wholesome deed to awakening and pay respect to the complete bodhisattvas. Such a person who is skilled in the ways of the profound and the vast will progressively achieve the spiritual level of Great Joy. Therefore, those who strive for that spiritual level should listen to this path.

2 THE SELFLESSNESS OF PHENOMENA

A. A Refutation of Production

An effect cannot arise from itself, but how could it come from something inherently other than itself? It cannot come from both, yet how could it exist without a cause?

---

*Reprinted with permission from Geshe Rabten, *Echoes of Voidness*, translated and edited by Stephen Batchelor (London: Wisdom Publications, 1983). *Translator's note:* What follows is a translation of the entire sixth chapter of Chandrakīrti's *Guide to the Middle Way.* The text is presented in prose form and has been clarified and explained according to the interpretation of Tsong Khapa as found in his commentarial work, the *Clear Illumination of the Intention.* . . . The paragraph formation has been made according to the topical outline of Tsong Khapa.

The translation of the text was brought to completion in 1980, in conjunction with oral explanations of Tsong Khapas's commentary given by Geshé Thubten Ngawang in the Tibetisches Zentrum, Hamburg. The sections in italics are the translator's gloss.

1. Refutation of the Sāṃkhya doctrine of production from self

The non-Buddhist Sāṃkhya school maintains that a causal relation between two things could only be possible if the effect were in some way essentially identical with its cause. Without such identity there would be no grounds upon which to affirm any relationship. Therefore, they posit the view of production from self, i.e. production from a cause that is essentially identical to its effect. . . .

There is no point at all for something to arise from itself. It is also quite unreasonable for something that has been produced to be produced again. If it is maintained that a seed that has already been produced is later produced again, then the production of such things as sprouts would never be found on this earth, and until the end of conditional existence seeds alone would be abundantly produced. For how could the sprout ever come to destroy the seed?

One consequence of the Sāṃkhya doctrine of production from self would be that the shape, colour, taste, potency and ripening of a sprout could not be distinct from those of its creative cause, a seed. If, upon discarding the very nature it had before, a seed then becomes the nature of something other than itself, namely a sprout, how could it still have the nature of a seed? If the seed and the sprout are not of different natures, then just as the seed is not apprehended at the time of the sprout, likewise one should not apprehend the sprout. Alternatively, since they are of an identical nature, when one apprehends the sprouts one should also apprehend the seed. Therefore, it is impossible to uphold this position of production from self.

Furthermore, even the people of the world do not maintain that a seed and a sprout have the same nature because they see the effects of a seed only when the cause itself has perished. Therefore, this firm conviction that things arise from themselves is unreasonable both in terms of suchness and in terms of the world.

When one asserts production from self, the product, the producer, the act and the agent all become identical. However, they are not identical. Therefore, one should not maintain this view of production from self, because in doing so the faults explained at length both here and in Nāgārjuna's *Fundamental Stanzas on Wisdom* will follow.

2. Refutation of production from other

In contrast to the Sāṃkhya doctrine of production from self, most Buddhist schools assert the otherness of, i.e. the essential difference between a cause and its effect. If a cause and its effect were not inherently distinct from one another, there would, for them, be no grounds upon which to establish causal relationships. . . .

a. *General refutation*

If an inherently other effect could arise in dependence upon inherently other causes, then the densest gloom should be able to arise even from flames. In fact, anything should be able to be produced from anything else, because even non-productive phenomena such as space are similar in their otherness.

However, the following objection may be raised: "A thing is called with certainty an effect only because something was actually able to create it. Likewise, that which had the ability to produce it—irrespective of its being other than the effect—is the cause. Moreover, because it must be produced from a seed that belongs to the same continuum as itself and is its producer, a rice sprout, for example, will never be produced from a grain of barley."

But because they are *other* than rice sprouts, such things as barley, stamens of flowers and evergreen trees (a) are not asserted to be the producers of rice sprouts, (b) do not have the ability to produce them, (c) do not belong to the same continuum as them and (d) are not at all similar to them. Likewise, because it too is said to be *other* than a rice-sprout, a rice seed could also conceivably lack those four qualities in relation to its sprout.

Otherness should be visible, as it is between two simultaneously present people, but a sprout does not exist simultaneously with its seed because it does not exist until the seed has ceased to be evident. So when there is no otherness between them, how can a seed become other than a sprout? Thus the production of a sprout from a seed is not inherently established. And therefore, one should reject the position which states that one thing is produced from an inherently other thing.

Some may argue that just as the movements of the higher and lower pans of a balance are seen to be simultaneous, so are the production of the product and the cessation of the producer simultaneous.

Although the movement of the balance pans may be simultaneous, there is no such simultaneity in the case of a seed and a sprout. For the sprout that is in the process of being produced is *yet* to be produced and thus is not yet existent, whereas the seed that is in the process of ceasing is asserted as an entity which is *yet* to perish, and thus is still existent. So in that case how could the production of a sprout from a seed be similar to the movement of the pans of a balance? Moreover, without a sprout as the agent, i.e. that in relation to which something else is determined to be an act, the act of producing a sprout is not an entity that can be reasonably asserted.

If one considers visual consciousness to be simultaneous with its producers, namely the eyes as well as the discernments and so forth that arise in conjunction with them, then although it would be quite other than those things, what would be the need for it to arise into existence again? However, even if one now accepts that an effect must be non-existent at the time of its causes, one should still bear in mind the possible errors on this point as explained above.

If the producer is a cause that produces a product other than itself, one should consider whether the effect it produces is inherently existent, non-existent, both of these or neither. If the effect were inherently existent, what need would there be of a producer? And if it were non-existent, what could act as a cause for it? Furthermore, what could act as a cause for something both existent and non-existent? Likewise, what could act as a cause for something neither existent nor non-existent?

We assert that the cognitions of people of the world are valid as long as they remain within their own ordinary views. Therefore, one might ask, what can be achieved through stating reasons to prove this point of production from other. Surely the people of the world understand that entities arise from entities other than themselves. So what need is there for reasoning to prove the existence of production from other?

b. *A presentation of the two truths*

In order to answer the above questions it is necessary to clarify the precise extent of the validity of an ordinary person's cognition. This is achieved through explaining the notion of the two truths.

For all things two natures are apprehended: one found through seeing their reality and another found through seeing their deceptive character. The object of the mind that sees reality is suchness, i.e. the ultimate truth, and that of the mind that sees deceptive entities is the conventional truth.

Vision of deceptive entities is of two kinds: perception based upon non-defective senses and perception based on defective senses. The perceptions of those who have defective senses are regarded as mistaken in comparison with the perceptions of those with good senses. Whatever is apprehended by the perceptions of one of the six senses not adversely affected by a cause for distortion is validly cognized by the world. But it is *true* for the world alone. Likewise, in terms of the world, everything else, e.g. a magician's illusion, is posited as mistaken.

A fundamental nature—in the way it is considered by the non-Buddhist Tīrthikas, who are entirely motivated by the sleep of nescience—is utterly non-existent, even in terms of the world. So too are such things as magician's illusions considered to be horses and mirages considered to be water.

Just as the non-existent objects seen by eyes affected with cataracts do not invalidate a consciousness unaffected with cataracts, similarly a mind devoid of stainless wisdom does not invalidate a stainless mind.

Because bewilderment obstructs one from seeing the nature of phenomena, it is said to be deceived. And the Mighty One taught that whatever objects are artificially affected by it and thus appear to be true are deceptive, i.e. conventional, truths. For those who have abandoned the apprehension of inherent existence, however, things which are so artificially affected are seen as merely deceptive but not as true.

Upon searching for fallacious entities such as the hairs seen by someone through the force of his cataracts, a person with good eyesight will see no hairs at all in the place where those very hairs are supposed to be. In a similar fashion should the perception of suchness be understood here.

If the perceptions of the world were valid cognitions of reality, the world would perceive suchness. In that case what would be the need for the āryas to perceive it? What would be achieved by the ārya's path? It is also unreasonable for the foolish to be regarded as valid authorities on reality. In all respects the perceptions of the world are invalid cognitions with regard to reality. Therefore, when suchness is under consideration the views of the world cannot contradict one. Nevertheless, simply because something that is established in the world is well-known to the world, one is contradicted by the world when one denies it.

Just because they inseminated their wives, the men of the world announce, "I produced this son." And just because they sowed a seed, they think, "I planted this tree." The notion of "production from other" does not exist for the world.

At the time of the sprout there is no destruction of the seed, i.e. no severance of its generic continuity, because the sprout is not something inherently other than the seed. Nevertheless, at the time of the sprout one cannot say that the seed exists, because the sprout and the seed do not exist as one thing.

If the inherent characteristics of things were produced in dependence upon causes and conditions, by denying those characteristics in the perception of voidness the things would thereby be destroyed. Thus, the perception of voidness would become a cause for the destruction of the nature of things. But such a notion is unreasonable; therefore, inherent characteristics of things cannot exist.

One should not analyze the nominal truths of the world to see whether they are produced from self or other and so forth, because when things such as forms and feelings are subjected to such analysis, they are not found to exist in any way other than that of having the nature of suchness.

When making an ultimate analysis of suchness, production from both self and other is proved to be unreasonable. Likewise, those very proofs show such production to be unreasonable even nominally. Thus, what valid means of knowledge can establish this inherent production?

Void, i.e. deceptive, things such as reflections are well known in the world to arise in dependence upon a collection of causes and conditions. And just as perceptions are produced from these void reflections bearing their image, likewise, although all things are void of inherent characteristics, void effects are definitely produced from void causes.

Moreover, the two truths are neither inherently permanent nor subject to annihilation, because they have no inherent nature.

An action does not inherently cease. Therefore, even without having recourse to such things as a foundation consciousness (*ālaya vijñāna*), effects are still able to arise from actions. Although, in certain cases, a long time may have elapsed since the action ceased, it should be understood that a corresponding effect will still occur.

Even when they are awake, foolish men continue to have desire for objects such as beautiful women that they saw in their dreams. Similarly, effects arise from actions which have ceased and have no inherent existence.

A person with cataracts sees the appearance of non-existent hairs and the like but he does not see the appearance of other things such as hares' horns and the offspring of barren women, even though those objects are equally non-existent. Likewise, it should be understood that although actions are equally devoid of inherent existence, those that have already come to fruition will not bear fruit again, whereas those that have not yet ripened will produce effects. Therefore, it is seen that unpleasant ripening effects arise from black deeds and pleasant ripening effects from what is wholesome. However, he who perceives the lack of inherent existence of wholesome and unwholesome actions will be liberated from samsara. Thus analytical thought comes to a standstill when confronted with the relation between actions and their effects.

The doctrines that propound the existence of a foundation consciousness, the substantial existence of the person and that the aggregates alone are inherently existent, are intended by the Buddha for those who cannot at present understand the meaning of the profound truth of voidness that he explains.

Moreover, although the Buddha is free from the view of the transitory composite, i.e. the view of an inherently existent self, he still uses the terms "I" and "mine" in order to communicate the dharma to others. Likewise, although things have no inherent nature, he may teach, in a way that is to be interpreted, that they do have such a nature. For he is able, by these means, to lead others gradually to the higher view of voidness.

c. *Refutation of the Chittamātra position*

The Chittamātra, or Mind-only, philosophy was initially formulated by the Buddhist sage Asaṅga in the third century A.D. *Its principal contention is that all phenomena are in essence solely of the nature of mind. Therefore, they deny an external reality that is essentially distinct from the nature of mind. Unlike the Mādhyamika they do not interpret the concept of voidness as meaning the mere absence of inherent existence. On the contrary, they maintain that mind, as the basis of all phenomena,* must *inherently exist. . . .*

i. *Refuting the notion of an inherently existent consciousness that has no external referent*

The Chittamātra school maintains that since there are no apprehensible objects of a substance other than mind, the bodhisattva abiding in wisdom, i.e. on the sixth spiritual level, does not see any subjective apprehensions which are of a nature other than them, and fully understands the three realms of existence to be merely consciousness. Therefore, he understands suchness to be merely consciousness. Just as waves emerge from the great ocean when it is stirred by wind, so, for the Chittamātra, do dependent phenomena, which are merely consciousness, emerge through the ripening of potencies previously placed on the foundation consciousness, the common basis for the seeds of all things. Therefore, they assert that the inherently existent nature of dependent phenomena should be accepted because they are the causes, i.e. the bases, for imputedly existent things. Furthermore, dependent phenomena arise from their own potencies without there being any external apprehensibles. They inherently exist and have the nature of not being the objects of any conceptual fabrication.

But what examples are there of a mind that inherently exists without an external object? The Chittamātra might well give the example of a dreaming mind. Now, this should be given some consideration. In our tradition, just as the object of the dream is non-existent, an inherently existent mind is also non-existent when one is dreaming. In that case, the inherently existent dreaming mind that they give as their example could not exist. If, upon waking, such a mind is established as existent from one's recollection of the experience of the dream, external objects could likewise be established as existent. Because, just as one recollects "I saw . . . ," and thereby establishes the existence of that mind, likewise the recollection of an external object in the dream should establish the existence of such an object.

However, the Chittamātra would argue that since visual perception is impossible during sleep, there can be no visual-forms existent at that time. Thus only mental consciousness can be existent. But, they would add, the aspect of what appears is mistakenly conceived to be externally existent. And just as consciousness occurs without any external objects during a dream, so does it occur now during the waking period.

In the same way that for them external objects are not produced during a dream, similarly the mind too is not inherently produced. During a dream the eyes, the visual objects and the perceptions they produce are, all three of them, equally deceptive. Similarly the three components of auditory and other perceptual situations are also not inherently produced during dreams. And just as the objects, sense organs and perceptions in a dream are deceptive, so are all things deceptive now even while we are awake. The mind does not inherently exist; likewise, the experienced objects are non-inherently existent, and the sense organs too are not inherently produced. In this world, as long as people are asleep, the objects, sense-organs and perceptions of their dreams seem to them to exist in the same way as they do when they are awake. But upon waking they realize all three component elements of their dreams to have been non-existent. It is a similar experience when one wakes from the sleep of bewilderment.

A further example put forth by the Chittamātra is that of the perception of non-existent hairs that occurs for someone with cataracts. In this case they maintain that an inherently existent perception occurs there without there being an external object. But this example is also invalid. The mind of someone whose eyes are affected by cataracts does perceive non-existent hairs through the force of his cataracts, and *in terms of his mind* the visual perception of those hairs and what it is that appear to be hairs are both true, i.e. existent. But for someone who sees things clearly, they are both deceptive. If an inherently existent perception of a non-existent object could exist for a person with cataracts, by directing our vision to the place where he sees non-existent hairs, we who have no cataracts should also perceive them because the non-existence of the object is the same for both of us. However, this does not happen. Therefore, an objectless, inherently existent perception cannot exist.

The Chittamātra explain that a perception of hairs does not occur for us because we who are looking in that place have no ripe potentials on our minds to see hairs there, not because an existent object of knowledge is absent. But since an inherently existent potential does not exist, such a perception cannot be established. Moreover, it is impossible that the potential for a particular perception could be present with that perception once it has been produced.

However, there can also exist no potential for something that is not yet produced. For when a quality, in this case the perception, is non-existent, there can exist no possessor of that quality, in this case the potential. If that were not the case, it would follow that the potential for the son of a barren woman could also exist. It may be asserted that one can speak of a potential for perception by referring to a perception that is in the process of coming to be. But since an inherently existent perception that is yet to be could *never* exist, its potential would be utterly non-existent. Furthermore, it may be argued that the perception that is coming to be and the potential for it exist in mutual dependence. But in that case the wise would proclaim them to have no inherent existence at all.

If a perception in the process of coming to be emerges from the ripening of a potential deposited by another perception that has already ceased, the resultant perception will be emerging from a potential belonging to a perception inherently other than itself. According to the Chittamātra this would be so because in their successive emergence the individual instances of a continuum are inherently distinct from one another. Therefore, all things should be able to arise from all things that are other than themselves.

The Chittamātra would argue that this fault is not applicable, because although the individual instances of a continuum are inherently distinct, the instances do not possess distinct continuums, but are all instances of the same continuum. But this is something that remains to be proved, because in fact it is unreasonable for sequential entities that are inherently distinct to share the same continuum. For example, the individual qualities of John and Bill are not included in the same continuum because they are quite distinct things belonging to different people. Likewise, it is unreasonable for all entities, which by their own characteristics are distinct from one another, to belong to the same continuum.

However, Chittamātrins may attempt to clarify their position as follows: "The production of visual perception arises from its very own potential, which previously has been placed on the foundation consciousness, as soon as that potential ripens. However, in bewilderment, people recognize the physical eye-organ to be the basis that has the potential for the visual perception. In fact, there exists no eye-organ distinct from consciousness. In this world people maintain that the mind apprehends external objects because they do not understand that perceptions that arise from sense organs occur as simple "blue-awareness" and so forth from the ripening of their own seeds, which have been placed on the foundation consciousness, not from the apprehension of anything external. While dreaming, a perception bearing the aspect of a material form arises from the ripening of its own potential without there being a distinct material object present. Similarly, during this waking state too, perception exists without there being any external objects."

But just as mental perceptions that behold objects such as blue colours occur in the dream state without the assistance of an eye-organ, likewise why can they not be produced from the ripening of the seeds of mental perception for awake blind people, who also have no functioning eye-organs? If, as the Chittamātra assert, the ripening of the potential for such mental perceptions exists while one is dreaming but ceases to exist when one is awake, then just as the ripening of the potential for mental perceptions that behold forms and so forth is non-existent for the blind during the waking state, why would it be unreasonable to say that it is non-existent during the dream state? Just as the lack of eyes is not the cause for the ripening of the potential that would enable a blind person to see forms while awake, likewise in the dream state, sleep cannot be the cause for the ripening of the potential to see forms. Therefore, even in the dream state, we maintain that things such as forms are the causes for the deceptive perceptions of forms, and that dream-eyes are also causes for such perceptions.

No matter what replies the Chittamātrins give us, we see their basic theses to be equally incapable of proof. Thus the arguments of this school are dispelled. The refutation of their system is also not in contradiction with scriptural authority, because the buddhas have never declared that things inherently exist.

Furthermore, a ground covered with skeletons, which is beheld by the yogī who is following the instructions of his guru to meditate on the foul aspect of the body, is also beheld without inherent production of the object, the sense-organ and the perception, because it is taught that such a concentration is a mistaken state of attention, i.e. one that does not apprehend suchness. If that perception of skeletons inherently existed, whatever appeared to it would have to exist in the way it appeared. Thus, the perception would be a state of attention which apprehends suchness. If, according to the Chittamātra, the objects of the mind contemplating the foul are just like the objects of all sensory perception, then, should someone else who is not a yogī direct his mind to the place where the yogī is meditating, he also should perceive skeletons there. And in that case, the concentration of the yogī could no longer be considered false, i.e. as a mistaken state of attention. Moreover, a ghost's valid perception of a stream of running water's being pus would have to be equated with the invalid perceptions of someone whose eyes are affected by cataracts.

In short, the point to be understood is this: just as the objects of consciousness have no inherent existence, neither does the mind have any inherent existence.

ii. *Refuting the notion of apperception, a self-cognizing aspect of consciousness that the Chittamātra assert in order to establish inherently existent dependent entities*

If there exist such things as dependent entities that, since there are no external objects to apprehend, are separate from being apprehensions that are essentially other than external objects, and thus are void of being either apprehensibles or apprehensions that are substantially distinct from one another, what consciousness can know of their existence? One cannot say that they exist without being apprehended by consciousness, and it cannot be established, as the Chittamātra maintain, that they are experienced by themselves through apperception (*rang.rig*).

It is claimed that apperception is established from recollections that occur at a later time. But the unestablished inherently existent recollections that the Chittamātra speak of in order to prove an as yet unestablished apperception are no proof at all for apperception. For even if apperception were established, it would still be unreasonable for the memory to recollect the objects of a previous apperception. Why? Because it is maintained that the later recollection and the previous object of apperception are inherently other phenomena. This would be like the memory recollecting something one never experienced. This argument, "because they are inherently other," effectively eliminates any possibility of inclusion within one continuum, or of causal relationship.

For us a recollection does not exist as inherently other than the consciousness that previously experienced the object. Thus one simply recollects, "I saw. . . ." This is the way it conventionally occurs in the world.

Therefore, if apperception does not exist, what consciousness is there to apprehend the dependent entities asserted by the Chittamātra? Since the three components of any action—the agent, the acted upon and the act—can never be one undifferentiated entity, it is not reasonable for consciousness to apprehend itself.

Although it may be asserted that there exist things established by their own nature that are inherently unproduced and unknown to valid cognition, the existence of such things cannot be proven by any reasoning. So how can the offspring of barren women have any effect at all on those who maintain the Chittamātra position?

When dependent entities such as consciousness do not have a trace of inherent existence, how can they be the cause, i.e. the substantial basis, for conventional phenomena? By being attached like the Chittamātra to the inherent existence of mere consciousness as the substance of dependent entities, all that is commonly known in the world breaks down.

Those who remain outside the path shown by the venerable master Nāgārjuna lack the principal means for attaining peace. For they fail to uphold effectively the distinction between conventional truths and the truth of suchness. And because of this failure they will not find liberation. Why is this so? Because a flawless presentation of nominal, or conventional, truths is the means for a correct understanding of ultimate truth and thus an understanding of ultimate truth arises from those means. But those who do not know how to distinguish between these two truths enter upon an unfortunate course because of their mistaken conceptions.

We do not accept even as *conventional* truths the inherently existent dependent entities that the Chittamātra assert. However, for the sake of leading others to the goal, we sometimes say to the world that the aggregates and so forth inherently exist, whereas in fact they have no inherent existence. If conventional phenomena were non-existent for the world in the same way as they are non-existent for arhats who have discarded their aggregates and entered the peace of nirvana, then, just as we would not say that such phenomena existed for those arhats, we would also not say that they existed for the world. If the Chittamātra think that they are not contradicted by the world, let them go and deny to the people of the world conventionally accepted phenomena such as external existence. Let us see them and the world argue on these points. After this debate we shall rely upon whoever shows himself to be the stronger.

iii. *The word "only" in the term "Mind-only" (Chittamātra) does not deny the existence of external phenomena*

The bodhisattva on the Approach who is nearing the sphere of reality is said to understand the three worlds to be consciousness, i.e. mind, only. He has realized that a permanent self is not the creator of the world and therefore now understands mind alone to be the creator.

In order to further develop the minds of the intelligent, the Omniscient One made, in the *Descent into Laṅkā Sutra*, certain adamantine proclamations destroying the high mountain peaks of the non-Buddhists' wrong views. These statements serve to clarify the meaning he intended with the notion "mind-only." In some of their treatises, the non-Buddhists claim that such things as a person are the creator of the aggregates and so forth. It was upon seeing that such things are not the creator that the Conqueror declared mind alone to be the creator of the world.

Just as the Awakened One (Buddha) is so called from his being awakened to suchness, likewise, while meaning that between mind and form only mind is of principal importance, the notion "mind-only" is taught to the world in some sutras. But it is not the aim of those sutras to deny thereby the external existence of form and to assert that mind alone is inherently existent. According to the Chittamātra, in the *Ten Grounds Sutra* the Buddha denies the existence of external forms on the basis of his understanding that the three worlds are only inherently existent mind. If this were so, why, in the same sutra, does the Magnanimous One go on to say that mind is produced from bewilderment and actions and is thus dependently and not inherently existent? Moreover, the mind itself creates living beings and constructs the various worlds in which they live. It is also taught that every form of life is produced from actions; but without the mind those actions would not exist. Indeed form exists; but unlike mind, it does not exist as the creator of life. Therefore, although we deny that there is a creator other than mind, we do not deny that external forms exist.

For those who dwell amidst the realities of the world, *all* the five aggregates, both mental and physical, exist because they are commonly known to the world. But for the yogī who assents to what appears to the wisdom that directly cognizes suchness, *none* of the five aggregates occur. Therefore, if one asserts the non-existence of external forms, one should not maintain that mind exists; and if one asserts the existence of mind, one should not maintain that external forms are non-existent. In the *Perfection of Wisdom Sutras* the Buddha denied equally the inherent existence of mind *and* form, whereas in the *Abhidharma* he affirmed equally the characteristics of each. Even were these two levels of truth to perish, the substantially existent dependent entities of the Cittamātra would not be established because they would still be refuted by our previous arguments. Therefore, as has been progressively explained above, one should understand that primordially things are ultimately unproduced, although in terms of worldly convention they are produced.

Furthermore, it is said in the *Descent into Laṅkā Sutra* that externally appearing entities do not exist; rather, it is the mind that appears as all those diverse forms. But this is taught in order to turn away from forms those who are extremely attached to them. The meaning of the statement is to be interpreted. Such passages as this were not only said by the Teacher to be of an interpretative meaning, but can be proved to be such by reasoning. Moreover, this passage makes it clear that other sutras which take a similar position are also to be interpreted and not taken literally.

The buddhas have also said that if the non-existence of externally existent objects of consciousness is taught first, it will be easier subsequently to discover the absence of inherently existent consciousness. Thus, first externally existent objects of consciousness should be negated because, if their non-existence is understood, the refutation of consciousness, i.e. the understanding of its selflessness, can be easily realized.

Hence one should understand that some statements are to be interpreted whereas others are to be taken literally. Sutras whose subject matter deals with what is not actually suchness are said to be of interpretative meaning; having understood them to be so we should interpret them accordingly. Sutras whose subject matter deals explicitly with voidness are said to be of definitive meaning and thus we should take them literally.

3. Refutation of production from both self and other

Production from both self and other together is not something reasonable because the faults of production from self or other individually, which we explained above, would be just as applicable to production from self and other together. Such a mode of production neither exists in the world nor can be asserted as suchness for the simple reason that neither production from self nor from other can be individually established.

4. Refutation of the Hedonist (Chārvāka) doctrine of production from no cause

If it were the case that things are produced from no cause at all, all things could always be produced from anything else. In that case people in the world would not have to undergo the many hardships of gathering seeds and so forth in order to produce their crops. If living beings were devoid of causes they would be simply inapprehensible, like the scent and the colour of a sky-lotus. But because these extremely diverse beings *are* apprehensible, one should understand them to be produced from their own causes, just as one's own perception of blueness, for example, arises in dependence upon a blue patch of colour.

If the four material elements of earth, water, fire and air do not have the nature of being the ultimate suchness—i.e. the nature ascribed to them in the Chārvāka scriptures and thus the way that the Chārvākas perceive them—how, when there exists such darkness in the mind concerning such gross things, can the Chārvākas correctly understand the very subtle phenomenon of future lives? Moreover, when they deny the existence of future lives, they have a mistaken understanding of the nature of a knowable phenomenon, because they take the physical body as the correlate upon the basis of which they put forth such views. This is likewise the case when they assert the inherently existent nature of the elements. However, we have already explained how the elements have no inherent existence, for we have now refuted in general production from self, from other, from both self and other together and from no cause. Thus the elements, although they were not specifically mentioned above, can be understood to have no inherent existence.

B. Concluding Remarks

Since they are not produced from self, from other, from both self and other and are not independent of any causes, all things are devoid of inherent existence.

The people of the world are subject to great bewilderment as dense as a mass of clouds, hence the nature of objects appears to them in a mistaken way. Through the force of their cataracts some people mistakenly see hairs where in fact there are none, two moons in the sky, and imaginary peacock feathers, flies and so forth. Similarly, through the power of the fallacious character of bewilderment, ordinary unwise people cognize a variety of conditioned phenomena with their minds. When the Buddha taught that formative actions arise in dependence upon bewildered ignorance but do not occur without that bewilderment, it was certainly intended that this be so understood only by the unwise. But the wise, whose noble sun-like minds dispel the dense gloom of ignorance, upon hearing such teachings only experience the voidness of inherent existence of conditioned phenomena and thereby are liberated from samsara.

It might be thought that if things did not ultimately, i.e. inherently, exist, they could not exist conventionally either, like the son of a barren woman. Therefore, it may be concluded, they must exist inherently, by their own nature.

To begin with one should, for a while, argue only with those who have cataracts: "Since the hairs which appear to you are unproduced, why do you not also see sons of barren women, for they too are unproduced?" Only later should one bring such analysis to bear on the condition of those whose perceptions are distorted by the cataracts of ignorance. One should ask of them: "If you can see such unproduced things as houses in your dreams, cities of gandharvas, the water of a mirage, the illusory creations of a magician and a face in a reflection, why do you say that it is unreasonable to see the son of a barren woman, which is as nonexistent as them?" Therefore, although forms and so forth are likewise unproduced, unlike the son of a barren woman they are not invisible to the people of the world. Hence the objection raised above — that if things did not ultimately exist they could not be seen even conventionally, like the son of a barren woman — is not justified.

The inherent production of the son of a barren woman exists neither ultimately nor for the world, i.e. conventionally. Similarly, all things are not inherently produced either ultimately or for the world. Therefore, the Teacher has said that all phenomena are pacified from the very beginning, they lack inherent production and by their very nature are completely beyond sorrow (lit: in nirvana). Hence inherent production never takes place. Things such as jugs do not ultimately exist yet they are well known to the world and thus conventionally exist. All things in fact exist in this way; thus it does not follow that just because they are ultimately non-existent they are similar to the offspring of barren women.

Things are not produced without causes, nor from causes such as Ishvara, nor from self, other, or both self and other together. Therefore, they can be produced only *dependently.* And since things arise only dependently, these conceptions that they arise from self, other and so forth are unable to understand the matter correctly. Hence the entire fabric of evil views is cut to pieces by the reasoning of dependent arising. Only if things are apprehended as inherently existent do such conceptions come about. But we have made a thorough analysis which has determined how things do *not* inherently exist. Thus when an apprehension of inherently existent things is absent, those conceptions will not occur, as, for example, without fuel there will be no fire.

Ordinary beings, i.e. those who do not understand voidness, are bound by their extreme conceptions, but the yogī who has gained a nonconceptual insight into voidness is thereby liberated. Therefore, the wise have taught that the goal of the Mādhyamaka analysis is a reversal of conception that comes about through an utter negation of whatever is apprehended by extreme conceptions. Nāgārjuna did not compose his treatises on Mādhyamaka because of an attachment to logical analysis and polemic. He taught suchness in order to lead others to liberation. However, there is no contradiction if, in explaining suchness, the ideas expounded in the texts of others are refuted through logical analysis and argument. Nevertheless, any attachment to one's own views and likewise any aversion to the views of others are simply conceptions that keep one in bondage. Therefore, dispel such attachment and anger and use analysis for the swift attainment of liberation.

3 THE SELFLESSNESS OF THE PERSON

Having refuted the notion of inherent existence in general, Chandrakīrti now turns his attention to an analysis of the person in particular. It is the understanding of the voidness of inherent existence of the person that has the greatest initial effect in uprooting unwholesome modes of thought and behaviour.

The yogī perceives that all the disturbing conceptions and negative aspects of existence arise from the view of the transitory composite . . . i.e. the disturbing conception of an inherently existent I and mine. Upon understanding the self to be an objective referent of this view, he proceeds to negate such an inherently existent self.

A. Refutation of an Inherently Existent "I"

1. *Refutation of the self posited by non-Buddhists to be essentially distinct from the aggregates*

The non-Buddhist Sāṃkhya school considers the self to be the experiencer of pleasure and pain, something permanent, not a creator, devoid of the qualities, (i.e. *sattva, rajaḥ* and *tamaḥ*) and inactive. The other non-Buddhist traditions, such as the Vaisheshika school, differ from the Sāṃkhya school as well as from one another according to various slight distinctions they make concerning the specific qualities of the self.

However, such a self is non-existent because it is unproduced, like the son of a barren woman. It is also unreasonable for it to be the basis for the innate apprehension of I. Even conventionally it cannot be asserted to exist. All the characteristics of that self, which are described by the non-Buddhists in their various scriptures, are refuted by reason of their non-production, a quality that they themselves attribute to the self. Hence, all those characteristics are non-existent. Therefore, there exists no self that is essentially other than the aggregates because, apart from apprehensions of the aggregates, no apprehension of an independent self can be established. Furthermore, such a self is not even asserted as the basis, i.e. the referent, of the world's innate apprehension of I because the world still has a view of the self even though it does not know of the self posited by non-Buddhist philosophers. Likewise, beings who have spent many aeons as animals also do not behold an unproduced and permanent self, although it is clear that they are involved in the apprehension of a self-identity. Thus there can be no self at all existing as something other than the aggregates.

2. *Refutation of certain Buddhist schools who regard the aggregates to be the self*

Some Buddhists maintain that because the self is not established as essentially other than the aggregates, the aggregates alone must be the referent for the view of the self, i.e. the view of the transitory composite. Certain adherents of the Sammitīya school, for example, assert all five aggregates to be the basis, i.e. the referent, for the view of the self, whereas other adherents of this school assert the mind alone to be the self.

But, if the aggregates were the self, since they are many, one person would have many selves. Furthermore, since the aggregates are substances, the self too would have to be a substance. In that case, the view of the transitory composite would apprehend a substance and therefore, just like a perception of blue or yellow, it would not be mistaken. Moreover, upon passing into the state of non-residual nirvana, the self would definitely cease, because it is asserted by some Buddhist schools that at this time the five aggregates cease. But at the moments prior to the attainment of nirvana the self would inherently arise and perish just like the aggregates. Furthermore, upon perishing the agent would cease to exist and therefore there would be no basis upon which the impressions of an action could remain. In that case there could be no results of an action. Alternatively, the results of an action accumulated by one person would be experienced by someone else.

One may reply that there is no contradiction here as long as it is asserted that ultimately the individual instances exist in one continuum. But in our previous analyses we explained the logical faults in the notion of such a continuum. Therefore, it is unreasonable to assert that the aggregates or the mind are the self.

Furthermore, the Buddha refused to comment on certain questions such as, "Does the world have an end?" Therefore, to assert that the aggregates are the self would imply that the Buddha committed himself on certain points (such as whether the tathāgata continues after death or not) when in fact he did not.

In the view of these Buddhists, a yogī who directly perceives the absence of a self would definitely perceive the absence of things, i.e. the aggregates, too. However, they themselves would not accept this. They would reply that when he perceived the absence of a self, he rejected, i.e. perceived the absence of, a *permanent* self. Thus it would follow that the mind and the aggregates could not be the self. Hence, in their view, a yogī who perceived the absence of a self did not understand the suchness of such things as forms. Therefore, he would apprehend forms and so forth as inherently existent. In that case, attachment towards those things could still occur because he would lack an understanding of their nature.

It may be asserted that the aggregates are the self because the Teacher himself taught that the aggregates are the self. However, in those instances the Buddha was denying that there is a self that is essentially other than the aggregates because, in other sutras, he stated that form and the other aggregates are *not* self. He declared quite clearly that forms and feelings are not the self; neither are discernments, formative elements or consciousness. Therefore, we can conclude that he did not assert the aggregates to be the self.

It might be argued that when the aggregates are described as the self, what is actually meant is that the *collection* of the aggregates is the self, not the individual aggregates themselves. However, the self is also spoken of as the "master," the "controller" and the "witness"—but a mere collection can be neither a master, controller nor witness, because it has no substantial existence. Therefore, the self cannot be the collection of the aggregates.

In this case, it would be like saying that the piled-up collection of the parts of a cart could be the cart itself. This would follow since a cart and the self would be similar in their being posited as the collection of their parts.

Moreover, in some sutras it is taught that the self is imputed in *dependence upon* the collection of the aggregates. Therefore, the mere collection of the aggregates cannot be the self.

Some would say that the shape of the aggregates is the self. In that case one could only call the material elements the self, because they alone have shape; the collection of the mental elements could not be posited as the self, because they are devoid of any shape.

It is unreasonable for the grasper, i.e. the self, to be something which is identical with what it grasps, i.e. the aggregates. In that case the agent and what is acted upon would become identical. This would be equivalent to identifying a potter with his pot. It would be fallacious then to imagine that the agent, i.e. the self, is non-existent, whereas what is acted upon, i.e. the aggregates, exists: if there is no agent, there can also be nothing that is acted upon.

In the *Meeting of Father and Son Sutra* the Buddha taught clearly that the self is dependent upon the six elements—earth, water, fire, air, consciousness and space—and the six bases—the sense fields of visual, auditory, olfactory, gustatory, tactile and mental contact. Likewise he stated that the self is imputed in dependence upon the phenomena of the mind and the mental events, which are apprehended as the basis for that imputation. Therefore, the self is neither the various elements individually nor their mere collection. And the mind that instinctively apprehends I does *not* refer to them.

Some maintain that when the lack of self is understood one merely rejects, i.e. perceives the lack of, a permanent self. But they do not assert that this permanent self is the basis for the innate apprehension of I. Therefore, it is most peculiar to say that this knowledge of the lack of a permanent self can uproot the primordial view of self. Imagine a frightened person who has noticed a snake living in a hole in the wall of his house. Others would simply laugh at him if he tried to dispel his fear of the snake by thinking, "There is no elephant in my house."

3. *Refutation of other misconceptions concerning the nature of the relationship between the self and the aggregates*

The self does not exist in inherent dependence upon the aggregates and neither do the aggregates exist in inherent dependence upon the self. Only if the self and the aggregates were essentially other could such conceptions be correct. But because such an inherent otherness does not exist, these conceptions are mistaken. The self is not asserted to inherently possess form because it does not exist as either inherently identical with or distinct from form. Therefore, there exists no inherent relationship of possession between the self and the aggregates. A person can possess something essentially other than himself, such as a cow, and he can possess something that is not essentially other than himself, such as form. But it is impossible for the self inherently to possess form, because it is neither identical with nor other than form.

Therefore, form is not the self; the self does not inherently possess form; the self does not inherently exist in form; and form does not inherently exist in the self. Likewise, these four aspects of the view of the transitory composite should be understood with regard to the other four aggregates. Thus we assert twenty views of the self. The thunderbolt of understanding selflessness shatters the mountain of views about the self. And together with the view of the self are destroyed these twenty high peaks that rise up out of the huge mountain of the view of the transitory composite.

4. *Refutation of the notion of a substantially existent self that is neither identical with nor other than the aggregates*

Some adherents of the Saṃmitīya school assert the person, i.e. the self, to be substantially existent yet indescribable. For them it cannot be spoken of as either identical with or other than the aggregates, neither permanent nor impermanent and so forth. However, they also assert it to be an object known by the six senses, as well as the basis for the apprehension of I.

Just as one does not regard the mind's relation to the body as indescribable, it is incomprehensible how the relation between any substantially existent things can be indescribable. If the self were substantially existent, then being something just like the mind it could not be indescribable in relation to the aggregates. It would follow for these Saṃmitīyas that a jug, the nature of which they regard as not being a self-sufficient thing, would be indescribable in relation to its parts such as its form. Therefore, they should not regard this self, which they claim to be indescribable in relation to the aggregates, as existing by its own nature. They assert that consciousness is not other than itself but that it is something other than such things as form. Thus they definitely see these two aspects of identity and difference among things. Therefore, the self they posit cannot exist substantially because it is devoid of the qualities of being identical or different that characterize all things.

5. *Showing how the self is merely a dependent imputation by referring to the analogy of the cart*

Hence the basis for the apprehension of I is not something inherently existent. The self is neither essentially other than the aggregates nor of the nature of the aggregates. It is not the basis of the aggregates nor does it inherently possess them. Rather, the self is established in dependence upon the aggregates. In this respect it is similar to a cart, for a cart is not asserted either (1) to be essentially other than its parts, or (2) to be identical with them, or (3) inherently to possess them, or (4) to be inherently dependent upon them, or (5) to be the basis upon which they inherently depend, or (6) to be the mere collection of them, or (7) to be their shape.

If the mere collection of the parts were the cart, the collection of the same parts placed in a heap should also be the cart.

Some Buddhist schools maintain that not the cart but the collection of its parts is the part-bearer. But if the part-bearer is not the cart, the parts will also not be it. Therefore, it is also unreasonable for the mere shape, as well as for the mere collection of the parts, to be the cart.

However, some people do assert that the mere shape of the parts is the cart. First, let us assume that the shape of the individual parts prior to the assemblage of the cart exists in the same way as it does when the parts are subsequently assembled into a cart. Since the shape of the parts is not the cart when the parts are dispersed, there is no reason for them to be the cart when they are assembled. Now, if when assembled as a cart, the wheels and so forth have a shape different from the shape they had before, such a difference should be observable visually. However, it is not. Therefore, the mere shape of the individual parts cannot be the cart. According to such people, a substantially existent collection does not exist in the slightest. Hence for them the shape cannot be imputed upon the basis of the collection of the parts, because they believe that a basis for imputation must be substantially existent. So how, when it depends upon something that has no substantial existence, could the shape which is posited as the cart even be seen?

According to their assertion of the non-substantial existence of the collection, they should understand that *all* effects with an untrue nature are produced in dependence upon causes which are also untrue. It is likewise unreasonable to maintain, as many Buddhist schools do, that, since the qualities of form and so forth when placed in a particular way constitute the jug, a perception of a jug occurs with regard to them. Furthermore, since their lack of inherent *production* has now been explained, forms and so forth must also lack inherent *existence*. For this reason too it is unreasonable for substantially existent jugs to be the shape of the forms and so forth which are their parts.

Indeed, through this seven-fold analysis, the cart is found to be established neither ultimately nor in terms of worldly convention. However, *without* such analysis it is, in accordance with the conventions of the world, imputed in dependence upon its parts.

In the world it is acknowledged that a cart *has* parts and *has* pieces. It is likewise said that a cart *possesses* those parts. Furthermore, in relation to the bodies and minds that they possess, people are also established as possessors. One should not destroy these conventional phenomena well known in the world.

Something which cannot be found through the seven-fold analysis cannot be said to exist inherently. Thus the yogī does not find the very existence of the cart and in this way he easily penetrates suchness. However, it should be asserted here that, without analysis, the cart *is* established.

If the cart does not inherently exist, the part-possessor is not inherently existent. Therefore, the parts too cannot inherently exist. If, for example, the cart were burned, its parts would also cease to exist. Likewise, when the inherent existence of the part-possessor is burned away by the mental fire of wisdom, so is the inherent existence of the parts consumed.

Similarly, on the basis of what is well known in the world, we maintain that the self too depends upon the aggregates, the elements and the six sense-fields and, just like the cart, is the possessor of its parts. In this case the aggregates and so forth, which are possessed, are the objects of the act of possession, and self is the agent of possession.

Once the self has been posited as a dependent imputation it cannot be established as the basis for any extreme conceptions. Thus such conceptions are easily dismissed. The self is not an inherently existent thing. Therefore, it is neither inherently stable nor unstable, neither inherently produced nor destroyed, neither inherently identical with nor distinct from the aggregates, and neither inherently permanent nor impermanent and so forth.

The self in reference to which the mind that apprehends I constantly arises in sentient beings and in reference to whose possessions the mind that apprehends mine occurs is, in terms of what is well known and unanalyzed, established by bewilderment, not by its own intrinsic nature.

B. Refutation of an Inherently Existent Mine

There exist no objects of action for an agent who does not exist. Therefore, an inherently existent mine cannot exist when there is no inherently existent self. Hence the yogī who beholds the voidness of an inherently existent self and mine is liberated from samsara.

C. Concluding Remarks

Things such as jugs, cloth, tents, armies, forests, rosaries, trees, houses, trolleys and guest-houses should be understood to exist in the way they are commonly spoken of by people because the Buddha did not argue with the world over these matters. Furthermore, by applying the analysis of the cart to part-possessors and their parts, quality-possessors and their qualities, people with attachment and their desires, bases of characteristics and their characteristics and fire and the fuel it burns, one finds that they do not exist in any of the seven ways. But as long as they are not subjected to such analysis, they do exist in another way: namely, in terms of their being well known to the world.

Only if a cause has produced a product can it be a cause. But if a result has not been produced, since production is lacking there can be no causes for it. Likewise for results: they can only be produced when their causes exist. Therefore, cause and result are *mutually* dependent. Now, if they inherently existed, which would arise in dependence upon the other? And which would precede the other? If causes inherently produced results, would they be contiguous with their results or not? If they were contiguous with the results they produced, cause and result would become one identical force. One would then be unable to distinguish between them, because the producer and its result would no longer be distinct. But, on the other hand, if they were distinct and not contiguous, that which was asserted to be the cause for a particular result would really be no different from whatever else was not its cause. There are no other ways to conceive of this phenomenon once these two alternatives have been eliminated. Therefore, an inherently existent cause could not produce any results. Hence, what are called "results" have no inherent existence and, since there is no reason for positing something as a cause when it has produced no results, causes too have no inherent existence. Both cause and result are similar to a magician's illusion in their not being inherently produced. Therefore, for us these problems of contiguity and so forth do not arise. We simply accept as existent whatever things are well known in the world.

However, the following argument may be raised: "But what about the refutation stated above? Does it effect its refutation through being contiguous with what it refutes or not? Do not exactly the same faults apply to the Mādhyamikas themselves? In pronouncing their refutations they only destroy their own position. Thus they are unable to refute the positions of others that they claim to refute. With fallacious arguments, the consequences of which are equally applicable to their own pronouncements, they quite illogically deny and negate everything. Therefore, no wise or saintly people would ever assert what they do. Since they have no position of their own, they are merely engaged in sophistry."*

This objection, "Does the refutation effect its refutation through being contiguous with what it refutes or not?" would only be applicable to someone who has a definite position, i.e. someone who asserts inherent existence. But we do not have such a position. It is therefore impossible to ascribe such logical consequences to us.

At the time of an eclipse one can observe what is happening to the shape of the sun by looking at its reflection. Yet although it is illogical to say that the sun and its reflection are either contiguous or not contiguous, nevertheless, merely through the power of convention one can affirm that the reflection arises in dependence upon the sun. Even though a reflection is not true it can still establish whether or not one's face is clean. Thus it is capable of performing a function. Likewise here, although our reasoning may lack any inherent validity, it is seen to be capable of cleaning the face of wisdom. One should recognize that it can lead to an understanding of what we are trying to prove: the lack of any inherent nature.

The logical objections of contiguity and so forth would be applicable to us only if we were to maintain that the nature of the reasoning—that which gives rise to the understanding of what is proved—and the nature of that which is actually understood—that which is proved—were inherently existent. But we assert that they have no inherent existence. Therefore, the objections our critics make against us are utterly in vain.

One can very easily gain the understanding that all things lack an inher-

---

*Here, one engaged in sophistry is defined as someone who takes no position of his own and only criticizes the positions of others.

ent thingness. But for others, such as ourselves, a similar comprehension of an inherent nature in things is not at all easy to gain for the simple reason that such an inherent nature is unfindable. So why, when the people of the world request one's help, should one entangle them in a web of harmful ideation?

First one should understand these additional refutations of the Realist position given above. Having done so one should then reject the arguments that we stated in order to present the answers that the opponents gave to our objections of contiguity and so forth. By no means are we merely engaged in sophistry; the additional refutations stated above are for the sake of our opponents' own understanding.

4 THE DIVISIONS OF VOIDNESS

It must be emphasized that in classifying voidness the author is not speaking of qualitatively different forms of voidness but of different bases, i.e. internal entities, external entities etc., to which the characteristic of voidness applies. Voidness itself, i.e. the lack of inherent existence, does not differ in quality from one object to another.

In order to lead beings of different capacities to liberation, the Buddha taught two kinds of selflessness: the selflessness of phenomena and the selflessness of persons. The Teacher further divided these two selflessnesses into many different kinds in accordance with the varied inclinations of his disciples. In an extensive classification he spoke of sixteen voidnesses; in a more concise form he spoke of just four. He also regarded these voidnesses as the great vehicle.

A. The Sixteen Voidnesses

1. *The voidness of internal entities*

The eye is void of being an inherently existent eye because its very nature is that of being void of inherent existence. The ears, the nose, the tongue, the body and the mind are also described in a similar way. All these things are void because ultimately they neither remain fixed and static nor do they perish. This very lack of inherent existence of the six senses is regarded as the voidness of internal entities.

2. *The voidness of external entities*

Visual-forms are void of being inherently existent visual-forms because their very nature is that of being void. Sounds, smells, tastes, tactile sensations and mental phenomena should be understood in the same way. The very lack of inherent existence of visual-forms and so forth is asserted to be the voidness of external entities.

3. *The voidness of the internal and external*

The lack of inherent existence of those entities that are both internal and external, such as the gross physical bases of the senses, is the voidness of the internal and external.

4. *The voidness of voidness*
The wise call the lack of inherent existence of such phenomena voidness. But they also maintain that this voidness too is void of being an inherently existent voidness. This voidness of the so-called voidness is regarded as the voidness of voidness. The Buddha spoke of this in order to counteract the tendency of the mind to apprehend voidness as inherently existent.

5. *The voidness of immensity*
The directions are immense because they pervade every single physical world as well as the sentient beings who abide there and because, by taking their immeasurability as an example, the four immeasurable states of love and so forth are thus regarded as boundless. Therefore, the voidness of inherent existence of these ten directions is the voidness of immensity. It is taught in order to counteract the tendency of apprehending the directions as inherently immense.

6. *The voidness of the ultimate*
Here the ultimate means nirvana because nirvana is the supreme necessity. Thus the voidness of inherent existence of nirvana is the voidness of the ultimate. The Knower of the Ultimate, i.e. the Buddha, likewise taught the voidness of the ultimate in order to counteract the tendency of the mind to apprehend nirvana as an inherently existent thing.

7. *The voidness of the conditioned*
The three worlds are declared to be conditioned because they arise from causal conditions. And their voidness of inherent existence is taught as the voidness of the conditioned.

8. *The voidness of the unconditioned*
Phenomena that lack production—i.e. the quality of changing into something else once they have come into existence—and impermanence—i.e. destructibility—are unconditioned. Their voidness of inherent existence is the voidness of the unconditioned.

9. *The voidness of that which is beyond extremes*
Whatever lacks the extremes of permanence and annihilation is described as being beyond extremes. Its mere voidness of inherent existence is called the voidness of that which is beyond extremes.

10. *The voidness of that which has neither beginning nor end*
Samsara is described as having neither beginning nor end because it has no first beginning and no final end. The scriptures declare that the sheer absence of inherent existence of this state of conditioned existence—which is like a dream because it lacks any inherent coming or going—is the voidness of that which has neither beginning nor end.

11. *The voidness of that which is not to be discarded*
To discard something means to cast it away or to forsake it, whereas not to discard something means not to give it up. Here it refers to the Mahāyāna: that which is not to be discarded under any circumstances. The voidness that is the very lack of inherent existence of that which is not to be discarded is said to be the voidness of that which is not to be discarded because such voidness is its very nature.

12. *The voidness of a phenomenon's own nature*
The very essence, i.e. the suchness, of conditioned phenomena is said to be their very own nature because this very essence of theirs is not something that has been created by either the shrāvakas, the pratyekabuddhas, the bodhisattvas or the tathāgatas. Its voidness of inherent existence is thus the voidness of a phenomenon's own nature.

13. *The voidness of all phenomena*
"All phenomena" refers to the eighteen elements, the six contacts, the six feelings that arise from those contacts and all other material and immaterial, conditioned and unconditioned phenomena. The voidness that is the absence of inherent existence of all these phenomena is the voidness of all phenomena.

14. *The voidness of defining characteristics*
The lack of inherent thingness of such defining characteristics as something's being fit to be form is the voidness of defining characteristics.

Form has the defining characteristic of being fit to be form; feeling has the nature of experiencing; discernment apprehends the characteristics of things; the formative elements actually constitute conditioned phenomena; consciousness has the defining characteristic of cognizing particular objects; the aggregates have the defining characteristic of unsatisfactoriness; and the nature of the elements is likened to that of a poisonous snake. The Buddha taught that the sense-fields are the very gateways to birth. And whatever arises dependently has the defining characteristics of being formed and compounded by causes and conditions.

The six perfections have the following defining characteristics: the perfection of generosity is the intention to give away; moral discipline is a state of being untormented by disturbing conceptions; patience is a state of not being angry; enthusiasm is a state devoid of the unwholesome; absorption gathers the attention to one point; and wisdom is a state of non-attachment. The Omniscient One taught that the defining characteristic of the four absorptions, the four immeasurable states and likewise the four formless states of absorption is that of imperturbability. The thirty-seven facets of enlightenment have the defining characteristic of causing one definitely to go forth to liberation. The first of the three doors to liberation, voidness, has the defining characteristic of absence, because it is not defiled by the stains of the conceptual apprehension of inherent existence. The second door, signlessness, is sheer tranquility; and the defining characteristic of the third door, wishlessness, is the lack of suffering and bewilderment. The defining characteristic of the eight forms of liberation is that of causing total freedom from the obstructions to absorption.

The ten powers of the Buddha have the nature of utter certainty, and the four states of fearlessness that the Lord possesses are of the nature of extreme firmness. His perfect knowledge of individual phenomena, i.e. of dharmas, meanings, words and confident speech, has the defining characteristic of unapproachability. His direct bestowal of benefit to the world is what is known as his great love; his affording complete protection to those who suffer is his great compassion; his great joy is his being supremely joyful; and his great equanimity has the defining characteristic of being unmixed with either attachment or hatred. What are asserted as the eighteen unmixed qualities of the Buddha have the defining characteristic of unassailability, because the Teacher can never be assailed by confusion and so forth. The wisdom of omniscience is regarded as bearing the defining characteristic of being a direct perception of all phenomena. All cognitions other than it are not called direct perceptions of all phenomena because they have only a partial apprehension of their objects.

Thus the voidness of defining characteristics is the voidness of just the inherent existence of the defining characteristics of all conditioned and unconditioned phenomena.

15. *The voidness of the non-apprehensible*

The three times do not inherently exist because the present does not remain, the past is gone and the future has not yet come. In whichever of these three respects they are not apprehended, in that respect each of the three times is said to be non-apprehensible. Since the non-apprehensible neither remains fixed and static nor perishes, its sheer absence of an inherent nature is the voidness of the non-apprehensible.

16. *The voidness of non-things*

Because things arise from causes and conditions they lack the nature of being inherently compounded. Therefore they can be called non-things. Thus the voidness of inherent existence of what is compounded is the voidness of non-things.

B. The Four Voidnesses

1. *The voidness of things*

Generally speaking, the term "things" simply denotes the five aggregates. Their voidness of inherent existence is explained as the voidness of things.

2. *The voidness of non-things*

In brief, the term "non-things" denotes all unconditioned phenomena. The voidness of inherent existence of those very non-things is said to be the voidness of non-things.

3. *The voidness of nature*
The nature of phenomena, i.e. their suchness, is said to be their nature because it is not created by anyone. The lack of an inherent essence in this nature is the voidness of nature.

4. *The voidness that is the other nature*
Whether buddhas appear in the world or not, the natural voidness of all things is proclaimed to be their other, i.e. supreme or transcendent, nature. The perfect end, i.e. the nirvana which is the exhaustion of samsara, and suchness are said to constitute the voidness that is the other nature.

These different aspects of voidness as they have been explained here were originally proclaimed in the *Perfection of Wisdom Sutras.*

C. Conclusion

With rays of wisdom emerging from such analyses the bodhisattva on the sixth spiritual level creates a brilliant light that enables him to understand the primordial lack of inherent production of the three realms of existence as clearly as he would see a fresh olive resting in the palm of his hand. Thus in terms of conventional truth he proceeds towards cessation. But although his thought is constantly directed towards cessation, his compassion for the protectorless world continues to develop. Subsequently his mind will come to outshine even the shrāvakas, who are born from the Sugata's speech, as well as all the pratyekabuddhas. This king of swans with his broad white outstretched wings of the paths of conventional and ultimate truth soars ahead of the swans of ordinary beings. Through the force of the mighty winds of virtue he flies to the magnificent shores of the ocean of buddha-qualities.

III
Tsong Khapa: The Chief Reason for Negation of Ultimate Status*

1. DESCRIPTION OF THE CHIEF REASON

Which does this system take to be the chief reason negating the ultimate status of things?

Chandrakīrti states, in the *Introduction Commentary*: "Nāgārjuna did not execute the analyses in the *Treatise* out of a love for debate, but taught the

*Reprinted with permission from Robert A.F. Thurman, *Tsong Khapa's Speech of Gold* in "The Essence of True Eloquence" (Princeton: Princeton University Press, 1984).

facts in order to liberate (living beings)." All analytical reasonings in the *Wisdom* have as their sole aim the attainment of liberation by living beings. Living beings are chained in cyclic life by their habitual adherence to personal and objective selves. And since the chief cause of bondage is this habitual adherence to the two selves, in the person, object for the arisal of the thought "I," and in the things that (constitute) his process (of existence), those two are the chief bases of rational negation of habitual selfhood. Therefore, (all) reasonings are categorized as negating the two selves.

In the passage in the *Introduction Commentary* where the reasonings determining reality in the *Introduction* are categorized as determining the two selflessnesses, Chandra states that the reasonings refuting four-extreme-production are demonstrations of objective selflessness. He also states that the Master (Nāgārjuna), in beginning (the *Wisdom*) with "not from self, not from other . . . etc.," demonstrated with reasoning only the equality of the non-production of all things, from among the ten equalities stated in the *Ten Stages* (to be contemplated) in entering the sixth stage, thinking that the other (nine) equalities were easier to demonstrate. Therefore, the chief reasoning proving the selflessness of things is the reasoning negating four-extreme-production.

Furthermore, this reasoning proving (selflessness) boils down to the cutter of the whole trap of false views, the royal reason of relativity itself. For, the very fact of the inter-relative occurrence of inner things such as mental creations and outer things such as sprouts, dependent on causes and conditions such as misknowledge and seeds, (corroborates) the negations "their production is empty with reference to any intrinsically identifiable intrinsic reality" and "they are not produced from self, other, both, or neither." As Chandra states in the *Introduction*:

> Things will never be produced from self, other, or both, or from a creator, or causelessly (randomly); thus, they are produced relatively. Thus, since things occur relatively these constructs cannot (withstand) analysis, and hence this reason of relativity cuts open the whole network of bad views.

As for the chief reasoning negating personal self, Chandra states in the *Introduction:*

> While that (self) will never be established, either ultimately or conventionally, via seven modes, still, through social conventions without analysis, it is designated depending on its components.

Although no chariot is found when sought in seven ways, as identical with its components, different from them, possessing them, mutually dependent in two ways (with them), the mere composite (of them), or as the structure of their composite, it still is presented as designatively existent, designated depending on its components. In the same way, the person is presented. (He also) states that very (reasoning) to be the method for the easy finding of the view of the profound, and hence those reasonings should be acknowledged as the chief reasonings negating personal self.

Chandra also states in the *Introduction*:

> "How could it exist, if not in these seven ways?" The yogi finds no existence of this (self), and thereby easily penetrates reality as well—so here its status should thus be acknowledged.

Since this (example of the chariot) is easier to understand at first than the non-discovery of the person when seeking in seven ways, as well as its designative status dependent on its aggregates, such is the sequence in practice. And this (reasoning) also boils down to the reason of relativity, since the import of the selflessness of the person is the non-discovery of any person in those seven ways because of the fact of its (mere) designation depending on the aggregates. Such being the case, the very negation of self-production, etc., four (extremes) and of intrinsic sameness or different, etc., in seven (ways), by the reasons of relative production and dependent designation should be upheld as the principally significant of reasonings.

2. THE PROCESS OF REFUTING INTRINSIC IDENTIFIABILITY THEREBY

Well then, since this negation of intrinsically identifiable status (of anything) even in the superficial by those reasons of relativity appears to be the distinctive specialty of this system in elucidating the intention of the Holy Ones, how do they execute such an exceptional negation?

As this is extremely crucial, let us explain it. This (exceptional negation) is executed in the *Central Way Introduction* by three reasonings given in the basic verses and one given in the commentary.

The first of these (is called) "the consequence that the holy equipoise would destroy phenomena," (and it runs as follows): if things had an intrinsically identifiable reality, when the yogi realized directly the unreality of all things, his intuitive knowledge would annihilate things such as forms and sensations, since they should be apprehended (if they were real), yet they are not. A thing that formerly exists and later does not is called "destroyed," and (in this case) the cause of its destruction would be taken to be that intuitive knowledge. Since it is irrational for that (wisdom) to be a cause of destruction, intrinsically identifiable production is inadmissible at all times. Chandra states in the *Introduction:* "If things stood on intrinsic identifiability, its repudiation would be their destruction and emptiness would be the destructive cause. Such being irrational, things do not exist (identifiably)."

Here one (Dogmaticist) might object that mere intrinsically identifiable existence does not entail that intuitive wisdom apprehend things, and, although ultimate existence does entail such apprehension, he does not assert such (existence of things), since intrinsically identifiable status is only conventional.

Although this is a direct rebuttal, it cannot evade Chandra's consequence, as we will explain in the context of the next reasoning.

(The second of the four exceptional reasonings is called) the "consequence that conventional reality could withstand analysis," (and it runs as follows): if things were intrinsically identifiable, then if, for example, one were to analyze the objective referent of the conventional designation "production"—"Is this 'produced' sprout really the same as the seed? Or really different?"—it is necessary that the analytic (cognition) find (those things). Otherwise, they would become established merely on the strength of conventions since there would be no intrinsically identifiable objective referents.

However, when one analyzes things by investigating them in such a way, one does not find any such thing as production apart from that the nature of which is ultimate reality, where there is no production and no cessation.[1] Therefore, superficial things should not be asserted to be objects discovered by such analysis. (Chandra formulates this consequence) in the *Introduction* (as follows):

> When one analyzes these (mundane) things, they are not found to stand anywhere short of that with ultimate nature. Therefore, social conventional reality should not be analyzed.

Here, as explained above, a certain Dogmaticist claims (that this consequence does him) no damage, the essence of his disagreement being his drawing a line between reasoning analytic of ultimacy and non-ultimacy and the method of analysis merely (seeking referents of designations) explained above, since, although conventional reality does withstand analysis by the latter type of analysis, he never claimed that it withstands analysis by reasoning analytic of the ultimacy or non-ultimacy (of things). This rebuttal is the fundamental one, and is essentially the same (in thrust) as the previous rebuttal (given to the first consequence).

As for the reason why they cannot evade the damage of those (consequences), it is—as repeatedly explained above, and as given in Chandra's statements in this context and in many others that superficial existence is (equivalent to) social conventional existence—the very statement that whatever persons and things are established by social conventions are only established without the slightest analysis as to the mode of existence of the referents of the conventions; and thus that which, on the contrary, is analytically established to exist is ultimately existent. Therefore, if (something) is intrinsically identifiably existent, it must of necessity withstand analysis by rational cognition and must of necessity be apprehended by the intuitive wisdom that directly encounters the ultimate.

[1]This rather odd locution derives from Chandra's own in the succeeding quote, and is a rather indirect way of saying that through analysis one finds only the ultimate nature of things, which is to say one finds their ultimate unfindability.

(Again the Dogmaticist) objects that ultimate existence of something is its existence on the strength of its own actual condition, not merely established on the strength of its appearance in non-defective cognitions such as sense-cognitions, and hence social conventional existence is not that established on the strength of verbal conventions, but is existence on the strength of appearance in non-defective cognition, while still not being existence established on the strength of a thing's own objective condition.

(We answer that) if such were the case, it would contradict the (scriptural) statement that all things are mere names, signs, and designations, and the statement that "(things) exist by social conventions and usages, and not in the ultimate sense." (For), if there were some object found by analysis of the mode of existence of the referents of conventional designations, what would the word "merely" (in the former statement) exclude? And how could it be correct to say (in the latter statement) "it exists by social conventions," etc.? (And here finally,) while being completely out of touch with the way in which a common person accepts the referents of conventional designations, if one nevertheless says "(such and such) exists as a social convention," this is no more than empty talk, since one does not (in fact) accept the meaning.

The sevenfold analysis, (which proves) the impossibility of establishing as person any object found by analysis seeking the referent of the convention "person," and the reasonings such as the negation of production from other even conventionally, (which prove) the impossibility of establishing as production, etc., any objects found by analysis seeking the referents of conventions for things such as "production"—these should be understood from the detailed examinations (I have given them) elsewhere.

Thus, there is no difference between the conventions for persons and things, such as "I saw" and "the sprout grows," and the conventions (of philosophy) such as "my substantial self saw" and "the sprout grows from a substantially different seed," in the sense that investigation of the mode of existence of the referents of (both-types of) conventions finds nothing (ultimately). Nevertheless, there is an extremely great difference (between them) with regard to whether or not their existence corresponding to their designations is faulted by other (conventional) validating cognitions; the former pair (of conventional objects) being conventionally existent, the latter pair not being existent even conventionally. And further, this (point) depends on the thorough discrimination of the difference between (a thing's) being faulted by rational cognition and its being unable to withstand analysis, as well as the extremely great difference between rational cognition's not finding the existence (of something) and its seeing the non-existence (of something). But I have already explained these extensively elsewhere.

Here, someone, who has not accomplished the analysis of fine discrimination between the above (apparently similar types of conventions) yet negates ultimate status by a few likely reasons and maintains the existence of superficial things by means of a few erroneous cognitions, might think that (those conventions) can be established merely by their existence according to erroneous cognition, since their referents merely exist according to error.

This (kind of attitude) ends up (as the position that) if (the propositions that) "happiness and suffering arise from the creator and from nature, etc." and "happiness and suffering arise from good and evil actions" are right, they are both equally right, and if wrong, are both equally wrong; since analytic cognition will not find (the referent of) even the latter when analyzing it as above, and even the former exists according to erroneous cognition. Therefore, (such a person holds that Chandra's statements) in the *Introduction*: "This self is irrational even as the ground of the 'I'-process, nor do we assent even to its superficial existence"; and also, "What the fundamentalists, disturbed by sleep of ignorance, imagine respectively as real each in their own theory, and what people imagine in illusions and mirages—these are just what do not exist, even conventionally"; (that is, to the effect that) the imaginative constructions of the special theories of our own and others' schools and the objects such as horses and elephants apprehended in illusions or water apprehended in mirages are non-existent even superficially; both become incorrect. For, (unless they exist superficially) not even erroneous cognitions could apprehend them; since they do exist according to erroneous cognitions, they should become conventionally existent; and otherwise the rational negations such as "production from self or other is not established even conventionally" would become incapable of refuting anything at all.[2]

Here, (the above holder of the confused attitude about the status of conventions) cannot claim immunity (from the unacceptable consequences of his position) by asserting that he establishes superficial existence, not as those errors which belong to unreflective living beings from beginningless time, but merely as existence according to the error derived from the beginningless continuum of failure to analyze (the nature of reality). For, if such were the case (that is, that superficial existence is constituted by the specific error of lack of analysis), then even the conceptual objects of notions of permanence that hold prior and posterior as identical, (as well as the objects) of unconscious self-habits that adhere to the intrinsic identifiability of persons and things, would become conventionally existent.

Therefore, granting that (something's) conventional existence precludes its discovery by rational cognition investigating its mode of existence, still it is definitely necessary that it not be refuted by validating rational cognition, and it is also necessary that it not be faulted by any other conventional validating cognition, because it is necessary that (a thing's) conventional existence be established by validating cognition.

Here, if one objects that such (a position) contradicts (the doctrine that) conventionally existent things are merely established on the strength of verbal conventions, we respond that this does not fault our position. The word

[2]This very subtle passage may be confusing if we forget that Tsong Khapa is here drawing out the absurd conclusions of the position that the superficial, conventional reality is merely established according to erroneous cognition, which position makes its holder unable to distinguish between the genuinely superficially real, and the totally unreal.

"merely" in the expression "superficially existent things such as persons are merely established on the strength of verbal conventions" excludes (the possibility that) the person is not established on the strength of verbal conventions, and does not exclude (the possibility that) the person is also established by validating cognition; nor does it give any indication that everything established on the strength of verbal conventions is (in fact) superficially existent.

If you wonder what sort of non-conventional status of things is excluded (by the above expression, we can explain that) if the referent designated by the convention "person" were to have intrinsically identifiable status, this would entail its having an existence by virtue of its own intrinsic reality and would not allow it to have existence (merely) by virtue of the subjective convention ("person"). (Thus,) this is the kind of (non-conventional status, that is, intrinsically identifiable status) that is ruled out (by "merely"). Although such a kind (of non-conventional status) is negated by rational cognition, the (conventional) existence of the referents of conventional expressions such as "Yajña sees" is (nonetheless) established, since, if a conventional expression had no referent (at all), it would be faulted (even) by conventional validating cognition. And, in the context of a verbal convention and its referent, when a referent is found not to exist by its own intrinsic reality, its existence on the strength of convention is automatically established. Therefore, if one analyzes the mode of existence of the ultimate reality, it finally ends up as just the same. And so we assert that its existence is also established on the strength of convention, although we do not assert that the ultimate reality is established by conventional validating cognition. Furthermore, we say that the ultimate reality exists according to conventional cognition because of the fact that the notion of the existence of the ultimate is absent from the habit-pattern of rational cognition, which is not the same as saying that ultimate reality is established by that (conventional validating cognition).

Buddhapalita also explains that the Victor spoke of production, etc., on the strength of conventions and that "production," etc., were established as mere expressions. Whereas the Dogmaticists assert that the non-defective cognition that establishes conventional existence is non-erroneous with regard to the intrinsically identifiable thing that is its perceptual or conceptual object, in this (Dialecticist system) there are a great many things that can be established as objective by cognitions erroneous about their apparent objects. Hence there is a great difference in (the determination of what is) defective and non-defective in the non-defective cognitions of these two (systems).[3]

---

[3]That is to say, "defective" cognition for the Dogmaticist is cognition that suffers from organic malfunction, that is, vision distorted by hallucinations, and so forth, whereas for the Dialecticist all conventional cognitions are defective in that they perceive things as apparently objective while the things are actually only designatively objective, but nevertheless these intrinsically defective cognitions may successfully establish the conventional, designative existence of objects. The difference here again turns on the Dogmaticist assertion of intrinsic identifiability of the conventional, which is anathema to the Dialecticist.

Although Chandra calls this sort of existence on strength of convention "designative existence," it is definitely not the sort of designative existence where something is designated in the absence of any phenomenon. Thus, all things such as Buddhas and living beings as defined, and bondage and liberation as defined, are viable in this (interpretation of conventional existence), and are not at all viable in any other system. (Finally), in the face of the elucidation of this very fact by the two masters (Buddhapalita and Chandrakirti) as the ultimate intention of the Holy Father and Son, if one can see no ground for establishing (all empirical) systems with (all their) attributes, it is the result of the predominance of the ingrained habit of associating all normal causalities, etc., with intrinsically identifiable status. And since it means that still the import of relativity has not yet dawned as the import of emptiness by intrinsic reality, you should realize that you are standing at the point of greatest resistance to this system.

(The third of the four exceptional reasonings is called) "the consequence of the non-negation of ultimate production," (and it runs as follows): if things' intrinsically identifiable status is not negated by the negation through analysis of whether production is from self or other, then negation of ultimate status also will not be accomplished through such analysis. Since that is irrational, intrinsically identifiable status can also be negated conventionally. By the essential point that intrinsic identifiability necessarily entails ultimacy, the reasonings negating ultimate production also negate conventional intrinsic identifiability. Therefore, intrinsically identifiable production does not exist in either of the two realities, as Chandra states in the *Introduction*:

> The very reasons (proving) the irrationality of self- and other-production in the ultimate sense also (prove) their irrationality in the conventional reality —so whereby will your production come to pass?

(The fourth of the four exceptional reasonings is called the consequence of) "the wrongness of the (scriptural) statement that things are empty by intrinsic reality." Chandra in comment on the first (exceptional) reasoning in the *Introduction* cites the *Kashyapa Chapter*[4] to prove emptiness with respect to intrinsic identifiability:

> Kashyapa, furthermore, the central way is the genuine insight into things; it does not make things empty by means of emptiness, but (realizes that) the very things themselves are emptiness . . . likewise it does not make things signless, wishless, performanceless, non-produced, and non-occurrent by means of signlessness . . . and non-occurrence, (but realizes that) the very things themselves are signlessness . . . the very things themselves are non-occurrence. . . .

[4]Of the Ratnakūta.

Chandra also explains that this scriptural reference teaches the incorrectness of the (interpretation of) emptiness by the Idealist system. (Thus,) if things had an intrinsically identifiable reality, they would not be empty in their own nature, and "the very things themselves are emptiness" would be wrong. And if existence by a thing's own intrinsic reality were not refuted, then it would be necessary to demonstrate emptiness through an emptiness with respect to something else, which contradicts "it does not makes things empty because of emptiness." In short, (intrinsic identifiability of things) would mean that there is no self-emptiness which is emptiness by a thing's own nature. Therefore, if one does not assent to the emptiness of things with respect to the intrinsic reality which is intrinsic identifiability, though one may call it "self-emptiness," it does not get beyond "other-emptiness," and (Chandra means that) the Idealist doctrine that the relative is free of substantial subject-object-dichotomy does not negate (intrinsic identifiability) by taking the import of the relative to be intrinsic realitylessness.

Although (the various positions on the subtle objective selflessness) are similar insofar as they are modes of emptiness where the negation-ground does not exist as a actuality of the negatee, and where that ground is empty with respect to the negatee, only the emptiness (of things) with respect to intrinsic identifiability means their emptiness in their own right, all other modes of emptiness not being emptiness of things in themselves. The reason is that, with the former type of emptiness, as long as there is no loss of concentration on the previously attained establishment by validating cognition, it is impossible for reifications to occur which, under the influence of theories, hold that ground as truly existent or existent in a way tantamount to that. Whereas, even when the latter (Idealist and Dogmaticist systems) do not lose the establishment by validating cognition of their objectives, this does not prevent reifications (holding) theoretically to (existence in) truth or (in something with) the meaning of truth.

CHAPTER 13

YOGĀCĀRA

The origins of the Yogācāra School ("The School that Practices the Way of Yoga") are obscure, though tradition regards a third-century thinker by the name of Maitreyanatha as the founder. It is likely that Yogācāra was already several centuries old by the time it reached its definitive formulation by the brothers Asaṅga and Vasubandhu in the fourth to fifth centuries. Asaṅga's fame, first in India, later in China and Tibet, was secured by his monumental work, *Stages of Yoga Practice* (*Yogācārabhūmi*), of which the Bodhisattva Stages (*Bodhisattvabhūmi*), from which the "Knowing Reality" chapter has been selected, is a part. In this chapter—our first selection—Asaṅga explains that the emptiness of things is not their nonexistence but their perfect (or absolute) existence.

Nāgārjuna's earlier critique has been misunderstood by many as advocating metaphysical nihilism, a misunderstanding that Asaṅga attempted to overcome by distinguishing among the three natures of things. First, there is the nature that the mind imposes on things as it attempts to know them. This is the mentally constructed and illusory nature, recognized by the wise to be empty of intrinsic reality. Second, there is the relative nature of things as they depend on each other and on the mind. When this nature is recognized, things are seen to be relatively real (although devoid of separate and independent reality). Finally, there is the third nature, the absolute perfection of things, which is precisely their relative existence, seen with the eye of wisdom when the meditational insight of yoga practice has gone beyond all conceptual dualities. In the "Knowing Reality" chapter Asaṅga explains how the different kinds of knowledge correspond to the three natures of things, offering a bridge between rational knowledge and the wisdom of meditational insight that sees things just as they are.

Vasubandhu, a great Sautrāntika thinker and expert in Abhidharma, was converted to Yogācāra by Asaṅga, his brother, probably in the late fourth century, and promptly produced an authoritative systematization of the school through his impressive commentaries and independent treatises. The first selection, *A Discussion of the Five Aggregates* (*Pañcaskandha Pra-*

karaṇa) by Vasubandhu, is both a commentary on, and a critique of, the Abhidharma analysis of the five aggregates constituting an individual existence. It provides a good example of typical Abhidharma analysis, even though it was evidently composed after Vasubandhu's conversion to Mahāyāna. Since this is a revision of his brother's work, and Asaṅga was a Mahīśāsaka before converting to Yogācāra, we may assume the Abhiddharma view being considered to be that of the Mahīśāsaka school. As commentary on this school's teachings, it is faithful for the most part to the Sarvāstivāda tenets, although its critique appears to reflect Vasubandhu's conversion to the Yogācāra Mahāyāna.

Vasubandhu's *Twenty Verses and Commentary* (*Viṃśatikā Kārikā [Vṛtti]*) is one of his later works and reveals him at his philosophical best, vigorously advancing his own views and refuting those of his opponents. Although frequently interpreted as a work advocating philosophical idealism, the text itself makes no claims that the things of the world are the creations of consciousness. Its main emphasis is on the fact that whatever is experienced is known only to the extent that it affects consciousness in some way at some level. But this is not to claim either that external things are created by consciousness or that all experience is illusory. For Vasubandhu, the very notion of knowable things existing independently of consciousness is an illusion. Put differently, Vasubandhu argues against the assumption that we can adopt a perspective beyond our actual experience. The autocommentary shows Vasubandhu's skill in bringing out the subtle philosophical issues implicit in the ordinary human situation and the fundamental problems of human life.

The *Thirty Verses* (*Triṃśikā Kārikā*) is Vasubandhu's famous attempt to relate the motivating dispositions to the six stages of consciousness evolving from the store consciousness. Identifying the motivating dispositions associated with each stage is important for freeing consciousness from these dispositions and from the underlying, latent impressions. Although only meditational yogic practice can free consciousness from its latent impressions and dispositions, Vasubandhu's analysis is useful for setting the stage for meditational insight and for loosening the grip that conceptual entification has on ordinary consciousness.

Janice Dean Willis, *On Knowing Reality: The Tattvārtha Chapter of Asaṅga's Bodhisattvabhūmi* (New York: Columbia University Press, 1979), the work from which the Asaṅga selection was taken, provides an excellent introduction to Yogācāra philosophy, locating Asaṅga within the larger Buddhist philosophical framework. Because of space limitations we have reproduced the translation without commentary, but Willis's running commentary is extremely helpful for someone approaching this text for the first time. Stefan Anacker, *Seven Works of Vasubandhu* (Delhi: Motilal Banarsidass, 1984), from which the Vasubandhu translations have been taken, provides an overall introduction to the place of Vasubandhu's thought within the larger framework of Yogācāra, as well as useful introductions to each of the works translated. Lewis Lancaster and Luis Gomez, editors, *Prajñāpāramitā and*

Related Systems (Berkeley: Berkeley Buddhist Studies Series, 1977), contains a number of essays helpful in understanding Yogācāra and Mādhyamaka thought. D. T. Suzuki, *Studies in the Laṅkāvatāra Sūtra* (London: Routledge and Kegan Paul, 1930), remains the authoritative study of one of the most important foundational Yogācāra texts and is an excellent companion to his (Suzuki's) translation of *The Laṅkāvatāra Sūtra: A Mahāyāna Text* (London: Routledge and Kegan Paul, 1932).

I
Asaṅga: On Knowing Reality*

[I]

What is knowledge of reality? Concisely, there are two sorts: (1) that sort which consists of [knowing] the noumenal aspect of dharmas,[1] or the true state of dharmas as they are in themselves, and (2) that sort which consists of [knowing] the phenomenal aspect of dharmas, as they are in totality. In short, knowledge of reality should be understood as [knowledge of] "dharmas as they are, and as they are in totality."

Further, knowledge of reality may be given a fourfold analysis, as follows:

(1) what is universally accepted by ordinary beings;

(2) what is universally accepted by reason, or logic;

(3) that which is the sphere of cognitive activity completely purified of the obscurations of defilement and

(4) that which is the sphere of cognitive activity completely purified of obscurations to the knowable.

Of these four, the first may be defined as follows: The shared opinion of all worldly beings—because their minds are involved with and proceed according to signs and conventions, out of habit with respect to any "given thing", is like so: "Earth is earth alone, and not fire." And as with earth, just so fire, water, wind, forms, sounds, smells, tastes, tactiles, food, drink, conveyance, clothes, ornaments, utensils, incense, garlands, ointments, dance, song, music, illumination, sexual intercourse, fields, shops, household objects, happiness, and suffering are viewed accordingly. "This is suffering, not happiness." "This is happiness, not suffering." In short, "This is this, and not that." And likewise, "This is this, and not any other."

Whatever given thing is taken hold of and becomes established for all

---

*Reprinted with permission from Janice Dean Willis, *On Knowing Reality: The* Tattvārtha *Chapter of Asaṅga's* Bodhisattvabhūmi (New York: Columbia University Press, 1979).

[1] The *dharmas* are the fundamental constituents of reality.

ordinary beings owing merely to their own discursive thought by means of associations arising one after another in the sphere of foregone conclusions, without having been pondered, without having been weighed and measured, and without having been investigated, that is said to be the reality which is universally accepted by ordinary beings, or which is established by worldly consent.

What is that reality universally accepted by reason? It is that which is known from the personal eloquence of those at the stage of being governed by reason, who are learned in the meaning of logical principles, and who have intelligence, reasoning power, and skill in investigation. Also, it is that knowledge arising in ordinary beings which is based on the authority of those engaged in investigation, namely, the proofs of the logicians: direct perception, inference, and the testimony of trustworthy persons. That is the sphere of well-analyzed knowledge wherein the knowable given thing is proven and established by demonstration-and-proof reason. That is said to be the reality which is universally accepted by reason.

What is the reality which is the sphere of cognitive activity completely purified of the obscurations of defilement? It is that domain and sphere of cognitive activity attained by putting an end to the outflows which is the "putting an end to the outflows" of all the śrāvakas and pratyekabuddhas, as well as that mundane knowledge which puts an end to the outflows at some future time. That reality is said to be the sphere of cognitive activity that is completely purified of the obscurations of defilement. When knowledge becomes purified of the obscurations of defilement, i.e., of those three mental supports [the three defilements], one dwells in nonobscuration. Therefore, it is called reality which is the sphere of cognitive activity completely purified of the obscurations of defilement.

Moreover, what is that reality? The Four Noble Truths, namely: (1) suffering, (2) its origin, (3) its cessation, and (4) the path leading to its cessation. It is that knowledge which arises in those having clear comprehension who, after thorough investigation, arrive at the understanding of these Four Noble Truths. Further, it is the understanding of those truths on the part of those śrāvakas and pratyekabuddhas who have apprehended that there are only aggregates [in what is commonly assumed to be a person] and who have not apprehended a self as a separate entity apart from the aggregates. By means of insight properly applied to the arising and passing away of all dependently arisen conditioned states, clear vision arises from the repetition of the view that "apart from the aggregates there is no 'person.'"

What is the reality which is the sphere of cognitive activity completely purified of the obscurations to the knowable? That which prevents knowledge of a knowable is said to be an "obscuration." Whatever sphere of cognitive activity is completely freed from all obscurations to the knowable, just that should be understood to be the domain and sphere of cognitive activity completely purified of the obscurations to the knowable.

Again, what is that? It is the domain and the sphere of cognitive activity that belongs to the Buddha-Bhagavans and bodhisattvas who, having penetrated the non-self of dharmas and having realized, because of that pure understanding, the inexpressible nature of all dharmas, know the sameness of the essential nature of verbal designation and the nondiscursive knowable. That is the supreme Suchness, there being none higher, which is at the extreme limit of the knowable and for which all analyses of the dharmas are accomplished, and which they do not surpass.

Furthermore, it should be understood that the correctly determined characteristic of reality is its not-two nature, or constitution. The two are said to be "being" and "nonbeing."

With regard to those two, "being" is whatever is determined to have essential nature solely by virtue of verbal designation and as such is clung to by the worldly for a long time. For ordinary beings, this [notion of being] is the root of all discursive thought and proliferation whether "form," "feeling," "ideation," "motivation," or "perception"; "eye," "ear," "nose," "tongue," "body," or "mind"; "earth," "water," "fire," or "wind"; "form," "sound," "smell," "taste," or "contact"; "skillful," "unskillful," or "indeterminate" acts; "birth" or "passing away" or "dependent arising"; "past," "future," or "present"; "compounded" or "uncompounded"; "This is a world, and beyond is a world," "There are both the sun and moon," and whatever is "seen," "heard," "believed," or "perceived"; what is "attained or striven for," what is "adumbrated" or "thought with signs" by the mind; even up to "Nirvāṇa." Everything in this category has a nature established by verbal designation only. This is said [by ordinary beings] to be "being."

With regard to those two, "nonbeing" is when the base of the verbal designation "form," and so on up to "Nirvāṇa," is absent or noncharacterizable; when the basis of verbal designation, with recourse to which verbal designation operates, is insubstantial, nonascertainable, nonexistent, or nonpresent in any way whatsoever. This is said to be "nonbeing."

Moreover, the given thing, comprised of dharma characteristics, that is completely freed from both "being" and "nonbeing"—i.e., from the "being" and "nonbeing" described above—is "not-two." Now, what is not-two, just that is said to be the incomparable Middle Path which avoids the two extremes; and concerning that reality the knowledge of all the Buddha-Bhagavans should be understood to be exceedingly pure. Further, it should be understood that that knowledge for the bodhisattvas constitutes the Path of Instruction.

That insight is the bodhisattva's great means for reaching the Incomparable Perfect Enlightenment. And why? Because of the bodhisattva's firm conviction in voidness, practicing in these and those births and circling in saṃsāra for the sake of thoroughly ripening the Buddhadharmas for himself and other sentient beings, he comes to know saṃsāra as it really is. And moreover, he does not weary his mind with the aspects of impermanence and so forth which pertain to that saṃsāra. Should he not experience the true nature of saṃsāra, he would be unable, owing to all the defilements—of lust, hatred, delusion, and so forth—to render his mind equable; and not being equable, his defiled mind, circling in saṃsāra, would mature neither the Buddhadharmas nor the sentient beings.

Again, if he should weary his mind with the aspects of saṃsāra, impermanence, and so forth, being thus [wearied] that bodhisattva would very quickly enter Parinirvāṇa. But the bodhisattva thus entering very quickly into Parinirvāṇa would mature neither the Buddhadharmas nor the sentient beings. Again, how would he become awakened to the Incomparable Perfect Enlightenment?

On account of his firm conviction in voidness, that bodhisattva, continuously applying himself, is neither frightened by Nirvāṇa nor does he strive toward Nirvāṇa. If that bodhisattva should be frightened by Nirvāṇa, he would not store up his equipment for Nirvāṇa hereafter; but rather, not seeing the benefits which lie in Nirvāṇa, owing to fear of it, that bodhisattva would give up the faith and conviction which sees the excellent qualities in that.

On the other hand, if that bodhisattva should frequently fix [his or her mind] zealously on Parinirvāṇa, he would speedily enter Parinirvāṇa. But as a result of quickly entering Parinirvāṇa, he would mature neither the Buddhadharmas or the sentient beings.

In summary, whoever does not thoroughly experience saṃsāra as it really is circles in saṃsāra with a defiled mind. And whoever is wearied in mind by saṃsāra quickly enters Nirvāṇa. Whoever possesses a mind of fear with respect to Nirvāṇa does not store up equipment for it. And whoever fixed [his mind] zealously on Nirvāṇa quickly enters Parinirvāṇa. But it should be understood that these are not the bodhisattva's means for attaining Incomparable Perfect Enlightenment.

Again, whoever thoroughly experiences saṃsāra as it really is circles in saṃsāra with an undefiled mind. And whoever has a mind which is unwearied by the aspects of impermanence and so forth of saṃsāra, that one does not quickly enter Nirvāṇa. And whoever has a mind which is unfrightened by Nirvāṇa stores up equipment for it, and though seeing the good qualities and benefits in Nirvāṇa still does not exceedingly long for it, and so does not quickly enter Nirvāṇa. This is the bodhisattva's great means for attaining the Incomparable Perfect Enlightenment. And this means is well grounded in that firm conviction in supreme voidness. Therefore for the bodhisattva who has well taken hold of the Path of Instruction, cultivating conviction in supreme voidness is said to be the "Great Means" for reaching the knowledge of the Tathāgata.

Now you should know that that bodhisattva, because of his long-time engagement with the knowledge of dharma-selflessness, having understood the inexpressibility of all dharmas as they really are, does not at all imagine any dharma; otherwise he would not [truly] grasp "given thing only" as precisely "Suchness only." It does not occur to him, "This is the given thing only, and this other, the Suchness only." In clear understanding the bodhisattva courses, and coursing in this supreme understanding with insight into Suchness, he sees all dharmas as they really are, i.e., as being absolutely the same. And seeing everywhere sameness, his mind likewise, he attains to supreme equanimity.

Taking recourse in that equanimity, while greatly applying himself toward skill in all the sciences, that bodhisattva does not turn away from his goal because of fatigue, or because of any suffering. Unwearied in body and unwearied in mind, he quickly achieves skillfulness in those [sciences], and he reaches the stage of attaining the great power of mindfulness. He is not puffed up by virtue of his skill, nor does he have a teacher's closed-fistedness toward others. Not only does his mind not shrink from any skills, but also, with enthusiasm, he proceeds without hindrance. Practicing with steadfast mental armor:

to the extent that circling in saṃsāra he experiences diverse sufferings, to that extent he generates enthusiasm toward Incomparable Perfect Enlightenment;

to the extent that he experiences diverse bodies, to that extent he lacks pride toward any sentient being;

to the extent that he experiences diverse acquaintances[?], to that extent when associated with others seeking brawls and disputes, who are garrulous, have great and lesser defilements, and who practice unbridled and mistaken ways, as he experiences those ones, even to greater measure his mind stays in equanimity;

and to the extent that he grows in virtue, to that extent his goodness is unabated.

He does not seek to know from others nor does he seek gain or reverence [for himself]. These and numerous other benefits of the same category, i.e., the Wings of Enlightenment dharmas and all things consistent with Enlightenment, accrue for the bodhisattva who has that knowledge [of dharma-selflessness] as his excellent basis. Therefore, whoever sets out to attain Enlightenment, whoever will attain it, and those who do attain it, all these have as their basis that very same knowledge — not another knowledge, whether superior or inferior.

Having thus entered upon the practical application of the method without proliferation, the bodhisattva has many benefits: he rightly engages in thoroughly ripening the Buddhadharmas for himself, and for others, in thoroughly ripening the Dharma of the Three Vehicles. Moreover, thus rightly engaged, he is without craving for possessions or even for his own body.

He trains himself in noncraving so that he is able to give to sentient beings his possessions and even his own body. For the sake of sentient beings alone is he restrained, and well restrained, in body and speech. He trains himself in restraint so that he naturally takes no pleasure in sin, and so that he becomes wholesome and good by nature. He is forbearing toward all injury and wrongdoing on the part of others. He trains himself in forbearance so that he has little anger and so that he does no injury to others.

He becomes skillful and expert in all the sciences in order to dispel the doubts of sentient beings and to manage to assist them, and for himself, to embrace the cause of omniscience. His mind abides within, equipoised. And he trains himself in the fixing of his mind, so as to completely purify the Four Sublime Abodes, and to sport in the Five Supernormal Faculties in order to perform his duty toward all sentient beings, and in order to clear away all the fatigue that arose from his exertions to become expert. And he becomes wise, knowing the Supreme Reality. He trains himself to know the Supreme Reality, so that in the future he will himself, in the Great Vehicle, enter Parinirvāṇa.

You should know that the bodhisattva thus rightly engaged carefully attends all virtuous beings with worship and reverence. And all unvirtuous beings he carefully attends with a mind of sympathy and a mind of supreme compassion.

Insofar as he can and has the strength, he is engaged in dispersing their faults. He carefully attends all harmful beings with a mind of love. And insofar as he can and has the strength, being himself without trickery and without deceit, he works for their benefit and happiness, to eliminate the hostile consciousness of those who do evil because of their faults of expectation and practice. Unto helpful beings, after showing gratitude, he carefully attends them in return with more than equal helpfulness. And he fulfills their pious aspirations as much as he can and has the strength. Even when he is unable, not having been asked, he displays respectful endeavor toward these and those duties to be done. Never once does he reject duty. How should the notion occur to him, "I, being incapable, do not wish to do this"? This, and other actions of the same category, should be understood as the right procedure for the bodhisattva who, having taken up the way of nonproliferation, is well based in knowledge of Supreme Reality.

[II]

Now by what philosophical reasoning is the inexpressible character of all dharmas to be understood? As follows: Whatever is a designation for the individual characteristics of the dharmas, for example, "form" or "feeling" or the other personality aggregates, or, as before explained, even up to "Nirvāṇa," that should be understood to be only a designation. It is neither the essential nature of that dharma, nor is it wholly other than that. That [essential nature] is neither the sphere of speech nor the object of speech; nor is it altogether different from these. That being the case, the essential nature of dharmas is not found in the way in which it is expressed. But further, neither is absolutely nothing found. Again, the essential nature is absent and yet not absolutely absent. One might ask: "How is it found?" It is found by avoiding grasping both the view which affirms the existence of what is nonexistent and the view which denies existence altogether. Moreover, one should understand that only the sphere of cognitive activity which is completely freed of discursive thought is the domain of knowledge of the supreme essential nature of all dharmas.

Again, if with regard to any dharma or any given thing it is assumed that it becomes just like its expression, then those dharmas and that given thing would be that expression itself. But if that were the case, then for a single dharma and a single given thing there would be very many kinds of essential nature. And why? It is like this: to a single dharma and to a single given thing, various men will attach many different designations by virtue of numerous expressions of various kinds. That dharma and that given thing ought to have identity with, be made up of, and have the essential nature of some one verbal designation, but not of the other remaining verbal designations. But there being no fixed determination, which of the very many kinds of verbal designation would hold as the correct one? Therefore, the use of any and all verbal designations, however complete or incomplete, for any and all given things does *not* mean that the latter are identical to, made up of, or receive essential nature through those verbal designations.

Now, to view it in another way, suppose the dharmas themselves, of form and so forth as previously expounded, should become the essential nature of their verbal designations. If this were the case, then, first there would be just the given thing alone, i.e., completely disassociated from names, and only afterward would there be the desire to attach to that given thing a verbal designation. But this would mean that before a verbal designation was attached, at the time just prior to attaching the designation, that very dharma and that very given thing would be without essential nature. But if there were no essential nature, there would be no given thing at all; and hence, a designation would not be called for. And since no verbal designation would be attached, the essential nature of the dharma and of the given thing could not be proved.

Again, suppose that just prior to the attaching of a verbal designation, that dharma and that given thing should be identical with the designation. This being the case, even without the verbal designation "form," the idea of form would occur whenever there was a dharma with the name "form," and whenever there was a given thing with the name "form." But such does not occur.

Now, through employing reasoning like this, one should understand that the essential nature of all dharmas is inexpressible, i.e., completely beyond the reach of expression. And one should understand that just as with regard to form, so with feelings, etc., as previously expounded, even up to Nirvāṇa itself.

It should be understood that these two views have fallen away from our Dharma-Vinaya: (1) that one which clings to affirming the existence of what are nonexistent individual characteristics, having essential nature only through verbal designations for a given thing, form, etc., or for the dharmas, form and so forth; and also (2) that one which, with respect to a given thing, denies the foundation for the sign of verbal designation, and the basis for the sign of verbal designation, which exists in an ultimate sense owing to its inexpressible essence, saying "absolutely everything is nonexistent."

The faults which result from affirming the existence of what is nonexistent have been examined, laid out, clarified and illumined immediately above. Because of these faults which arise from affirming the existence of nonexistents with respect to the given thing of form, etc., one should understand that view as having fallen away from our Dharma-Vinaya.

Likewise, denying the bare given thing, which is a universal denial, has fallen away from our Dharma-Vinaya. I say, then: "Neither reality nor designation is known when the bare given thing, form and so forth, is denied. Both these views are incorrect."

Thus, if the aggregates of form exist, then the designation "person" is valid. But if they do not, the designation "person" is groundless. Attaching a verbal designation to the dharmas, form, etc., and to the bare given thing of form, etc., is valid when they are existent. When they are not existent, the attaching of a verbal designation is groundless. And again, if there is no given thing present to be designated then since there is no foundation, there is also no designation.

Therefore, certain persons who have heard the abstruse sūtra passages associated with the Mahāyāna and associated with profound voidness, and that evince only an indirect meaning, do not understand the meaning of the teaching as it really is. Those ones, imagining it superficially, thus have views posited merely by logic, without cogency, and speak as follows: "All this reality is just designation only. And whoever sees accordingly, that one sees rightly." According to those, the given thing itself, which is the foundation for designation, is lacking. But if this were so, no designations would occur at all! How should reality, then, come to be solely designation?

Accordingly, they deny both these two, reality as well as designation. One should understand that the denial of both reality and designation is the position of the chief nihilist. Because his views are like this, the nihilist is not to be spoken with and not to be associated with by those intelligent ones who live the pure life. Such a one, i.e., the nihilist, brings disaster even unto himself, and worldly ones who follow his view also fall into misfortune. In connection with this, the Lord has declared: "Indeed, better it is for a being to have the view of a 'person' than for one to have wrongly conceptualized voidness." And why? Because men who have the view of a "person" are deluded only with respect to a single knowable, but they do not deny all knowables. And not for that reason alone would they be born among hell-beings.

Nor should another bring disaster to the seeker of Dharma, the seeker of liberation from suffering, nor deceive him. Rather, he should establish him in righteousness and in Truth and he should not be lax concerning the points of instruction. Because of the nihilist's wrongly conceptualized voidness, he is confused with respect to the knowable given thing of dharmas to the point of denying all knowables; and on that account one does get born among hell-beings. The nihilist would bring disaster to the righteous man, the seeker of liberation from suffering, and he would become lax concerning the points of instruction. Therefore, denying the given thing as it really is, he has strayed far from our Dharma-Vinaya.

Again, how is voidness wrongly conceptualized? There are some śramaṇas, as well as brāhmaṇas, who do not agree concerning "owing to what there is a void"; nor do they agree concerning "that which is void." But such formulations as these are evidence of what is said to be "voidness wrongly conceptualized." And why? Voidness is logical when one thing is void of another because of that [other's] absence and because of the presence of the void things itself. But how and for what reason would the void come to be from universal absence [i.e., from complete nonexistence]? Hence, the conception of voidness these describe is not valid. And therefore, in this manner voidness is wrongly conceptualized.

Now, how is voidness rightly conceptualized? Wherever and in whatever place something is not, one rightly observes that [place] to be void of that [thing]. Moreover, whatever remains in that place one knows as it really is, that "here there is an existent." This is said to be engagement with voidness as it really is and without waywardness. For example, when a given thing, as indicated, is termed "form," etc., there is no dharma identical to the verbal designation "form" and so on. Hence, whenever a dharma is termed "form" etc., that given thing is void of identity with the verbal designation "form," etc. Then what remains in that place when a given thing is termed "form," etc.? As follows: just the basis of the verbal designation "form," etc. When one knows both those as they really are—namely, that there is just a given thing and there is just a designation for just a given thing—then he neither affirms the existence of what is nonexistent nor denies what is existent. He neither makes it in excess nor makes it in deficiency. He neither minimizes nor adds.

And when he knows Suchness, as it really is, with its inexpressible essential nature, as it really is, this is called "voidness rightly conceptualized," and called "well-discerned right insight." By this means, and others consistent with demonstration-and-proof reasoning, he will come to judge that the essential nature of all dharmas is inexpressible.

[III]

Moreover, one should understand that all dharmas have an inexpressible essential nature from the scriptures of a trustworthy person. This very meaning was expressed by the Lord through an elucidating verse in the "Discourse on Transference in Phenomenal Life" (*Bhavasaṃkrāntisūtra*):

> Indeed, by whatsoever name whatsoever dharma is mentioned, that dharma is not found therein. For that is the true nature of all dharmas.

How does this verse elucidate our very meaning? When a dharma has the name "form" and so on, whatever the name be, i.e., "form," etc., by means of that name the dharmas are referred to with the names "form" etc., whether form or feeling and so on up to Nirvāṇa. But the dharmas having those names "form" etc. are themselves not identical with the designations "form," etc. Nor is there any dharma found outside of those that is identical to "form," etc. Again, for those dharmas having the names "form," etc., one should understand that what does exist there in the ultimate sense, with an inexpressible meaning, is the true mode of essential nature. And it was spoken by the Lord in the discourse treating the categories of dharmas [the *Arthavargīya*]:

> Whatever conventions there be among the worldly, all those the Muni does not take up. And verily not participating, how could he indulge, since he takes no pleasure in what is seen or heard?

How does this verse elucidate our very meaning? Whatever be the designations, such as "form," etc., applied to a dharma of form, etc., those are said to be "conventions." He does not accept that dharmas are identical with those designations. In this respect, he does not accept those conventions. And why? Because his view is neither that of exaggeration nor of underestimation. Now because he does not have a wayward view, he is said to not participate. Thus not participating, how is he to indulge? Without that wayward view, he neither affirms nor denies that given thing; and not indulging, he rightly sees in the knowable what is to be seen of it. And what he hears spoken of the knowable was indeed heard of it. In regard to what is seen and heard, he neither originates nor increases craving. Not otherwise would he rid himself of the object of consciousness and dwell with equanimity; and having equanimity, he does not create desire.

And again, such was declared by the Lord in the discourse beginning with the story of the "Saṃtha Kātyāyana." In this account, the monk having the title "Saṃtha" meditates neither upon the base earth, water, fire, nor wind; neither upon the bases space, perception, or nothing-at-all, nor ideation nor nonideation; neither upon this world nor the other; neither upon the sun nor the moon; nor upon what is seen, heard, thought, perceived, obtained, striven for, inquired about, or concluded about by the mind. None of these does he employ as a meditative base. Now since he does not meditate upon the base earth, etc., nor all the rest, upon what does he meditate? Here, for the saṃtha monk, whatever the idea of "earth" regarding earth, that idea is lost. Whatever the idea of "water" with regard to water, and with regard to all the rest, that idea is lost. Thus this monk meditates, not using earth as a meditative base nor any of the others. Using none of them at all as a meditative base, he meditates. Therefore do all the gods along with Indra, along with the Īśānas, and along with Prajāpati, bow down near the monk thus meditating, saying,

> Salutations to this noble man. Salutations to the best of men. To you for whom there is nothing further to know, resorting to what will you meditate?

Again, how does this sūtra verse elucidate our very intent? For given things named "earth," etc., "earth" and so on are only nominal designations. For those given things named "earth," etc., the idea of them arises with exaggeration, or the idea of them arises with underestimation. The idea with "exaggeration" posits the essential nature of the given thing as consisting of that name; and the idea with "underestimation" posits the destruction of the ultimate basis of the given thing itself. When these two erroneous views are abandoned and eliminated, the idea of any meditative base is said to be "lost."

Therefore from the scriptures and also from the Tathāgata's supreme lineage of trustworthy successors, one should understand that all dharmas have an inexpressible essential nature. Now, since all dharmas have thus inexpressible essential nature, why is expression applicable at all? Verily, because without expression, the inexpressible true nature could not be told to others, nor heard by others. And if it were neither spoken nor heard, then the inexpressible essential nature could not become known. Therefore, expression is applicable for producing knowledge through hearing.

[IV]

Precisely because that Suchness is not thoroughly known, the eight kinds of discursive thought arise for immature beings and operate so as to create the three bases which further produce the receptacle worlds of all sentient beings. The eight are as follows: (1) discursive thought concerning essential nature; (2) discursive thought concerning particularity; (3) discursive thought concerning grasping whole shapes; (4) discursive thought concerning "I"; (5) discursive thought concerning "mine"; (6) discursive thought concerning the agreeable; (7) discursive thought concerning the disagreeable; and (8) discursive thought contrary to both these.

Further, these eight kinds of discursive thought create what three bases? The discursive thought concerning essential nature, the discursive thought concerning particularity, and the discursive thought concerning grasping whole shapes, these three engender the [perceivable] base which is named "form," etc., i.e., the base which serves as the foundation of discursive proliferation and as its mental support. With that [perceivable] base as its foundation, discursive thought—saturated with words, ideas, and names and enveloped in words, ideas, and names—proliferates and ranges on that base in many ways.

Of these eight, the discursive thought concerning "I" and the discursive thought concerning "mine" engender the reifying view and the root of all other views, namely: the root of pride, the root of egoism, and the root of all other self-centered views.

Among those eight, discursive thought concerning the agreeable and the disagreeable, as well as discursive thought which is contrary to both these, engender, according to the circumstances, desire, hatred, or delusion. Thus do these eight kinds of discursive thought serve to manifest the three kinds of bases, namely: (1) the [perceivable] base which serves as the foundation of discursive thought and its proliferation; (2) the base of the reifying view, egoism, and pride; and (3) the base of lust, hatred, and delusion. With regard to those, when the [perceivable] base of discursive thought together with proliferation exist, then the reifying view and the "I am" pride have a support; and when the reifying view and the "I am" pride exist, then lust, hatred, and delusion have a support. Further, these three bases explain completely the manifold evolution of all the worlds [of saṃsāra].

1. Among those eight, what is discursive thought concerning essential nature? It is that discursive thought which designates "form," etc., when there is a given thing of form, etc. This is said to be discursive thought concerning essential nature.

2. What is discursive thought concerning particularity? It is that discursive thought which, when there is a given thing named "form," etc., thinks, "This has form," "This is formless," "This is shown," "This is not shown," "This has hindrance," "This is unhindered," "This is outflow," "This is not outflow," "This is compounded," "This is uncompounded," "virtuous," "unvirtuous," "indeterminate," "past," "future," "present"; and by way of immeasurable distinctions of the same category, whatever discursive thought is founded upon the discursive thought concerning essential nature, with the object of particularizing it, this is said to be discursive thought concerning particularity.

3. What is discursive thought concerning grasping whole shapes? When there is a given thing named "form," etc., whatever operates to grasp whole shapes with respect to the multiple dharmas taken together, adding to given things nominal designations like "self," "life," and "sentient being"; and adding nominal designations like "house," "army," and "forest," "food," "drink," "conveyance," and "clothes," etc., this is said to be discursive thought concerning grasping whole shapes.

4. 5. What is discursive thought concerning "I" and "mine"? When a given thing has outflow, is graspable, and for a long time has been familiar, clung to and thought of as "self" or as "what belongs to self" so by intimacy with that errant way of conceptualizing, discursive thought wrongly takes the given thing, which has arisen dependently, as having been placed there by one's own view. This is said to be discursive thought concerning "I" and "mine."

6. What is discursive thought concerning the agreeable? It is that discursive thought which has as its mental support a given thing which is pleasant and captivating to the mind.

7. What is discursive thought concerning the disagreeable? It is that discursive thought which has as its mental support a given thing which is unpleasant and revolting to the mind.

8. What is discursive thought which is contrary to both the agreeable and the disagreeable? It is that discursive thought which has as its mental support a given thing which is neither pleasant nor unpleasant, neither captivating nor revolting to the mind.

And this whole process is composed of two elements only: discursive thought, and the given thing which then becomes the mental support of discursive thought and the foundation of discursive thought. It should be understood that these two are mutually caused and without beginning in time. A previous discursive thought is the cause which generates a present given thing which, in turn, becomes the mental support of discursive thought. And again, the generated given thing which is the present mental support for discursive thought is the cause which generates the future discursive thought, having that as its mental support.

Now, with respect to this, it is precisely from lack of understanding that the discursive thought of the present is the cause which generates the given thing in the future—and that this given thing in turn becomes the mental support of discursive thought in the future—that there is the inevitable generation of discursive thought in the future, having that thing as its foundation and as its basis.

But now how does thorough knowledge of discursive thought arise? It arises by means of the four thorough investigations and by means of the four kinds of knowing precisely and in detail. What are the four thorough investigations? They are the investigation of the name, the investigation of the given thing, the investigation of the designations for essential nature, and the investigation of the designations for particularity.

With respect to these, investigation of the name means that the bodhisattva sees with regard to a name that it is just a name. Likewise, with regard to a given thing, seeing that it is just a given thing is the investigation of the given thing. With respect to designations for essential nature, clearly seeing those as just designations for essential nature is the investigation of designations for essential nature; and with regard to designations for particularity, seeing those as just designations for particularity is the investigation of designations for particularity. He sees names and given things as having distinct characteristics and as having connected characteristics, and he realizes that designations for essential nature and designations for particularity are based upon the connected characteristics of the name and the given thing.

What are the four kinds of knowing precisely, in detail? They are knowing in detail the investigated name, the investigated given thing, the designations for essential nature, and designations for particularity—knowing all these precisely, in detail.

What is knowing precisely, in detail the investigated name? You should know that the bodhisattva, having investigated name as name only, knows that name just as it really is; to wit, he determines that "This name is the linguistic unit for a given thing"; likewise "the linguistic unit for conceptualizing, the linguistic unit for viewing, and the linguistic unit for attributing. If, for a given thing ordinarily conceived of as form, etc., a name 'form," is not decided upon, no one would thus conceive that given thing as form; and not conceiving it, he would not exaggerate or cling to it. And not clinging to it, he could not express it. Thus he knows it precisely, in detail. This is said to be knowing the investigated name precisely, in detail.

What is knowing precisely, in detail, the investigated given thing? For any given thing, the bodhisattva, having investigated it as given thing only, sees that that given thing, while conceived of as "form," etc., and while associated with all the expressions [for it], is in itself inexpressible. This is the second knowing in detail, namely, knowing precisely, in detail the investigated given thing.

What is knowing precisely, in detail the investigated designations for essential nature? It is that knowing whereby the bodhisattva, with regard to a given thing conceived of as "form," etc., after having investigated its designations for essential nature as designations only, knows and well knows in detail that in designations relating to that given thing there is only the mere semblance of essential nature, and that in truth essential nature is lacking there. for him, seeing that "essential nature" as but a magical creation, a reflected image, an echo, a hallucination, the moon's reflection in the waters, a dream and an illusion, he knows that this semblance is not made up of that essential nature. This is the third knowing precisely, in detail, which is the sphere of most profound knowledge.

What is knowing precisely, in detail, the investigated designations for particularity? It is that knowing whereby the bodhisattva, after having investigated the designations for particularity as designations only attached to the given things called "form," etc., sees designations for particularity as having a not-two meaning. The given thing is neither completely present nor completely absent [neither existent nor nonexistent]. It is not present, since it is not "perfected" owing to its expressible self. And it is not altogether absent, since in fact it is determined to have an inexpressible essence. Thus from the stance of absolute truth, it is not formed, yet from the stance of relative truth it is not formless, since form is attributed to it. As with presence and absence, and formed and formless, just so is whatever is shown or not shown, etc. All the enumerations of designations for particularity should be understood in just this same manner. He [the bodhisattva] knows in detail as having a not-two meaning, whatever be the designations for particularity. This is knowing precisely, in detail the investigated designations for particularity.

Now it should be understood that those eight kinds of errant discursive thought which belong to immature beings and which engender the three bases and cause the continual return to the world, operate through weakness of, and nonengagement with, these four kinds of knowing precisely, in detail. Moreover, from errant discursive thought defilement arises; from defilement, circling in saṃsāra; from circling in saṃsāra, the consequences of saṃsāra, i.e., the sufferings of birth, old age, disease, and death.

But whenever the bodhisattva resorts to the four kinds of knowing precisely, in detail, he knows the eight kinds of discursive thought. And because of his right knowledge, in his lifetime there is no generation, now or in the future, of a given thing associated with proliferation which could serve as a mental support and as a foundation for discursive thought. And because discursive thought does not arise, there is no generation in the future of a given thing having that as its support. Thus for him that discursive thought, along with the given thing, ceases. This should be understood as the cessation of all proliferation.

Therefore, one should understand the complete cessation of proliferation as the bodhisattva's "Parinirvāṇa of the Great Vehicle." Because of the complete purity of his knowledge, now the sphere of the most splendid knowledge of reality, in this lifetime that bodhisattva attains the mastery of power everywhere; for example, he attains the mastery of multiform magical creation owing to the magical power of creating; of multiform transformation owing to the magical power of transformation; of knowledge of all knowables; of remaining in the world as long as he wishes, and of departing from the world at his pleasure, without hindrance.

Thus, that one, with that mastery of power, is best of and incomparable among all beings. And you should understand that this bodhisattva has five superior benefits which control in all circumstances, namely: (1) he attains supreme peace of mind, because he attains the tranquil stations, and not by reason of pacifying defilement; (2) his knowledge and vision with respect to all the sciences are unimpeded, extremely pure, and perfectly clear; (3) he is unwearied by his circling in saṃsāra for the sake of beings; (4) he understands all the speech with "veiled intention" of the Tathāgatas; and (5) because he is self-reliant, not depending on others, he is not led away from his zealous devotion to the Great Vehicle.

Now it should be understood that there are five kinds of actions concomitant with those five kinds of benefits. Namely, it should be understood that the action that goes along with the benefit of a peaceful mind is dwelling in the present life in the supreme station of happiness, i.e., that station of the bodhisattva familiar with praxis that leads to Enlightenment and destroys the physical and mental weariness of exertion.

It should be understood that the action for the bodhisattva that goes along with the benefit of possessing unimpeded knowledge in all the sciences is the maturation of all the Buddhadharmas, and that the action going along with the benefit of being unwearied by saṃsāra is the maturation of beings.

It should be understood that the action going along with understanding all the speech with "veiled intention" is that of removing the doubts that have arisen among the candidates of holding them together, and of upholding the rule of Dharma for a long time, by recognizing, exposing, and dispelling the fictitious resemblances to the True Dharma that cause the Teaching to disappear. And lastly, it should be understood that the action for the bodhisattva that goes along with the benefit of not depending on others and so not being led astray is his victory over all heretical arguments by others, his steadfast striving, and his not falling away from his vow.

Accordingly, whatever the bodhisattva duty of the bodhisattva may be, all that is encompassed by these five actions going along with the benefits. Again, what is that duty? It consists of undefiled personal happiness, maturing the Buddhadharmas, maturing the beings, upholding the True Dharma, and defeating opposing theories, by one whose striving is fierce and whose vow does not waver.

With regard to all the foregoing, it should be understood that of the four sorts of knowledge of reality, the first two are inferior, the third is middling, but the fourth is the best.

Here ends the Chapter on Knowing Reality, being the fourth [chapter] in the first division of the *Bodhisattvabhūmi.*

II
Vasubandhu: Discussion of the Five Aggregates*

1. The five aggregates are the aggregate of materialities, the aggregate of feelings, the aggregate of cognitions, the aggregate of motivational dispositions, and the aggregate of consciousnesses.

What is *materiality*? Materiality is whatever has dimensionality, and consists of all of the four great elements, and everything that is derived from the four great elements. And what are the four great elements? The earth-element, water-element, fire-element, and wind-element. Among these, what is the earth-element? It is solidity. What is the water-element? It is liquidity. What is the fire-element? It is heat. What is the wind-element? It is gaseousness. What is derived from them? The sense-organ of the eye, the sense-organ of the ear, the sense-organ of the nose, the sense-organ of the tongue, the sense-organ of the body, visibles, sounds, smells, tastes, everything that can be subsumed under tactile sensations, and unmanifest action. And among these, what is the sense-organ of the eye? It is sentient materiality which has color as its sense-object. What is the sense-organ of the ear? It is sentient materiality which has sounds as its sense-object. What is the sense-organ of the nose? It is sentient materiality which has smells as its sense-object. What is the sense-organ of the tongue? It is sentient materiality which has tastes as its sense-object. What is the sense-organ of the body? It is sentient materiality which has tactile sensations as its sense-object. And what are visibles? They are the sense-objects of the eye: color, configuration, and manifest action. And what are sounds? They are the sense-objects of the ear, having as their causes great elements appropriated by the body, or great elements unappropriated. And what are smells? They are the sense-objects of the nose: pleasant smells, unpleasant smells, and those which are neither. And what are tastes? They are the sense-objects of the tongue: sweet, sour, salty, sharp, bitter, and stringent. What is everything that can be subsumed under tactile sensations? They are the sense-objects of the body: the great elements themselves, softness, hardness, heaviness, lightness, coldness, hunger, and thirst. What is unmanifest action? It is materiality which has arisen from manifest action or meditational concentration: it is invisible and exercises no resistance.

2. And what are *feelings*? They are experiences, and are of three kinds: pleasure, suffering, and that which is neither pleasure nor suffering. Pleasure is whatever there arises a desire to be connected with again, once it has stopped. Suffering is whatever there arises a desire to be separated from, once it has arisen. That which is neither pleasure nor suffering is whatever towards which neither desire arises, once it has arisen.

3. And what are *cognitions*? They are the grasping of signs in a sense-object. They are of three kinds: indefinite, definite, and immeasurable.

---

*Reprinted with permission from Stefan Anacker, *Seven Works of Vasubandhu* (Delhi: Motilal Banarsidass, 1984).

4. And what are *motivational dispositions*? They are events associated with cittas (mental states), other than feelings and cognitions, and those that are disassociated from cittas. Among these, what are the events associated with cittas? They are whatever events are associated with cittas. And what are they? They are contact, mental attention, feelings, cognitions, volitions, zest, confidence, memory or mindfulness, meditational concentration, insight, faith, inner shame, dread of blame, the root-of-the-beneficial of lack of greed, the root-of-the-beneficial of lack of hostility, the root-of-the-beneficial of lack of confusion, vigor, tranquility, carefulness, equanimity, attitude of nonharming, attachment, aversion, pride, ignorance, views, doubt, anger, malice, hypocrisy, maliciousness, envy, selfishness, deceitfulness, guile, mischievous exuberance, desire to harm, lack of shame, lack of dread of blame, mental fogginess, excitedness, lack of faith, sloth, carelessness, loss of mindfulness, distractedness, lack of recognition, regret, torpor, initial mental application, and subsequent discursive thought.

Among these, the first five occur in every citta. The next five are certain only with specific objects-of-sense. The next eleven are beneficial. The next six are afflictions. The rest are secondary afflictions. The last four also become different (i.e. they are capable of being either afflictions or beneficial).

And what is *contact*? It is the distinguishing which comes after the three (sense-organ, object-of-sense, and corresponding consciousness) have met together. And what is *mental attention*? It is the entering into done by a citta. What is *volition*? It is mental action, which impels a citta towards good qualities, flaws, and that which is neither. And what is *zest*? It is desire towards a range of events of which there is consciousness. And what is *confidence*? It is holding to certainty in regard to a range of events of which there is certainty. What is *memory*? It is the non-forgetting of a range of events towards which there is acquaintance, and is a certain kind of discourse of citta. What is *meditational concentration*? It is one-pointedness of citta towards an examined range of events. What is *insight*? It is discernment as regards the same, and is either understanding, that which has arisen from not having understood, or that which is different from these two. What is *faith*? It is firm conviction, desire, and serenity of citta towards action, its results, the beneficial, and the Gems. What is *inner shame*? It is a shame coming about through a committed offense, in which the self, or rather the (psychological) event responsible, is predominant. And what is *dread of blame*? It is that shame towards others that comes about through a committed offense, in which the outer world is predominant. What is *lack of greed*? It is the antidote to greed, a non-attachment to that which is arising in *manas* (mind). What is *lack of hostility*? It is the antidote to hostility, and is loving kindness. What is *lack of confusion*? It is the antidote to confusion, and is right recognition. And what is *vigor*? It is the antidote to sloth, and is enthusiasm of citta towards the beneficial. And what is *tranquility*? It is the antidote to a situation of susceptibility to harm, and is a skill in bodily and mental action. And what is *carefulness*? It is the antidote to carelessness, a cultivation of those beneficial events which are antidotes, and abandoning unbeneficial events through continuing in those beneficial factors: lack of greed, up to vigor. What is *equanimity*? It is whatever evenness of citta, remaining in a tranquil state of citta, total tranquility in citta continuing in those factors—lack of greed up to vigor, through which there is continuity in a state without afflictions through the clearing away of afflicted events. And what is an *attitude of non-harming*? It is the antidote to an attitude of harming, and is compassion. And what is *attachment*? It is adherence to any fixed intent in appropriating aggregates. And what is *aversion*? It is a tormented volition towards sentient beings. And what is *pride*? There are seven kinds of pride: basic pride, greater pride, the pride that is more than pride, the pride of thinking "I am," conceit, the pride of thinking deficiency, and false pride. Basic pride is any inflation of citta which considers, through a smallness, either "I am greater," or "I am equal." What is greater pride? Greater pride is any inflation of citta which considers, through an equality, that "I am greater" or "I am endowed with greatness." And what is pride that is more than pride? It is any inflation of citta which is connected with the view of either "I am" or "mine" in regard to appropriating aggregates. And what is conceit? It is any inflation of citta which considers, in regard to an excellence which was previously obtained in another moment, but is no longer, "I've attained it." And what is the pride of thinking deficiency? It is any inflation of citta which considers, "I am only a little bit inferior to those of greatly excellent qualities." And what is false pride? It is any inflation of citta which considers "I am endowed with good qualities" when good qualities have not been acquired. And what is *ignorance*? It is lack of knowledge regarding action, results of action, the Truths, and the Gems, and also the mentally constructed that rises together with it. In the realm of desires, there are three roots-of-the-unbeneficial: attachment, aversion, and ignorance, and these are the same as the roots-of-the-unbeneficial greed, hostility, and confusion. And what are *views*? These views are generally of five kinds: the view of a fixed self in the body, views regarding the permanence or impermanence of the elements constituting personality, false views, adherence to particular views, and adherence to mere rule and ritual. And what is the view of a fixed self in the body? It is an afflicted judgment viewing either an "I" or "mine" in the appropriating aggregates. And what are views regarding the permanence or the impermanence of the elements constituting personality? They relate to these same elements (the appropriating aggregates), and are afflicted judgments viewing them as either lasting or discontinuous. And what are false views? They are any afflicted judgments which involve fear towards the elements of existence, and which cast aspersions on the efficacy of cause and effect. What is adherence to particular views? It is any afflicted judgment viewing these same three views, and the aggregates which continue in them, as being the best, the most excellent, attained, and most exalted. And what is attachment to mere rules and rituals? It is any afflicted judgment seeing in rules and rituals, and in the aggregates continuing in them, purity, liberation, and a leading to Nirvāṇa. And what is *doubt*? It is any two-mindedness as regards the Truths, etc. The latter three of those afflicted views mentioned above, and doubt, are the basic mentally constructed. The rest of these views are the mentally constructed that often arise together with those. What is *anger*? It is any tormented volition of citta which all of a sudden becomes intent on doing harm. What is *malice*? It is taking hold of a hostility. What is *hypocrisy*? It is unwillingness to recognize one's own faults. What is *maliciousness*? It is being enslaved by unpleasant speech. What is *envy*? It is an agitation of citta at the attainments of another. What is *selfishness*? It is a holding fast to a citta which is not in accord with giving. What is *deceitfulness*? It is attempting to show forth to another an unreal object through an action of decoying. What is *guile*? It is a deceitfulness of citta which seizes an opportunity for making secret one's own flaws. What is *mischievous exuberance*? It is holding fast to a delighted citta unconnected with internal good qualities. What is an *attitude of harming*? It is an intention unbeneficial towards sentient beings. And what is *lack of shame*? It is a lack of internal shame at offenses one has committed. And what is *lack of dread of blame*? It is a lack of dread towards others at offenses one has committed. What is *mental fogginess*? It is a lack of skill in mental action, and is thickheadedness. What is *excitedness*? It is lack of calm in citta. What is *lack of faith*? It is a lack of trust in a citta, which is not in accord with faith, towards action and its results, the Truths and the Gems. What is *sloth*? It is a lack of enthusiasm towards the beneficial in a citta, and is that which is not in accord with vigor. What is *carelessness*? It is any non-guarding of citta from afflictions, and non-cultivation of the beneficial, which comes about by being linked with greed, hostility, confusion, or sloth. What is *loss of mindfulness*? It is an afflicted mindfulness, an unclarity as to the beneficial. What is *distractedness*? It is any diffusion of citta on the five sense-qualities of the realm of desires, which partakes of greed, hostility, or confusion. What is *lack of recognition*? It is a judgment connected with afflictions, by which there is entry into not knowing what has been done by body, voice, or manas. What is *regret*? It is remorse, a piercing sensation in manas. What is *torpor*? It is a contraction of citta which is without capacity for entering down into anything. What is *initial mental application*? A discourse of inquiry by manas, a certain kind of volition and discernment, which can be characterized as an indistinct state of citta. What is *(subsequent) discursive thought*? A discourse of examination by manas, which in the same way can be characterized as a more precise state of citta.

And what are the *motivating dispositions disassociated from cittas* (mental states)? These are pure designations for situations in materialities, cittas, and events associated with cittas, and are designations only for these, and not for anything else. And what are they? *Prāpti*, the attainment without cognitions, the attainment of the cessation of cognitions and feelings, any non-meditative state without cognitions, life-force, taking part in an organism, birth, decrepitude, continuity, lack of duration, the collection of words, the collection of phrases, the collection of syllables, the state of being separate from Dharma, and other factors like these.

Among these, what is *prāpti*? It is becoming connected with something attained. Actually, it is a "seed," a capacity, an approachment, and an adjustment to circumstances. And what is an *attainment free from cognitions*? It is any cessation of non-stable events: cittas and events associated with cittas, which is totally clear and separate from attainments, and which comes about through a mental attention dispensing with cognitions about to arise, where former cognitions do not exist. And what is the *attainment of the cessation of cognitions, and feelings*? It is any cessation of non-stable and more stable events, cittas and events associated with cittas, which comes about through a mental attention dispensing with cognitions, continuing in which comes after the summits of existence have been practiced, and which is separate from those attainments present in the stage-of-nothing-whatever. And what is a *non-meditative state without cognitions*? It is the cessation of non-stable events: cittas and events associated with cittas, which takes place, for instance, within those groups of gods which are sentient, but do not have cognitions. What is *life-force*? It is, as regards any events taking part in an organism, any continuity, for a certain time, of motivating dispositions which have been projected by past action. And what is *taking part in an organism*? It is any close interrelationship of bodily parts as regards sentient beings. What is *birth*? It is any arising of a stream of motivating dispositions which has not already arisen, as regards any collection of events taking part in an organism. And what is *decrepitude*? It is an alteration in the stream of those like that (i.e. events taking part in an organism). What is *continuity*? It is the serial propagation in the stream of those like that. What is *lack of duration*? It is the discontinuity in the stream of those like that. What is the *collection of words*? It is denotations for the own-beings of events. What is the *collection of phrases*? It is denotations for the particularities of events. What is the *collection of syllables*? They are the syllables of actual sound through which the other two are disclosed. Though these all refer to speech, meanings are communicated dependent on words and phrases. For the same syllable does not arise with another synonym. And what is the *state of being separate from Dharma*? It is the non-attainment of noble psychological events.

These all are called "the aggregate of motivational dispositions."

5. And what is *consciousness*? It is awareness of an object-of-consciousness, visibles, etc. "Citta" and "manas" are the same as consciousness. They are so designated because of their variety, and because of their providing a mental basis, respectively. Actually, the store consciousness is also citta, as it accumulates the seeds for all motivating dispositions. Its objects-of-consciousness and aspects are undiscerned. It joins an assemblage pertaining to an organism into a felt relationship, and continues as a series of moment-events. Thus, though there is awareness of a sense-object immediately upon emerging from the attainment of cessation of cognitions and feelings, the attainment free from cognitions, or a non-meditative state without cognitions, it arises as the consciousness of the attainments themselves; it is the state of evolvement into another aspect once there has been perception dependent upon any object-of-consciousness; it is the state of citta's arising again even after the consciousness-stream has been severed; it is entry into Saṃsāra[1] and transmigration in it. This same store-consciousness is the support of all the seeds, the basis and causality for the body, and the state of continuance in a body. It is also called "the appropriating consciousness," because it appropriates a body. Used in the sense of a specific entity, *manas* is an object-of-consciousness, within the store-consciousness, a consciousness always connected with confusion of self, the view of a self, pride of self, love of self, etc. It also joins an assemblage pertaining to an organism into a felt relationship, and continues as a series of moment-events, but does not exist in a saint, the Noble Path, or at the time of the attainment of cessation.

Why are the aggregates thus designated? It is through their collectivity, i.e. various kinds of materialities, etc., being heaped up together that "times," "series," "aspects," "developments," and "sense-objects" seem to occur.

The twelve *sense-fields* are the sense-field of the eye and the sense-field of visibles, the sense-field of the ear and the sense-field of sounds, the sense-field of the nose and the sense-field of smells, the sense-field of the tongue and the sense-field of tastes, the sense-field of the body and the sense-field of tactile sensations, the sense-field of *manas* and the sense-field of mentally cognizables. The eye, visibles, the ear, sounds, the nose, smells, the tongue, tastes have all been discussed previously. The sense-field of the tactile is the four great elements and everything (all the incredibly numerous various sensations) which can be subsumed under tactile sensations. The sense-field of *manas* is any aggregate of consciousness. The sense-field of mentally cognizables is feelings, cognitions, motivating dispositions, unmanifest action, and the uncompounded. And what is the uncompounded? Space, the cessation not through contemplation, the cessation through contemplation, and Suchness. Among these, what is *space*? It is any interval separating materialities. What is a *cessation not through contemplation*? It is any non-separation from cessation without antidotes to afflictions figuring in. And what is *cessation through contemplation*? It is any non-separation from cessation, any constant non-arising of aggregates through antidotes to afflictions. What is *Suchness*? It is the "inherent nature (*dharmatā*) of any event," and is the selflessness of events.

Why are these called "sense-fields"? Because they are the doors to the rising of consciousness. The eighteen *sensory domains* are the domain of the eye, the domain of the visible, the domain of the visual consciousness; the domain of the ear, the domain of sounds, the domain of audial consciousness; the domain of the nose, the domain of smells, the domain of olfactory consciousness; the domain of the tongue, the domain of tastes, the domain of gustatory consciousness; the domain of the body, the domain of the tactile, the domain of tactile consciousness, the domain of the *manas*, the domain of mentally cognizables, and the domain of the mental consciousness. The domains of the eye, etc., and the domains of visibles, etc., are the same as the sense-fields. The domains of the six consciousnesses are awarenesses with

[1] The world of change.

objects-of-consciousness in visibles, etc., and which are dependent on the eye, etc. The domain of *manas* is any of these consciousness-moments which are past immediately afterwards, because of the continuity of the sixth consciousness. In this way, the sensory domains have been determined as eighteen.

Ten of those sense-fields and domains (the sensory organs and their objects) and that part of the sense-field of mentally cognizables which may be subsumed under it (unmanifest action) constitute whatever is the aggregate of materiality. The sense-field of *manas* and the seven domains of citta (the visual, olfactory, gustatory, tactile, and mental consciousnesses, and the domain of mentally cognizables) constitute whatever is the aggregate of consciousness. The sense-fields and domains of mentally cognizables also constitute whatever are the other three aggregates (feelings, cognitions, and motivating dispositions), one part of the aggregate of materiality which may be subsumed under it (manifest action), and the uncompounded. Why are these called "domains"? Because they grasp an "own-characteristic," though without a "doer." As to why they are called "aggregates," etc., this serves as an antidote to the three kinds of grasping after self, in order. The three kinds of grasping after self are grasping for one central entity, grasping for an "enjoyer," and grasping for a "doer."

Among these eighteen sensory domains, which contain materiality? Whatever has the own-being of the aggregate of materiality. Which do not contain materiality? The rest of them. Which can be seen? Only the sensory domain of visibles is an object-of-sense which can be seen. Which are invisible? The rest of them. Which exercise resistance? The ten which contain materiality, which exercise resistance on each other. Which do not exercise resistance? The rest of them. Which are liable to be connected with afflictions? Fifteen (i.e. the sensory domains of the eye to tactile consciousness), and part of the last three (*manas*, mentally cognizables, and mental consciousness). Which are unliable to be connected with afflictions? Part of the last three. Those because of having a scope allowing for the direct perception of the arising of afflictions. Which are without afflictions? Part of the last three. Which occur in the realm of desires? All of them. Which occur in the realm of simple images? Fourteen: all of them except smells, tastes, olfactory-consciousness, and gustatory-consciousness. Which occur in the imageless sphere? Part of the last three. Which are included within the aggregates? All of them except the uncompounded. Which are included within the appropriating aggregates? Those constituting a "personality." Which are beneficial, which unbeneficial, and which indeterminate? Ten may belong to any of the three categories: the seven sensory domains of citta, and the sensory domains of visibles, sounds and mentally cognizables. The rest of them are all indeterminate. Which are "internal"? Twelve of them: all of them except visibles, sounds, smells, tastes, tactile sensations and mentally cognizables. Which are "external"? Six of them: those not included in the preceding. Which have an object-of-consciousness? The seven sensory domains of citta, and one part of the sensory domain of mentally cognizables, namely, whatever events are associated with cittas. Which are without an object-of-consciousness? The ten others and most of the sensory domains of mentally cognizables. Which contain discrimination? The sensory domains of *manas*, mental consciousness, and mentally cognizables. Which do not contain discrimination? The rest of them. Which are appropriated? Five of the "internal" (organs I-V) and part of the "external" (i.e. part of visibles, sounds, smells, tastes, and tactile sensations). Which are unappropriated? Part of the four (all visibles, smells, tastes and tactile sensations not integral parts of the sensory organism). Which are similar in what they show? The five internal material ones (organs I-V), their respective consciousnesses and sensory domains, inasmuch as they have something in common. What is their similarity? These are all, by means of their respective consciousnesses, empty, because of a conformity of each to understanding.

III
Vasubandhu: Twenty Verses and Commentary*

In the Great Vehicle, the three realms of existence are determined as being perception-only. As it is said in the sūtra[1], "The three realms of existence are citta-only." Citta, manas, consciousness, and perception are synonyms. By the word 'citta," citta along with its associations is intended here. "Only" is said to rule out any (external) object of sense or understanding.

1. All this is perception-only, because of the appearance of non-existent objects,
just as there may be the seeing of non-existent nets of hair by someone afflicted with an optical disorder.

Here it is objected:

2. "If perception occurs without an object,
any restriction as to place and time becomes illogical,
as does non-restriction as to moment-series
and any activity which has been performed."

What is being said? If the perception of visibles, etc. arises without any object of visibles, etc. why is it that it arises only in certain places, and not everywhere, and even in those places, why is it that it arises only sometimes, and not all the time? And why is it that it arises in the moment-series of all that are situated in that time and place, and not just in the moment-

*Reprinted with permission from Stefan Anacker, *Seven Works of Vasubandhu* (Delhi: Motilal Banarsidass, 1984).

[1] *Avataṃsaka-sūtra: Daśa-bhūmika* VI.

series of one, just as the appearance of hair, etc. arises in the moment-series of those afflicted by an optical disorder, and not in the moment-series of others? Why is it that the hair, bees, etc. seen by those afflicted by an optical disorder don't perform the functions of hair, etc. while it is not the case that other hair, etc. don't perform them? Food, drink, clothes, poison, weapons, etc. that are seen in a dream don't perform the functions of food, etc. while it is not the case that other food, etc. don't perform them. An illusory town does not perform the functions of a town, because of its non-existence, while it is not the case that other towns don't perform them. Therefore, with the non-being of an object, any restriction as to place and time, any non-restriction as to moment-series, and any activity which has been performed, would be illogical.

Reply:

3a. No, they are not illogical, because
Restriction as to place, etc. is demonstrated as in a dream.

Now how is this? In a dream, even without an (external) object of sense or understanding, only certain things are to be seen: bees, gardens, women, men, etc. and these only in certain places, and not everywhere. And even there in those places, they are to be seen only sometimes, and not all the time. In this way, even without an (external) object of sense or understanding, there may be restriction as to place and time.

3b. And non-restriction as to moment series
is like with the *pretas*[2].

The phrase "is demonstrated" continues to apply here (to make the verse read: "And non-restriction as to moment-series is demonstrated as with the pretas.*"). How is it demonstrated?*

3c. In the seeing of pus-rivers, etc. by all of them

all together. A "pus-river" is a river filled with pus. Just as one says "a ghee pot." For all the pretas *who are in a similar situation due to a similar retribution for action, and not just one of them, see a river filled with pus. With the expression "etc." rivers full of urine and feces, guarded by men holding clubs or swords, and other such perceptions, are included also. Thus, non-restriction as to moment-series in regard to perceptions is demonstrated even with an (external) object of sense or understanding being non-existent.*

4a. And activity which has been performed
is just like being affected in a dream.

---

[2] Ghosts.

A case of being affected in a dream is like where semen is released even without a couple's coming together. So, by these various examples, the four-fold restriction as to place and time, and so on, is demonstrated.

4b. And as in a hell-state,
all of these are demonstrated.

"In a hell-state" means "among those experiencing a hell-state." How are they demonstrated?

4c. In the seeing of hell-guardians, etc.
and in being tormented by them.

Just as the seeing of hell-guardians, etc. by those experiencing a hell-state (and with the expression "etc." the seeing of dogs, crows, moving mountains, and so on, is included) is demonstrated with a restriction as to place and time for all of those experiencing a hell-state, and not just for one of them, and just as their torment inflicted by them is demonstrated through the sovereignty of the common retribution for their individual actions, even though the hell-guardians, and so on, are really non-existent. So the four-fold restriction as to place and time is to be known as demonstrated in yet another way.

Objection: But for what reason is the existence of hell-guardians, dogs, and crows (experienced in hell-states) not accepted?

Reply: Because they are illogical. For to assume that these kinds of hell-beings have an external existence is not logical. This is so because they don't feel the sufferings there themselves, or if they tormented each other mutually, there would be no difference in situation between those experiencing a hell-state and the hell-guardians, and if they mutually tormented each other having equal make-ups, sizes, and strengths, there would be no fear in those experiencing a hell-state, and since they couldn't stand the burning suffering of standing on a ground made of heated iron, how could they be tormenting others? And how could there be an arising of those not experiencing a hell-state, together with those who are?

Objection: How is this? The arising of animals in a heaven-state may occur, so in the same way, there may be the arising of hell-guardians, etc. which have the distinct qualities of animals or pretas, *in hell-states.*

5. There is no arising of animals in hell-states,
as there is in heaven-states,
nor is there any arising of *pretas*,
since they don't experience the sufferings that are engendered there.

Those animals which arise in heaven-states experience all the pleasure that is engendered there because of (past) actions bringing pleasure to their environment. But hell-guardians, etc. don't experience hellish suffering in the same way. So the arising of animals (in hell-states) is not logical, and neither is the arising of pretas *there.*

An opinion: Then it's because of the actions of those experiencing a hell-state that special material elements arise, which have special qualities as to color, make-up, size, and strength, and are cognized as hell-guardians, etc. That's why they are constantly transforming in various ways, and appear to be shaking their hands, etc. in order to instill fear, just as mountains that look like sheep appear to be coming and going, and just as thorns in forests of iron silk-cotton trees appear to be bowing down and rising up again. And yet it isn't that (these phenomena) aren't arising.

Reply:

6. If the arising and transformation of material elements due to the actions of those is accepted,
why isn't (such arising and transformation) of a consciousness accepted?

Why is a transformation of consciousness itself due to (past) actions not accepted, and why instead are material elements constructed? And furthermore,

7. It's being constructed that the process of impressions from actions takes place elsewhere than does its effect,
and it is not being accepted that it exists there where the impressions take place: Now what is your reason for this?

Because it is through their action that such an arising and transformation of material elements is constructed for those experiencing a hell-state, and inasmuch as impressions through actions enter together into their consciousness-series, and not anywhere else, why is it that that effect is not accepted as being such a transformation of consciousness taking place just where the impressions themselves do? What is the reason for an effect being constructed where there is no process of impression?

(You may say): By reason of scriptural authority. If consciousness were only the appearance of visibles, etc. and there were no (external) object of visibles, etc. the existence of the sense-fields of visibles, etc. would not have been spoken of by the Exalted One.

Reply:

8. This is no reason, because
Speaking of sense-fields of visibles, etc.
was intended for those to be introduced to Dharma,
just as in the case of spontaneously-generated beings.

It's just like in the case where spontaneously generated beings were discussed by the Exalted One. This was done with the intention of indicating the non-discontinuity of the citta-series in the future. "There is neither a sentient being, or a self, but only events along with their causes," has been stated by the Exalted One.[3] *Thus, statements were made by the Exalted One regarding the existence of the sense-fields of visibles, etc. with an intention directed at people to be introduced to the Dharma. And what was the intention there?*

9. Because their appearances continue as perceptions,
because of (consciousnesses') own seeds,
the Sage spoke in terms of states of two-fold sense-fields."

What was said? The Exalted One spoke of sense-fields of the eye and of visibles in those cases where a perception with the appearance of visibles arises from the attainment of a special transformation (in the consciousness-series) through its own seeds, and when this seed and perception become manifest with this appearance, respectively. In the same way, in those cases where a perception with the appearance of tactile sensations arises from the attainment of a special transformation (in the consciousness-series) through its own seeds, and when this seed and that appearance become manifest, the Exalted One spoke of sense-fields of the body and of tactile sensations, respectively. This is the intention.

10a. What is the advantage of teaching with such an intention?
In this way, there is entry into the selflessness of personality.

If the sense-fields are taught in this way, people will enter into an understanding of the selflessness of personality. The group of six consciousnesses evolves because of duality. But when it is known that there is not any one seer (any one hearer, any one smeller, any one taster, any one toucher), or any one thinker, those to be introduced to Dharma through the selflessness of personality will enter into an understanding of the selflessness of personality.

10b. And in yet another way, this teaching is entry into the selflessness of events.

"And in yet another way," etc. is in reference to how the teaching of perception-only is entry into the selflessness of events, when it becomes known that this perception-only makes an appearance of visibles, etc. arise, and that there is no experienced event with the characteristics of visibles, etc. But if there isn't an event in any way, then perception-only also isn't, so how can it be demonstrated? But it's not because there isn't an event in any way that there is entry into the selflessness of events. Rather, it's

[3] *Majjhima* I, 138.

10c. in regard to a constructed self.

It is selflessness in reference to a constructed self, i.e. all those things that constitute the "own-being" believed in by fools, that is the constructed with its "objects apprehended" and "subjects apprehendors," etc. and not in reference to the ineffable Self, which is the scope of Buddhas. In the same way, one penetrates the selflessness of perception-only itself in reference to a "self" constructed by another perception, and through this determination of perception-only, there is entry into the selflessness of all events, and not by a denial of their existence. Otherwise, there would be an object for this other perception because of a perception itself (i.e. either "perception-only" or "the perception of self" would be a real object), there would be at least one perception which has an object consisting of another perception, and the state of perception-only wouldn't be demonstrated, because of the perception's state of having objects.

But how is it to be understood that the existence of the sense-fields of visibles, etc. was spoken of by the Exalted One not because those things which singly become sense-objects of the perceptions of visibles, etc. really exist, but rather with a hidden intention? Because

11. A sense-object is neither a single thing,
nor several things,
from the atomic point of view,
nor can it be an aggregate (of atoms),
so atoms can't be demonstrated.

What is being said? The sense-field of visibles, etc. which consists (in a moment) of a single sense-object of a perception of visibles, etc. is either a unity, like the composite whole constructed by the Vaiśeṣikas,[4] or it is several things, from the atomic point of view, or it is an aggregation of atoms. Now, the sense-object can't be a single thing, because one can nowhere apprehend a composite whole which is different from its component parts. Nor can it be plural, because of atoms, since they can't be apprehended singly. Nor does an aggregation of atoms become a sense-object, because an atom as one entity can't be demonstrated, either.

12a. How is it that it can't be demonstrated? Because
Through the simultaneous conjunction of six elements,
the atom has six parts.

If there is a simultaneous conjunction of six elements in six directions, the atom comes to have six parts. For that which is the locus of one can't be the locus of another.

---

[4] Philosophers belonging to a non-Buddhist school holding that all things are constituted by fundamentally different constituents.

12b. If there were a common locus for the six,
the agglomeration would only be one atom.

It might be maintained that the locus for each single atom is the locus of all six elements. But then, because of the common locus for all of them, the agglomeration would be only one atom, because of the mutual exclusion of occupants of a locus. And then, no agglomeration would become visible. Nor, for that matter, can atoms join together at all, because of their state of having no parts. The Vaibhāṣikas[5] *of Kashmir say, "We aren't arguing such an absurdity. It's just when they're in aggregation, that they can join together." But the question must be asked: Is then an aggregation of atoms not an object different from the atoms themselves?*

13. When there is no conjunction of atoms,
how can there be one for their aggregations?
Their conjunction is not demonstrated,
for they also have no parts.

So the aggregations themselves can't mutually join together, either. For there is no conjunction of atoms, because of their state of having no parts. That is to say, such a thing can't be demonstrated. So even in the case of an aggregation, which does have parts, its conjunction becomes inadmissible (because there can be no aggregation of atoms unless individual atoms conjoin. And so the atoms as one entity can't be demonstrated. And whether the conjunction of atoms is accepted, or isn't

14a. (To assume) the singleness of that which has divisions as to directional dimensions, is illogical.

For one atom, there may be the directional dimension of being "in front," for another, of being "on the bottom," and if there are such divisions as to directional dimensions, how can the singleness of an atom, which partakes of such divisions, be logical?

14b. Or else, how could there be shade and blockage?

If there were no divisions as to directional dimensions in an atom, how could there be shade in one place, light in another, when the sun is rising? For there could be no other location for the atom where there would be no light. And how could there be an obstruction of one atom by another, if divisions as to directional dimensions are not accepted? For there would be no other part for an atom, where, through the arrival of another atom, there would be a collision with this other atom. And if there is no collision, then

---

[5] A Buddhist philosophical school holding that the unity of things comprises many different actual components.

the whole aggregation of all the atoms would have the dimensions of only one atom, because of their common locus, as has been stated previously.

It may be argued: Why can't it be accepted that shade and blockage refer to an agglomeration, and not to a single atom?

Reply: But in that case, is it being admitted that an agglomeration is something other than the atoms themselves? Objector: No, that can't be admitted.

14c. If the agglomeration isn't something other,
then they can't refer to it.

If it is not accepted that the agglomeration is something other than the atoms, then shade and blockage can't be demonstrated as occurring in reference to the agglomeration only. This is simply an attachment to mental construction. "Atoms" or "aggregations": what's the point of worrying with those, if "their basic characteristics of being visibles, etc." are not refuted?

What then is their characteristic? That they are in a state of being sense-objects of the eye etc., in a state of being blue, etc. It is just this which should be investigated. If a sense-object for the eye, and so on, is accepted in the form of blue, yellow, etc. then are these one entity, or several? Now what follows from this? The flaw inherent in assuming their severalness has already been discussed (in relation to the arguments on atomic aggregation).

15. If their unity existed, one couldn't arrive at anything gradually,
there couldn't be apprehension and non-apprehension simultaneously
there couldn't be separate, several, developments,
and there would be no reason for the non-seeing of the very subtle.

If one entity as a sense-object for the eye, with no separations, and no severalness, were constructed, then one couldn't arrive at anything gradually on the Earth: that is, there could be no act of going. For, even with placing down a foot once, one would go everywhere. There could be no apprehension of a nearer "part of something" and a non-apprehension of a more removed "part," simultaneously. For a concurrent apprehension and non-apprehension of the same thing isn't logical. There would be no special development for species that are separate, such as elephants, horses, etc. and since they would all be one in that case, how could their separation be accepted? And how can they be accepted as single, anyway, since there is the apprehension of an empty space between two of them? And there would be no reason for the non-seeing of subtle water-beings, since they would be visible in common with the more apparent.

An otherness in entities is constructed if there is a division of characteristics, and not otherwise, so when speaking from the atomic point of view, one must by necessity construct divisions, and it cannot be demonstrated that they (the atoms) are in any way of one kind. With their unity undemonstrated, visibles', etc.'s state of being sense-objects of the eye, etc., is also undemonstrated, and thus perception-only is *demonstrated.*

If the existence and non-existence of objects of sense or understanding are being investigated by force of the means-of-cognition (direct perception, inference, appeal to reliable authority), direct perception must be recognized as being the most weighty of all means-of-cognition. But with an object of sense or understanding not existing, how can there be any cognizing which can be termed "direct perception"?

16a. Cognizing by direct perception is like in a dream, etc.

For it is without an object of sense or understanding, as has been made known previously.

16b. And when it occurs, the object is already not seen,
so how can it be considered a state of direct perception?

When a cognition through direct perception arises in the form "This is my direct perception," the object itself is already not seen, since this distinguishing takes place only through a mental consciousness, and the visual consciousness has already ceased by that time, so how can its being a direct perception be accepted? This is especially true for a sense-object, which is momentary, for that visible, or taste, etc. has already ceased by that time. It may be said that nothing which hasn't been experienced (by other consciousnesses) is remembered by the mental consciousness, and that this takes place by necessity as it is brought about by the experience of an object of sense or understanding, and that those can be considered to be a state of direct perception of sense-objects, visibles, etc. in this way. But this remembering of an experienced object of sense or understanding is not demonstrated, either. Because

17a. It has been stated how perception occurs with its appearance.

It has already been stated how perceptions in the shape of eye-consciousnesses, etc. arise with the appearance of an object, even without there being any (external) object of sense or understanding.

17b. And remembering takes place from that.

"From that" means "from the perception." A mental perception arises with the discrimination of a visible, etc. when that appearance is linked with memory, so an experience of an (external) object can't be demonstrated through the arising of a memory.

Objection: If, even when one is awake, perception has sense-objects which weren't, like in a dream, then people would understand their nonbeing by themselves. But that isn't the case. So it's not that the apprehen-

sion of objects is like in a dream, and all perceptions are really without an (external) object.

Reply: This argument won't bring us to the cognition you wish, because

17c. Somebody who isn't awake doesn't understand the non-being of the visual sense-objects in a dream.

Just as people when they are asleep in a dream have their faculties concentrated on impressions of appearances of discriminations which appear differently than they do later, and, as long as they aren't awake, don't understand the non-being of objects of sense and understanding that weren't just so when they become awakened by the attainment of a supermundane knowledge free from discriminations, which is the antidote to these (discriminations), then they truly understand the non-being of these sense-objects through meeting with a clear worldly subsequently attained knowledge. So their situations are similar.

Objection: If, through a special transformation of "their own" moment-series, perceptions with the appearance of (external) objects of sense or understanding arise for beings, and not through special objects themselves, then how can any certainty as regards perceptions be demonstrated from association with bad or good friends, or from hearing about existent and non-existent events, since there can exist neither association with the good or bad, nor any real teaching?

Reply:

18a. The certainty of perceptions takes place mutually,
by the state of their sovereign effect on one another.

For all beings there is certainty of perception through a mutual sovereign effect of perceptions on one another, according to circumstances. "Mutually" means "each affecting the other." So one special perception arises within a moment-series through a special perception within the moment-series, and not because of a special object.

Objection: If a perception is without an (external) object, just like in a dream, even for those who are awake, why is it that in the practice of the beneficial and unbeneficial there won't be an equal result from desirable and undesirable efforts, for those who are asleep and those who aren't?

Reply: Because

18b. Citta is affected by torpor in a dream,
so their results are different.

This is the reason, not the existing being of an (external) object.

Objection: If all this is perception-only, there can't be body or speech for anybody. So how can the dying of sheep who have been attacked by shepherds, take place? If their dying takes place without the shepherds having done anything, how can the shepherds be held responsible for the offense of taking life?

Reply:

19. Dying may be a modification resulting from a special perception by another,
just like losses of memory, etc. may take place through the mental control of spirits, etc.

Just as there may be modifications in others, such as loss of memory, the seeing of dreams, or being taken possession of by spirits, by the mental control of psychic powers, as in the case of Sāraṇa's seeing dreams through Mahā-Kātyāyana's mental force, or, as in the case of the vanquishing of Vemacitra through mental harming coming from the forest-dwelling seers. In the same way, through the force of a special perception of another, a certain modification of the aggregate-series, destroying its life-force, may arise, through which dying, which is to be known as a name for a discontinuity in the aggregate-series taking part in an organism takes place.

20a. Or else, how was it that the Daṇḍaka Forest became empty because of the anger of seers?

If it isn't accepted that the dying of beings can occur through the force of a special perception in others, how is it that the Exalted One, in order to demonstrate that mental hạrm constitutes a great offense, questioned Upāli when he was still a householder, as follows: "Householder! Through what agency were the Daṇḍaka, Mataṅga, and Kaliṅga Forests made empty and sacred, as has been reported?," and Upāli replied, "I heard that it happened through the mental harming of seers, Gautama."[6]

20b. If not, how could it be demonstrated that mental harm constitutes a great offense?

If this situation were constructed as not taking place through a mental harming, and it were to be said that those sentient beings that were living in that forest were destroyed by non-human spirits that had been propitiated as if they were seers, how could it be demonstrated by this passage that mental harm through mental action is a greater offense than bodily or verbal harm? This passage demonstrates that the dying of so many sentient beings came about only through a mental harming.

Objection: But if all this is perception-only, do those who understand the cittas of others really know the cittas of others, or don't they?

Reply:

What about this?

---

[6] *Majjhima* I, 37–38.

Objector: If they don't know them, how can they be "those who understand the cittas of others"?

Reply: They know them.

21a. The knowledge of those who understand others' cittas is not like an object.
And how is this? As in the case of a knowledge of one's own citta.

Objector: And how is that *knowledge (of one's own citta) not like an object?*

Reply:

21b. Because of non-knowledge, as in the case of the scope of Buddhas.

It's just like in the case of the scope of Buddhas, which comes about through the ineffable Self. Thus both of these knowledges, because of their inherent non-knowledge, are not like an object, because it is through the state of an appearance of something which appears differently than it does later that there is a state of non-abandonment of the discrimination between object apprehended and subject apprehendor.

Though perception-only has unfathomable depth, and there are limitless kinds of ascertainments to be gained in it,

22a. I have written this demonstration of perception-only according to my abilities,
but in its entirety it is beyond the scope of citta.

It is impossible for people like me to consider it in all its aspects, because it is not in the range of dialectics. And in order to show by whom it is known entirely as a scope of insight, it is said to be

22b. the scope of Buddhas.

In all its modes, it is the scope of Buddhas, Exalted Ones, because of their lack of impediment to the knowledge of everything that can be known in all aspects.

IV
Vasubandhu: Thirty Verses*

1. The metaphors of "self" and "events" which develop in so many different ways
Take place in the transformation of consciousness: and this transformation is of three kinds:

---

*Reprinted with permission from Stefan Anacker, *Seven Works of Vasubandhu* (Delhi: Motilal Banarsidass, 1984).

2. Maturation, that called "always reflecting," and the perception of sense-objects.
Among these, "maturation" is that called "the store-consciousness" which has all the seeds.

3. Its appropriations, states, and perceptions are not fully conscious,
Yet it is always endowed with contacts, mental attentions, feelings, cognitions, and volitions.

4. Its feelings are equaniminous: it is unobstructed and indeterminate.
The same for its contacts, etc. It develops like the currents in a stream.

5. Its de-volvement takes place in a saintly state: Dependent on it there develops
A consciousness called "manas," having it[1] as its object-of-consciousness, and having the nature of always reflecting;

6. It is always conjoined with four afflictions, obstructed-but-indeterminate,
Known as view of self, confusion of self, pride of self, and love of self.

7. And wherever it arises, so do contact and the others. But it doesn't exist in a saintly state,
Or in the attainment of cessation, or even in a supermundane path.

8. This is the second transformation. The third is the apprehension
of sense-objects of six kinds: it is either beneficial, or unbeneficial, or both.

9. It is always connected with motivating dispositions, and sometimes with factors that arise specifically,
With beneficial events associated with citta, afflictions, and secondary afflictions: its feelings are of three kinds.

10. The first[2] are contact, etc.; those arising specifically are
zest, confidence, memory, concentration, and insight;

11. The beneficial are faith, inner shame, dread of blame,
The three starting with lack of greed,[3] vigor, tranquility, carefulness, and non-harming;

12. The afflictions are attachment, aversion, and confusion, pride, views, and doubts.
The secondary afflictions are anger, malice, hypocrisy, maliciousness, envy, selfishness, deceitfulness,

13. Guile, mischievous exuberance, desire to harm, lack of shame, lack of dread of blame, mental fogginess, excitedness,
lack of faith, sloth, carelessness, loss of mindfulness,

14. Distractedness, lack of recognition, regret, and torpor,
initial mental application, and subsequent discursive thought: the last two pairs are of two kinds.

---

1. The store-consciousness.
2. Feelings, cognitions, and volitions.
3. Lack of greed, lack of hostility, lack of confusion.

15. In the root-consciousness, the arising of the other five takes place according to conditions,
Either all together or not, just as waves in water.

16. The co-arising of a mental consciousness takes place always except in a non-cognitional state,
Or in the two attainments,[4] or in torpor, or fainting, or in a state without citta.

17. This transformation of consciousness is a discrimination, and
As it is discriminated, it does not exist, and so everything is perception-only.

18. Consciousness is only all the seeds, and transformation takes place in such and such a way,
According to a reciprocal influence, by which such and such a type of discrimination may arise.

19. The residual impressions of actions, along with the residual impressions of a "dual" apprehension,
Cause another maturation (of seeds) to occur, where the former maturation has been exhausted.

20. Whatever range of events is discriminated by whatever discrimination
Is just the constructed own-being, and it isn't really to be found.

21. The interdependent own-being, on the other hand, is the discrimination which arises from conditions,
And the fulfilled is its[5] state of being separated always from the former.[6]

22. So it is to be spoken of as neither exactly different nor non-different from the interdependent,
Just like impermanence, etc., for when one isn't seen, the other is.

23. The absence of own-being in all events has been taught with a view towards
The three different kinds of absence of own-being in the three different kinds of own-being.

24. The first is without own-being through its character itself, but the second
Because of its non-independence, and the third *is* absence of own-being.

25. It is the ultimate truth of all events, and so it is "Suchness," too, since it is just so all the time, and it is just perception-only.

26. As long as consciousness is not situated within perception-only,
The residues of a "dual" apprehension will not come to an end.

27. And so even with the consciousness: "All this is perception only," because this also involves an apprehension,
For whatever makes something stop in front of it isn't situated in "this-only."

---

[4]Forms of concentration.
[5]The interdependent's.
[6]The constructed.

28. When consciousness does not apprehend any object-of-consciousness,
It's situated in "consciousness-only," for with the non-being of an object apprehended, there is no apprehension of it.

29. It is without citta, without apprehension, and it is super-mundane knowledge;
It is revolution at the basis, the ending of two kinds of susceptibility to harm.

30. It is the inconceivable, beneficial, constant Ground, not liable to affliction,
It is bliss, the liberation-body called the Dharma-body of the Sage.

CHAPTER 14

ZEN

Zen has its origins in the Mahāyāna thought and practice of the Yogācāra and Mādhyamaka as these were understood in China in the third to fifth centuries. It is generally agreed that Dōgen (1200 - 1253), founder of the Sōtō Zen School in Japan, is Japan's greatest Zen thinker, and that the *Shōbōgenzō* ("Treasury of the Eye of True Teaching") is his greatest work. Having first studied Tendai and Rinzai Zen in Japan under Myōzen, at age twenty-five Dōgen began practicing under Master Nyojō (Ju-ching, 1163 - 1228) in China, who two years later certified Dōgen's realization. His profound realization, great erudition, creativity with language, and subtle teaching devices shine through the ninety-five essays of his masterpiece, the *Shōbōgenzō*. The majority of these essays were composed between 1240 and 1243 at the Kyoto Kōshō Hōrin temple where Dōgen presided from 1234 until 1243, at which time he moved to the Eiheiji temple where he presided until 1253, the year of his death.

Although the *Shōbōgenzō* essays contain traditional teachings and acute analysis of these teachings, their overall thrust is not to present theoretical analysis or a metaphysical view of reality, but to lead the reader into a self-awakening. Toward this end, teachings are often "presented sideways and used upside down," deconstructing the traditional doctrines so that the underlying truth can be grasped directly. It was naturally assumed that these essays, born out of learning realized in meditational practice, would be incorporated into the totality of the reader's own Zen practice.

Thomas Cleary, *Shōbōgenzō: Zen Essays by Dōgen* (Honolulu: University of Hawaii Press, 1986), from which these selections have been taken, contains a total of thirteen *Shōbōgenzō* chapters, each prefaced by an excellent brief commentary. These commentaries along with the extremely helpful introductory chapters make this book the best place to begin one's reading of Dōgen. Recently three fine collections of translations from the *Shōbōgenzō* have become available: Hee-Jin Kim, *Flowers of Emptiness: Selections from Dōgen's Shōbōgenzō* (Lewiston, N.Y.: Mellen, 1989); Carl Bielfeldt, *Dōgen's Manuals of Zen Meditation* (Berkeley: University of California Press, 1988);

and Francis H. Cook, editor, *Sounds of Valley Streams: Enlightenment in Dōgen's Zen: Translation of Nine Essays from Shōbōgenzō* (Albany: State University of New York Press, 1988). The best book-length study of Dōgen is Hee-Jin Kim, *Dōgen Kigen: Mystical Realist*, revised edition, (Tucson: University of Arizona Press, 1987), which places Dōgen's thought in the context of his life.

Zenkei Shibayama, Zen Master of the Kyoto Nanzenji Monastery from 1948 to 1967 and head of the Nanzenji Organization of Rinzai Temples, is among the most recent masters to comment on the *koans* in the classic collection called the *Mumonkan*. *Koans* are sayings presented to Zen students as puzzles to help them let go of the dualistic grasping characteristic of ordinary thinking. The forty-eight *koans* collected in the *Mumonkan* are sayings of many earlier Zen masters to which Master Mumon added his own commentaries in the thirteenth century. Joshu's *Mu*, the most famous *koan* in this collection, is presented here with the traditional commentaries as well as the commentary Master Shibayama composed to help his own students break the barrier of dualistic knowledge and gain direct insight into reality. The selection is taken from Zenkei Shibayma, *Zen Comments on the Mumonkan* (New York: New American Library, 1975), which has a very short but helpful introduction. Philip Kapleau, *The Three Pillars of Zen* (New York: Harper & Row, 1969), remains one of the best introductions to both the thought and the practice of Zen. For an overall history of Zen, from its Indian beginnings to its recent developments in Japan, Heinrich Dumoulin, *Zen Buddhism: A History*, volumes 1 and 2 (New York: Macmillan Publishing Company, 1988 and 1989), is unsurpassed. The second volume has an excellent chapter on Dōgen, placing his thought within the larger context of the history of Zen thought. Masao Abe, *Zen and Western Thought* (Honolulu: University of Hawaii Press, 1985), is a penetrating study of Zen in comparison with Western philosophy. Thomas P. Kasulis, *Zen Action, Zen Person* (Honolulu: University of Hawaii, 1981), explores the core of Zen realization from the perspective of personhood and action within Japanese culture. Paul Reps, compiler, *Zen Flesh, Zen Bones* (Garden City: Doubleday Anchor, 1961), is a delightful collection of Zen teachings that conveys the authentic flavor of Zen.

I
Essays from Dōgen's *Shōbōgenzō**

GREAT TRANSCENDENT WISDOM

The time when the Independent Seer practices profound transcendent wisdom is the whole body's clear vision that the five clusters are all empty. The five clusters are physical form, sensations, perceptions, conditionings, and consciousness. They are five layers of wisdom. *Clear vision*[1] is wisdom.

*Reprinted with permission from Thomas Cleary, *Shōbōgenzō: Zen Essays by Dōgen* (Honolulu: University of Hawaii Press, 1986).

[1] The translator has italicized words and phrases for which the original Chinese was used in the Japanese text.

In expounding and manifesting this fundamental message, we would say form is empty, emptiness is form, form is form, emptiness is empty. It is *the hundred grasses*, it is myriad forms.

Twelve layers of wisdom are the twelve sense-media. There is also eighteen-layer wisdom — eye, ear, nose, tongue, body, intellect, form, sound, smell, taste, touch, phenomena, as well as the consciousness of the eye, ear, nose, tongue, body, and intellect. There is also four layered wisdom, which is suffering, its accumulation, its extinction, and the path to its extinction. Also there is six-layered wisdom which is charity, morality, forbearance, vigor, meditation, and wisdom. There is also one-layer wisdom, which is manifest in the immediate present, which is unexcelled complete perfect enlightenment. There are also three layers of wisdom, which are past, present, and future. There are also six layers of wisdom, which are earth, water, fire, air, space, and consciousness. Also, four-layered wisdom is constantly being carried out — it is walking, standing, sitting,and reclining.

> In the assembly of Shakyamuni Buddha was a monk who thought to himself, "I should pay obeisance to most profound transcendent wisdom. Though there is no origination or extinction of phenomena herein, yet there are available facilities of bodies of precepts, meditation, wisdom, liberation, and knowledge and insight of liberation. Also there are available facilities of the fruit of the stream-enterer, the fruit of the once-returner, the fruit of the nonreturner, and the fruit of the saint. Also there are available facilities of self-enlightenment and enlightening beings. Also there is the available facility of unexcelled true enlightenment. Also there are the available facilities of the Buddha, Teaching, and Community. Also there are the available facilities of the turning of the wheel of the sublime teaching and liberating living beings." The Buddha, knowing what he was thinking, said to the monk, "It is so, it is so. Most profound transcendent wisdom is extremely subtle and hard to fathom."

As for the present monk's *thinking to himself*, where all phenomena are respected, wisdom which still *has no origination or extinction* is *paying obeisance*. Precisely at the time of their obeisance, accordingly wisdom with *available facilities* has become manifest: that is what is referred to as precepts, meditation, wisdom, and so on, up to the liberation of living beings. This is called nothing. The facilities of *nothing* are available in this way. This is transcendent wisdom which is most profound, extremely subtle, and hard to fathom.

> The king of gods asked the honorable Subhūti, "O Great Worthy, if great bodhisattvas want to learn most profound transcendent wisdom, how should they learn it?" Subhūti answered, "If great bodhisattvas want to learn most profound transcendent wisdom, they should learn it like space."

So learning wisdom is space, space is learning wisdom.

> The king of gods also said to the Buddha, "World Honored One, if good men and women accept and hold this most profound transcendent wisdom you have explained, repeat it, reflect upon it in truth, and expound it to others, how should I offer protection?" Then Subhūti said to the king of gods, "Do you see that there is something to protect?" The king said, "No, I do not see that there is anything to protect." Subhūti said, "If good men and women live according to most profound transcendent wisdom as they are taught, that is protection. If good men and women abide in most profound transcendent wisdom as taught here, and never depart from it, no humans or nonhumans can find any way to harm them. If you want to protect the bodhisattvas who live in most profound transcendent wisdom as taught, this is no different from wanting to protect space."

We should know that receiving, holding, repeating, and reflecting reasonably are none other than protecting wisdom? Wanting to protect is receiving and holding and repeating and so on.

My late teacher said, "The whole body is like a mouth hung in space; without question of east, west, south, or north winds, it equally tells others of wisdom. Drop after drop freezes." This is the speaking of wisdom of the lineage of Buddhas and Zen adepts. It is whole body wisdom, whole other wisdom, whole self wisdom, whole east west south north wisdom.

> Shakyamuni Buddha said, "Shariputra, living beings should abide in this transcendent wisdom as Buddhas do. They should make offerings, pay obeisance, and contemplate transcendent wisdom just as they make offerings and pay obeisance to the Blessed Buddha. Why? Because transcendent wisdom is not different from the Blessed Buddha, the Blessed Buddha is not different from transcendent wisdom. Transcendent wisdom *is* Buddha, Buddha *is* transcendent wisdom. Why? It is because all those who realize thusness, worthies, truly enlightened ones, appear due to transcendent wisdom. It is because all great bodhisattvas, self-enlightened people, saints, nonreturners, once-returners, stream-enterers, and so on, appear due to transcendent wisdom. It is because all manner of virtuous action in the world, the four meditations, four formless concentrations, and five spiritual powers all appear due to transcendent wisdom."

Therefore the Buddha, the Blessed One, is transcendent wisdom. Transcendent wisdom is all things. These "all things" are the characteristics of emptiness, unoriginated, imperishable, not defiled, not pure, not increasing, not decreasing. The manifestation of this transcendent wisdom is the manifestation of the Buddha. One should inquire into it, investigate it, honor and pay homage to it. This is attending and serving the Buddha, it is the Buddha of attendance and service.

THE ISSUE AT HAND

When all things are Buddha-teachings, then there is delusion and enlightenment, there is cultivation of practice, there is birth, there is death, there are Buddhas, there are sentient beings. When myriad things are all not self, there is no delusion, no enlightenment, no Buddhas, no sentient beings, no birth, no death. Because the Buddha Way originally sprang forth from abundance and paucity, there is birth and death, delusion and enlightenment, sentient beings and Buddhas. Moreover, though this is so, flowers fall when we cling to them, and weeds only grow when we dislike them.

Acting on and witnessing myriad things with the burden of oneself is "delusion." Acting on and witnessing oneself in the advent of myriad things is enlightenment. Great enlightenment about delusion is Buddhas; great delusion about enlightenment is sentient beings. There are also those who attain enlightenment on top of enlightenment, and there are those who are further deluded in the midst of delusion. When the Buddhas are indeed the Buddhas, there is no need to be self-conscious of being Buddhas; nevertheless it is realizing buddhahood—Buddhas go on realizing.

In seeing forms with the whole body-mind, hearing sound with the whole body-mind, though one intimately understands, it isn't like reflecting images in a mirror, it's not like water and the moon—when you witness one side, one side is obscure.

Studying the Buddha Way is studying oneself. Studying oneself is forgetting oneself. Forgetting oneself is being enlightened by all things. Being enlightened by all things is causing the body-mind of oneself and the body-mind of others to be shed. There is ceasing the traces of enlightenment, which causes one to forever leave the traces of enlightenment which is cessation.

When people first seek the Teaching, they are far from the bounds of the Teaching. Once the Teaching is properly conveyed in oneself, already one is the original human being.

When someone rides in a boat, as he looks at the shore he has the illusion that the shore is moving. When he looks at the boat under him, he realizes the boat is moving. In the same way, when one takes things for granted with confused ideas of body-mind, one has the illusion that one's own mind and own nature are permanent; but if one pays close attention to one's own actions, the truth that things are not self will be clear.

Kindling becomes ash, and cannot become kindling again. However, we should not see the ash as after and the kindling as before. Know that kindling abides in the normative state of kindling, and though it has a before and after, the realms of before and after are disconnected. Ash, in the normative state of ash, has before and after. Just as that kindling, after having become ash, does not again become kindling, so after dying a person does not become alive again. This being the case, not saying that life becomes death is an established custom in Buddhism—therefore it is called *unborn*. That death does not become life is an established teaching of the Buddha; therefore we say *imperishable.* Life is an individual temporal state, death is an individual temporal state. It is like winter and spring—we don't think winter becomes spring, we don't say spring becomes summer.

People's attaining enlightenment is like the moon reflected in water. The moon does not get wet, the water isn't broken. Though it is a vast expansive light, it rests in a little bit of water—even the whole moon, the whole sky, rests in a dewdrop on the grass, rests in even a single droplet of water. That enlightenment does not shatter people is like the moon not piercing the water. People's not obstructing enlightenment is like the drop of dew not obstructing the moon in the sky. The depth is proportionate to the height. As for the length and brevity of time, examining the great and small bodies of water, you should discern the breadth and narrowness of the moon in the sky.

Before one has studied the Teaching fully in body and mind, one feels one is already sufficient in the Teaching. If the body and mind are replete with the Teaching, in one respect one senses insufficiency. For example, when one rides a boat out onto the ocean where there are no mountains and looks around, it only appears round, and one can see no other, different characteristics. However, this ocean is not round, nor is it square—the remaining qualities of the ocean are inexhaustible. It is like a palace, it is like ornaments, yet as far as our eyes can see, it only seems round. It is the same with all things—in the realms of matter, beyond conceptualization, they include many aspects, but we see and comprehend only what the power of our eye of contemplative study reaches. If we inquire into the "family ways" of myriad things, the qualities of seas and mountains, beyond seeming square or round, are endlessly numerous. We should realize there exist worlds everywhere. It's not only thus in out of the way places—know that even a single drop right before us is also thus.

As a fish travels through water, there is no bound to the water no matter how far it goes; as a bird flies through the sky, there's no bound to the sky no matter how far it flies. While this is so, the fish and birds have never been apart from the water and the sky—it's just that when the need is large the use is large, and when the requirement is small the use is small. In this way, though the bounds are unfailingly reached everywhere and tread upon in every single place, the bird would instantly die if it left the sky and the fish would instantly die if it left the water. Obviously, water is life; obviously the sky is life. There is bird being life. There is fish being life. There is life being bird, there is life being fish. There must be progress beyond this—there is cultivation and realization, the existence of the living one being like this. Under these circumstances, if there were birds or fish who attempted to traverse the waters or the sky after having found the limits of the water or sky, they wouldn't find a path in the water or the sky—they won't find any place. When one finds this place, this action accordingly manifests as the issue at hand; when one finds this path, this action accordingly manifests as the issue at hand. This path, this place, is not big or small, not self or other, not preexistent, not now appearing—therefore it exists in this way. In this way, if someone cultivates and realizes the Buddha Way, it is *attaining a principle, mastering the principle;* it is *encountering a practice, cultivating the practice.* In this there is a place where the path has been accomplished, hence the unknowability of the known boundary is born together and studies along with the thorough investigation of the Buddha Teaching of this knowing—therefore it is thus. Don't get the idea that the attainment necessarily becomes one's own knowledge and view, that it would be known by discursive knowledge. Though realizational comprehension already takes place, implicit being is not necessarily obvious—*why necessarily* is there obvious becoming?

Zen Master Hōtetsu of Mt. Mayoku was using a fan. A monk asked him about this: "The nature of wind is eternal and all-pervasive—why then do you use a fan?" The master said, "You only know the nature of wind is eternal, but do not yet know the principle of its omnipresence." The monk asked, "What is the principle of its omniscience?" The master just fanned. The monk bowed.

The experience of the Buddha Teaching, the living road of right transmission, is like this. To say that since (the nature of wind) is permanent one should not use a fan, and that one should feel the breeze even when not using a fan, is not knowing permanence and not knowing the nature of the wind either. Because the nature of wind is eternal, the wind of Buddhism causes the manifestation of the earth's being gold and by participation develops the long river into butter.

THE NATURE OF THINGS

In meditation study, whether following scripture or following a teacher, one *becomes enlightened alone without a teacher.* Becoming *enlightened alone without a teacher* is the activity of the nature of things. Even though one be *born knowing*, one should seek a teacher to inquire about the Path. Even in the case of *knowledge of the birthless* one should definitely direct effort to mastering the Path. Which individuals are not *born knowing?* Even up to enlightenment, the fruit of buddhahood, it is a matter of following scriptures and teachers. Know that encountering a scripture or a teacher and attaining *absorption in the nature of things* is called the *born knowing* that attains *absorption in the nature of things* on encountering *absorption in the nature of things.* This is attaining knowledge of past lives, attaining the three superknowledges, realizing unexcelled enlightenment, encountering inborn knowledge and learning inborn knowledge, encountering teacherless knowledge and spontaneous knowledge and correctly conveying teacherless knowledge and spontaneous knowledge.

If one were not *born knowing*, even though might encounter scriptures and teachers one could not hear of the *nature of things*, one could not witness the *nature of things.* The *Great Path* is not the principle of *like someone drinking water knows for himself whether it's warm or cool.* All Buddhas as well as all bodhisattvas and all living beings clarify the Great Path of the nature of all things by the power of inborn knowledge. To clarify the *Great Path* of the *nature of things* following scriptures or teachers is called clarifying the *nature of things* by oneself. Scriptures are the nature of things, are oneself. Teachers are the *nature of things*, are oneself. The *nature of things* is the teacher, the *nature of things* is oneself. Because the *nature of things* is oneself, it is not the self misconceived by heretics and demons. In the *nature of things* there are no heretics or demons—it is only *eating breakfast, eating lunch, having a snack.* Even so, those who claim to have studied for a long time, for twenty or thirty years, pass their whole life in a daze when they read or hear talk of the *nature of things.* Those who claim to have fulfilled Zen study and assume the rank of teacher, while they hear the voice of the *nature of things* and see the forms of the *nature of things*, yet their body and mind, objective and subjective experience, always just rise and fall in the pit of confusion. What this is like is wrongly thinking that the *nature of things* will appear when the whole world we perceive is obliterated, that the *nature of things* is not the present totality of phenomena. The principle of the *nature of things* cannot be like this. This *totality of phenomena* and the *nature of things* are far beyond any question of sameness or difference, beyond talk of distinction or identity. It is not past, present, or future, not annihilation or eternity, not form, sensation, conception, conditioning, or consciousness—therefore it is the *nature of things.*

Zen Master Baso said, "All living beings, for infinite eons, have never left absorption in the nature of things: they are always within absorption in the nature of things, wearing clothes, eating, conversing—the functions of the six sense organs, and all activities, all are the nature of things."

The *nature of things* spoken of by Baso is the *nature of things* spoken of by the *nature of things.* It learns from the same source as Baso, is a fellow student of the *nature of things*: since hearing of it takes place, how could there not be speaking of it? The fact is that *the nature of things rides Baso*; it is *people eat food, food eats people.* Ever since the *nature of things*, it has never left *absorption in the nature of things.* It doesn't leave the *nature of things* after the *nature of things*, it doesn't leave the *nature of things* before the *nature of things.* The *nature of things*, along with *infinite eons*, is *absorption in the nature of things*; the *nature of things* is called *infinite eons.* Therefore the *here* of the immediate present is the *nature of things*; the *nature of things* is the *here* of the immediate present. *Wearings clothes and eating food* is the *wearing clothes and eating food of absorption in the nature of things.* It is the manifestation of the *nature of things* of food, it is the manifestation of the *nature of things* of eating, it is the manifestation of the *nature of things* of clothing, it is the manifestation of the *nature of things* of wearing. If one does not dress or eat, does not talk or answer, does not use the senses, does not act at all, it is not the *nature of things*, it is *not entering the nature of things.*

The manifestation of the Path of the immediate present was transmitted by the Buddhas, reaching Shakyamuni Buddha; correctly conveyed by the Zen adepts, it reached Baso. Buddha to Buddha, adept to adept, correctly conveyed and handed on, it has been correctly communicated in *absorption in the nature of things.* Buddhas and Zen adepts, *not entering*, enliven the *nature of things.* Though externalist scholars may have the term *nature of things*, it is not the *nature of things* spoken of by Baso. Though the power to propose that *living beings* who *don't leave the nature of things* are not the *nature of things* may achieve something, this is three or four new layers of the *nature of things*. To speak, reply, function, and act as if it were not the *nature of things* must be the *nature of things*. The days and months of *infinite eons* are the passage of the *nature of things*. The same is so of past, present, and future. If you take the limit of body and mind as the limit of body and mind and think it is far from the *nature of things*, this thinking still is the *nature of things*. If you don't consider the limit of body and mind as the limit of body and mind and think it is not the *nature of things*, this thought too is the *nature of things*. Thinking and not thinking are both the *nature of things*. To learn that since we have said *nature* (it means that) water must not flow and trees must not bloom and wither, is heretical.

Shakyamuni Buddha said, "Such characteristics, such nature." So *flowers blooming* and *leaves falling* are *such nature*. Yet ignorant people think that there could not be *flowers blooming and leaves falling* in the realm of the *nature of things*. For the time being one should not question another. You should model your doubt on verbal expression. Bringing it up as others have said it, you should investigate it over and over again—there will be escape from before. The aforementioned thoughts are not wrong thinking, they are just thoughts while not yet having understood. It is not that this thinking will be caused to disappear when one understands. Flowers blooming and leaves falling are of themselves flowers blooming and leaves falling. The thinking that is thought that there can't be flowers blooming or leaves falling in the *nature of things* is the *nature of things*. It is thought which has fallen out according to a pattern; therefore it is thought of the *nature of things*. The whole thinking of thinking of the *nature of things* is such an appearance.

Although Baso's statement *all is the nature of things* is truly an *eighty or ninety percent* statement, there are many points which Baso has not expressed. That is to say, he doesn't say *the natures of all things do not leave the nature of things*, he doesn't say *the natures of all things are all the nature of things*. He doesn't say *all living beings do not leave living beings*, he doesn't say *all living beings are a little bit of the nature of things*, he doesn't say *all living beings are a little bit of all living beings*, he doesn't say *the natures of all things are a little bit of living beings*. He doesn't say *half a living being is half the nature of things*. He doesn't say *nonexistence of living beings is the nature of things*, he doesn't say *the nature of things is not living beings*, he doesn't say *the nature of things exudes the nature of things*, he doesn't say *living beings shed living beings*. We only hear that living beings do not leave absorption in the nature of things—he doesn't say that the nature of things cannot leave absorption in living beings, there is no statement of absorption in the nature of things exiting and entering absorption in living beings. Needless to say, we don't hear of the attainment of buddhahood of the *nature of things*, we don't hear *living beings realize the nature of things*, we don't hear *the nature of things* realizes the nature of things, there is no statement of how *inanimate beings don't leave the nature of things.* Now one should ask Baso, what do you call "living beings"? If you call the *nature of things* living beings, it is *what thing comes thus*? If you call living beings living beings, it is *if you speak of it as something, you miss it.* Speak quickly, speak quickly!

BEING TIME

An ancient Buddha said, *At a time of being, standing on the summit of the highest peak; at a time of being, walking on the bottom of the deepest ocean; at a time of being, three-headed and eight-armed; at a time of being, sixteen feet and eight feet; at a time of being, staff and whisk; at a time of being, pillar and lamp; at a time of being, the average man; at a time of being, earth and sky.*

So-called *time of being* means time is already being; all being is time. The *sixteen foot tall golden body* is time; because it is time, it has the adornments and radiance of time. You should study it in the twenty-four hours of the present. *Three-headed, eight-armed* is time; because it is time, it must be *one suchness* in the twenty-four hours of the present. The length and brevity of the twenty-four hours, though not as yet measured, is called twenty-four hours. Because the direction and course of their going and coming are obvious, people don't doubt them—yet though they don't doubt them, this is not to say that they know them. Because sentient beings' doubting of things which they don't know is not fixed, the future course of their doubting does not necessarily accord with their doubts of the present. It's just that doubting is for the moment *time.*

Self is arrayed as the whole world. You should perceive that each point, each thing of this *whole world* is an individual *time.* The mutual noninterference of things is like the mutual noninterference of *times.* For this reason there is *arousal of minds at the same time,* there is *arousal of times in the same mind.* Cultivating practice and achieving enlightenment are also like this. Arraying self, self sees this—such is the principle of *self* being *time.*

Because it is the principle of *being such,* there are *myriad forms, a hundred grasses* on *the whole earth.* You should learn that each *single blade of grass,* each *single form,* is on *the whole earth.* Such *going and coming* is the starting point of cultivation of practice. When one reaches the state of *suchness,* it is *one blade of grass, one form*; it is *understanding forms, not understanding forms,* it is *understanding grasses, not understanding grasses.* Because it is only *right at such a time,* therefore *being time* is all *the whole time. Being grass* and *being form* are both time. In the time of *time's time* there is *the whole of being, the whole world.* For a while try to visualize whether or not there is *the whole being, the whole world* apart from the present time.

In spite of this, when people are ordinary folk who have not studied the Buddha's teaching, the views they have are such that when they hear the expression *a time of being,* they think at some time one had become *three-*

headed and eight-armed, at some time one had become *sixteen feet tall, eight feet seated,* like having crossed rivers and crossed mountains. They think, "Even though those mountains and rivers may exist still, I have passed them and am now in the vermillion tower of the jewel palace—the mountains and rivers and I are as far apart as sky and earth." However, the truth is not just this one line of reasoning alone. In the time one climbed the mountains and crossed the rivers, there was oneself. There must be *time* in oneself. Since oneself exists, *time* cannot leave. If time is not the appearances of going and coming, the time of climbing a mountain is the *immediate present* of *being time.* If time preserves the appearances of going and coming, there is in oneself the *immediate present of being time*—this is *being time.* Does not that *time* of *climbing mountains and crossing rivers* swallow up this *time* of the *vermillion tower of the jewel palace*? Does it not spew it forth?

Three-headed, eight-armed is yesterday's *time; sixteen feet, eight feet* is today's *time.* However, the principle of *yesterday and today* is just the time of directly entering the mountains and gazing out over the thousand peaks, the myriad peaks—it is not a matter of having passed. *Three-headed, eight-armed* too *transpires* as one's own *being time; sixteen feet, eight feet* too *transpires* as one's own *being time.* Though it seems to be elsewhere, it is *right now.* So pines are *time* too; bamboo is *time* too.

One should not understand time only as flying away; one should not only get the idea that flying away is the function of time. If time only were to fly, then there would be gaps. Not having heard of the path of *being time* is because of learning only that it has passed. To tell the gist of it, all existences in the whole world, while being lined up, are individual times. Because it is *being time,* it is *my being time.*

In *being time* there is the quality of passage. That is, it passes from today to tomorrow, it passes from today to yesterday, it passes from yesterday to today, it passes from today to today, it passes from tomorrow to tomorrow.

Because passage is a quality of time, past and present time doesn't pile up, doesn't accumulate in a row—nevertheless Seigen is *time,* Ōbaku too is *time,* Baso and Sekitō also are *time.* Since self and others are *time,* cultivation and realization are times. *Going into the mud, going into the water* is similarly *time.*

Though the present views and the conditions of views of ordinary people are what ordinary people see, they are not the norm of ordinary people. It is merely that the norm temporarily conditions ordinary people. Because of learning that this *time,* this *being,* are not the norm, they take the *sixteen foot tall golden body* as not themselves. Trying to escape by claiming that oneself is not the *sixteen foot tall golden body* is also itself bits of *being time*; it is the *looking* of *those who have not yet verified it.*

Even causing the horses and sheep now arrayed in the world to exist is the *rising and falling, ups and downs* which are the *suchness* of *remaining in the normal position.* The *rat* is time, the *tiger* is time too. Living beings are time. Buddhas are time too. This *time* witnesses the whole world with *three heads and eight arms,* it witnesses the whole world with *the sixteen foot tall golden body.*

Now exhausting the limits of the whole world by means of the whole world is called investigating exhaustively. To actualize being *the sixteen foot golden body* by means of *the sixteen foot golden body* as determination, cultivating practice, enlightenment, and nirvana, is *being*, is *time*. Just investigating exhaustively *all time* as *all being*, there is nothing left over. Because leftovers are leftovers, even the *being time* of half-exhaustive investigation is the exhaustive investigation of half *being time*.

Even forms which seem to slip by are *being*. Furthermore, if you leave it at that, being the period of manifestation of *slipping by*, it is the *abiding in position of being time*. Don't stir it as nonexistence, don't insist on it as existence. Only conceiving of time as passing one way, one doesn't understand it as not yet having arrived. Though understanding is *time*, it has no relation drawn by another. Only recognizing it as coming and going, no skin bag has seen through it as *being time* of *abiding in position*—how much less could there be a time of *passing through the barrier*? Even recognizing *remaining in position*, who can express the preservation of *already being such*? Even if they have long expressed it as *such*, still everyone gropes for the appearance of its countenance. If we leave ordinary people's being *being time* at that, then even enlightenment and nirvana are only *being time* which is merely the appearances of going and coming.

In sum, it cannot be ensnared or arrested—it is the manifestation of *being time*. The celestial monarchs and celestial beings manifesting in the regions right and left are *being time* now exerting their whole strength. The other myriad *being times* of water and land are now manifesting exerting their whole strength. The various species and objects that are *being time* in darkness and light are all the manifestation of their whole strength, they are the passage of their total strength. If they were not the present *passage of whole strength*, not one single thing would become manifest, there would be no passage—you should study it this way. You should not have been learning about passage as like the wind and rain's going east and west. The *whole world* is not *inactive*, it is not *neither progressing nor regressing*: it is *passage*.

Passage is, for example, like spring: in spring there are numerous appearances—this is called *passage*. You should learn that it *passes through* without any external thing. For example, the *passage* of spring necessarily *passes through* spring. Though *passage* is not spring, because it is the *passage* of spring, *passage* has *accomplished the Way* in this *time* of spring. You should examine thoroughly in whatever you are doing. In speaking of *passage*, if you think that the objective realm is outside and the phenomenon which *passes through* passes a million worlds to the east through a billion eons, in thinking thus you are not concentrating wholly on the study of the Buddha Way.

Yakuzan, at the direction of the Zen master Sekitō, went to call on the Zen master Baso. He said, "As far as the Buddhist canon is concerned, I pretty much understand its message—what is the living meaning of Zen?" When Yakuzan asked this, Baso said, "Sometimes I have him raise the eyebrows and blink the eyes. Sometimes I don't have him raise the eyebrows and blink the eyes. Sometimes having him raise the eyebrows and blink the eyes is it, sometimes having him raise the eyebrows and blink the eyes is not it." Hearing this, Yakuzan was greatly enlightened. He said to Baso, "When I was with Sekitō, I was like a mosquito climbing on an iron ox."

What Baso says is not the same as others. *Eyebrows and eyes* must be *mountains and oceans,* because *mountains and oceans* are *eyebrows and eyes.* That *having him raise* must see the *mountains,* that *having him blink* must have its source in the *ocean.* It is conditioned by *him, he* is induced by causation. *Not it* is not *not having him, not having him* is not *not it.* These are all *being time.* The mountains are *time,* the oceans are *time* too. If they were not *time,* the mountains and oceans could not be. You should not think there is no *time* in the *immediate present* of the mountains and oceans. If *time* disintegrates, mountains and oceans too disintegrate; if *time* is indestructible, mountains and oceans too are indestructible. On this principle *the morning star* appears, *the Buddha* appears, *the eye* appears, *the raising of the flower* appears. This is *time.* If it were not *time,* it would not be thus.

Zen Master Kisei of Sekken was a religious descendant of Rinzai, and was the heir of Shuzan. One time he said to the community, "Sometimes the intent arrives but the expression doesn't arrive: sometimes the expression arrives but the intent doesn't arrive. Sometimes intent and expression both arrive, sometimes neither intent nor expression arrive." *Intent* and *expression* are both *being time; arriving* and *not arriving* are both *being time.* Though *the time of arrival is incomplete,* yet *the time of nonarrival has come. Intent* is a donkey, *expression* is a horse; the horse is considered the expression, the donkey is considered the intent. *Arriving* is not *coming; not arriving* is not *yet to come.* This is the way *being time* is. *Arriving* is blocked by *arriving,* not blocked by *not arriving. Not arriving* is blocked by *not arriving,* not blocked by *arriving. Intent* blocks *intent* and sees *intent; expression* blocks *expression* and sees *expression. Blocking* blocks *blocking* and sees *blocking. Blocking* blocks *blocking*—this is *time.* Though *blocking* is used by *other things,* there is never any *blocking* which blocks *other things.* It is *oneself meeting other people,* it is *other people meeting other people,* it is *oneself meeting oneself,* it is *going out* meeting *going out.* If these do not have *time,* they are not *so.*

Also, *intent* is the *time* of *the issue at hand; expression* is the *time* of *the key of transcendence. Arriving* is the *time* of *the whole body; not arriving* is the *time* of *one with this, detached from this.* In this way should you correctly understand and *be time.*

Though the aforementioned adepts have all spoken as mentioned, is there nothing further to say? We should say *intent and expression half arriving too is being time; intent and expression half not arriving too is being time.* There should be study like this. *Having him raise his eyebrows and blink his eyes is half being time; having him raise his eyebrows and blink his eyes is amiss being time. Not having him raise his eyebrows and blink his eyes is half being time; not having him raise his eyebrows and blink his eyes is amiss being time.* To investigate thus, coming and going, investigating arriving and investigating not arriving, is the *time* of *being time.*

THE EIGHT AWARENESSES OF GREAT PEOPLE

The Buddhas are great people. As these are what is realized by great people, they are called the awareness of great people. Realizing these principles is the basis of nirvana. This was the final teaching of our original teacher, Shakyamuni Buddha, on the night he passed away into final extinction.

1. Having few desires

Not extensively seeking objects of desire not yet attained is called having few desires.

Buddha said, "You monks should know that people with many desires seek to gain a lot, and therefore their afflictions are also many. Those with few desires have no seeking and no craving, so they don't have this problem. You should cultivate having few desires even for this reason alone, to say nothing of the fact that having few desires can produce virtues. People with few desires are free from flattery and deviousness whereby they might seek to curry people's favor, and they also are not under the compulsion of their senses. Those who act with few desires are calm, without worry or fear. Whatever the situation, there is more than enough—there is never insufficiency. Those who have few desires have nirvana."

2. Being content

To take what one has got within bounds is called being content.

Buddha said, "O monks, if you want to shed afflictions, you should observe contentment. The state of contentment is the abode of prosperity and happiness, peace and tranquility. Those who are content may sleep on the ground and still consider it comfortable; those who are not content would be dissatisfied even in heaven. Those who are not content are always caught up in sensual desires; they are pitied by those who are content."

3. Enjoying quietude

Leaving the clamor and staying alone in deserted places is called enjoying quietude.

Buddha said, "O monks, if you wish to seek the peace and happiness of quietude and nonstriving, you should leave the clamor and live without clutter in a solitary place. People in quiet places are honored by the gods. Therefore you should leave your own group as well as other groups, stay alone in a deserted place, and think about extirpating the root of suffering. Those who like crowds suffer the vexations of crowds, just as a big tree will suffer withering and breakage when flocks of birds gather on it. Worldly ties and clinging sink you into a multitude of pains, like an old elephant sunk in the mud, unable to get itself out."

4. Diligence

Diligently cultivating virtues without interruption is called diligence, pure and unalloyed, advancing without regression.

Buddha said, "O monks, if you make diligent efforts, nothing is hard. Therefore you should be diligent. It is like even a small stream being able to pierce rock if it continually flows. If the practitioner's mind flags and gives up time and gain, that is like drilling for fire but stopping before heat is produced — though you want to get fire, fire can hardly be gotten this way."

5. Unfailing recollection

This is also called keeping right mindfulness; keeping the teachings without loss is called right mindfulness, and also called unfailing recollection.

Buddha said, "O monks, if you seek a good companion and seek a good protector and helper, nothing compares to unfailing recollection. Those who have unfailing recollection cannot be invaded by the thieving afflictions. Therefore you should concentrate your thoughts and keep mindful. One who loses mindfulness loses virtues. If one's power of mindfulness is strong, even if one enters among the thieving desires one will not be harmed by them. It is like going to the front lines wearing armor — then one has nothing to fear."

6. Cultivating meditation concentration

Dwelling on the teaching without distraction is called meditation concentration.

Buddha said, "O monks, if you concentrate the mind, it will be in a state of stability and you will be able to know the characteristics of the phenomena arising and perishing in the world. Therefore you should energetically cultivate and learn the concentrations. If you attain concentration, your mind will not be distracted. Just as a household careful of water builds a dam, so does the practitioner, for the sake of the water of knowledge and wisdom, cultivate meditation concentration well, to prevent them from leaking."

7. Cultivating wisdom

Developing learning, thinking, and application, the realization is wisdom.

Buddha said, "O monks, if you have wisdom, you will have no greedy attachment. Always examine yourselves and do not allow any heedlessness. Then you will be able to attain liberation from ego and things. Otherwise, you are neither people of the Way nor laypeople — there is no way to refer to you. True wisdom is a secure ship to cross the sea of aging, sickness, and death. It is also a bright lamp in the darkness of ignorance, good medicine for all the ailing, a sharp axe to fell the trees of afflictions. Therefore you should use the wisdom of learning, thinking, and application, and increase it yourself. If anyone has the illumination of wisdom, this is a person with clear eyes, even though it be the mortal eye."

8. Not engaging in vain talk

Realizing detachment from arbitrary discrimination is called not engaging in vain talk; when one has fully comprehended the character of reality, one will not engage in vain talk.

Buddha said, "O monks, if you indulge in various kinds of vain talk, your mind will be disturbed. Even if you leave society you will still not attain liberation. Therefore you should immediately give up vain talk which disturbs the mind. If you want to attain bliss of tranquility and dispassion, you should extinguish the affliction of vain talk."

These are the eight awarenesses of great people. Each one contains the eight, so there are sixty-four. If you expand them, they must be infinite; if you summarize them, there are sixty-four. After the final speech of the great teacher Shakyamuni, made for the instruction of the Great Vehicle, the ultimate discourse at midnight on the fifteenth day of the second month, he didn't preach anymore and finally became utterly extinct.

Buddha said, "You monks always should single-mindedly seek the path of emancipation. All things in the world, mobile and immobile, are unstable forms which disintegrate. Stop now and don't talk anymore. The time is about past, and I am going to cross over into extinction. This is my last instruction."

Therefore students of the Buddha definitely should learn these principles. Those who do not learn them, who do not know them, are not students of Buddha. These awarenesses are the Buddha's treasury of the eye of true teaching, the sublime heart of nirvana. The fact that many now nevertheless do not know them and few have read or heard of them is due to the interference of demons. Also, those who have cultivated little virtue in the past do not hear of or see them.

In the past, during the periods of the true teaching and the imitation teaching, all Buddhists knew them, and practiced and studied them. Now there are hardly one or two among a thousand monks who know the eight awarenesses of great people. What a pity—the decline in the degenerate age is beyond compare. While the true teaching of the Buddha is still current in the world and goodness has not yet perished, one should hasten to learn them. Don't be lazy. It is difficult to encounter the Buddha's teaching even in countless eons. It is also difficult to get a human body. And even if one gets a human body, it is preferable to live as a human where it is possible to see a Buddha, hear the teaching, leave the mundane, and attain enlightenment. Those who died before the Buddha's final extinction didn't hear of these eight awarenesses of great people, and didn't learn them. Now we have heard of them and learn them—this is the power of virtue cultivated in the past. Now, learning and practicing them, developing them life after life, we will surely reach unexcelled enlightenment. Explain them to people the same as Shakyamuni Buddha.

BIRTH AND DEATH

"Because there is Buddha in birth and death, there is no birth and death." Also, "because there is no Buddha in birth and death, one is not deluded by birth and death." These are the words of two Zen teachers called Kassan and Jōsan. Being the words of enlightened people, they were surely not uttered without reason. People who want to get out of birth and death should understand what they mean.

If people seek Buddha outside of birth and death, that is like heading north to go south, like facing south to try to see the north star: accumulating causes of birth and death all the more, they have lost the way to liberation. Simply understanding that birth and death is itself nirvana, there is nothing to reject as birth and death, nothing to seek as nirvana. Only then will one have some measure of detachment from birth and death.

It is a mistake to assume that one moves from birth to death. Birth, being one point in time, has a before and after; therefore in Buddhism birth is called unborn. Extinction too, being one point in time, also has before and after, so it is said that extinction is nonextinction. When we say "birth" there is nothing but birth, and when we say "extinction" there is nothing but extinction. Therefore when birth comes it is just birth, and when extinction comes it is just extinction. In facing birth and extinction, don't reject, don't long.

This birth and death is the life of the Buddha. If we try to reject or get rid of this, we would lose the life of the Buddha. If we linger in this and cling to birth and death, this too is losing the life of the Buddha; it is stopping the Buddha's manner of being. When we have no aversion or longing, only then do we reach the heart of the Buddha.

However, don't figure it in your mind, don't say it in words. Just letting go of and forgetting body and mind, casting them into the house of Buddha, being activated by the Buddha—when we go along in accord with this, then without applying effort or expending the mind we part from birth and death and become Buddhas. Who would linger in the mind?

There is a very easy way to become a Buddha: not doing any evil, having no attachment to birth and death, sympathizing deeply with all beings, respecting those above, sympathizing with those below, not feeling aversion or longing for anything, not thinking or worrying—this is called Buddha. Don't seek it anywhere else.

II
Shibayama: Commentary on the *Mumonkan**

JOSHU'S "MU"

A monk once asked Master Joshu, "Has a dog the Buddha Nature or not?" Joshu said, "Mu!"

MUMON'S COMMENTARY

In studying Zen, one must pass the barriers set up by ancient Zen Masters. For the attainment of incomparable satori, one has to cast away his discriminating mind. Those who have not passed the barrier and have not cast away the discriminating mind are all phantoms haunting trees and plants.

Now, tell me, what is the barrier of the Zen Masters? Just this "Mu"—it is

---

*Reprinted with permission from Zenkei Shibayama, *Zen Comments on the Mumonkan*, translated by Sumiko Kudo (New York: New American Library, 1975).

the barrier of Zen. It is thus called "the gateless barrier of Zen." Those who have passed the barrier will not only see Joshu clearly, but will go hand in hand with all the Masters of the past, see them face to face. You will see with the same eye that they see with and hear with the same ear. Wouldn't it be wonderful? Don't you want to pass the barrier? Then concentrate yourself into this "Mu," with your 360 bones and 84,000 pores, making your whole body one great inquiry. Day and night work intently at it. Do not attempt nihilistic or dualistic interpretations. It is like having bolted a red hot iron ball. You try to vomit it but cannot.

Cast away your illusory discriminating knowledge and consciousness accumulated up to now, and keep on working harder. After a while, when your efforts come to fruition, all the oppositions (such as in and out) will naturally be identified. You will then be like a dumb person who has had a wonderful dream: he only knows it personally, within himself. Suddenly you break through the barrier; you will astonish heaven and shake the earth.

It is as if you have snatched the great sword of General Kan. You kill the Buddha if you meet him; you kill the ancient Masters if you meet them. On the brink of life and death you are utterly free, and in the six realms and the four modes of life you lie, with great joy, a genuine life in complete freedom.

Now, how should one strive? With might and main work at this "Mu," and *be* "Mu." If you do not stop or waver in your striving, then behold, when the Dharma candle is lighted, darkness is at once enlightened.

MUMON'S POEM

The dog! The Buddha Nature!
The Truth is manifested in full.
A moment of yes-and-no:
Lost are your body and soul.

TEISHO[1] ON THE KOAN

This koan is extremely short and simple. Because of this simplicity, it is uniquely valuable and is an excellent koan.

Joshu is the name of a place in northern China, and Master Junen (778–897) who lived in Kannon-in Temple at Joshu, is now generally known as Master Joshu. He was an exceptionally long-lived Zen Master who died at the age of one hundred and twenty years.

Joshu was fifty-seven years old when his teacher Nansen died. The great persecution of Buddhism by Emperor Bu-so (845) took place in Joshu's sixty-seventh year, Master Rinzai Gigen died (867) in Joshu's ninetieth year, and Master Gyozan died when he was in his one hundred and fifteenth year.

---

1. *Teisho* is a teaching or commentary on a prior teaching. Here it is Shibayama's commentary on Joshu's teaching and on Mumon's commentary on that teaching.

This means that Joshu lived toward the end of the T'ang dynasty when Zen with its creative spirits flourished in China. At that time Joshu was one of the leading figures in Zen circles. People who described his Zen said, "His lips give off light," and greatly respected him.

Joshu was born in a village near Soshufu in the southwestern part of Santosho and entered a Buddhist temple when he was a young boy. Later, while he was still young, he came to Chishu to study under Master Nansen. When he first met Nansen, the latter was resting in bed. Nansen asked him, "Where have you been recently?" "At Zuizo [literally 'auspicious image'], Master," replied Joshu. "Did you then see the Auspicious Image?" the Master asked. Joshu said, "I did not see the Image, but I have seen a reclining Tathagata." Nansen then got up and asked, "Do you already have a Master to study under or not?" Joshu replied, "I have." Nansen asked, "Who is he?" At this, Joshu came closer to Nansen and, bowing to him, said, "I am glad to see you so well in spite of such a severe cold." Nansen recognized in him unusual character and allowed him to be his disciple. After that, Joshu steadily carried on his Zen studies under Nansen.

When Joshu was fifty-seven years old, his Master Nansen died, and four years later Joshu started on a pilgrimage with the determination: "Even a seven-year-old child, if he is greater than I am, I'll ask him to teach me. Even a hundred-year-old man, if I am greater than he is, I'll teach him." He continued on the pilgrimage to deepen and refine his Zen spirituality until he reached his eightieth year. Later he stayed at Kannon-in Temple, in Joshu, and was active as a leading Zen Master of the time in northern China, together with Rinzai.

In the biography of Joshu a series of mondo are recorded, from which this koan is extracted. There have been many attempts to interpret these mondo and to explain the koan in relation to them. We do not have to worry about such attempts here but should directly grip the koan itself. Knowing well its context, Master Mumon presents a simple, direct, and clear koan. Its simplicity plays an important role.

"A monk once asked Master Joshu, 'Has a dog the Buddha Nature or not?'" This monk was well aware that all sentient beings have the Buddha Nature without exception. This is therefore a piercingly effective and unapproachable question which would not be answered if the Master were to say Yes or No. The monk is demanding that Joshu show him the real Buddha Nature, and he is not asking for its interpretation or conceptual understanding. What a cutting question!

Joshu, like the genuine capable Master that he was, answered "Mu!" without the least hesitation. He threw himself—the whole universe—out as "Mu" in front of the questioner. Here is no Joshu, no world, but just "Mu." This is the koan of Joshu's "Mu."

The experience of the Buddha Nature itself is creatively expressed here by "Mu." Although literally "Mu" means No, in this case it points to the incomparable satori which transcends both yes and no, to the religious experience of the Truth one can attain when he casts away his discriminating mind. It has nothing to do with the dualistic interpretation of yes and no, being and nonbeing. It is Truth itself, the Absolute itself.

Joshu, the questioning monk, and the dog are however only incidental to the story, and they do not have any vital significance in themselves. Unless one grasps the koan within himself as he lives here and now, it ceases to be a real koan. We should not read it as an old story; you yourself have to *be* directly "Mu" and make not only the monk, but Joshu as well, show the white feather. Then the Buddha Nature is "Mu"; Joshu is "Mu." Not only that, you yourself and the whole universe are nothing but "Mu." Further, "Mu" itself falls far short, it is ever the unnamable "it."

Master Daie says, "Joshu's 'Mu'—work directly at it. Be just it." He is telling us to be straightforwardly no-self, be "Mu," and present it right here. This is a very inviting instruction indeed.

Once my own teacher, Master Bukai, threw his nyoi (a stick about fifty centimeters long which a Zen Master always carries with him) in front of me and demanded, "Now, transcend the yes-and-no of this nyoi!" and he did not allow me even a moment's hesitation. Training in Zen aims at the direct experience of breaking through to concrete Reality. That breaking through to Reality has to be personally attained by oneself. Zen can never be an idea or knowledge, which are only shadows of Reality. You may reason out that "Mu" transcends both yes and no, that it is the Absolute Oneness where all dualistic discrimination is exhausted. While you are thus conceptualizing, real "Mu" is lost forever.

My teacher also asked me once, "Show me the form of 'Mu'!" When I said, "It has no form whatsoever," he pressed me, saying "I want to see that form which has no-form." How cutting and drastic! Unless one can freely and clearly present the form of "Mu," it turns out to be a meaningless corpse.

In the biography of Master Hakuin we read the following moving story of his first encounter with his teacher, Master Shoju. Shoju asked Hakuin, 'Tell me, what is Joshu's 'Mu'?" Hakuin elatedly replied, "Pervading the universe! Not a spot whatsoever to take hold of!" As soon as he had given that answer, Shoju took hold of Hakuin's nose and gave it a twist. "I am quite at ease to take hold of it," said Shoju, laughing aloud. The next moment he released it and abused Hakuin, "You! Dead monk in a cave! Are you self-satisfied with such 'Mu'?" This completely put Hakuin out of countenance.

We have to realize that this one word "Mu" has such exhaustive depth and lucidity that once one has really grasped it as his own he has the ability to penetrate all Zen koans.

Often people remark that "Mu" is an initial koan for beginners, which is a great mistake. A koan in Zen is fundamentally different from questions and problems in general. Etymologically the term *koan* means "the place where the truth is." In actual training its role is to smash up our dualistic consciousness and open our inner spiritual eye to a new vista. In actual cases there may be differences in the depth of the spirituality and ability of Zen students who break through a koan. This is inevitable for human beings living in this world. For any koan, however, there should be no such discrimination or gradation as an initial koan for beginners or difficult ones for the advanced. And old Zen Master said, "If you break through one koan, hundreds and thousands of koan have all been penetrated at once." Another Master said, "It is like cutting a reel of thread: one cut, and all is cut."

The use of a koan in Zen training developed spontaneously in the southern Sung dynasty in China when a reminiscent, traditionalist tendency began to prevail in Zen circles. In the early period of the southern Sung, Joshu's "Mu" was already being used widely as a koan. Mumon himself was driven into the abyss of Great Doubt by this koan and finally had the experience of breaking through it. Out of his own training and experience, he must have extracted the most essential part from several mondo and presented it to his disciples as simple, direct koan.

This koan is taken from a mondo between Joshu and a monk, and *Joshu Zenji Goroku* ("Sayings of Master Joshu") and a few other books record similar mondo. In the chapter "Joshu Junen" in *Goto Egen*, volume 4, we read, "A monk asked Joshu, 'Has a dog the Buddha Nature or not?' The Master said, 'Mu.' The monk asked, 'From Buddhas above down to creeping creatures like ants, all have the Buddha Nature. Why is it that a dog has not?' 'Because he has ignorance and attachment,' the Master replied."

Joshu Zenji Goroku had the following mondo: "A monk asked, 'Has a dog the Buddha Nature or not?' The Master said, 'Mu.' Monk: 'Even creeping creatures all have the Buddha Nature. Why is it that the dog has not?' Master: 'Because he has ignorance and attachment.'"

Another monk asked Joshu, "Has a dog the Buddha Nature or not?" The Master said, "U" (Yes). The monk asked, "Having the Buddha Nature, why is he in such a dog-body?" Master: "Knowingly he dared to be so."

Although generally Joshu is supposed to have originated this mondo on the Buddha Nature, we read the following mondo in the biography of Master Ikan (755–817) of Kozenji at Keicho: Monk: "Has a dog the Buddha Nature or not?" Master: "Yes" (U). Monk: "Have you, O Master, the Buddha Nature or not?" Master: "I have not." Monk: "All sentient beings have the Buddha Nature. Why is it that you alone, Master, have not?" Master: "I am not among all sentient beings." Monk: "If you are not among sentient beings, are you then a Buddha or not?" Master: "I am not a Buddha." Monk: "What kind of thing are you after all?" Master: "I am not a thing either." Monk: "Can it be seen and thought of?" Master: "Even if you try to think about it and know it, you are unable to do so. It is therefore called 'unknowable.'" (*Keitoku Dento-roku*, volume 7)

Let us put aside for the time being historical studies of the koan. "Mu" as a koan is to open our spiritual eye to Reality, to "Mu," that is, to Joshu's Zen—this is the sole task of this koan, and everything else is just complementary and not of primary importance. We may simply read about it for our information.

All sentient beings without exception have the Buddha Nature. This is the fundamental Truth of nondualism and equality. On the other hand, this actual world of ours is dualistic and full of discriminations. The above mondo presents to us the basic contradiction between the fundamental Truth of nondualism and actual phenomena. The ancient Masters made us face the fact that we human beings from the very beginning have been living in this fundamental contradiction. It was the compassion of the Masters that led them to try thus to intensify their disciples' Great Doubt, their spiritual quest, and finally lead them to satori by breaking through it. If here one really breaks through this koan, which uniquely presents before him the core of human contradiction, he can clearly see for himself with his genuine Zen eye what these mondo are trying to tell us.

TEISHO ON MUMON'S COMMENTARY

Mumon comments: "In studying Zen, one must pass the barriers set up by ancient Zen Masters. For the attainment of incomparable satori, one has to cast away his discriminating mind. Those who have not passed the barrier and have not cast away the discriminating mind are all phantoms haunting trees and plants.

"Now, tell me, what is the barrier of the Zen Masters? Just this 'Mu'—it is the barrier of Zen. It is thus called 'the gateless barrier of Zen.' Those who have passed the barrier will not only see Joshu clearly, but will go hand in hand with all the Masters of the past, see them face to face. You will see with the same eye that they see with and hear with the same ear. Wouldn't it be wonderful? Don't you want to pass the barrier? Then concentrate yourself into this 'Mu,' with your 360 bones and 84,000 pores, making your whole body one great inquiry. Day and night work intently at it. Do not attempt nihilistic or dualistic interpretations. It is like having bolted a red hot iron ball. You try to vomit it but cannot.

"Cast away your illusory discriminating knowledge and consciousness accumulated up to now, and keep on working harder. After a while, when your efforts come to fruition, all the oppositions (such as in and out) will naturally be identified. You will then be like a dumb person who has had a wonderful dream: he only knows it personally, within himself. Suddenly you break through the barrier; you will astonish heaven and shake the earth.

"It is as if you have snatched the great sword of General Kan. You kill the Buddha if you meet him; you kill the ancient Masters if you meet them. On the brink of life and death you are utterly free, and in the six realms and the four modes of life you live, with great joy, a genuine life in complete freedom.

"Now, how should one strive? With might and main work at this 'Mu,' and *be* 'Mu.' If you do not stop or waver in your striving, then behold, when the Dharma candle is lighted, darkness is at once enlightened."

According to Master Mumon's biography, he stayed in a cave in a mountain where he practiced zazen and disciplined himself for six long years. In spite of such hard training he could not fundamentally satisfy his spiritual quest. It was this koan of "Joshu's 'Mu'" that made him plunge into the abyss of Great Doubt and finally attain satori, breaking through it as if the bottom had fallen out of a barrel. His commentary on this koan is therefore especially kind and detailed. He tells us most frankly of the hard training he himself went through and tries to guide Zen students on the basis of his own experiences.

"In studying Zen, one must pass the barriers set up by ancient Zen Masters. For the attainment of incomparable satori, one has to cast away his discriminating mind."

First Mumon tells us what must be the right attitude for a Zen student, that is, what is fundamentally required of him in studying Zen. As Master Daiye says, "Satori is the fundamental experience in Zen." One has to cast his ordinary self away and be reborn as a new Self in a different dimension. In other words, the student must personally have the inner experience called satori, by which he is reborn as the True Self. This fundamental experience of awakening is essential in Zen. Although various different expressions are used when talking about the fact of this religious awakening, it cannot be real Zen without it. Mumon therefore declares at the very beginning that "in studying Zen one must pass the barriers set up by the ancient Zen Masters." The barrier of the ancient Zen Masters is the barrier to Zen, and the obstacle to transcend is the dualism of yes and no, subject and object. Practically, the sayings of ancient Masters, which are called koan, are such barriers.

The phrase "incomparable satori" indicates the eternal emancipation or absolute freedom that is attained by directly breaking through the Zen barrier. In order to break through it, Mumon stresses that one must once and for all cast away his discriminating mind completely. "Discriminating mind" is our ordinary consciousness, which is dualistic, discriminating, and the cause of all sorts of illusions. Mumon asks us to cast this away. To get rid of it requires that one's whole being must be the koan. There should be nothing left, and the secret of Zen lies in this really throwing oneself away. One does not have to ask what would be likely to happen after that; whatever happens would naturally and automatically come about without any seeking for it. What is important here is for him to actually do it himself.

"Those who have not passed the barrier and have not cast away the discriminating mind are all phantoms haunting trees and plants."

There is a superstition that the phantoms of those who after death are not in peace haunt trees and plants and cast evil spells on people. Here it means those people who do not have a fundamental spiritual basis, those who cling to words and logic and are enslaved by dualistic views, without grasping the subjective point of view.

Mumon says that anyone who is unable to pass the barrier of the old Masters or to wipe out his discriminating mind—that is, if his Zen mind is not awakened—is like a phantom, without reality. There is no significance in such an existence. Thus by using extreme and abusive language Mumon tries to make us ashamed of our unenlightened existence and to arouse in us the great spiritual quest.

"Now, tell me," Mumon demands, "what is the barrier of the Zen Masters?" Having aroused our interest, he answers himself that this "Mu" is the ultimate barrier of Zen. If once one has broken through it, he is the master of all the barriers and the forty-eight koan and commentaries of the *Mumonkan* are all his tools. This is therefore called "The Gateless Barrier of Zen," Mumon remarks. We should remember however that it is not only the first koan, but that any of the forty-eight koan of the *Mumonkan* is the barrier of Zen.

"Those who have passed the barrier will not only see Joshu clearly, but will go hand in hand with all the Masters in the past, see them face to face. You will see with the same eye that they see with and hear with the same ear. Wouldn't it be wonderful?"

Mumon tells us how wonderful it is to experience breaking through the barrier and to live the life of satori. Once the Gate is broken through, ultimate peace is attained. You can get hold of old Joshu alive. Further, you will live in the same spirituality with all the Zen Masters, see them face to face, and enjoy the Truth of Oneness. How wonderful, how splendid! He praises the life of satori in the highest terms. There are no ages in satori; no distinctions of I and you, space and time. Wherever it may be and whenever it may be, just here and now you see and you hear—it is Joshu, it is your Self, and "Mu." There can be no greater joy. To experience this is to attain eternal peace.

"Don't you want to pass the barrier? Then concentrate yourself into this 'Mu' with your 360 bones and 84,000 pores, making your whole body one great inquiry."

Having described the great joy of satori, Mumon now turns to his disciples and speaks directly to them, "Are there any among you who want to pass this barrier of the ancient Masters?" He then goes on to give practical instructions as to how they should carry on their training in order to break through the barrier—how to attain satori. He tells them to inquire, with their heart and soul, what it is to transcend yes and no, you and I. They are to cast their whole being, from head to foot, into this inquiry and carry on with it. There will be no world, no self, but just one Great Doubt. This is "Mu." "Just be 'Mu'!" Mumon urges the disciples.

"To concentrate" is to be unified and identified. "To concentrate oneself into 'Mu'" is for "Mu" and the self to be one—to be one and then to transcend both "Mu" and the self.

"Day and night work intently at it; do not attempt nihilistic or dualistic interpretations."

Mumon's instructions continue: never be negligent, even for a short while, but do zazen and devote yourself to the koan day and night. An old Master described this training process, saying, "Work like a mother hen trying to hatch her eggs." Do not misunderstand "Mu" as nihilistic emptiness. Never in the world take it as a dualistic No in opposition to Yes. Needless to say, it has nothing to do with intellectual discrimination or dualistic reasoning. It is utterly beyond all description.

"It is like having bolted a red hot iron ball; you try to vomit it but cannot. Cast away your illusory discriminating knowledge and consciousness accumulated up to now, and keep on working harder. After a while, when your efforts come to fruition, all the oppositions (such as in and out) will naturally be identified. You will then be like a dumb person who has had a wonderful dream: he only knows it personally, within himself."

"Like having bolted a red hot iron ball" describes the one who, with his whole being, body and soul, has plunged into the Great Doubt, the spiritual quest. All the emotions are exhausted, all the intellect has come to its extremity; there is not an inch for the discrimination to enter. This is the state of utmost spiritual intensification. When it is hot, the whole universe is nothing but the heat; when you see, it is just one pure act of seeing — there is no room there for any thought to come in. In such a state, Mumon warns us, never give up but straightforwardly carry on with your striving. In such a state no thought of discrimination can be present. "Illusory discriminating knowledge and consciousness accumulated up to now" refers to our dualistically working mind we have had before. No trace of it is now left. You are thoroughly lucid and transparent like a crystal. Subject and object, in and out, being and nonbeing are just one, and this very one ceases to be one any longer. Rinzai said, describing this state, "The whole universe is sheer darkness." Hakuin said, "It was like sitting in an ice cave a million miles thick." This is the moment when the I and the world are both altogether gone. This is exactly the moment when one's discriminating mind is emptied and cast away. When one is in the abyss of absolute "Mu" in actual training, the inexpressible moment comes upon him — the moment when "Mu" is awakened to "Mu," that is, when he is revived as the self of no-self. At this mysterious moment, he is like a dumb person who has had a wonderful dream, for he is fully aware of it, but is unable to use words to express it. The Absolute Nothingness ("Mu") is awakened to itself. This is the moment of realization when subject-object opposition is altogether transcended. To describe it we have to use such words as inexpressible or mysterious. 'You will then be like a dumb person who has had a wonderful dream: he only knows it personally, within himself."

Then Mumon tries again to describe the experience of the one who has just broken through the barrier: "Suddenly you break through the barrier; you will astonish heaven and shake the earth." I myself, however, should like to reverse the order of these two sentences and say, "Suddenly you break through the barrier; you will astonish heaven and shake the earth. You will then be like a dumb person who has had a wonderful dream: he only knows it personally, within himself." This would be more faithful to actual experience. Zen calls this experience "incomparable satori," or "to die a Great Death once and to revive from death." Mumon described his experience of attaining satori by saying that "all beings on earth have opened their eyes." This is the most important and essential process one has to go through in Zen training.

"It is as if you have snatched the great sword of General Kan. You kill the Buddha if you meet him; you kill the ancient Masters if you meet them. On the brink of life and death, you are utterly free, and in the six realms and the four modes of life you live, with great joy, a genuine life in complete freedom."

General Kan was a brave general famous in ancient China. With his great sword he used to freely cut and conquer his enemies. Once one attains the satori of this "Mu," his absolute inner freedom can be compared to the man who has the great sword of that famous strong general in his own hand.

Having experienced this exquisite moment of breaking through the barrier, one's self, the world, and everything change. It is just like one who was born blind getting his sight. Here Mumon tells us how absolutely free he now is. He sees, he hears, and everything, as it is, is given new life. Mumon in his own poem speaks of this wonder, "Mount Sumeru jumps up and dances." Only those who have actually experienced it themselves can really appreciate what Mumon sings here.

"You kill the Buddha if you meet him; you kill the ancient Masters if you meet them."

This expression is often misunderstood. Zen postulates absolute freedom in which all attachments and restraints are completely wiped away. The Buddha therefore is to be cast away and so are the Patriarchs. Any restraints whatsoever in the mind are to be cast away. For the one who has passed through the abyss of Great Doubt, transcending subject and object, you and I, and has been revived as the True Self, can there be anything to disturb him? The term "to kill" should not be interpreted in our ordinary ethical sense. "To kill" is to transcend names and ideas. If you meet the Buddha, the Buddha is "Mu." If you meet ancient Masters, they are "Mu." Therefore he says that if you pass the barrier you will "not only see Joshu clearly, but go hand in hand with all the Masters in the past, see them face to face. You will see with the same eye that they see with and hear with the same ear."

To live is an aspect of "Mu"; to die is also an aspect of "Mu." If you stand, your standing is "Mu." If you sit, your sitting is "Mu." The six realms refer to the six different stages of existence, i.e., the celestial world, human world, fighting world, beasts, hungry beings, and hell. The four modes are four different forms of life, i.e., viviparous, oviparous, from moisture, and metamorphic. Originally the phrase referred to various stages of life in transmigration, depending on the law of causation. The reference to the six realms and the four modes of life means, "under whatever circumstances you may live, in whatever situation you may find yourself." Both favorable conditions and adverse situations are "Mu," working differently as you live, at any time, at any place. How wonderful it is to live such a serene life with perfect freedom, the spiritual freedom of the one who has attained religious peace!

"Now, how should one strive? With might and main work at this 'Mu,' and *be* 'Mu.'"

Mumon once again gives his direct instruction on how one should carry out his Zen training in order to break through the barrier of the Zen Masters to attain incomparable satori and his Zen personality. How should he work at "Mu"? All that can be said is: "Be just 'Mu' with might and main." To be "Mu" is to cast everything—yourself and the universe—into it.

"If you do not stop or waver in your striving, then behold, when the Dharma candle is lighted, the darkness is at once enlightened."

This can be simply taken as a candle on the altar. Once one's mind bursts open to the truth of "Mu," the ignorance is at once enlightened, just as all darkness is gone when a candle is lighted.

Mumon warns his disciples that they should not stop or waver in their striving. In other words, he says that with might and main you must be "Mu" through and through, and never stop striving to attain that. An old Japanese Zen Master has a waka poem:

When your bow is broken and your arrows are exhausted,
There, shoot!
Shoot with your whole being!

A Western philosopher has said, "Man's extremity is God's opportunity." When man is at his very extremity and still goes on striving with his whole being, without stopping, the moment to break through suddenly comes to him. This is the moment of fundamental change when one is reborn as a True Self. It is as if a candle were lighted in darkness. Darkness is at once illumined.

Master Engo has a poem in the *Hekigan-roku*:

It is like cutting a reel of thread:
One cut, and all is cut.
It is like dyeing of a reel of thread:
One dip and all is dyed.

I join Mumon in saying, "Wouldn't it be wonderful!" In his commentary Mumon has tried his best to tell us how exquisite and wonderful true Zen attainment is, and pointed out the way to experience it.

TEISHO ON MUMON'S POEM

The dog! the Buddha Nature!
The Truth is manifested in full.
A moment of yes-and-no
Lost are your body and soul.

Following his detailed commentary on Joshu's "Mu," Mumon wrote this poem to comment on it once more, so that he might clearly and simply present the essence of satori.

He first presents the koan itself directly to us: "The dog! the Buddha Nature!" What else is needed here? As it is, it is "Mu." As they are, they are "Mu." Those who really know it will fully understand it all by this.

The second line says, "The Truth is manifested in full." The original Chinese term used for Truth literally means "True Law," that is, the Buddha's fundamental command. It is nothing but "Mu" itself. Look, it is right in front of you, Mumon says. A blind person fails to see the sunlight, but it is not the fault of the sun.

"A moment of yes-and-no: lost are your body and soul." Out of his compassion Mumon adds the last two lines, which say that if even a thought of discrimination comes, the truth of "Mu" is altogether gone. When one is really "Mu" through and through, to call it "Mu" is already incorrect, for that belongs to the dualistic world of letters. "Mu" here is just temporarily used in order to transcend U (yes) and Mu (no). If one is afraid of losing his body and soul, what can be accomplished? The secret here can be communicated only to those who have once died the Great Death.

CHAPTER 15

MODERN BUDDHIST THOUGHT

Traditional Buddhist thought and practice as well as modern studies and interpretations of Buddhism are flourishing in this century. The three selections from K. N. Jayatilleke; Tenzin Gyatso, the Dalai Lama; and Kelji Nishitani, chosen to conclude this anthology of Buddhist texts, exemplify the vigor of recent Buddhist thinking in Theravāda, Tibetan, and Japanese Zen Buddhism. Jayatilleke, late professor at the University of Ceylon, was recognized around the world for his profound understanding of Theravāda Buddhism. The selection here, "The Buddhist Ethical Ideal of the Ultimate Good," is taken from his posthumous book, *The Message of the Buddha* (New York: The Free Press, 1974), an edited (by Ninian Smart) version of a series of radio talks given shortly before his untimely death in 1969. In this essay Jayatilleke shows how pleasure, righteousness, and duty constitute dimensions of the ultimate good, the ideal of realizing complete perfection, bliss, and freedom.

"The Key to the Middle Way" is by Tenzin Gyatso, the fourteenth Dalai Lama. It is excerpted from the essay by the same title in Tenzin Gyatso, *The Buddhism of Tibet and the Key to the Middle Way* (New York: Harper & Row, 1975). In it the Dalai Lama explains the meaning of emptiness and its importance in meditational practice. The whole essay, emphasizing the practice of emptying oneself of the constructions of consciousness, is a contemporary commentary on the Middle Way thought of Nāgārjuna.

The final selection is from Keiji Nishitani, *Religion and Nothingness* (Berkeley: University of California Press, 1982), a work in which Nishitani plumbs the depths of emptiness (*śūnyatā*), finding in the primordial reality denoted by this term a basis for overcoming the nihilism implicit in Western thought. It is a fine example of Buddhist thought seeking self-understanding through encounter with Western thought, showing us not only the profundity of Buddhist thought but its practicality as a way of self-realization. The selection is excerpted from chapter 4, "The Standpoint of *Śūnyatā*," where Nishitani is seeking to understand the emptiness of self (*anātman*) by going beyond the self as either object or subject to an experiential reality preceding this dichotomy. Only in the experiential realization of this prior reality in which one's self falls away is one truly oneself, or, in Nishitani's words, there one encounters "that which is self in not being self."

I
K. N. Jayatilleke: The Buddhist Ethical Ideal of the Ultimate Good*

Moral philosophers use the term "good" in two important senses. There is the sense in which we speak of what is "good as an end" or what is "intrinsically good." There is also the sense in which we speak of what is "good as a means" or what is "instrumentally good." The two senses are interrelated. For what is instrumentally good, or good as a means, is necessary to bring about what is intrinsically good, or good as an end.

When the *Dhammapada* says that "health is the greatest gain" it is, in a sense, treating the state of health as being what is good as an end. For whatever our gains may be, most people are prepared to lose them or use them in order to recover their health if they fall ill. Besides, it is only if we are healthy that we can adopt the means to gain material or even spiritual riches. If health is a desirable end to achieve or is good as an end, then what is instrumental in achieving this state of health is good as a means. Since medicines, even when they are bitter, are often useful as a means to the cure of illnesses, they are deemed to be good as a means, or instrumentally good.

Although some people would regard a state of physical health in the above sense as being good as an end, others may say that good health is only a relative end since the ultimate end or goal that we should seek is happiness, and good health is only a necessary condition for happiness. So while no one would say that bitter medicine is good as an end, many people would regard a state of health as being good as an end only in a relative sense, as contributing to one's well-being and happiness. One's well-being and happiness would, therefore, be for them an ultimate end in a sense in which even physical health is not. Besides, in the world in which we live, we can enjoy a state of physical health only in a relative sense since we may fall ill from time to time and even healthy men eventually die.

In this chapter we shall be concerned only with what is ultimately good from the Buddhist point of view. Buddhism presents a clear conception of what is ultimately good, and what is instrumentally good in order to achieve it. What is instrumentally good to achieve this end is regarded as good as a means. This consists mainly of right actions and the other factors that help in bringing about what is ultimately good.

---

*Reprinted with permission from K. N. Jayatilleke, *The Message of the Buddha* (New York: The Free Press, 1974).

These right actions may often be called good as opposed to evil actions. But we shall avoid the phrase "good actions" and consistently use the phrase "right actions" (as opposed to "wrong actions") in speaking about what is primarily necessary in order to achieve what is good as an end.

In the Buddhist texts, the terms that are most often used to denote "right actions" are kusala or puñña. Kusala means "skillful" and denotes the fact that the performance of right actions requires both theoretical understanding as well as practice. The person who has attained the ideal or the highest good is referred to as a person of "accomplished skill or the highest skill." Akusala, its opposite, means the "unskillful." Puñña, as used of right actions, means what is "meritorious," as opposed to pāpa, which means "demeritorious." It is not a term that is employed to denote the highest good. In fact, the person who has attained the highest good is said to have "cast aside both meritorious and demeritorious actions."

As we shall see in examining the nature of right actions, this does not imply that meritorious actions (as opposed to demeritorious) ones are not necessary for the attainment of the highest good, nor that those who have attained are amoral. The path to salvation or the path leading to the highest good in Buddhism is a gradual path, and although we may start with our egoistic or self-centered desires as a motive for self-advancement, they have progressively to be cast aside until eventually the goodness of the actions alone remains without the personal motivation for doing good.

If we acquaint ourselves with the nature of the ethical ideal or the conception of what is intrinsically good or good as an end, we would be in a better position to understand the Buddhist conception of right and wrong.

Moral philosophers have conceived of the ethical ideal in various ways. Some have thought of it as pleasure and others as happiness. Yet others considered the notion of duty or obligation as central to ethics, while others again think of the goal as perfection.

What is the Buddhist conception of the ideal? Buddhism conceives of the ethical idea as one of Happiness, Perfection, Realization and Freedom. These ethical goals, in fact, coincide, and the highest good is at the same time one of ultimate Happiness, moral Perfection, final Realization and perfect Freedom. This is the goal to be attained in the cosmic or personal dimension of existence.

This is a goal for one and all to attain, each in his own interest as well as that of others. Besides, there is a social ideal which it is also desirable to bring into existence. This is broadly conceived of as "the well-being or happiness of the multitude or mankind." Here "well-being and happiness" is conceived of both materially as well as spiritually. The ideal society in which this well-being and happiness will prevail in an optimum form is conceived of as both socialistic, being founded on the principle of equality, and democratic, as affording the best opportunities for the exercise of human freedom. Such a society is also just, as it is based on principles of righteousness.

We shall explore the nature of these conceptions in greater detail in examining the social philosophy of Buddhism. We shall also examine in Chapter 15 the relationship that exists between the social ideal and the personal ideal. Although from an individualistic point of view "the path to the acquisition of wealth is one, while the path to Nirvana is another" even the social ideal can be attained, it is said, only by people who are motivated to act in accordance with the Ten Virtues in a society built on firm economic, political and moral foundations.

What is the role of pleasure and the performance of one's duties in relation to the Buddhist ethical ideal? Let us first take the role of pleasure. Buddhism recognizes the importance of the hedonistic principle that man is predominantly motivated to act out of "his desire for happiness and his repulsion for unhappiness." In fact, the central truths of Buddhism, "the four truths concerning unhappiness" are formulated in the manner set forth so as to appeal to man's intrinsic desire for happiness and the desire to escape from or transcend his unhappiness.

Pleasure is classified in the Buddhist texts according to its different grades, and it is stated that "the most refined and sublimest form of pleasure" is the bliss of Nirvana. This "experience of the bliss of freedom" is so different from the conditioned pleasure and happiness of worldly existence that there is a reluctance on the part of the texts to use the word *vedanā* (feeling) of it since *vedanā* as represented in the formula of conditioning is always conditioned.

The attitude to pleasure in the Buddhist texts is a realistic one. It does not deny the fact or value of pleasure. The limited good as well as the evil consequences of even the gross forms of pleasure are recognized. The Buddha did not advocate a form of asceticism whereby we should shun all pleasures by closing our eyes and ears (and becoming like the blind and the deaf) to objects which arouse sensuous pleasure. Instead the Buddha wanted those who were addicted to such pleasures to realize their limitations.

One form of pleasure that we experience is by the gratification of our desires. We get satisfaction from time to time by gratifying our desire for sensuous pleasures and sex. We get such temporary satisfaction, again, by gratifying our egoistic instincts, such as the desire for self-preservation, for security, for possessions, for power, for fame, for personal immortality, etc. We also get satisfaction by gratifying our desire for destruction or aggression or the elimination of what we dislike. The enjoyment of these pleasures is often accompanied by rationalizations or erroneous beliefs, such as, for instance, that we have been created for a life of enjoyment of this sort or that we should eat, drink and be merry today for tomorrow we die.

What is important is not to shun pleasure or torment the body, but to realize for oneself the limitations of pleasures and the diminishing returns they afford, so that eventually we can transcend them by a life of temperance and restraint and enjoy the immaterial or spiritual forms of pleasure which accompany selfless and compassionate activity based on understanding. One must give up the gross forms of pleasure for the more refined and superior kinds of happiness. As the *Dhammapada* states, "If by renouncing a little pleasure we can find a great deal of happiness, then the prudent man should relinquish such trifling pleasures on discovering an abundant happiness" (Dh. 290).

This is only an extension of the hedonistic principle that man has a tendency to seek pleasure and to recoil from pain, and therefore that he ought to do what is both rational and possible by giving up the gross forms of pleasure for the more sublime forms until he eventually attains the supreme bliss of Nirvana.

These more sublime forms of pleasure are correlated with forms of activity which are spiritually elevating and socially desirable. It is not always necessary that one should literally renounce the worldly life in order to cultivate them. Both laymen and monks can attain the first stage of spiritual progress as well as some of the later stages. A person who can perform the duties associated with his livelihood, provided it is a right mode of living with a sense of selfless service to his fellow men out of concern, compassion and understanding, can act without a narrowly selfish motivation and derive happiness from his work. The Buddha compared the spiritual gains to be had from the lay life and the life of the monk to agriculture and trade. Agriculture gives slow but steady returns, while trade gives quicker returns though it is more risky. According to the Buddha, nothing could be worse than the outward renunciation of the lay life in order to live a life of corruption and hypocrisy as a recluse. Such a person, apart from the disservice he would be doing to the community, would be digging his own grave.

However, the ignorance that clouds the judgment of man is such that a man who enjoys the grosser forms of pleasure cannot experience anything more refined or more sublime, since he is addicted to them. So what often happens is that he experiences less and less of both pleasure and happiness because of his reluctance to go against the current until eventually he becomes a slave to his passions, losing both his freedom and happiness as well as every other quality which can bring him closer to the ethical ideal.

While Buddhist ethics recognizes and appeals to the hedonistic, it does not fall into the error of hedonism by asserting that pleasure alone, abstracted from everything else, is what is worth achieving. The hedonistic ideal of supreme happiness, for example, is also identical with the therapeutic goal of perfect mental health.

So the path to happiness is also the path to mental stability, serenity, awareness, integration and purity of mind. The Buddha classified diseases as bodily and mental and it is said that while we have bodily diseases from time to time, mental illness is almost continual until arahantship is attained, so that only the saint or a person with a Nirvanic mind can be said to have a perfectly healthy mind.

While the four noble truths, as we have pointed out, on the one hand indicate the path from unhappiness to perfect happiness, it is also in the form of a medical diagnosis. From this point of view, the truths give an account of (1) the nature of the illness, its history and prognosis, (2) the causes of the illness, (3) the nature of the state of health that we ought to achieve and (4) the remedial measures to be taken in order to achieve it.

This diseased state of the mind is due to the unsatisfied desires and the conflicts caused by the desires that rage within our minds both at the conscious and unconscious levels. Thus the desire for sense pleasures and selfish pursuits is found as a subliminal or latent tendency as well. It is the same with our hatred or aggression. Mental serenity, stability and sanity can be achieved neither by free indulgence in our desires nor by ascetic repression and self-torment. When we become more aware of the way these desires operate in us by the exercise or practice of awareness, we gradually attain a level of consciousness in which there is a greater degree of serenity and stability. The culmination of this development, when the mind is purged of all its defilements, is the perfect state of mental health, which coincides with the experience of the highest bliss.

Buddhism points to the source of unhappiness, or the causes of suffering, not to make us unhappy or brood over our lot, but in order that we may emerge from our condition with stronger, happier and healthier minds. Such people could say in the words of the *Dhammapada*:

> "So happily we live, free from anger among those who are angry" (197)
> "So happily we live in good health amongst the ailing" (198)
> "So happily we live relaxed among those who are tense" (199).

The person who has attained the ideal is said to have fulfilled all his obligations since the greatest obligation of everyone, whatever else he may do, is the attainment of the goal of Nirvana. But, till he does this, man has all his social duties to perform towards the various classes of people in society. The duties and obligations of parents and children, employers, husbands and wives, religious men and their followers, etc., are given in the *Sigālovāda Sutta,* while the duties and rights of a king or state and its citizens are recorded in the *Aggañña* and *Cakkavatti-sīhanāda Suttas.* Even such duties and obligations are to be performed in a spirit of selfless service, love and understanding, so that we are treading the path to Nirvana in the exercise of these obligations.

So while the ultimate end is one of perfect happiness and mental health, it is not one in which one is obliged to perform one's duties for duty's sake. Likewise, when the Arahant serves society as the several enlightened monks and nuns mentioned in the *Thera-* and *Therīgathā* did, they did so out of a spontaneous spirit of selflessness, compassion and understanding.

It is, therefore, a mistaken notion to hold, as some scholars have held, that the Arahant is amoral and could even do evil with impunity. It is true that an Arahant "casts aside both meritorious and demeritorious actions." By this is meant only that he does not do any acts, whether they be good or evil, with the expectation of reward, nor do these acts have any efficacy for bringing about karmic consequences in the future. They are mere acts of goodness, which flow spontaneously from a transcendent mind, which shines with its natural luster with the elimination of craving, hatred and delusion and is wholly filled with selflessness, loving-kindness and wisdom.

The following passage illustrates the process and nature of this attainment:

> "In whatever monk who was covetous, covetousness is got rid of . . . wrath, grudging, hypocrisy, spite, jealousy, stinginess, treachery, craftiness, . . . who was of evil desires, evil desire is got rid of, who was of wrong view, wrong view is got rid of. . . . He beholds himself purified of all these unskilled states and sees himself freed. . . . When he beholds himself freed, delight is born; rapture is born from delight; when he is in rapture, the body is impassible; when the body is impassible, he experiences joy; being joyful the mind is concentrated. He dwells, suffusing one direction with a mind of loving-kindness, likewise the second, third and fourth; just so, above, below, across; he dwells having suffused the whole world everywhere, in every way with a mind of friendliness that is far-reaching, widespread, immeasurable, without enmity, without malevolence. He abides with a mind full of pity . . . sympathetic joy . . . equanimity . . . without enmity, without malevolence. It is as if there were a lovely lotus pond with clear water, sweet water, cool water, limpid, with beautiful banks; and a man were to come along from the east, west, north, or south, overcome and overpowered by the heat, exhausted, parched and thirsty. On coming to that lotus pond he might quench his thirst with water and quench his feverish heat. Even so . . . one who has come into this Dhamma and discipline taught by the Buddha, having thus developed loving-kindness, pity, sympathetic joy and equanimity, attains inward calm" (M. I. 283).

We find it expressly stated of the saint that he is a "person of accomplished skill, of the highest skill, who has attained the highest attainment, an invincible recluse," who is endowed with "right aspirations such as compassion, which do not require to be further disciplined. The Arahant's state is, therefore, one of moral perfection, though it is not one of "conditioned morality but natural or spontaneous morality"; he is said to be "naturally virtuous and not virtuous through conditioning."

This state of bliss or ultimate happiness, perfect mental health and moral perfection, is also described as a state of supreme freedom and realization. The mind is master of itself and one has supreme control over it. The inflowing impulses do not disturb it.

The criticism has been made that the quest for Nirvana is a form of escapism. But this criticism is without basis since the person who attains Nirvana does so with full understanding of the nature of the world as well as of himself. If he ceases to be henceforth attracted by the pleasures of the world, it is because he can assess their worth and their limitations. The real escapists are the people who cannot, in fact, face reality as a whole and try to drown their fears, anxieties and sorrows by indulging in their passions. They are easily upset by their circumstances and find consolation in some form of neurosis. But the person who has a Nirvanic mind, or is anywhere near it, is "unruffled by the ups and downs of the world, is happy, unstained and secure."

In such a state one has "no fear or anxiety" at all. The highest good or the ethical ideal for each person is, therefore, conceived of as a state of bliss, mental health, perfection, freedom and realization. It is a state that is stable and ineffable as well.

II
The Dalai Lama: *The Key to the Middle Way**

Homage to the perfection of wisdom.

I respectfully bow down to the Conqueror,
Protector of all beings through boundless compassion,
With dominion over glorious wisdom and deeds, but who
Like an illusion is only designated by words and thoughts.

I will explain here in brief terms the essence
Of the ambrosia of his good speech,
The mode of the union of emptiness and dependent-arising,
To increase the insight of those with burgeoning intellect.

We all want happiness and do not want suffering. Moreover, achieving happiness and eliminating suffering depend upon the deeds of body, speech and mind. As the deeds of body and speech depend upon the mind, we must therefore constructively transform the mind. The ways of constructively transforming the mind are to cause mistaken states of consciousness not to be generated and good states of consciousness to be both generated and increased.

What are the determinants, in this context, of a bad state of consciousness? A state of consciousness, once produced, may initially cause ourselves to become unhappy and our previously calm mind suddenly to become excited or tense. This may then act as the cause of hard breathing, nervous sweating, illness, and so forth. From these, in turn, bad deeds of body and speech may arise, which directly or indirectly may also cause hardship for others. All states of consciousness that give rise to such a causal sequence are assigned as bad. The determinants of good states of consciousness, on the other hand, are just the opposite. All states of consciousness that cause the

*Reprinted with permission from Tenzin Gyatso, *The Buddhism of Tibet and the Key to the Middle Way* (New York: Harper & Row, 1975).

bestowal of the fruit of happiness and peace upon ourselves or others, either superficially or in depth, are assigned as good.

As for ways of causing mistaken states of consciousness not to be generated, there are such means as undergoing brain operations, ingesting various types of drugs, making our awareness dull as if overcome with drowsiness, and making ourselves senseless as if in deep sleep. However, apart from only occasional superficial help, these mostly do more harm than good from the point of view of deep solutions.

Therefore, the way of beneficially transforming the mind is as follows. First we must think about the disadvantages of bad states of consciousness, identifying them from our own personal experience. Then we must recognize the good states of consciousness. If familiarity with them is developed through thinking again and again about their advantages and about their supporting validators, then the various types of good states of consciousness will become stronger. This occurs through the force of familiarity and through these good states of consciousness having valid foundations and being qualities dependent on the mind [and thus capable of limitless development]. Then, it is natural that the defective states of consciousness will decrease in strength. Thereby, in time, sure signs of goodness will appear in the mind.

Many such different methods of transforming the mind have been taught by the many great teachers of this world, in accordance with individual times and places and in accordance with the minds of individual trainees. Among these, many methods of taming the mind have been taught in the books of the Buddhists. From among these, a little will be said here about the view of emptiness.

Views of selflessness are taught in both Buddhist vehicles, the Mahāyāna and the Hīnayāna, and with respect to the Mahāyāna in both sūtra and tantra divisions. When a Buddhist and a non-Buddhist are differentiated by way of behaviour, the difference is whether or not the person takes refuge in the Three Jewels. When they are differentiated by way of view, the difference is whether or not the person asserts the views which are the four seals testifying to a doctrine's being the word of the Buddha. The four seals are:

> All products are impermanent.
> All contaminated things are miserable.
> All phenomena are empty and selfless.
> Nirvāṇa is peace.

Therefore, all Buddhists assert that all phenomena are empty and selfless.

With respect to the meaning of selflessness, there is a selflessness of persons, that is the non-existence of persons as substantial entities or self-sufficient entities. This is asserted by all four Buddhist schools of tenets: Vaibhāṣika, Sautrāntika, Cittamātra and Mādhyamika. The Cittamātrins asserts, in addition, a selflessness of phenomena that is an emptiness of objects and subjects as different entities. The Mādhyamikas assert a selflessness of phenomena that is an emptiness of inherent existence.

The meaning of the views of the lower and higher schools of tenets differs greatly in coarseness and subtlety. However, if understanding is developed with respect to the lower systems, this serves as a means of deep ascertainment of the higher views; therefore, it is very helpful to do so. Here, selflessness is to be discussed in accordance with the Mādhyamika system, and within the division of the Mādhyamika into Svātantrika and Prāsaṅgika, in accordance with the Prāsaṅgika system.

Question: Did the Blessed One set forth all these different schools of tenets? If he did, on what sūtras do each rely? Also, does the difference of status and depth of the schools of tenets necessarily depend on scriptural authority?

Answer: The different views of the four schools of tenets were set forth by the Blessed One himself in accordance with the mental capacities of his trainees, whether superior, middling, or low. Some trainees were likely to fall into views of nihilism or were in danger of losing faith if taught selflessness. For them Buddha even taught the existence of a self in some sūtras. Also, some trainees were likely to go either to the extreme of eternity or to the extreme of annihilation if Buddha answered their questions in the positive or the negative. For them Buddha did not say either "exists" or "does not exist," but remained silent, as in the case of the fourteen inexpressible views. Also, with respect to the modes of selflessness, Buddha set forth many forms as was briefly explained above.

The sūtras on which each of the schools relies are as follows. The Vaibhāṣika and Sautrāntika schools of tenets rely mainly on the sūtras of the first wheel of doctrine, such as the *Sūtra on the Four Truths* (*Catuḥsatya*). The Cittamātra school of tenets relies mainly on the sūtras of the last wheel of doctrine, such as the *Unravelling of the Thought Sūtra* (*Saṃdhinirmocana*). The Mādhyamika school relies mainly on the sūtras of the middle wheel of doctrine, such as the *Hundred Thousand Stanza Perfection of Wisdom Sūtra* (*Śatasāhasrikāprajñāpāramitā*). There are ways of presenting the three series of wheels of doctrine from the point of view of place, time, subject and trainee [but this is not a place for such a lengthy discussion].

If it were necessary to differentiate the status and depth of the schools' different views in dependence on scriptural authority, then, since the individual sūtras each say that the system which it teaches is the superior system, we may wonder which scripture should be held as true. If one scripture were held to be true, we would then wonder how the other discordant sūtras should be considered. But, if the modes of truth of one sūtra and the non-truth of the others were necessarily provable only by scriptural authority, then the process would be endless. Therefore, the differentiation of the superiority and inferiority of views must rely only on reasoning.

Thus, the Mahāyāna sūtras say that it is necessary to distinguish what requires interpretation and what is definitive. Thinking of this, Buddha says in a sūtra:

Monks and scholars should
Well analyse my words,
Like gold [to be tested through] melting, cutting and polishing,
And then adopt them, but not for the sake of showing me respect.

In his *Ornament of the Mahāyāna Sūtras* (*Mahāyānasūtrālaṃkāra*), Maitreya commented well on the meaning of Buddha's thought in that state and set forth the four reliances:

1. One should not rely on the person of a teacher, but on the tenets or doctrines that he teaches.
2. One should not rely merely on the euphony and so forth of his words, but on their meaning.
3. With respect to the meaning, one should not rely on those teachings that require interpretation. Such interpretation would be necessary if there were some other non-explicit base in the teacher's thought, if there were a purpose for the teaching's being stated in interpretable form, and if the explicit words of the teaching were susceptible to refutation. One should rely, rather, on those teachings that have definitive meaning, that is, which do not require interpretation.
4. With respect to the definitive meaning, one should not rely on a dualistic consciousness, but on a non-conceptual wisdom.

With respect to a non-conceptual wisdom that apprehends a profound emptiness, one first cultivates a conceptual consciousness that apprehends an emptiness, and when a clear perception of the object of meditation arises, this becomes a non-conceptual wisdom. Moreover, the initial generation of that conceptual consciousness must depend solely on a correct reasoning. Fundamentally, therefore, this process traces back solely to a reasoning, which itself must fundamentally trace back to valid experiences common to ourselves and others. Thus, it is the thought of Dignāga and Dharmakīrti, the kings of reasoning, that fundamentally a reasoning derives from an obvious experience.

Question: For the sake of improving the mind what is the use of developing valid cognisers and states of consciousness that realize the presentations of views of emptiness? What practioners need is a sense of practical application and goodness; it is the scholars who need to be learned.

Answer: There are many stages in the improvement of the mind. There are some in which analysis of reasons is not necessary, such as when trusting faith alone is to be cultivated single-pointedly. Not much strength, however, is achieved by just that alone. Especially for developing the mind into limitless goodness, it is not sufficient merely to familiarize the mind with its object of meditation. The object of meditation must involve reasoning. Further, it is not sufficient for the object to have reasons in general; the meditator himself must know them and have found a conviction in them. Therefore, it is impossible for the superior type of practitioner not to have intelligence.

Still, if we were forced to choose between a sense of practical application and learnedness, a sense of practical application would be more important, for one who has this will receive the full benefit of whatever he knows. The mere learnedness of one whose mind is not tamed can produce and increase bad states of consciousness, which cause unpleasantness for himself and others instead of the happiness and peace of mind that were intended. One could become jealous of those higher than oneself, competitive with equals and proud and contemptuous towards those lower and so forth. It is as if medicine had become poison. Because such danger is great, it is very important to have a composite of learnedness, a sense of practical application and goodness, without having learnedness destroy the sense of practical application or having the sense of practical application destroy learnedness.

Concerning the improvement of the mind, in order to ascertain the meaning of a selflessness or of an emptiness, it is necessary to ascertain first the meaning of just what a phenomenon is empty of when we refer to "an emptiness." The Bodhisattva Śāntideva says in his *Engaging in the Bodhisattva Deeds* (*Bodhicaryāvatāra*, IX. 140):

> Without identifying the imputed thing
> Its non-existence cannot be apprehended.

Just so, without ascertaining that of which a phenomenon is empty, an understanding of its emptiness does not develop.

Question: Of what is it that a phenomenon is empty?

Answer: [When we Prāsaṅgikas speak of an emptiness, we are not referring to the situation in which one object is empty of some other existent entity. Thus] though we may commonly speak of an "empty rainbow," since the rainbow is empty of anything tangible, this type of an emptiness is not what we have in mind. [This is because anything tangible can exist separate from an empty rainbow; and, moreover, there is still something positive about this rainbow empty of anything tangible, such as its having color.] Though we may also speak of "empty space," since space is empty of anything physical, this too is not an example of what we mean by an emptiness [although here there is nothing else positive implied about space, which is the mere absence of anything physical. This is because here too anything physical can exist separate from empty space]. Rather, when we speak of a phenomenon as being empty, we are referring to its being empty of its own inherent existence [which does not exist at all, let alone exist separate from the phenomenon. In one respect, then, there is a similarity here in that just as a rainbow is naturally empty of anything tangible—it never has been tangible—so too, a phenomenon is naturally empty of its own inherent existence—it never has had inherent existence]. Further, it is not that the object of the negation [inherent existence] formerly existed and is later eliminated, like the forest which existed yesterday and which is burned by fire today, with the result that the area is now empty of the forest. Rather, this is an emptiness of an object of negation [inherent existence], which from beginningless time has never been known validly to exist.

Also, with respect to the way in which a phenomenon is empty of the object of negation, it is not like a table top being empty of flowers. [There, the object of the negation, flowers, is an entity separate from the base of the negation, the table top. With the object of the negation being inherent existence, however, we are not negating an entity separate from the base of the negation, a phenomenon, but rather we are negating a mode of existence of the base of the negation itself. Thus] we mean that the base of the negation, a phenomenon, does not exist in the manner of the object of the negation, its own inherent existence. Therefore, without ascertaining just what the object of the negation is of which phenomena are empty, that is, without ascertaining the measure of what self is in the theory of selflessness, we cannot understand the meaning of an emptiness. A mere vacuity without any sense of "The object of the negation is this" and "It is not that" is utterly not the meaning of emptiness.

Question: What is the use of going to all the trouble of first understanding what something definitely non-existent [inherent existence] would mean if it were existent; and then, after that, viewing it as definitely non-existent?

Answer: It is common worldly knowledge that by believing untrue information to be true we fall into confusion and are harmed. Similarly, by believing phenomena to be inherently existent when in fact they are not inherently existent, we are also harmed. For example, with respect to the different ways in which there can be a consciousness of "I," there is a definite difference between the way the "I" is apprehended when desire, hatred, pride and so forth are generated based on this "I," and the way the "I" is apprehended when we are relaxed without any of those attitudes being manifest. Similarly, there is the mere consciousness that apprehends an article in a store before we buy it, and there is the consciousness apprehending that article after it has been bought, when it is adhered to as "mine" and grasped with attachment. Both these consciousnesses have the same object, and in both cases the mode of appearance of the article is the appearance of it as inherently existent. However, there is the difference of the presence or absence of our adhering to it as inherently or independently existent.

Also, when we see ten men, just from merely seeing them it appears to us that ten men exist there objectively or inherently; however, there is no certainty that we will go on to adhere at that time to this appearance of ten objectively or inherently existent men and posit truth to it. [If we were to posit truth to the appearance of these men as being inherently existent, the process of doing so would be as follows.] For either right or wrong reasons, a strong thought [based on having conceived these ten men to be inherently existent] will be generated, which incorrectly considers one from among these ten men as good or bad. At that time, our intellect will falsely superimpose on the appearance of this man a goodness or badness that exceeds what actually exists. Desire and hatred will then be generated, and consequently we will adhere at that time to this object [the appearance of an inherently existent good or bad man] tightly from the depths of our mind as true, most true.

Therefore, a consciousness conceiving inherent existence precedes any bad consciousness, leading it on by the nose, and also accompanies, or aids, many other bad consciousnesses as well. Thus, if there were no ignorance conceiving inherent existence, then there would be no chance for desire, hatred and so forth to be generated. Since that is so, it is important to identify the beginningless emptiness of the object of the negation, which is to say, it is important to identify as non-existent that non-existent entity [inherent existence] which has never validly been known to exist. Once we have made this identification, it is necessary to generate conviction in it as well. The purpose of this process is to cease the arising of incorrect thoughts, inexhaustible like ripples on an ocean, which arise through the force of the appearance of inherent existence as existent, even though it is non-existent, and through the force of the adherence to that false appearance as true. As Nāgārjuna says in the eighteenth chapter of his *Fundamental Text Called "Wisdom"* (*Prajñā-nāma-mūlamadhyamakakārikā*, XVIII. 4–5):

> When the thought of the internal
> And the external as "I" and "mine"
> Has perished, grasping ceases
> And through that cessation birth ceases.
>
> When actions and afflictions cease, there is liberation;
> They arise from false conceptions, these arise
> From the elaborations [of false views on inherent
> Existence]; elaborations cease in emptiness.

Inherent existence has never been validly known to exist; therefore, it is impossible for there to be any phenomenon that exists through its own power. Since it is experienced that mere dependent-arisings, which are in fact empty of inherent existence, do cause all forms of help and harm, these are established as existent. Thus, mere dependent-arisings do exist. Therefore, all phenomena exist in the manner of appearing as varieties of dependent-arisings. They appear this way without passing beyond the sphere or condition of having just this nature of being utterly non-inherently existent. Therefore, all phenomena have two entities: one entity that is its superficial mode of appearance and one entity that is its deep mode of being. These two are called respectively conventional truths and ultimate truths.

The Superior (Ārya) Nāgārjuna says in his *Fundamental Text Called "Wisdom"* (XXIV. 8):

Doctrines taught by the Buddhas
Rely wholly on the two truths,
Conventional and worldly truths
And truths that are ultimate.

Also, the glorious Candrakīrti says in his *Supplement to (Nāgārjuna's) "Treatise on the Middle Way"* (*Madhyamakāvatāra*, VI. 23):

[Buddha] said that all phenomena have two entities,
Those found by perceivers of the true and of the false;
Objects of perceivers of the true are realities,
Objects of perceivers of the false are conventional truths.

The divisions of ultimate truths will be briefly explained below. Conventional truths themselves are divided into the real and the unreal just from the point of view of an ordinary worldly consciousness. Candrakīrti says (*Supplement*, VI. 24–25):

Also those which perceive falsities are said to be of two types,
Those with clear senses and those having defective ones.
A consciousness having a defective sense is said to be
Wrong in relation to one with a sense that is sound.

Objects realised by the world and apprehended
By the six non-defective senses are only true
From a worldly point of view, the rest are presented
As unreal only from the viewpoint of the world.

The purpose of knowing thus the presentation of the two truths is as follows. Since it is utterly necessary to be involved with these appearances which bring about varieties of good and bad effects, it is necessary to know the two natures, superficial and deep, of these objects to which we are related. For example, there may be a cunning and deceptive neighbor with whom it is always necessary for us to interact and to whom we have related by way of an estimation of him that accords only with his [pleasant] external appearance. The various losses that we have sustained in this relationship are not due to the fault of our merely having interacted with that man. Rather, the fault lies with our mistaken manner of relating to him. Further, because of not knowing the man's nature, we have not estimated him properly and have thereby been deceived. Therefore, if that man's external appearance and his fundamental nature had both been well known, we would have related to him with a reserve appropriate to his nature and with whatever corresponded to his capacities, and so forth. Had we done this, we would not have sustained any losses.

Similarly, if phenomena had no deep mode of being other than their external or superficial mode of being, and if thus the way they appeared and the way they existed were in agreement, then it would be sufficient to hold that conventional modes of appearance are true just as they appear, and to place confidence in them. However, this is not so. Though phenomena appear as if true, most true, ultimately they are not true. Therefore, phenomena abide in the middle way, not truly or inherently existent and also not utterly non-existent. This view, or way of viewing — the knowledge of such a mode of being, just as it is — is called the view of the middle way.

With respect to this, the way in which there is no inherent existence or self is as follows. Whatever objects appear to us now — forms, sounds and so forth which are cognised by the eyes, ears and so on, or objects cognised by the mind, or objects of experience and so forth — these objects are the bases of negation, in relation to which the object of that negation, inherent existence, is negated. They appear to be inherently existent, or existing as independent entities, or existing objectively. Therefore, all consciousnesses are mistaken except for the wisdom that directly cognises emptiness.

Question: [If all those consciousnesses that are not directly cognising emptiness are mistaken, does this mean that] there are no valid cognisers which could certify the existence of conventionally existent phenomena, such as forms and so on? Or, does this mean that since the criterion for a phenomenon's existing conventionally would have to be its existing for a mistaken, perverse consciousness [rather than its existing for a valid cogniser], it would follow that the non-existence of any phenomenon could not occur [because any phenomenon could be cognised by a mistaken consciousness]?

Answer: It is not contradictory for a consciousness to be mistaken, on the one hand, because objects appear to it as if they inherently existed, and, on the other, for it to be valid, because it is not deceived with respect to its main object. For example, a visual consciousness perceiving a form is indeed a mistaken consciousness because the form appears to it as inherently existent. However, to the extent that it perceives the form as a form and does not *conceive* the form to be inherently existent, it is a valid cogniser. Not only that, but a visual consciousness perceiving a form is also a valid cogniser with respect to the appearance of the form and even with respect to the appearance of the form's seeming to be inherently existent. All dualistic consciousnesses, therefore, are valid direct cognisers with respect to their own objects of perception, because in the expression, "a consciousness knowing its object," a consciousness refers to a clear knower which is generated in the image of its object through the force of the appearance of its object.

Further, the criterion for a phenomenon's existing conventionally is not merely its existing for a mistaken, perverse consciousness. For example, an appearance of falling hairs manifestly appears to the visual consciousness of someone with cataract. Because his consciousness has been generated in the image of falling hairs, it is a valid, direct cogniser with respect to that object of perception. However, since the falling hairs, which are the basis of such an appearance, are utterly nonexistent, the consciousness is deceived with respect to its main object. Thus, because this consciousness of falling hairs is directly contradicted by a consciousness with a valid mode of perception, it is asserted to be a wrong consciousness. How could existing for this mistaken consciousness be the criterion for a phenomenon's existing conventionally?

In short, it is said that though there is no phenomenon that is not posited by the mind, whatever the mind posits is not necessarily existent.

When a phenomenon appears thus to be inherently existent, if the phenomenon existed in the same way as it appeared, then the entity of its inherent existence would necessarily become clearer when its mode of existence was carefully analyzed. For example, even in terms of what is widely known in the world, if something is true, it becomes clearer and its foundation more firm the more one analyses it. Therefore, when sought, it must definitely be findable. If, on the contrary, it is false, then when it is analyzed and sought, it becomes unclear, and in the end it cannot stand up. Nāgārjuna's *Precious Garland* (*Ratnāvalī*, 52–53) says:

> A form seen from a distance
> Is seen clearly by those nearby.
> If a mirage were water, why
> Is water not seen by those nearby?
>
> The way this world is seen
> As real by those afar
> Is not so seen by those nearby,
> [For whom it is] signless like a mirage.

Let us give an example. When it is said and thought that human beings should have happiness, a human who is one who should have happiness appears boldly to our mind as if existing in his own right. To create human happiness, one must achieve the favorable circumstances for physical pleasures such as food, clothing, shelter, medicines and transportation for the body, and the favorable circumstances for mental pleasures such as higher education, respectability, good disposition and tranquility for the mind. It is necessary to create a human's happiness through physical and mental pleasures. That being so, if we search, wondering what the real human is, we find that his body and mind individually are not the human, and there is also no identifying, "This is the human," separately from these two.

Similarly, when we have met an acquaintance named "Lucky," we say, for instance, "I saw Lucky," "Lucky has become old," or "Lucky has become fat." Without analyzing or examining those statements, seeing Lucky's body is said to be seeing Lucky; seeing his body weaker is said to be seeing Lucky weaker; and seeing his body larger is said to be seeing Lucky larger. A consciousness that perceives such without analysis is not a wrong consciousness, and these statements also are not false. [However] when analysis is done, a real Lucky himself who is the possessor of the body is not to be seen, and his aging and becoming fat also cannot stand up to analysis. Further, with respect to the goodness or badness of Lucky's mind, Lucky is designated as a good man or a bad man. But Lucky's mind itself is not Lucky. In short, there is not the slightest part which is Lucky among the mere collection of Lucky's mind and body, his continuum, or individual parts. Therefore, dependent on the mere collection of Lucky's body and mind, we designate "Lucky." As Nāgārjuna says in his *Precious Garland* (80):

> The person is not earth, not water,
> Not fire, not wind, not space,
> Not consciousness and not all of them;
> What person is there other than these?

Further, with respect to the statement, "I saw Lucky's body," seeing merely the external skin from among the many parts of the body, flesh, skin, bones and so forth, functions as seeing his body. Even if the blood, bones and so forth are not seen, it does not mean that the body is not seen. To see a body it is not necessary to see all of the body; seeing even a small part can function as seeing the body. However, sometimes by the force of general custom, if a certain amount is not seen, it cannot function as a seeing of the body. As above, if the body is divided into its individual parts, legs, arms and so on, a body is not found. Also, the legs and arms can be divided into toes and fingers, the toes and fingers into joints and the joints into upper and lower portions; these can be divided into small parts and even the smallest parts into parts corresponding with the directions. When they are divided in this way, none of these entities are findable. Also, if the smallest particle were directionally partless, that is, if it had no sides, then no matter how many directionally partless particles were collected, they could never be arranged side by side to form a mass.

Furthermore, Lucky is said to be happy or unhappy according to whether his mind is at ease or not. What is this mind which is the basis of this determination? It does not exist as anything physical, it lacks anything tangible, any object can appear to it, and it exists as an entity of mere knowing. Further, it is like this when it is not analyzed; but when it is analyzed, it is unfindable. When Lucky's mind is happy, the entity of that mind is what is to be analyzed. If it is divided into individual moments, there is no mass that is a composite of the many former and later moments. At the time of the later moments, the former moments have ceased; therefore, the former ones have gone and their conscious entity has disappeared. Because the future moments have not yet been produced, they are not existing now. Also, the single present moment is not separate from what has already been produced and what has not yet been produced. Therefore, when it is sought thus, one is unable to establish a present consciousness. When the happy mind, which is the object discussed in "His mind is happy," is sought, it is utterly unfindable. In short, happy and unhappy minds and so forth are designated to a mere collection of their own former and future moments. Even the shortest moment is imputed to its own parts; it has the individual parts of a beginning and an end. If a moment were partless, there could be no continuum composed of them.

Similarly, when an external object such as a table appears to the mind, a naturally existent or independent table appears. Let us analyze this table by dividing it into a whole and parts. In general, the table is put as the base of its qualities, and by examining its qualities such as shape, color, material and size, we can speak of its value, quality and so forth. For example, when we say "This table is good, but its color is not good," there is a table that is the base of the estimation of the quality of its color. A base of qualities that possesses these qualities does [conventionally] exist, but the qualities and parts individually are not themselves the base of the qualities. Also, after eliminating the qualities and parts, a base of these qualities is not findable. If there is no such base, then since qualities are necessarily established in dependence on a base of qualities and, moreover, since a base of qualities is necessarily established in dependence on qualities, the qualities also will not exist.

Let us illustrate this with the example of a rosary which has one hundred and eight beads. The whole, the one rosary, has one hundred and eight beads as its parts. The parts and the whole are [conventionally] different; yet, when the parts are eliminated, a rosary cannot be found. Because the rosary is one and its parts are many, the rosary is not the same as its parts. When the parts are eliminated, there is no rosary which exists separately; therefore, it is not inherently or fundamentally different from its parts. Because the rosary does not exist separate from its parts, it does not inherently depend on its parts, nor do the parts inherently depend on it. Also, the beads do not inherently belong to the rosary. Similarly, since the shape of the rosary is one of its qualities, this shape is not the rosary. Also, the collection of the beads and the string is the basis in dependence on which the rosary is imputed; therefore, it is not the rosary. If it is sought in this way, a rosary is unfindable as any of the seven extremes. Further, if the individual beads are sought as above, that is, as one with their parts, or different from their parts and so forth, they are unfindable as well. Furthermore, since forests, armies, continents, and countries are imputed to aggregations of many parts, when each is analyzed as to whether it is this or not that, it is utterly unfindable.

Further, it is extremely clear that good and bad, tall and short, big and small, enemy and friend, father and son and so forth are all imputations of the one based on the other. Also earth, water, fire, wind and so on are each imputed in dependence on their parts. Space is imputed in dependence on its parts, which pervade the directions. Also, Buddhas and sentient beings, cyclic existence and nirvāṇa and so forth are only just imputed in dependence on their parts and their bases of imputation.

Just as it is widely known that, "An effect is produced from causes," so production does exist [conventionally]. However, let us analyze the meaning of production. If effects were produced causelessly, they would either always be produced or would never be produced. If they were produced from themselves, it would be purposeless for what has already attained its own entity to be produced again; and if what had already been produced is produced again, then there is the consequent fallacy that its reproduction would be endless. If effects were produced from entities other than themselves, they would be produced from everything, both from what are considered conventionally to be their causes and from what are not [since both are equally other]. Or, it would be contradictory for effects to depend on causes [for, being totally separate, they could not be inter-related]. Production from both self and others is not possible either [because of the faults in both these positions demonstrated separately above]. Thus, if the meaning of the designation "production" is sought, production is not capable of being established. As the Superior Nāgārjuna says in his *Fundamental Text Called "Wisdom"* (I. 1):

> There is never production
> Anywhere of any phenomenon
> From itself, from others,
> From both, or without cause.

Though it is widely known [and conventionally correct] that causes do produce effects, let us analyze these effects. If the produced effect inherently existed, how could it be correct for what already exists to be produced newly? For, causes are not needed to create it anew. In general, causes conventionally do newly create that which has not been produced or which is non-existent at the time of its causes. However, if the non-produced were inherently true as non-produced, it would be no different from being utterly non-existent; therefore, how could it be fit for production by causes? As Nāgārjuna says in his *Seventy Stanzas on Emptiness* (*Śūnyatāsaptati*):

> Because it exists, the existent is not produced;
> Because it does not exist, the non-existent is not produced.

In short, once the existence of something is necessarily dependent on causes and conditions and on others, then it is contradictory for it to exist independently. For, independence and dependence on others are contradictory. The *Questions of the King of Nāgas, Anavatapta, Sūtra* (*Anavataptanāgarājaparipṛcchā*) says:

> That which is produced from causes is not [inherently] produced,
> It does not have an inherent nature of production.
> That which depends on causes is said to be
> Empty; he who knows emptiness is aware.

Nāgārjuna's *Fundamental Text Called "Wisdom"* (XXIV. 19) says:

> Because there are no phenomena
> Which are not dependent-arisings,
> There are no phenomena
> Which are not empty.

Āryadeva says in his *Four Hundred* (*Cathuḥśataka*, XIV. 23):

That which has dependent-arising
Cannot be self-powered; since all these
Lack independence there can be
No self [no inherent existence].

If phenomena were not empty of a fundamental basis or of inherent existence, it would be utterly impossible for the varieties of phenomena to be transformed in dependence on causes. If they existed by way of their own fundamental basis, then no matter what type of entity they were, good, bad and so on, how could they be changed? If a good fruit tree, for instance, were inherently existent by way of its own entity or its own inner basis, how would it be true that it could become bare and ugly? If the present mode of appearance of these things to our minds were their own inner mode of being, how could we be deceived? Even in the ordinary world many discrepancies are well known between what appears and what actually is. Therefore, although beginninglessly everything has appeared as if it were inherently existent to the mind that is contaminated with the errors of ignorance, if those objects were indeed inherently existent, their inner basis would be just as they appear. In that case, when the consciousness searching for the inner basis of a phenomenon performed analysis, that inner basis would definitely become clearer. Where does the fault lie, that when sought, phenomena are not found and seemingly disappear?

Further, if things inherently existed, it would be as Candrakīrti says in his *Supplement* (VI. 34–36):

> If the inherent existence [of phenomena] depended [on causes, the yogī
> Realising emptiness], by denying that, would be destroying phenomena;
> Therefore, [seeing] emptiness would be a cause which destroys phenomena, but since
> This is not reasonable, phenomena do not [inherently exist].
>
> When these phenomena are analysed, they are not found
> To abide as other than phenomena with the nature
> Of reality [having no inherently existent production or cessation];
> Therefore, worldly conventional truths are not to be analysed.
>
> When reality [is analysed] production
> From self and other is not admissible,
> Through the same reasoning [inherently existent production] also is not admissible
> Conventionally; how then could your [inherently existent] production be [established]?

Thus, Candrakīrti is saying that if phenomena existed naturally or inherently, it would follow that a Superior's meditative equipoise realizing emptiness would cause the destruction of these phenomena. Also, it would follow that conventional truths would be able to stand up to a reasoned analysis. Further, it would follow that production would not be ultimately refuted, and that many sūtras which teach that phenomena are empty of themselves in the sense that they are empty of their own natural inherent existence would be wrong. For instance, a Mother Sūtra, the *Twenty-Five Thousand Stanza Perfection of Wisdom Sūtra* (*Pañcaviṃśatisāhasrikāprajñāpāramitā*) says, "With respect to this, Śāriputra, when a Bodhisattva, a great being, practises the perfection of wisdom, he does not see a Bodhisattva as real. . . . Why? Śāriputra, it is like this: a Bodhisattva is empty of being an inherently existent Bodhisattva. A Bodhisattva's name also is empty of being a Bodhisattva's name. Why? That is their nature. It is like this: it is not that a form is empty on account of emptiness; emptiness is not separate from a form. A form itself is [that which is] empty; just [that which is] empty is also the form." Further, the *Kāśyapa Chapter* in the *Pile of Jewels Sūtra* (*Ratnakūṭa*) says, "Phenomena are not made empty by emptiness, the phenomena themselves are empty." Therefore, all phenomena lack inherent existence or their own basic foundation. . . .

III
Nishitani: "The Self as Śūnyatā"*

. . . . "Being self in not being self" means that the being of the self as a personal, conscious, corporeal human and the existence of the self as subject are essentially illusory appearances. It means, moreover, that the various phenomena of human body and human mind, and all of reflective knowledge wherein the self knows the self and objects, are essentially illusory appearances: what the ancients called "vain discernment" (*vikalpa*) No matter how objectively true these phenomena are in themselves (for instance, as scientific cognition), in this very truth they are essentially illusory appearances. Or, put the other way around, it is precisely on the field of śūnyatā that these phenomena, at one with emptiness, are nothing less than actual reality at an essential level. It is what we spoke of earlier as "true suchness" (*tāthatā*). Or again, if you will, it is the "likeness" contained in the assertion "the bird flies and it is like a bird."

---

*Reprinted with permission from Keiji Nishitani, *Religion and Nothingness*, translated, with an introduction by Jan Van Bragt (Berkeley: University of California Press, 1982).

In another context, I have spoken of this same thing as "primal fact," remarking there:

> Goethe says that things that will pass are metaphors of the Eternal . . . yet so long as there is nothing like an eternal thing to serve as its archetype, the metaphor as such is the primal reality or fact. It is metaphor even as primal fact, and primal fact even as metaphor. A Zen master extends his staff and says: "If you call this a staff you cling to it; if you do not call it a staff you depart from the facts. So what should you call it then?" The staff he has in mind is not the sensible wooden object, but neither is it not the sensible object. The staff is always the staff, but at the same time it is not the staff. Even though we say of it "form is emptiness, emptiness is form," our words are not spoken from a contemplative standpoint. . . . The fact that this staff is this staff is a fact in such a way as to involve at the same time a deliverance of the self. In this the fact appears as a primal factuality. The point at which this fact can be comprehended in a primal manner is the point of deliverance where one becomes a Son of God, a Son of Buddha.
>
> It is not that it is *not* the world of sense perception, matter, and life, but only that it is the *primal* world of these things. It is the world of these things brought back to what is primal, stripped of the discerning intellect that infiltrates our ordinary talk of sense perception, matter, and life without our realizing it.

When a fact is on its own home-ground, it is a fact without bottom. There it rises above anything that might provide a roothold of support. On whatever dimension one seeks to make a ground of its "cause," or "reason," or "purpose"—not only in matter, sensibility, life, and so on, but also in discursive understanding with its categories, speculative reason with its Ideas, or even the Will to Power as a metaphysical principle—one is unable to reach the facts themselves on their own home-ground.

On the field of śūnyatā, fact as primal fact, that is fact as the very fact it is in its own true reality, is groundlessly itself. It is simultaneously the far side and the near side of every roothold and every ground, on every dimension. It is simply itself, cut off from every How and Why and Wherefore. And this being, a being bottomlessly on the field of śūnyatā, is precisely what we have been calling illusory appearance. Our subjective existence and all its facts can also be called a "likeness" of that sort.

"Not being self in being self," on the other hand, means that on the field of śūnyatā the selfness of the self has its being in the home-ground of all other things. On the field of śūnyatā, the center is everywhere. Each and every thing in its nonobjective and "middle" selfness is an absolute center. To that extent, it is impossible for the self on the field of śūnyatā to be self-centered like the "self" seen as ego or subject. Rather, the absolute negation of that very self-centeredness enables the field of śūnyatā to open up in the first place.

To the extent that the being of the self is present in the home-ground of all other things, the self is not the self. The self is not a small, self-centered circle. Together with emptiness it is free of all outer limits. It is, so to speak, something with no circumference whatsoever. This is elemental self-awareness.

As a being in unison with emptiness, then, the self is one absolute center, and, to that extent, all things are in the home-ground of the self. And so far as our self is at the home-ground of all things, that is, on the field of śūnyatā, all things are also at the home-ground of the self. Such a circuminsessional interpenetration, as we said before, can only come about when all things, including ourselves, are in a nonobjective, "middle" mode of being. As we also noted there, through this circuminsessional interpenetration, all things are gathered together, and as such render possible an order of being, a "world," and consequently enable the existence of things as well.

The "force" by virtue of which each and every thing is able to exist, or perhaps better, the force by virtue of which all things make one another exist—the primal force by virtue of which things that exist appear as existing things—emanates from this circuminsessional relationship. All things "are" in the home-ground of any given thing and make it to "be" what it is. With that thing as the absolute center, all things assemble at its home-ground. This assembly is the force that makes the thing in question be, the force of the thing's own ability to be. In that sense, we also said that when a thing *is*, the world *worlds*, and that as the field of circuminsessional interpenetration, the field of śūnyatā is a field of force.

Now this field can also open up in the self when the self is truly in the self's home-ground. It lies at the home-ground of the self. It is, as it were, directly underfoot, directly at hand for the self. The roothold of the possibility of the world and of the existence of things, namely, the place where the world and the existence of things "take hold of their ground," can be said to lie in the home-ground of each man, underfoot and right at hand.

In this way, the selfness of the self—insofar as the self is said to "be a self"—lies radically in *time*, or, rather, is bottomlessly in time. At the same time, on the field of śūnyatā—insofar as the being of the self is at bottom only being in unison with emptiness, insofar as the self is said "not to be a self"—the self is, at every moment of time, ecstatically outside of time. It was in this sense that we spoke above of the self of each man as at bottom preceding the world and things.

We are born in time and we die in time. "To be in time" means to be constantly within the cycle of birth-and-death. But we are not merely within time and within the cycle of birth-and-death. On our own home-ground, we are not simply drifting about in birth-and-death: we live and die birth-and-death. We do not simply live in time: we live time. From one moment in time to the next we are making time to be time, we are bringing time to the "fullness of time." That is the sense of what we referred to earlier as "being bottomlessly in time."

But now, thus to be bottomlessly within time and within the cycle of birth-and-death means to stand ecstatically outside of time and outside of that cycle. It means to precede the world and things, to be their master. This, at bottom, is the sort of thing we "are" in our home-ground, in our selfness. And when we become aware of that fact, namely, when we truly *are* in our own home-ground, we stand from one moment of time to the next *outside* of time, even as we rest from one moment to the next bottomlessly *inside* of time. Even as we stand radically, or rather bottomlessly (groundlessly and with nothing to rely on), inside the world, we stand at the same time outside of it. In this case, having nothing to rely on means absolute freedom.

Passing out of time and onto the field of śūnyatā is no different from radicalizing the mode of being in time, that is, from living *positively* in the vicissitudes of time. This means that our existence goes beyond all possible things to rely on. This "reliance on nothing" is absolute freedom.

Precisely as the absolute freedom that bottomlessly makes being and time to be being and time, emptiness is also a knowledge. It is the standpoint of an insight that knows everything in its true suchness. But similar to what we have noted often enough before, this suchness can be spoken of as phantom-like. This knowledge is a "phantom-like Wisdom."

In the words of the *Avatamsaka Sutra*:

> The phantom-like Wisdom of the Buddha, without hindrance, completely penetrates with its light all dharmas of the three worlds, and enters into the mental activities of all sentient beings. Here is it the domain of the Good Heavenly Being of the North. Its all-inclusiveness knows no limits at all. . . . Here, it is the deliverance of the Great Light.

A little further on, the sutra compares the dwelling of the Tathāgata in "phantom-like Wisdom" to a magician's magic (literally, the phantom acts of the phantom master):

> It is as with the magician accomplished in his art who dwells at the cross-roads, producing all kinds of magical effects. On one day, a fleeting instant, he conjures up a full day or a full night, even seven days or seven nights, a fortnight, a month, a year, a hundred years. And always everything is there: cities and hamlets, wells, rivulets, rivers and seas, sun and moon, clouds and rain, palaces and houses. The original day or hour is not done away with simply because a great stretch of years has been shown in that time; and the days, months, and years of the phantasmagoria are not destroyed simply because the original time was so very short.

What this passage says is that in a fleeting instant, in the twinkling of an eye, the temporal span of a whole day or a hundred years appears phantasmally, and this phantasm is the day or the hundred years in actuality. At the same time, since the phantasmal span is revealed here in its suchness, this actual instant does not cease to be this actual instant. "With a single thought, ten thousand years. And with ten thousand years, a single thought."

On the field of emptiness, all time enters into each moment of time passing from one moment to the next. In this circuminsessional interpenetration of time, or in time itself that only comes about as such an interpenetration, namely, in the *absolute relativity* of time on the field of śūnyatā, the whole of time is phantom-like, and the whole of the being of things in time is no less phantom-like.

But in spite of this, on the field of śūnyatā, each time, in its very actuality, is the suchness of this time or that time. We might say, in other words, that because in the field of śūnyatā each time is bottomlessly in time, all times enter into each time. And only as something bottomless that all times can enter into does each time actually emerge in its manifestation as this or that time, such as it is. This suchness and phantom-likeness must needs be one. Therein, to be sure, lies the essence of time.

Should one be inclined to dismiss this view of time as a mere fantasy, one might recall, for example, that Kierkegaard speaks of a "transcendence" in the "moment," and along with that of a "simultaneity" coming to be in the "moment." In fact, past and present can be simultaneous without "destroying" the temporal sequence of before and after. Without such a field of simultaneity not even culture, let alone religion, could come into being. We can encounter Sakyamuni and Jesus, Bashō and Beethoven in the present. That religion and culture can arise within and be handed down historically through time points to the very essence of time.

The *Avatamasaka Sūtra* speaks of the same idea not only in connection with time but also with place:

> The magician, staying in one place, produces all kinds of magical effects of magical places; but he does not thereby destroy his original place. . . . He does not destroy this one world by the fact that those worlds are many, nor are those many worlds destroyed by the fact that this world is one.

That time and place consist of a circuminsessional interpenetration in which all enter into each, in other words, the absolute relativity of time and space, means that all things have their being temporally and spatially; "earth, water, fire, air, oceans and mountains, towns and hamlets," and the very "halls of heaven"—in short, the "world"—arise in the interpenetration in the being of each and every thing, in the elemental relativity of existence.

In addition, that the world comes into being as a single totality, as a single "world," means that it originates in a circuminsessional interpenetration with many "worlds." This world of ours is one relative world. Any number of other possible or actual (in Leibniz's idiom, *possible* or *compossible*) worlds are conceivable. On the field of śūnyatā, where they can be conceived, each such world is able to reflect all the others without ceasing to be the real world that it is of itself. The one world itself comes into being on the field of śūnyatā as a field of absolute relativity.

(On the field of śūnyatā, we can also find a point from which to conceive of the workings of reason in fixing its "ideas" and "ideals" representationally from within itself; or to conceive of the workings of the creative power of the artist—what the seventeenth-century haiku poet Kikaku, in speaking of one of the poems of his master, Bashō, calls the "phantom technique." The poem reads:

> The first wintry shower—
> Even the monkeys seem to long
> For a small straw coat.

Indeed, these words seem to conjure up the image of the poet himself in his straw raincoat, winding his way along a solitary mountain pass. Here, however, we restrict our concerns to the field of śūnyatā as a "knowing.")

In brief, the totality of things in the world, and also the world itself, have their being bottomlessly on the field of śūnyatā and, therefore, *are* in their phantomness-*sive*-suchness by virtue of the circuminsessional interpenetration whereby all are in each. Here the suchness of the bird consists in the fact that "The bird flies and it is like a bird." And the mode of being of we who stand on that field, namely, our selfness returned to its own home-ground, comes about at the point where "to dwell in the world is to dwell in the void." As it is written, "One does not enter the world outside of the void, nor enter the void outside of the world. And why? Because there is no difference between void and world." This is what it is "to dwell, with a boundless heart, in the phantom-like Wisdom of the Tathāgata," "to know everything such as it is," and "to know that all dharmas are without ego."

To know things such as they are is to restore things to their own home-ground. And if the fact that the bird looks like a bird when it is flying points to the fact that the bird is flying, and is thus precisely what we called above its primal factuality, then knowing its suchness is no different from knowing that "this fact is this fact" and "this fact has its being as this fact." The identity of "being" and "knowing" is more primal than traditional metaphysics has taken it to be.

As we said above, on the field of śūnyatā, our self is at bottom prior to the world and things, and therein lies the roothold of the possibility of the world and the existence of things. This does not mean, as in Kant's philosophy, that the cognition of objects (and, consequently, of phenomena insofar as they are objects of cognition) would be a construction from a priori formalities of sensation and understanding. I speak here of the nonobjective "selfness" of things prior to any separation between materiality and formality or between matter and eidetic form, and prior to any consideration of the distinction between the phenomenon and the thing-in-itself. The point where the manifestation of things as they are in themselves "takes hold" rests in our own home-ground: on the field of śūnyatā.

Such knowledge of things in themselves (the knowing of non-knowing) means precisely that in truly returning to our own home-ground, we return to the home-ground of things that become manifest in the world. This knowledge is a realization (apprehension) in the sense of a reentry to the home-ground where things are manifest in their suchness. This reentry to the point where things in themselves realize themselves nonobjectively and posit themselves (on their *position* or samādhi-being), means for the self a direct reentry to the home-ground of the self itself. This is a knowing of non-knowing.

In a word, it is the nonobjective knowing of the nonobjective thing as it is in itself that we speak of. It is not a knowledge, therefore, that depends on rational capacity. As remarked earlier, reason has traditionally been called the "natural light," but the true "natural light" is not reason. If we call nature a *force* that gathers all things into one and arranges them into an order to bring about a "world," then this force belongs to the field of śūnyatā, which renders possible a circuminsessional interpenetration among all things. Returning to take a stand there means returning to the home-ground of the world and of things; and this, in turn, means a return of the self to the home-ground of the self. Therefore, once we grant that this is where the knowing of non-knowing originates, *this* knowledge has to be the true "natural light."

As opposed to reason, this light is not something apart from the very "being" of all things themselves. On the field of śūnyatā, the very being of all things, each of which becomes manifest as itself even as it is being gathered into unison with every other thing, is the being of the light of our knowledge (a knowing of non-knowing) returned to its own home-ground through its reentry into the field where all things are manifest. This is why the "natural light" within us was spoken of earlier as the light of the things themselves coming to us from all things. The light that illumines us from our own home-ground and brings us back to an elemental self-awareness is but the nonobjective being of things as they are in themselves on the field where all things are manifest from their own home-ground. It is also the reason why we could say, with Dōgen: "To practice and confirm all things by conveying one's self to them, is illusion; for all things to advance forward and practice and confirm the self, is enlightenment"; and with Musō Kokushi: "Hills and rivers, the earth, plants and trees, tiles and stones, all of these are the self's own original part."

The field of śūnyatā is a field whose center is everywhere. It is the field in which each and everything—as an absolute center, possessed of an absolutely unique individuality—becomes manifest as it is in itself. To say that each thing is an absolute center means that wherever a thing *is*, the world *worlds*. And this, in turn, means that each thing, by being in its own home-ground is in the home-ground of all beings; and, conversely, that in being on the home-ground of all, each is in its own home-ground. (As I have stated repeatedly, this relationship is inconceivable except in the nonobjective mode of being of things where they are what they are in themselves.)

To claim, then, that a thing is such as it is, and is really itself, is no different from saying that all things are essentially one with one another and gathered together as a world. This is the "One and All," not as it is contemplated on the field of reason, but as it is comprehended on the field of śūnyatā. This is, as noted earlier, not simply "being," but being at one with emptiness; and, consequently, it is not an absolute unity abstracted from all multiplicity and differentiation in the world, but an absolute unity on the field where multiplicity and differentiation are absolutely radicalized. It means that an All that is nothingness-*sive*-being, being *sive*-nothingness is One; it means that on the field of śūnyatā all centers, each of which is absolutely independent, are essentially one.

In the nonobjective, "middle" mode of being where each thing in itself is concentrated in itself, all things of necessity concentrate themselves into one. For in the middle mode of being, it is necessary to the very essence of being that a thing be in the home-ground of every other thing in being in its own home-ground. Moreover, for the field of śūnyatā to open up in the return to our own home-ground, our self—in which the possibility of the world and of the existence of things takes hold—has to be what we termed above a self in itself: a self that is not itself in being itself, a self that is not a self.

We spoke of the selfness of things as the mode that we see, for example, in fire not burning fire, in the eye not seeing the eye, and so forth; and that can only be expressed paradoxically in statements such as, "Fire is not fire, therefore it is fire." Borrowing a term usually reserved for a state of mental concentration, we called this samādhi-being.

Now the same can be said with regard to the self that was spoken of as "confirmed by all things" in that mode of being, namely, the self that is not a self. The mode of being of the self that I have in mind in saying that emptiness is self, or that the self is not self because it is self, can also be expressed as what the ancients called "emptiness samādhi" or the "samādhi of non-mind Form." Samādhi is not simply a psychological concept but an *ontological* one. The point at which the non-objective mode of being of things as they are in themselves takes hold of its ground lies at the home-ground of our self ("in hand" and "underfoot"). In its own home-ground, the being of the self is essentially a sort of samādhi. No matter how dispersed the conscious self be, its self as it is in itself is ever in samādhi. Indeed, when we look back at it again from its home-ground, that dispersed mode of being, such as it is, is in samādhi.

I have called this nonobjective mode of being of things as they are in themselves—namely, the mode of being wherein things rest in the complete uniqueness of what they themselves are—a "middle"; I cited the saying, "If you try to explain something by comparing it with something else, you fail to hit the middle." If we grant that the field of śūnyatā, on which the possibility of the existence of the selfness of things takes hold of its ground, opens for us only when we return to our own home-ground, these words would apply in their most original sense to our own self in itself. Our self in itself is most elementally "middle." It resists all explanation because it is a being in unison with emptiness; because it is a being united with emptiness in a self-awareness according to which emptiness is self; and because, by virtue of that self-awareness, which is nearer to the elemental than anything else, it precedes the world and all things. Every human being in its selfness contains the field of that force by virtue of which the selfness of all things are gathered into one as a world. This field contains a roothold for the possibility of all things that become manifest in the world. And yet each human being, as such, is but one illusory thing in the world among others.

When we say that our self in itself is most elementally "middle," we are not thinking in terms of the "middle" that Aristotle, for instance, spoke of as the "mean" between too much and too little. Nor are we thinking of the role of go-between that Hegel attributed to reason as a "mediation" between contradictories. Whereas these are both "middles" projected on the field of reason, the "middle" seen as a mode of being on the field of emptiness cannot be projected on any other field whatsoever. It is immediately present —and immediately realized as such—at the point that we ourselves actually are. It is "at hand" for us and "underfoot." Just as no one else can see for us or hear for us, so too *none* of our actions can be performed by proxy. All actions imply, as it were, an absolute immediacy. And it is there that what we are calling the "middle" appears.

Now this insistence that we do not hit the "middle" of the self when we come at it through some other thing may seem to contradict the words cited earlier about hills and rivers, grass and trees, and so on being the self's original part. But this difficulty stems from the fact that hills and rivers, grass and trees, as well as the self itself, are being represented in a merely objective manner. On the field of the opposition between the subjective and the objective, the subject is still represented in a self-conscious manner such that it can never be objectified. But at a deeper level we find a relationship in which all things are in our home-ground and we ourselves are in the home-ground of all things. What we have in mind here is not a unification of subject and object, but what we called before a circuminsessional relationship. Therefore, even though we speak of hills and rivers as the self's original part, hills and rivers are here hills and rivers in *not* being hills and rivers, just as the self is the self in *not* being the self. And yet it is only here that hills and rivers are real hills and rivers in their suchness, only here that the self is the real self in its suchness. It is on this field that our self is the "self-presentation" of the most elemental "middle."

The same *Muchū mondō* that speaks of hills and rivers, grass and trees, and so on as the self's original part also contains the following example:

> The ancients tell us that every man possesses a spiritual light. When the *Sutra of Perfect Enlightenment* speaks of the samādhi of the Storehouse of the Great Light, it means this spiritual light that belongs to the nature of all sentient beings. What is called the body-light, the wisdom-light, and the miracle-light of all the Buddhas, all are born out of this Storehouse of the Great Light. Down to the ordinary man's distinguishing of east from west and black from white, there is nothing that is not the marvellous work of that spiritual light. But fools forget this original light and turn to the outside in search of a worldly light.

We noted earlier that the "natural light" is not the light of reason but the light of all things. What is here called "spiritual light" does not mean the light of the "soul" or the "spirit" in the ordinary sense of those words. It is rather a "samādhi of the Storehouse of the Great Light" out of which the light of all things (namely, the being itself of all things) is coming to birth; it belongs to the nature of every human being. When we say that our self in itself is the original and most elemental "middle," we are pointing to nothing other than just this.

PART III

CHINESE TEXTS

Chinese philosophy is made up of three main strands: Confucianism, Taoism, and Buddhism. Each of these complex ways of thought has interacted with the others over the centuries, leading to a rich and diverse philosophical tradition. But the diversity of Chinese philosophy grows out of a shared concern of Chinese thinkers over the ages to find the Way (*Tao*) of life that will provide for a full and tranquil life in a peaceful and harmonious society. The Confucian way is concerned with establishing correct human relationships as the key to achieving harmony with Heaven and Earth; the Taoist way emphasizes the naturalness and spontaneity of Nature as the model for human action; and the Buddhist way focuses on the ultimate nature of mind as the key to enlightenment.

The development of Chinese philosophy occurred in four stages. In the earliest period, from the sixth to the second centuries B.C., there was lively interaction among a number of different philosophies, the so-called hundred schools. Chief among these were Confucianism and Taoism, which were challenged by Mohism and Legalism. The Yin-Yang school, which emphasized the polarity of yin and yang and the five agencies of change, and the I-Ching school, which emphasized the emergence of structure out of the Great Ultimate through the interaction of yin and yang, contributed to Chinese metaphysics. In the environment of debate and dialogue created by these early interactions, Confucianism incorporated features of its rival systems, thus making it sufficiently attractive that Tung Chung-shu (ca. 179–104 B.C.) was able to persuade Emperor Han Wu-ti to adopt it as the state ideology in 136 B.C. This favored treatment lasted until 1905, guaranteeing the supremacy of Confucianism for two thousand years.

The second stage occurred with the introduction of Buddhism from India during the first century A.D., Buddhism borrowed Taoist thought and language as it gradually moved to religious and philosophical center stage, which it shared with Taoism and Confucianism as one of the three ways of thought dominating China until the ascendancy of Neo-Confucianism in the eleventh and twelfth centuries. Although Confucianism continued to serve as the official ideology, China under the Sui and T'ang dynasties (589 - 906) was dominated by Buddhist thought.

Although Buddhism arrived in China during the first century, its main development began in the fourth, fifth, and sixth centuries, and its full flowering came during the Sui and T'ang dynasties. The Chinese acceptance of Buddhism from the fourth century onward occurred at a time when political and military disarray, the near collapse of traditional Confucian norms and virtues, and the Neo-Taoist attitude of retreat and seclusion from public life combined to create a kind of spiritual vacuum. The Mahāyāna Buddhism that attracted the Chinese glorified the ideal of Buddhahood; it assured the faithful that they already possessed the beginnings of this perfected condition of being, and that by accepting the help of innumerable Bodhisattvas, who for countless eons had been working tirelessly in all the regions of this vast universe, they, too, could enjoy the radiant splendor of being so attractively depicted in the *Lotus Sūtra*.

The Chinese transformed the Middle Way philosophy's emphasis on the absence of selfhood in persons and things from what was understood to be a dominantly negative notion of emptiness into a positive notion emphasizing the dynamic interconnectedness of all existence. In this positive emphasis the Chinese found inherent Buddhahood to be the ground of existence itself, not restricted to Heaven or a Divine Being, but the fundamental aspect of the myriad processes constituting reality. Furthermore, the manifest differences characterizing different things and persons suggested that the means of realizing the Buddhahood that constituted the most fundamental dimension of reality had to be adapted to the specific characteristics and conditions of the individual. In this absence of fixed doctrine and authority, Chinese Buddhism presented itself as a wonderfully adaptive spirituality, able to take on many forms and respond to many needs. It borrowed methods and ideas from Taoism, and incorporated the Confucian emphasis on learning and self-cultivation.

The third stage of philosophical development, coincident with the decline of Buddhism, was characterized by the development of Neo-Confucianism, a development that occurred in the context of centuries of dialogue with Buddhism and Taoism, as well as with the older Confucian traditions and the philosophy of change that developed out of the Yin-yang tradition. By the tenth century, with the simultaneous decline of Buddhism and the T'ang dynasty, the revival of Confucianism that had begun with Han Yü (768 - 824) and Li Ao (early tenth century) took hold. Inspired by the comprehensive metaphysical visions of Buddhism and Taoism, eleventh-century interpreters of Confucianism revitalized the tradition, providing it with broad metaphysical foundations. Like the seed of Buddhahood inherent in all things, the seed of perfected humanness, *jen*, was now seen as the fundamental nature, inherent in all persons. And as Buddhists sought enlightenment by following the way of the Buddha, Neo-Confucians emphasized practicing the way of learning of the Sage.

Chu Hsi (1130 - 1200) stands out as the greatest Neo-Confucian thinker and chief architect of Neo-Confucianism. He was able to integrate the thought of his predecessors through a profound re-visioning of principle (*li*), enabling him to understand that humanness is the principle of love and the fundamental character of the human mind, binding the human community together and making possible realization of the fullness of human existence in peace and harmony. Chu's vision enabled him to select and interpret the *Analects*, the *Mencius*, the *Great Learning*, and the *Central Harmony* as the Four Books that were to provide the foundation of learning and the basis for the civil service exams from 1313 to 1905. It was also Chu's vision that inspired the reinvigoration of the Confucian tradition in Korea and Japan.

The fourth stage was marked by influence from the West. Modern Western ideas of historical progress and scientific knowledge catalyzed nineteenth- and twentieth-century Chinese thought. The well-received lectures by Bertrand Russell and John Dewey early in the twentieth century paved the way for deeper encounters with Western philosophy. Marxist-Leninist thought, as interpreted by Mao Tse-tung, came to dominate Chinese philosophy by the middle of the century. As the twentieth century draws to a close Maoist-Marxist thought continues to dominate, but in a more pluralistic environment there is also a serious revival of Taoist and Confucian scholarship, and significant comparative philosophical work is beginning to flourish.

For a succinct introduction to the main ideas and movements of Chinese philosophy the reader may consult John M. Koller, *Oriental Philosophies*, 2nd edition (New York: Macmillan Publishing Company, 1985), part 3: "Chinese Philosophies." Wm. Theodore De Bary, *East Asian Civilizations: A Dialogue in Five Stages* (Cambridge, Mass.: Harvard University Press, 1988), is a good overall account of the development and influence of Chinese thought in China, Korea, and Japan. Fung Yu-lan, *History of Chinese Philosophy*, two volumes, translated by Derk Bodde (Princeton: Princeton University Press, 1952), is generally accepted as the most authoritative history available in English. Wing-tsit Chan, *A Source Book in Chinese Philosophy* (Princeton: Princeton University Press, 1963), is an outstanding collection of source material by an acknowledged master scholar and translator. The translations are accompanied by helpful introductory remarks as well as a commentary on the most difficult and important passages. Charles Wei-hsun Fu and Wing-tsit Chan, *Guide to Chinese Philosophy* (Boston: G. K. Hall, 1978), arranged both topically and historically, is an excellent annotated guide to the literature up to 1976.

CHAPTER 16

THE VISION OF CONFUCIUS

The Confucian vision, which has tended to dominate Chinese thought, finds its first recorded expression in the early Chou classics compiled before the sixth century B.C. This vision, especially as revealed through the *Book of Documents* and *The Book of Poetry*, was renewed and transmitted by Confucius (551–479 B.C.) through his teachings. These teachings were then transmitted by successive generations of Confucianists, undergoing various modifications along the way, so that when we speak of Confucianism it is to an entire tradition rather than the thought of one person that we refer. Despite a long history of creative development, there is a relatively stable core vision that anchors the Confucian tradition, a core that Confucius saw in the ancient teachings.

This core envisions a complete normative ordering of human affairs harmonizing the feelings and thoughts of individual members of the community with each other by following the way of Heaven. Moral virtue, music, and the rules (*li*) that regulate personal behavior combine to shape the conduct of human affairs in accord with the way of Heaven, bringing about full and harmonious human and social development. "Heaven" refers to the sacred foundation of all things, especially human beings and human relationships, and the "way of Heaven" to the divinely ordained operations of all things, with the Confucian emphasis primarily on the ordering of human affairs. Thus, although Confucius emphasized the way of human beings, this way was regarded as being grounded in the way of Heaven.

There is general agreement that the *Analects* (*Lun-Yü*) contains Confucius' own thought, as recorded by his students. The *Central Harmony* (*Chung-yung*) and the *Great Learning* (*Ta-hsüeh*) are regarded as later compilations of teachings, frequently ascribed to Confucius or to his grandson, Tzu-ssu, a contemporary of Mo-tzu and teacher of Mencius. Chu Hsi attributes the core of the *Great Learning* to Confucius' disciple, Tseng-tzu. Although many scholars regard the *Central Harmony* and the *Great Learning* as later than the works of Mencius and Mo-tzu, they are included here with the *Analects* because the Neo-Confucian tradition regards them as part of the central teachings of Confucius.

The selections from Confucius are from D. C. Lau, *Confucius: The Analects* (Harmondsworth: Penguin Books, 1979), which contains a good introduction and helpful notes. David L. Hall and Roger T. Ames, *Thinking Through Confucius* (Albany; State University of New York Press, 1987), is by far the most helpful analysis of the thought of Confucius for contemporary Western readers, presupposing no specialized knowledge of Chinese philosophy. The most philosophical passages of the *Analects* are translated and commented upon in a careful and sensitive way that provides a coherent and unified Confucian vision. Through carefully developed comparisons with Western thought, the authors help us get into the spirit of Confucian thinking about fundamental human questions. H. G. Creel, *Confucius and the Chinese Way* (New York: Harper & Row, 1960), originally published in 1949, remains one of the better studies of Confucius. Herbert Fingarette, *Confucius: The Secular as Sacred* (New York: Harper & Row Torchbook, 1972), is an excellent philosophical study of ritual (*li*) in the *Analects.*

A.C. Graham, *Disputers of the Tao: Philosophical Argument in Ancient China* (La Salle, Ill.: Open Court, 1989), is the single best introduction to philosophical thought in China during the classical period (500–200 B.C.). The basic ideas and arguments of each of the major thinkers and schools are clearly set out in their historical relationship to each other. Extensive quotations from primary sources coupled with careful analysis give the reader first-hand acquaintance with Chinese philosophy. Benjamin I. Schwartz, *The World of Thought in Ancient China* (Cambridge, Mass.: Harvard University Press, 1985), is a deeply reflective and sophisticated work, presupposing some acquaintance with Chinese thought and considerable ability to think abstractly. But because of its masterly treatment of the interactions between the main ways of thought in ancient China, it is worth the struggle required of most undergraduates to come to grips with this text.

The *Ta-hsüeh,* usually translated as the *Great Learning,* but as the *Greater Learning* by Daniel K. Gardner, is presented here in its entirety, along with the preface and comments of Chu Hsi (1130–1200), the great Neo-Confucian thinker responsible for arranging the text in its modern form and making it one of the Four Books on which civil service exams were based. Translated by Daniel K. Gardner, *Chu Hsi and the Ta-hsüeh* (published by the Council on East Asian Studies, Harvard University Press, 1986) contains an excellent introduction and extensive annotations and notes that make this the best book on the *Great Learning.*

The *Chung-yung,* usually translated as the *Central Harmony,* but as the *Doctrine of the Mean* by Wing-tsit Chan, is also presented in its entirety. Chu Hsi's introduction and comments, omitted here, can be found in Wing-tsit Chan's translation in *A Source Book in Chinese Philosophy* (Princeton: Princeton University Press, 1963), which accompany the translation reprinted here. The single best book on this classic text is Wei-ming Tu's *Centrality and Commonality* (Albany: State University of New York Press, 1989), which follows Chan's translation. Tu interprets the text in terms of three basic ideas: (1) the profound person (*chün-tzu*), who is continually engaged in a quest for self-realization that is essentially a process of deepening her humanity through self-cultivation; (2) the politics (*cheng*) of social transformation in a society seen as a "fiduciary community" rather than an adversarial system; and (3) sincerity (*ch'eng*). The regulation of human relationships and, thereby, the quest for self-realization, is grounded in human nature. But human nature, as the opening line of *Chung-yung* says, is given by Heaven, and following what is given by Heaven is the Way. Therefore, to succeed in the transformative process of self-realization it is necessary to be *ch'eng*—true to the Way.

I
CONFUCIUS: THE ANALECTS (*LUN-YÜ*)*

BOOK I

1. The Master said, "Is it not a pleasure, having learned something, to try it out at due intervals? Is it not a joy to have friends come from afar? Is it not gentlemanly not to take offence when others fail to appreciate your abilities?"

2. Yu Tzu said, "It is rare for a man whose character is such that he is good as a son and obedient as a young man to have the inclination to transgress against his superiors; it is unheard of for one who has no such inclination to be inclined to start a rebellion. The gentleman devotes his efforts to the roots, for once the roots are established, the Way will grow therefrom. Being good as a son and obedient as a young man is, perhaps, the root of a man's character."

3. The Master said, "It is rare, indeed, for a man with cunning words and an ingratiating face to be benevolent."

4. Tseng Tzu said, "Every day I examine myself on three counts. In what I have undertaken on another's behalf, have I failed to do my best? In my dealings with my friends have I failed to be trustworthy in what I say? Have I passed on to others anything that I have not tried out myself?"

5. The Master said, "In guiding a state of a thousand chariots, approach your duties with reverence and be trustworthy in what you say; avoid excesses in expenditure and love your fellow men; employ the labour of the common people only in the right seasons."

6. The Master said, "A young man should be a good son at home and an obedient young man abroad, sparing of speech but trustworthy in what he says, and should love the multitude at large but cultivate the friendship of his fellow men. If he has any energy to spare from such action, let him devote it to making himself cultivated."

*From D. C. Lau, *Confucius: The Analects* (Harmondsworth: Penguin Books, 1979).

7. Tzu-hsia said, "I would grant that a man has received instruction who appreciates men of excellence where other men appreciate beautiful women, who exerts himself to the utmost in the service of his parents and offers his person to the service of his lord, and who, in his dealings with his friends, is trustworthy in what he says, even though he may say that he has never been taught."

8. The Master said, "A gentleman who lacks gravity does not inspire awe. A gentleman who studies is unlikely to be inflexible.

"Make it your guiding principle to do your best for others and to be trustworthy in what you say. Do not accept as friend anyone who is not as good as you.

"When you make a mistake, do not be afraid of mending your ways."

11. The Master said, "Observe what a man has in mind to do when his father is living, and then observe what he does when his father is dead. If, for three years, he makes no changes to his father's ways, he can be said to be a good son."

12. Yu Tzu said, "Of the things brought about by the rites, harmony is the most valuable. Of the ways of the Former Kings, this is the most beautiful, and is followed alike in matters great and small, yet this will not always work: to aim always at harmony without regulating it by the rites simply because one knows only about harmony will not, in fact, work."

14. The Master said, "The gentleman seeks neither a full belly nor a comfortable home. He is quick in action but cautious in speech. He goes to men possessed of the Way to be put right. Such a man can be described as eager to learn."

BOOK II

1. The Master said, "The rule of virtue can be compared to the Pole Star which commands the homage of the multitude of stars without leaving its place."

2. The Master said, "The *Odes* are three hundred in number. They can be summed up in one phrase,

> Swerving not from the right path."

3. The Master said, "Guide them by edicts, keep them in line with punishments, and the common people will stay out of trouble but will have no sense of shame. Guide them by virtue, keep them in line with the rites, and they will, besides having a sense of shame, reform themselves."

4. The Master said, "At fifteen I set my heart on learning; at thirty I took my stand; at forty I came to be free from doubts; at fifty I understood the Decree of Heaven; at sixty my ear was atuned; at seventy I followed my heart's desire without overstepping the line."

5. Meng Yi Tzu asked about being filial. The Master answered, "Never fail to comply."

Fan Ch'ih was driving. The Master told him about the interview, saying, "Meng-sun asked me about being filial. I answered, 'Never fail to comply.'"

Fan Ch'ih asked, "What does that mean?"

The Master said, "When your parents are alive, comply with the rites in serving them; when they die, comply with the rites in burying them; comply with the rites in sacrificing to them."

6. Meng Wu Po asked about being filial. The Master said, "Give your father and mother no other cause for anxiety than illness."

7. Tzu-yu asked about being filial. The Master said, "Nowadays for a man to be filial means no more than that he is able to provide his parents with food. Even hounds and horses are, in some way, provided with food. If a man shows no reverence, where is the difference?"

12. The Master said, "The gentleman is no vessel."[1]

13. Tzu-kung asked about the gentleman. The Master said, "He puts his words into action before allowing his words to follow his action."

14. The Master said, "The gentleman enters into associations but not cliques; the small man enters into cliques but not associations."

15. The Master said, "If one learns from others but does not think, one will be bewildered. If, on the other hand, one thinks but does not learn from others, one will be in peril."

BOOK IV

1. The Master said, "Of neighbourhoods benevolence is the most beautiful. How can the man be considered wise who, when he has the choice, does not settle in benevolence?"

2. The Master said, "One who is not benevolent cannot remain long in straitened circumstances, nor can he remain long in easy circumstances.

"The benevolent man is attracted to benevolence because he feels at home in it. The wise man is attracted to benevolence because he finds it to his advantage."

3. The Master said, "It is only the benevolent man who is capable of liking or disliking other men."

4. The Master said, "If a man sets his heart on benevolence, he will be free from evil."

5. The Master said, "Wealth and high station are what men desire but unless I got them in the right way I would not remain in them. Poverty and low

---

[1]I.e., he is no specialist, as every vessel is designed for a specific purpose only.

station are what men dislike, but even if I did not get them in the right way I would not try to escape from them.[1]

"If the gentleman forsakes benevolence, in what way can he make a name for himself? The gentleman never deserts benevolence, not even for as long as it takes to eat a meal. If he hurries and stumbles one may be sure that it is in benevolence that he does so."

6. The Master said, "I have never met a man who finds benevolence attractive or a man who finds unbenevolence repulsive. A man who finds benevolence attractive cannot be surpassed. A man who finds unbenevolence repulsive can, perhaps, be counted as benevolent, for he would not allow what is not benevolent to contaminate his person.

"Is there a man who, for the space of a single day, is able to devote all his strength to benevolence? I have not come across such a man whose strength proves insufficient for the task. There must be such cases of insufficient strength, only I have not come across them."

9. The Master said, "There is no point in seeking the views of a Gentleman who, though he sets his heart on the Way, is ashamed of poor food and poor clothes."

10. The Master said, "In his dealings with the world the gentleman is not invariably for or against anything. He is on the side of what is moral."

11. The Master said, "While the gentleman cherishes benign rule, the small man cherishes his native land. While the gentleman cherishes a respect for the law, the small man cherishes generous treatment.

12. The Master said, "If one is guided by profit in one's actions, one will incur much ill will."

13. The Master said, "If a man is able to govern a state by observing the rites and showing deference, what difficulties will he have in public life? If he is unable to govern a state by observing the rites and showing deference, what good are the rites to him?"

14. The Master said, "Do not worry because you have no official position. Worry about your qualifications. Do not worry because no one appreciates your abilities. Seek to be worthy of appreciation."

15. The Master said, "Ts'an! There is one single thread binding my way together."

Tseng Tzu assented.

After the Master had gone out, the disciples asked, "What did he mean?"

Tseng Tzu said, "The way of the Master consists in doing one's best and in using oneself as a measure to gauge others. That is all."

16. The Master said, "The gentleman understands what is moral. The small man understands what is profitable."

---

[1]This sentence is most likely to be corrupt. The negative is probably an interpolation and the sentence should read: "Poverty and low station are what men dislike, but if I got them in the right way I would not try to escape from them."

17. The Master said, "When you meet someone better than yourself, turn your thoughts to becoming his equal. When you meet someone not as good as you are, look within and examine your own self."

BOOK V

16. The Master said of Tzu-ch'an that he had the way of the gentleman on four counts: he was respectful in the manner he conducted himself; he was reverent in the service of his lord; in caring for the common people, he was generous and, in employing their services, he was just.

26. Yen Yüan and Chi-lu were in attendance. The Master said, "I suggest you each tell me what it is you have set your hearts on."

Tzu-lu said, "I should like to share my carriage and horses, clothes and furs with my friends, and to have no regrets even if they become worn."

Yen Yüan said, "I should like never to boast of my own goodness and never to impose onerous tasks upon others."

Tzu-lu said, "I should like to hear what you have set your heart on."

The Master said, "To bring peace to the old, to have trust in my friends, and to cherish the young."

BOOK VII

1. The Master said, "I transmit but do not innovate; I am truthful in what I say and devoted to antiquity. I venture to compare myself to our Old P'eng."

2. The Master said, "Quietly to store up knowledge in my mind, to learn without flagging, to teach without growing weary, these present me with no difficulties."

3. The Master said, "It is these things that cause me concern: failure to cultivate virtue, failure to go more deeply into what I have learned, inability, when I am told what is right, to move to where it is, and inability to reform myself when I have defects."

6. The Master said, "I set my heart on the Way, base myself on virtue, lean upon benevolence for support and take my recreation in the arts."

8. The Master said, "I never enlighten anyone who has not been driven to distraction by trying to understand a difficulty or who has not got into a frenzy trying to put his ideas into words.

"When I have pointed out one corner of a square to anyone and he does not come back with the other three, I will not point it out to him a second time."

20. The Master said, "I was not born with knowledge but, being fond of antiquity, I am quick to seek it."

22. The Master said, "Even when walking in the company of two other men, I am bound to be able to learn from them. The good points of the one I copy; the bad points of the other I correct in myself."

23. The Master said, "Heaven is author of the virtue that is in me. What can Huan T'ui do to me?"

24. The Master said, "My friends, do you think I am secretive? There is nothing which I hide from you. There is nothing I do which I do not share with you, my friends. There is Ch'iu for you."

25. The Master instructs under four heads: culture, moral conduct, doing one's best and being trustworthy in what one says.

30. The Master said, "Is benevolence really far away? No sooner do I desire it than it is here."

37. The Master said, "The gentleman is easy of mind, while the small man is always full of anxiety."

38. The Master is cordial yet stern, awe-inspiring yet not fierce, and respectful yet at ease.

BOOK VIII

2. The Master said, "Unless a man has the spirit of the rites, in being respectful he will wear himself out, in being careful he will become timid, in having courage he will become unruly, and in being forthright he will become intolerant.

"When the gentleman feels profound affection for his parents, the common people will be stirred to benevolence. When he does not forget friends of long standing, the common people will not shirk their obligations to other people."

7. Tseng Tzu said, "A Gentleman must be strong and resolute, for his burden is heavy and the road is long. He takes benevolence as his burden. Is that not heavy? Only with death does the road come to an end. Is that not long?"

8. The Master said, "Be stimulated by the *Odes*, take your stand on the rites and be perfected by music."

9. The Master said, "The common people can be made to follow a path but not to understand it."

BOOK IX

4. There were four things the Master refused to have anything to do with: he refused to entertain conjectures or insist on certainty; he refused to be inflexible or to be egotistical.

5. When under siege in K'uang, the Master said, "With King Wen dead, is not culture (*wen*) invested here in me? If Heaven intends culture to be destroyed, those who come after me will not be able to have any part of it. If Heaven does not intend this culture to be destroyed, then what can the men of K'uang do to me?"

11. Yen Yüan, heaving a sigh, said, "The more I look up at it the higher it appears. The more I bore into it the harder it becomes. I see it before me. Suddenly it is behind me.

"The Master is good at leading one on step by step. He broadens me with culture and brings me back to essentials by means of the rites. I cannot give up even if I wanted to, but, having done all I can, it[1] seems to rise sheer above me and I have no way of going after it, however much I may want to."

14. The Master wanted to settle amongst the Nine Barbarian Tribes of the east. Someone said, "But could you put up with their uncouth ways?" The Master said, "Once a gentleman settles amongst them, what uncouthness will there be?"

24. The Master said, "One cannot but give assent to exemplary words, but what is important is that one should rectify oneself. One cannot but be pleased with tactful words, but what is important is that one should reform oneself. I can do nothing with the man who gives assent but does not rectify himself or the man who is pleased but does not reform himself."

BOOK XI

12. Chi-lu asked how the spirits of the dead and the gods should be served. The Master said, "You are not able even to serve man. How can you serve the spirits?"

"May I ask about death?"

"You do not understand even life. How can you understand death?"

BOOK XII

1. Yen Yüan asked about benevolence. The Master said, "To return to the observance of the rites through overcoming the self constitutes benevolence. If for a single day a man could return to the observance of the rites through overcoming himself, then the whole Empire would consider benevolence to be his. However, the practice of benevolence depends on oneself alone, and not on others."

Yen Yüan said, "I should like you to list the items." The Master said, "Do not look unless it is in accordance with the rites; do not listen unless it is in accordance with the rites; do not speak unless it is in accordance with the rites; do not move unless it is in accordance with the rites."

Yen Yüan said, "Though I am not quick, I shall direct my efforts towards what you have said."

2. Chung-kung asked about benevolence. The Master said, "When abroad behave as though you were receiving an important guest. When employing the services of the common people behave as though you were officiating at an important sacrifice. Do not impose on others what you

---

[1]The way (*Tao*).

yourself do not desire. In this way you will be free from ill will whether in a state or in a noble family."

Chung-kung said, "Though I am not quick, I shall direct my efforts towards what you have said."

7. Tzu-kung asked about government. The Master said, "Give them enough food, give them enough arms, and the common people will have trust in you."

Tzu-kung said, "If one had to give up one of these three, which should one give up first?"

"Give up arms."

Tzu-kung said, "If one had to give up one of the remaining two, which should one give up first?"

"Give up food. Death has always been with us since the beginning of time, but when there is no trust, the common people will have nothing to stand on."

10. Tzu-chang asked about the exaltation of virtue and the recognition of misguided judgement. The Master said, "Make it your guiding principle to do your best for others and to be trustworthy in what you say, and move yourself to where rightness is, then you will be exalting virtue. When you love a man you want him to live and when you hate him you want him to die. If, having wanted him to live, you then want him to die, this is misguided judgement.

> If you did not do so for the sake of riches,
> You must have done so for the sake of novelty."

11. Duke Ching of Ch'i asked Confucius about government. Confucius answered, "Let the ruler be a ruler, the subject a subject, the father a father, the son a son." The Duke said, "Splendid! Truly, if the ruler be not a ruler, the subject not a subject, the father not a father, the son not a son, then even if there be grain, would I get to eat it?"

12. The Master said, "If anyone can arrive at the truth in a legal dispute on the evidence of only one party, it is, perhaps, Yu."

Tzu-lu never put off the fulfilment of a promise to the next day.

13. The Master said, "In hearing litigation, I am no different from any other man. But if you insist on a difference, it is, perhaps, that I try to get the parties not to resort to litigation in the first place."

16. The Master said, "The gentleman helps others to realize what is good in them; he does not help them to realize what is bad in them. The small man does the opposite."

17. Chi K'ang Tzu asked Confucius about government. Confucius answered, "To govern (*cheng*) is to correct (*cheng*).[1] If you set an example by being correct, who would dare to remain incorrect?"

---

[1]In other words, if you did not set an example by stealing from the people.

19. Chi K'ang Tzu asked Confucius about government, saying, "What would you think if, in order to move closer to those who possess the Way, I were to kill those who do not follow the Way?"

Confucius answered, "In administering your government, what need is there for you to kill? Just desire the good yourself and the common people will be good. The virtue of the gentleman is like wind; the virtue of the small man is like grass. Let the wind blow over the grass and it is sure to bend.

BOOK XIII

3. Tzu-lu said, "If the Lord of Wei left the administration (*cheng*) of his state to you, what would you put first?"

The Master said, "If something has to be put first, it is, perhaps, the rectification (*cheng*) of names."

Tzu-lu said, "Is that so? What a roundabout way you take! Why bring rectification in at all?"

The Master said, "Yu, how boorish you are. Where a gentleman is ignorant, one would expect him not to offer any opinion. When names are not correct, what is said will not sound reasonable; when what is said does not sound reasonable, affairs will not culminate in success; when affairs do not culminate in success, rites and music will not flourish; when rites and music do not flourish, punishments will not fit the crimes; when punishments do not fit the crimes, the common people will not know where to put hand and foot. Thus when the gentleman names something, the name is sure to be usable in speech, and when he says something this is sure to be practicable. The thing about the gentleman is that he is anything but casual where speech is concerned."

18. The Governor of She said to Confucius, "In our village there is a man nicknamed 'Straight Body.' When his father stole a sheep, he gave evidence against him." Confucius answered, "In our village those who are straight are quite different. Fathers cover up for their sons, and sons cover up for their fathers. Straightness is to be found in such behaviour."

19. Fan Ch'ih asked about benevolence. The Master said, "While at home hold yourself in a respectful attitude; when serving in an official capacity be reverent; when dealing with others do your best. These are qualities that cannot be put aside, even if you go and live among the barbarians."

20. Tzu-kung asked, "What must a man be like before he can be said truly to be a Gentleman?" The Master said, "A man who has a sense of shame in the way he conducts himself and, when sent abroad, does not disgrace the commission of his lord can be said to be a Gentleman."

"May I ask about the grade below?"

"Someone praised for being a good son in his clan and for being a respectful young man in the village."

"And the next?"

"A man who insists on keeping his word and seeing his actions through to the end can, perhaps, qualify to come next, even though he shows a stubborn petty-mindedness."

"What about men who are in public life in the present day?"

The Master said, "Oh, they are of such limited capacity that they hardly count."

BOOK XIV

1. Hsien asked about the shameful. The Master said, "It is shameful to make salary your sole object, irrespective of whether the Way prevails in the state or not."

"Standing firm against the temptation to press one's advantage, to brag about oneself, to harbour grudges or to be covetous may be called 'benevolent'?"

The Master said, "It may be called 'difficult,' but I don't know about its being benevolent."

28. The Master said, "There are three things constantly on the lips of the gentleman none of which I have succeeded in following: 'A man of benevolence never worries, a man of wisdom is never in two minds; a man of courage is never afraid.'" Tzu-kung said, "What the Master has just quoted is a description of himself."

34. Someone said,

> "Repay an injury with a good turn.

What do you think of this saying?"

The Master said, "What, then, do you repay a good turn with? You repay an injury with straightness, but you repay a good turn with a good turn."

42. Tzu-lu asked about the gentleman. The Master said, "He cultivates himself and thereby achieves reverence."

"Is that all?"

"He cultivates himself and thereby brings peace and security to his fellow men."

"Is that all?"

"He cultivates himself and thereby brings peace and security to the people. Even Yao and Shun would have found the task of bringing peace and security to the people taxing."

BOOK XV

3. The Master said, "Ssu, do you think that I am the kind of man who learns widely and retains what he has learned in his mind?"

"Yes, I do. Is it not so?"

"No. I have a single thread binding it all together."

4. The Master said, "Yu, rare are those who understand virtue."

8. The Master said, "To fail to speak to a man who is capable of benefiting is to let a man go to waste. To speak to a man who is incapable of benefiting is to let one's words go to waste. A wise man lets neither men nor words go to waste."

9. The Master said, "For Gentlemen of purpose and men of benevolence while it is inconceivable that they should seek to stay alive at the expense of benevolence, it may happen that they have to accept death in order to have benevolence accomplished."

18. The Master said, "The gentleman has morality as his basic stuff and by observing the rites puts it into practice, by being modest gives it expression, and by being trustworthy in word brings it to completion. Such is a gentleman indeed!"

19. The Master said, "The gentleman is troubled by his own lack of ability, not by the failure of others to appreciate him."

21. The Master said, "What the gentleman seeks, he seeks within himself; what the small man seeks, he seeks in others."

22. The Master said, "The gentleman is conscious of his own superiority without being contentious, and comes together with other gentlemen without forming cliques."

23. The Master said, "The gentleman does not recommend a man on account of what he says, neither does he dismiss what is said on account of the speaker."

24. Tzu-kung asked, "Is there a single word which can be a guide to conduct throughout one's life?" The Master said, "It is perhaps the word '*shu*.' Do not impose on others what you yourself do not desire."

29. The Master said, "It is Man who is capable of broadening the Way. It is not the Way that is capable of broadening Man."

32. The Master said, "The gentleman devotes his mind to attaining the Way and not to securing food. Go and till the land and you will end up by being hungry, as a matter of course; study, and you will end up with the salary of an official, as a matter of course. The gentleman worries about the Way, not about poverty."

33. The Master said, "What is within the reach of a man's understanding but beyond the power of his benevolence to keep is something he will lose even if he acquires it. A man may be wise enough to attain it and benevolent enough to keep it, but if he does not rule over them with dignity, then the common people will not be reverent. A man may be wise enough to attain it, benevolent enough to keep it and may govern the people with dignity, but if he does not set them to work in accordance with the rites, he is still short of perfection."

34. The Master said, "The gentleman cannot be appreciated in small things but is acceptable in great matters. A small man is not acceptable in great matters but can be appreciated in small things."

35. The Master said, "Benevolence is more vital to the common people than even fire and water. In the case of fire and water, I have seen men die by stepping on them, but I have never seen any man die by stepping on benevolence."

36. The Master said, "When faced with the opportunity to practise benevolence do not give precedence even to your teacher."

37. The Master said, "The gentleman is devoted to principle but not inflexible in small matters."

BOOK XVI

4. Confucius said, "He stands to benefit who makes friends with three kinds of people. Equally, he stands to lose who makes friends with three other kinds of people. To make friends with the straight, the trustworthy in word and the well-informed is to benefit. To make friends with the ingratiating in action, the pleasant in appearance and the plausible in speech is to lose."

5. Confucius said, "He stands to benefit who takes pleasure in three kinds of things. Equally, he stands to lose who takes pleasure in three other kinds of things. To take pleasure in the correct regulation of the rites and music, in singing the praises of other men's goodness and in having a large number of excellent men as friends is to benefit. To take pleasure in showing off, in a dissolute life and in food and drink is to lose."

8. Confucius said, "The gentleman stands in awe of three things. He is in awe of the Decree of Heaven. He is in awe of great men. He is in awe of the words of the sages. The small man, being ignorant of the Decree of Heaven, does not stand in awe of it. He treats great men with insolence and the words of the sages with derision."

9. Confucius said, "Those who are born with knowledge are the highest. Next come those who attain knowledge through study. Next again come those who turn to study after having been vexed by difficulties. The common people, in so far as they make no effort to study even after having been vexed by difficulties, are the lowest."

10. Confucius said, "There are nine things the gentleman turns his thought to: to seeing clearly when he uses his eyes, to hearing acutely when he uses his ears, to looking cordial when it comes to his countenance, to appearing respectful when it comes to his demeanour, to being conscientious when he speaks, to being reverent when he performs his duties, to seeking advice when he is in doubt, to the consequences when he is enraged, and to what is right at the sight of gain."

BOOK XVII

6. Tzu-chang asked Confucius about benevolence. Confucius said, "There are five things and whoever is capable of putting them into practice in the Empire is certainly 'benevolent.'"

"May I ask what they are?"

"They are respectfulness, tolerance, trustworthiness in word, quickness and generosity. If a man is respectful he will not be treated with insolence. If he is tolerant he will win the multitude. If he is trustworthy in word his fellow men will entrust him with responsibility. If he is quick he will achieve results. If he is generous he will be good enough to be put in a position over his fellow men.";

8. The Master said, "Yu, have you heard about the six qualities and the six attendant faults?"

"No."

"Be seated and I shall tell you. To love benevolence without loving learning is liable to lead to foolishness. To love cleverness without loving learning is liable to lead to deviation from the right path. To love trustworthiness in word without loving learning is liable to lead to harmful behaviour. To love forthrightness without loving learning is liable to lead to intolerance. To love courage without loving learning is liable to lead to insubordination. To love unbending strength without loving learning is liable to lead to indiscipline."

21. Tsai Wo asked about the three-year mourning period, saying, "Even a full year is too long. If the gentleman gives up the practice of the rites for three years, the rites are sure to be in ruins; if he gives up the practice of music for three years, music is sure to collapse. A full year's mourning is quite enough. After all, in the course of a year, the old grain having been used up, the new grain ripens, and fire is renewed by fresh drilling."

The Master said, "Would you, then, be able to enjoy eating your rice and wearing your finery?"

"Yes. I would."

"If you are able to enjoy them, do so by all means. The gentleman in mourning finds no relish in good food, no pleasure in music, and no comforts in his own home. That is why he does not eat his rice and wear his finery. Since it appears that you enjoy them, then do so by all means."

After Tai Wo had left, the Master said, "How unfeeling Yü is. A child ceases to be nursed by his parents only when he is three years old. Three years' mourning is observed throughout the Empire. Was Yü not given three years' love by his parents?"

BOOK XVIII

10. The Duke of Chou said to the Duke of Lu, "The gentleman does not treat those closely related to him casually nor does he give his high officials occasion to complain because their advice was not heeded. Unless there are grave reasons, he does not abandon officials of long standing. He does not look for all-round perfection in a single person."

II
THE *GREATER LEARNING* (*TA-HSÜEH*), WITH CHU HSI'S PREFACE*

PREFACE TO THE *GREATER LEARNING IN CHAPTERS AND VERSES*

This book, the *Greater Learning*, explains the system by which people were taught in the school for greater learning in ancient times.

Since heaven first gave birth to the people down below, it has granted them all the same nature of benevolence, righteousness, propriety, and wisdom. Yet their psychophysical endowments often prove unequal; so not all are able to know the composition of their natures and thus to preserve them whole. Should there appear among the people one who is bright and wise, capable of fulfilling the capacity of his nature, heaven would certainly ordain him to act as sovereign and instructor to the multitudes, commissioning him to govern and teach them so that their natures be restored.

Thus, Fu Hsi, Shen Nung, Huang Ti, Yao, and Shun carried on for heaven and established the highest point of excellence; and these were the reasons for which the office of the Minister of Education and the post of the Director of Music were founded.

Amidst the glory of the Three Dynasties, regulations were gradually perfected, and thereafter schools were found everywhere, from the Imperial Palace and the state capitals on down to the villages. At the age of eight, all the male children, from the sons of kings and dukes to the sons of commoners, entered the school of lesser learning; there they were instructed in the chores of cleaning and sweeping, in the formalities of polite conversation and good manners, and in the refinements of ritual, music, archery, charioteering, calligraphy, and mathematics. At the age of fifteen, the Son of Heaven's eldest son and other imperial sons on down to the eldest legitimate sons of dukes, ministers, high officials, and officers of the chief grade, together with the gifted from among the populace, all entered the school of greater learning; there they were instructed in the Way of probing principle, setting the mind in the right, cultivating oneself, and governing others. This was the way instruction in the schools was divided into programs of greater and lesser learning.

Such was the scope of the establishment of schools; such too were the details of the sequence and program of instruction. As for the content of the instruction, it was based entirely on principles drawn from the sovereign's personal experience and deep understanding, and yet it consisted of nothing more than the standards of right conduct to be followed by the people in their daily lives. Thus all in that age advanced in learning, and, in their advancement, they all came to know the primal constitution of their natures, and at the same time, the duties that were demanded of each of them. Each man

---

*Reprinted with permission from Daniel K. Gardner, *Chu Hsi and the Ta-Hsüeh* (published by the Council on East Asian Studies, Harvard University, 1986). Reprinted here without Gardner's extensive annotations and notes.

was diligent and put forth his utmost effort. This is why in the heyday of antiquity good government flourished above and excellent customs prevailed below—it was a period never equaled by later generations.

As the Chou declined, worthy and sage sovereigns did not arise, administration of schools was not kept up, education deteriorated, mores degenerated. Though a Sage like Confucius appeared in such times, he did not attain the position of sovereign-instructor, the position from which he could enact his politics and teachings. Alone, he took the ways of the former kings, recited and passed them on to his disciples; to proclaim them to later generations.

Chapters such as the "Ch'ü-li" "Shao-i," "Nei-tse," and "Ti-tzu chih" originally were only ancillary writings on lesser learning. But this chapter [the "Ta-hsüeh"] prominently sets forth the brilliant system of greater learning for those who have already completed the program of lesser learning: it develops the design of greater learning in all its magnitude and at the same time explores fully the details of the program of instruction.

We may presume that every one of the three thousand disciples heard this doctrine, yet only the tradition from the school of Tseng Tzu had the full authority of it. The school thus wrote a commentary to bring out its meaning. With the death of Mencius the transmission ceased, and, though the book was preserved, there were few who understood it. From then on, vulgar Confucians devoted twice as much effort to memorization and recitation, and to the composition of ornate verse and essays as they did to lesser learning, yet what they achieved was of no use. The heterodox teachings of emptiness and inaction, of calmness and extinction seemed "loftier" than great learning, yet they were without application to the real world. In addition, there appeared all manner of intrigues and strategems—that is, counsels designed to lead to great success and fame—together with the sects of the "hundred schools" and the "multitudinous experts," which confuse the world, deceive the people, and obstruct the path of benevolence and righteousness. These caused the ruler misfortune, unable to hear the essentials of the Great Way; these caused the common people misfortune, unable to enjoy the best government. Like a chronic disease, gloom and obstruction persisted, until decay and chaos reached their peak with the end of the Five Dynasties.

Heaven moves in cycles: nothing goes that does not come back to its origins. So the virtuous force of the Sung appeared in all its glory, and instruction flourished. At this time, the two Ch'eng brothers of Honan appeared, and found it within their capacity to take up again the tradition of Mencius. Indeed, they were the first to give due honor to the *Greater Learning* and to make it known to the world; and, after putting the text in order, they explicated its essential points. Only then was the system of teaching employed in the school for greater learning in antiquity—the subject of the Sage's Classic and the worthies' commentary—brilliantly illuminated for the world again. Though I acknowledge my ignorance, I was still fortunate to have learned indirectly [from the Ch'eng brothers through their disciples and writings], so share in having heard [the tradition].

Still, the text of the *Greater Learning* contained some errata and lacunae and hence, forgetting my rusticity, I edited it. At times also I took the liberty of appending my own ideas and filling in the lacunae—these await [the criticism] of superior men of the future. I know full well that I have overstepped my bounds and that there is no way for me to escape blame. Yet, in explaining how the state should educate the people and perfect the customs, how the student should cultivate himself and govern others, this work need not be without some small benefit.

Preface done by Chu Hsi of Hsin-an on the *chia-tzu* day of the second month of the *chi-yu* year of the Ch'un-hsi period [20 February 1189].

THE *GREATER LEARNING* (*TA-HSÜEH*)*

*INTRODUCTORY NOTE BY CHU HSI, REFERRING TO HIS MASTERS, THE CH'ENG BROTHERS: *The masters Ch'eng-tzu said,* 'The Greater Learning *is a work handed down from Confucius; it is the gate through which beginning students enter into virtue. It is only through the preservation of this work that we can now see the sequence of the learning process among the ancients.* The Analects *and the* Mencius *should be read next. Students must follow this order in their studies; then they may approach the point where they are free from error.*"

1. The way of greater learning lies in keeping one's inborn luminous Virtue unobscured, in renewing the people, and in coming to rest in perfect goodness.

2. Knowing where to come to rest, one becomes steadfast; being steadfast, one may find peace of mind; peace of mind may lead to serenity; this serenity makes reflection possible; only with reflection is one able to reach the resting place.

3. Things have their roots and branches [i.e., their fundamentals and what derives from them and depends on them]; affairs have a beginning and an end. One comes near the Way in knowing what to put first and what to put last.

4. Those of antiquity who wished that all men throughout the empire keep their inborn luminous Virtue unobscured put governing their states well first; wishing to govern their states well, they first established harmony in their households; wishing to establish harmony in their households, they first cultivated themselves; wishing to cultivate themselves, they first set their minds in the right; wishing to set their minds in the right, they first made their thoughts true; wishing to make their thoughts true, they first extended their knowledge to the utmost; the extension of knowledge lies in fully apprehending the principle in things.

5. Only after the principle in things is fully apprehended does knowledge become complete; knowledge being complete, thoughts may become true; thoughts being true, the mind may become set in the right; the mind being so set, the person becomes cultivated; the person being cultivated, harmony is established in the household; household harmony established, the state becomes well-governed; the state being well-governed, the empire becomes tranquil.

6. From the Son of Heaven on down to the commoners, all without exception should regard self-cultivation as the root.

7. It is impossible that the root be unhealthy and the branches healthy. Never should the important be treated as trivial; never should the trivial be treated as important.*

*NOTE BY CHU HSI: *This, the Classic portion in one chapter, may be taken as the words of Confucius, transmitted by Tseng Tzu. The ten chapters of commentary contain the ideas of Tseng Tzu, recorded by his disciples. In the old version [of the* Greater Learning*] there were passages out of place. Now, availing myself of Ch'eng-tzu's arrangement, and having reexamined the text of the Classic, I have ordered it as follows:*

THE COMMENTARY OF TSENG TZU

Chapter I

1. In the "Announcement to the Prince of K'ang" it is said, "[King Wen] was able to keep his Virtue unobscured."

2. In the "T'ai-chia" it is said, "[T'ang's] attention was constantly on his heaven-given luminous Virtue."

3. In the "Canon of Emperor Yao" it is said, "He was able to keep his lofty Virtue unobscured."

4. All [these passages speak of] keeping one's own inborn Virtue unobscured.

Chapter II

1. The inscription on T'ang's basin read, "If one day you truly renew yourself, day after day you should renew yourself; indeed, renew yourself every day."

2. In the "Announcement to the Prince of K'ang" it is said, "You shall give rise to a renewed people."

3. In the *Book of Poetry* it is said, "Though Chou is an old state, the charge it holds is new."

4. For this purpose, the superior man exerts himself to the utmost in everything.

Chapter III

1. In the *Book of Poetry* it is said, "The royal domain of a thousand *li* / Is where the people come to rest."

2. In the *Book of Poetry* it is said, "Min-man, the orioles sing / Resting on the peak's foliage." The Master said, "They rest—and they know where to come to rest. Can a man be less than these birds?"

3. In the *Book of Poetry* it is said, "Profound was King Wen / Ah! continuously bright and deeply attentive—he came to rest [in perfect goodness]." As a sovereign, he came to rest in benevolence; as a subject, he came to rest in reverence. As a son, he came to rest in filial piety; as a father, he came to rest in affection. In intercourse with countrymen, he came to rest in fidelity.

4. In the *Book of Poetry* it is said,

> Look to the coves in the banks of the Ch'i
> With green bamboo, so lush and fine;
> There is our elegant and accomplished prince—
> As if cutting and filing,
> As if chiselling and polishing,
> [So he cultivates himself!]
> How grave is he and resolute!
> How commanding and distinguished!
> Our elegant and accomplished prince—
> Never can he be forgotten!

"As if cutting and filing" speaks to the process of learning; "as if chiselling and polishing" to the process of self-cultivation. "How grave is he and resolute" involves a feeling of trepidation; "how commanding and distinguished" is of an imposing demeanor. "Our elegant and accomplished prince,— / Never can he be forgotten" speaks to his abundant virtue and perfect goodness which the people cannot forget.

5. In the *Book of Poetry* it is said, "Ah! the former kings are not forgotten!" Superior men [of later generations] have esteemed their worthiness and have treated their descendants with the affection due kinsmen. Commoners [of later generations] have delighted in the prosperity passed on by them and have profited from their benefactions. Therefore, after coming to the end of their days they have not been forgotten.

Chapter IV

1. "The Master said, 'In hearing litigations, I am no different from others. But what is necessary is to create conditions where there are no litigations.'" Then those whose accusations are baseless will not be able to pour out all their lies—so greatly shall the people's will be kept in awe. This is called "knowing the root."

Chapter V

1. This is called "knowing the root."

2. This is called "the completion of knowledge."*

*CHU HSI'S COMMENT: *It would appear that the preceding, the fifth chapter of commentary [by Tseng Tzu], elucidated the meaning of "fully apprehending the principle in things" and "the extension of knowledge," but it is now lost. Recently, I made bold to use the ideas of Ch'eng-tzu to supplement it as follows: what is meant by "the extension of knowledge lies in fully apprehending the principle in things" is that, if we wish to extend our knowledge to the utmost, we must probe thoroughly the principle in those things we encounter. It would seem that every man's intellect is possessed of the capacity for knowing and that every thing in the world is possessed of principle. But, to the extent that principle is not yet thoroughly probed, man's knowledge is not yet fully realized. Hence, the first step of instruction in greater learning is to teach the student, whenever he encounters anything at all in the world, to build upon what is already known to him of principle and to probe still further, so that he seeks to reach the limit. After exerting himself in this way for a long time, he will one day become enlightened and thoroughly understand [principle]; then, the manifest and the hidden, the subtle and the obvious qualities of all things will all be known, and the mind, in its whole substance and vast operations, will be completely illuminated. This is called "fully apprehending the principle in things." This is called "the completion of knowledge."*

Chapter VI

1. "Becoming true in one's thoughts" is allowing no self-deception—as one hates the hateful smell, as one loves the lovely color. And this in turn means that one may keep one's self-respect. Therefore, the superior man will always be watchful over himself when he is alone.

2. The petty man, when alone, practices evil, stopping at nothing. But, as soon as he sees the superior man, he draws back and disguises himself, concealing evil and making a display of good. If, when others look at him, it is as though they see his [very] lungs and liver—of what benefit [is the disguise]? This is called what is true within being manifested without. Therefore, the superior man will always be watchful over himself when he is alone.

3. Tseng Tzu said, "It will be seen by ten eyes, pointed at by ten hands. How awesome!"

4. As wealth enriches the house, so virtue enriches the person; [for with virtue] the mind will be magnanimous and the body relaxed. It is for this reason that the superior man must make his thoughts true.

Chapter VII

1. What is meant by "the cultivation of the person depends upon setting the mind in the right" is this: neither in rage, nor in terror, nor in doting, nor in misery can the mind achieve its right balance.

2. If the mind is not present [i.e., attending], one looks but does not see, listens but does not hear, eats but does not appreciate the flavor.

3. This is what is meant by "the cultivation of the person depends upon setting the mind in the right."

Chapter VIII

1. What is meant by "establishing harmony in the household depends upon the cultivation of the person" is this: men are biased in favor of what they hold dear; biased against what they despise; biased in favor of what they revere; biased in favor of what they pity; and biased against what they scorn. Therefore, under heaven there are few who love something and yet appreciate its faults, who hate something and yet appreciate its virtues.

2. Hence, as the proverb says, "No one recognizes his son's evils, and no one recognizes the full ear in his sprout of grain."

3. This is what is meant by "if one's person is not cultivated, one cannot establish harmony in the household."

Chapter IX

1. What is meant by "to govern the state well, it is necessary first to establish harmony in the household" is this: no one is able to teach others who cannot teach his own household. Therefore, the superior man does not leave his household yet his teachings are accomplished throughout the state. Filial piety becomes the means to serve the ruler; fraternal respect becomes the means to serve the elders; parental kindness becomes the means to treat the multitude.

2. In the "Announcement to the Prince of K'ang" it is said, "[Deal with the people] as if you were taking care of an infant." Though you may not hit the mark exactly, if you try sincerely in your heart, you will not be far off. There has never been a woman who would marry only after studying how to rear a child.

3. If one household is humane, the whole state will be stirred to a sense of humaneness; if one household is courteous, the whole state will be stirred to a sense of courtesy. If the One Man is avaricious and perverse, the whole state will be led to rebellious disorder. Such are the springs of action. This is what is meant by "One word may ruin the affairs [of state]; the One Man may put the state in order."

4. Yao and Shun led the empire with benevolence, and the people followed their example; Chieh and Chou led the empire with violence, and the people followed their example. If what one decrees for others is contrary to what one loves oneself, the people will not obey. Hence, only after the superior man possesses goodness himself will he demand it of others; only after he is himself free of evil will he condemn it in others. No one has ever been able to teach others unless he himself was able to put himself in the position of those others.

5. Therefore, governing the state well depends upon establishing harmony in the household.

6. In the *Book of Poetry* it is said:

> The peach tree is young and elegant;
> Luxuriant are its leaves.
> This young lady is going to her future home,
> And will order well her household.

Only after ordering one's own household well can one teach the people of the state.

7. In the *Book of Poetry* it is said, "May relations between their brothers be as they should be!" Only after relations between one's brothers are as they should be can one teach the people of the state.

8. In the *Book of Poetry* it is said, "There is no fault in his behavior / Thus all the state is in its right balance." Only when one is a worthy model as father, son, elder brother, and younger brother, will the people model themselves after him.

9. This is what is meant by "governing the state well depends upon establishing harmony in the household."

Chapter X

1. What is meant by "bringing tranquility to the empire depends upon good governance of the state" is this: when the ruler treats the aged of his own family in a manner befitting their venerable age the people will be stirred to a sense of filial piety; when in his own family the ruler treats those who are older than himself in a manner befitting their elderly status the people will be stirred to a sense of fraternal respect; when the ruler takes pity on the young and fatherless the people will not be disobedient. To bring this about, the ruler must follow the principle of the "measuring-square"—having the proper measure in one's own mind to measure the minds of others.

2. In dealing with subordinates, do not practice what you hate in your superiors; in serving superiors, do not practice what you hate in your subordinates. In leading those behind you, do not practice what you hate in those ahead of you; in following those ahead of you, do not practice what you hate in those behind you. In intercourse with those on your left, do not practice what you hate in those on your right; in intercourse with those on your right, do not practice what you hate in those on your left. This is what is called the principle of having the proper measure in one's own mind to measure the minds of others.

3. In the *Book of Poetry* it is said, "You are to be rejoiced in, O prince / Father and mother to the people." What the people love he loves; what the people hate he hates. This is called being father and mother to the people.

4. In the *Book of Poetry* it is said:

> Lofty is that southern hill,
> With its masses of rocks!
> Awe-inspiring are you, O [Grand-] master Yin,
> And the people all look to you!

Whoever has charge of the state must take care, for, if he shows partiality, he will be a disgrace in the eyes of the world.

5. In the *Book of Poetry* it is said:

> When the rulers of Yin had not yet lost the multitude,
> They were able to be a counterpart to Shang Ti.
> Observe closely the fate of Yin;
> The great Mandate is not easy to keep.

This implies that to gain the multitude is to gain the state, to lose the multitude is to lose the state.

6. Therefore, the ruler puts watchfulness over his (inborn luminous) Virtue first. In having the (luminous) Virtue he will have the people with him; and with the people, territory, and with territory, wealth, and with wealth, resources for expenditure.

7. (The inborn luminous) Virtue is the root; wealth is the branch.

8. But, should the ruler regard the root as secondary and the branch as primary, he will contend with the people and teach them to plunder.

9. Therefore, when wealth is gathered the people disperse; when wealth is dispersed the people gather.

10. Therefore, words uttered by the ruler in a manner contrary to right come back to him in a manner contrary to right; wealth come to him by means contrary to right leaves him by means contrary to right.

11. In the "Announcement to the Prince of K'ang" it is said, "The Mandate of Heaven is not constant." That is to say, when the ruler is good he obtains it, when he is not good he loses it.

12. In the *Book of Ch'u* it is said, "The state of Ch'u treasures no object; it treasures only good men."

13. [Ch'ung-erh's] Uncle Fan said, "Our fugitive prince treasures no object; he treasures only love of kin."

14. In the "Speech of the Duke of Ch'in" it is said:

> Let me have but one minister, sincere and devoted, without other abilities; a man whose mind is broad and upright and possessed of generosity; who esteems the talents of others as if he himself possessed them; and who, upon finding accomplished and sage-like men, loves them in his heart more than his speech expresses, truly showing himself able to accept them. Such a minister would be able to preserve my descendants and my people. Would that I might have such a benefit.
>
> But a minister who, upon finding men of ability, is jealous and hates them, who upon finding accomplished and sage-like men, opposes them and does not allow their advancement, showing himself really not able to accept them—such a man will not be able to protect my descendants and people, and furthermore will be dangerous.

15. Only the humane man will banish such a jealous man, driving him out among the barbarian tribes beyond the four borders. He will not dwell together with him in the Middle Kingdom. This is what is meant by "only the humane man is able to love others and to hate others."

16. It is negligence to see a worthy man but not to raise him to office or to raise him to office but not to do so at once. Likewise, it is a mistake to see an evil man but not to remove him from office or to remove him from office but not to do so to a distant region.

17. To love what men hate or to hate what men love goes against human nature. One who does so will surely meet with calamity.

18. Thus, there is a great course to be followed by the ruler: to gain the multitude he must be true to his nature and true to others; through arrogance and wantonness he will lose it.

19. There is a great course to be followed in the generation of wealth: let producers be many and consumers few; let production be speedy and expenditure unhurried. Then wealth will always be sufficient.

20. The humane man disperses his wealth and thereby distinguishes himself (i.e., gains the people); the inhumane man destroys himself that he might increase his wealth.

21. Never has a ruler loved humaneness without his subordinates loving righteousness. Never have they loved righteousness without completely fulfilling their duties. Never in such a state has the wealth stored in the treasury soon departed.

22. Meng Hsien-tzu said,

> He who keeps a team of four horses does not tend to fowl and pigs. The household that uses ice [in funeral rites and sacrifices] does not keep cattle and sheep. The household of one hundred chariots does not keep a minister

> who collects excessive revenue from the people—rather than such a man it would be better to have a minister who pilfers the household treasury.

This is what is meant by "a state gains by righteousness and not by interest in gain."

23. The head of a state or household who makes wealth and its expenditure his chief cares is certain to be under the influence of petty men. . . . If petty men are employed in governing the state or household, calamity and misfortune together will result. And, though there be an able man, he will be of no avail. This is what is meant by "a state gains by righteousness and not by interest in gain."

CHU HSI'S COMMENT: . . . *There are, in all, ten chapters of commentary [by Tseng Tzu], the first four of which discuss in general terms the gist of the principia, the latter six of which discuss in detail the effort required in each of the particular steps. The fifth chapter contains what is essential for "understanding goodness," and the sixth what is fundamental in "making oneself true." These two chapters deal with especially urgent matters that demand the attention of the beginning student. The reader should not neglect them on account of their simplicity.*

CHU HSI'S POSTSCRIPT

The preceding, the *Greater Learning*, with a Classic portion of two hundred and five characters and a commentary of ten chapters, may presently be found in Tai [Sheng's] book on rites; but the text there is in disarray and the commentary has to some degree lost its proper order. Master Ch'eng-tzu corrected the *Greater Learning*; without considering my ability, I have ventured to rearrange the text, following his views. Now, the first chapter of commentary elucidates "keeping the inborn luminous Virtue unobscured"; the second chapter, "renewing the people"; the third chapter, "coming to rest in perfect goodness"; the fourth chapter "the roots and the branches"; the fifth chapter, "the extension of knowledge"; the sixth chapter, "making the thoughts true"; the seventh chapter, "setting the mind in the right" and "cultivation of the person"; the eighth chapter, "cultivation of the person" and "establishing harmony in the household"; and the ninth chapter, "establishing harmony in the household," "governing the state well," and "bringing tranquility to the empire." There is a natural order to the work, and the ideas are all interrelated; it would seem that I have reconstructed the original form of the text. I have respectfully recorded it above in its proper order. The superfluous passages and the mistaken characters, which the former worthy [Ch'eng I] corrected, are all preserved [in the text] in their original form; I have placed circles above them and noted the corrections. These corrections together with my present doubts concerning the text may be found in my commentary.

Respectfully, Chu Hsi of Hsin-an.

III
Doctrine of the Mean (Chung-yung)*

1. What Heaven imparts to man is called human nature. To follow our nature is called the Way. Cultivating the Way is called education. The Way cannot be separated from us for a moment. What can be separated from us is not the Way. Therefore the superior man is cautious over what he does not see and apprehensive over what he does not hear. There is nothing more visible than what is hidden and nothing more manifest than what is subtle. Therefore the superior man is watchful over himself when he is alone.

Before the feelings of pleasure, anger, sorrow, and joy are aroused it is called equilibrium (*chung*, centrality, mean). When these feelings are aroused and each and all attain due measure and degree, it is called harmony. Equilibrium is the great foundation of the world, and harmony its universal path. When equilibrium and harmony are realized to the highest degree, heaven and earth will attain their proper order and all things will flourish.

2. Chung-ni (Confucius) said, "The superior man exemplifies the Mean (*chung-yung*). The inferior man acts contrary to the Mean. The superior man exemplifies the Mean because, as a superior man, he can maintain the Mean at any time. The inferior man acts contrary to the Mean because, as an inferior man, he has no caution."

3. Confucius said, "Perfect is the Mean. For a long time few people have been able to follow it."

4. Confucius said, "I know why the Way is not pursued. The intelligent go beyond it and the stupid do not come up to it. I know why the Way is not understood. The worthy go beyond it and the unworthy do not come up to it. There is no one who does not eat and drink, but there are few who can really know flavor."

5. Confucius said, "Alas! How is the Way not being pursued!"

6. Confucius said, "Shun was indeed a man of great wisdom! He loved to question others and to examine their words, however ordinary. He concealed what was bad in them and displayed what was good. He took hold of their two extremes, took the mean between them, and applied it in his dealing with the people. This was how he became Shun (the sage-emperor)."

7. Confucius said, "Men all say, 'I am wise'; but when driven forward and taken in a net, a trap, or a pitfall, none knows how to escape. Men all say, 'I am wise'; but should they choose the course of the Mean, they are not able to keep it for a round month."

8. Confucius said, "Hui was a man who chose the course of the Mean, and when he got hold of one thing that was good, he clasped it firmly as if wearing it on his breast and never lost it."

---

*Reprinted with permission from Wing-tsit, Chan, *A Source Book in Chinese Philosophy* (Princeton: Princeton University Press, 1963).

9. Confucius said, "The empire, the states, and the families can be put in order. Ranks and emolument can be declined. A bare, naked weapon can be tramped upon. But the Mean cannot easily be attained."

10. Tzu-lu asked about strength. Confucius said, "Do you mean the strength of the South, the strength of the North, or the strength you should cultivate yourself? To be genial and gentle in teaching others and not to revenge unreasonable conduct—this is the strength of the people of the South. The superior man lives by it. To lie under arms and meet death without regret—this is the strength of the people of the North. The strong man lives by it. Therefore the superior man maintains harmony in his nature and conduct and does not waver. How unflinching is his strength! He stands in the middle position and does not lean to one side. How unflinching is his strength! When the Way prevails in the state, if he enters public life, he does not change from what he was in private life. How unflinching is his strength! When the Way does not prevail in the state, he does not change even unto death. How unflinching is his strength!"

11. "There are men who seek for the abstruse, and practice wonders. Future generations may mention them. But that is what I will not do. There are superior men who act in accordance with the Way, but give up when they have gone half way. But I can never give up. There are superior men who are in accord with the Mean, retire from the world and are unknown to their age, but do not regret. It is only a sage who can do this."

12. "The Way of the superior man functions everywhere and yet is hidden. Men and women of simple intelligence can share its knowledge; and yet in its utmost reaches, there is something which even the sage does not know. Men and women of simple intelligence can put it into practice; and yet in its utmost reaches there is something which even the sage is not able to put into practice. Great as heaven and earth are, men still find something in them with which to be dissatisfied. Thus with the Way of the superior man, if one speaks of its greatness, nothing in the world can contain it, and if one speaks of its smallness, nothing in the world can split it. The *Book of Odes* says, 'The hawk flies up to heaven; the fishes leap in the deep.' This means that the Way is clearly seen above and below. The Way of the superior man has its simple beginnings in the relation between man and woman, but in its utmost reaches, it is clearly seen in heaven and on earth."

13. Confucius said, "The Way is not far from man. When a man pursues the Way and yet remains away from man, his course cannot be considered the Way. The *Book of Odes* says, 'In hewing an axe handle, the pattern is not far off.' If we take an axe handle to hew another axe handle and look askance from the one to the other, we may still think the pattern is far away. Therefore the superior man governs men as men, in accordance with human nature, and as soon as they change what is wrong, he stops. Conscientiousness (*chung*) and altruism (*shu*) are not far from the Way. What you do not wish others to do to you, do not do to them.

"There are four things in the Way of the superior man, none of which I have been able to do. To serve my father as I would expect my son to serve me: that I have not been able to do. To serve my ruler as I would expect my ministers to serve me: that I have not been able to do. To serve my elder brothers as I would expect my younger brothers to serve me: that I have not been able to do. To be the first to treat friends as I would expect them to treat me: that I have not been able to do. In practicing the ordinary virtues and in the exercise of care in ordinary conversation, when there is deficiency, the superior man never fails to make further effort, and when there is excess, never dares to go to the limit. His words correspond to his actions and his actions correspond to his words. Isn't the superior man earnest and genuine?"

14. The superior man does what is proper to his position and does not want to go beyond this. If he is in a noble station, he does what is proper to a position of wealth and honorable station. If he is in a humble station, he does what is proper to a position of poverty and humble station. If he is in the midst of barbarian tribes, he does what is proper in the midst of barbarian tribes. In a position of difficulty and danger, he does what is proper to a position of difficulty and danger. He can find himself in no situation in which he is not at ease with himself. In a high position he does not treat his inferiors with contempt. In a low position he does not court the favor of his superiors. He rectifies himself and seeks nothing from others, hence he has no complaint to make. He does not complain against Heaven above or blame men below. Thus it is that the superior man lives peacefully and at ease and waits for his destiny (*ming*) while the inferior man takes to dangerous courses and hopes for good luck. Confucius said, "In archery we have something resembling the Way of the superior man. When the archer misses the center of the target, he turns around and seeks for the cause of failure within himself."

15. The Way of the superior man may be compared to traveling to a distant place: one must start from the nearest point. It may be compared to ascending a height: one must start from below. The *Book of Odes* says, "Happy union with wife and children is like the music of lutes and harps. When brothers live in concord and at peace, the harmony is sweet and delightful. Let your family live in concord, and enjoy your wife and children." Confucius said, "How happy will parents be!"

16. Confucius said, "How abundant is the display of power of spiritual beings! We look for them but do not see them. We listen to them but do not hear them. They form the substance of all things and nothing can be without them. They cause all people in the world to fast and purify themselves and put on the richest dresses to perform sacrifices to them. Like the spread of overflowing water they seem to be above and to be on the left and the right. The *Book of Odes* says, 'The coming of spiritual beings cannot be surmised. How much less can we get tired of them?' Such is the manifestation of the subtle. Such is the impossibility of hiding the real (*ch'eng*)."

17. Confucius said, "Shun was indeed greatly filial! In virtue he was a sage; in honor he was the Son of Heaven (emperor); and in wealth he owned all within the four seas (China). Temple sacrifices were made to him, and his descendants preserved the sacrifices to him. Thus it is that he who possesses great virtue will certainly attain to corresponding position, to corresponding wealth, to corresponding fame, and to corresponding long life. For Heaven, in the production of things, is sure to be bountiful to them, according to their natural capacity. Hence the tree that is well taken care of is nourished and that which is about to fall is overthrown. The *Book of Odes* says, 'The admirable, amiable prince displayed conspicuously his excellent virtue. He put his people and his officers in concord. And he received his emolument from Heaven. It protected him, assisted him, and appointed him king. And Heaven's blessing came again and again.' Therefore he who possesses great virtue will surely receive the appointment of Heaven."

18. Confucius said, "King Wen was indeed the only one without sorrow! He had King Chi for father and King Wu for son. His father laid the foundation of the great work of the Chou dynasty and his son carried it on. King Wu continued the enterprise of King T'ai, King Chi, and King Wen. Once he buckled on his armor and revolted against wicked King Chou of Shang, the world came into his possession, and did not personally lose his great reputation throughout the empire. In honor he was the Son of Heaven, and in wealth he owned all within the four seas. Temple sacrifices were made to him, and his descendants preserved the sacrifices to him.

"King Wu received Heaven's Mandate to rule in his old age. Duke Chou carried to completion the virtue of King Wen and King Wu. He honored T'ai and Chi with the posthumous title of king. He sacrificed to the past reigning dukes of the house with imperial rites. These rites were extended to the feudal lords, great officers, officers, and the common people. If the father was a great officer, and the son a minor officer, when the father died, he was buried with the rite of a great officer but afterward sacrificed to with the rite of a minor officer. If the father was a minor officer and the son was a great officer, then the father was buried with the rite of a minor officer but afterward sacrificed to with the rite of a great officer. The rule of one year of mourning for relatives was extended upward to include great officers, but the rule for three years of mourning was extended upward to include the Son of Heaven. In mourning for parents, there was no difference for the noble or the commoner. The practice was the same."

19. Confucius said, "King Wu and Duke Chou were indeed eminently filial. Men of filial piety are those who skillfully carry out the wishes of their forefathers and skillfully carry forward their undertakings. In spring and autumn they repaired their ancestral temple, displayed their ancestral vessels and exhibited the ancestral robes, and presented the appropriate offerings of the season. The ritual of the ancestral temple is in order to place the kindred on the left or on the right according to the order of descent. This order in rank meant to distinguish the more honorable or humbler stations. Services in the temple are arranged in order so as to give distinction to the worthy [according to their ability for those services]. In the pledging rite the inferiors present their cups to their superiors, so that people of humble stations may have something to do. In the concluding feast, honored places were given people with white hair, so as to follow the order of seniority. To occupy places of their forefathers, to practice their rites, to perform their music, to reverence those whom they honored, to love those who were dear to them, to serve the dead as they were served while alive, and to serve the departed as they were served while still with us: this is the height of filial piety.

"The ceremonies of sacrifices to Heaven and Earth are meant for the service of the Lord on High, and the ceremonies performed in the ancestral temple are meant for the service of ancestors. If one understands the ceremonies of the sacrifices to Heaven and Earth and the meaning of the grand sacrifice and the autumn sacrifice to ancestors, it would be as easy to govern a kingdom as to look at one's palm."

20. Duke Ai asked about government. Confucius said, "The governmental measures of King Wen and King Wu are spread out in the records. With their kind of men, government will flourish. When their kind of men are gone, their government will come to an end. When the right principles of man operate, the growth of good government is rapid, and when the right principles of soil operate, the growth of vegetables is rapid. Indeed, government is comparable to a fast-growing plant. Therefore the conduct of government depends upon the men. The right men are obtained by the ruler's personal character. The cultivation of the person is to be done through the Way, and the cultivation of the Way is to be done through humanity. Humanity (*jen*) is the distinguishing characteristic of man, and the greatest application of it is in being affectionate toward relatives. Righteousness (*i*) is the principle of setting things right and proper, and the greatest application of it is in honoring the worthy. The relative degree of affection we ought to feel for our relatives and the relative grades in the honoring of the worthy give rise to the rules of propriety.

"Therefore the ruler must not fail to cultivate his personal life. Wishing to cultivate his personal life, he must not fail to serve his parents. Wishing to serve his parents, he must not fail to know man. Wishing to know man, he must not fail to know Heaven.

"There are five universal ways in human relations, and the way by which they are practiced is three. The five are those governing the relationship between ruler and minister, between father and son, between husband and wife, between elder and younger brothers, and those in the intercourse between friends. These five are universal paths in the world. Wisdom, humanity, and courage, these three are the universal virtues. The way by which they are practiced is one.

"Some are born with the knowledge of these virtues. Some learn it through study. Some learn it through hard work. But when the knowledge is acquired, it comes to the same thing. Some practice them naturally and easily. Some practice them for their advantage. Some practice them with effort and difficulty. But when the achievement is made, it comes to the same thing."

Confucius said, "Love of learning is akin to wisdom. To practice with vigor is akin to humanity. To know to be shameful is akin to courage. He who knows these three things knows how to cultivate his personal life. Knowing how to cultivate his personal life, he knows how to govern other men. And knowing how to govern other men, he knows how to govern the empire, its states, and the families.

"There are nine standards by which to administer the empire, its states, and the families. They are: cultivating the personal life, honoring the worthy, being affectionate to relatives, being respectful toward the great ministers, identifying oneself with the welfare of the whole body of officers, treating the common people as one's own children, attracting the various artisans, showing tenderness to strangers from far countries, and extending kindly and awesome influence on the feudal lords. If the ruler cultivates his personal life, the Way will be established. If he honors the worthy, he will not be perplexed. If he is affectionate to his relatives, there will be no grumbling among his uncles and brothers. If he respects the great ministers, he will not be deceived. If he identifies himself with the welfare of the whole body of officers, then the officers will repay him heavily for his courtesies. If he treats the common people as his own children, then the masses will exhort one another to do good. If he attracts the various artisans, there will be sufficiency of wealth and resources in the country. If he shows tenderness to strangers from far countries, people from all quarters of the world will flock to him. And if he extends kindly and awesome influence over the feudal lords, then the world will stand in awe of him.

"To fast, to purify, and to be correct in dress at the time of solemn sacrifice, and not to make any movement contrary to the rules of propriety—this is the way to cultivate the personal life. To avoid slanderers, keep away seductive beauties, regard wealth lightly, and honor virtue—this is the way to encourage the worthy. To give them honorable position, to bestow on them ample emoluments, and to share their likes and dislikes—this is the way to encourage affection for relatives. To allow them many offers to carry out their functions—this is the way to encourage the great ministers. To deal with them loyally and faithfully and to give them ample emoluments—this is the way to encourage the body of officers. To require them for service only at the proper time and to tax them lightly—this is the way to encourage the common masses. To inspect them daily and examine them monthly and to reward them according to the degree of their workmanship—this is the way to encourage the various artisans. To welcome them when they come and send them off when they go and to commend the good among them and show compassion to the incompetent—this is the way to show tenderness to strangers from far countries. To restore lines of broken succession, to revive states that have been extinguished, to bring order to chaotic states, to support those states that are in danger, to have fixed times for their attendance at court, and to present them with generous gifts while expecting little when they come—this is the way to extend kindly and awesome influence on the feudal lords.

"There are nine standards by which to govern the empire, its states, and the families, but the way by which they are followed is one. In all matters if there is preparation they will succeed; if there is no preparation, they will fail. If what is to be said is determined beforehand, there will be no stumbling. If the business to be done is determined beforehand, there will be no difficulty. If action to be taken is determined beforehand, there will be no trouble. And if the way to be pursued is determined beforehand, there will be no difficulties. If those in inferior positions do not have the confidence of their superiors, they will not be able to govern the people. There is a way to have the confidence of the superiors: If one is not trusted by his friends, he will not have the confidence of his superiors. There is a way to be trusted by one's friends: If one is not obedient to his parents, he will not be trusted by his friends. There is a way to obey one's parents: If one examines himself and finds himself to be insincere, he will not be obedient to his parents. There is a way to be sincere with oneself: If one does not understand what is good, he will not be sincere with himself. Sincerity is the Way of Heaven. To think how to be sincere is the way of man. He who is sincere is one who hits upon what is right without effort and apprehends without thinking. He is naturally and easily in harmony with the Way. Such a man is a sage. He who tries to be sincere is one who chooses the good and holds fast to it.

"Study it (the way to be sincere) extensively, inquire into it accurately, think over it carefully, sift it clearly, and practice it earnestly. When there is anything not yet studied, or studied but not yet understood, do not give up. When there is any question not yet asked, or asked but its answer not yet known, do not give up. When there is anything not yet thought over, or thought over but not yet apprehended, do not give up. When there is anything not yet sifted, or sifted but not yet clear, do not give up. When there is anything not yet practiced, or practiced but not yet earnestly, do not give up. If another man succeed by one effort, you will use a hundred efforts. If another man succeed by ten efforts, you will use a thousand efforts. If one really follows this course, though stupid, he will surely become intelligent, and though weak, will surely become strong."

21. It is due to our nature that enlightenment results from sincerity. It is due to education that sincerity results from enlightenment. Given sincerity, there will be enlightenment, and given enlightenment, there will be sincerity.

22. Only those who are absolutely sincere can fully develop their nature. If they can fully develop their nature, they can then fully develop the nature of others. If they can fully develop the nature of others, they can then fully develop the nature of things. If they can fully develop the nature of things, they can then assist in the transforming and nourishing process of Heaven and Earth. If they can assist in the transforming and nourishing process of Heaven and Earth, they can thus form a trinity with Heaven and Earth.

23. The next in order are those who cultivate to the utmost a particular goodness. Having done this, they can attain to the possession of sincerity. As there is sincerity, there will be its expression. As it is expressed, it will become conspicuous. As it becomes conspicuous, it will become clear. As it becomes clear, it will move others. As it moves others, it changes them. As it changes them, it transforms them. Only those who are absolutely sincere can transform others.

24. It is characteristic of absolute sincerity to be able to foreknow. When a nation or family is about to flourish, there are sure to be lucky omens. When a nation or family is about to perish, there are sure to be unlucky omens. These omens are revealed in divination and in the movements of the four limbs. When calamity or blessing is about to come, it can surely know beforehand if it is good, and it can also surely know beforehand if it is evil. Therefore he who has absolute sincerity is like a spirit.

25. Sincerity means the completion of the self, and the Way is self-direction. Sincerity is the beginning and end of things. Without sincerity there would be nothing. Therefore the superior man values sincerity. Sincerity is not only the completion of one's own self, it is that by which all things are completed. The completion of the self means humanity. The completion of all things means wisdom. These are the character of the nature, and they are the Way in which the internal and the external are united. Therefore whenever it is employed, everything done is right.

26. Therefore absolute sincerity is ceaseless. Being ceaseless, it is lasting. Being lasting, it is evident. Being evident, it is infinite. Being infinite, it is extensive and deep. Being extensive and deep, it is high and brilliant. It is because it is extensive and deep that it contains all things. It is because it is high and brilliant that it overshadows all things. It is because it is infinite and lasting that it can complete all things. In being extensive and deep, it is a counterpart of Earth. In being high and brilliant, it is a counterpart of Heaven. In being infinite and lasting, it is unlimited. Such being its nature, it becomes prominent without any display, produces changes without motion, and accomplishes its ends without action.

The Way of Heaven and Earth may be completely described in one sentence: They are without any doubleness and so they produce things in an unfathomable way. The Way of Heaven and Earth is extensive, deep, high, brilliant, infinite, and lasting. The heaven now before us is only this bright, shining mass; but when viewed in its unlimited extent, the sun, moon, stars, and constellations are suspended in it and all things are covered by it. The earth before us is but a handful of soil; but in its breadth and depth, it sustains mountains like Hua and Yüeh without feeling their weight, contains the rivers and seas without letting them leak away, and sustains all things. The mountain before us is only a fistful of straw; but in all the vastness of its size, grass and trees grow upon it, birds and beasts dwell on it, and stores of precious things (minerals) are discovered in it. The water before us is but a spoonful of liquid, but in all its unfathomable depth, the monsters, dragons, fishes, and turtles are produced in them, and wealth becomes abundant because of it [as a result of transportation]. The *Book of Odes* says, "The Mandate of Heaven, how beautiful and unceasing." This is to say, this is what makes Heaven to be Heaven. Again, it says, "How shining is it, the purity of King Wen's virtue!" This is to say, this is what makes King Wen what he was. Purity likewise is unceasing.

27. Great is the Way of the sage! Overflowing, it produces and nourishes all things and rises up to the height of heaven. How exceedingly great! [It embraces] the three hundred rules of ceremonies and the three thousand rules of conduct. It waits for the proper man before it can be put into practice. Therefore it is said, "Unless there is perfect virtue, the perfect Way cannot be materialized." Therefore the superior man honors the moral nature and follows the path of study and inquiry. He achieves breadth and greatness and pursues the refined and subtle to the limit. He seeks to reach the greatest height and brilliancy and follows the path of the Mean. He goes over the old so as to find out what is new. He is earnest and deep and highly respects all propriety. Therefore when occupying a high position, he is not proud, and when serving in a low position, he is not insubordinate. When the Way prevails in the country, he can rise to official position through his words. When the Way does not prevail in the country, he can preserve himself through silence. The *Book of Odes* says. "Intelligent and wise, he protects his person." This is the meaning.

28. Confucius said, "To be stupid and like to use his own judgment, to be in a humble station and like to dictate, to live in the present world and go back to the ways of antiquity—people of this sort bring calamity on themselves. Unless one is the Son of Heaven, he does not decide on ceremonies, make regulations, or investigate the form and pronunciation of characters. In the world today, all carriages have wheels of the same size, all writing is done with the same characters, and all conduct is governed by the same social relations. Although a man occupies the throne, if he has not the corresponding virtue, he may not dare to institute systems of music and ceremony. Although a man has the virtue, if he does not occupy the throne, he may not dare to institute systems of music and ceremony either."

Confucius said, "I have talked about the ceremonies of the Hsia dynasty (2183 - 1752 B.C.?), but what remains in the present state of Ch'i (descendant of Hsia) does not provide sufficient evidence. I have studied the ceremonies of the Shang dynasty (1751 - 1112 B.C.). They are still preserved in the present state of Sung (descendant of Shang). I have studied the ceremonies of the [Western] Chou dynasty (1111 - 770 B.C.). They are in use today. I follow the Chou."

29. If he who attains to the sovereignty of the world has three important things [ceremonies, regulations, and the form and pronunciation of characters], he will make few mistakes. However excellent may have been the regulations of former times, there is no evidence for them. Without evidence, they cannot command credence, and not being credited, the people would not follow them. However excellent might be the regulations made by one in a low position, his position is not an honored one. The position not being honored does not command credence, and not being credited, the people would not follow them. Therefore the Way of the true ruler is rooted in his own personal life and has its evidence in the following of the common people. It is tested by the experience of the Three Kings and found without error, applied before Heaven and Earth and found to be without contradiction in their operation, laid before spiritual beings without question or fear, and can wait a hundred generations for a sage to confirm it without a doubt. Since it can be laid before spiritual beings without question or fear, it shows that he knows Heaven. Since it can wait for a hundred generations for a sage without a doubt, it shows that he knows the principles of man. Therefore every move he makes becomes the way of the world, every act of his becomes the model of the world, and every word he utters becomes the pattern of the world. Those who are far away look longingly for him, and those who are near do not get weary of him. The *Book of Odes* says, "There they do not dislike him, here they do not get tired of him. Thus from day to day and night to night, they will perpetuate their praise." There has never been a ruler who did not answer this description and yet could obtain early renown throughout the world.

30. Chung-ni (Confucius) transmitted the ancient traditions of Yao and Shun, and he modeled after and made brilliant the systems of King Wen and King Wu. He conformed with the natural order governing the revolution of the seasons in heaven above, and followed the principles governing land and water below. He may be compared to earth in its supporting and containing all things, and to heaven in its overshadowing and embracing all things. He may be compared to the four seasons in their succession, and to the sun and moon in their alternate shining. All things are produced and developed without injuring one another. The courses of the seasons, the sun, and moon are pursued without conflict. The lesser forces flow continuously like river currents, while the great forces go silently and deeply in their mighty transformations. It is this that makes heaven and earth so great.

31. Only the perfect sage in the world has quickness of apprehension, intelligence, insight, and wisdom, which enable him to rule all men; magnanimity, generosity, benignity, and tenderness, which enable him to embrace all men; vigor, strength, firmness, and resolution, which enable him to maintain a firm hold; orderliness, seriousness, adherence to the Mean, and correctness, which enable him to be reverent; pattern, order, refinement, and penetration, which enable him to exercise discrimination. All embracing and extensive, and deep and unceasingly springing, these virtues come forth at all times. All embracing and extensive as heaven and deep and unceasingly springing as an abyss! He appears and all people respect him, speaks and all people believe him, acts and all people are pleased with him. Consequently his fame spreads overflowingly over the Middle Kingdom and extends to barbarous tribes. Wherever ships and carriages reach, wherever the labor of man penetrates, wherever the heavens overshadow and the earth sustains, wherever the sun and moon shine, and wherever frosts and dew fall, all who have blood and breath honor and love him. Therefore we say that he is a counterpart of Heaven.

32. Only those who are absolutely sincere can order and adjust the great relations of mankind, establish the great foundations of humanity, and know the transforming and nourishing operations of heaven and earth. Does he depend on anything else? How earnest and sincere—he is humanity! How deep and unfathomable—he is abyss! How vast and great—he is heaven! Who can know him except he who really has quickness of apprehension, intelligence, sageliness, and wisdom, and understands character of Heaven?

33. The *Book of Odes* says, "Over her brocaded robe, she wore a plain and simple dress, for she disliked the loudness of its color and patterns. Thus the way of the superior man is hidden but becomes more prominent every day, whereas the way of the inferior man is conspicuous but gradually disappears. It is characteristic of the superior man to be plain, and yet people do not get tired of him. He is simple and yet rich in cultural adornment. He is amiable and yet systematically methodical. He knows what is distant begins with what is near. He knows where the winds (moral influence) come from. And he knows the subtle will be manifested. Such a man can enter into virtue.

The *Book of Odes* says, "Although the fish dive and lie at the bottom, it is still quite clearly seen." Therefore the superior man examines his own heart and sees that there is nothing wrong there, and that he is not dissatisfied with himself. The superior man is unequaled in the fact that he is cautious in those things which people do not see. The *Book of Odes* says, "Though the ceiling looks down upon you, be free from shame even in the recesses of your own house." Therefore the superior man is reverent without any movement and truthful without any words. The *Book of Odes* says, "Throughout the sacrifice not a word is spoken, and yet the worshipers are influenced and transformed without the slightest contention." Therefore the superior man does not resort to rewards and the people are encouraged to virtue. He does not resort to anger and the people are awed. The *Book of Odes* says, "He does not display his virtue, and yet all the princes follow him." Therefore when the superior man is sincere and reverent, the world will be in order and at peace. The *Book of Odes* says, "I cherish your brilliant virtue, which makes no great display in sound or appearance." Confucius said, "In influencing people, the use of sound or appearance is of secondary importance." The *Book of Odes* says, "His virtue is as light as hair." Still, a hair is comparable. "The operations of Heaven have neither sound nor smell."

CHAPTER 17

THE TAOIST VISION

The classical Taoist vision is set forth in two texts, the *Lao-tzu* and the *Chuang-tzu.* The *Lao-tzu,* the older of the two, is probably from the sixth or fifth century B.C., and the *Chuang-tzu* from a century or two later. It is likely that these two collections of sayings actually contain the sayings of the two persons after whom they are named, but as there is practically no reliable knowledge about either person, when talking about Taoist views it is better to talk about the views presented in the texts than the views of the historical persons after whom the texts are named. Although some scholars regard these texts as responses to earlier Mohist and Legalist thought, more commonly the Taoist vision is regarded as an earlier way of thought, dating at least to the time of Confucius.

The Taoist vision is made up of three strands. First is the emphasis on preserving oneself by skillful adaptation to circumstances and avoidance of unnecessary risks, a strand sometimes attributed to the legendary Yang Chu. A second strand emphasizes the way of natural things in their spontaneity and naturalness. A third strand is the conviction that language and conceptual thought cannot grasp the deepest truth of reality. Only through a direct and immediate realization—a mystical experiential unity—can the ultimate be known, and only through this knowledge can one be transformed by the power of the ultimate. The Tao emphasized in the *Lao-tzu* is this unfathomable dynamic unity of the myriad processes making up reality, the inner unity that gives them their being and direction.

The selections from the *Lao-tzu* are taken from D. C. Lau, *Tao Te Ching* (Hong Kong: Chinese University Press, 1982), part 2. This is a translation of the Ma Wang Tui *Lao-tzu,* the oldest authentic version of the text available, and is accompanied by an excellent introduction and useful comparisons with the Wang Pi text, which is translated in part 1.

The selection from Chuang-tzu, "Chapter 2: The Sorting Which Evens Things Out," is from A. C. Graham, *Chuang-tzu: The Seven Inner Chapters and Other Writings from the Book "Chuang-tzu"* (London: George Allen & Unwin, 1981). This is the most reliable translation of the Chuang-tzu and it contains a helpful introduction and useful notes. "The Sorting Which Evens Things Out" is a brilliant protest against the logicians and utilitarians whose rigid categorizations and emphasis on utility mistake the superficialities of human artifice for the deep and profound mysteries of the Tao.

Chung-yuan Chang has written two extremely interesting and provocative books on Taoism. His *Tao: A New Way of Thinking. A Translation of the "Tao Te Ching," with an Introduction and Commentaries* (New York: Harper & Row, 1975), relates Taoist thought to a wide range of Western and Eastern thinkers, with a special focus on Martin Heidegger. *Creativity and Taoism* (New York: Harper & Row, 1970), focuses on aesthetic experience, East and West. Kuang-ming Wu's *Chuang-tzu: World Philosopher at Play* (New York: Crossroad Publishing, 1982) explores the relevance of Chuang-tzu's thought for today's world. Robert E. Allinson, in an important recent book on the *Chuang-tzu, Chuang-tzu for Spiritual Transformation: An Analysis of the Inner Chapters* (Albany: State University of New York Press, 1989), argues clearly and convincingly that the style of Chuang-tzu is consistent with his commitment to the fundamental importance of achieving spiritual transformation. Max Kaltenberg, *Lao-Tzu and Taoism* (Stanford: Stanford University Press, 1969), remains a reliable study of the *Lao-tzu.*

Lao Tzu: *Tao Te Ching**

(I)

The way can be spoken of,
But it will not be the constant way;
The name can be named,
But it will not be the constant name.
The nameless was the beginning of the myriad creatures;
The named was the mother of the myriad creatures.
Hence constantly rid yourself of desires in order to observe its subtlety;
But constantly allow yourself to have desires in order to observe what it is after.
These two have the same origin but differ in name.
    They are both called dark,
    Darkness upon darkness
    The gateway to all that is subtle.

(II)

The whole world knows the beautiful as the beautiful, and this is only the ugly; it knows the good as the good and this is, indeed, the bad.

*Reprinted with permission from D. C. Lau, *Tao Te Ching,* Part Two, the Ma Wang Tui *Lao Tzu* (Hong Kong: Chinese University Press, 1982).

Something and Nothing producing each other;
The difficult and the easy complementing each other;
The long and the short off-setting each other;
The high and the low filling out each other;
Note and sound harmonizing with each other;
Before and after following each other—

These are in accordance with what is constant.

Hence the sage dwells in the deed that consists in taking no action and practises the teaching that uses no words.

The myriad creatures it makes without causing them to begin,
It benefits them without exacting any gratitude for this;
It accomplishes its task without claiming any merit for this.
It is because it lays no claim to merit
That its merit never deserts it.

(III)

Not to honour men of excellence will keep the people from contention; not to value goods that are hard to come by will keep the people from theft; not to display what is desirable will keep the people from being unsettled.

Hence in his rule, the sage empties their minds but fills their bellies, weakens their purpose but strengthens their bones. He constantly keeps the people innocent of knowledge and free from desire, and causes the clever not to dare.

He simply takes no action and everything is in order.

(IV)

The way is empty, yet when used there is something that does not make it full.
Deep, it is like the ancestor of the myriad creatures.
Blunt the sharpness;
Untangle the knots;
Soften the glare;
Follow along old wheel tracks.
Darkly visible, it only seems as if it were there.
I know not whose son it is.
It images the forefather of God.

(V)

Heaven and earth are ruthless; they treat the myriad creatures as straw dogs. The sage is ruthless; he treates the people as straw dogs.

Is not the space between heaven and earth like a bellows?

It is empty without being exhausted;
The more it works the more comes out.
To hear much will lead only to a dead end.
Better to hold fast to what is within.

(VI)

The spirit of the valley never dies;
This is called the dark female.
The entry into the dark female
Is called the root of heaven and earth.
Tenuous, it seems as if it were there,
Yet use will never exhaust it.

(XI)

Thirty spokes
Share one hub.

Make the nothing therein appropriate, and you will have the use of the cart. Knead clay in order to make a vessel. Make the nothing therein appropriate, and you will have the use of the clay vessel. Cut out doors and windows in order to make a room. Make the nothing therein appropriate, and you will have the use of the room.

Thus we gain by making it Something, but we have the use by making it Nothing.

(XVI)

I attain the utmost emptiness;
I keep to extreme stillness.
The myriad creatures all rise together
And I watch thereby their return.
The teeming creatures
All return to their separate roots.
Returning to one's roots is known as stillness.
Stillness is what is called returning to one's destiny.
Returning to one's destiny is normal.
Knowledge of the normal is discernment.

Not to know the normal is to be without basis.
To innovate without basis bodes ill.
To know the normal is to be tolerant.
Tolerance leads to impartiality,
Impartiality to kingliness,
Kingliness to heaven,
Heaven to the way,
The way to perpetuity,
And to the end of one's days one will meet with no danger.

(XVII)

The best of all rulers is but a shadowy presence to his subjects.
Next comes the ruler they love and praise;

Next comes one they fear;
Last comes one they treat with impertinence.
Only when there is not enough faith is there a lack of faith.
Hesitant, he does not utter words lightly.
When his task is accomplished and his work done
The people all say, "It happened to us naturally."

(XVIII)

Thus when the great way falls into disuse
There are benevolence and rectitude;
When cleverness emerges
There is great hypocrisy;
When the six relations are at variance
There are the filial;
When the state is benighted
There are true subjects.

(XXV)

There is a thing confusedly formed,
Born before heaven and earth.
Silent and void
It stands alone and does not change,
Goes round and does not weary.
It is capable of being the mother of heaven and earth.
As yet I do not know its name.
I style it "the way."
I give it the makeshift name of "great."
Being great, it is described as receding,
Receding, it is described as far away,
Being far away, it is described as turning back.
The way is great; heaven is great; earth is great, and the king is great.
Within the realm there are four greats and the king counts as one.
Man models himself on earth,
Earth on heaven,
Heaven on the way,
And the way on that which is naturally so.

(XXVIII)

Know the male
But keep to the role of the female
And be a ravine to the empire.
If you are a ravine to the empire,
The constant virtue will not desert you.
When the constant virtue does not desert you,
You will again return to being a babe.

Know the white
But keep to the role of the sullied.
And be a valley to the empire.
If you are a valley to the empire,
The constant virtue will be sufficient.
When the constant virtue is sufficient,
You will again return to being the uncarved block.
Know the white
But keep to the role of the black
And be a model to the empire.
If you are a model to the empire,
The constant virtue will not deviate.
When the constant virtue does not deviate,
You will again return to the infinite.

When the uncarved block shatters it becomes vessels. When the sage is employed he becomes the chief of the officials.

Now the greatest cutting
Never severs.

(XLIII)

The most submissive thing in the world can ride roughshod over the most unyielding in the world—that which is without substance entering that which has no gaps.

That is why I know the benefit of resorting to no action. The teaching that uses no words, the benefit of resorting to no action, these are beyond the understanding of all but a very few in the world.

(XLVI)

When the way prevails in the empire, fleet-footed horses are relegated to providing manure for the fields; when the way does not prevail in the empire, war-horses breed on the border.

There is no crime greater than being desirable;
There is no disaster greater than not being content;
There is no misfortune more painful than being covetous:

Hence in knowing the sufficiency of being content, one will constantly have sufficient.

(XLVII)

By not setting foot outside the door
One knows the whole world;
By not looking out of the window
One knows the way of heaven.
The further one goes
The less one knows.
Hence the sage knows without having to stir,

Identifies without having to see,
Accomplishes without having to do it.

(XLVIII)

One who pursues learning gains every day; one who gets to hear about the way loses every day. One loses every day until one resorts to no action. One resorts to no action nor has one any ulterior motive for action. If you wished to gain the empire your success would constantly be through not being meddlesome. By the time you meddle, you are not equal to the task of gaining the empire.

(LX)

Governing a large state is like boiling a small fish.
When the empire is ruled in accordance with the way, the spirits are not potent. Or, rather, it is not that they are not potent, but that in their potency they do not harm men. It is not only they who, in their potency, do not harm men, the sage, too, does not harm them. Now as neither does any harm, each attributes the merit to the other.

(LXXVIII)

In the world there is nothing more submissive and weak than water.
Yet for attacking that which is unyielding and strong nothing can take precedence over it. This is because there is nothing that can take its place.
    The weak overcomes the unbending,
And the submissive overcomes the strong,
This every one in the world knows yet no one can put it into practice.
Hence in the words of the sage,
    One who takes on himself the abuse hurled against the state
    Is called a ruler worthy of offering sacrifices to the gods of earth and millet;
    One who takes on himself the calamities of the state
    Is called a king worthy of dominion over the entire empire.
Straightforward words seem paradoxical.

Chuang-tzŭ: Chapter 2:

THE SORTING WHICH EVENS THINGS OUT*†

Tzŭ-ch'i of Nan-kuo reclined elbow on armrest, looked up at the sky and exhaled, in a trance as though he had lost the counterpart of himself. Yen-ch'eng Tzŭ-yu stood in waiting before him.

---

*Reprinted with permission from A. C. Graham, *Chuang-tzŭ: The Seven Inner Chapters and Other Writings from the Book "Chuang-tzŭ"* (London: George Allen & Unwin, 1981).

†[*Translator's footnote*] The last word in the title *Ch'i wu lun* is sometimes understood as "discourse" ("The discourse on evening things out"), sometimes in its more basic sense of "sort out (in coherent discourse)."

"What is this?" he said. "Can the frame really be made to be like withered wood, the heart like dead ashes? The reclining man here now is not the reclining man of yesterday."

"You do well to ask that, Tzŭ-yu! This time I had lost my own self, did you know it? You hear the pipes of men, don't you, but not yet the pipes of earth, the pipes of earth but not yet the pipes of Heaven?"

"I venture to ask the secret of it."

"That hugest of clumps of soil[1] blows out breath, by name the 'wind.' Better if it were never to start up, for whenever it does ten thousand hollow places burst out howling, and don't tell me you have never heard how the hubbub swells! The recesses in mountain forests, the hollows that pit great trees a hundred spans round, are like nostrils, like mouths, like ears, like sockets, like bowls, like mortars, like pools, like puddles. Hooting, hissing, sniffing, sucking, mumbling, moaning, whistling, wailing, the winds ahead sing out AAAH!, the winds behind answer EEEH!, breezes strike up a tiny chorus, the whirlwind a mighty chorus. When the gale has passed, all the hollows empty, and don't tell me you have never seen how the quivering slows and settles!"

"The pipes of earth, these are the various hollows; the pipes of men, these are rows of tubes. Let me ask about the pipes of Heaven."[2]

"Who is it that puffs out the myriads which are never the same, who in their self-ending is sealing them up, in their self-choosing is impelling the force into them?

"Heaven turns circles, yes!
Earth sits firm, yes!
Sun and moon vie for a place, yes!
Whose is the bow that shoots them?
Whose is the net that holds them?
Who is it sits with nothing to do and gives them the push that sends them?

[Translator's footnote continued.]
Comparison with the three-word titles of the other *Inner chapters* favours the latter alternative. *Lun*, "sorting out," is the one kind of thinking always mentioned with approval in *Chuang-tzŭ*. Outside Taoism it suggests grading in superior and inferior categories, but Chuang-tzŭ detaches it from valuation, turns it into "the sorting which evens things out."

The theme of the chapter is the defence of a synthesising vision against Confucians, Mohists and Sophists, who analyse, distinguish alternatives and debate which is right or wrong. It contains the most philosophically acute passages in the *Inner chapters*, obscure, fragmented, but pervaded by the sensation, rare in ancient literatures, of a man jotting the living thought at the moment of its inception. It is a pity that the Syncretist who assembled the chapter seem to have been out of sympathy with these intellectual subtleties designed to discredit the intellect, for he has relegated a number of closely related passages to the *Mixed chapters*.

[1]"That hugest of clumps of soil," a phrase peculiar to the *Inner chapters*, seems to conjure up an image of the universe so far in the distance that it is no bigger than a clod you could hold in your hand.

[2]Chuang-tzŭ's parable of the wind compares the conflicting utterances of philosophers to the different notes blown by the same breath in the long and short tubes of the pan-pipes, and the noises made by the wind in hollows of different shapes. It is natural for differently constituted persons to think differently; don't try to decide between their opinions, listen to Heaven who breathes through them.

"Shall we suppose, yes, that something triggers them off, then seals them away, and they have no choice?

Or suppose, yes, that wheeling in their circuits they cannot stop themselves?

Do the clouds make the rain?
Or the rain the clouds?
Whose bounty bestows them?
Who is it sits with nothing to do as in ecstasy he urges them?

"The winds rise in the north,
Blow west, blow east,
And now again whirl high above.
Who breathes them out, who breathes them in?
Who is it sits with nothing to do and sweeps between and over them?"

"Great wit is effortless,
Petty wit picks holes.
Great speech is flavourless,
Petty speech strings words.

"While it sleeps, the paths of souls cross:
When it wakes, the body opens.
Whatever we sense entangles it:
Each day we use that heart of ours for strife."

The calm ones, the deep ones, the subtle ones.

"Petty fears intimidate,
The supreme fear calms.
It shoots like the trigger releasing the string on the notch,"

referring to its manipulation of "That's it, that's not."

"It ties us down as though by oath, by treaty,"

referring to its commitment to the winning alternative.

"Its decline is like autumn and winter,"

speaking of its daily deterioration. As it sinks, that which is the source of its deeds cannot be made to renew them.

"It clogs as though it were being sealed up,"

speaking of its drying up in old age. As the heart nears death, nothing can make it revert to the Yang.

Pleasure in things and anger against them, sadness and joy, forethought and regret, change and immobility, idle influences that initiate our gestures—music coming out of emptiness, vapour condensing into mushrooms—alternate before it day and night and no one knows from what soil they spring. Enough! The source from which it has these morning and evening, is it not that from which it was born?[3]

"Without an Other there is no Self, without Self no choosing one thing rather than another."

This is somewhere near it, but we do not know in whose service they are being employed. It seems that there is something genuinely in command, and that the only trouble is we cannot find a sign of it. That as "Way" it can be walked is true enough, but we do not see its shape; it has identity but no shape. Of the hundred joints, nine openings, six viscera all present and complete, which should I recognise as more kin to me than another? Are you people pleased with them all? Rather, you have a favourite organ among them. On your assumption, does it have the rest of them as its vassals and concubines? Are its vassals and concubines inadequate to rule each other? Isn't it rather that they take turns as each other's lord and vassals? Or rather than that, they have a genuine lord present in them. If we seek without success to grasp what its identity might be, that never either adds to nor detracts from its genuineness.[4]

Once we have received the completed body we are aware of it all the time we await extinction. Is it not sad how we and other things go on stroking or jostling each other, in a race ahead like a gallop which nothing can stop? How can we fail to regret that we labour all our lives without seeing success, wear ourselves out with toil in ignorance of where we shall end? What use is it for man to say that he will not die, since when the body dissolves the heart dissolves with it? How can we not call this our supreme regret? Is man's life really as stupid as this? Or is it that I am the only stupid one, and there are others not so stupid? But if you go by the completed heart and take it as your authority, who is without such an authority? Why should it be only the man who knows how things alternate and whose heart approves its own judgments who has such an authority? The fool has one just as he has. For there to be "That's it, that's not" before they are formed in the heart would be to "go to Yüeh today and have arrived yesterday." This would be crediting with existence what has no existence; and if you do that even the daemonic Yü could not understand you, and how can you expect to be understood by me?

---

[3]Chuang-tzŭ might be either the author or the annotator of these verses about the heart, the organ of thought. The "supreme fear" which calms would be the fear of death, reconciliation with which is Chuang-tzŭ's central concern.

[4]Chuang-tzŭ starts from a quotation or a provisional formulation of his own. His theme is again the heart, the organ of thought. Should it be allowed to take charge of our lives? Isn't it merely one of many organs each with its own functions within an order which comes from beyond us, from the Way?

Saying is not blowing breath, saying says something; the only trouble is that what it says is never fixed. Do we really say something? Or have we never said anything? If you think it different from the twitter of fledgelings, is there proof of the distinction? Or isn't there any proof? By what is the Way hidden, that there should be a genuine or a false? By what is saying darkened, that sometimes "That's it" and sometimes "That's not"? Wherever we walk how can the Way be absent? Whatever the standpoint how can saying be unallowable? The Way is hidden by formation of the lesser, saying is darkened by its foliage and flowers. And so we have the "That's it, that's not" of Confucians and Mohists, by which what is *it* for one of them for the other is not, what is *not* for one of them for the other is. If you wish to affirm what they deny and deny what they affirm, the best means is Illumination.

No thing is not "other," no thing is not "it." If you treat yourself too as "other" they do not appear, if you know of yourself you know of them. Hence it is said:

> "'Other' comes out from 'it,' 'it' likewise goes by 'other,'

the opinion that "it" and "other" are born simultaneously. However,

> "Simultaneously with being alive one dies,"

and simultaneously with dying one is alive, simultaneously with being allowable something becomes unallowable and simultaneously with being unallowable it becomes allowable. If going by circumstance that's it then going by circumstance that's not, if going by circumstance that's not then going by circumstance that's it. This is why the sage does not take this course, but opens things up to the light of Heaven; his too is a "That's it" which goes by circumstance.[5]

What is It is also Other, what is Other is also It. There they say "That's it, that's not" from one point of view, here we say "That's it, that's not" from another point of view. Are there really It and Other? Or really no It and Other? Where neither It nor Other finds its opposite is called the axis of the Way. When once the axis is found at the centre of the circle there is no limit to responding with either, on the one hand no limit to what is *it*, on the other no

---

[5]In disputation if an object fits the name "ox" one affirms with the demonstrative word *shih*, "(That) is it"; if it is something other than an ox one denies with a *fei*, "(That) is not." Here Chuang-tzŭ tries to discredit disputation by the objection that at any moment of change both alternatives will be admissible. He appeals to a paradox of Hui Shih, "The sun is simultaneously at noon and declining, a thing is simultaneously alive and dead," and generalises to the conclusion that any statement will remain inadmissible at the moment when it has just become admissible. It was also recognised in current disputation (as we find it in the Mohist *Canons*) that one can say both "Y is long" (in relation to X) and "Y is short" (in relation to Z), and that even with words such as "black" and "white" which are not comparative one has to decide whether to "go by" (*yin*) the black parts or the white when deeming someone a "black man." Chuang -tzŭ sees it as the lesson of disputation that one is entitled to affirm or deny anything of anything. He thinks of Confucians and Mohists who stick rigidly to their affirmations and denials as lighting up little areas of life and leaving the rest in darkness; the Illumination of the sage is a vision which brings everything to light.

limit to what is not. Therefore I say: "The best means is Illumination." Rather than use the meaning to show that

"The meaning is not the meaning,"

use what is *not* the meaning. Rather than use a horse to show that

"A horse is not a horse"

use what is *not* a horse. Heaven and earth are the one meaning, the myriad things are the one horse.[6]

Allowable?—allowable. Unallowable?—unallowable. The Way comes about as we walk it; as for a thing, call it something and that's so. Why so? By being so. Why not so? By not being so. It is inherent in a thing that from somewhere that's so of it, from somewhere that's allowable of it; of no thing is it not so, of no thing is it unallowable. Therefore when a "That's it" which deems picks out a stalk from a pillar, a hag from beautiful Hsi Shih, things however peculiar or incongruous, the Way interchanges them and deems them one. Their dividing is formation, their formation is dissolution; all things whether forming or dissolving in reverting interchange and are deemed to be one. Only the man who sees right through knows how to interchange and deem them one; the "That's it" which deems he does not use, but finds for them lodging-places in the usual. The "usual" is the usable, the "usable" is the interchangeable, to see as "interchangeable" is to grasp; and once you grasp them you are almost there. The "That's it" which goes by circumstance comes to an end; and when it is at an end, that of which you do not know what is so of it you call the "Way."

To wear out the daemonic-and-illumined in you deeming them to be one without knowing that they are the same I call "Three every morning." What do I mean by "Three every morning?" A monkey keeper handing out nuts said, "Three every morning and four every evening." The monkeys were all in a rage. "All right then," he said, "four every morning and three every evening." The monkeys were all delighted. Without anything being missed out either in name or in substance, their pleasure and anger were put to use; his too was the "That's it" which goes by circumstance. This is why the sage smooths things out with his "That's it, that's not," and stays at the point of rest on the potter's wheel of Heaven. It is this that is called "Letting both alternatives proceed."

The men of old, their knowledge had arrived at something: at what had it arrived? There were some who thought there had not yet begun to be

[6]There are extant essays by the Sophist Kung-sun Lung arguing that "A white horse is not a horse" and "When no thing is not the meaning the meaning is not the meaning." Chuang-tzŭ thinks he was wasting his time; since all disputation starts from arbitrary acts of naming, he had only to pick something else as the meaning of the word, name something else "horse," and then for him what the rest of us call a horse would not be a horse.

things—the utmost, the exhaustive, there is no more to add. The next thought there were things but there had not yet begun to be borders. The next thought there were borders to them but there had not yet begun to be "That's it, that's not." The lighting up of "That's it, that's not" is the reason why the Way is flawed. The reason why the Way is flawed is the reason why love becomes complete. Is anything really complete or flawed? Or is nothing really complete or flawed? To recognise as complete or flawed is to have as model the Chao when they play the zither; to recognise as neither complete nor flawed is to have as model the Chao when they don't play the zither. Chao Wen strumming on the zither, Music-master K'uang propped on his stick, Hui Shih leaning on the sterculia, had the three men's knowledge much farther to go? They were all men in whom it reached a culmination, and therefore was carried on to too late a time. It was only in being preferred by them that what they knew about differed from an Other; because they preferred it they wished to illumine it, but they illumined it without the Other being illumined, and so the end of it all was the darkness of chop logic: and his own son too ended with only Chao Wen's zither string, and to the end of his life his musicianship was never completed. May men like this be said to be complete? Then so am I. Or may they not be said to be complete? Then neither am I, nor is anything else.

Therefore the glitter of glib implausibilities is despised by the sage. The "That's it" which deems he does not use, but finds for things lodging-places in the usual. It is this that is meant by "using Illumination."[7]

> "Now suppose that I speak of something, and do not know whether it is of a kind with the 'it' in question or not of a kind. If what is of a kind and what is not are deemed of a kind with one another, there is no longer any difference from an 'other.'"

However, let's try to say it.

There is "beginning," there is "not yet having begun having a beginning."

—There is "there not yet having begun to be that 'not yet having begun having a beginning.'"

There is "something," there is "nothing."

—There is "not yet having begun being without something."

—There is "there not yet having begun to be that 'not yet having begun being without something.'"

All of a sudden "*there is* nothing," and we do not yet know of something and nothing really which there is and which there is not. Now for my part I have already referred to something, but do not yet know whether my reference really referred to something or really did not refer to anything.

---

[7]Systems of knowledge are partial and temporary like styles on the zither, which in forming sacrifice some of the potentialities of music, and by their very excellence make schools fossilise in decline. Take as model Chao Wen *not* playing the zither, not yet committed, with all his potentialities intact.

> "Nothing in the world is bigger than the tip of an autumn hair, and Mount T'ai is small; no one lives longer than a doomed child, and P'eng-tsu died young; heaven and earth were born together with me, and the myriad things and I are one."

Now that we are one, can I still say something? Already having called us one, did I succeed in not saying something? One and the saying makes two, two and one make three. Proceeding from here even an expert calculator cannot get to the end of it, much less a plain man. Therefore if we take the step from nothing to something we arrive at three, and how much worse if we take the step from something to something! Take no step at all, and the "That's it" which goes by circumstance will come to an end.

The Way has never had borders, saying has never had norms. It is by a "That's it" which deems that a boundary is marked. Let me say something about the marking of boundaries. You can locate as there and enclose by a line, sort out and assess, divide up and discriminate between alternatives, compete over and fight over: these I call our Eight Powers. What is outside the cosmos the sage locates as there but does not sort out. What is within the cosmos the sage sorts out but does not assess. The records of the former kings in the successive reigns in the Annals the sage assesses, but he does not argue over alternatives.

To "divide," then, is to leave something undivided: to "discriminate between alternatives" is to leave something which is neither alternative. "What?" you ask. The sage keeps it in his breast, common men argue over alternatives to show it to each other. Hence I say: "To 'discriminate between alternatives' is to fail to see something."

The greatest Way is not cited as an authority,
The greatest discrimination is unspoken,
The greatest goodwill is cruel,
The greatest honesty does not make itself awkward,
The greatest courage does not spoil for a fight.

When the Way is lit it does not guide,
When speech discriminates it fails to get there,
Goodwill too constant is at someone's expense,
Honesty too clean is not to be trusted,
Courage that spoils for a fight is immature.

These five in having their corners rounded off come close to pointing the direction. Hence to know how to stay within the sphere of our ignorance is to attain the highest. Who knows an unspoken discrimination, an untold Way? It is this, if any is able to know it, which is called the Treasury of Heaven. Pour into it and it does not fill, bale out from it and it is not drained, and you do not know from what source it comes. It is this that is called our Benetnash Star.[8]

Therefore formerly Yao asked Shun

"I wish to smite Tsung, K'uai and Hsü-ao. Why is it that I am not at ease on the south-facing throne?"

"Why be uneasy," said Shun, "if these three still survive among the weeds? Formerly ten suns rose side by side and the myriad things were all illumined, and how much more by a man in whom the Power is brighter than the sun!"

Gaptooth put a question to Wang Ni.

"Would you *know* something of which all things agreed 'That's it'?"

"How would I know that?"

"Would you know what you did not know?"

"How would I know that?"

"Then does no thing know anything?"

"How would I know that? However, let me try to say it—"How do I know that what I call knowing is not ignorance? How do I know that what I call ignorance is not knowing?"[9]

"Moreover, let me try a question on you. When a human sleeps in the damp his waist hurts and he gets stiff in joints; is that so of the loach? When he sits in a tree he shivers and shakes; it that so of the ape? Which of these three knows the right place to live? Humans eat the flesh of hay-fed and grain-fed beasts, deer eat the grass, centipedes relish snakes, owls and crows crave mice; which of the four has a proper sense of taste? Gibbons are sought by baboons as mates, elaphures like the company of deer, loaches play with fish. Mao-ch'iang and Lady Li were beautiful in the eyes of men; but when the fish saw them they plunged deep, when the birds saw them they flew high, when the deer saw them they broke into a run. Which of these four knows what is truly beautiful in the world? In my judgment the principles of Goodwill and Duty, the paths of 'That's it, that's not,' are inextricably confused; how could I know how to discriminate between them?"

"If you do not know benefit from harm, would you deny that the utmost man knows benefit from harm?"

"The utmost man is daemonic. When the wide woodlands blaze they cannot sear him, when the Yellow River and the Han freeze they cannot chill him, when swift thunderbolts smash the mountains and whirlwinds shake the

---

[8]The standard text has the obscure *Pao kuang* ("Shaded light"(?)), but there is a plausible variant, *Yao-kuang*, "Benetnash," the star at the far end of the handle of the Dipper. The Dipper by turning its handle up, down, east and west, marks the progress of the four seasons. As a metaphor for the prime mover of things Chuang-tzŭ chooses not the stationary North Star but the circumpolar star which initiates the cyclic motions.

[9]In the opening exchange Gaptooth is pressing for an admission that there must be something which is knowable: (1) Would you know something which everyone agrees on? Wang Ni denies it, perhaps because there could be no independent viewpoint from which to judge a universally shared opinion. (2) Then at least one knows what one does not know. But that is a contradiction, or so Chuang-tzŭ thinks. . . . (3) Then one knows that no one knows anything—another contradiction.

seas they cannot startle him. A man like that yokes the clouds to his chariot, rides the sun and moon and roams beyond the four seas; death and life alter nothing in himself, still less the principles of benefit and harm!"

Ch'ü-ch'üeh-tzŭ asked Ch'ang-wu-tzŭ

"I heard this from the Master: 'The sage does not work for any goal, does not lean towards benefit or shun harm, does not delight in seeking, does not fix a route by a Way, in saying nothing says something and in saying something says nothing, and roams beyond the dust and grime.' The Master thought of the saying as a flight of fancy, but to me it seemed the walking of the most esoteric Way. How does it seem to you?"

"This is a saying which would have puzzled the Yellow Emperor, and what would old Confucius know about it? Moreover you for your part are counting your winnings much too soon; at the sight of the egg you expect the cock-crow, at the sight of the bow you expect a roasted owl. Suppose I put it to you in abandoned words, and you listen with the same abandon:

> 'Go side by side with the sun and moon,
> Do the rounds of Space and Time.
> Act out their neat conjunctions,
> Stay aloof from their convulsions.
> Dependents each on each, let us honour one another.
> Common people fuss and fret,
> The sage is a dullard and a sluggard.
> Be aligned along a myriad years, in oneness, wholeness, simplicity.
> All the myriad things are as they are,
> And as what they are make up totality.'

How do I know that to take pleasure in life is not a delusion? How do I know that we who hate death are not exiles since childhood who have forgotten the way home? Lady Li was the daughter of a frontier guard at Ai. When the kingdom of Chin first took her the tears stained her dress; only when she came to the palace and shared the King's square couch and ate the flesh of hay-fed and grain-fed beasts did she begin to regret her tears. How do I know that the dead do not regret that ever they had an urge to life? Who banquets in a dream at dawn wails and weeps, who wails and weeps in a dream at dawn goes out to hunt. While we dream we do not know that we are dreaming, and in the middle of a dream interpret a dream within it; not until we wake do we know that we were dreaming. Only at the ultimate awakening shall we know that this is the ultimate dream. Yet fools think they are awake, so confident that they know what they are, princes, herdsmen, incorrigible! You and Confucius are both dreams, and I who call you a dream am also a dream. This saying of his, the name for it is 'a flight into the extraordinary'; if it happens once in ten thousand ages that a great sage knows its explanation it will have happened as though between morning and evening."

You and I have been made to argue over alternatives, if it is you not I that wins, is it really you who are on to it, I who am not? If it is I not you that wins, is it really I who am on to it, you who are not? Is one of us on to it and the other of us not? Or are both of us on to it and both of us not? If you and I are unable to know where we stand, others will surely be in the dark because of us. Whom shall I call in to decide it? If I get someone of your party to decide it, being already of your party how can he decide it? If I get someone of my party to decide it, being already of my party how can he decide it? If I get someone of a party different from either of us to decide it, being already of a party different from either of us how can he decide it? If I get someone of the same party as both of us to decide it, being already of the same party as both of us how can he decide it? Consequently you and I and he are all unable to know where we stand, and shall we find someone else to depend on?

It makes no different whether the voices in their transformations have each other to depend on or not. Smooth them out on the whetstone of Heaven, use them to go by and let the stream find its own channels; this is the way to live out your years. Forget the years, forget duty, be shaken into motion by the limitless, and so find things their lodging-places in the limitless.

What is meant by "Smooth them out on the whetstone of Heaven"? Treat as "it" even what is not, treat as "so" even what is not. If the "it" is really it, there is no longer a difference for disputation from what is not it; if the "so" is really so, there is no longer a difference for disputation from what is not so.

The penumbra asked the shadow:

"Just then you were walking, now you stop; just then you were sitting, now you stand. Why don't you make up your mind to do one thing or the other?"

"Is it that there is something on which I depend to be so? And does what I depend on too depend on something else to be so? Would it be that I depend on snake's scales, cicada's wings? How would I recognise why it is so, how would I recognise why it is not so?"

Last night Chuang Chou dreamed he was a butterfly, spirits soaring he was a butterfly (is it that in showing what he was he suited his own fancy?), and did not know about Chou. When all of a sudden he awoke, he was Chou with all his wits about him. He does not know whether he is Chou who dreams he is a butterfly or a butterfly who dreams he is Chou. Between Chou and the butterfly there was necessarily a dividing; just this is what is meant by the transformations of things.

CHAPTER 18

UTILITARIAN AND LEGALIST CHALLENGES

The main challenges to both Confucianism and Taosim in pre-Buddhist China came from the Utilitarians and the Legalists. Mo-tzu, who lived sometime in the fifth century, B.C., nearly a century after Confucius, is the acknowledged founder of the Mohist school. This school's emphasis on usefulness measured by reason eventually led to the development of logic and scientific canons of evidence. Extremely critical of the Confucianists of his day for their social passivism and ritual extravagances, Mo-tzu nevertheless praised the insights of Confucius and was strongly committed to their mutual goal of bringing peace and harmony to the world and to their shared vision of an organic hierarchical social order in which only the top leadership could direct and guide the process of human and social self-transformation.

But Mo-tzu rejects the Confucian and Taoist visions of a preestablished order of things (*tao*) that simply needs to be followed to find perfection. The Mohist vision saw an original chaos at the foundation of existence, a chaos on which order must be imposed by vigilant and unrelenting effort. Although this order required the cooperative effort of Heaven, the spirits, and human beings, such cooperation was not given in the nature of things but had to be achieved through intelligent effort. Furthermore, this order was very fragile, constantly threatened by the tendency to disintegration and the chaos inherent in things.

Before any government existed there was constant strife among the people, according to Mo-tzu, for there was no shared vision of life and each individual pursued his or her own self-interest. The way from this chaotic strife to a peaceful and prosperous society was to show that one's self-interest depended on the interests of the entire society, and only through efforts to improve society could one improve oneself. This is the basis of Mo-tzu's idea of universal love, for only through loving all humanity can the motivation of self-love lead to fulfillment and peace. The utilitarian aspect of his thought regards those actions that make useful contributions to the well-being of society as good, and those that do not as useless or bad.

The chapter from the *Mo-tzu*, entitled "Universal Love," reprinted here, presents the core of Mo-tzu's utilitarianism. It is translated by Burton Watson in *The Basic Writings of Mo Tzu, Hsun Tzu, and Han Fei Tzu* (New York: Columbia University Press, 1967), which contains a short but helpful introduction to Mo-tzu's thought and other important selections from the *Mo-tzu.* Chapter 4, "Mo-tzu's Challenge," in Benjamin Schwartz, *The World of Thought in Ancient China,* (Cambridge, Mass.: Harvard University Press, 1985), is an excellent study of Mo-tzu's philosophy. Angus Graham, *Later Mohist Logic, Ethics, and Science* (Hong Kong: Chinese University Press, 1978), is the best book-length study of Mohism available in English.

Legalist thought, which probably predates Confucius, challenges the Confucian conviction that personal virtue and the sincere practice of traditional ceremonial forms of action (*li*) can preserve the perfection of society. Instead, it proposes strengthening the power of central authority and using this authority to establish necessary laws and secure enforcement through a system of punishment. Han Fei-tzu (ca. 280–233 B.C.), the great synthesizer and theoretician of the Legalist school, argued that to achieve specific social goals it was necessary to combine a system of laws and punishments for controlling society with effective bureaucratic organization.

The selection from Han Fei-tzu entitled "The Way of the Ruler" presents the view that political authority results ultimately from the office of the ruler; kingship embodies the way of ultimate authority from which all power flows. The selection "Wielding Power" discusses how the power of the ruler is to be used in achieving societal goals. Both selections are from Burton Watson, *Basic Writings of Mo Tzu, Hsun Tzu,and Han Fei Tzu.* Benjamin Schwartz, *The World of Thought in Ancient China* provides an excellent historical overview of Legalist thought, with a focus on Han Fei-tzu. A. C. Graham, *Disputers of the Tao* (La Salle, Illinois: Open Court, 1989), identifies the main philosophical issues and arguments of Legalism.

I
Mo-tzu: Universal Love*

Mo Tzu said: It is the business of the benevolent man to try to promote what is beneficial to the world and to eliminate what is harmful. Now at the present time, what brings the greatest harm to the world? Great states attacking small ones, great families overthrowing small ones, the strong oppressing the weak, the many harrying the few, the cunning deceiving the stupid, the eminent lording it over the humble—these are harmful to the world. So too are rulers

*Reprinted with permission from Burton Watson, *Basic Writings of Mo-tzu, Hsün Tzu, and Han Fei Tzu* (New York: Columbia University Press, 1967).

who are not generous, ministers who are not loyal, fathers who are without kindness, and sons who are unfilial, as well as those men who, with weapons, knives, poison, fire, and water, seek to injure and undo each other.

When we inquire into the cause of these various harms, what do we find has produced them? Do they come about from loving others and trying to benefit them? Surely not! They come rather from hating others and trying to injure them. And when we set out to classify and describe those men who hate and injure others, shall we say that their actions are motivated by universality or partiality? Surely we must answer, by partiality, and it is this partiality in their dealings with one another that gives rise to all the great harms in the world. Therefore we know that partiality is wrong.

Mo Tzu said: Whoever criticizes others must have some alternative to offer them. To criticize and yet offer no alternative is like trying to stop flood with flood or put out fire with fire. It will surely have no effect. Therefore Mo Tzu said: Partiality should be replaced by universality.

But how can partiality be replaced by universality? If men were to regard the states of others as they regard their own, then who would raise up his state to attack the state of another? It would be like attacking his own. If men were to regard the cities of others as they regard their own, then who would raise up his city to attack the city of another? It would be like attacking his own. If men were to regard the families of others as they regard their own, then who would raise up his family to overthrow that of another? It would be like overthrowing his own. Now when states and cities do not attack and make war on each other and families and individuals do not overthrow or injure one another, is this a harm or a benefit to the world? Surely it is a benefit.

When we inquire into the cause of such benefits, what do we find has produced them? Do they come about from hating others and trying to injure them? Surely not! They come rather from loving others and trying to benefit them. And when we set out to classify and describe those men who love and benefit others, shall we say that their actions are motivated by partiality or by universality? Surely we must answer, by universality, and it is this universality in their dealings with one another that gives rise to all the great benefits in the world. Therefore Mo Tzu has said that universality is right.

I have said previously that it is the business of the benevolent man to try to promote what is beneficial to the world and to eliminate what is harmful. Now I have demonstrated that universality is the source of all the great benefits in the world and partiality is the source of all the great harm. It is for this reason that Mo Tzu has said that partiality is wrong and universality is right.

Now if we seek to benefit the world by taking universality as our standard, those with sharp ears and clear eyes will see and hear for others, those with sturdy limbs will work for others, and those with a knowledge of the Way will endeavor to teach others. Those who are old and without wives or children will find means of support and be able to live out their days; the young and orphaned who have no parents will find someone to care for them and look after their needs. When all these benefits may be secured merely by taking universality as our standard, I cannot understand how the men of the world can hear about this doctrine of universality and still criticize it!

And yet the men of the world continue to criticize it, saying, "It may be a good thing, but how can it be put to use?"

Mo Tzu said: If it cannot be put to use, even I would criticize it. But how can there be a good thing that still cannot be put to use? Let us try considering both sides of the question. Suppose there are two men, one of them holding to partiality, the other to universality. The believer in partiality says, "How could I possibly regard my friend the same as myself, or my friend's father the same as my own?" Because he views his friend in this way, he will not feed him when he is hungry, clothe him when he is cold, nourish him when he is sick, or bury him when he dies. Such are the words of the partial man, and such his actions. But the words and actions of the universal-minded man are not like these. He will say, "I have heard that the truly superior man of the world regards his friend the same as himself, and his friend's father the same as his own. Only if he does this can he be considered a truly superior man." Because he views his friend in this way, he will feed him when he is hungry, clothe him when he is cold, nourish him when he is sick, and bury him when he dies. Such are the words and actions of the universal-minded man.

So the words of these two men disagree and their actions are diametrically opposed. Yet let us suppose that both of them are determined to carry out their words in action, so that word and deed agree like the two parts of a tally and nothing they say is not put into action. Then let us venture to inquire further. Suppose that here is a broad plain, a vast wilderness, and a man is buckling on his armor and donning his helmet to set out for the field of battle, where the fortunes of life and death are unknown; or he is setting out in his lord's name upon a distant mission to Pa or Yüeh, Ch'i or Ching, and his return is uncertain. Now let us ask, to whom would he entrust the support of his parents and the care of his wife and children? Would it be to the universal-minded man, or to the partial man? It seems to me that, on occasions like these, there are no fools in the world. Though one may disapprove of universality himself, he would surely think it best to entrust his family to the universal-minded man. Thus people condemn universality in words but adopt it in practice, and word and deed belie each other. I cannot understand how the men of the world can hear about this doctrine of universality and still criticize it!

And yet the men of the world continue to criticize, saying, "Such a principle may be all right as a basis in choosing among ordinary men, but it cannot be used in selecting a ruler."

Let us try considering both sides of the question. Suppose there are two rulers, one of them holding to universality, the other to partiality. The partial ruler says, "How could I possibly regard my countless subjects the same as I regard myself? That would be completely at variance with human nature! Man's life on earth is as brief as the passing of a team of horses glimpsed through a crack in the wall." Because he views his subjects in this way, he will not feed them when they are hungry, clothe them when they are cold, nourish them when they are sick, or bury them when they die. Such are the words of the partial ruler, and such his actions. But the words and actions of the universal-minded ruler are not like these. He will say, "I have heard that the truly enlightened ruler must think of his subjects first, and of himself last. Only then can he be considered a truly enlightened ruler." Because he views his subjects in this way, he will feed them when they are hungry, clothe them when they are cold, nourish them when they are sick, and bury them when they die. Such are the words and actions of the universal-minded ruler.

So the words of these two rulers disagree and their actions are diametrically opposed. Yet let us suppose that both of them speak in good faith and are determined to carry out their words in action, so that word and deed agree like the two parts of a tally and nothing they say is not put into action. Then let us venture to inquire further. Suppose this year there is plague and disease, many of the people are suffering from hardship and hunger, and the corpses of countless victims lie tumbled in the ditches. If the people could choose between these two types of ruler, which would they follow? It seems to me that, on occasions like this, there are no fools in the world. Though one may disapprove of universality himself, he would surely think it best to follow the universal-minded ruler. Thus people condemn universality in words but adopt it in practice, and word and deed belie each other. I cannot understand how the men of the world can hear about this doctrine of universality and still criticize it!

And yet the men of the world continue to criticize, saying, "This doctrine of universality is benevolent and righteous. And yet how can it be carried out? As we see it, one can no more put it into practice than one can pick up Mount T'ai and leap over a river with it! Thus universality is only something to be longed for, not something that can be put into practice."

Mo Tzu said: As for picking up Mount T'ai and leaping over rivers with it, no one from ancient times to the present, from the beginning of mankind to now, has ever succeeded in doing that! But universal love and mutual aid were actually practiced by four sage kings of antiquity. How do we know that they practiced these?

Mo Tzu said: I did not live at the same time as they did, nor have I in person heard their voices or seen their faces. Yet I know it because of what is written on the bamboo and silk that has been handed down to posterity, what is engraved on metal and stone, and what is inscribed on bowls and basins.

The "Great Oath" says: "King Wen was like the sun or moon, shedding his bright light in the four quarters and over the western land."[1] That is to say, the universal love of King Wen was so broad that it embraced the whole world, as the universal light of the sun and the moon shines upon the whole world without partiality. Such was the universality of King Wen, and the universality which Mo Tzu has been telling you about is patterned after that of King Wen.

---

[1]The "Great Oath," supposedly a speech by King Wu, the son of King Wen, was a section of the *Book of Documents.*

Not only the "Great Oath" but the "Oath of Yü"[2] also expresses this idea. Yü said: "All you teeming multitudes, listen to my words! It is not that I, the little child, would dare to act in a disorderly way. But this ruler of the Miao, with his unyielding ways, deserves Heaven's punishment. So I shall lead you, the lords of the various states, to conquer the ruler of the Miao." When Yü went to conquer the ruler of the Miao, it was not that he sought to increase his wealth or eminence, to win fortune or blessing, or to delight his ears and eyes. It was only that he sought to promote what was beneficial to the world and to eliminate what was harmful. Such was the universality of Yü, and the universality which Mo Tzu has been telling you about is patterned after that of Yü.

And not only the "Oath of Yü" but the "Speech of T'ang"[3] also expresses this idea. T'ang said: "I, the little child, Lü, dare to sacrifice a dark beast and make this announcement to the Heavenly Lord above, saying, 'Now Heaven has sent a great drought and it has fallen upon me, Lü. But I do not know what fault I have committed against high or low. If there is good, I dare not conceal it; if there is evil, I dare not pardon it. Judgment resides with the mind of God. If the myriad regions have any fault, may it rest upon my person; but if I have any fault, may it not extend to the myriad regions.'" This shows that, though T'ang was honored as the Son of Heaven and possessed all the riches of the world, he did not hesitate to offer himself as a sacrifice in his prayers and entreaties to the Lord on High and the spirits. Such was the universality of T'ang, and the universality which Mo Tzu has been telling you about is patterned after that of T'ang.

This idea is expressed not only in the "Speech of T'ang" but in the odes of Chou as well. In the odes of Chou it says:

> Broad, broad is the way of the king,
> Neither partial nor partisan.
> Fair, fair is the way of the king,
> Neither partisan nor partial.
>
> It is straight like an arrow,
> Smooth like a whetstone.
> The superior man treads it;
> The small man looks upon it.

So what I have been speaking about is no mere theory of action. In ancient times, when Kings Wen and Wu administered the government and assigned each person his just share, they rewarded the worthy and punished the wicked without showing any favoritism toward their own kin or brothers. Such was the universality of Kings Wen and Wu, and the universality which

---

[2]A section of the *Book of Documents*, now lost.
[3]A section of the *Book of Documents*, now lost.

Mo Tzu has been telling you about is patterned after that of Wen and Wu. I cannot understand how the men of the world can hear about this doctrine of universality and still criticize it!

And yet the men of the world continue to criticize, saying, "If one takes no thought for what is beneficial or harmful to one's parents, how can one be called filial?"

Mo Tzu said: Let us examine for a moment the way in which a filial son plans for the welfare of his parents. When a filial son plans for his parents, does he wish others to love and benefit them, or does he wish others to hate and injure them? It stands to reason that he wishes others to love and benefit his parents. Now if I am a filial son, how do I go about accomplishing this? Do I first make it a point to love and benefit other men's parents, so that they in return will love and benefit my parents? Or do I first make it a point to hate and injure other men's parents, so that they in return will love and benefit my parents? Obviously, I must first make it a point to love and benefit other men's parents, so that they in return will love and benefit my parents. So if all of us are to be filial sons, can we set about it any other way than by first making a point of loving and benefiting other men's parents? And are we to suppose that the filial sons of the world are all too stupid to be capable of doing what is right?

Let us examine further. Among the books of the former kings, in the "Greater Odes" of the *Book of Odes*, it says:

> There are no words that are not answered,
> No kindness that is not requited.
> Throw me a peach,
> I'll requite you a plum.

The meaning is that one who loves will be loved by others, and one who hates will be hated by others. So I cannot understand how the men of the world can hear about this doctrine of universality and still criticize it!

Do they believe that it is too difficult to carry out? Yet there are much more difficult things that have been carried out. In the past King Ling of the state of Ching loved slender waists. During his reign, the people of Ching ate no more than one meal a day, until they were too weak to stand up without a cane, or to walk without leaning against the wall. Now reducing one's diet is a difficult thing to do, and yet people did it because it pleased King Ling. So within the space of a single generation the ways of the people can be changed, for they will strive to ingratiate themselves with their superiors.

Again in the past King Lou-chien of Yüeh admired bravery and for three years trained his soldiers and subjects to be brave. But he was not sure whether they had understood the true meaning of bravery, and so he set fire to his warships and then sounded the drum to advance. The soldiers trampled each other down in their haste to go forward, and countless numbers of them perished in the fire and water. At that time, even though he ceased to drum them forward, they did not retreat. The soldiers of Yüeh were truly astonishing. Now consigning one's body to the flames is a difficult thing to do, and yet they did it because it pleased the king of Yüeh. So within the space of a single generation the ways of the people can be changed, for they will strive to ingratiate themselves with their superiors.

Duke Wen of Chin liked coarse clothing, and so during his reign the men of the state of Chin wore robes of coarse cloth, wraps of sheepskin, hats of plain silk, and big rough shoes, whether they were appearing before the duke in the inner chamber or walking about in the outer halls of the court. Now bringing oneself to wear coarse clothing is a difficult thing to do, and yet people did it because it pleased Duke Wen. So within the space of a single generation the ways of the people can be changed, for they will strive to ingratiate themselves with their superiors.

To reduce one's diet, consign one's body to the flames, or wear coarse clothing are among the most difficult things in the world to do. And yet people will do them because they know their superiors will be pleased. So within the space of a single generation the ways of the people can be changed. Why? Because they will strive to ingratiate themselves with their superiors.

Now universal love and mutual benefit are both profitable and easy beyond all measure. The only trouble, as I see it, is that no ruler takes any delight in them. If the rulers really delighted in them, promoted them with rewards and praise, and prevented neglect of them by punishments, then I believe that people would turn to universal love and mutual benefit as naturally as fire turns upward or water turns downward, and nothing in the world could stop them.

The principle of universality is the way of the sage kings, the means of bringing safety to the rulers and officials and of assuring ample food and clothing to the people. Therefore the superior man can do no better than to examine it carefully and strive to put it into practice. If he does, then as a ruler he will be generous, as a subject loyal, as a father kind, as a son filial, as an older brother comradely, and as a younger brother respectful. So if the superior man wishes to be a generous ruler, a loyal subject, a kind father, a filial son, a comradely older brother, and a respectful younger brother, he must put into practice this principle of universality. It is the way of the sage kings and a great benefit to the people. (Chapter 16.)

II
Han Fei-tzu: The Way of the Ruler*

The Way is the beginning of all beings and the measure of right and wrong. Therefore the enlightened ruler holds fast to the beginning in order to understand the wellspring of all beings, and minds the measure in order to know

*Reprinted with permission from Burton Watson, *Basic Writings of Mo Tzu, Hsün Tzu, and Hanfei Tzu.* (New York: Columbia University Press, 1967).

the source of good and bad. He waits, empty and still, letting names define themselves and affairs reach their own settlement. Being empty, he can comprehend the true aspect of fullness; being still, he can correct the mover. Those whose duty it is to speak will come forward to name themselves; those whose duty it is to act will produce results. When names and results[1] match, the ruler need do nothing more and the true aspect of all things will be revealed.

Hence it is said: The ruler must not reveal his desires; for if he reveals his desires his ministers will put on the mask that pleases him. He must not reveal his will; for if he does so his ministers will show a different face. So it is said: Discard likes and dislikes and the ministers will show their true form; discard wisdom and wile and the ministers will watch their step. Hence, though the ruler is wise, he hatches no schemes from his wisdom, but causes all men to know their place. Though he has worth, he does not display it in his deeds, but observes the motives of his ministers. Though he is brave, he does not flaunt his bravery in shows of indignation, but allows his subordinates to display their valor to the full. Thus, though he discards wisdom, his rule is enlightened; though he discards worth, he achieves merit; and though he discards bravery, his state grows powerful. When the ministers stick to their posts, the hundred officials have their regular duties, and the ruler employs each according to his particular ability, this is known as the state of manifold constancy.

Hence it is said: "So still he seems to dwell nowhere at all; so empty no one can seek him out." The enlightened ruler reposes in nonaction above, and below his ministers tremble with fear.

This is the way of the enlightened ruler: he causes the wise to bring forth all their schemes, and he decides his affairs accordingly; hence his own wisdom is never exhausted. He causes the worthy to display their talents, and he employs them accordingly; hence his own worth never comes to an end. Where there are accomplishments, the ruler takes credit for their worth; where there are errors, the ministers are held responsible for the blame; hence the ruler's name never suffers. Thus, though the ruler is not worthy himself, he is the leader of the worthy; though he is not wise himself, he is the corrector of the wise. The ministers have the labor; the ruler enjoys the success. This is called the maxim of the worthy ruler.

The Way lies in what cannot be seen, its function in what cannot be known. Be empty, still, and idle, and from your place of darkness observe the defects of others. See but do not appear to see; listen but do not seem to listen; know but do not let it be known that you know. When you perceive the trend of a man's words, do not change them, do not correct them, but examine them and compare them with the results. Assign one man to each office and do not let men talk to each other, and then all will do their utmost.

[1]Literally, "forms" or "realities." But Han Fei Tzu is discussing concrete problems of political science, i.e., do the officials really do what they say they are going to do? Does their actual performance match the title they hold?

Hide your tracks, conceal your sources, so that your subordinates cannot trace the springs of your action. Discard wisdom, forswear ability, so that your subordinates cannot guess what you are about. Stick to your objectives and examine the results to see how they match; take hold of the handles of government carefully and grip them tightly.[2] Destroy all hope, smash all intention of wresting them from you; allow no man to covet them.

If you do not guard the door, if you do not make fast the gate, then tigers will lurk there. If you are not cautious in your undertakings, if you do not hide their true aspect, then traitors will arise. They murder their sovereign and usurp his place, and all men in fear make common cause with them: hence they are called tigers. They sit by the ruler's side and, in the service of evil ministers, spy into his secrets: hence they are called traitors. Smash their cliques, arrest their backers, shut the gate, deprive them of all hope of support, and the nation will be free of tigers. Be immeasurably great, be unfathomably deep; make certain that names and results tally, examine laws and customs, punish those who act willfully, and the state will be without traitors.

The ruler of men stands in danger of being blocked in five ways. When the ministers shut out their ruler, this is one kind of block. When they get control of the wealth and resources of the state, this is a second kind of block. When they are free to issue orders as they please, this is a third kind. When they are able to do righteous deeds in their own name, this is a fourth kind. When they are able to build up their own cliques, this is a fifth kind. If the ministers shut out the ruler, then he loses the effectiveness of his position. If they control wealth and resources, he loses the means of dispensing bounty to others. If they issue orders as they please, he loses the means of command. If they are able to carry out righteous deeds in their own name, he loses his claim to enlightenment. And if they can build up cliques of their own, he loses his supporters. All these are rights that should be exercised by the ruler alone; they should never pass into the hands of his ministers.

The way of the ruler of men is to treasure stillness and reserve. Without handling affairs himself, he can recognize clumsiness or skill in others; without laying plans of his own, he knows what will bring fortune or misfortune. Hence he need speak no word, but good answers will be given him; he need exact no promises, but good works will increase. When proposals have been brought before him, he takes careful note of their content; when undertakings are well on their way, he takes careful note of the result; and from the degree to which proposals and results tally, rewards and punishments are born. Thus the ruler assigns undertakings to his various ministers on the basis of the words they speak, and assesses their accomplishments according to the way they have carried out the undertaking. When accomplishments match the undertaking, and the undertaking matches what was said about it, then he rewards the man; when these things do not match, he punishes the man. It is the way of the enlightened ruler never to allow his ministers to speak words that cannot be matched by results.

---

[2]On the two handles of government—punishment and favor.

The enlightened ruler in bestowing rewards is as benign as the seasonable rain; the dew of his bounty profits all men. But in doling out punishment he is as terrible as the thunder; even the holy sages cannot assuage him. The enlightened ruler is never overliberal in his rewards, never overlenient in his punishments. If his rewards are too liberal, then ministers who have won merit in the past will grow lax in their duties; and if his punishments are too lenient, then evil ministers will find it easy to do wrong. Thus if a man has truly won merit, no matter how humble and far removed he may be, he must be rewarded; and if he has truly committed error, no matter how close and dear to the ruler he may be, he must be punished. If those who are humble and far removed can be sure of reward, and those close and dear to the ruler can be sure of punishment, then the former will not stint in their efforts and the latter will not grow proud. (Chapter 5.)

Han Fei-tzu: Wielding Power[1]

Both Heaven [Nature] and man have their fixed destinies. Fragrant aromas and delicate flavors, rich wine and fat meat delight the palate but sicken the body. Fair lineaments and pearly teeth warm the heart but waste the spirit. Therefore renounce riot and excess, for only then can you keep your health unharmed.

Do not let your power be seen; be blank and actionless. Government reaches to the four quarters, but its source is in the center. The sage holds to the source and the four quarters come to serve him. In emptiness he awaits them, and they spontaneously do what is needed. When all within the four seas have been put in their proper places, he sits in darkness to observe the light. When those to his left and right have taken their places, he opens the gate to face the world. He changes nothing, alters nothing, but acts with the two handles of reward and punishment, acts and never ceases: this is what is called walking the path of principle.

Things have their proper place, talents their proper use. When all are in their proper place, then superior and inferior may be free from action. Let the cock herald the dawn, let the cat catch rats. When each exercises his ability, the ruler need do nothing. If the ruler tries to excel, then nothing will go right. If he boasts of an eye for the abilities of others, he will invite deceit among his subordinates. If he is lenient and fond of sparing lives, his subordinates will impose upon his kind nature. If superior and inferior try to change roles, the state will never be ordered.

Use the single Way and make names the head of it. When names are correct, things stay in place; when names are twisted, things shift about. Hence the sage holds to unity in stillness; he lets names define themselves and affairs reach their own settlement. He does not reveal his nature, and his

[1]In this chapter, Han Fei-tzu borrows the laconic language of Taoist quietism to express his political philosophy, using short, neatly balanced phrases with frequent end rhymes. Because of the deliberately arcane mode of expression he employs, commentators disagree at many points on exactly what he is saying.

subordinates are open and upright. He assigns them tasks according to their ability and lets them settle things for themselves; he hands out rewards according to the results and lets them raise their own station. He establishes the standard, abides by it, and lets all things settle themselves. On the basis of names he makes his appointments, and where the name is not clear, he looks to the actual achievement it applies to. According to how achievement and name tally, he dispenses the reward or punishment deserved. When rewards and punishments are certain to be handed out, then subordinates will bare their true nature.

Attend diligently to these matters, await the decree of Heaven, do not lose hold of the vital point, and you may become a sage. Discard wisdom and wile, for, if you do not, you will find it hard to remain constant. When the people use wisdom and wile, they bring grave danger to themselves; when the ruler uses them, his state faces peril and destruction. Follow the way of Heaven, reflect on the principle behind human affairs; investigate, examine, and compare these things, and when you come to the end, begin again. Be empty, quiet, and retiring; never put yourself forward. All the worries of the ruler come about because he tries to be like others. Trust others but never be like them, and then the myriad people will follow you as one man.

The Way is vast and great and without form; its Power is clear and orderly and extends everywhere. Since it extends to all living beings, they may use it proportionately; but, though all things flourish through it, it does not rest among things. The Way pervades all affairs here below. Therefore examine and obey the decrees of Heaven and live and die at the right time; compare names, differentiate events, comprehend their unity, and identify yourself with the Way's true nature.

Thus it is said: The Way does not identify itself with the myriad beings; its Power does not identify itself with the yin and yang, any more than a scale identifies itself with heaviness or lightness, a plumb line with bumps and hollows, a reed organ with dampness or dryness,[2] or a ruler with his ministers. All these [the myriad beings, the yin and yang, heaviness and lightness, etc.] are products of the Way; but the Way itself is never plural—therefore it is called a unity. For this reason the enlightened ruler prizes solitariness, which is the characteristic of the Way. The ruler and his ministers do not follow the same way. The ministers name their proposals, the ruler holds fast to the name, and the ministers come forward with results. When names and results match, then superior and inferior will achieve harmony.

The way to listen to the words of the ministers is to take the statements that come from them and compare them with the powers that have been invested in them. Therefore you must examine names carefully in order to establish ranks, clarify duties in order to distinguish worth. This is the way to listen to the words of others: be silent as though in a drunken stupor. Say to

[2]A kind of reed musical instrument whose pitch was said to remain unaffected by changes of humidity; it could therefore be used to set the pitch for other instruments.

yourself: Lips! teeth! do not be the first to move; lips! teeth! be thicker, be clumsier than ever! Let others say their piece — I will gain knowledge thereby.

Though right and wrong swarm about him, the ruler does not argue with them. Be empty, still, inactive, for this is the true nature of the Way. Study, compare, and see what matches, for this will reveal how much has been accomplished. Compare with concrete results; check against empty assertions. Where the root and base of the affair are unshaken, there will be no error in movement or stillness. Whether you move or remain still, transform all though inaction. If you show delight, your affairs will multiply; if you show hatred, resentment will be born. Therefore discard both delight and hatred and with an empty mind become the abode of the Way.

The ruler does not try to work side by side with his people, and they accordingly respect the dignity of his position. He does not try to tell others what to do, but leaves them to do things by themselves. Tightly he bars his inner door, and from his room looks out into the courtyard; he has provided the rules and yardsticks, so that all things know their place. Those who merit reward are rewarded; those who deserve punishment are punished. Reward and punishment follow the deed; each man brings them upon himself. Therefore, whether the result is pleasant or hateful, who dares to question it? When compass and rule have marked out one corner of truth, the other three corners will become evident of themselves.

If the ruler is not godlike in his isolation, his subordinates will find ways to move him. If his management of affairs is not impartial, they will guess at his inclinations. Be like Heaven, be like earth, and all coils will be untangled. Be like Heaven, be like earth; then who will be close to you, who will be distant? He who can model himself on Heaven and earth may be called a sage.

Would you order the affairs of the palace? Delegate them and be intimate with no one. Would you order outside affairs? Appoint one man to each office. Let no one do as he pleases, and never permit men to change office or to hold two offices at the same time. Take warning when there are many men gathered at the gates of the high ministers! The height of good government is to allow your subordinates no means of taking advantage of you. Make certain that name and result match, and then the people will stick to their posts. If you discard this and look for some other method to rule, you will win the name of one who is profoundly deluded; wily men will only increase, and evil ministers fill your ranks. Hence it is said: Never enrich a man to the point where he can afford to turn against you, never ennoble a man to the point where he becomes a threat; never put all your trust in a single man and thereby lose your state.

When the shin grows stouter than the thigh, it is hard to run; when the ruler loses his godlike qualities, tigers prowl behind him. If the ruler fails to take notice of them, then he and his ministers, who should be tigers themselves, become as impotent as dogs. If the ruler fails to check the danger, then the dogs will continue to increase in number; the tigers will form a band and assassinate their master. A ruler who has no ministers — how can he keep possession of a state? Let the ruler apply the laws, and the greatest tigers will tremble; let him apply punishments, and the greatest tigers will grow docile. If laws and punishments are justly applied, then tigers will be transformed into men again and revert to their true form.

If you wish to govern the state, you must make certain to destroy conclaves; if you do not do so, they will only grow more numerous. If you wish to govern the land, you must make certain that your bestowals pass into the right hands; if you do not do so, then unruly men will come seeking gain. If you grant what they seek, you will be lending a battle-ax to your enemies; this you must not do, for it will only be used against you.

The Yellow Emperor used to say, "Superior and inferior fight a hundred battles a day." The subordinates hide their private desires and see what they can get from the ruler; the ruler employs his standards and measures to weigh what they are up to. Thus the standards and measures that are set up are the ruler's treasures; and the parties and cliques that are formed are the ministers' treasures. The only reason the ministers do not assassinate their sovereign is that their parties and cliques are not strong enough. Hence, if the ruler loses an inch, his subordinates gain a yard.

The ruler who knows how to govern his state does not let his cities grow too large; the ruler who understands the Way does not enrich the powerful families nor ennoble his ministers. Were he to enrich and ennoble them, they would turn about and try to overthrow him. Guard against danger, fear peril, make haste to designate your heir, and misfortune will have no means to arise.

In ferreting out evil within the palace and controlling it outside, you yourself must hold fast to your standards and measurements. Whittle away from those who have too much, enhance those who have too little, but let the taking and the giving be according to measure. Never allow men to form cliques or join together to deceive their superiors. Let your whittling be as gradual as the slimming moon, your enhancing like a slow-spreading heat. Simplify the laws and be cautious in the use of penalties but, where punishments are called for, make certain they are carried out. Never loosen your bow, or you will find two cocks in a single roost, squawking in fierce rivalry. When wildcat and wolf break into the fold, the sheep are not likely to increase. When one house has two venerables, its affairs will never prosper. When husband and wife both give orders, the children are at a loss to know which one to obey.

The ruler of men must prune his trees from time to time and not let them grow too thick for, if they do, they will block his gate; while the gates of private men are crowded with visitors, the ruler's courts will stand empty, and he will be shut in and encircled. He must prune his trees from time to time and not let them obstruct the path for, if they do, they will impinge upon his dwelling. He must prune his trees from time to time and not let the branches grow larger than the trunk for, if they do, they will not be able to bear up under the spring wind, and will do injury to the heart of the tree. When cadet houses become too numerous, the royal family will face anxiety and grief.

The way to prevent this is to prune your trees from time to time and not let the branches grow too luxurious. If the trees are pruned from time to time, cliques and parties will be broken up. Dig them up from the roots, and then the trees cannot spread. Fill up the pools, and do not let water collect in them. Search out the hearts of others, seize their power from them. The ruler himself should possess the power, wielding it like lightning or like thunder. (Chapter 8.)

CHAPTER 19

CONFUCIAN DEVELOPMENTS: MENCIUS AND HSÜN-TZU

Mencius (390–305 B.C.) and Hsün-tzu (between 340–145 B.C.) represent further developments in Confucianism, energized in part by Mohist and Legalist challenges. Their work brought the classical Confucian vision to its definitive form, enabling Tung Chung-shu to present a synthesis of ancient learning, in which Confucianism predominated, to the emperor for adoption as the official ideology in 136 B.C. The *Book of Mencius* may be roughly contemporaneous with the writings of Mo-tzu and is, in part, a response to the latter's critique of Confucianism. Mencius rejects Mo-tzu's utilitarian morality because it is based on interest, whereas true morality is based on virtue. But by positing self-interest as an original inherent tendency, the Mohists and Legalists had challenged Confucius' assumption of an innate inclination to virtue, thus requiring Mencius to provide an ontological basis for human virtue. This he does by establishing the mind-and-heart (*hsin*) as the locus of the innate moral tendency that is revealed in the moral sensitivities that incline a person to virtue. Evil in the world does not prove a lack of inherent virtue, but only shows that its realization can be frustrated by the effect of environmental factors on the psychophysical energies called *ch'i*.

The selections from Mencius begin with Book 6, which is the fullest statement of his view of human nature as originally virtuous, and then include portions of the other books dealing with this central topic. The translation is by D. C. Lau, in *Mencius*, volume 2 (Hong Kong: Chinese University Press, 1984), which has notes and an excellent introduction. Donald Munro, *The Concept of Man in Early China* (Stanford: Stanford University Press, 1969), is an outstanding philosophical account of Chinese thinking about human nature in Mencius and other early thinkers.

The work of Hsün-tzu is later than Mencius and, although probably earlier than the writings of Han Fei-tzu, it clearly represents a Confucian response to the Legalist thought that Han Fei-tzu synthesized and championed so forcefully. Hsün-tzu denies any innate moral nature, claiming instead, quite in opposition to Mencius, that humans have an inherent tendency toward evil. This inclination to evil, which arises out of the efforts to satisfy unlimited desires, can be overcome, however, for although moral consciousness is not innate in humans, intelligence is, and intelligence can be used to acquire knowledge that in turn can be used to achieve the goals that define the good life. Because intelligence is fundamental to human nature, learning to use it to overcome the tendency to evil is the way to the goal of full development of a harmonious and peaceful society. The learning involved is profound; it is simultaneously a process of self-understanding and a mastery of the moral-cultural tradition (the social embodiment of *li* and righteousness) that serves to replace evil inclinations with virtue. Like the Utilitarians, Hsün-tzu is concerned with the total welfare of society and is willing to measure the goodness of various means of achieving this welfare by their effectiveness. However, the ideal person, the sage, acts to further neither personal nor societal interest but to serve the *li* that reveal the way of Heaven. In this emphasis on the sage as moral exemplar and the *li* as instruments of Heaven, Hsün-tzu is profoundly Confucian.

The selections from Hsün-tzu, "A Discussion of Heaven" and "Man's Nature Is Evil," present key features of his unique synthesis. They are reprinted from Burton Watson, *Basic Writings of Mo Tzu, Hsun Tzu and Han Fei Tzu* (New York: Columbia University Press, 1967), which has a good introduction. A. S. Cua, *Ethical Argumentation: A Study in Hsün Tzu's Moral Epistemology* (Honolulu: University of Hawaii Press, 1985), is an excellent comparative study of the moral grounding of learning in Hsün-tzu's philosophy.

I
Mencius*

BOOK VI · PART A

1. Kao Tzu said, "Human nature is like the *ch'i* willow. Dutifulness is like cups and bowls. To make morality out of human nature is like making cups and bowls out of the willow."

"Can you," said Mencius, "make cups and bowls by following the nature of the willow? Or must you mutilate the willow before you can make it into cups and bowls? If you have to mutilate the willow to make it into cups and bowls, must you, then, also mutilate a man to make him moral? Surely it will be these words of yours men in the world will follow in bringing disaster upon morality."

2. Kao Tzu said, "Human nature is like whirling water. Give it an outlet in

---

*Reprinted with permission from D. C. Lau, *Mencius*, volume 2 (Hong Kong: Chinese University Press, 1984).

the east and it will flow east; give it an outlet in the west and it will flow west. Human nature does not show any preference for either good or bad just as water does not show any preference for either east or west."

"It certainly is the case," said Mencius, "that water does not show any preference for either east or west, but does it show the same indifference to high and low? Human nature is good just as water seeks low ground. There is no man who is not good; there is no water that does not flow downwards.

"Now in the case of water, by splashing it one can make it shoot up higher than one's forehead, and by forcing it one can make it stay on a hill. How can that be the nature of water? It is the circumstances being what they are. That man can be made bad shows that his nature is no different from that of water in this respect."

3. Kao Tzu said, "The inborn is what is meant by 'nature.'"

"Is that," said Mencius, "the same as 'white is what is meant by "white"'?'[1]

"Yes."

"Is the whiteness of white feathers the same as the whiteness of white snow and the whiteness of white snow the same as the whiteness of white jade?"

"Yes."

"In that case, is the nature of a hound the same as the nature of an ox and the nature of an ox the same as the nature of a man?"

4. Kao Tzu said, "Appetite for food and sex is nature. Benevolence is internal, not external; rightness is external, not internal."

"Why do you say," said Mencius, "that benevolence is internal and rightness is external?"

"That man there is old and I treat him as elder. He owes nothing of his elderliness to me, just as in treating him as white because he is white I only do so because of his whiteness which is external to me. That is why I call it external."

"The case of rightness is different from that of whiteness. 'Treating as white' is the same whether one is treating a horse as white or a man as white. But I wonder if you would think that 'treating as old' is the same whether one is treating a horse as old or a man as elder? Furthermore, is it the one who is old that is dutiful, or is it the one who treats him as elder that is dutiful?"

"My brother I love, but the brother of a man from Ch'in I do not love. This means that the explanation lies in me. Hence I call it internal. Treating an elder of a man from Ch'u as elder is no different from treating an elder of my own family as elder. This means that the explanation lies in their elderliness. Hence I call it external."

"My enjoyment of the roast provided by a man from Ch'in is no different from my enjoyment of my own roast. Even with inanimate things we can find

---

[1]In "*sheng chih wei hsing*" ("the inborn is what is meant by 'nature'"), the two words "*sheng*" and "*hsing*," though slightly different in pronunciation, were probably written by the same character in Mencius' time. This would make the statement at least tautological in written form and so parallel to "*pai chih wei pai*" ("white is what is meant by 'white'").

cases similar to the one under discussion. Are we, then, to say that there is something external even in the enjoyment of roast?"

5. Meng Chi-tzu asked Kung-tu Tzu, "Why do you say that rightness is internal?"

"It is the respect in me that is being put into effect. That is why I say it is internal."

"If a man from your village is a year older than your eldest brother, which do you respect?"

"My brother."

"In filling their cups with wine,[2] which do you give precedence to?"

"The man from my village."

"The one you respect is the former; the one you treat as elder is the latter. This shows that it is in fact external, not internal."

Kung-tu Tzu was unable to find an answer and gave an account of the discussion to Mencius.

Mencius said, "[Ask him,] 'Which do you respect, your uncle or your younger brother?' He will say, 'My uncle.' 'When your younger brother is impersonating an ancestor at a sacrifice, then which do you respect?' He will say, 'My younger brother.' You ask him, 'What has happened to your respect for your uncle?' He will say, 'It is because of the position my younger brother occupies.' You can then say, '[In the case of the man from my village] it is also because of the position he occupies. Normal respect is due to my elder brother; temporary respect is due to the man from my village.'"

When Meng Chi-tzu heard this, he said, "It is the same respect whether I am respecting my uncle or my younger brother. It is, as I have said, external and does not come from within."

"In winter," said Kung-tu Tzu, "one drinks hot water, in summer cold. Does that mean that even food and drink can be a matter of what is external?"

6. Kung-tu Tzu said, "Kao Tzu said, 'There is neither good nor bad in human nature,' but others say, 'Human nature can become good or it can become bad, and that is why with the rise of King Wen and King Wu, the people were given to goodness, while with the rise of King Yu and King Li, they were given to cruelty.' Then there are others who say, 'There are those who are good by nature, and there are those who are bad by nature. For this reason, Hsiang could have Yao as prince, and Shun could have the Blind Man as father, and Ch'i, Viscount of Wei and Prince Pi Kan could have Tchou as nephew as well as sovereign.''[3] Now you say human nature is good. Does this mean that all the others are mistaken?"

"As far as what is genuinely in him is concerned, a man is capable of becoming good," said Mencius. "That is what I mean by good. As for his

---

[2]I.e., at a village gathering where precedence is in accordance with seniority.

[3]According to the *Shi chi* (Records of the Historian), (1607) the Viscount of Wei was an elder brother of Tchou, and son of a concubine of low rank. For this reason, it has been pointed out that the description of having Tchou as nephew applies only to Pi Kan. Cf. the coupling of the name of Chi with that of Yü in IV. B. 29.

becoming bad, that is not the fault of his native endowment. The heart of compassion is possessed by all men alike; likewise the heart of shame, the heart of respect, and the heart of right and wrong. The heart of compassion pertains to benevolence, the heart of shame to dutifulness, the heart of respect to the observance of the rites, and the rites, and the heart of right and wrong to wisdom. Benevolence, dutifulness, observance of the rites, and wisdom do not give me a lustre from the outside, they are in me originally. Only this has never dawned on me. That is why it is said, 'Seek and you will find it; let go and you will lose it.' There are cases where one man is twice, five times or countless times better than another man, but this is only because there are people who fail to make the best of their native endowment. The *Odes* say,

> Heaven produces the teeming masses,
> And where there is a thing there is a norm.
> If the people held on to their constant nature,
> They would be drawn to superior virtue.

Confucius commented, 'The author of this poem must have had knowledge of the Way.' Thus where there is a thing there is a norm, and because the people hold on to their constant nature they are drawn to superior virtue."

8. Mencius said, "There was a time when the trees were luxuriant on the Ox Mountain, but as it is on the outskirts of a great metropolis, the trees are constantly lopped by axes. Is it any wonder that they are no longer fine? With the respite they get in the day and in the night, and the moistening by the rain and dew, there is certainly no lack of new shoots coming out, but then the cattle and sheep come to graze upon the mountain. That is why it is as bald as it is. People, seeing only its baldness, tend to think that it never had any trees. But can this possibly be the nature of a mountain? Can what is in man be completely lacking in moral inclinations? A man's letting go of his true heart is like the case of the trees and the axes. When the trees are lopped day after day, is it any wonder that they are no longer fine? If, in spite of the respite a man gets in the day and in the night and of the effect of the morning air on him, scarcely any of his likes and dislikes resembles those of other men, it is because what he does in the course of the day once again dissipates what he has gained. If this dissipation happens repeatedly, then the influence of the air in the night will no longer able to preserve what was originally in him, and when that happens, the man is not far removed from an animal. Others, seeing his resemblance to an animal, will be led to think that he never had any native endowment. But can that be what a man is genuinely like? Hence, given the right nourishment there is nothing that will not grow, while deprived of it there is nothing that will not wither away. Confucius said, 'Hold on to it and it will remain; let go of it and it will disappear. One never knows the time it comes or goes, neither does one know the direction.' It is perhaps to the heart this refers."

15. Kung-tu Tzu asked, "Though equally human, why are some men greater than others?"

"He who is guided by the interests of the parts of his person that are of greater importance is a great man; he who is guided by the interests of the parts of his person that are of smaller importance is a small man."

"Though equally human, why are some men guided one way and others guided another way?"

"The organs of hearing and sight are unable to think and can be misled by external things. When one thing acts on another, all it does is to attract it. The organ of the heart can think. But it will find the answer only if it does think; otherwise, it will not find the answer. This is what Heaven has given me. If one makes one's stand on what is of greater importance in the first instance, what is of smaller importance cannot displace it. In this way, one cannot but be a great man."

16. Mencius said, "No man is devoid of a heart sensitive to the suffering of others. Such a sensitive heart was possessed by the Former Kings and this manifested itself in compassionate government. With such a sensitive heart behind compassionate government, it was as easy to rule the Empire as rolling it on your palm.

"My reason for saying that no man is devoid of a heart sensitive to the suffering of others is this. Suppose a man were, all of a sudden, to see a young child on the verge of falling into a well. He would certainly be moved to compassion, not because he wanted to get in the good graces of the parents, nor because he wished to win the praise of his fellow villagers or friends, nor yet because he disliked the cry of the child. From this it can be seen that whoever is devoid of the heart of compassion is not human, whoever is devoid of the heart of shame is not human, whoever is devoid of the heart of courtesy and modesty is not human, and whoever is devoid of the heart of right and wrong is not human. The heart of compassion is the germ of benevolence; the heart of shame, of dutifulness; the heart of courtesy and modesty, of observance of the rites; the heart of right and wrong, of wisdom. Man has these four germs just as he has four limbs. For a man possessing these four germs to deny his own potentialities is for him to cripple himself; for him to deny the potentialities of his prince is for him to cripple his prince. If a man is able to develop all these four germs that he possesses, it will be like a fire starting up or a spring coming through. When these are fully developed, he can tend the whole realm within the Four Seas, but if he fails to develop them, he will not be able even to serve his parents."

BOOK III · PART A

1. Duke Wen of T'eng, while still crown prince, was once going to Ch'u. While passing through Sung, he saw Mencius who talked to him about the goodness of human nature, always citing as his authorities Yao and Shun.

On the way back from Ch'u the crown prince again saw Mencius.

"Does Your Highness doubt my words?" asked Mencius. "There is one Way and one only. Ch'eng Chien said to Duke Ching of Ch'i, 'He is a man and I am a man. Why should I be in awe of him?' Similarly, Yen Hui said, 'What sort of a man was Shun? And what sort of a man am I? Anyone who can make anything of himself will be like that.' Kung-ming Yi said, 'When he said that he modelled himself on King Wen, surely the Duke of Chou was not trying to take us in?'

"Now if you reduce T'eng to a regular shape, it would have a territory of almost fifty *li* square. It is big enough for you to do good.

"The *Book of History* says,

> If the medicine does not make the head swim, the illness will not be cured.

4. There was a man by the name of Hsü Hsing who preached the teachings of Shen Nung.[1] He came to T'eng from Ch'u, went up to the gate and told Duke Wen, "I, a man from distant parts, have heard that you, my lord, practise benevolent government. I wish to be given a place to live and become one of your subjects."

The Duke gave him a place.

His followers, numbering several score, all wore unwoven hemp, and lived by making sandals and mats.

Ch'en Hsiang and his brother Hsin, both followers of Ch'en Liang, came to T'eng from Sung, carrying ploughs on their backs. "We have heard," said they, "that you, my lord, practise the government of the sages. In that case you must yourself be a sage. We wish to be the subjects of a sage."

Ch'en Hsiang met Hsü Hsing and was delighted with his teachings, so he abjured what he had learned before and became a follower of Hsü Hsing.

Ch'en Hsiang saw Mencius and cited the words of Hsü Hsing. "The prince of T'eng is a truly good and wise ruler. However, he has never been taught the Way. To earn his keep a good and wise ruler shares the work of tilling the land with his people. He rules while cooking his own meals. Now T'eng has granaries and treasuries. This is for the prince to inflict hardship on the people in order to keep himself. How can he be a good and wise prince?"

"Does Hsü Tzu only eat grain he has grown himself?" asked Mencius.

"Yes."

"Does Hsü Tzu only wear cloth he has woven himself?"

"No. He wears unwoven hemp."

"Does Hsü Tzu wear a cap?"

"Yes."

"What kind of cap does he wear?"

"Plain raw silk."

"Does he weave it himself?"

"No. He trades grain for it."

"Why does Hsü Tzu not weave it himself?"

---

[1]The legendary Emperor credited with the invention of agriculture.

"Because it interferes with his work in the fields."

"Does Hsü Tzu use an iron pot and an earthenware steamer for cooking rice and iron implements for ploughing the fields?"

"Yes."

"Does he make them himself?"

"No. He trades grain for them."

"To trade grain for implements is not to inflict hardship on the potter and the blacksmith. The potter and the blacksmith, for their part, also trade their wares for grain. In doing this, surely they are not inflicting hardship on the farmer either. Why does Hsü Tzu not be a potter and a blacksmith as well so that he can get everything he needs from his own house? Why does he indulge in such multifarious trading with men who practise the hundred crafts? Why does Hsü Tzu go to so much bother?"

"It is naturally impossible to combine the work of tilling the land with that of a hundred different crafts."

"Now, is ruling the Empire such an exception that it can be combined with the work of tilling the land? There are affairs of great men, and there are affairs of small men. Moreover, it is necessary for each man to use the products of all the hundred crafts. If everyone must make everything he uses, the Empire will be led along the path of incessant toil. Hence it is said, 'There are those who use their minds and there are those who use their muscles. The former rule; the latter are ruled. Those who rule are supported by those who are ruled.' This is a principle accepted by the whole Empire.

"In the time of Yao, the Empire was not yet settled. The Flood still raged unchecked, inundating the Empire; plants grew thickly; birds and beasts multiplied; the five grains did not ripen; birds and beasts encroached upon men, and their trail criss-crossed even the Central Kingdoms. The lot fell on Yao to worry about this situation. He raised Shun to a position of authority to deal with it. Shun put Yi in charge of fire. Yi ringed off the mountains and valleys and set them alight, and birds and beasts went into hiding. Yü dredged the Nine Rivers, cleared the courses of the Chi and the T'a to channel the water into the Sea, deepened the beds of the Ju and the Han, and raised the dykes of the Huai and the Ssu to empty them into the River. Only then were the people of the Central Kingdoms able to find food for themselves. During this time Yü spent eight years abroad and passed the door of his own house three times without entering. Even if he had wished to plough the fields, could he have done it?

"Hou Chi taught the people how to farm and grow the five kinds of grain. When these ripened, the people multiplied. This is the way of the common people: once they have a full belly and warm clothes on their back they degenerate to the level of animals if they are allowed to lead idle lives, without education and discipline. This gave the sage King further cause for concern, and so he appointed Hsieh as the Minister of Education whose duty was to teach the people human relationships: love between father and son, duty between ruler and subject, distinction between husband and wife, precedence of the old over the young, and faith between friends. Fang Hsün said,

> Encourage them in their toil,
> Put them on the right path,
> Aid them and help them,
> Make them happy in their station,
> And by bountiful acts further relieve them of hardship.

The Sage worried to this extent about the affairs of the people. How could he have leisure to plough the fields? Yao's only worry was that he should fail to find someone like Shun, and Shun's only worry was that he should fail to find someone like Yü and Kao Yao. He who worries about his plot of a hundred *mu* not being well cultivated is a mere farmer.

"To share one's wealth with others is generosity; to teach others to be good is conscientiousness; to find the right man for the Empire is benevolence. Hence it is easier to give the Empire away than to find the right man for it.

"Confucius said, 'Great indeed was Yao as a ruler! It is Heaven that is great, and it was Yao who modelled himself upon it. He was so boundless that the people were not able to put a name to his virtues. What a ruler Shun was! He was so lofty that while in possession of the Empire he held aloof from it.'

"It is not true that in ruling the Empire Yao and Shun did not have to use their minds. Only they did not use their minds on ploughing the fields.

"I have heard of the Chinese converting barbarians to their ways, but not of their being converted to barbarian ways. Ch'en Liang was a native of Ch'u. Being delighted with the way of the Duke of Chou and Confucius, he came north to study in the Central Kingdoms. Even the scholars in the north could not surpass him in any way. He was what one would call an outstanding scholar. You and your brother studied under him for scores of years, and now that your teacher is dead, you turn your back on him.

"When Confucius died and the three-year mourning period had elapsed, his disciples packed their bags and prepared to go home. They went in and bowed to Tzu-kung and facing one another they wept until they lost their voices before setting out for home. Tzu-kung went back to build a hut in the burial grounds and remained there on his own for another three years before going home. One day, Tzu-hsia, Tzu-chang and Tzu-yu wanted to serve Yu Jo as they had served Confucius because of his resemblance to the Sage. They tried to force Tseng Tzu to join them, but Tseng Tzu said, 'That will not do. Washed by the River and the river Han, bleached by the autumn sun, so immaculate was he that his whiteness could not be surpassed.'

"Now you turn your back on the way of your teacher in order to follow the southern barbarian with the twittering tongue, who condemns the way of the Former Kings. You are indeed different from Tseng Tzu. I have heard of coming out of the dark ravine and going up to settle on a tall tree, but not of forsaking the tall tree to go down into the dark ravine. The *Lu sung* says,

> It was the barbarians that he attacked;
> It was Ching and Shu that he punished.

It is these people the Duke of Chou was going to punish and you want to learn from them. That is not a change for the better, is it?"

"If we follow the way of Hsü Tzu there will only be one price in the market, and dishonesty will disappear from the capital. Even if you send a mere boy to the market, no one will take advantage of him. For equal lengths of cloth or silk, for equal weights of hemp, flax or raw silk, and for equal measures of the five grains, the price will be the same; for shoes of the same size, the price will also be the same."

"That things are unequal is part of their nature. Some are worth twice or five times, ten or a hundred times, even a thousand and ten thousand times, more than others. If you reduce them to the same level, it will only bring confusion to the Empire. If a roughly finished shoe sells at the same price as a finely finished one, who would make the latter? If we follow the way of Hsü Tzu, we will be showing one another the way to being deceitful. How can one govern a state in this way?"

BOOK IV · PART A

27. Mencius said, "The content of benevolence is the serving of one's parents; the content of dutifulness is obedience to one's elder brothers; the content of wisdom is to understand these two and to hold fast to them; the content of the rites is the regulation and adornment of them; the content of music is the joy that comes of delighting in them. When joy arises how can one stop it? And when one cannot stop it, then one begins to dance with one's feet and wave one's arms without knowing it.

BOOK IV · PART B

12. Mencius said, "A great man is one who retains the heart of a new-born babe."

19. Mencius said, "Slight is the difference between man and the brutes. The common man loses this distinguishing feature, while the gentleman retains it. Shun understood the way of things and had a keen insight into human relationships. He followed the path of morality. He did not just put morality into practice."

26. Mencius said, "In the theories about human nature put forth by the world there is nothing else other than resort to precedents. The primary thing in any resort to precedents is ease of explanation. What one dislikes in clever men is their tortuosity. If clever men could act as Yü did in guiding the flood waters, then there would be nothing to dislike in them. Yü guided the water by imposing nothing on it that was against its natural tendency. If clever men can also do this, then great indeed will their cleverness be. In spite of the height of the heavens and the distance of the heavenly bodies, if one seeks out former instances, one can calculate the solstices of a thousand years hence without stirring from one's seat."

BOOK VII · PART A

1. Mencius said, "For a man to give full realization to his heart is for him to understand his own nature, and a man who knows his own nature will know Heaven. By retaining his heart and nurturing his nature he is serving Heaven. Whether he is going to die young or to live to a ripe old age makes no difference to his steadfastness of purpose. It is through awaiting whatever is to befall him with a perfected character that he stands firm on his proper Destiny."

4. Mencius said, "All the ten thousand things are there in me. There is no greater joy for me than to find, on self-examination, that I am true to myself. Try your best to treat others as you would wish to be treated yourself, and you will find that this is the shortest way to benevolence."

9. Mencius said to Sung Kou-chien, "You are fond of travelling from state to state, offering advice. I shall tell you how this should be done. You should be content whether your worth is recognized by others or not."

"What must a man be before he can be content?"

"If he reveres virtue and delights in rightness, he can be content. Hence a Gentleman never abandons rightness in adversity, nor does he depart from the Way in success. By not abandoning rightness in adversity, he finds delight in himself; by not departing from the Way in success, he remains an example the people can look up to. Men of antiquity made the people feel the effect of their bounty when they realized their ambition, and, when they failed to realize their ambition, were at least able to show the world an exemplary character. In obscurity a man makes perfect his own person, but in prominence he makes perfect the whole Empire as well."

21. Mencius said, "An extensive territory and a huge population are things a gentleman desires, but what he delights in lies elsewhere. To stand in the centre of the Empire and bring peace to the people within the Four Seas is what a gentleman delights in, but that which he follows as his nature lies elsewhere. That which a gentleman follows as his nature is not added to when he holds sway over the Empire, nor is it detracted from when he is reduced to straitened circumstances. This is because he knows his allotted station. That which a gentleman follows as his nature, that is to say, benevolence, rightness, the rites and wisdom, is rooted in his heart, and manifests itself in his face, giving it a sleek appearance. It also shows in his back and extends to his limbs, rendering their message intelligible without words."

30. Mencius said, "Yao and Shun had it as their nature. T'ang and King Wu embodied it. The Five Leaders of the feudal lords borrowed it.[4] But if a man borrows a thing and keeps it long enough, how can one be sure that it will not become truly his?"

---

[4]Cf. II. A. 3. The "it" here would seem to refer to benevolence.

BOOK VII • PART B

32. Mencius said, "Words near at hand but with far-reaching import are good words. The way of holding on to the essential while giving it wide application is a good way. The words of a gentleman never go as far as below the sash, yet in them is to be found the Way. What the gentleman holds on to is the cultivation of his own character, yet this brings order to the Empire. The trouble with people is that they leave their own fields to weed the fields of others. They are exacting towards others but indulgent towards themselves."

33. Mencius said, "Yao and Shun had it as their nature; T'ang and King Wu returned to it.[5] To be in accord with the rites in every movement is the highest of virtue. When one mourns sorrowfully over the dead it is not to impress the living. When one follows unswervingly the path of virtue it is not to win advancement. When one invariably keeps one's word it is not to establish the rectitude of one's actions. A gentleman merely follows the norm and awaits his destiny."

II
Hsün-tzu: A Discussion of Heaven*

Heaven's ways are constant. It does not prevail because of a sage like Yao; it does not cease to prevail because of a tyrant like Chieh. Respond to it with good government, and good fortune will result; respond to it with disorder, and misfortune will result. If you encourage agriculture and are frugal in expenditures, then Heaven cannot make you poor. If you provide the people with the goods they need and demand their labor only at the proper time, then Heaven cannot afflict you with illness. If you practice the Way and are not of two minds, then Heaven cannot bring you misfortune. Flood or drought cannot make your people starve, extremes of heat or cold cannot make them fall ill, and strange and uncanny occurrences cannot cause them harm. But if you neglect agriculture and spend lavishly, then Heaven cannot make you rich. If you are careless in your provisions and slow to act, then Heaven cannot make you whole. If you turn your back upon the Way and act rashly, then Heaven cannot give you good fortune. Your people will starve even when there are no floods or droughts; they will fall ill even before heat or cold come to oppress them; they will suffer harm even when no strange or uncanny happenings occur. The seasons will visit you as they do a well-ordered age, but you will suffer misfortunes that a well-ordered age does not know. Yet you must not curse Heaven, for it is merely the natural result of your own actions. Therefore, he who can distinguish between the activities of Heaven and those of mankind is worthy to be called the highest type of man.

---

[5]Cf. VII. A. 30. The "it" here must also be referring to benevolence.

*Reprinted with permission from Burton Watson, *Basic Writings of Mo Tzu, Hsün Tzu, and Han Fei Tzu.* (New York: Columbia University Press, 1967).

To bring to completion without acting, to obtain without seeking—this is the work of Heaven. Thus, although the sage has deep understanding, he does not attempt to exercise it upon the work of Heaven; though he has great talent, he does not attempt to apply it to the work of Heaven; though he has keen perception, he does not attempt to use it on the work of Heaven. Hence it is said that he does not compete with Heaven's work. Heaven has its seasons; earth has its riches; man has his government. Hence man may form a triad with the other two. But if he sets aside that which allows him to form a triad with the other two and longs for what they have, then he is deluded. The ranks of stars move in progression, the sun and moon shine in turn, the four seasons succeed each other in good order, the yin and yang go through their great transformations, and the wind and rain pass over the whole land. All things obtain what is congenial to them and come to life, receive what is nourishing to them and grow to completion. One does not see the process taking place, but sees only the results. Thus it is called godlike. All men understand that the process has reached completion, but none understands the formless forces that bring it about. Hence it is called the accomplishment of Heaven. Only the sage does not seek to understand Heaven.

When the work of Heaven has been established and its accomplishments brought to completion, when the form of man is whole and his spirit is born, then love and hate, delight and anger, sorrow and joy find lodging in him. These are called his heavenly emotions. Ears, eyes, nose, mouth, and body all have that which they perceive, but they cannot substitute for one another. They are called the heavenly faculties. The heart dwells in the center and governs the five faculties, and hence it is called the heavenly lord. Food and provisions are not of the same species as man, and yet they serve to nourish him and are called heavenly nourishment. He who accords with what is proper to his species will be blessed; he who turns against it will suffer misfortune. These are called the heavenly dictates. To darken the heavenly lord, disorder the heavenly faculties, reject the heavenly nourishment, defy the heavenly dictates, turn against the heavenly emotions, and thereby destroy the heavenly accomplishment is called dire disaster. The sage purifies his heavenly lord, rectifies his heavenly faculties, cherishes the heavenly nourishment, obeys the heavenly dictates, nourishes the heavenly emotions, and thereby preserves the heavenly accomplishment. In this way he understands what is to be done and what is not to be done. Hence Heaven and earth too perform their functions and all things serve him. His actions are completely ordered; his nourishment of the people is completely appropriate; his life is without injury. This is what it means to truly understand Heaven. Hence the really skilled man has things which he does not do; the really wise man has things that he does not ponder.[1]

When he turns his thoughts to Heaven, he seeks to understand only

[1]In this passage, which I fear goes rather ponderously into English, Hsün Tzu uses the word *t'ien* in the sense of "Nature" or "natural." I have translated it as "Heaven" or "heavenly" throughout, however, in order to make clear the connection with what has gone before.

those phenomena which can be regularly expected. When he turns his thoughts to earth, he seeks to understand only those aspects that can be taken advantage of. When he turns his thoughts to the four seasons, he seeks to understand only the changes that will affect his undertakings. When he turns his thoughts to the yin and yang, he seeks to understand only the modulations which call for some action on his part. The experts may study Heaven; the ruler himself should concentrate on the Way.

Are order and disorder due to the heavens? I reply, the sun and moon, the stars and constellations revolved in the same way in the time of Yü as in the time of Chieh. Yü achieved order; Chieh brought disorder. Hence order and disorder are not due to the heavens.

Are they then a matter of the seasons? I reply, the crops sprout and grow in spring and summer, and are harvested and stored away in autumn and winter. It was the same under both Yü and Chieh. Yü achieved order; Chieh brought disorder. Hence order and disorder are not a matter of the seasons.

Are they due to the land? I reply, he who acquires land may live; he who loses it will die. It was the same in the time of Yü as in the time of Chieh. Yü achieved order; Chieh brought disorder. Hence order and disorder are not due to the land. This is what the *Odes* means when it says:

> Heaven made a high hill;
> T'ai Wang opened it up.
> He began the work
> And King Wen dwelt there in peace.

Heaven does not suspend the winter because men dislike cold; earth does not cease being wide because men dislike great distances; the gentleman does not stop acting because petty men carp and clamor. Heaven has its constant way; earth has its constant dimensions; the gentleman has his constant demeanor. The gentleman follows what is constant; the petty man reckons up his achievements. This is what the *Odes* means when it says:

> If you have no faults of conduct,
> Why be distressed at what others say?

The king of Ch'u has a retinue of a thousand chariots, but not because he is wise. The gentleman must eat boiled greens and drink water, but not because he is stupid. These are accidents of circumstance. To be refined in purpose, rich in virtuous action, and clear in understanding; to live in the present and remember the past — these are things which are within your own power. Therefore the gentleman cherishes what is within his power and does not long for what is within the power of Heaven alone. The petty man, however, puts aside what is within his power and longs for what is within the power of Heaven. Because the gentleman cherishes what is within his power and does not long for what is within Heaven's power, he goes forward day by day. Because the petty man sets aside what is within his power and longs for what is within Heaven's power, he goes backward day by day. The same cause impels the gentleman forward day by day, and the petty man backward. What separates the two originates in this one point alone.

When stars fall or trees make strange sounds,[2] all the people in the country are terrified and go about asking, "Why has this happened?" For no special reason, I reply. It is simply that, with the changes of Heaven and earth and the mutations of the yin and yang, such things once in a while occur. You may wonder at them, but you must not fear them. The sun and moon are subject to eclipses, wind and rain do not always come at the proper season, and strange stars occasionally appear. There has never been an age that was without such occurrences. If the ruler is enlightened and his government just, then there is no harm done even if they all occur at the same time. But if the ruler is benighted and his government ill-run, then it will be no benefit to him even if they never occur at all. Stars that fall, trees that give out strange sounds—such things occur once in a while with the changes of Heaven and earth and the mutations of the yin and yang. You may wonder at them, but do not fear them.

Among all such strange occurrences, the ones really to be feared are human portents. When the plowing is poorly done and the crops suffer, when the weeding is badly done and the harvest fails; when the government is evil and loses the support of the people; when the fields are neglected and the crops badly tended; when grain must be imported from abroad and sold at a high price, and the people are starving and die by the roadside—these are what I mean by human portents. When government commands are unenlightened, public works are undertaken at the wrong season, and agriculture is not properly attended to, these too are human portents. When the people are called away for *corvée* labor at the wrong season, so that cows and horses are left to breed together and the six domestic animals produce prodigies; when ritual principles are not obeyed, family affairs and outside affairs are not properly separated, and men and women mingle wantonly, so that fathers and sons begin to doubt each other, superior and inferior become estranged, and bands of invaders enter the state—these too are human portents. Portents such as these are born from disorder, and if all three types occur at once, there will be no safety for the state. The reasons for their occurrence may be found very close at hand; the suffering they cause is great indeed. You should not only wonder at them, but fear them as well.

An old text says, "Strange occurrences among the creatures of nature are not discussed in the *Documents*." Useless distinctions, observations which are not of vital importance—these may be left aside and not tended to. But when it comes to the duties to be observed between ruler and subject, the affection between father and son, and the differences in station between husband and wife—these you must work at day after day and never neglect.

You pray for rain and it rains. Why? For no particular reason, I say. It is

---

[2]Hsün Tzu is probably referring in particular to the sacred trees planted around the altar of the soil, whose rustlings and creakings were believed to have deep significance.

just as though you had not prayed for rain and it rained anyway. The sun and moon undergo an eclipse and you try to save them,[3] a drought occurs and you pray for rain; you consult the arts of divination before making a decision on some important matter. But it is not as though you could hope to accomplish anything by such ceremonies. They are done merely for ornament. Hence the gentleman regards them as ornaments, but the common people regard them as supernatural. He who considers them ornaments is fortunate; he who considers them supernatural is unfortunate.

In the heavens nothing is brighter than the sun and moon; on earth nothing is brighter than fire and water; among natural objects nothing is brighter than pearls and jewels; among men nothing is brighter than ritual principles. If the sun and moon did not rise high in the sky, their splendor would not be seen; if fire and water did not accumulate into a mass, their glow and moisture would not spread abroad; if pearls and jewels did not come to light, then kings and lords would not prize them. So if ritual principles are not applied in the state, then its fame and accomplishment will not become known. The fate of man lies with Heaven; the fate of the nation lies in ritual. If the ruler of men honors rites and promotes worthy men, he may become a true king. If he relies upon laws and loves the people, he may become a dictator. If he cares only for profit and engages in much deceit, he will be in danger. And if he engrosses himself in plots and schemes, subversion and secret evil, he will be destroyed.

Is it better to exalt Heaven and think of it,
Or to nourish its creatures and regulate them?
Is it better to obey Heaven and sing hymns to it,
Or to grasp the mandate of Heaven and make use of it?
Is it better to long for the seasons and wait for them,
Or to respond to the seasons and exploit them?
Is it better to wait for things to increase of themselves,
Or to apply your talents and transform them?
Is it better to think of things but regard them as outside you,
Or to control things and not let them slip your grasp?
Is it better to long for the source from which things are born,
Or to possess the means to bring them to completion?

Hence if you set aside what belongs to man and long for what belongs to Heaven, you mistake the nature of all things.

What the hundred kings of antiquity never departed from — this may serve as the abiding principle of the Way. To the ups and downs of history, respond with this single principle. If you apply it well, there will be no disorder; but if you do not understand it, you will not know how to respond to change. The essence of this principle has never ceased to exist. Disorder is

[3]According to *Tso chuan*, Duke Wen 15th year, when an eclipse occurs, the king should beat a drum at the altar of the soil and the feudal lords should beat drums in their courts in order to drive it away.

born from misunderstanding of it; order consists in applying it thoroughly. If you harmonize with what is best in the Way, all will go well; if you distort what is best in the Way, you cannot govern effectively; if you mistake what is best in the Way, you will be led into grave error.

When men wade across a river, they mark the deep places; but if the markers are not clear, those who come after will fall in. He who governs the people marks the Way; but if the markers are not clear, disorder will result. Rites are the markers. He who does away with rites blinds the world; and when the world is blinded, great disorder results. Hence, if the Way is made clear in all its parts, different marks set up to indicate the outside and inside, and the dark and light places are made constant, then the pits which entrap the people can be avoided.

The ten thousand beings are only one corner of the Way. One species of being is only one corner of the ten thousand beings. The stupid man is only one corner of one species. He himself believes that he understands the Way, though of course he does not. Shen Tzu[4] could see the advantages of holding back, but not the advantages of taking the lead. Lao Tzu could see the advantages of humbling oneself, but not the advantages of raising one's station. Mo Tzu could see the advantages of uniformity, but not those of diversity. Sung Tzu[5] could see the advantages of having few desires, but not those of having many. If everyone holds back and no one takes the lead, then there will be no gate to advancement for the people. If everyone humbles himself and no one tries to improve his station, then the distinctions between eminent and humble will become meaningless. If there is only uniformity and no diversity, then the commands of government can never be carried out. If there is only a lessening of desires and never an increase, then there will be no way to educate and transform the people.[6] This is what the *Documents* means when it says: "Do not go by what you like, but follow the way of the king; do not go by what you hate, but follow the king's road." (Chapter 17.)

III
Hsün-tzu: Man's Nature Is Evil

Man's nature is evil; goodness is the result of conscious activity. The nature of man is such that he is born with a fondness for profit. If he indulges this fondness, it will lead him into wrangling and strife, and all sense of courtesy and humility will disappear. He is born with feelings of envy and hate, and if he indulges these, they will lead him into violence and crime, and all sense of loyalty and good faith will disappear. Man is born with the desires of the eyes and ears, with a fondness for beautiful sights and sounds. If he indulges these,

[4]Shen Tao, a Taoist-Legalist thinker who, according to the "T'ien-hsia" chapter of *Chuang Tzu*, preached a doctrine of passivity.
[5]Sung Chien, a philosopher who, according to the same source, taught a life of frugality and few desires.
[6]Because they will not be attracted by the hope of reward.

they will lead him into license and wantonness, and all ritual principles and correct forms will be lost. Hence, any man who follows his nature and indulges his emotions will inevitably become involved in wrangling and strife, will violate the forms and rules of society, and will end as a criminal. Therefore, man must first be transformed by the instructions of a teacher and guided by ritual principles, and only then will he be able to observe the dictates of courtesy and humility, obey the forms and rules of society, and achieve order. It is obvious from this, then, that man's nature is evil, and that his goodness is the result of conscious activity.

A warped piece of wood must wait until it has been laid against the straightening board, steamed, and forced into shape before it can become straight; a piece of blunt metal must wait until it has been whetted on a grindstone before it can become sharp. Similarly, since man's nature is evil, it must wait for the instructions of a teacher before it can become upright, and for the guidance of ritual principles before it can become orderly. If men have no teachers to instruct them, they will be inclined towards evil and not upright; and if they have no ritual principles to guide them, they will be perverse and violent and lack order. In ancient times the sage kings realized that man's nature is evil, and that therefore he inclines toward evil and violence and is not upright or orderly. Accordingly they created ritual principles and laid down certain regulations in order to reform man's emotional nature and make it upright, in order to train and transform it and guide it in the proper channels. In this way they caused all men to become orderly and to conform to the Way. Hence, today any man who takes to heart the instructions of his teacher, applies himself to his studies, and abides by ritual principles may become a gentleman, but anyone who gives free rein to his emotional nature, is content to indulge his passions, and disregards ritual principles becomes a petty man. It is obvious from this, therefore, that man's nature is evil, and that his goodness is the result of conscious activity.

Mencius states that man is capable of learning because his nature is good, but I say that this is wrong. It indicates that he has not really understood man's nature nor distinguished properly between the basic nature and conscious activity. The nature is that which is given by Heaven; you cannot learn it, you cannot acquire it by effort. Ritual principles, on the other hand, are created by sages; you can learn to apply them, you can work to bring them to completion. That part of man which cannot be learned or acquired by effort is called the nature; that part of him which can be acquired by learning and brought to completion by effort is called conscious activity. This is the difference between nature and conscious activity.

It is a part of man's nature that his eyes can see and his ears can hear. But the faculty of clear sight can never exist separately from the eye, nor can the faculty of keen hearing exist separately from the ear. It is obvious, then, that you cannot acquire clear sight and keen hearing by study. Mencius states that man's nature is good, and that all evil arises because he loses his original nature. Such a view, I believe, is erroneous. It is the way with man's nature that as soon as he is born he begins to depart from his original naïveté and simplicity, and therefore he must inevitably lose what Mencius regards as his original nature.[1] It is obvious from this, then, that the nature of man is evil.

Those who maintain that the nature is good praise and approve whatever has not departed from the original simplicity and naïveté of the child. That is, they consider that beauty belongs to the original simplicity and naïveté and goodness to the original mind in the same way that clear sight is inseparable from the eye and keen hearing from the ear. Hence, they maintain that [the nature possesses goodness] in the same way that the eye possesses clear vision or the ear keenness of hearing. Now it is the nature of man that when he is hungry he will desire satisfaction, when he is cold he will desire warmth, and when he is weary he will desire rest. This is his emotional nature. And yet a man, although he is hungry, will not dare to be the first to eat if he is in the presence of his elders, because he knows that he should yield to them, and although he is weary, he will not dare to demand rest because he knows that he should relieve others of the burden of labor. For a son to yield to his father or a younger brother to yield to his elder brother, for a son to relieve his father of work or a young brother to relieve his elder brother—acts such as these are all contrary to man's nature and run counter to his emotions. And yet they represent the way of filial piety and the proper forms enjoined by ritual principles. Hence, if men follow their emotional nature, there will be no courtesy or humility; courtesy and humility in fact run counter to man's emotional nature. From this it is obvious, then, that man's nature is evil, and that his goodness is the result of conscious activity.

Someone may ask: if man's nature is evil, then where do ritual principles come from? I would reply: all ritual principles are produced by the conscious activity of the sages; essentially they are not products of man's nature. A potter molds clay and makes a vessel, but the vessel is the product of the conscious activity of the potter, not essentially a product of his human nature. A carpenter carves a piece of wood and makes a utensil, but the utensil is the product of the conscious activity of the carpenter, not essentially a product of his human nature. The sage gathers together his thoughts and ideas, experiments with various forms of conscious activity, and so produces ritual principles and sets forth laws and regulations. Hence, these ritual principles and laws are the products of the conscious activity of the sage, not essentially products of his human nature.

Phenomena such as the eye's fondness for beautiful forms, the ear's fondness for beautiful sounds, the mouth's fondness for delicious flavors, the mind's fondness for profit, or the body's fondness for pleasure and ease—these are all products of the emotional nature of man. They are instinctive and spontaneous; man does not have to do anything to produce them. But that which does not come into being instinctively but must wait for some activity

[1]Mencius, it will be recalled, stated: "The great man is he who does not lose his child's-heart" (*Mencius* IVB, 12). If I understand Hsün Tzu correctly, he is arguing that this "child's-heart," i.e., the simplicity and naïveté of the baby, will inevitably be lost by all men simply in the process of growing up, and therefore it cannot be regarded as the source of goodness.

to bring it into being is called the product of conscious activity. These are the products of the nature and of conscious activity respectively, and the proof that they are not the same. Therefore, the sage transforms his nature and initiates conscious activity; from this conscious activity he produces ritual principles, and when they have been produced he sets up rules and regulations. Hence, ritual principles and rules are produced by the sage. In respect to human nature the sage is the same as all other men and does not surpass them; it is only in his conscious activity that he differs from and surpasses other men.

It is man's emotional nature to love profit and desire gain. Suppose now that a man has some wealth to be divided. If he indulges his emotional nature, loving profit and desiring gain, then he will quarrel and wrangle even with his own brothers over the division. But if he has been transformed by the proper forms of ritual principle, then he will be capable of yielding even to a complete stranger. Hence, to indulge the emotional nature leads to the quarreling of brothers, but to be transformed by ritual principles makes a man capable of yielding to strangers.

Every man who desires to do good does so precisely because his nature is evil. A man whose accomplishments are meager longs for greatness; an ugly man longs for beauty; a man in cramped quarters longs for spaciousness; a poor man longs for wealth; a humble man longs for eminence. Whatever a man lacks in himself he will seek outside. But if a man is already rich, he will not long for wealth, and if he is already eminent, he will not long for greater power. What a man already possesses in himself he will not bother to look for outside. From this we can see that men desire to do good precisely because their nature is evil. Ritual principles are certainly not a part of man's original nature. Therefore, he forces himself to study and to seek to possess them. An understanding of ritual principles is not a part of man's original nature, and therefore he ponders and plans and thereby seeks to understand them. Hence, man in the state in which he is born neither possesses nor understands ritual principles. If he does not possess ritual principles, his behavior will be chaotic, and if he does not understand them, he will be wild and irresponsible. In fact, therefore, man in the state in which he is born possesses this tendency towards chaos and irresponsibility. From this it is obvious, then, that man's nature is evil, and that his goodness is the result of conscious activity.

Mencius states that man's nature is good, but I say that this view is wrong. All men in the world, past and present, agree in defining goodness as that which is upright, reasonable, and orderly, and evil as that which is prejudiced, irresponsible, and chaotic. This is the distinction between good and evil. Now suppose that man's nature was in fact intrinsically upright, reasonable, and orderly—then what need would there be for sage kings and ritual principles? The existence of sage kings and ritual principles could certainly add nothing to the situation. But because man's nature is in fact evil, this is not so. Therefore, in ancient times the sages, realizing that man's nature is evil, that it is prejudiced and not upright, irresponsible and lacking in order, for this reason established the authority of the ruler to control it, elucidated ritual principles to transform it, set up laws and standards to correct it, and meted out strict punishments to restrain it. As a result, all the world achieved order and conformed to goodness. Such is the orderly government of the sage kings and the transforming power of ritual principles. Now let someone try doing away with the authority of the ruler, ignoring the transforming power of ritual principles, rejecting the order that comes from laws and standards, and dispensing with the restrictive power of punishments, and then watch and see how the people of the world treat each other. He will find that the powerful impose upon the weak and rob them, the many terrorize the few and extort from them, and in no time the whole world will be given up to chaos and mutual destruction. It is obvious from this, then, that man's nature is evil, and that his goodness is the result of conscious activity.

Those who are good at discussing antiquity must demonstrate the validity of what they say in terms of modern times; those who are good at discussing Heaven must show proofs from the human world. In discussions of all kinds, men value what is in accord with the facts and what can be proved to be valid. Hence if a man sits on his mat propounding some theory, he should be able to stand right up and put it into practice, and show that it can be extended over a wide area with equal validity. Now Mencius states that man's nature is good, but this is neither in accord with the facts, nor can it be proved to be valid. One may sit down and propound such a theory, but he cannot stand up and put it into practice, nor can he extend it over a wide area with any success at all. How, then, could it be anything but erroneous?

If the nature of man were good, we could dispense with sage kings and forget about ritual principles. But if it is evil, then we must go along with the sage kings and honor ritual principles. The straightening board is made because of the warped wood; the plumb line is employed because things are crooked; rulers are set up and ritual principles elucidated because the nature of man is evil. From this it is obvious, then, that man's nature is evil, and that his goodness is the result of conscious activity. A straight piece of wood does not have to wait for the straightening board to become straight; it is straight by nature. But a warped piece of wood must wait until it has been laid against the straightening board, steamed, and forced into shape before it can become straight, because by nature it is warped. Similarly, since man's nature is evil, he must wait for the ordering power of the sage kings and the transforming power of ritual principles; only then can he achieve order and conform to goodness. From this it is obvious, then, that man's nature is evil, and that his goodness is the result of conscious activity.

Someone may ask whether ritual principles and concerted conscious activity are not themselves a part of man's nature, so that for that reason the sage is capable of producing them. But I would answer that this is not so. A potter may mold clay and produce an earthen pot, but surely molding pots out of clay is not a part of the potter's human nature. A carpenter may carve wood and produce a utensil, but surely carving utensils out of wood is not a part of the carpenter's human nature. The sage stands in the same relation to ritual principles as the potter to the things he molds and produces. How, then, could ritual principles and concerted conscious activity be a part of man's basic human nature?

As far as human nature goes, the sages Yao and Shun possessed the same nature as the tyrant Chieh or Robber Chih, and the gentleman possesses the same nature as the petty man. Would you still maintain, then, that ritual principles and concerted conscious activity are a part of man's nature? If you do so, then what reason is there to pay any particular honor to Yao, Shun, or the gentleman? The reason people honor Yao, Shun, and the gentleman is that they are able to transform their nature, apply themselves to conscious activity, and produce ritual principles. The sage, then, must stand in the same relation to ritual principles as the potter to the things he molds and produces. Looking at it this way, how could ritual principles and concerted conscious activity be a part of man's nature? The reason people despise Chieh, Robber Chih, or the petty man is that they give free rein to their nature, follow their emotions, and are content to indulge their passions, so that their conduct is marked by greed and contentiousness. Therefore, it is clear that man's nature is evil, and that his goodness is the result of conscious activity.

Heaven did not bestow any particular favor upon Tseng Tzu, Min Tzu-ch'ien, or Hsiao-i that it withheld from other men. And yet these three men among all others proved most capable of carrying out their duties as sons and winning fame for their filial piety. Why? Because of their thorough attention to ritual principles. Heaven has not bestowed any particular favor upon the inhabitants of Ch'i and Lu which it has withheld from the people of Ch'in. And yet when it comes to observing the duties of father and son and the separation of roles between husband and wife, the inhabitants of Ch'in cannot match the filial reverence and respect for proper form which marks the people of Ch'i and Lu. Why? Because the people of Ch'in give free rein to their emotional nature, are content to indulge their passions, and are careless of ritual principles. It is certainly not due to any difference in human nature between the two groups.

The man in the street can become a Yü. What does this mean? What made the sage emperor Yü a Yü, I would reply, was the fact that he practiced benevolence and righteousness and abided by the proper rules and standards. If this is so, then benevolence, righteousness, and proper standards must be based upon principles which can be known and practiced. Any man in the street has the essential faculties needed to understand benevolence, righteousness, and proper standards, and the potential ability to put them into practice. Therefore it is clear that he can become a Yü.

Would you maintain that benevolence, righteousness, and proper standards are not based upon any principles that can be known and practiced? If so, then even a Yü could not have understood or practiced them. Or would you maintain that the man in the street does not have the essential faculties needed to understand them or the potential ability to put them into practice? If so, then you are saying that the man in the street in his family life cannot understand the duties required of a father or a son and in public life cannot comprehend the correct relationship between ruler and subject. But in fact this is not true. Any man in the street *can* understand the duties required of a father or a son and *can* comprehend the correct relationship between ruler and subject. Therefore, it is obvious that the essential faculties needed to understand such ethical principles and the potential ability to put them into practice must be a part of his make-up. Now if he takes these faculties and abilities and applies them to the principles of benevolence and righteousness, which we have already shown to be knowable and practicable, then it is obvious that he can become a Yü. If the man in the street applies himself to training and study, concentrates his mind and will, and considers and examines things carefully, continuing his efforts over a long period of time and accumulating good acts without stop, then he can achieve a godlike understanding and form a triad with Heaven and earth. The sage is a man who has arrived where he has through the accumulation of good acts.

You have said, someone may object, that the sage has arrived where he has through the accumulation of good acts. Why is it, then, that everyone is not able to accumulate good acts in the same way? I would reply: everyone is capable of doing so, but not everyone can be made to do so. The petty man is capable of becoming a gentleman, yet he is not willing to do so; the gentleman is capable of becoming a petty man but he is not willing to do so. The petty man and the gentleman are perfectly capable of changing places; the fact that they do not actually do so is what I mean when I say that they are capable of doing so but they cannot be made to do so. Hence, it is correct to say that the man in the street is *capable* of becoming a Yü but it is not necessarily correct to say that he will in fact find it possible to do so. But although he does not find it possible to do so does not prove that he is incapable of doing so.

A person with two feet is theoretically capable of walking to every corner of the earth, although in fact no one has ever found it possible to do so. Similarly, the artisan, the carpenter, the farmer, and the merchant are theoretically capable of exchanging professions, although in actual practice they find it impossible to do so. From this we can see that, although someone may be theoretically capable of becoming something, he may not in practice find it possible to do so. But although he does not find it possible to do so, this does not prove that he is not capable of doing so. To find it practically possible or impossible to do something and to be capable or incapable of doing something are two entirely different things. It is perfectly clear, then, that a man is theoretically capable of becoming something else.

Yao asked Shun, "What are man's emotions like?" Shun replied, "Man's emotions are very unlovely things indeed! What need is there to ask any further? Once a man acquires a wife and children, he no longer treats his parents as a filial son should. Once he succeeds in satisfying his cravings and desires, he neglects his duty to his friends. Once he has won a high position and a good stipend, he ceases to serve his sovereign with a loyal heart. Man's emotions, man's emotions—they are very unlovely things indeed! What need is there to ask any further? Only the worthy man is different from this."

There is the understanding of the sage, the understanding of the gentleman and man of breeding, the understanding of the petty man, and the understanding of the menial. He speaks many words but they are graceful and well ordered; all day he discourses on his reasons, employing a thousand different and varied modes of expression, and yet all that he says is united around a single principle: such is the understanding of the sage. He speaks little but what he says is brief and to the point, logical and clearly presented, as though laid out with a plumb line: such is the understanding of the gentleman and man of breeding. His words are all flattery, his actions irresponsible; whatever he does is shot through with error: such is the understanding of the petty man. His words are rapid and shrill but never to the point; his talents are varied and many but of no practical use; he is full of subtle distinctions and elegant turns of phrase that serve no practical purpose; he ignores right or wrong, disdains to discuss crooked or straight, but seeks only to overpower the arguments of his opponent: such is the understanding of the menial.[2]

There is superior valor, there is the middle type of valor, and there is inferior valor. When proper standards prevail in the world, to dare to bring your own conduct into accord with them; when the Way of the former kings prevails, to dare to follow its dictates; to refuse to bow before the ruler of a disordered age, to refuse to follow the customs of the people of a disordered age; to accept poverty and hardship if they are in the cause of benevolent action; to reject wealth and eminence if they are not consonant with benevolent action; if the world recognizes you, to share in the world's joys; if the world does not recognize you, to stand alone and without fear: this is superior valor. To be reverent in bearing and modest in intention; to value honor and make light of material goods; to dare to promote and honor the worthy, and reject and cast off the unworthy: such is the middle type of valor. To ignore your own safety in the quest for wealth; to make light of danger and try to talk your way out of every difficulty; to rely on lucky escapes; to ignore right and wrong, just and unjust, and seek only to overpower the arguments of your opponents: such is inferior valor.

Fan-jo and Chü-shu were famous bows of ancient times, but if they had not first been subjected to presses and straighteners, they would never have become true of themselves. Ts'ung of Duke Huan of Ch'i, Ch'üeh of T'ai-kung of Ch'i, Lu of King Wen of the Chou, Hu of Lord Chuang of Ch'u, and Kan-chiang, Mu-yeh, Chü-ch'üeh, and Pi-lü of King Ho-lü of Wu were all famous swords of antiquity, but if they had not been subjected to the grindstone, they would never have become sharp, and if men of strength had not wielded them, they would never have been able to cut anything. Hua-liu, Ch'i-chi, Hsien-li, and Lu-erh were famous horses of antiquity, but if they had not been subjected to the restraint of bit and bridle and the threat of the whip, and driven by a master driver like Tsao-fu, they would never have succeeded in traveling a thousand *li* in one day.

---

[2]This last is of course aimed at the logicians.

In the same way a man, no matter how fine his nature or how keen his mind, must seek a worthy teacher to study under and good companions to associate with. If he studies under a worthy teacher, he will be able to hear about the ways of Yao, Shun, Yü, and T'ang, and if he associates with good companions, he will be able to observe conduct that is loyal and respectful. Then, although he is not aware of it, he will day by day progress in the practice of benevolence and righteousness, for the environment he is subjected to will cause him to progress. But if a man associates with men who are not good, then he will hear only deceit and lies and will see only conduct that is marked by wantonness, evil, and greed. Then, although he is not aware of it, he himself will soon be in danger of severe punishment, for the environment he is subjected to will cause him to be in danger. An old text says, "If you do not know a man, look at his friends; if you do not know a ruler, look at his attendants." Environment is the important thing! Environment is the important thing! (Chapter 23.)

CHAPTER 20

CHINESE BUDDHISM

Although Confucianism was securely established as the official philosophy from the Han dynasty on, it continued to be challenged—not only by the Taoist developments known as Neo-Taoism, but also, beginning in the third and fourth centuries, by Buddhism, which had found its way to China several centuries earlier. Indeed, Buddhism became the dominant way of thought in the Sui and T'ang dynasties (589-906), temporarily eclipsing both Confucianism and Taoism. The interactions of Buddhism, Taoism, and Confucianism produced the unique forms of Chinese Buddhist thought and practice known as T'ien Tai, Pure Land (Ching-tu), Hua-yen, and Ch'an.

Although all the schools of Indian Buddhism found their way to China, it was the Middle Way philosophy of Mahāyāna that eventually provided the basis for the Chinese transformation of Buddhism into the highly successful Hua-yen and Ch'an schools. *Śūnyatā* (emptiness), the core idea of Middle Way thought, came to be seen as an essentially positive notion, the omnipresence of Buddhahood, the true reality of all things, realizable when separation and permanence were overcome. The Chinese transformation of the Middle Way philosophy can be seen most clearly in the Hua-yen school, which borrows freely from T'ien Tai, whereas its practical side can be seen most clearly in Ch'an thought and practice. For this reason we have chosen texts from these two schools to represent Chinese Buddhism.

The Hua-yen ("Flower Splendor") school was founded by Tu-shun (557-640) but owes its prominence to Fa-tsang (643-712), who developed it into one of the most profound of all the schools of Chinese Buddhism. Starting with an understanding of *śūnyatā* as the dynamic and interrelated nature of existence, Fa-tsang develops this idea through an analysis of the mutual interpenetration and identity of all elements of existence (*dharmas*). The totally and dynamic interrelated nature of existence flows from the fact that each element of existence manifests six characteristics: (1) universality, (2) particularity, (3) difference, (4) identity, (5) integration, and (6) disintegration. Because the whole universe is nothing other than the totality of *dharmas*, and because *dharmas* have no being of their own, their existence

—and that of everything in the universe—consists of their mutual, reciprocal implication, their compete interpenetration. One of the clearest discussions of this complete interpenetration of things is found in Fa-tsang's *Hua-yen Treatise* (*Hua-yen i-ch'eng chiao i fen-ch'i chang*), where the teaching is illustrated with the analogy of the identity of a rafter and building. The translation is by Francis H. Cook, *Hua-yen Buddhism: The Jewel Net of Indra* (University Park, Pa.: Pennsylvania State University Press, 1977), chapter 6, which also provides a running commentary; chapters 4 and 5 explain the central concepts of Hua-yen. Thomas Cleary, *Entry Into the Inconceivable: An Introduction to Hua-yen Buddhism* (Honolulu: University of Hawaii Press, 1983), is the best introduction to Hua-yen. It includes clear and readable translations of the major thinkers and an appendix that summarizes and highlights the Hua-yen scripture on which the school is based.

Ch'an Buddhism is practice oriented, and its most important teachings have to do with the practices facilitating enlightenment, especially meditation. Because Buddha-nature is present in everyone and everything, anyone can become enlightened, and anything can serve as an occasion for realizing enlightenment. Meditative sitting, in which all concerns, distractions, and dualities are allowed to fall away, was emphasized by Bodhidharma (fifth century), who was traditionally regarded as the founder of this school. Although sitting meditation remained the primary practice, Ch'an added koan (*kung-an*) practice as a way of discovering the original, enlightened mind. Koans are paradoxical sayings that are to be taken seriously, as announcing truth. But the student trying to understand the truth of the saying comes to realize that conceptualization cannot grasp this truth, and is therefore driven beyond the conceptualizing mind to a deeper, spontaneous, and undivided awareness. Not only sayings, but shouts and slaps as well, can help a student move beyond ordinary understanding to deeper insight, to a deeper level of being. In the Ch'an selections from Hui-neng and I-hsüan, sayings, shouts, and beatings are all referred to as means of awakening the enlightened mind.

The *Platform Sutra* of Hui-neng (638–713) represents the full flowering of Ch'an Buddhism. Made famous by Hui-neng's disciple, Shen-hui, this text is one of the most important of the Ch'an school. The translation by Philip B. Yampolsky, *The Platform Sutra of the Sixth Patriarch* (New York: Columbia University Press, 1967), contains the text of the Tun-huang manuscript, an extensive introduction, and copious notes. The selections from Master I-hsüan (d. 867), regarded as the founder of the Lin-chi (Rinzai), school, which emphasized sudden ("Lightning") enlightenment, are from Wing-tsit Chan, *A Source Book in Chinese Philosophy* (Princeton: Princeton University Press, 1963). Heinrich Dumoulin, *Zen Buddhism: A History*, volume 1 (New York: Macmillan Publishing Company, 1988), part 2 ("Origins and Blossoming in China"), is the best historical account of Ch'an (zen), with considerable emphasis on the substance of the various schools and teachings.

I
Fa-tsang: Hua-yen Treatise*

THE PERFECT INTERPENETRATION OF THE SIX CHARACTERISTICS

The interdependent origination of the six characteristics will be divided into three parts. First, the names of the six characteristics will be briefly explained; second, the concepts which have given rise to this doctrine will be shown; third, this teaching will be elucidated by means of questions and answers.

First, the names: they are the characteristics of universality, particularity, identity, difference, integration, and disintegration. "Universality" means that the one includes many qualities. "Particularity" means that the many qualities are not identical, because the universal is necessarily made up of many dissimilar particulars. "Identity" means that the many elements are not different, because they are identical in forming the one universal. "Difference" means that each element is different from the standpoint of any other element. "Integration" means that the totality of interdependent origination is formed as a result of these elements. "Disintegration" means that each element remains what it is [as an individual with its own characteristics] and is not disturbed [in its own nature].

Second, the concepts which have given rise to this teaching [of the six characteristics]: this teaching attempts to show such things as the interdependent origination of the *dharma-dhātu*, which is the perfect doctrine of the one vehicle, the infinite interpenetration of all things, the unimpeded identity of all things, and all other matters including the infinite interrelationship of noumenon and phenomenon and so on, shown in the symbol of the net of Indra. When these concepts are manifested then when one of the many obstacles is overcome, all are overcome, and one acquires the destruction of faults the nine times and ten times. In practicing the virtues, when one is perfected, all are perfected, and with regard to reality, when one part is revealed, everything is revealed. All things are endowed with universality and particularity, beginning and end are the same, and when one first arouses the aspiration for enlightenment, one also becomes perfectly enlightened. Indeed, the interdependent origination of the *dharma-dhātu* results from the interfusion of the six characteristics, the simultaneity of cause and result, perfectly free identity, and the fact that the goal is inherent in causal practice. The cause of enlightenment is the comprehension and practice, as well as enlightenment, of Samantabhadra, and the result is the infinitude which is revealed in the realm of the ten Buddhas, all the details of which can be found in the *Avantaṁsaka Sūtra*.

---

*Reprinted with permission from Francis H. Cook, *Hua-yen Buddhism: The Jewel Net of Indra* (University Park, Pa.: Pennsylvania State University Press, 1977).

Third, the elucidation by means of questions and answers. Now, the law of interdependent origination is common to all situations, but here, briefly, I shall discuss this through the use of the analogy of a building formed by conditions.

Question: what is the universal? *Answer:* it is the building. *Question:* that is nothing but various conditions, such as a rafter; what is the building itself? *Answer:* the rafter is the building. Why? Because the rafter by itself totally makes the building. If you get rid of the rafter, the building is not formed. When there is a rafter, there is a building.

Question: if the rafter all by itself totally creates the building, then if there are still no roof tiles and other things, how can it create the building? *Answer:* when there are no tiles and such things, the rafter is not a rafter, so it does not create the building. A nonrafter is a rafter which does not create a building. Now, when I say that the rafter does create it, I am only discussing the ability of a real rafter to create it. I am not saying that a nonrafter makes it. Why is that? A rafter is a condition. When it has not yet created the building, it is not yet a condition, and therefore it is not a rafter. If it is a real rafter, it totally forms the building. If it does not totally form it, it is not called a rafter.

Question: if all the various conditions such as the rafter each exerts its own partial power, thus creating the building together and not through total power, what would be the error? *Answer:* there would be the errors of eternalism and annihilationism. If each part does not wholly cause the building to be made and only exerts partial power, then each condition would have only partial power. They would consist simply of many individual partial powers and would not make one whole building. This is annihilationism [because there could be no building]. Also, the various conditions cannot completely make the building if they each possess partial power, so that if you maintain that there is a whole building, then since it exists without a cause, this is eternalism. Also, if the rafter does not wholly create the building, then when the one rafter is removed, the whole building should remain. However, since the total building is not formed, then you should understand that the building is not formed by the partial power of a condition such as the rafter but by its total power.

Question: why would there be no building if a single rafter is lacking? *Answer:* that would only be a spoiled building, not a perfect building. Therefore, you should know that the perfect building is inherent in the one rafter. Since it is inherent in this one rafter, you should know therefore that the rafter is the building. *Question:* since the building is identical with the rafter, then the remaining planks, tiles, and so on, must be identical with the rafter, aren't they? *Answer:* generally speaking, they are all identical with the rafter. The reason is that if you take away a rafter, there is no building, because if there is no rafter, the building is spoiled. And when you have a spoiled building, you cannot speak of planks, tiles, and so on. Therefore, the planks, tiles, and so on, are identical with the rafter. If they are not the rafter, then the building is not formed, for planks, tiles, and so on, do not become formed either. Now, since they all are formed together, you should know that they are identical. Since this is so of the one rafter, the other rafters are the same. Therefore, if all the *dharmas* which constitute interdependent origination are not formed as an integrated totality of interdependence, then they cease. If they are all formed together, then they are all identical with each other, interfused, completely free in their interrelationships, extremely difficult to conceive, and surpass commonsense notions. The nature of things, which is interdependent origination, is universal, so you can understand everything else by analogy with the above example.

Second, the characteristic of particularity: all the conditions such as the rafter are parts in the whole. If they were not parts, they could not form a whole, because without parts, there is no whole. What this means is that intrinsically the whole is formed of parts, so that without parts, there can be no whole. Therefore, the parts become parts by means of the whole. *Question:* if the whole is identical with the parts, how can it be a whole? *Answer:* it can be a whole precisely because it is identical with the parts. Just as the rafter is identical with the building, which is called the characteristic of universality [possessed by the rafter-part], so also because it is a rafter, we speak of the characteristic of particularity. If the rafter is not identical with the building, it is not a rafter; if the building is not identical with the rafter, it is not a building. The universal and the particular are identical. This is how you should understand it.

Question: if they are identical, how can you speak of parts? *Answer:* because parts become parts on the basis of their identity with the whole. If they [i.e., part and whole] were not identical, the whole would exist outside the parts, and could not then be a whole; the parts would exist outside the whole and could not then be parts. If you think about it, it is clear.

Question: what would the error be if they are not parts? *Answer:* the errors of annihilationism and eternalism. If there were no parts, there would be no distinct rafters, tiles, and so on. This would be annihilationism, because without distinct parts such as rafters, tiles, and so on, there would be no building. If it is maintained that there can still be a building without distinct rafters, tiles, and the like, this is eternalism.

Third, the characteristic of identity: the various conditions such as the rafter all combine and create the building. Because there is no difference among them [as conditions], all are called "conditions of the building." This is called the characteristic of identity because they are all identically conditions within the context of the building which they create. *Question:* what is the difference between this and the above characteristic of universality? *Answer:* the characteristic of universality is spoken of only from the standpoint of the one whole building; the characteristic of identity concerns all the various conditions such as the rafter. Even though each part is different in its own nature, they each possess the characteristic of identity because they are all identical in their power of creation. *Question:* what is the error if they are not identical? *Answer:* the errors of annihilationism and eternalism. If they are not identical, the conditions such as the rafter would oppose each other, and thus would not be able to create the building identically. This is annihilationism, because there would be no building. If they cannot create the building, because each is different, and you still say that there is a building, this is eternalism, because there is a building without any cause.

Fourth, the characteristic of difference: the various conditions such as the rafter are different from each other in conformity with their own individual species. *Question:* if they are different, how can they be identical? *Answer:* they are identical precisely because they are different. If they were not different, then since the rafter is eleven feet long, the tiles would be the same, and since this would destroy the original condition then, as before, they could not function identically as conditions for the building. Now, since there is a building, they must all function identically as conditions, and so you can understand that they are different.

Question: what is the difference between this and the characteristic of particularity? *Answer:* particularity means that all the conditions, such as the rafter, are distinct within the one building. Now, when we speak of difference, we mean that each of the various conditions, such as the rafter, are different from each other.

Question: what is the error if they are not different? *Answer:* there would be the errors of annihilationism and eternalism. If they are not different, then the roof tiles would be eleven feet long, like the rafter. This would destroy the original condition of the tile and the building could not be formed. Therefore, you have annihilationism. Eternalism results from attachment to the existence of a building which has no conditions, because if the various conditions are not different, then the necessary conditions for the building do not exist.

Fifth, the characteristic of integration: because the building is created as a result of these various conditions, the rafter and other parts are called conditions. If this were not so, neither of the two [i.e., forming conditions or formed result] would come to be. Now, since they actually form the building, you should know that this is the characteristic of integration.

Question: when we actually see the various conditions such as the rafter, each retains its own character and does not literally become a building; how is it able to form the building? *Answer:* simply because the various conditions such as the rafter do not become the building, and retain their own character, they are able to create the building. The reason for this is that if the rafter becomes the building, it loses its intrinsic character of being a rafter, and therefore the building cannot come into being. Now, because it does not become [the building], conditions such as the rafter and so on are manifested. Because they are manifested [as being just what they are], the building is created. Also, if they do not make the building, the rafters and so on are not to be called conditions. However, since they can be said to be conditions, you should know that they definitely create the house.

Question: if they do not become integrated, what is the error? *Answer:* the errors of annihilationism and eternalism. Why? The building is created originally as a result of the various conditions such as the rafter. Now, if they do not create the building all together [in their integration], the existence of the building is not possible, and this is annihilationism. Originally, the conditions create the building, and thus they are called rafters and so on. Now, since they do not create the building, they are not rafters, and this is annihilationism. If they do not become integrated, then because a building exists without a cause, this is eternalism. It is also eternalism if the rafters do not create the building but are still called rafters.

Sixth, the characteristic of disintegration: each of the various conditions such as the rafter retains its own separate character and does not become the building. *Question:* if you see the various conditions such as the rafter right in front of you, creating and perfecting the building, how can you say that they do not intrinsically become the building? *Answer:* simply because they do not become the building, the *dharma* or building can be formed. If they become the building and do not retain their own characters, then the building cannot come into being. Why? Because if they become the building, they lose their [individual] characters, and the building cannot be formed. Now, since the building is formed, you should know that they do not become the building.

Question: if they were to become the building, what would be the error? *Answer:* there would be the errors of annihilationism and eternalism. If it is claimed that the rafter becomes the building, the character of rafterness is lost. Because the character of the rafter is lost, the building has no conditions for its existence and cannot exist. This is annihilationism. If the character of the rafter is lost, and yet a building were able to exist, this would be eternalism, because the building would exist without conditions.

Also, universality is the one building, particularity consists of the various conditions, identity is the nondifference [of the parts as conditions for the whole], difference is the difference of the various conditions [from the standpoint of each other], integration means that the various conditions create the result, the disintegration means that each [condition] retains its own character. To summarize this in a verse:

The many in the one is the characteristic of universality;
The many not being the one is the characteristic of particularity;
The universal is formed by many species which are in themselves identical;
Their identity is shown in the difference of each in its own essence;
The principle of the interdependent origination of the one and the many is wonderful integration;
Disintegration means that each retains its own character and does not become [the whole].
This all belongs to the realm of [Buddha-] wisdom and is not said from the standpoint of worldly knowledge.
By means of this skillful device [of the teaching of the six characteristics], you can understand Hua-yen.

II
Hui-neng: The Platform Sūtra*

1. The Master Hui-neng ascended the high seat at the lecture hall of the Ta-fan Temple and expounded the Dharma[1] of the Great Perfection of Wisdom, and transmitted the precepts of formlessness. At that time over ten thousand monks, nuns, and lay followers sat before him. The prefect of Shao-chou, Wei Ch'ü, some thirty officials from various departments, and some thirty Confucian scholars all begged the Master to preach on the Dharma of the Great Perfection of Wisdom. The prefect then had the monk-disciple Fa-hai record his words so that they might become known to later generations and be of benefit to students of the Way, in order that they might receive the pivot of the teaching and transmit it among themselves, taking these words as their authority.

2. The Master Hui-neng said: "Good friends, purify your minds and concentrate on the Dharma of the Great Perfection of Wisdom."

The Master stopped speaking and quieted his own mind. Then after a good while he said: "Good friends, listen quietly. My father was originally an official at Fan-yang. He was later dismissed from his post and banished as a commoner to Hsin-chou in Ling-nan. While I was still a child, my father died and my old mother and I, a solitary child, moved to Nan-hai. We suffered extreme poverty and here I sold firewood in the market place. By chance a certain man bought some firewood and then took me with him to the lodging house for officials. He took the firewood and left. Having received my money and turning towards the front gate, I happened to see another man who was reciting the Diamond Sutra. Upon hearing it my mind became clear and I was awakened.

"I asked him: 'Where do you come from that you have brought this sutra with you?'

"He answered: 'I have made obeisance to the Fifth Patriarch, Hung-jen, at the East Mountain, Feng-mu shan, in Huang-mei hsien in Ch'i-chou. At present there are over a thousand disciples there. While I was there I heard the Master encourage the monks and lay followers, saying that if they recited just the one volume, the Diamond Sutra, they could see into their own natures and with direct apprehension become Buddhas.'

"Hearing what he said, I realized that I was predestined to have heard him. Then I took leave of my mother and went to Feng-mu shan in Huang-mei and made obeisance to the Fifth Patriarch, the priest Hung-jen.

3. "The priest Hung-jen asked me: 'Where are you from that you come to this mountain to make obeisance to me? Just what is it that you are looking for from me?'

---

*Reprinted with permission from Philip B. Yampolsky, *The Platform Sūtra of the Sixth Patriarch* (New York: Columbia University Press, 1967).

[1]Dharma is the true teaching.

"I replied: 'I am from Ling-nan, a commoner from Hsin-chou. I have come this long distance only to make obeisance to you. I am seeking no particular thing, but only the Buddhadharma.'

"The Master then reproved me, saying: 'If you're from Ling-nan then you're a barbarian. How can you become a Buddha?"

"I replied: 'Although people from the south and people from the north differ, there is no north and south in Buddha nature. Although my barbarian's body and your body are not the same, what difference is there in our Buddha nature?'

"The Master wished to continue his discussion with me; however, seeing that there were other people nearby, he said no more. Then he sent me to work with the assembly. Later a lay disciple had me go to the threshing room where I spent over eight months treading the pestle.

4. "Unexpectedly one day the Fifth Patriarch called his disciples to come, and when they had assembled, he said: 'Let me preach to you. For people in this world birth and death are vital matters. You disciples make offerings all day long and seek only the field of blessings, but you do not seek to escape from the bitter sea of birth and death. Your own self-nature obscures the gateway to blessings; how can you be saved? All of you return to your rooms and look into yourselves. Men of wisdom will of themselves grasp the original nature of their *prajñā* intuition. Each of you write a verse and bring it to me. I will read your verses, and if there is one who is awakened to the cardinal meaning, I will give him the robe and the Dharma and make him the Sixth Patriarch. Hurry, hurry!'

6. "The head monk Shen-hsiu thought: 'The others won't present mind-verses because I am their teacher. If I don't offer a mind-verse, how can the Fifth Patriarch estimate the degree of understanding within my mind? If I offer my mind to the Fifth Patriarch with the intention of gaining the Dharma, it is justifiable; however, if I am seeking the patriarchship, then it cannot be justified. Then it would be like a common man usurping the saintly position. But if I don't offer my mind then I cannot learn the Dharma.' For a long time he thought about it and was very much perplexed.

"At midnight, without letting anyone see him, he went to write his mind-verse on the central section of the south corridor wall, hoping to gain the Dharma. 'If the Fifth Patriarch sees my verse and says that it . . . and there is a weighty obstacle in my past karma, then I cannot gain the Dharma and shall have to give up. The honorable Patriarch's intention is difficult to fathom.'

"Then the head monk Shen-hsiu, at midnight, holding a candle, wrote a verse on the central section of the south corridor, without anyone else knowing about it. The verse read:

> The body is the Bodhi tree,
> The mind is like a clear mirror.
> At all times we must strive to polish it,
> And must not let the dust collect.

"The Fifth Patriarch said: 'This verse you wrote shows that you still have not reached true understanding. You have merely arrived at the front of the gate but have yet to be able to enter it. If common people practice according to your verse they will not fall. But in seeking the ultimate enlightenment (*bodhi*) one will not succeed with such an understanding. You must enter the gate and see your own original nature. Go and think about it for a day or two and then make another verse and present it to me. If you have been able to enter the gate and see your own original nature, then I will give you the robe and the Dharma.' The head monk Shen-hsiu left, but after several days he was still unable to write a verse.

8. "One day an acolyte passed by the threshing room reciting this verse. As soon as I heard it I knew that the person who had written it had yet to know his own nature and to discern the cardinal meaning. I asked the boy: 'What's the name of the verse you were reciting just now?'

"The boy answered me, saying: 'Don't you know? The Master said that birth and death are vital matters, and he told his disciples each to write a verse if they wanted to inherit the robe and the Dharma, and to bring it for him to see. He who was awakened to the cardinal meaning would be given the robe and the Dharma and be made the Sixth Patriarch. There is a head monk by the name of Shen-hsiu who happened to write a verse on formlessness on the walls of the south corridor. The Fifth Patriarch had all his disciples recite the verse, saying that those who awakened to it would see into their own self-natures, and that those who practiced according to it would attain emancipation.'

"I said: 'I've been treading the pestle for more than eight months, but haven't been to the hall yet. I beg you to take me to the south corridor so that I can see this verse and make obeisance to it. I also want to recite it so that I can establish causation for my next birth and be born in a Buddha-land.'

"The boy took me to the south corridor and I made obeisance before the verse. Because I was uneducated I asked someone to read it to me. As soon as I had heard it I understood the cardinal meaning. I made a verse and asked someone who was able to write to put it on the wall of the west corridor, so that I might offer my own original mind. If you do not know the original mind, studying the Dharma is to no avail. If you know the mind and see its true nature, you then awaken to the cardinal meaning. My verse said:

Bodhi originally has no tree,
The mirror also has no stand.
Buddha nature is always clean and pure;
Where is there room for dust?

"Another verse said:

The mind is the Bodhi tree,
The body is the mirror stand.
The mirror is originally clean and pure;
Where can it be stained by dust?

"The followers in the temple were all amazed when they heard my verse. Then I returned to the threshing room. The Fifth Patriarch realized that I had a splendid understanding of the cardinal meaning. Being afraid lest the assembly know this, he said to them: 'This is still not complete understanding.'

9. "At midnight the Fifth Patriarch called me into the hall and expounded the Diamond Sutra to me. Hearing it but once, I was immediately awakened, and that night I received the Dharma. None of the others knew anything about it. Then he transmitted to me the Dharma of Sudden Enlightenment and the robe, saying: 'I make you the Sixth Patriarch. The robe is the proof and is to be handed down from generation to generation. My Dharma must be transmitted from mind to mind. You must make people awaken to themselves.'

"The Fifth Patriarch told me: 'From ancient times the transmission of the Dharma has been as tenuous as a dangling thread. If you stay here there are people who will harm you. You must leave at once.'

12. "I was predestined to come to live here and to preach to you officials, monks, and laymen. My teaching has been handed down from the sages of the past; it is not my own personal knowledge. If you wish to hear the teachings of the sages of the past, each of you must quiet his mind and hear me to the end. Please cast aside your own delusions; then you will be no different from the sages of the past. What follows below is the Dharma.

The Master Hui-neng called, saying: "Good friends, enlightenment (*bodhi*) and intuitive wisdom (*prajñā*) are from the outset possessed by men of this world themselves. It is just because the mind is deluded that men cannot attain awakening to themselves. They must seek a good teacher to show them how to see into their own natures. Good friends, if you meet awakening, [Buddha]-wisdom will be achieved.

13. "Good friends, my teaching of the Dharma takes meditation (*ting*) and wisdom (*hui*) as its basis. Never under any circumstances say mistakenly that meditation and wisdom are different; they are a unity, not two things. Meditation itself is the substance of wisdom; wisdom itself is the function of meditation. At the very moment when there is wisdom, then meditation exists in wisdom; at the very moment when there is meditation, then wisdom exists in meditation. Good friends, this means that meditation and wisdom are alike. Students, be careful not to say that meditation gives rise to wisdom, or that wisdom gives rise to meditation, or that meditation and wisdom are different from each other. To hold this view implies that things have duality—if good is spoken while the mind is not good, meditation and wisdom will not be alike. If mind and speech are both good, then the internal and the external are the same and meditation and wisdom are alike. The practice of self-awakening does not lie in verbal arguments. If you argue which comes first, meditation or wisdom, you are deluded people. You won't be able to settle the argument and instead will cling to objective things, and will never escape from the four states of phenomena.

15. "Good friends, how then are meditation and wisdom alike? They are like the lamp and the light it gives forth. If there is a lamp there is light; if there is no lamp there is no light. The lamp is the substance of light; the light is the function of the lamp. Thus, although they have two names, in substance they are not two. Meditation and wisdom are also like this.

16. "Good friends, in the Dharma there is no sudden or gradual, but among people some are keen and others dull. The deluded recommend the gradual method, the enlightened practice the sudden teaching. To understand the original mind of yourself is to see into your own original nature. Once enlightened, there is from the outset no distinction between these two methods; those who are not enlightened will for long kalpas be caught in the cycle of transmigration.

17. "Good friends, in this teaching of mine, from ancient times up to the present, all have set up no-thought as the main doctrine, non-form as the substance, and non-abiding as the basis. Non-form is to be separated from form even when associated with form. No-thought is not to think even when involved in thought. Non-abiding is the original nature of man.

"Successive thoughts do not stop; prior thoughts, present thoughts, and future thoughts follow one after the other without cessation. If one instant of thought is cut off, the Dharma body separates from the physical body, and in the midst of successive thoughts there will be no place for attachment to anything. If one instant of thought clings, then successive thoughts cling; this is known as being fettered. If in all things successive thoughts do not cling, then you are unfettered. Therefore, non-abiding is made the basis.

"Good friends, being outwardly separated from all forms, this is non-form. When you are separated from form, the substance of your nature is pure. Therefore, non-form is made the substance.

"To be unstained in all environments is called no-thought. If on the basis of your own thoughts you separate from environment, then, in regard to things, thoughts are not produced. If you stop thinking of the myriad things, and cast aside all thoughts, as soon as one instant of thought is cut off, you will be reborn in another realm. Students, take care! Don't rest in objective things and the subjective mind. [If you do so] it will be bad enough that you yourself are in error, yet how much worse that you encourage others in their mistakes. The deluded man, however, does not himself see and slanders the teachings of the sutras. Therefore, no-thought is established as a doctrine. Because man in his delusion has thoughts in relation to his environment, heterodox ideas stemming from these thoughts arise, and passions and false views are produced from them. Therefore this teaching has established no-thought as a doctrine.

"Men of the world, separate yourselves from views; do not activate thoughts. If there were no thinking, then no-thought would have no place to exist. 'No' is the 'no' of what? 'Thought' means 'thinking' of what? 'No' is the separation from the dualism that produces the passions. 'Thought' means thinking of the original nature of True Reality. True Reality is the substance of thoughts; thoughts are the function of True Reality. If you give rise to thoughts from your self-nature, then, although you see, hear, perceive, and know, you are not stained by the manifold environments, and are always free. The

Vimalakīrti Sūtra says: 'Externally, while distinguishing well all the forms of the various *dharmas*, internally he stands firm within the First Principle.'

18. "Good friends, in this teaching from the outset sitting in meditation does not concern the mind nor does it concern purity; we do not talk of steadfastness. If someone speaks of 'viewing the mind,' then I would say that the 'mind' is of itself delusion, and as delusions are just like fantasies, there is nothing to be seen. If someone speaks of 'viewing purity,' then I would say that man's nature is of itself pure, but because of false thoughts True Reality is obscured. If you exclude delusions then the original nature reveals its purity. If you activate your mind to view purity without realizing that your own nature is originally pure, delusions of purity will be produced. Since this delusion has no place to exist, then you know that whatever you see is nothing but delusion. Purity has no form, but, nonetheless, some people try to postulate the form of purity and consider this to be Ch'an practice. People who hold this view obstruct their own original natures and end up by being bound by purity. One who practices steadfastness does not see the faults of people everywhere. This is the steadfastness of self-nature. The deluded man, however, even if he doesn't move his own body, will talk of the good and bad of others the moment he opens his mouth, and thus behave in opposition to the Tao. Therefore, both 'viewing the mind' and 'viewing purity' will cause an obstruction to Tao.

19. "Now that we know that this is so, what is it in this teaching that we call 'sitting in meditation' (*tso-ch'an*)? In this teaching 'sitting' means without any obstruction anywhere, outwardly and under all circumstances, not to activate thoughts. 'Meditation' is internally to see the original nature and not become confused.

"And what do we call Ch'an meditation (*ch'an-ting*)? Outwardly to exclude form is 'ch'an'; inwardly to be unconfused is meditation (*ting*). Even though there is form on the outside, when internally the nature is not confused, then, from the outset, you are of yourself pure and of yourself in meditation. The very contact with circumstances itself causes confusion. Separation from form on the outside is 'ch'an'; being untouched on the inside is meditation (*ting*). Being 'ch'an' externally and meditation (*ting*) internally, it is known as ch'an meditation (*ch'an-ting*). The *Vimalakīrti Sūtra* says: 'At once, suddenly, you regain the original mind.' The *P'u-sa-chieh* says: 'From the outset your own nature is pure.'

"Good friends, see for yourselves the purity of your own natures, practice and accomplish for yourselves. Your own nature is the *Dharmakāya* and self-practice is the practice of Buddha; by self-accomplishment you may achieve the Buddha Way for yourselves.

20. "Good friends, you must all with your own bodies receive the precepts of formlessness and recite in unison what I am about to say. It will make you see the threefold body of the Buddha in your own selves. 'I take refuge in the pure *Dharmakāya* Buddha in my own physical body. I take refuge in the ten thousand hundred billion *Nirmāṇakāya* Buddhas in my own physical body. I take refuge in the future perfect *Sambhogakāya* Buddha in my own physical body.' (Recite the above three times). The physical body is your own home; you cannot speak of turning to it. The threefold body which I just mentioned is within your own self-natures. Everyone in the world possesses it, but being deluded, he cannot see it and seeks the threefold body of the Tathāgata on the outside. Thus he cannot find the threefold Buddha body in his own physical body.

"Good friends, listen! I shall make you see that there is a threefold Buddha body of your own self-natures in your own physical bodies. The threefold Buddha body is produced from your own natures.

"What is the pure *Dharmakāya* Buddha? Good friends, although the nature of people in this world is from the outset pure in itself, the ten thousand things are all within their own natures. If people think of all the evil things, then they will practice evil; if they think of all the good things, then they will practice good. Thus it is clear that in this way all the dharmas are within your own natures, yet your own natures are always pure. The sun and the moon are always bright, yet if they are covered by clouds, although above they are bright, below they are darkened, and the sun, moon, stars, and planets cannot be seen clearly. But if suddenly the wind of wisdom should blow and roll away the clouds and mists, all forms in the universe appear at once. The purity of the nature of man in this world is like the blue sky; wisdom is like the sun, knowledge like the moon. Although knowledge and wisdom are always clear, if you cling to external environments, the floating clouds of false thoughts will create a cover, and your own natures cannot become clear. Therefore, if you meet a good teacher, open up the true Dharma, and waft aside your delusions and errors; inside and outside will become clear. Within your own natures the ten thousand things will all appear, for all things of themselves are within your own natures. Given a name, this is the pure *Dharmakāya* Buddha. Taking refuge in oneself is to cast aside all actions that are not good; this is known as taking refuge.

"What are the ten thousand hundred billion *Nirmāṇakāya* Buddhas? If you do not think, then your nature is empty; if you do think, then you yourself will change. If you think of evil things then you will change and enter hell; if you think of good things then you will change and enter heaven. If you think of harm you will change and become a beast; if you think of compassion you will change and become a Bodhisattva. If you think of intuitive wisdom you will change and enter the upper realms; if you think of ignorance you will change and enter the lower quarters. The changes of your own natures are extreme, yet the deluded person is not himself conscious of this. [Successive thoughts give rise to evil and evil ways are always practiced]. But if a single thought of good evolves, intuitive wisdom is born. This is called the *Nirmāṇakāya* Buddha of your own nature. What is the perfect *Sambhogakāya* Buddha? As one lamp serves to dispel a thousand years of darkness, so one flash of wisdom destroys ten thousand years of ignorance. Do not think of the past; always think of the future; if your future thoughts are always good, you may be called the *Sambhogakāya* Buddha. An instant of thought of evil will result in the destruction of good which has continued a thousand years; an instant of thought of good compensates for a thousand years of evil and destruction. If from the timeless beginning future thoughts have always been good, you may be called the *Sambhogakāya* Buddha. Observed from the standpoint of the Dharmakāya, this is none other than the *Nirmāṇakāya.* When successive thoughts are good, this then is the *Sambhogakāya.* Self-awakening and self-practice, this is 'to take refuge.' Skin and flesh form the physical body; the physical body is the home. This has nothing to do with taking refuge. If, however, you awaken to the threefold body, then you have understood the cardinal meaning.

29. "When people of shallow capacity hear the Sudden Doctrine being preached they are like the naturally shallow-rooted plants on this earth, which, after a deluge of rain, are all beaten down and cannot continue their growth. People of shallow capacity are like such plants. Although these people have *prajñā* wisdom and are not different from men of great knowledge, why is it that even though they hear the Dharma they are not awakened? It is because the obstructions of their heterodox views are heavy and the passions deep-rooted. It is like the times when great clouds cover the sun; unless the wind blows the sun will not appear. There is no large and small in *prajñā* wisdom. Because all sentient beings have of themselves deluded minds, they seek the Buddha by external practice, and are unable to awaken to their own natures. But even these people of shallow capacity, if they hear the Sudden Doctrine, and do not place their trust in external practices, but only in their own minds always raise correct views in regard to their own original natures; even these sentient beings, filled with passions and troubles, will at once gain awakening. It is like the great sea which gathers all the flowing streams, and merges together the small waters and the large waters into one. This is seeing into your own nature. Such a person does not abide either inside or outside; he is free to come or go. Readily he casts aside the mind that clings [to things], and there is no obstruction to his passage. If in the mind this practice is carried out, then your own nature is no different from the *prajñāpāramitā.*

30. "All the sūtras and written words, Hīnayāna, Mahāyāna, the twelve divisions of the canon, all have been postulated by men. Because of the nature of wisdom [within man] it has been possible, therefore, to postulate them. If we were without this wisdom, all things would, from the outset, have no existence in themselves. Therefore it is clear that all things were originally given rise to by man, and that all the sutras exist because they are spoken by man. Among men there are the stupid and the wise. The stupid are insignificant, the wise, great men. Should deluded people ask the wise, the wise will expound the Dharma for the stupid and enable them to understand and gain a deep awakening. If the deluded person understands and his mind is awakened, then there is no difference between him and the man of wisdom. Therefore we know that, unawakened, even a Buddha is a sentient being, and that even a sentient being, if he is awakened in an instant of thought, is a Buddha. And thus we know that the ten thousand dharmas are all within our own minds. Why not from your own natures make the original nature of True

Reality suddenly appear? The *P'u-sa-chieh ching* says: 'From the outset our own nature is pure.' If we perceive the mind and see our own natures, then of ourselves we have achieved the Buddha Way. 'At once, suddenly, we regain our original mind.'

31. "Good friends, when I was at Priest Jen's place, hearing it [the *Diamond Sūtra*] just once, I immediately gained the great awakening and saw suddenly that True Reality was my original nature. Therefore, I have taken this teaching and, passing it on to later generations, shall make you students of the Way suddenly awaken to enlightenment, and let each of you see into your own minds, and suddenly awaken to your own original natures. If you cannot gain enlightenment for yourselves, you must seek a great teacher to show you the way to see into your own self-natures. What is a great teacher? He is a man who understands at once that the *Dharma* of the Supreme Vehicle is indeed the correct path. This is a great teacher. This is the great causal event, the so-called conversion which will enable you to see Buddha. All the good *dharmas* are activated by a great teacher. Therefore, although the Buddhas of the three worlds and all the twelve divisions of the canon are from the beginning within the nature of man, if he cannot gain awakening with his own nature, he must obtain a good teacher to show him how to see into his own self-nature. But if you awaken by yourself, do not rely on teachers outside. If you try to seek a teacher outside and hope to obtain deliverance, you will find it impossible. If you have recognized the good teacher within your own mind, you have already obtained deliverance. If you are deluded in your own mind and harbor erroneous thoughts and contrary concepts, even though you go to an outside teacher you will not be able to obtain salvation. If you are not able to obtain self-awakening, you must give rise to *prajñā* and illuminate with it, and then in one instant false thoughts will be destroyed. Once you have awakened to the fact that you yourself are your own true good teacher, in one awakening you will know the Buddha. If, standing upon your own nature and mind, you illuminate with wisdom and make inside and outside clear, you will know your own original mind. If you know your original mind, this then is deliverance. Once you have attained deliverance this then is the *prajñā samādhi*. If you have awakened to the *prajñā samādhi*, this then is no-thought. What is no-thought? The *Dharma* of no-thought means: even though you see all things, you do not attach to them, but, always keeping your own nature pure, cause the six thieves to exit through the six gates. Even though you are in the midst of the six dusts, you do not stand apart from them, yet are not stained by them, and are free to come and go. This is the *prajñā samādhi*, and being free and having achieved release is known as the practice of no-thought. If you do not think of the myriad things, but always cause your thoughts to be cut off, you will be bound in the *Dharma*. This is known as a biased view. If you awaken to the *Dharma* of no-thought, you will penetrate into all things thoroughly, and will see the realm of the Buddha. If you awaken to the sudden doctrine of no-thought, you will have reached the status of the Buddha.

III
I-hsüan: Recorded Conversations*

1. The Prefect, Policy Advisor Wang, and other officials requested the Master to lecture. The Master ascended the hall and said, "Today it is only because I, a humble monk, reluctantly accommodate human feelings that I sit on this chair. If one is restricted to one's heritage in expounding the fundamental understanding [of salvation], one really cannot say anything and would have nothing to stand on. However, because of the honorable general advisor's strong request today, how can the fundamental doctrines be concealed? Are there any talented men or fighting generals to hurl their banners and unfold their strategy right now? Show it to the group!"

A monk asked, "What is the basic idea of the Law preached by the Buddha?" Thereupon the Master shouted at him. The monk paid reverence. The Master said, "The Master and the monk can argue all right."

Question: "Master, whose tune are you singing? Whose tradition are you perpetuating?"

The Master said, "When I was a disciple of Huang-po, I asked him three times and I was beaten three times."

As the monk hesitated about what to say, the master shouted at him and then beat him, saying, "Don't nail a stick into empty space."

2. The Master ascended the hall and said, "Over a lump of reddish flesh there sits a pure man who transcends and is no longer attached to any class of Buddhas or sentient beings. He comes in and out of your sense organs all the time. If you are not yet clear about it, look, look!"

At that point a monk came forward and asked, "What is a pure man who does not belong to any class of Buddhas or sentient beings?" The Master came right down from his chair and, taking hold of the monk, exclaimed, "Speak! Speak!" As the monk deliberated what to say, the Master let him go, saying, "What dried human excrement-removing stick is the pure man who does not belong to any class of Buddhas or sentient beings!" Thereupon he returned to his room.

3. The Master ascended the hall. A monk asked, "What is the basic idea of the Law preached by the Buddha?" The Master lifted up his swatter. The monk shouted, and the Master beat him.

The monk asked again, "What is the basic idea of the Law preached by the Buddha?" The Master again lifted up his swatter. The monk shouted, and the Master shouted also. As the monk hesitated about what to say, the Master beat him.

Thereupon the Master said, "Listen, men. Those who pursue after the Law will not escape from death. I was in my late Master Huang-po's place for

---

*Reprinted with permission from Wing-tsit Chan, *A Source Book in Chinese Philosophy* (Princeton: Princeton University Press, 1963).

twenty years. Three times I asked him about the basic idea of the Law preached by the Buddha and three times he bestowed upon me the staff. I felt I was struck only by a dried stalk. Now I wish to have a real beating. Who can do it to me?"

One monk came out of the group and said, "I can do it."

The Master picked up the staff to give him. As he was about to take it over, the Master beat him.

4. The Master ascended the hall and said, "A man stands on top of a cliff, with no possibility of rising any further. Another man stands at the crossroad, neither facing nor backing anything. Who is in the front and who is in the back? Don't be like Vimalakīrti (who was famous for his purity), and don't be like Great Gentleman Fu (who benefited others). Take care of yourselves."

5. The Master told the congregation: "Seekers of the Way. In Buddhism no effort is necessary. All one has to do is to do nothing, except to move his bowels, urinate, put on his clothing, eat his meals, and lie down if he is tired. The stupid will laugh at him, but the wise one will understand. An ancient person said, 'One who makes effort externally is surely a fool.'"

6. *Question:* "What is meant by the mind's not being different at different times?"

The Master answered, "As you deliberated to ask the question, your mind has already become different. Therefore the nature and character of dharmas have become differentiated. Seekers of the Way, do not make any mistake. All mundane and supramundane dharmas have no nature of their own. Nor have they the nature to be produced [by causes]. They have only the name Emptiness, but even the name is empty. Why do you take this useless name as real? You are greatly mistaken! . . . If you seek after the Buddha, you will be taken over by the devil of the Buddha, and if you seek after the patriarch, you will be taken over by the devil of the patriarch. If you seek after anything, you will always suffer. It is better not to do anything. Some unworthy priests tell their disciples that the Buddha is the ultimate, and that he went through three infinitely long periods, fulfilled his practice, and then achieved Buddhahood. Seekers of the Way, if you say that the Buddha is the ultimate, why did he die lying down sidewise in the forest in Kuśinagara after having lived for eighty years? Where is he now? . . . Those who truly seek after the Law will have no use for the Buddha. They will have no use for the bodhisattvas or arhats. And they will have no use for any excellence in the Three Worlds (of desires, matter, and pure spirit). They will be distinctly free and not bound by material things. Heaven and earth may turn upside down but I shall have no more uncertainty. The Buddhas of the ten cardinal directions may appear before me and I shall not feel happy for a single moment. The three paths (of fire, blood, and swords) to hell may suddenly appear, but I shall not be afraid for a single moment. Why? Because I know that all dharmas are devoid of characters. They exist when there is transformation [in mind] and cease to exist when there is no transformation. The Three Worlds are but the mind, and all dharmas are consciousness only.

Therefore [they are all] dreams, illusions, and flowers in the air. What is the use of grasping and seizing them? . . .

"Seekers of the Way, if you want to achieve the understanding according to the Law, don't be deceived by others and turn to [your thoughts] internally or [objects] externally. Kill anything that you happen on. Kill the Buddha if you happen to meet him. Kill a patriarch or an arhat if you happen to meet him. Kill your parents or relatives if you happen to meet them. Only then can you be free, not bound by material things, and absolutely free and at ease. . . . I have no trick to give people. I merely cure disease and set people free. . . . My views are few. I merely put on clothing and eat meals as usual, and pass my time without doing anything. You people coming from the various directions have all made up your minds to seek the Buddha, seek the Law, seek emancipation, and seek to leave the Three Worlds. Crazy people! If you want to leave the Three Worlds, where can you go? 'Buddha' and 'patriarchs' are terms of praise and also bondage. Do you want to know where the Three Worlds are? They are right in your mind which is now listening to the Law."

7. Ma-ku came to participate in a session. As he arranged his seating cushion, he asked, "Which face of the twelve-face Kuan-yin faces the proper direction?"

The Master got down from the rope chair. With one hand he took away Ma-ku's cushion and with the other he held Ma-ku, saying, "Which direction does the twelve-face Kuan-yin face?"

Ma-ku turned around and was about to sit in the rope chair. The Master picked up the staff and beat him. Ma-ku having grasped the staff, the two dragged each other into the room.

8. The Master asked a monk: "Sometimes a shout is like the sacred sword of the Diamond King. Sometimes a shout is like a golden-haired lion squatting on the ground. Sometimes a shout is like a rod or a piece of grass [used to attract fish]. And sometimes a shout is like one which does not function as a shout at all. How do you know which one to use?"

As the monk was deliberating what to say, the Master shouted.

9. When the Master was among Huang-po's congregation, his conduct was very pure. The senior monk said with a sigh, "Although he is young, he is different from the rest!" He then asked, "Sir, how long have you been here?"

The Master said, "Three years."

The senior monk said, "Have you ever gone to the head monk (Huang-po) and asked him questions?"

The Master said, "I have not. I wouldn't know what to ask."

The senior monk said, "Why don't you go and ask the head monk what the basic idea of the Law preached by the Buddha clearly is?"

The Master went and asked the question. But before he finished, Huang-po beat him. When he came back, the senior monk asked him how the conversation went. The master said, "Before I finished my question, he already had beaten me. I don't understand." The senior monk told him to go and ask again.

The Master did and Huang-po beat him again. In this way he asked three times and got beaten three times. . . . Huang-po said, "If you go to Ta-yü's place, he will tell you why."

The Master went to Ta-yü, who asked him, "Where have you come from?"

The Master said, "I am from Huang-po's place."

Ta-yü said, "What did Huang-po have to say?"

The Master said, "I asked three times about the basic idea of the Law preached by the Buddha and I was beaten three times. I don't know if I was mistaken."

Ta-yü said, "Old kindly Huang-po has been so earnest with you and you still came here to ask if you were mistaken!"

As soon as the Master heard this, he understood and said, "After all, there is not much in Huang-po's Buddhism."

CHAPTER 21

NEO-CONFUCIAN FOUNDATIONS

Neo-Confucianism is the resurgence and full flowering of the Confucian tradition that dominated Chinese thought from the twelfth through the nineteenth centuries. In their attacks on Buddhism and Taoism and their insistence on returning to Confucian thought, Han Yü (768-824) and Li Ao (early ninth century) prepared the way for the Sung revival of Confucianism. Chou Tun-i (1017-1073) is the real pioneer of Neo-Confucianism, however, for by incorporating I-Ching and Taoist thought he provided its metaphysical basis. His very influential short treatise, "An Explanation of the Diagram of the Great Ultimate," reprinted from Wing-tsit Chan, *A Source Book in Chinese Philosophy* (Princeton: Princeton University Press, 1963) synthesizes ideas from the *I-Ching,* Taoist sources, and the Confucian tradition in a highly original way.

Shao Yung (1011-1077) further developed the idea of the Great Ultimate as providing the source and the principles of all forms of existence, which arise through a natural process of evolutionary change. Yin and Yang, the tranquil and the active, which by their unceasing transformations produce the concrete things, are not separate from the Great Ultimate, which inheres in all things as their fundamental principle. Thus, to learn the way of being human one must learn from objective things their inherent principle, for humanity is the perfection of nature not separate from it. The selections here are from Shao Yung's work, *Supreme Principles Governing the World,* as translated by Wing-tsit Chan in *A Source Book in Chinese Philosophy.*

Chang Tsai (1020-1077) gave the Great Ultimate a naturalistic and rational interpretation by regarding it as none other than material force itself. By spiritualizing material force, Chang was able to see it as the foundation for for a deep and pervasive love embracing all things, making of them a single family. This idea, presented in "The Western Inscription," became the basis for the Neo-Confucian way of human perfection. In the selection "Nature and Goodness" (excerpted from *Correcting Youthful Ignorance*), Chang presents his view that evil originates in the physical nature, for in physical nature is found imbalance and opposition. If this imbalance and opposition is not transformed it produces evil; when it is transformed it produces goodness.

With the brothers Ch'eng Hao (1032–1085) and Ch'eng I (1033–1107), students of Chou Tun-i and nephews of Chang Tsai, Neo-Confucianism finds its first full statement. Building on the idea of principle (*li*) as the origin and unity of things, they focused on its human and moral implications, reinterpreting Confucianism as the way of realizing principle. The notion of principle is subtle and profound, not easily characterized. For the Ch'engs it functions as a unifying factor, identifying the many with the one, mind with nature, and as the inherent truth of things that, when realized, brings a thing or person to perfection. Although the Ch'engs shared a common philosophical perspective, their views and emphases differed on important topics. Ch'eng Hao laid great stress on being true to one's humanity (*jen*) as the fundamental realization of principle. Ch'eng I stressed the importance of learning principle through the investigations of concrete events and things, for all these are manifestations of principle and serve as a guide to the way of becoming a sage. Frequently, however, their philosophies are not sharply distinguished from each other; Chu Hsi, for example, often cites both as "Master Ch'eng."

The selections from both Ch'eng Hao and Ch'eng I are from *The Complete Works of the Two Ch'engs* (*Erh-Ch'eng Ch'uan-shu*) as translated by Wing-tsit Chan in *A Source Book in Chinese Philosophy.* Wing-tsit Chan, *Reflections on Things at Hand: The Neo-Confucian Anthology Compiled by Chu Hsi and Lu Tsu-ch'ien* (New York: Columbia University Press, 1967), is the single most important collection of Neo-Confucian thought, bringing together the works of Chou Tun-i, Chang Tsai, and Chu Hsi's teachers, the brothers Ch'eng Hao and Ch'eng I. Carsun Chang, *The Development of Neo-Confucian Thought* (New Haven: College and University Press, 1963), is the best book on the historical development of Neo-Confucian thought.

I
Chou Tun-i: An Explanation of the Diagram of the Great Ultimate*

The Ultimate of Non-being and also the Great Ultimate (*T'ai-chi*)! The Great Ultimate through movement generates yang. When its activity reaches its limit, it becomes tranquil. Through tranquility the Great Ultimate generates yin. When tranquillity reaches its limit, activity begins again. So movement

*Reprinted with permission from Wing-tsit Chan, *A Source Book in Chinese Philosophy* (Princeton: Princeton University Press, 1963).

and tranquillity alternate and become the root of each other, giving rise to the distinction of yin and yang, and the two modes are thus established.

By the transformation of yang and its union with yin, the Five Agents of Water, Fire, Wood, Metal, and Earth arise. When these five material forces (*ch'i*) are distributed in harmonious order, the four seasons run their course.

The Five Agents constitute one system of yin and yang, and yin and yang constitute one Great Ultimate. The Great Ultimate is fundamentally the Non-ultimate. The Five Agents arise, each with its specific nature.

When the reality of the Ultimate of Non-being and the essence of yin, yang, and the Five Agents come into mysterious union, integration ensues. *Ch'ien* (Heaven) constitutes the male element, and *k'un* (Earth) constitutes the female element. The interaction of these two material forces engenders and transforms the myriad things. The myriad things produce and reproduce, resulting in an unending transformation.

It is man alone who receives the Five Agents in their highest excellence, and therefore he is most intelligent. His physical form appears, and his spirit develops consciousness. The five moral principles of his nature (humanity or *jen*, righteousness, propriety, wisdom, and faithfulness) are aroused by, and react to, the external world and engage in activity; good and evil are distinguished; and human affairs take place.

The sage settles these affairs by the principles of the Mean, correctness, humanity, and righteousness (for the way of the sage is none other than these four), regarding tranquillity as fundamental. Having no desire, there will therefore be tranquillity. Thus he establishes himself as the ultimate standard for man. Hence the character of the sage is "identical with that of Heaven and Earth; his brilliancy is identical with that of the sun and moon; his order is identical with that of the four seasons; and his good and evil fortunes are identical with those of spiritual beings." The superior man cultivates these moral qualities and enjoys good fortune, whereas the inferior man violates them and suffers evil fortune.

Therefore it is said that "yin and yang are established as the way of Heaven, the weak and the strong as the way of Earth, and humanity and righteousness as the way of man." It is also said that "if we investigate the cycle of things, we shall understand the concepts of life and death." Great is the *Book of Changes!* Herein lies its excellence!

Only the intelligent can understand the manifestations and concealments (of the operations of yin and yang). Strength may be good or it may be evil. The same is true of weakness. The ideal is the Mean.

The myriad things are created and transformed out of the two material forces and the Five Agents. These Five Agents are the basis of their differentiation while the two material forces constitute their actuality. The two forces are fundamentally one. Consequently, the many are [ultimately] one and the one is actually differentiated in the many. The one and the many each has its own correct state of being. The great and the small each has its definite function.

II
Shao Yung:
The Great Ultimate*

A. Everything follows the evolutionary order of the Great Ultimate, the Two Modes (of yin and yang), the Four Forms, and the Eight Elements. Everything also possesses the two forms of time, the past and the present. As form is externalized in physical form, the result is physical substance, for substance is derived from physical form. As form contains the dormant nature of things, the result is their manifested nature, for manifested nature is the expression of dormant nature. In fire, the nature is fundamental, while its physical substance is secondary, whereas in water the opposite is true. Each of the Eight Elements has its own nature and physical substance, but none can exist outside of the operation of *ch'ien* and *k'un.* Thus all things receive their nature from Heaven but the nature of each is peculiar to it. In man it becomes human nature. In animals and plants it becomes the nature of animals and plants.

B. Our nature views things as they are, but our feelings cause us to see things subjectively and egotistically. Our nature is impartial and enlightened, but our feelings are partial and deceived. When the material endowment in man is characterized by equilibrium and harmony, the elements of strength and weakness in him will be balanced. If yang predominates, he will be off balance toward strength, and if yin predominates, he will be off balance toward weakness. As knowledge directed toward the nature of man increases, the knowledge directed toward things will decrease.

Man occupies the most honored position in the scheme of things because he combines in him the principles of all species. If he honors his own position and enhances his honor, he can make all species serve him.

The nature of all things is complete in the human species.

The spirit of man is the same as the spirit of Heaven and Earth. Therefore, when one deceives himself, he is deceiving Heaven and Earth. Let him beware!

Spirit is nowhere and yet everywhere. The perfect man can penetrate the minds of others because he is based on the One. Spirit is perforce called the One and the Way. It is best to call it spirit.

C. Without physical substance, the nature (of man and things) cannot be complete. Without nature, physical substance cannot be produced. The yang has the yin as its physical substance and the yin has the yang as its nature. Nature is active but physical substance is tranquil. In heaven, yang is active while yin is tranquil, whereas in earth yang is tranquil while yin is active. When nature is given physical substance, it becomes tranquil. As physical substance follows nature, it becomes active. Hence yang is at ease with itself but yin is fast moving without control.

---

*Reprinted with permission from Wing-tsit Chan, *A Source Book in Chinese Philosophy* (Princeton: Princeton University Press, 1963).

D. The Great Ultimate is the One. It produces the two (yin and yang) without engaging in activity. The two (in their wonderful changes and transformations) constitute the spirit. Spirit engenders number, number engenders form, and form engenders concrete things.

E. The mind is the Great Ultimate. The human mind should be as calm as still water. Being calm, it will be tranquil. Being tranquil, it will be enlightened.

In the study of prior existence sincerity is basic. Perfect sincerity can penetrate all spirits. Without sincerity, the Way cannot be attained.

Our nature comes from Heaven, but learning lies with man. Our nature develops from within, while learning enters into us from without. "It is due to our nature that enlightenment results from sincerity," but it is due to learning that sincerity results from intelligence.

The learning of a superior man aims precisely at enriching his personality. The rest, such as governing people and handling things, is all secondary.

Without sincerity, one cannot investigate principle to the utmost.

Sincerity is the controlling factor in one's nature. It is beyond space and time.

He who acts in accordance with the Principle of Nature will have the entire process of creation in his grip. When the Principle of Nature is achieved, not only his personality, but his mind also, are enriched. And not only his mind but his nature and destiny are enriched. To be in accord with principle is normal, but to deviate from principle is abnormal.

III
Chang Tsai*

1. THE WESTERN INSCRIPTION

Heaven is my father and Earth is my mother, and even such a small creature as I finds an intimate place in their midst.

Therefore that which fills the universe I regard as my body and that which directs the universe I consider as my nature.

All people are my brothers and sisters, and all things are my companions.

The great ruler (the emperor) is the eldest son of my parents (Heaven and Earth), and the great ministers are his stewards. Respect the aged—this is the way to treat them as elders should be treated. Show deep love toward the orphaned and the weak—this is the way to treat them as the young should be treated. The sage identifies his character with that of Heaven and Earth, and the worthy is the most outstanding man. Even those who are tired, infirm, crippled, or sick; those who have no brothers or children, wives or husbands, are all my brothers who are in distress and have no one to turn to.

*Reprinted with permission from Wing-tsit Chan, *A Source Book in Chinese Philosophy* (Princeton: Princeton University Press, 1963).

When the time comes, to keep himself from harm—this is the care of a son. To rejoice in Heaven and to have no anxiety—this is filial piety at its purest.

He who disobeys [the Principle of Nature] violates virtue. He who destroys humanity is a robber. He who promotes evil lacks [moral] capacity. But he who puts his moral nature into practice and brings his physical existence into complete fulfillment can match [Heaven and Earth].

One who knows the principles of transformation will skillfully carry forward the undertakings [of Heaven and Earth], and one who penetrates spirit to the highest degree will skillfully carry out their will.

Do nothing shameful in the recesses of your own house and thus bring no dishonor to them. Preserve your mind and nourish your nature and thus (serve them) with untiring effort.

The Great Yü hated pleasant wine but attended to the protection and support of his parents. Border Warden Ying brought up and educated the young and thus extended his love to his own kind.

Shun's merit lay in delighting his parents with unceasing effort, and Shen-sheng's reverence was demonstrated when he awaited punishment without making an attempt to escape.

Tsang Ts'an received his body from his parents and reverently kept it intact throughout life, while Po-ch'i vigorously obeyed his father's command.

Wealth, honor, blessing, and benefits are meant for the enrichment of my life, while poverty, humble station, and sorrow are meant to help me to fulfillment.

In life I follow and serve [Heaven and Earth]. In death I will be at peace.

2. NATURE AND GOODNESS

Nature in man is always good. It depends on whether man can skillfully return to it or not. To exceed the transforming operation of Heaven and Earth (such as food and sex) means not to return skillfully. Destiny in man is always correct. It depends on whether or not one obeys it. If one takes to dangerous courses and hopes for good luck, he is not obeying his destiny.

With the existence of physical form, there exists physical nature. If one skillfully returns to the original nature endowed by Heaven and Earth, then it will be preserved. Therefore in physical nature there is that which the superior man denies to be his original nature.

Man's strength, weakness, slowness, quickness, and talent or lack of talent are due to the one-sidedness of the material force. Heaven (Nature) is originally harmonious and not one-sided. If one cultivates this material force and returns to his original nature without being one-sided, one can then fully develop his nature and [be in harmony with] Heaven. Before man's nature is formed, good and evil are mixed. Therefore to be untiring in continuing the good which issues [from the Way] is good. If all evil is removed, good will also disappear [for good and evil are relative and are necessary to reveal each other]. Therefore avoid just saying "good" but say, "That which realizes it (the Way) is the individual nature."

When moral character does not overcome the material force, our nature and destiny proceed from the material force. But when moral character overcomes the material force, then our nature and destiny proceed from moral character. If one investigates principle to the utmost and fully develops his nature, then his nature will be in accord with the character of Heaven and his destiny will be in accord with the Principle of Heaven (Nature). Only life, death, and longevity and brevity of life are due to the material force and cannot be changed.

Therefore, in discussing life and death, Confucius said that they "are the decree of Heaven," referring to material force, and in discussing wealth and honor he said that they "depend on Heaven" referring to principle. This is why a man of great virtue (the sage ruler) always receives the Mandate of Heaven (*T'ien-ming*). He is in accord with the easy and simple Principle of Heaven and Earth, and occupies the central position in the universe. What is meant by the Principle of Heaven is the principle which can make the hearts of all people happy and give free expression to the will of the whole world. As it can make the world happy and free in their expression, the world will all turn to him. If some do not do so, it would be because of differences in circumstances and opportunities, as in the cases of Confucius [who never had a chance to be a ruler] and those rulers who succeeded [sage rulers in spite of their own wickedness].

Confucius said, "Shun and Yü held possession of the empire as if it were nothing to them." This was because they achieved the Principle of Heaven through moral effort and not because they were entitled to rule because of their endowment in physical nature or because they obtained it through their ambition. Shun and Yü were mentioned by Confucius because the rest of the rulers did not come to the throne through natural tendencies but because they sought it.

IV
Ch'eng Hao: Selected Writings*

1. ON UNDERSTANDING THE NATURE OF JEN (HUMANITY)

The student must first of all understand the nature of *jen*. The man of *jen* forms one body with all things without any differentiation. Righteousness, propriety, wisdom, and faithfulness are all [expressions of] *jen*.

One's duty is to understand this principle (*li*) and preserve *jen* with sincerity and seriousness (*ching*), that is all. There is no need for caution and

---

*Reprinted with permission from Wing-tsit Chan, *A Source Book in Chinese Philosophy* (Princeton: Princeton University Press, 1963).

control. Nor is there any need for exhaustive search. Caution is necessary when one is mentally negligent, but if one is not negligent, what is the necessity for caution? Exhaustive search is necessary when one has not understood principle, but if one preserves *jen* long enough, it will automatically dawn on him. Why should he have to depend on exhaustive search?

Nothing can be equal to this Way. It is so vast that nothing can adequately explain it. All operations of the universe are our operations. Mencius said that "all things are already complete in oneself" and that one must "examine oneself and be sincere (or absolutely real)" and only then will there be great joy. If one examines himself and finds himself not yet sincere, it means there is still an opposition between the two (the self and the non-self). Even if one tries to identify the self with the non-self, one still does not achieve unity. How can one have joy?

The purpose of (Chang Tsai's) "Western Inscription" is to explain this substance (of complete unity) fully. If one preserves it (*jen*) with this idea, what more is to be done? "Always be doing something without expectation. Let the mind not forget its objective, but let there be no artificial effort to help it grow." Not the slightest effort is exerted! This is the way to preserve *jen*. As *jen* is preserved, the self and the other are then identified.

For our innate knowledge of good and innate ability to do good are originally not lost. However, because we have not gotten rid of the mind dominated by habits, we must preserve and exercise our original mind, and in time old habits will be overcome. This principle is extremely simple; the only danger is that people will not be able to hold on to it. But if we practice it and enjoy it, there need be no worry of our being unable to hold to it. (*I-Shu*, 2A:3a-b)

2. REPLY TO MASTER HENG-CH'Ü'S LETTER ON CALMING HUMAN NATURE

I have received your letter in which you said that nature in the state of calmness cannot be without activity and must still suffer from the influence of external things. This problem has been ardently pondered by a worthy [like you]. What need is there for a humble person like myself to say anything? However, I have gone over the matter in my mind, and dare present my ideas to you. By calmness of nature we mean that one's nature is calm whether it is in a state of activity or in a state of tranquillity. One does not lean forward or backward to accommodate things, nor does he make any distinction between the internal and external. To regard things outside the self as external, and force oneself to conform to them, is to regard one's nature as divided into the internal and the external. Furthermore, if one's nature is conceived to be following external things, then, while it is outside what is it that is within the self? To conceive one's nature thus is to have the intention of getting rid of external temptations, but to fail to realize that human nature does not possess the two aspects of internal and external. Since one holds that things internal and things external form two different bases, how can one hastily speak of the calmness of human nature?

The constant principle of Heaven and Earth is that their mind is in all things, and yet they have no mind of their own. The constant principle of the sage is that his feelings are in accord with all creation, and yet he has no feelings of his own. Therefore, for the training of the superior man there is nothing better than to become broad and extremely impartial and to respond spontaneously to all things as they come. The *Book of Changes* says, "Firm correctness brings good fortune and prevents all occasions for repentance. If he is hesitant in his movements, only his friends will follow his purpose." If one merely attempts to remove external temptations, then no sooner do some disappear in the east than others will arise in the west. Not only is one's time limited, but the source of temptation is inexhaustible and therefore cannot be removed.

Everyone's nature is obscured in some way and as a consequence he cannot follow the Way. In general the trouble lies in resorting to selfishness and the exercise of cunning. Being selfish, one cannot take purposive action to respond to things, and being cunning, one cannot be at home with enlightenment. For a mind that hates external things to seek illumination in a mind where nothing exists, is to look for reflection on the back of a mirror. The *Book of Changes* says, "Stop in the back of a thing. See not the person. Walk in the hall and do not see the people in it." Mencius also said, "What I dislike in your wise men is their forced reasoning." Instead of looking upon the internal as right and the external as wrong, it is better to forget the distinction. When such a distinction is forgotten, the state of quietness and peace is attained. Peace leads to calmness and calmness leads to enlightenment. When one is enlightened, how can the response to things become an impediment? The sage is joyous because according to the nature of things before him he should be joyous, and he is angry because according to the nature of things before him he should be angry. Thus the joy and anger of the sage do not depend on his own mind but on things. Does not the sage in this way respond to things? Why should it be regarded wrong to follow external things and right to seek what is within? Compare the joy and anger of the selfish and cunning man to the correctness of joy and anger of the sage. What a difference! Among human emotions the easiest to arouse but the most difficult to control is anger. But if in time of anger one can immediately forget his anger and look at the right and wrong of the matter according to principle, he will see that external temptations need not be hated, and he has gone more than halfway toward the Way. My subtle ideas cannot be expressed in words. On top of my usual lack of skill in writing, my official duties have kept me busy, so that I have not given the finest thought to this matter. Whether I am correct or not, I pray you to let me know. However, I believe I am not far from the truth in essential points. The ancients considered it wrong to seek afar when the truth lies nearby. Will you, a man of wisdom and intelligence, draw your own conclusions. (*Ming-tao wen-chi*, 3:1a-b)

3. DISCUSSION OF PRINCIPLE

A. The student need not seek afar but search right here in himself. All he has to do is to understand the Principle of Nature and be serious. This is where restraint lies [as against extensive learning]. In the section on the *ch'ien* (Heaven) hexagram of the *Book of Changes*, the learning of the sage is discussed, and in the section on the *k'un* (Earth) hexagram the learning of the worthy is discussed. They only say that "seriousness is to straighten one's internal life and righteousness is to square one's external life" and that "as seriousness and righteousness are established, one's virtue will not be an isolated instance." Even for a sage this is all; there is no other way. To force things and to drag things along is naturally not to be in accord with the Way and principle. Therefore when the Way and principle are followed, Heaven and man will be one and can no longer be separable. The great moving power is my own power. If it is nourished and not injured, it fills up all between heaven and earth. However, as soon as it is obscured by selfish ideas, it will be diminished and feeble. From this we know it is is small. "Have no depraved thoughts." "Never lack seriousness." If one follows only these two teachings and puts them into practice, how can he make any mistake? Any mistake is due to the lack of seriousness and to incorrectness of thought.

B. "Change means production and reproduction." This is how Heaven becomes the Way. To Heaven, the Way is merely to give life. What follows from this principle of life-giving is good. Goodness involves the idea of origination (*yüan*), for origination is the chief quality of goodness. All things have the impulses of spring (spirit of growth) and this is goodness resulting from the principle of life. "That which realizes it is the individual nature." Realization is possible only when the myriad things fully realize their own nature.

C. The reason why it is said that all things form one body is that all have this principle, simply because they all have come from it. "Change means production and reproduction." In production, once a thing is produced, it possesses this principle complete. Man can extend this principle to others, but because their material force with which they are endowed is dark, things cannot do so. But we must not say that they do not share principle with others. Simply because of selfishness, man thinks in terms of his own person, and therefore, from the point of view of principle, belittles them. If he lets go this person of his and views all things in the same way, how much joy would there be! Because the Buddhists do not know this, they think in terms of the self. As they cannot cope with it, they become disgusted and want to get rid of sense-perception, and because the source of their mind is not calm, they want to be like dry wood and dead ashes. But this is impossible. It is possible only with death. The Buddhists say all that because they in reality love their own persons and cannot let go. They are like those worms that carry things on their backs which are already unable to bear their load, and still add more things on their bodies, or like a man who sinks in a river.

D. "All things are already complete in oneself." This is not only true of man but of things also. Everything proceeds from the self, only things cannot extend [the principle in them] to others whereas man can. However, although man can extend it, when has he augmented it to any extent? And although things cannot extend it, when have they diminished it to any extent? All principles exist in complete sufficiency and are openly laid before us. How can we say that (sage-emperor) Yao, in fulfilling the Way of the ruler, added anything to it, or Shun, in fulfilling the Way of the son, added anything to it? They are always there as ever before.

E. There is only one principle in the world. You may extend it over the four seas and it is everywhere true. It is the unchangeable principle that "can be laid before Heaven and Earth" and is "tested by the experience of the Three Kings." Therefore to be serious is merely to be serious with this principle. To be humane (*jen*) is to be humane with this principle. And to be faithful is to be faithful to this principle. (Confucius) said, "In times of difficulty or confusion, [a superior man] acts according to it." (His pupil) also said, "I do not yet have the confidence to do so." They could say this much. Principle is extremely difficult to describe.

V
Ch'eng I: Selected Writings*

1. A TREATISE ON WHAT YEN TZU[1] LOVED TO LEARN

In the school of Confucius, there were three thousand pupils. Yen Tzu alone was praised as loving to learn. It is not that the three thousand scholars had not studied and mastered the Six Classics such as the *Book of Odes* and the *Book of History*. Then what was it that Yen Tzu alone loved to learn? *Answer:* It was to learn the way of becoming a sage.

Can one become a sage through learning? *Answer:* Yes. What is the way to learn? *Answer:* From the essence of life accumulated in Heaven and Earth, man receives the Five Agents (Water, Fire, Wood, Metal, and Earth) in their highest excellence. His original nature is pure and tranquil. Before it is aroused, the five moral principles of his nature, called humanity, righteousness, propriety, wisdom, and faithfulness, are complete. As his physical form appears, it comes into contact with external things and is aroused from within. As it is aroused from within, the seven feelings, called pleasure, anger, sorrow, joy, love, hate, and desire, ensue. As feelings become strong and increasingly reckless, his nature becomes damaged. For this reason the enlightened person controls his feelings so that they will be in accord with the Mean. He rectifies his mind and nourishes his nature. This is therefore called

---

*Reprinted with permission from Wing-tsit Chan, *A Source book in Chinese Philosophy* (Princeton: Princeton University Press, 1963).

[1]Yen Hui, Confucius' favorite pupil. Confucius once remarked that the pupil loved learning more than anyone else. See *Analects*, 6:2.

turning the feelings into the [original] nature. The stupid person does not know how to control them. He lets them loose until they are depraved, fetter his nature, and destroy it. This is therefore called turning one's nature into feelings.

The way to learn is none other than rectifying one's mind and nourishing one's nature. When one abides by the Mean and correctness and becomes sincere, he is a sage. In the learning of the superior man, the first thing is to be clear in one's mind and to know where to go and then act vigorously in order that one may arrive at sagehood. This is what is meant by "sincerity resulting from enlightenment."

Therefore the student must exert his own mind to the utmost. If he does so, he will know his own nature. And if he knows his own nature, examines his own self and makes it sincere, he becomes a sage. Therefore the "Great Norm" says, "The virtue of thinking is penetration and profundity. . . . Penetration and profundity lead to sageness." The way to make the self sincere lies in having firm faith in the Way. As there is firm faith in the Way, one will put it into practice with determination. When one puts it into practice with determination, he will keep it securely. Then humanity, righteousness, loyalty, and faithfulness will never depart from his heart. In moments of haste, he acts according to them. In times of difficulty or confusion, he acts according to them. And whether he is at home or outside, speaking or silent, he acts according to them. As he holds on to them for a long time without fail, he will then be at home with them and in his movements and expressions, he will always be acting in a proper manner, and no depraved thought will arise in him. This is the reason why Yen Tzu, in his behavior, "did not see what was contrary to propriety, did not listen to what was contrary to propriety, did not speak what was contrary to propriety, and did not make any movement which was contrary to propriety." Confucius praised him, saying, "When he got hold of one thing that was good, he clasped it firmly, as if wearing it on his breast, and never lost it." He also said, "[Hui] did not transfer his anger; he did not repeat a mistake." "Whenever he did anything wrong, he never failed to realize it. Having realized it, he never did it again." This is the way he earnestly loved and learned.

All [Yen Hui's] seeing, listening, speaking, and movement were in accord with propriety. Therein he differed from a sage in that whereas a sage "apprehends without thinking, hits upon what is right without effort, and is easily and naturally in harmony with the Way," Yen Tzu had to think before apprehending, and had to make an effort before hitting upon what was right. Hence it has been said, "The difference between Yen Tzu and the sage is as little as a moment of breathing."

Mencius said, "He [whose goodness] is abundant and is brilliantly displayed is called a great man. When one is great and is completely transformed [to be goodness itself], he is called a sage. When a sage is beyond our knowledge, he is called a man of the spirit." The virtue of Yen Tzu may be said to be abundant and brilliantly displayed. What was lacking in him was that he held on to [goodness] but was not yet completely transformed [into goodness itself]. Since he loved to learn, had he lived longer, he would have achieved transformation in a short time. Therefore Confucius said, "[Hui] unfortunately lived a short life." Confucius was lamenting the fact that he did not reach the state of the sage.

What is meant by being transformed [to be goodness itself] is to enter into the spirit and be natural with it, so that one can apprehend without thinking and hit upon what is right without effort. When Confucius said, "At seventy I could follow my heart's desire without transgressing moral principles," he meant this.

Someone asks: A sage is one who is born with knowledge. Now you say that sagehood can be achieved through learning. Is there any basis for this contention? *Answer:* Yes, Mencius said, "Sage-emperors Yao and Shun [practiced humanity and righteousness] because of their nature, and Kings T'ang and Wu [practiced them] because of their effort to return (to their nature)." Those who do so by nature are those born with the knowledge (of the good), and those who return to their nature are those who obtain knowledge (of the good) through learning. It is also said, "Confucius was born with such knowledge but Mencius obtained it through learning." Not understanding the true meaning of this, in later years people thought that sagehood was basically due to inborn knowledge (of the good) and could not be achieved through learning. Consequently the way to learn has been lost to us. Men do not seek within themselves but outside themselves and engage in extensive learning, effortful memorization, clever style, and elegant diction, making their words elaborate and beautiful. Thus few have arrived at the Way. This being the case, the learning of today and the learning that Yen Tzu loved are quite different. (*I-ch'uan wen-chi*, 4:1a-2a)

2. LEARNING AND PRINCIPLE

A. The mind of one man is one with the mind of Heaven and Earth. The principle of one thing is one with the principle of all things. The course of one day is one with the course of a year.

B. True knowledge and ordinary knowledge are different. I once saw a farmer who had been wounded by a tiger. When someone said that a tiger was hurting people, everyone was startled. But in his facial expression the farmer reacted differently from the rest. Even a young boy knows that tigers can hurt people, but his is not true knowledge. It is true knowledge only if it is like the farmer's. Therefore when men know evil and still do it, this also is not true knowledge. If it were, they would surely not do it.

To devote oneself to investigate principle to the utmost does not mean that it is necessary to investigate the principle of all things in the world to the utmost nor does it mean that principle can be understood merely by investigating one particular principle. It is necessary to accumulate much and then one will naturally come to understand principle.

C. A thing is an event. If the principles underlying the event are investigated to the utmost, there all principles will be understood.

D. If one does not look, listen, speak, or move in violation of principle, that is propriety, for propriety is none other than principle. What is not of the Principle of Nature (*T'ien*, Heaven) is of human (selfish) desire. In that case, even if one has the intention to do good, it will still be contrary to propriety. When there is no human (selfish) desire, then all will be the Principle of Nature.

E. Where there is impartiality, there is unity, and where there is partiality, there is multiplicity. The highest truth is always resolved into a unity, and an essential principle is never a duality. If people's minds are as different as their faces are, it is solely due to partiality.

F. In nourishing the mind there is nothing better than having few desires. Without desires, there will be no delusion. One does not need to be submerged in desires. Merely to have the intention is already desire.

G. If we say that the material force which has already returned to Nature must be needed to become once more the expanding material force, such a theory would be entirely at odds with the transformation of Heaven and Earth. The transformation of Heaven and Earth naturally produces and reproduces without end. What is the need for any physical form that has perished or material force that has returned to Nature to constitute creation? Let us take an example near at hand in our own body. The opening and closing, going and coming [of the material or vital force] can be seen in breathing. It is not necessary to depend on inhaling the already exhaled breath for the second time in order to breathe out. Material (vital) force naturally produces it. The material force of man is produced from the true source (*chen-yüan*, true origin). The material force of Nature also naturally produces and reproduces without end. Take, for example, the case of tides. They dry up because yang (the sun) is very strong. When yin (the moon) is strong and tides are produced, it is not that the dried-up water is used to produce them. They are produced by themselves. Going and coming, and expansion and contraction, are but principle. As there is growth, there is decline; as there is morning, there is evening; and as there is going, there is coming. The universe is like a vast furnace. What cannot be burned up?

H. *Question:* Do observation of things and self examination mean returning to the self and seeing [principles] after [some principles] have been discovered in things? *Answer:* You do not have to say it in this way. Things and the self are governed by the same principle. If you understand one, you understand the other, for the truth within and the truth without are identical. In its magnitude it reaches the height of heaven and the depth of earth, but in its refinement it constitutes the reason of being in every single thing. The student should appreciate both. *Further question:* In the extension of knowledge, how about seeking first of all in the Four Beginnings (of our nature, namely, humanity, righteousness, propriety, and wisdom)? *Answer:* To seek in our own nature and feelings is indeed to be concerned with our own moral life. But every blade of grass and every tree possesses principle and should be examined.

I. All things under heaven can be understood in the light of their principle. As there are things, there must be their specific principles. One thing necessarily has one principle.

J. The investigation of principle to the utmost, the full development of the nature, and the fulfillment of destiny are only one thing. As principle is investigated to the utmost, one's nature is fully developed, and as one's nature is fully developed, destiny is fulfilled.

K. *Question:* In the investigation of things, should these be external things or things within our nature and function? *Answer:* It does not matter. All that is before our eyes is nothing but things, and all things have principle. For example, from that by which fire is hot or water is cold to the relations between ruler and minister, and father and son, are all principle. *Further question:* If one investigates only one thing, does he understand only one thing or does he understand the various principles? *Answer:* We must seek to understand all. However, even Yen Tzu could understand only ten points when he heard one. When one finally understands principle, even millions of things can be understood.

L. Nature comes from Heaven, whereas capacity comes from material force. When material force is clear, capacity is clear. When material force is turbid, capacity is turbid. Take, for instance, wood. Whether it is straight or crooked is due to its nature. But whether it can be used as a beam or as a truss is determined by its capacity. Capacity may be good or evil, but the nature is always good.

M. Principle in the world is one. Although there are many roads in the world, the destination is the same, and although there are a hundred deliberations, the result is one. Although things involve many manifestations and events go through infinite variations, when they are united by the one, there cannot be any contradiction.

N. According to the principle of the world, nothing can last forever without activity. With activity, a thing will begin again when it ends, and can therefore last forever without limit. Among things in the universe, even as solid and dense as huge mountains, nothing can remain unchanged. Thus being long lasting does not mean being in a fixed and definite state. Being fixed and definite, a thing cannot last long. The way to be constant is to change according to circumstances. This is a common principle. . . . Unless one knows the Way, how can he understand the constant and lasting way of the universe and the constant and lasting principle of the world?

O. That which is inherent in things is principle. That by which things are managed is moral principles.

P. The mind embraces all principles and all principles are complete in this single entity, the mind. If one is not able to preserve the mind, he will be unable to investigate principle to the utmost. If he is unable to investigate principle to the utmost, he will be unable to exert his mind to the utmost.

(From the *I-shu* (Surviving Works))

CHAPTER 22

THE TWO WINGS OF NEO-CONFUCIANISM

Chu Hsi (1130 - 1200) and Wang Yang-ming (1472 - 1529) represent the two great developments in Neo-Confucian thought after the Ch'engs. Chu integrated the thought of his Neo-Confucian predecessors, particularly the Ch'engs, into a unified system that reaffirmed the basic teachings of Confucianism as they had developed over the centuries. His understanding of *jen* as "the character of the human mind and principle of love" is the culmination of a profound and systematic understanding of human nature and human action. The foundation of Chu's system is provided by his understanding of principle (*li*), which is present in all things as their unity as well as their difference. From the perspective of things, it is their way of being and acting; from the perspective of human action, it is the inherent and fundamental human nature. Human nature considered simply as principle is inherently good, as Mencius had insisted. But the physical form embodying human nature is inclined to evil, as Hsün-tzu has insisted. Thus, both goodness and evil are recognized, but since principle is fundamental and physical form is secondary, evil can be prevented and removed through the cultivation of *jen*, which as principle is primary.

The selections from Chu Hsi are from Wing-tsit Chan, *A Source Book in Chinese Philosophy* (Princeton: Princeton University Press, 1963), which contains a good introduction to Chu Hsi and helpful comments on the texts. Wing-Tsit Chan is the leading authority on Chu Hsi and has written extensively on his philosophy. Chan's new book, the culmination of a lifetime of profound scholarship, *Chu Hsi: New Studies* (Honolulu: University of Hawaii Press, 1989), is the definitive work on China's most influential thinker since Mencius. Chan shows us a complete picture of Chu as a person and thinker, discusses the intellectual and religious environment that shaped Chu's thought, and explains his main ideas in their interrelationship with each other and with events in his life. *Chu Hsi and Neo-Confucianism* (Honolulu: University of

Hawaii Press, 1986), edited by Chan, is an outstanding collection of interpretations of Chu Hsi's thought by leading scholars. Wm. Theodore de Bary has written two masterful books on Neo-Confucian thought, *Neo-Confucian Orthodoxy and the Learning of Mind-and-Heart* and *The Message of the Mind in Neo-Confucianism*, both published in New York by Columbia University Press, the first in 1981, the second in 1989. Together, they follow the development of Neo-Confucianism down to the nineteenth century. The focus is on the "Learning of the Mind-and-Heart"—rather than on the other fundamental Neo-Confucian idea, that of principle (*li*)—and shows its origins in the Ch'eng-Chu school, its modifications in the Lu-Wang school, and the continuing debates marking the interpretive effort over the centuries. Donald J. Munro, *Images of Human Nature: A Sung Portrait* (Princeton: Princeton University Press, 1988), is a fascinating and rewarding philosophical reconstruction of Chu Hsi's concept of human nature, a reconstruction based on analysis of the pictorial images used by Chu Hsi himself. What emerges is a portrait of human nature in which the innate moral sense possessed by everyone is dominant. The obstructions of the moral nature are depicted, and ways of removing these obstructions—so that personal tranquillity and harmonious social order can be achieved—are clearly delineated. Although the focus is primarily on Chu Hsi's thought, occasionally explicit comparisons with Western structural images are made in a way that forces one to reexamine one's own basic methods and images of thought.

The other wing of Neo-Confucianism, championed by Wang Yang-ming, stresses moral development through extension of the innate knowledge of the good that constitutes fundamental human nature. This knowledge cannot be separated from action, for moral knowledge and action are ultimately one. This insistence on the unity of knowledge and action, a trademark of Wang's thought, is seen clearly in his interpretation of the "learning of the great man" as "abiding in the highest good." Wang's most important work, his essay "Inquiry on the Great Learning," is included here in its entirety. The translation is from Wing-tsit Chan, *A Source Book in Chinese Philosophy*. Chan's *Instructions for Practical Living and Other Neo-Confucian Writings by Wang Yang-ming* (New York: Columbia University Press, 1984), contains translations of all of Wang's major works along with excellent introductions and helpful notes. Three collections of scholarly essays edited by Wm. Theodore de Bary, *Self and Society in Ming Thought*, *The Unfolding of Neo-Confucianism*, and, with Irene Bloom, *Principle and Practicality: Essays in Neo-Confucian Practicality*, all published in New York by Columbia University Press, in 1970, 1975, and 1979, respectively, can be recommended for their insights into Neo-Confucianism in general and the thought of Wang Yang-ming in particular. Julia Ching, *To Acquire Wisdom: The Way of Wang Yang-ming* (New York: Columbia University Press, 1976), is a helpful account of Wang's concept of moral learning. Wei-ming Tu's *Neo-Confucian Thought in Action: Wang Yang-ming's Youth (1472-1509)* (Berkeley: University of California Press, 1976) is very insightful, as are his later writings.

I
Chu Hsi: Selected Writings*

1. A TREATISE ON *JEN*

"The mind of Heaven and Earth is to produce things."[1] In the production of man and things, they receive the mind of Heaven and Earth as their mind. Therefore, with reference to the character of the mind, although it embraces and penetrates all and leaves nothing to be desired, nevertheless, one word will cover all of it, namely, *jen* (humanity). Let me try to explain fully.

The moral qualities of the mind of Heaven and Earth are four: origination, flourish, advantages, and firmness. And the principle of origination unites and controls them all. In their operation they constitute the course of the four seasons, and the vital force of spring permeates all. Therefore in the mind of man there are also four moral qualities—namely, *jen*, righteousness, propriety, and wisdom—and *jen* embraces them all. In their emanation and function, they constitute the feeling of love, respect, being right, and discrimination between right and wrong—and the feeling of commiseration pervades them all. Therefore in discussing the mind of Heaven and Earth, it is said, "Great is *ch'ien* (Heaven), the originator!" and "Great is *k'un* (Earth), the originator." Both substance and function of the four moral qualities are thus fully implied without enumerating them. In discussing the excellence of man's mind, it is said, "*Jen* is man's mind." Both substance and function of the four moral qualities are thus fully presented without mentioning them. For *jen* as constituting the Way (Tao) consists of the fact that the mind of Heaven and Earth to produce things is present in everything. Before feelings are aroused this substance is already existent in its completeness. After feelings are aroused, its function is infinite. If we can truly practice love and preserve it, then we have in it the spring of all virtues and the root of all good deeds. This is why in the teachings of the Confucian school, the student is always urged to exert anxious and unceasing effort in the pursuit of *jen*. In the teachings (of Confucius, it is said), "Master oneself and return to propriety." This means that if we can overcome and eliminate selfishness and return to the Principle of Nature, (*T'ien-li*, Principle of Heaven), then the substance of this mind (that is, *jen*) will be present everywhere and its function will always be operative. It is also said, "Be respectful in private life, be serious in handling affairs, and be loyal in dealing with others." These are also ways to preserve this mind. Again, it is said, "Be filial in serving parents," "Be respectful in serving elder brothers," and "Be loving in dealing with all things." These are ways to put this mind into practice. It is again said, "They sought *jen* and found it," for (Po-i) declined a kingdom and left the country (in favor of his younger brother, Shu-ch'i) and they both remonstrated their superior against

---

*Reprinted with permission from Wing-tsit Chan, *A Source Book on Chinese Philosophy* (Princeton: Princeton University Press, 1963).

[1] Ch'eng Hao or Ch'eng I.

a punitive expedition and chose retirement and hunger, and in doing so, they prevented losing this mind. Again it is said, "Sacrifice life in order to realize *jen*." This means that we desire something more than life and hate something more than death, so as not to injure this mind. What mind is this? In Heaven and Earth it is the mind to produce things infinitely. In man it is the mind to love people gently and to benefit things. It includes the four virtues (of humanity, righteousness, propriety, and wisdom) and penetrates the Four Beginnings (of the sense of commiseration, the sense of shame, the sense of deference and compliance, and the sense of right and wrong).

Someone said: According to our explanation, is it not wrong for Master Ch'eng to say that love is feeling while *jen* is nature and that love should not be regarded as *jen*?

Answer: Not so. What Master Ch'eng criticized was the application of the term to the expression of love. What I maintain is that the term should be applied to the principle of love. For although the spheres of man's nature and feelings are different, their mutual penetration is like the blood system in which each part has its own relationship. When have they become sharply separated and been made to have nothing to do with each other? I was just now worrying about students' reciting Master Ch'eng's words without inquiring into their meaning, and thereby coming to talk about *jen* as clearly apart from love. I have therefore purposely talked about this to reveal the hidden meaning of Master Ch'eng's words, and you regard my ideas as different from his. Are you not mistaken?

Someone said: The followers of Master Ch'eng have given many explanations of *jen*. Some say that love is not *jen*, and regard the unity of all things and the self as the substance of *jen*. Others maintain that love is not *jen* but explain *jen* in terms of the possession of consciousness by the mind. If what you say is correct, are they all wrong?

Answer: From what they call the unity of all things and the self, it can be seen that *jen* involves love for all, but unity is not the reality which makes *jen* a substance. From what they call the mind's possession of consciousness, it can be seen that *jen* includes wisdom, but that is not the real reason why *jen* is so called. If you look up Confucius' answer to (his pupil) Tzu-kung's question whether conferring extensive benefit on the people and bringing salvation to all (will constitute *jen*) and also Master Ch'eng's statement that *jen* is not to be explained in terms of consciousness, you will see the point. How can you still explain *jen* in these terms?

Furthermore, to talk about *jen* in general terms of the unity of things and the self will lead people to be vague, confused, neglectful, and make no effort to be alert. The bad effect—and there has been—may be to consider other things as oneself. To talk about love in specific terms of consciousness will lead people to be nervous, irascible, and devoid of any quality of depth. The bad effect—and there has been—may be to consider desire as principle. In one case, (the mind) forgets (its objective). In the other (there is artificial effort to) help (it grow). Both are wrong. Furthermore, the explanation in terms of consciousness does not in any way approach the manner of (a man of *jen* who) "delights in mountains" (while a man of wisdom delights in water) or the idea that (*jen* alone) "can preserve" (what knowledge has attained), as taught his pupil by Confucius. How then can you still explain love in those terms? I hereby record what they said and write this treatise on *jen*. (*Chu Tzu wen-chi*, or "Collection of Literary Works of Chu Hsi," CTTC, 67:20a-21b)

2. A TREATISE ON CH'ENG MING-TAO'S DISCOURSE ON THE NATURE

Master Ch'eng Hao also said, "What is inborn is called nature. . . . They (nature and material force, *ch'i*) are both inborn." [His meaning is this]: What is imparted by Heaven (Nature) to all things is called destiny (*ming*, mandate, fate). What is received by them from Heaven is called nature. But in the carrying out of the Mandate of Heaven, there must first be the interaction, mutual influence, consolidation, and integration of the two material forces (yin and yang) and the Five Agents (of Metal, Wood, Water, Fire, and Earth) before things can be produced. Man's nature and destiny exist before physical form [and are without it], while material force exists after physical form [and is with it]. What exists before physical form is the one principle harmonious and undifferentiated, and is invariably good. What exists after physical form, however, is confused and mixed, and good and evil are thereby differentiated. Therefore when man and things are produced, they have in them this material force, with the endowment of which they are produced. But the nature endowed by Heaven is therein preserved. This is how Master Ch'eng elucidated the doctrine of Kao Tzu that what is inborn is called nature, and expressed his own thought by saying that "One's nature is the same as material force and material force is the same as nature."

Master Ch'eng also said. "[According to principle, there are both good and evil] in the material force with which man is endowed at birth. . . . [Nature is of course good], but it cannot be said that evil is not nature." It is the principle of nature that the material force with which man is endowed necessarily has the difference of good and evil. For in the operation of material force, nature is the controlling factor. In accordance with its purity or impurity, material force is differentiated into good and evil. Therefore there are not two distinct things in nature opposing each other. Even the nature of evil material force is good, and therefore evil may not be said to be not a part of nature. The Master further said, "Good and evil in the world are both the Principle of Nature. What is called evil is not original evil. It becomes evil only because of deviation from the mean." For there is nothing in the world which is outside of one's nature. All things are originally good but degenerated into evil, that is all.

The Master further said, "For what is inborn is called one's nature. . . . The fact that whatever issues from the Way is good may be compared to water always flowing downward." Nature is simply nature. How can it be described in words? Therefore those who excel in talking about nature only do so in terms of the beginning of its emanation and manifestation, and what is involved in the concept of nature may then be understood in silence, as when Mencius spoke of the Four Beginnings (of humanity, righteousness, propriety, and wisdom). By observing the fact that water necessarily flows downward, we know the nature of water is to go downward. Similarly, by observing the fact that the emanation of nature is always good, we know that nature involves goodness.

The Master further said, "Water as such is the same in all cases. . . . Although they differ in being turbid or clear, we cannot say that the turbid water ceases to be water. . . . The original goodness of human nature is like the original clearness of water. Therefore it is not true that two distinct and opposing elements of good and evil exist in human nature and that each issues from it." This is again using the clearness and turbidity of water as an analogy. The clearness of water is comparable to the goodness of nature. Water flowing to the sea without getting dirty is similar to one whose material force with which he is endowed is pure and clear and who is good from childhood. In the case of a sage it is his nature to be so and he preserves his Heavenly endowment complete. Water that flows only a short distance and is already turbid is like one whose material endowment is extremely unbalanced and impure and is evil from childhood. Water that flows a long distance before becoming turbid is like one who, as he grows up, changes his character as he sees something novel and attractive to him, and loses his child's heart. That water may be turbid to a greater or smaller extent is similar to the fact that one's material force may be dark or clear and pure or impure in varying degrees. "We cannot say that the turbid water ceases to be water" means that it cannot be said that evil is not nature. Thus although man is darkened by material force and degenerates into evil, nature does not cease to be inherent in him. Only, if you call it nature, it is not the original nature, and if you say it is not nature, yet from the beginning it has never departed from it. Because of this, man must increase his effort at purification. If one can overcome material force through learning, he will know that this nature is harmonious and unified and from the beginning has never been destroyed. It is like the original water. Although the water is turbid, the clear water is nevertheless there, and therefore it is not that clear water has been substituted by turbid water. When it is clear, it is originally not turbid, and therefore it is not that turbid water has been taken out and laid in a corner. This being the case, the nature is originally good. How can there be two distinct, opposing, and parallel things existing in nature?

Master Ch'eng finally said, "This principle is the Mandate of Heaven. To obey and follow it is the Way. . . . One can neither augment nor diminish this function which corresponds to the Way. Such is the case of Shun who, [obeying and following the Way], possessed the empire as if it were nothing to him. The sentence "This principle is the Mandate of Heaven" includes the beginning and ending, and the fundament and the secondary. Although the cultivation of the Way is spoken of with reference to human affairs, what is cultivated is after all nothing but the Mandate of Heaven as it originally is and is nothing man's selfishness or cunning can do about it. However, only the sage can completely fulfill it. Therefore the example of Shun is used to make the meaning clear. (*Chu Tzu wen-chi*, 67:16b-18a)

3. FIRST LETTER TO THE GENTLEMEN OF HUNAN ON EQUILIBRIUM AND HARMONY

Concerning the meaning in the *Doctrine of the Mean* that equilibrium (*chung*, centrality, the Mean) is the state before the feelings of pleasure, anger, sorrow, and joy are aroused and that harmony is that state after they are aroused, because formerly I realized the substance of the operation of the mind, and, furthermore, because Master Ch'eng I had said that "whenever we talk about the mind, we refer to the state after the feelings are aroused," I looked upon the mind as the state after the feelings are aroused and upon nature as the state before the feelings are aroused. However, I have observed that there are many incorrect points in Master Ch'eng's works. I have therefore thought the matter over, and consequently realized that in my previous theory not only are the [contrasting] terms "mind" and "nature" improper but the efforts in my daily task also completely lack a great foundation. Therefore the loss has not been confined to the meanings of words.

The various theories in Master Ch'eng's *Wen-chi* (Collection of Literary Works) and *I-shu* (Surviving Works) seem to hold that before there is any sign of thought or deliberation and prior to the arrival of [stimulus] of external things, there is the state before the feelings of pleasure, anger, sorrow, and joy are aroused. At this time, the state is identical with the substance of the mind, which is absolutely quiet and inactive, and the nature endowed by Heaven should be completely embodied in it. Because it is neither excessive nor insufficient, and is neither unbalanced nor one-sided, it is called equilibrium. When it is acted upon and immediately penetrates all things, the feelings are then aroused. In this state the functioning of the mind can be seen. Because it never fails to attain the proper measure and degree and has nowhere deviated from the right, it is called harmony. This is true because of the correctness of the human mind and the moral character of the feelings and nature.

However, the state before the feelings are aroused cannot be sought and the state after they are aroused permits no manipulation. So long as in one's daily life the effort at seriousness and cultivation is fully extended and there are no selfish human desires to disturb it, then before the feelings are aroused it will be as clear as a mirror and as calm as still water, and after the feelings are aroused it will attain due measure and degree without exception. This is the essential task in everyday life. As to self-examination when things occur and seeking understanding through inference when we come into contact with things, this must also serve as the foundation. If we observe the state after the feelings are aroused, what is contained in the state before the feelings are aroused can surely be understood in silence. This is why in his answers to Su Chi-ming, Master Ch'eng discussed and argued back and forth in the greatest detail and with extreme care, but in the final analysis what he said was no more than the word "seriousness' (*ching*). This is the reason why he said, "Seriousness without fail is the way to attain equilibrium," and "For entering the Way there is nothing better than seriousness. No one can ever extend knowledge to the utmost without depending on seriousness," and again, "Self-cultivation requires seriousness; the pursuit of learning depends on the extension of knowledge."

Right along, in my discussions and thinking, I have simply considered the mind to be the state after the feelings are aroused, and in my daily efforts I have also merely considered examining and recognizing the clues [of activities of feelings] as the starting points. Consequently I have neglected the effort of daily self-cultivation, so that the mind is disturbed in many ways and lacks the quality of depth or purity. Also, when it is expressed in speech or action, it is always characterized by a sense of urgency and an absence of reserve, and there is no longer any disposition of ease or profoundness. For a single mistake in one's viewpoint can lead to as much harm as this. This is something we must not overlook.

When Master Ch'eng said that "whenever we talk about the mind, we refer to the state after the feelings are aroused," he referred [only] to the mind of an infant [whose feelings have already been aroused]. When he said "whenever we talk about the mind," he was mistaken in the way he expressed it and therefore admitted the incorrectness and corrected himself by saying, "This is of course incorrect, for the mind is one. Sometimes we refer to its substance (namely, the state of absolute quietness and inactivity) and sometimes we refer to its function (namely, its being acted on and immediately penetrating all things). It depends on one's point of view." We should not hold on to his saying which he had already corrected and on that basis doubt the correctness of his various theories, or simply dismiss it as incorrect without examining the fact that he was referring to something else. What do you gentlemen think about this? (*Chu Tzu wen-chi*, 64:28b-29b)

4. THE EXAMINATION OF THE SELF AND THINGS

A. There is dead seriousness and there is living seriousness. If one merely adheres to seriousness in concentrating on one thing and, when things happen, does not support it with righteousness to distinguish between right and wrong, it will not be living seriousness. When one becomes at home with it, then wherever there is seriousness, there is righteousness, and wherever there is righteousness, there is seriousness. When tranquil, one examines himself as to whether one is serious or not, and when active, one examines himself as to whether he is righteous or not. Take, for example, the cases of "going abroad and behaving to everyone as if you were receiving a guest and employing the people as if you were assisting at a great sacrifice." What would happen if you were not serious? Or the cases of "sitting as if one is impersonating an ancestor, and standing as if one is sacrificing." What would happen if you were not serious? Righteousness and seriousness must support each other, one following the other without beginning or end, and then both internal and external life will be thoroughly penetrated by them. (*Complete Works*, 3:1b-2a)

B. If the Principle of Nature exists in the human mind, human selfish desires will not, but if human selfish desires win, the Principle of Nature will be destroyed. There has never been a case where both the Principle of Nature and human selfish desires are interwoven and mixed. This is where the student must realize and examine for himself. (3:3a)

C. "Thinking alone can check passionate desires." What do you think of the saying? *Answer:* Thinking is the same as examining. It means that when one is angry, if one can directly forget his anger and examine the right and wrong according to principle, then right and wrong will be clearly seen and desires will naturally be unable to persist. (3:3b)

D. To say that one must examine at the point where the feelings are about to be aroused means to be careful when thoughts and deliberations are just beginning, and to say that one must examine after the feelings have been aroused means that one must examine one's words and actions after they have taken place. One must of course be careful about thoughts and deliberations when they begin, but one must not fail to examine his words and action after they have taken place. (3:7a)

5. KNOWLEDGE AND ACTION

A. Knowledge and action always require each other. It is like a person who cannot walk without legs although he has eyes, and who cannot see without eyes although he has legs. With respect to order, knowledge comes first, and with respect to importance, action is more important. (*Complete Works*, 3:8a)

B. The efforts of both knowledge and action must be exerted to the utmost. As one knows more clearly, he acts more earnestly, and as he acts more earnestly, he knows more clearly. Neither of the two should be unbalanced or discarded. It is like a person's two legs. If they take turn to walk, one will be able gradually to arrive at the destination. If one leg is weak and soft, then not even one forward step can be taken. However, we must first know before we can act. This is why the *Great Learning* first talks about the extension of knowledge, the *Doctrine of the Mean* puts wisdom ahead of humanity and courage, and Confucius first of all spoke of knowledge being sufficient to attain its objective. But none of extensive study, accurate inquiry, careful thinking, clear sifting, and vigorous practice can be omitted. (3:8b)

C. When one knows something but has not yet acted on it, his knowledge is still shallow. After he has experienced it, his knowledge will be increasingly clear, and its character will be different from what it was before. (3:12b)

D. Generally speaking, in any matter there is only one right or wrong. When the right or wrong is determined, one should choose the right and keep acting on it. How can one expect that by wavering he can win approval from everyone? Whether a thing is right or wrong will eventually become definite of itself. For the moment what is important is that one is satisfied within himself, so that looking up, he has no occasion for shame, and looking down, he has no occasion to blush. Never mind whether other people say they like it or not. (3:12b-13a)

E. Throughout a person's handling of affairs and dealing with things, there is no point at which moral principles are not present. Although one cannot know all of them, in all likelihood he has heard the great essentials. The important point is to put into action vigorously what he has already known and make efforts to go beyond it. In this way he can go from the near to the far and from the coarse to the refined, methodically and in an orderly manner, and observable effect can be achieved every day. (3:22b-23a)

6. THE EXTENSION OF KNOWLEDGE

A. What sages and worthies call extensive learning means to study everything. From the most essential and most fundamental about oneself to every single thing or affair in the world, even the meaning of one word or half a word, everything should be investigated to the utmost, and none of it is unworthy of attention. Although we cannot investigate all, still we have to keep on devoting our attention to them in accordance with our intelligence and ability, and in time there will necessarily be some accomplishment. Is this not better than not to pay attention at all? If we absolutely pay no attention, even ignoring things passing before us whose names are unknown to us, is that the way to investigate things to the utmost? (*Complete Works*, 3:26a)

B. Ch'i-yüan asked: In investigating the principles of things and affairs to the utmost, should one investigate exhaustively the point where all principles converge? What do you think? *Answer:* There is no need to talk about the converging point. All that is before our eyes is things and affairs. Just investigate one item after another somehow until the utmost is reached. As more and more is done, one will naturally achieve a far and wide penetration. That which serves as the converging point is the mind. (3:26a-b)

C. Moral principles are quite inexhaustible. No matter what past scholars have said, they have not necessarily exhausted the subject. We must examine them this way and that way ourselves. The more deeply we go into them, the more we shall discover. (3:27a)

D. Pay no attention to names. We must investigate into the reason things are as they are. (3:27b)

E. There is no other way to investigate principle to the utmost than to pay attention to everything in our daily reading of books and handling of affairs. Although there may not seem to be substantial progress, nevertheless after a long period of accumulation, without knowing it one will be saturated with principle and achieve an extensive harmony and penetration. Truly, one cannot succeed if one wants to hurry. (3:33b)

F. To investigate principle to the utmost means to seek to know the reason for which things and affairs are as they are and the reason according to which they should be, that is all. If we know why they are as they are, our will will not be perplexed, and if we know what they should be, our action will not be wrong. It does not mean to take the principle of something and put it in another. (3:34a)

7. THE GREAT ULTIMATE

A. The Great Ultimate is nothing other than principle. (*Complete Works*, 49:8b)

B. *Question:* The Great Ultimate is not a thing existing in a chaotic state before the formation of heaven and earth, but a general name for the principles of heaven and earth and the myriad things. Is that correct?

Answer: The Great Ultimate is merely the principle of heaven and earth and the myriad things. With respect to heaven and earth, there is the Great Ultimate in them. With respect to the myriad things, there is the Great Ultimate in each and every one of them. Before heaven and earth existed, there was assuredly this principle. It is the principle that "through movement generates the yang." It is also this principle that "through tranquillity generates the yin." (49:8b-9a)

C. *Question:* [You said,] "Principle is a single, concrete entity, and the myriad things partake it as their substance. Hence each of the myriad things possesses in it a Great Ultimate." According to this theory, does the Great Ultimate not split up into parts?

Answer: Fundamentally there is only one Great Ultimate, yet each of the myriad things has been endowed with it and each in itself possesses the Great Ultimate in its entirety. This is similar to the fact that there is only one moon in the sky but when its light is scattered upon rivers and lakes, it can be seen everywhere. It cannot be said that the moon has been split. (49:10b-11a)

D. The Great Ultimate has neither spatial restriction nor physical form or body. There is no spot where it may be placed. When it is considered in the state before activity begins, this state is nothing but tranquillity. Now activity, tranquillity, yin, and yang all exist only after physical form [and are with it]. However, activity is after all the activity of the Great Ultimate and tranquillity is also its tranquillity, although activity and tranquillity themselves are not the Great Ultimate. This is why Master Chou Tun-i only spoke of that state as Non-ultimate. While the state before activity begins cannot be spoken of as the Great Ultimate, nevertheless the principles of pleasure, anger, sorrow, and joy are already inherent in it. Pleasure and joy belong to yang and anger and sorrow belong to yin. In the initial stage the four are not manifested, but their principles are already there. As contrasted with the state after activity begins, it may be called the Great Ultimate. But still it is difficult to say. All this is but a vague description. The truth must be personally realized by each individual himself. (49:11a-b)

E. Someone asked about the Great Ultimate. *Reply:* The Great Ultimate is simply the principle of the highest good. Each and every person has in him the Great Ultimate and each and every thing has in it the Great Ultimate. What Master Chou calls the Great Ultimate is a name to express all the virtues and the highest good in Heaven and Earth, man, and things. (49:11b)

F. The Great Ultimate is similar to the top of a house or the zenith of the sky, beyond which point there is no more. It is the ultimate of principle. Yang is active and yin is tranquil. In these it is not the Great Ultimate that acts or remains tranquil. It is simply that there are the principles of activity and tranquillity. Principle is not visible; it becomes visible through yin and yang. Principle attaches itself to yin and yang as a man sits astride a horse. As soon as yin and yang produce the Five Agents, they are confined and fixed by physical nature and are thus differentiated into individual things each with its nature. But the Great Ultimate is in all of them. (49:14a)

G. The Great Ultimate contains all principles of the Five Agents and yin and yang. It is not an empty thing. If it were a void, it would approach the Buddhist theory of dharma-nature (which maintains that the nature of dharmas, that is, elements of existence, are void). (49:14a)

H. *Question:* Is the Great Ultimate the highest principle of the human mind?

Answer: There is an ultimate in every thing or event. That is the ultimate of principle.

Someone asked: Like humanity on the part of the ruler and respect on the part of ministers? These are ultimates.

Answer: These are ultimates of a particular thing or event. When all principles of heaven and earth and the myriad things are put together, that is the Great Ultimate. The Great Ultimate originally has no such name. It is merely a name to express its character. (49:14b-15a)

I. There is no other event in the universe except yin and yang succeeding each other in an unceasing cycle. This is called Change. However, for these activity and tranquillity, there must be the principles which make them possible. This is the Great Ultimate. (49:16a)

8. PRINCIPLE AND MATERIAL FORCE

A. *Question:* Man and things are all endowed with the principle of the universe as their nature, and receive the material force of the universe as their physical form. The difference in personality is of course due to the various degrees of purity and strength of the material force. But in the case of things, are they as they are because of the incompleteness of the principle with which they are endowed or because of the impurity and beclouding character of the material force endowed in them?

Answer: The principle received by things is precisely in the same degree as the material force received by them. For example, the physical constitution of dogs and horses being what it is, they know how to do only certain things. . . . (*Complete Works*, 42:26b–27a)

B. Question about the relation between principle and material force.

Answer: I-ch'uan (Ch'eng I) expressed it very well when he said that principle is one but its manifestations are many. When heaven, earth, and the myriad things are spoken of together, there is only one principle. As applied to man, however, there is in each individual a particular principle. (49:1b)

C. *Question:* What are the evidences that principle is in material force?

Answer: For example, there is order in the complicated interfusion of the yin and the yang and of the Five Agents. Principle is there. If material force does not consolidate and integrate, principle would have nothing to attach itself to. (49:2b)

D. *Question:* May we say that before heaven and earth existed there was first of all principle?

Answer: Before heaven and earth existed, there was after all only principle. As there is this principle, therefore there are heaven and earth. If there were no principle, there would also be no heaven and earth, no man, no things, and in fact, no containing or sustaining (of things by heaven and earth) to speak of. As there is principle, there is therefore material force to operate everywhere and nourish and develop all things.

Question: Is it principle that nourishes and develops all things?

Answer: As there is this principle, therefore there is this material force operating, nourishing, and developing. Principle itself has neither physical form nor body. (49:3a-b)

E. Throughout the universe there are both principle and material force. Principle refers to the Way, which exists before physical form [and is without it] and is the root from which all things are produced. Material force refers to material objects, which exists after physical form [and is with it]; it is the instrument by which things are produced. Therefore in the production of man and things, they must be endowed with principle before they have their nature, and they must be endowed with material force before they have physical form. (49:5b)

Wang Yang-ming: Inquiry on the *Great Learning**

Question: The *Great Learning* was considered by a former scholar [Chu Hsi] as the learning of the great man. I venture to ask why the learning of the great man should consist in "manifesting the clear character."

Master Wang said: The great man regards Heaven, Earth, and the myriad things as one body. He regards the world as one family and the country as one person. As to those who make a cleavage between objects and distinguish between the self and others, they are small men. That the great man can regard Heaven, Earth, and the myriad things as one body is not because he deliberately wants to do so, but because it is natural to the humane nature of his mind that he do so. Forming one body with Heaven, Earth, and the myriad things is not only true of the great man. Even the mind of the small man is no different. Only he himself makes it small. Therefore when he sees a child about to fall into a well, he cannot help a feeling of alarm and commiseration. This shows that his humanity forms one body with the child. It may be objected that the child belongs to the same species. Again, when he observes the pitiful cries and frightened appearance of birds and animals about to be slaughtered, he cannot help feeling an "inability to bear" their suffering. This shows that his humanity forms one body with birds and animals. It may be

---

*Reprinted with permission from Wing-tsit Chan, *A Source Book in Chinese Philosophy* (Princeton: Princeton University Press, 1963).

objected that birds and animals are sentient beings as he is. But when he sees plants broken and destroyed, he cannot help a feeling of pity. This shows that his humanity forms one body with plants. It may be said that plants are living things as he is. Yet, even when he sees tiles and stones shattered and crushed, he cannot help a feeling of regret. This shows that his humanity forms one body with tiles and stones. This means that even the mind of the small man necessarily has the humanity that forms one body with all. Such a mind is rooted in his Heaven-endowed nature, and is naturally intelligent, clear, and not beclouded. For this reason it is called the "clear character." Although the mind of the small man is divided and narrow, yet his humanity that forms one body can remain free from darkness to this degree. This is due to the fact that his mind has not yet been aroused by desires and obscured by selfishness. When it is aroused by desires and obscured by selfishness, compelled by greed for gain and fear of harm, and stirred by anger, he will destroy things, kill members of his own species, and will do everything. In extreme cases he will even slaughter his own brothers, and the humanity that forms one body will disappear completely. Hence, if it is not obscured by selfish desires, even the mind of the small man has the humanity that forms one body with all as does the mind of the great man. As soon as it is obscured by selfish desires, even the mind of the great man will be divided and narrow like that of the small man. Thus the learning of the great man consists entirely in getting rid of the obscuration of selfish desires in order by his own efforts to make manifest his clear character, so as to restore the condition of forming one body with Heaven, Earth, and the myriad things, a condition that is originally so, that is all. It is not that outside of the original substance something can be added.

Question: Why, then, does the learning of the great man consist in loving the people?

Answer: To manifest the clear character is to bring about the substance of the state of forming one body with Heaven, Earth, and the myriad things, whereas loving the people is to put into universal operation the function of the state of forming one body. Hence manifesting the clear character consists in loving the people, and loving the people is the way to manifest the clear character. Therefore, only when I love my father, the fathers of others, and the fathers of all men can my humanity really form one body with my father, the fathers of others, and the fathers of all men. When it truly forms one body with them, then the clear character of filial piety will be manifested. Only when I love my brother, the brothers of others, and the brothers of all men can my humanity really form one body with my brother, the brothers of others, and the brothers of all men. When it truly forms one body with them, then the clear character of brotherly respect will be manifested. Everything from ruler, minister, husband, wife, and friends to mountains, rivers, spiritual beings, birds, animals, and plants should be truly loved in order to realize my humanity that forms one body with them, and then my clear character will be completely manifested, and I will really form one body with Heaven, Earth, and the myriad things. This is what is meant by "manifesting the clear character throughout the world." This is what is meant by "regulation of the family," "ordering the state," and "bringing peace to the world." This is what is meant by "full development of one's nature."

Question: Then why does the learning of the great man consist in "abiding in the highest good"?

Answer: The highest good is the ultimate principle of manifesting character and loving people. The nature endowed in us by Heaven is pure and perfect. The fact that it is intelligent, clear, and not beclouded is evidence of the emanation and revelation of the highest good. It is the original substance of the clear character which is called innate knowledge of the good. As the highest good emanates and reveals itself, we will consider right as right and wrong as wrong. Things of greater or less importance and situations of grave or light character will be responded to as they act upon us. In all our changes and movements, we will stick to no particular point, but possess in ourselves the mean that is perfectly natural. This is the ultimate of the normal nature of man and the principle of things. There can be no consideration of adding or subtracting anything to or from it. Such a suggestion reveals selfish ideas and shallow cunning, and cannot be said to be the highest good. Naturally, how can anyone who does not watch over himself carefully when alone, and who has no refinement and singleness of mind, attain to such a state of perfection? Later generations fail to realize that the highest good is inherent in their own minds, but exercise their selfish ideas and cunning and grope for it outside their minds, believing that every event and every object has its own peculiar definite principle. For this reason the law of right and wrong is obscured; the mind becomes concerned with fragmentary and isolated details and broken pieces; the selfish desires of man become rampant and the Principle of Nature is at an end. And thus the learning of manifesting character and loving people is everywhere thrown into confusion. In the past there have, of course, been people who wanted to manifest their clear character. But simply because they did not know how to abide in the highest good, but instead drove their own minds toward something too lofty, they thereby lost them in illusions, emptiness, and quietness, having nothing to do with the work of the family, the state, and the world. Such are the followers of Buddhism and Taoism. There have, of course, been those who wanted to love their people. Yet simply because they did not know how to abide in the highest good, but instead sank their own minds in base and trifling things, they thereby lost them in scheming strategy and cunning techniques, having neither the sincerity of humanity nor that of commiseration. Such are the followers of the Five Despots and the pursuers of success and profit. All of these defects are due to a failure to know how to abide in the highest good. Therefore abiding in the highest good is to manifesting character and loving people as the carpenter's square and compass are to the square and the circle, or rule and measure to length, or balances and scales to weight. If the square and the circle do not abide by the compass and the carpenter's square, their standard will be wrong; if length does not abide by the rule and measure, its adjustment will be lost; if weight does not abide by the balances, its exactness will be gone; and if manifesting clear character and loving people do not abide by the highest good, their foundation will disappear. Therefore, abiding in the highest good so as to love people and manifest the clear character is what is meant by the learning of the great man.

Question: "Only after knowing what to abide in can one be calm. Only after having been calm can one be tranquil. Only after having achieved tranquillity can one have peaceful repose. Only after having peaceful repose can one begin to deliberate. Only after deliberation can the end be attained." How do you explain this?

Answer: People fail to realize that the highest good is in their minds and seek it outside. As they believe that everything or every event has its own definite principle, they search for the highest good in individual things. Consequently, the mind becomes fragmentary, isolated, broken into pieces; mixed and confused, it has no definite direction. Once it is realized that the highest good is in the mind and does not depend on any search outside, then the mind will have definite direction and there will be no danger of its becoming fragmentary, isolated, broken into pieces, mixed, or confused. When there is no such danger, the mind will not be erroneously perturbed but will be tranquil. Not being erroneously perturbed but being tranquil, it will be leisurely and at ease in its daily functioning and will attain peaceful repose. Being in peaceful repose, whenever a thought arises or an event acts upon it, the mind with its innate knowledge will thoroughly sift and carefully examine whether or not the thought or event is in accord with the highest good, and thus the mind can deliberate. With deliberation, every decision will be excellent and every act will be proper, and in this way the highest good will be attained.

Question: "Things have their roots and their branches." A former scholar considered manifesting the clear character as the root (or fundamental) and renovating the people as the branch (or secondary), and thought that they are two things opposing each other as internal and external. "Affairs have their beginnings and their ends." The former scholar considered knowing what to abide in as the beginning and the attainment of the highest good as the end, both being one thing in harmonious continuity. According to you, "renovating the people" (*hsin-min*) should be read as "loving the people" (*ch'in-min*). If so, isn't the theory of root and branches in some respect incorrect?

Answer: The theory of beginnings and ends is in general right. Even if we read "renovating the people" as "loving the people" and say that manifesting the character is the root and loving the people is the branches, it is not incorrect. The main thing is that root and branches should not be distinguished as two different things. The trunk of the tree is called the root, and the twigs are called the branches. It is precisely because the tree is one that its parts can be called root and branches. If they are said to be two different things, then since they are two distinct objects, how can we speak of them as root and branches of the same thing? Since the idea of renovating the people is different from that of loving the people, obviously the task of manifesting the character and that of loving the people are two different things. If it is realized that manifesting the clear character is to love the people and loving the people is to manifest the clear character, how can they be split in two? What the former scholar said is due to his failure to realize that manifesting the character and loving the people are basically one thing. Instead, he believed them to be two different things and consequently, although he knew that root and branches should be one, yet he could not help splitting them in two.

Question: The passage from the phrase, "The ancients who wished to manifest their clear character throughout the world" to the clause, "first [order their state . . . regulate their families . . .] cultivate their personal lives," can be understood by your theory of manifesting the character and loving the people. May I ask what task, what procedure, and what effort are involved in the passage from "Those who wished to cultivate their personal lives would first rectify their minds . . . make their will sincere . . . extend their knowledge" to the clause, "the extension of knowledge consists in the investigation of things"?

Answer: This passage fully explains the task of manifesting the character, loving the people, and abiding in the highest good. The person, the mind, the will, knowledge, and things constitute the order followed in the task. While each of them has its own place, they are really one thing. Investigating, extending, being sincere, rectifying, and cultivating are the task performed in the procedure. Although each has its own name, they are really one affair. What is it that is called the person? It is the physical functioning of the mind. What is it that is called the mind? It is the clear and intelligent master of the person. What is meant by cultivating the personal life? It means to do good and get rid of evil. Can the body by itself do good and get rid of evil? The clear and intelligent master must desire to do good and get rid of evil before the body that functions physically can do so. Therefore he who wishes to cultivate his personal life must first rectify his mind.

Now the original substance of the mind is man's nature. Human nature being universally good, the original substance of the mind is correct. How is it that any effort is required to rectify the mind? The reason is that, while the original substance of the mind is originally correct, incorrectness enters when one's thoughts and will are in operation. Therefore he who wishes to rectify his mind must rectify it in connection with the operation of his thoughts and will. If, whenever a good thought arises, he really loves it as he loves beautiful colors, and whenever an evil thought arises, he really hates it as he hates bad odors, then his will will always be sincere and his mind can be rectified.

However, what arises from the will may be good or evil, and unless there is a way to make clear the distinction between good and evil, there will be a confusion of truth and untruth. In that case, even if one wants to make his will sincere, he cannot do so. Therefore he who wishes to make his will sincere must extend his knowledge. By extension is meant to reach the limit. The word "extension" is the same as that used in the saying, "Mourning is to be carried to the utmost degree of grief." In the *Book of Changes* it is said: "Knowing the utmost, one should reach it." "Knowing the utmost" means knowledge and "reaching it" means extension. The extension of knowledge is not what later scholars understand as enriching and widening knowledge. It is simply extending one's innate knowledge of the good to the utmost. This innate knowledge of the good is what Mencius meant when he said, "The sense of right and wrong is common to all men." The sense of right and wrong requires no deliberation to know, nor does it depend on learning to function. This is why it is called innate knowledge. It is my nature endowed by Heaven, the original substance of my mind, naturally intelligent, shining, clear, and understanding.

Whenever a thought or a wish arises, my mind's faculty of innate knowledge itself is always conscious of it. Whether it is good or evil, my mind's innate knowing faculty itself also knows it. It has nothing to do with others. Therefore, although an inferior man may have done all manner of evil, when he sees a superior man he will surely try to disguise this fact, concealing what is evil and displaying what is good in himself. This shows that innate knowledge of the good does not permit any self-deception. Now the only way to distinguish good and evil in order to make the will sincere is to extend to the utmost the knowledge of the innate faculty. Why is this? When [a good] thought or wish arises, the innate faculty of my mind already knows it to be good. Suppose I do not sincerely love it but instead turn away from it. I would then be regarding good as evil and obscuring my innate faculty which knows the good. When [an evil] thought or wish arises, the innate faculty of my mind already knows it to be evil. If I did not sincerely hate it but instead carried it out, I would be regarding evil as good and obscuring my innate faculty which knows evil. In such cases what is supposed to be knowledge is really ignorance. How then can the will be made sincere? If what the innate faculty knows to be good or evil is sincerely loved or hated, one's innate knowing faculty is not deceived and the will can be made sincere.

Now, when one sets out to extend his innate knowledge to the utmost, does this mean something illusory, hazy, in a vacuum, and unreal? No, it means something real. Therefore, the extension of knowledge must consist in the investigation of things. A thing is an event. For every emanation of the will there must be an event corresponding to it. The event to which the will is directed is a thing. To investigate is to rectify. It is to rectify that which is incorrect so it can return to its original correctness. To rectify that which is not correct is to get rid of evil, and to return to correctness is to do good. This is what is meant by investigation. The *Book of History* says, "He [Emperor Yao] investigated (*ko*) heaven above and earth below"; "[Emperor Shun] investigated (*ko*) in the temple of illustrious ancestors"; and "[The ruler] rectifies (*ko*) the evil of his heart." The word "investigation" (*ko*) in the phrase "the investigation of things" combines the two meanings.

If one sincerely loves the good known by the innate faculty but does not in reality do the good as he comes into contact with the thing to which the will is directed, it means that the thing has not been investigated and that the will to love the good is not yet sincere. If one sincerely hates the evil known by the innate faculty but does not in reality get rid of the evil as he comes into contact with the thing to which the will is directed, it means that the thing has not been investigated and that the will to hate evil is not sincere. If as we come into contact with the thing to which the will is directed, we really do the good and get rid of the evil to the utmost which is known by the innate faculty, then everything will be investigated and what is known by our innate faculty will not be deficient or obscured but will be extended to the utmost. Then the mind will be joyous in itself, happy and without regret, the functioning of the will will carry with it no self-deception, and sincerity may be said to have been attained. Therefore it is said, "When things are investigated, knowledge is extended; when knowledge is extended, the will becomes sincere; when the will is sincere, the mind is rectified; and when the mind is rectified, the personal life is cultivated." While the order of the tasks involves a sequence of first and last, in substance they are one and cannot be so separated. At the same time, while the order and the tasks cannot be separated into first and last, their function must be so refined as not to be wanting in the slightest degree. This is why the doctrine of investigation, extension, being sincere, and rectification is a correct exposition of the true heritage of Sage-Emperors Yao and Shun and why it coincides with Confucius' own ideas.

CHAPTER 23

RECENT CHINESE THOUGHT

Recent Chinese philosophy can be divided into two periods: the modern period, dating from 1840 to 1949, and the contemporary period, from 1949 to the present. The philosophical model in the modern period was predominantly Confucian. Although Buddhist, Taoist, and Western thought also played a role, typically the interpretation of these ways of thought was along Confucian lines. In the contemporary period Marxism provides the dominant model, although since the Hanchow Conference on Neo-Confucianism in 1981 it seems clear that traditional philosophies, when restructured in line with Marxist thought, will play an increasingly important role in shaping China's public philosophy.

Among recent thinkers, five names stand out. K'ang Yu-wei (1858-1927), chief architect of the Hundred Days Reform of 1898, developed a utopian philosophy based on his interpretations of Western notions of historical progress and Confucian notions of humanity and the cultivation of fellow-feeling. Chang Tung-sun (1886-1962) is representative of a large number of philosophers who were greatly influenced by Western thought. His theory of knowledge was largely Kantian, and his philosophy of culture predominantly pragmatist, although in later life his thought became increasingly Marxist. Hsiung Shih-li (1883-1968) integrated a Buddhist philosophy of mind with a cosmology based on the *Book of Changes* in constructing a new interpretation of Confucianism. The two most influential thinkers, however, have been Fung Yu-lan (1895-) and Mao Tse-tung (1894-1976).

Mao's interpretation of Marxist-Leninist thought has established the basis of contemporary China's public philosophy. But, as numerous scholars have shown, Mao's reconstruction of Marxism is influenced considerably by traditional thought, both Taoist and Confucian. His most important philosophical writings are "On Practice" (1937), "On Contradiction" (1937), "On the People's Democratic Dictatorship" (1949), and "On the Correct Handling of Contradictions among the People" (1957). Of these, "On Practice" is the most important, for it establishes the unity of knowing and acting. Major portions of this essay are reproduced here, taken from *Mao Tse-tung: Four Essays on Philosophy* (Peking: Foreign Languages Press, 1968). Francis Y. K. Soo, *Mao Tse-tung's Theory of Dialectic* (Dordrecht: D. Reidel Publishing Company, 1968), is a fine cross-cultural analysis of Mao's understanding of the dialectical nature of reality.

Fung Yu-lan's prominence was established with the publication of his two-volume *History of Chinese Philosophy* in 1931 [English translation by Derk Bodde (Princeton: Princeton University Press, 1952–53)]. Almost immediately it became the standard history and, after his Marxist conversion, his revisions of this work became the main vehicle of his reconstruction of the history of Chinese philosophy. Before his Marxist conversion, Fung had established himself as the leading Confucian thinker in China with publication of *The New Rational Philosophy* in 1939. The selections from this work show him to be in the tradition of Chu Hsi. However, incorporating concepts and techniques from Western logic, he developed the idea of rational thought far beyond anything found previously in Confucian thought. "The Nature of the History of Chinese Philosophy," presented at the 1957 Peking conference, Discussions on Problems Concerning the History of Chinese Philosophy, provides insight into Fung's understanding of history and the criteria influencing his reconstructions of the history of Chinese philosophy.

The selections here are from Wing-tsit Chan, *A Source Book in Chinese Philosophy* (Princeton: Princeton University Press, 1963), which are preceded by brief introductions and accompanied by helpful comments. Fung Yu-lan, *A Short History of Chinese Philosophy*, edited by Derk Bodde (New York: Macmillan Publishing Company, 1948), chapter 28, presents a summary of Fung's philosophy in his own words. His *The Spirit of Chinese Philosophy*, translated by E. R. Hughes (London: Kegan Paul, 1947), is his assessment of the significance of the different schools of Chinese philosophy.

I
Mao Tse-tung: On Practice*

Before Marx, materialism examined the problem of knowledge apart from the social nature of man and apart from his historical development, and was therefore incapable of understanding the dependence of knowledge on social practice, that is, the dependence of knowledge on production and the class struggle.

Above all, Marxists regard man's activity in production as the most fundamental practical activity, the determinant of all his other activities. Man's knowledge depends mainly on his activity in material production, through

*From *Mao Tse-tung: Four Essays on Philosophy* (Peking: Foreign Languages Press, 1968).

which he comes gradually to understand the phenomena, the properties and the laws of nature, and the relations between himself and nature; and through his activity in production he also gradually comes to understand, in varying degrees, certain relations that exist between man and man. None of this knowledge can be acquired apart from activity in production. In a classless society every person, as a member of society, joins in common effort with the other members, enters into definite relations of production with them and engages in production to meet man's material needs. In all class societies, the members of the different social classes also enter, in different ways, into definite relations of production and engage in production to meet their material needs. This is the primary source from which human knowledge develops.

Man's social practice is not confined to activity in production, but takes many other forms — class struggle, political life, scientific and artistic pursuits; in short, as a social being, man participates in all spheres of the practical life of society. Thus man, in varying degrees, comes to know the different relations between man and man, not only through his material life but also through his political and cultural life (both of which are intimately bound up with material life). Of these other types of social practice, class struggle in particular, in all its various forms, exerts a profound influence on the development of man's knowledge. In class society everyone lives as a member of a particular class, and every kind of thinking, without exception, is stamped with the brand of a class.

Only social practice can be the criterion of truth. The standpoint of practice is the primary and basic standpoint in the dialectical-materialist theory of knowledge.

But how then does human knowledge arise from practice and in turn serve practice? This will become clear if we look at the process of development of knowledge.

In the process of practice, man at first sees only the phenomenal side, the separate aspects, the external relations of things. For instance, some people from outside come to Yenan on a tour of observation. In the first day or two, they see its topography, streets and houses; they meet many people, attend banquets, evening parties and mass meetings, hear talk of various kinds and read various documents, all these being the phenomena, the separate aspects and the external relations of things. This is called the perceptual stage of cognition, namely, the stage of sense perceptions and impressions. That is, these particular things in Yenan act on the sense organs of the members of the observation group, evoke sense perceptions and give rise in their brains to many impressions together with a rough sketch of the external relations among these impressions: this is the first stage of cognition. At this stage, man cannot as yet form concepts, which are deeper, or draw logical conclusions.

As social practice continues, things that give rise to man's sense perceptions and impressions in the course of his practice are repeated many times; then a sudden change (leap) takes place in the brain in the process of cognition, and concepts are formed. Concepts are no longer the phenomena, the separate aspects and the external relations of things; they grasp the essence, the totality and the internal relations of things. Between concepts and sense perceptions there is not only a quantitative but also a qualitative difference. Proceeding further, by means of judgement and inference one is able to draw logical conclusions. The expression in *San Kuo Yen Yi*, "knit the brows and a stratagem comes to mind," or in everyday language, "let me think it over," refers to man's use of concepts in the brain to form judgments and inferences. This is the second stage of cognition. When the members of the observation group have collected various data and, what is more, have "thought them over," they are able to arrive at the judgment that "the Communist Party's policy of the National United Front Against Japan is thorough, sincere and genuine." Having made this judgment, they can, if they too are genuine about uniting to save the nation, go a step further and draw the following conclusion, "The National United Front Against Japan can succeed." This stage of conception, judgment and inference is the more important stage in the entire process of knowing a thing; it is the stage of rational knowledge. The real task of knowing is, through perception, to arrive at thought, to arrive step by step at the comprehension of the internal contradictions of objective things, of their laws and of the internal relations between one process and another, that is, to arrive at logical knowledge. To repeat, logical knowledge differs from perceptual knowledge in that perceptual knowledge pertains to the separate aspects, the phenomena and the external relations of things, whereas logical knowledge takes a big stride forward to reach the totality, the essence and the internal relations of things and discloses the inner contradictions in the surrounding world. Therefore, logical knowledge is capable of grasping the development of the surrounding world in its totality, in the internal relations of all its aspects.

If you want knowledge, you must take part in the practice of changing reality. If you want to know the taste of a pear, you must change the pear by eating it yourself. If you want to know the structure and properties of the atom, you must make physical and chemical experiments to change the state of the atom. If you want to know the theory and methods of revolution, you must take part in revolution. All genuine knowledge originates in direct experience. But one cannot have direct experience of everything; as a matter of fact, most of our knowledge comes from indirect experience, for example, all knowledge from past times and foreign lands. To our ancestors and to foreigners, such knowledge was—or is —a matter of direct experience, and this knowledge is reliable if in the course of their direct experience the requirement of "scientific abstraction," spoken of by Lenin, was—or is—fulfilled and objective reality scientifically reflected; otherwise it is not reliable. Hence a man's knowledge consists only of two parts, that which comes from direct experience and that which comes from indirect experience. Moreover, what is indirect experience for me is direct experience for other people. Consequently, considered as a whole, knowledge of any kind is inseparable from direct experience. All knowledge originates in perception of the objective external world through man's physical sense organs. Anyone who denies such perception, denies direct experience, or denies personal participation in the practice that changes reality, is not a materialist. That is why the "know-all" is ridiculous. There is an old Chinese saying, "How can you catch tiger cubs without entering the tiger's lair?" This saying holds true for man's practice and it also holds true for the theory of knowledge. There can be no knowledge apart from practice.

Rational knowledge depends upon perceptual knowledge and perceptual knowledge remains to be developed into rational knowledge—this is the dialectical-materialist theory of knowledge. In philosophy, neither "rationalism" nor "empiricism" understands the historical or the dialectical nature of knowledge, and although each of these schools contains one aspect of the truth (here I am referring to materialist, not to idealist, rationalism and empiricism), both are wrong on the theory of knowledge as a whole. The dialectical-materialist movement of knowledge from the perceptual to the rational holds true for a minor process of cognition (for instance, knowing a single thing or task) as well as for a major process of cognition (for instance, knowing a whole society or a revolution).

But the movement of knowledge does not end here. If the dialectical-materialist movement of knowledge were to stop at rational knowledge, only half the problem would be dealt with. And as far as Marxist philosophy is concerned, only the less important half at that. Marxist philosophy holds that the most important problem does not lie in understanding the laws of the objective world and thus being able to explain it, but in applying the knowledge of these laws actively to change the world. From the Marxist viewpoint, theory is important, and its importance is fully expressed in Lenin's statement, "Without revolutionary theory there can be no revolutionary movement." But Marxism emphasizes the importance of theory precisely and only because it can guide action. If we have a correct theory but merely prate about it, pigeonhole it and do not put it into practice, then that theory, however good, is of no significance. Knowledge begins with practice, and theoretical knowledge is acquired through practice and must then return to practice. The active function of knowledge manifests itself not only in the active leap from perceptual to rational knowledge, but—and this is more important—it must manifest itself in the leap from rational knowledge to revolutionary practice. The knowledge which grasps the laws of the world, must be redirected to the practice of changing the world, must be applied anew in the practice of production in the practice of revolutionary class struggle and revolutionary national struggle and in the practice of scientific experiment. This is the process of testing and developing theory, the continuation of the whole process of cognition. The problem of whether theory corresponds to objective reality is not, and cannot be, completely solved in the movement of knowledge from the perceptual to the rational, mentioned above. The only way to solve this problem completely is to redirect rational knowledge to social practice, apply theory to practice and see whether it can achieve the objectives one has in mind. Many theories of natural science are held to be true not only because they were so considered when natural scientists originated them, but because they have been verified in subsequent scientific practice. Similarly, Marxism-Leninism is held to be true not only because it was so considered when it was scientifically formulated by Marx, Engels, Lenin and Stalin but because it has been verified in the subsequent practice of revolutionary class struggle and revolutionary national struggle. Dialectical materialism is universally true because it is impossible for anyone to escape from its domain in his practice. The history of human knowledge tells us that the truth of many theories is incomplete and that this incompleteness is remedied through the test of practice. Many theories are erroneous and it is through the test of practice that their errors are corrected. That is why practice is the criterion of truth and why "the standpoint of life, of practice, should be first and fundamental in the theory of knowledge." Stalin has well said, "Theory becomes purposeless if it is not connected with revolutionary practice, just as practice gropes in the dark if its path is not illumined by revolutionary theory."

When we get to this point, is the movement of knowledge completed? Our answer is: it is and yet it is not. When men in society throw themselves into the practice of changing a certain objective process (whether natural or social) at a certain stage of its development, they can, as a result of the reflection of the objective process in their brains and the exercise of their conscious dynamic role, advance their knowledge from the perceptual to the rational, and create ideas, theories, plans or programmes which correspond in general to the laws of that objective process. They then apply these ideas, theories, plans or programmes in practice in the same objective process. And if they can realize the aims they have in mind, that is, if in that same process of practice they can translate, or on the whole translate, those previously formulated ideas, theories, plans or programmes into fact, then the movement of knowledge may be considered completed with regard to this particular process. In the process of changing nature, take for example the fulfilment of an engineering plan, the verification of a scientific hypothesis, the manufacture of an implement or the reaping of a crop; or in the process of changing society, take for example the victory of a strike, victory in a war or the fulfilment of an educational plan. All these may be considered the realization of aims one has in mind. But generally speaking, whether in the practice of changing nature or of changing society, men's original ideas, theories, plans or programmes are seldom realized without any alteration. This is because people engaged in changing reality are usually subject to numerous limitations; they are limited not only by existing scientific and technological conditions but also by the development of the objective process itself and the degree to which this process has become manifest (the aspects and the essence of the objective process have not yet been fully revealed). In such a situation, ideas, theories, plans or programmes are usually altered partially and sometimes even wholly, because of the discovery of unforeseen circumstances in the course of practice. That is to say, it does happen that the original ideas, theories, plans or programmes fail to correspond with reality either in whole or in part and are wholly or partially incorrect. In many instances, failures have to be repeated many times before errors in knowledge can be corrected and correspondence with the laws of the objective process achieved, and consequently before the subjective can be transformed into the objective, or in other words, before the anticipated results can be achieved in practice. Nevertheless, when the point is reached, the movement of human knowledge regarding a certain objective process at a certain stage of its development may be considered completed.

However, so far as the progression of the process is concerned, the movement of human knowledge is not completed. Every process, whether in the realm of nature or of society, progresses and develops by reason of its internal contradiction and struggle, and the movement of human knowledge should also progress and develop along with it. As far as social movements are concerned, true revolutionary leaders must not only be good at correcting their ideas, theories, plans or programmes when errors are discovered, as has been indicated above; but when a certain objective process has already progressed and changed from one stage of development to another, they must also be good at making themselves and all their fellow-revolutionaries progress and change in their subjective knowledge along with it, that is to say, they must ensure that the proposed new revolutionary tasks and new working programmes correspond to the new changes in the situation. In a revolutionary period the situation changes very rapidly; if the knowledge of revolutionaries does not change rapidly in accordance with the changed situation, they will be unable to lead the revolution to victory.

In the present epoch of the development of society, the responsibility of correctly knowing and changing the world has been placed by history upon the shoulders of the proletariat and its party. This process, the practice of changing the world, which is determined in accordance with scientific knowledge, has already reached a historic moment in the world and in China, a great moment unprecedented in human history, that is, the moment for completely banishing darkness from the world and from China and for changing the world into a world of light such as never previously existed. The struggle of the proletariat and the revolutionary people to change the world comprises the fulfilment of the following tasks: to change the objective world and, at the same time, their own subjective world—to change their cognitive ability and change the relations between the subjective and the objective world. Such a change has already come about in one part of the globe, in the Soviet Union. There the people are pushing forward this process of change. The people of China and the rest of the world either are going through, or will go through, such a process. And the objective world which is to be changed also includes all the opponents of change, who, in order to be changed, must go through a stage of compulsion before they can enter the stage of voluntary, conscious change. The epoch of world communism will be reached when all mankind voluntarily and consciously changes itself and the world.

Discover the truth through practice, and again through practice verify and develop the truth. Start from perceptual knowledge and actively develop it into rational knowledge; then start from rational knowledge and actively guide revolutionary practice to change both the subjective and the objective world. Practice, knowledge, again practice, and again knowledge. This form repeats itself in endless cycles, and with each cycle the content of practice and knowledge rises to a higher level. Such is the whole of the dialectical-materialist theory of knowledge, and such is the dialectical-materialist theory of the unity of knowing and doing.

II
Fung Yu-lan: Selected Writings*

1. THE NEW RATIONAL PHILOSOPHY

A. Principle and Material Force

There are two aspects in every actually existing thing, namely, its "what" and that on which it depends for its existence or to become actually what it is. For example, every round thing has two aspects. One is that "it is round." The other is that on which it depends for existence, that is, to become actually round. This "what" is the thing's essential element in the class to which it belongs and the thing's nature. The reason that it exists is the foundation of the thing's existence. Its "what" depends on the principle it follows. That on which it depends for existence is the material which actualizes the principle. . . .

Material is either relative or absolute. Relative material has the two aspects just described. Absolute material, on the other hand, has only one of these aspects, namely, that it can be material simple and pure. Take a building, for example. . . . Bricks and tiles are material for the building, but they are relative and not absolute material. Earth is material for bricks and tiles, but it is still relative and not absolute material, for it still possesses the two aspects described above. . . .

When the nature of the building is removed, it will cease to be a building but only bricks and tiles. When the nature of bricks and tiles is removed, they will cease to be bricks and tiles but only earth. The nature of earth can also be removed, *ad infinitum.* At the end there is the absolute material. This material is called matter in the philosophies of Plato and Aristotle. . . . Matter itself has no nature. Because it has no nature whatsoever, it is indescribable, inexplicable in speech, and unrealizable in thought. . . .

We call this material *ch'i* (material force). . . . In our system material force is entirely a logical concept. It is neither a principle nor an actual thing. An actual thing is that which is produced by what we call material force in accordance with principle. Those who hold the theory of principle and material force should talk about material force in this way. But in the history

---

*Reprinted with permission from Wing-tsit Chan, *A Source Book in Chinese Philosophy* (Princeton: Princeton University Press, 1963).

of Chinese philosophy, those who held the theory of principle and material force in the past never had such a clear view of material force. In Chang Tsai's philosophy, material force is entirely a scientific concept. If there is the material force which he talked about, it is a kind of an actual thing. This point will be taken up in detail later. Even what Ch'eng I and Chu Hsi called material force does not seem to be a completely logical concept. For instance, they often described material force as clear or turbid. The way we look at the matter, the material force that can be described as clear or turbid is no longer material force [as such] but material force in accordance with the principle of clearness or turbidity. When they talked about material force as clear or turbid, they did not make clear whether they were talking about material force itself or about material force achieving the principle of clearness or turbidity.

We shall first discuss Chu Hsi's statement, "There has never been any material force without principle." This can very easily be proved. When we said that the material force of the true source has no nature whatsoever, we spoke entirely from the point of view of logic. From the point of view of fact, however, material force has at least the nature of existence. If not, it fundamentally does not exist. If material force does not exist, then there will not be any actual thing at all. If material force has the nature of existence, it means that it follows the principle of existence. Since it at least has to follow the principle of existence, therefore "There has never been any material force without principle."

Chu Hsi also said, "There has never been any principle without material force." This saying cannot be interpreted to mean that all principles are with material force, for if so, it would mean that all principles are actually exemplified and that there would be no principle which is only real but not actual. This statement merely says, "There must be some principles with material force," or "There has never been the time when all principles are without material force." This has been proved above, for at least the principle of existence is always followed by material force. (p. 75)

B. Tao, Substance and Function, and Universal Operation

What we call the material force of the true source is the Non-ultimate, and the totality of all principles is the Great Ultimate. The process from the Non-ultimate to the Great Ultimate is our world of actuality. We call this process "The Non-ultimate and also the Great Ultimate." The Non-ultimate, the Great Ultimate, and the Non-ultimate-and-also-the-Great-Ultimate are, in other words, the material force of the true source, the totality of principle, and the entire process from material force to principle, respectively. Collectively speaking, they are called Tao (the Way). . . .

Why have Tao in addition to the Great Whole or the universe? Our answer is that when we talk about the Great Whole or the universe, we speak from the aspect of tranquillity of all things, whereas when we talk about Tao, we speak from the aspect of activity of all things. . . .

The principle followed by "fact" (which includes all facts) is the Great Ultimate in its totality, and the material force depended on by "fact" is the Non-ultimate in its totality. (Actually the Non-ultimate has no totality to speak of. We merely say so.) In the first chapter we said that according to the old theory (of Sung Neo-Confucianists), principle is substance while actual things that actualize principle are function. But according to the concept of "the Non-ultimate and also the Great Ultimate," the Great Ultimate is substance and the "and also" is function. As all functions are included in this function, it is therefore (what Chu Hsi called) the total substance and great functioning. . . .

All things (meaning both things and events) go through the four stages of formation, flourish, decline, and destruction. Old things go out of existence this way and new things come into existence this way. This successive coming-into-existence and going-out-of-existence is the universal operation of the great functioning. The universal operation of the great functioning is also called the process of creation and transformation. The formation and flourish of things are creation, while their decline and destruction are transformation. The creation and transformation of all things are collectively called the process of creation and transformation. At the same time each thing or event is a process of creation and transformation. Since all things are each a process of creation and transformation, they are collectively called ten thousand transformations (all things). The term "transformation" may also involve both meanings of creation and transformation. Therefore the process is also called great transformation. The universal operation of the great transformation is the same as the universal operation of the great functioning. Our actual world is a universal operation.

The *Lao Tzu* and the "Appended Remarks" of the *Book of Changes* have a common idea, that is, that when things reach their limit, they return to their origin. . . . According to the law of circular movement described above, things in the universe come into existence and go out of existence at all times. They are always in the process of change. This is the daily renewal of the substance of Tao.

The daily renewal of the substance of Tao can be seen from four points of view. . . . (1) We can, from the point of view of classes, see the production and extinction of their actual members. Looked at this way, the daily renewal of the substance of Tao is cyclical. (2) We can, from the point of view of principle, see whether its actual exemplification tends to be perfect or not. Looked at this way, the daily renewal of the substance of Tao is one of progress and retrogression. (3) We can, from the point of view of the universe, see the increase or decrease of classes which have members in the actual world. Looked at this way, the daily renewal of the substance of Tao is one of increase and decrease. (4) And we can, from the point of view of an individual entity, see the process of its movement from one class to another. Looked at this way, the daily renewal of the substance of Tao is one of transformation and penetration.

C. Principle and the Nature

Principle is the moral nature of things. From one point of view, if the moral nature of things is perfectly good, then the physical nature of things is also good, for the physical nature of things is that by which things actually follow their principle. Their following may not be perfect, but since they are following the highest good, they should be good. They may be eighty percent good or seventy percent good or not very good, but we cannot say they are not good. . . .

If a thing can follow its principle perfectly, it can be said to have "investigated principle to the utmost." To get to the utmost of the principle which it follows means to develop its own nature fully. Therefore investigating principle to the utmost is the same as fully developing one's nature. According to the idea of destiny set forth in this chapter, investigating principle to the utmost and full development of one's nature are the same as getting to the point of fulfilling one's destiny. I-ch'uan (Ch'eng I) said, "The investigation of principle to the utmost, the full development of one's nature, and the fulfillment of destiny are only one thing. As principle is investigated to the utmost, one's nature is fully developed, and as soon as one's nature is fully developed, destiny is fulfilled." We also say the same. We further believe that this does not apply only to man but to things also.

D. Serving Heaven and Jen (Humanity)

From the point of view of Heaven (*T'ien*, Nature), every class of things has its own principle. Its principle is also its ultimate. With reference to the things in this class, their ultimate is the highest good, and their physical nature is that by which they actually follow principle. It is "what issues from the Way" and "is good." From the point of view of Heaven, what things in a given class should do in the great process of "the Non-ultimate and also the Great Ultimate" is to follow their principle completely. To be able to do so is to develop their nature fully and to investigate their principle to the utmost. This point has been discussed in chapter four. There the investigation of things means the use of my knowing faculty to know the principle of things. Here the term has a different meaning; it means to direct my conduct to realize fully the principle I am following. To use my knowing faculty to know the principle of things enables me to transcend experience and be free from the restriction of experience. This is transcendence of and freedom from experience. To direct my conduct to realize fully the principle I am following enables me to transcend myself and be free from self-bondage. This is transcendence and freedom from the self.

From the point of view of Heaven, men are also a class, and what they should do in the process of "the Non-ultimate and also the Great Ultimate" is also to follow their principle completely. Shao K'ang-chieh (Shao Yung, 1011–1077) said, "The sage is the ultimate of man." By the ultimate of man is meant the perfect man, one who can fully develop the nature of man and investigate the principle of man to the utmost.

Mencius said, "The sage is the ultimate standard of human relations." Human relations means to carry on the social relations, and to carry out human relations means the social activities of men. We said in chapter four that man's nature is social and that his social life issues from his nature. Therefore the full development of our nature and our investigation of principle to the utmost must be carried out in society.

In social life man's most social conduct is moral conduct. We can approach moral conduct in two different ways, one from the point of view of society and the other from the point of view of Heaven. From the point of view of society, man's moral conduct consists in fulfilling one's social duty. From the point of view of Heaven, one's moral conduct consists in fulfilling his universal duty, that is, fulfilling the way of man. From this point of view, in doing something moral, one is serving Heaven. . . .

We said previously that viewing things from the point of view of Heaven gives us a sympathetic understanding of them. In the sphere where the self is transcended, sympathy toward things is also increasingly enlarged until the sphere of what Sung and Ming Neo-Confucianists called "forming one body with all things" is reached. They call this sphere that of *jen*.

The word *jen* has two meanings. One is moral, the *jen* (humanity) in the (Five Constant Virtues) of humanity, righteousness, propriety, wisdom, and faithfulness discussed in chapter five. The other meaning refers to the sphere we are discussing. Ch'eng Ming-tao (Ch'eng Hao, 1032–1085) said, "The man of *jen* forms one body with all things without any differentiation. Righteousness, propriety, wisdom, and faithfulness are all [expressions of] *jen*." What he meant is this *jen*. In order to distinguish the two meanings, we shall call this *jen* "the great *jen*."

2. THE NATURE OF THE HISTORY OF CHINESE PHILOSOPHY

There are many struggles in social and political thought, which are in reality struggles between materialism and idealism. For example, in the history of Chinese philosophy, the question whether human nature is good or evil has continuously aroused extensive controversy from the pre-Ch'in (221–206 B.C.) period to modern times. In the pre-Ch'in period, Mencius held that nature is good, believing that inborn nature is good because there is originally a moral principle endowed by "Heaven." This is of course the view of idealism. Hsün Tzu (fl. 298–238 B.C.), on the other hand, held that human nature is evil, believing "Heaven" to be merely "Nature" in which there is no moral principle and that man's moral qualities are acquired through education. Such an idea directly negating Mencius' idealism should be regarded as materialistic.

Later, the Neo-Confucianism of Sung (960–1279) and Ming (1386–1644) distinguished the Principle of Nature and human desire and emphasized that the former should control the latter. What was called the Principle of Nature is really feudalistic moral principles objectified and made absolute. Philosophers who opposed the Neo-Confucianism of Sung and Ming like Ch'en Liang (1143 - 1194), Wang Fu-chih (Wang Ch'uan-shan, 1619 - 1692) and Tai Chen (Tai Tung-yüan, 1723 - 1777), regarded the Principle of Nature as the correct development of human desires, denied that the Principle of Nature had any right to control human desires, and placed man's desires and feelings in the position of first importance. This is a direct negation of the idealism of Sung-Ming Neo-Confucianism. This type of thought should also be regarded as materialistic. . . .

In the past several years in our effort to settle the problem of the struggle between materialism and idealism in the history of Chinese philosophy, we have only emphasized their conflicts and have paid no attention to their mutual influence and mutual penetration. Of course this side of the story is a relative one, but to ignore it is an error of onesidedness.

Let us take an example. In the beginning Sung-Ming Neo-Confucianism was fundamentally materialistic. In the philosophies of both Chou Tun-i (Chou Lien-hsi, 1017 - 1073) and Chang Tsai (Chang Heng-ch'ü, 1020 - 1077), material force was considered as primary. Later Ch'eng I (Ch'eng I-ch'uan, 1033 - 1107) and Chu Hsi (1130 - 1200) reverted to idealism. But Wang Fu-chih set aside the idealism of Ch'eng and Chu, directly continued the materialism of Chang Tsai, and thus established his great materialistic system of thought. This line of development is quite clear, and this is what we have said in instructing our students.

But this is only one side of the story. On the other side, while Wang continued Chang, he did not simply do so or revert to him without change. Similarly, while he set aside Ch'eng and Ch'u, he did not simply do so. What he did was to develop his own philosophy out of that of Ch'eng and Ch'u, then set them aside, and at the same time continued Chang Tsai. In the dialectical development of history and human knowledge, to go through something is not a simple matter. It involves absorbing its rational elements and throwing away its dregs. It involves an advance. . . .

In our recent work on the history of philosophy, we have generally employed the metaphysical and materialistic methods and have oversimplified and vulgarized the struggle between materialism and idealism in the history of philosophy, so that the history of philosophy, which is originally rich and active, has become poor and static. Actually the history of philosophy is what Lenin has described as a great development. . . .

To understand totally certain philosophical premises in the history of Chinese philosophy, we must pay attention to their two meanings, one abstract and the other concrete. In the past I have paid attention almost entirely to the abstract meaning of some of these premises. This, of course, is wrong. Only in the last several years have we paid attention to their concrete meaning. Without saying, it is correct to pay attention to their concrete meaning, but it would be wrong to pay attention to it alone. In trying to understand these premises in the history of philosophy we should of course place their concrete meaning in the position of first importance, for they have a direct relation to the concrete social conditions in which the authors of these premises lived. But their abstract meaning should also be taken into consideration. To neglect it would be to miss the total picture. . . .

Take for example Wang Yang-ming's doctrine of innate knowledge of the good (*liang-chih*). From the point of view of its concrete meaning, the content of what is called innate knowledge is the same as feudal morality and nothing new. The fact is that feudal morality at his time had become a dogma and not very effective. Wang therefore provided feudal morality with a new foundation. According to him, feudal morality was not imposed from the outside but something evolved from man's innate knowledge itself. . . .

Such a premise seems to advocate the emancipation of the individual, but the actual effect is that he is even more strongly bound by feudal morality. However, although this appraisal rests on a solid foundation, it concerns only one side of the matter, for aside from the concrete meaning of the premise, there is also its abstract meaning. . . . According to its abstract meaning, "Every one can become (sages) Yao and Shun," "People filling the street were all sages," and "All people are equal." That is to say, in their original nature all men are equal. . . . From this point of view, the philosophy of the school of Lu Hsiang-shan (Lu Chiu-yüan, 1139–1193) and Wang should not be simply denied in its entirety.

GLOSSARY

Abhidharma Canonical teachings that present the truth of Buddhist teachings in a systematic and analytical way. Focus is on analysis of experience.

Ācārāṅga Sūtra Foundational Jaina scripture.

Advaita Vedānta The school of Vedānta that emphasizes the nonduality of reality; Śaṅkara is the most famous Advaitin.

ahiṁsā The principle of nonhurting that is a hallmark of Jainism; also important in Buddhism and Hinduism.

Analects (Lun-yü) The collected sayings of Confucius.

anekāntavāda The Jaina view that knowledge is always from a particular perspective and no one perspective encompasses the whole truth.

Annambhaṭṭa Seventeenth century author of the *Tarkasaṁgraha*, a treatise combining Nyāya and Vaiśeṣika principles.

Āraṇayaka A set of texts appended to the Vedic verses that comment on the meaning of the verses.

arhant Buddhist ideal of perfect practitioner of the Path.

Arjuna The Pāṇḍava prince to whom Lord Krishna reveals the various paths to spiritual liberation in the *Bhagavad Gītā.*

āryan "Noble" The name by which the Indo-European culture that entered India around 1500 B.C. and produced the Vedic civilization is known.

āśrama In Hinduism, a stage of life; also a place to practice meditation.

Asaṅga His formulation of Yogacara Buddhism in the 4th or 5th century in *Stages of Yoga Practice* (*Yogācārabhumi*) secured its lasting form and fame.

Atharva Veda The fourth Veda, consisting mostly of formulas to ward off evil and achieve success in practical affairs.

Ātman Hindu term for the ultimate Self, which is held to be identical with Brahman, the ultimate reality.

Bādarāyaṇa Author of the *Brahma Sūtra.*

Bhagavad Gītā "Song of the Lord." A long devotional poem, constituting part of the *Mahābhārata*, in which Krishna teaches the secret of nonattached action.

Bhikkhu In Sanskrit, *Bhikṣu.* Pāli term for Buddhist monk.

Bodhidharma Traditionally regarded as the founder of the Ch'an school of Buddhism in China in the fifth century.

bodhisattva In Buddhism, an enlightened being who remains in the world to help others.

Book of Documents (Shu ching) One of the ancient classics that inspired the teachings of Confucius.

Book of Poetry (Shih ching) Chinese classic transmitted through the teachings of Confucius.

Brahma Sūtra A collection of key teachings of the Upanisads by Bādarāyaṇa in the second century B.C. One of the foundational texts of Vedānta.

Brahman Literally, "that which makes great." The Vedic and Hindu term for the ultimate reality.

Brāhmaṇa In the Vedic tradition, (1) prayer; (2) a class of people concerned with prayers (the *Brāhmaṇas*); (3) texts appended to the Vedic verses explaining the ritual significance of Vedic ritual.

Bṛhadāraṇyaka Upaniṣad The oldest Upaniṣad, ca. eighth century B.C., famous for Yājñavalkya's teachings of the supremacy of the Self (Ātman).

Buddha An enlightened being.

Buddhaghoṣa Great Sinhalese Buddhist commentator who produced the authoritative *Abhidharma* interpretation in the fifth century.

Buddhism A way of thought and practice that emphasizes moral practice, meditation, and enlightenment. Founded by Siddhārtha Gautama, the Buddha, in India, fifth century B.C., it soon spread throughout Asia.

Candrakīrti Illustrious commentator on Nāgārjuna. His seventh century work, *Mādhyamkāvatāra* ("Guide to the Middle Way") illumines the Mādhyamaka philosophy.

Cārvāka Indian system of philosophy that recognizes matter as the only reality. Also called *Lokāyata.*

Central Harmony (Chung-yung) One of the Four Books of Confucianism, emphasizes reciprocity.

Ch'an Chinese form of Mahāyāna Buddhism emphasizing meditative insight. Known in Japan and the West as Zen.

ch'eng Confucian virtue of sincerity.

Ch'eng Hao (1032 - 1085) Along with his brother, Ch'eng I, gave Neo-Confucianism its first full statement.

Ch'eng I (1033 - 1107) Younger of the famous Ch'eng brothers, who by developing the idea of Principle (*li*), gave Neo-Confucianism a secure ontological foundation.

ch'i Energy, especially the psychophysical energies through which full humanness (*jen*) can be achieved.

Chāndogya Upaniṣad One of the early Upaniṣads, famous for Uddālaka's teaching of the identity of Ātman and Brahman in the phrase, "You are That" (*Tat Tvam Asi*).

Chang Tsai (1020 - 1077) Neo-Confucian thinker who interpreted the Great Ultimate as material force; author of the "Western Inscription."

Chang Tung-sun (1886 - 1962) Modern Chinese comparative philosopher who combined Kantian epistemology, Pragmatist theory of culture, and Marxist ideas with traditional Chinese thought.

Chou dynasty The period from ca. 1123 - 221 B.C. during which the five classics and the six systems of philosophy were established.

Chou Tun-i (1017 - 1073) One of the founders of Neo-Confucianism; author of the influential "An Explanation of the Diagram of the Great Ultimate."

Chu Hsi (1130 - 1200) Neo-Confucian thinker who systematized the thought of his predecessors into a coherent and influential philosophy known as the Ch'eng-Chu school.

Chuang-tzu Fourth century B.C. Taoist philosopher, author of the text, *Chuang-tzu.*

citta Mind or mental state.

Confucianism Chinese tradition based on the teachings of Confucius and his followers, particularly Mencius and Hsün-tzu.

Confucius Latinized name of Master K'ung Fu-tzu, founder of Confucianism and China's most revered teacher.

Dalai Lama Title given to Tibet's spiritual and political ruler.

dependent origination Sanskrit, *pratītya samutpāda* (Pāli, *paticca samuppada*): the teaching that existence is of the nature of process and totally interconnected.

devotion (*bhakti*) One of the paths to liberation from the ignorance that mistakes the ego-self for the true Self (*Ātman*) according to Krishna in the *Bhagavad Gītā.*

Dhammapada Literally, "Path of Truth." Buddhist collection of wisdom sayings.

dharma Truth; virtue; righteousness.

dharmas In Buddhism, the true ultimate constituents of existence.

Diamond Sūtra Brief Mahāyāna scripture outlining the bodhisattva way.

Dōgen Thirteenth century founder of Sōtō Zen in Japan. His *Shōbōgenzō* is universally regarded as a masterpiece of Zen Buddhism.

dualism A metaphysical view that categorizes all existence into two fundamentally different kinds, e.g., into *prakṛti* and *puruṣa.*

duḥkka (Pali, *dukkha*) The defectiveness of life that underlies all forms of suffering according to Buddhism

Dvaita Vedānta The dualistic school of Vedānta championed by Madhva.

eight-fold path The Buddhist way of practice, namely, right knowledge, intention, speech, action, livelihood, effort, mindfulness, and meditation.

emptiness (*śūnyatā*) The Mahāyāna teaching that separate and permanent existence is devoid of reality.

enlightenment In Mahāyāna Buddhism, the direct seeing of the truth that liberates.

Fa-tsang (643–712) Foremost philosopher of the Hua-yen (Flower Splendor) school of Chinese Buddhism.

filial piety (*hsiao*) The love that exists naturally within a family; one of the grounds of respect and virtue in Confucianism.

five agents The agencies of change, namely water, fire, wood, metal, and earth, which through their interactions give form to all things.

five aggregates The five *skandhas* or groups of processes constituting a person, namely physical, feeling, perceptual, motivational, and consciousness processes.

five classics The Confucian canon from which Confucius drew much of his teaching, namely the Book of History (*Shu ching*), the Book of poetry (*shih ching*), The Book of Changes (*I ching*), the Book of Rites (*Li ching*), and the Spring and Autumn Chronicles (*Ch'un Ch'iu*).

five precepts The basic Buddhist moral precepts, namely to refrain from hurtful activity, from taking what is not given, from improper sexual activity, from wrong speech, and from alcohol and other drugs.

form (Sanskrit, *rūpa*) The physicality of existence; one of the five aggregates constituting a person.

four noble truths The kernel of the Buddha's message, namely, there is *duḥkha*, it is conditioned by ignorance and grasping, these conditions can be removed, and the eight-fold path is the way to remove them.

four signs The encounter with old age, sickness, death, and the contentment of a recluse that persuaded Siddhartha Gautama to seek enlightenment.

Fung Yu-lan (b. 1895) Influential modern Chinese philosopher whose *History of Chinese Philosophy* is the standard work in the field.

Gandhi, Mohandas (1869–1948) Moral leader of India's nationalist movement, championed the use of nonviolent resistance.

Gaṅgeśa Fourteenth century author of the *Tatvacintāmaṇi*, foundational text of the New Nyāya tradition.

Gautama Author of the foundational text of the Nyāya system, the *Nyāya Sūtra*, probably third century B.C.

Ghose, Aurobindo (1872–1950) Indian revolutionary and yogi who provided a new synthesis of yoga and vision of spiritual life.

Great Learning (Ta Hsüeh) One of the Four Books of Confucianism, emphasizing the way of moral development.

Great Ultimate (*T'ai-chi*) Neo-Confucian concept of the fundamental source and principle of existence that operates through the polarities of *yin* and *yang*.

guṇas The three strands, *sattva*, *rajas*, and *tamas*, that constitute the nature (*prakṛti*) of all things according to Sāṁkhya.

Han dynasty The Chinese dynasty during which Confucianism was adopted as state ideology and basis of education. Also, Buddhism entered China and religous Taoism developed during this period. (206 B.C. - 220 A.D.)

Han Fei-tzu Principal synthesizer and theoretician of the school of law (third century B.C.).

Heart Sūtra The encapsulation of Mahāyāna Buddhist teaching, emphasizing the emptiness of separate and permanent self-existence.

Heaven (*T'ien*) In Confucianism, the ultimate source of things; in the *I-ching*, the first hexagram, symbolizing the source and principle of all change.

Hsiung Shih-li (1883 - 1968) Developed an interpretation of Confucianism that incorporated *I-Ching* cosmology and Buddhist philosophy of mind.

Hsün-tzu (third century B.C) Confucian thinker who claimed innate human intelligence rather than inherent goodness to be the basis of virtue.

Hua-yen School of Chinese Buddhism based on Middle Way (Mādhyamaka) thought.

Hui-neng (638 - 713) Sixth patriarch of the Ch'an school, author of the *Platform Sutra.*

I-Ching Text of Changes; also school based on *I-Ching.*

I-hsüan (d.867) Founder of the Lin-chi (Rinzai) school of Ch'an.

Iqbal, Mohammed (1873 - 1938) Pakistan's national poet and modern Muslim philosopher.

Islam The religion of submission to Allah, the one true God, in accord with God's revelation to Mohammed in the Qu'ran.

Īśvara Brahman seen as God, the supreme Lord of the universe.

Īśvarakṛṣṇa Author of the *Sāṁkhya Kārikā,* third century foundational text of the Sāṁkhya system.

Jaimini Author of the *Mīmāṁsā Sūtra,* fourth century B.C..

Jainism Indian system of thought and practice founded before sixth century B.C. that stresses liberation from karmic bondage. Strong emphasis on knowledge and morality.

Jayatilleke Twentieth century Sinhalese Buddhist scholar.

jen The source and principle of humanity; what makes a person human.

Jina "Spiritual conqueror." Origin of *Jaina* and *Jainism.*

jīva The life-principle of a person.

K'ang Yu-wei (1858 - 1927) Modern utopian thinker responsible for the Hundred Days Reform of 1898.

Kaṇāda Author of the *Vaiśeṣika Sūtra,* third century B.C. foundational text of the Vaiśeṣika system.

karma Action, including the results of action that inevitably accrue to the agent, producing bondage.

knowledge Knowledge as the direct, unmediated insight into the true nature of ultimate reality is the key to liberation according to Hinduism, Buddhism, and Jainism.

kōan Lit. a "public case." Paradoxical saying used in Zen to break up dualistic thinking.

Krishna The God who teaches Arjuna the paths to liberation in the *Bhagavad Gīta.*

Kumārila Bhaṭṭa Important seventh century Mīmāṁsā philosopher.

Lao-tzu Sixth century B.C. Taoist sage, author of *Tao Te Ching*; also refers to the text, the *Lao-tzu*, another name for the *Tao Te Ching.*

Legalism Chinese school of law systematized by Han Fei-tzu that emphasized central authority backed with laws and punishments as key to an orderly society.

li (1) In Confucianism, the norm of propriety. (2) In Neo-Confucianism, principle; that which gives things their nature and connects them to each other. According to Chu Hsi, *jen* is the fundamental principle.

Lin-chi (*Rinzai*) School of Ch'an that emphasized sudden enlightenment and kōan practice.

Lokāyata Another name for Indian materialism (Cārvāka).

Lotus Sūtra Mahāyāna Buddhist scripture explaining the superiority of the Mahāyāna. A primary vehicle for the spread of Buddhism throughout East Asia.

Madhva Thirteenth century Dualistic Vedāntist who emphasized the differences between: God and self; God and matter; individual selves; self and matter; and between individual things.

Mādhyamaka The "Middle Way" philosophy of Mahāyāna Buddhism, established by Nāgārjuna (second century A.D.). Emphasizes the totally interconnected and dynamic nature of existence.

Mahāvīra Most recent of the Jina's (sixth century B.C.), according to Jaina tradition.

Mahāyāna Form of Buddhism prevalent in Tibet and East Asia. Emphasizes the Buddha's example of compassion and effort to bring all beings to enlightenment.

Malliṣeṇa Thirteenth century Jaina philosopher who wrote the *Syādavādamañjarī* to defend the Jaina theory of knowledge.

Mao Tse-tung (1894 – 1976) Communist leader of China who forged a new synthesis of Marxist-Leninist thought and traditional Chinese thought.

māyā The appearances of things, concealing the deeper reality.

Mencius The second great Confucian teacher who lived something more than a hundred years after Confucius. His work, known as the *Mencius*, was a key factor in the successful propogation of Confucianism throughout East Asia.

Middle Way Name given to Buddhism because it is middle between indulgence and asceticism, between being and nonbeing, and between determinism and indeterminism.

Milinda Indian name for the Greek king, Menander, who engaged the Buddhist Monk Nāgasena in a series of dialogues about Buddhism.

Mīmāṁsā Hindu philosophical system concerned with the interrelations between language, knowledge, and action.

Mīmāṁsā Sūtra Foundational text of the Mīmāṁsā tradition by Jaimini, fourth century B.C.

mind-and-heart (*hsin*) In Confucianism, the intelligence that combines feeling and thought; the locus of the innate moral nature;

Mind-only (*cittamātra*) The philosophy formulated by Asaṅga and Vasubhandhu, third century, according to which all phenomena are of the nature of mind.

Mo-tzu (Also Mo Ti) Founder of the Mohist school; argued for the principle of universal love and for benefitting the people as the criterion of the good (third century B.C.).

Mohism The Chinese school of Mo-tzu emphasizing utility and universal love.

mokṣa Liberation from all constraints, including the cycle of birth-and-death.

mu Famous kōan attributed to Joshu, who answered the question, "Does a dog have a Buddha-nature?" with the response, "Mu!"

Muhammed The prophet of Islam to whom God revealed his full message to humankind in the Qu'ran.

Mumon Thirteenth century Zen master who collected a set of famous kōans and added his own commentaries.

Mumonkan Classic collection of Zen kōans by Master Mumon in the thirteenth century.

Muslim Follower of Islam, one who has submitted to God.

mysticism The view that the ultimate can be directly experienced even though it cannot be known objectively.

Nāgārjuna Second century founder of the Mādhyamaka school, which sees *śūnyatā* as basis of Buddhist practice. Author of the *Mūlamādhyamakakārikā.*

Nāgasena Buddhist monk who engaged in a series of dialogues with the Greek king Menander (Milinda), recorded in the *Milindapanna.*

Neo-Confucianism The revival of Confucianism after centuries of Buddhist dominance. Ch'eng-Chu and Lu-Wang are the two main schools of Neo-Confucianism.

nikāyas Early canonical collections of the Buddha's teachings.

nirvāṇa In Pāli, *nibbana.* Elimination of all forms and conditions of suffering.

Nishitani Twentieth century Japanese Zen Buddhist thinker who focused on *śūnyatā.*

nonattachment Nonattachment to the fruits of action is the key to fulfilling one's duties without accumulating karmic bondage according to the *Bhagavad Gītā.*

non-Self (*anatta*) Buddhist teaching that there is no independent, self-existing self.

nonviolence Gandhi's way of moral resistance to evil and evildoers by holding fast to truth through personal suffering and sacrifice.

nyāya Argumentation; Hindu system that focuses on logic and epistemology.

Nyāya Sūtra Foundational text of the Nyāya system compiled by Gautama in the third century B.C..

Padārtha Dharma Saṁgraha Fourth century commentary by Praśastapāda on the *Vaiśeṣka Sūtra.*

Pāli The Indian vernacular language in which the Buddhist elders wrote the collected sayings of the Buddha.

pāramitās The surpassing virtues of generosity, enthusiasm, patience, morality, meditation, and wisdom that characterize the career of a bodhisattva.

Patañjali Author of the *Yoga Sūtras*, the collection of teachings on yoga compiled in the second century B.C.

Platform Sūtra Important text of the Ch'an school, by Hui-neng.

Prabhākara Important seventh century Mīmāṁsā philosopher.

prakṛti In Sāṁkhya, the "stuff" that is the evolutionary basis of all objects of existence. Constituted by the three *guṇas*, *sattva*, *rajas*, and *tamas.*

prāṇa Life-breath; the energy that makes life possible.

Praśastapāda Author of the *Padārtha Dharma Saṁgraha*, an important 4th c. commentary on the *Vaiésika Sūtra.*

Praśāstrasena Indian commentator, dates unknown, on the *Heart Sūtra.*

principle (*li*) Neo-Confucian concept of the source and inner nature of things.

Pure Land (*Ching-tu*) School of Chinese Buddhism that emphasizes devotion to Amitabha Buddha as a means to rebirth in the Pure Land paradise.

puruṣa Lit. "person." In Sāṁkhya, the self that is pure subject.

Radhakrishnan, Sarvapalli (1888 - 1975) India's philosopher-president. Provided modern interpretations of India's traditional wisdom.

rajas The aspect of nature (*prakṛti*) responsible for energy and movement in existence according to Sāṁkhya.

Rāmānuja Eleventh century Vedāntist whose qualified nondualism allowed him to regard Brahman as the soul and the world as the body of reality. Author of the *Vedārtha Saṁgraha.*

Rig Veda Oldest and philosophically most important of the Vedas, the sacred texts that form the foundation of Hinduism. Compiled between twelth and tenth centuries B.C.

righteousness (*i* or *yi*) What is morally right; the moral capacity to recognize what is right.

Śabara Author of important first century B.C. commentary on Jaimini's *Mīmāṁsā Sūtra.*

Sāma Veda The Veda that is sung at Vedic ritual performances. Comprised mainly of Rig Vedic verses.

samādhi In yoga, the intense concentration that absorbs one into one's ultimate being.

Sāṁkhya Hindu dualistic system rooted in the distinction of *puruṣa* and *prakṛti* that takes an evolutionary view of existence.

samsāra The cycle of repeated births and deaths.

saṅgha Buddhist community of monks and nuns.

Śaṅkara Most famous Advaita Vedānta philosopher, eighth century A.D.

Sarvāstivāda Buddhist philosophical school based on Abhidarma analysis that strongly affirms the reality of what is experienced. Two main branches are Vaibhāṣika and Sautrāntika.

sattva The aspect of nature (*prakṛti*) responsible for lightness and intelligence in existence according to Sāṁkhya.

Sautrāntika Buddhist philosophical school transitional between Theravāda and Mahāyāna. Emphasizes the representational and constructed nature of knowledge.

Shakyamuni The historical Buddha, sage (*muni*) of the Shakya clan.

Shao Yung (1011–1077) Early Neo-Confucian thinker who developed the idea of the Great Ultimate.

Siddhartha Gautama The historical Buddha, founder of Buddhism, born in northeast India in the sixth century B.C.

six characteristics According to Hua-yen Buddhism, existence has six fundamental characteristics: universality, particularity, identity, difference, integration, and disintegration.

Sōtō Zen School of Zen established in Japan by Dōgen which emphasizes *zazen*, sitting meditation.

Śruti The revelation of truth that has been heard by the pure and wise sages.

suchness (*tathātā*) Reality as it is in itself, dynamic and interrelated, prior to the imposition of mental constructions.

Sufi Islamic way emphasizing personal devotion and sincerity as key to realizing God's mystical presence.

Śūnyatā Buddhist teaching of dependent origination emphasizing the emptiness of separateness and permanence.

sūtra The aphoristic thread on which the teachings of a school hang.

Sūtrakṛtāṅga Foundational Jaina scrupture.

syādavāda Jaina theory of epistemological perspectivism.

Syādavādamañjarī Malliṣeṇa's thirteenth century commentary on Hemacandra's *Examination of the Other Systems.* Puts forth and defends the theory of perspectives.

T'ien Tai School of Chinese Buddhism based on the *Lotus Sūtra.*

Taittirīya Upaniṣad Contains the famous "five sheaths theory" of the self.

tamas The aspect of nature (*prakṛti*) responsible for inertia and dullness in existence according to Sāṁkhya.

Tantra A form of Mahāyāna that emphasizes integral unity of body and mind and bodily practices to achieve enlightenment.

Tao The way. In Taoism is refers to the way of nature, in Confucianism to the way of *jen.*

Tao Te Ching "Book of the Way and its Power." Foundational Taoist text written by Lao-tzu in the sixth century B.C.

Taoism Chinese tradition based on following the natural way (*tao*) as taught by Lao-tzu and Chuang-tzu.

Tarkasaṁgraha A seventeenth century treatise by Annambhaṭṭa that combines the essentials of Nyāya and Vaiśeṣika.

Tathāgata Title for the historical Buddha meaning "Thus-gone" (to *nirvāṇa*).

teisho In Zen, a commentary on a prior teaching.

Tenzin Gyatso The fourteenth and present Dalai Lama.

Theravāda The form of Buddhism prevalent in South and Southeast Asia. Emphasizes following the way taught by the Buddha in the early discourses.

Tīrthaṇkara Literally, "ford-maker." Another name for a Jina, emphasizing the conqueror's ability to find a way across the ocean of suffering.

Tseng-tzu Confucius' disciple, author of most of the *Great Learning* (*Ta-hsüeh*) according to Chu Hsi.

Tsong Khapa Fourteenth century founder of the dGe-lugs-pa sect of Tibetan Buddhism. Tibet's best known Mādhyamaka philosopher.

Tsu-ssu Grandson of Confucius, contemporary of Mo-tzu, and teacher of Mencius.

Tung Chung-shu Confucian scholar who persuaded Emperor Han Wu-ti to adopt Confucianism as the state ideology in 136 B.C..

universal love The ideal of Mo-tzu, aimed at overcoming the divisiveness of self-love and self-interest.

Upaniṣads Concluding portion of the Vedas containing sacred knowledge of reality.

Utilitarians The School of Mo-tzu, which regarded usefulness to society as the principal criterion of good.

Vaibhāṣika Buddhist philosophical school of the Theravāda tradition that regards the *dharmas*—ultimate units of existence—as both real and many.

Vaiśeṣika Differentiation; Hindu system that focuses on the metaphysics of difference; usually allied with the Nyāya system.

Vaiśeṣika Sāutra Third century B.C. text by Kaṇāda that is foundational for the Vaiśeṣika system.

Vasubandhu Great Sautrāntika and Abhidharmist who was converted to Yogācāra by his brother Asaṅga. Produced an authoritative systematization of Yogācāra.

Vedānta Hindu philosophical tradition rooted in the Upaniṣads; concerned to understand the relation between Brahman and the world.

Vedārtha Saṁgraha Rāmānuja's summary and interpretation of Vedic teachings.

Vedas Four foundational Indian religious texts—*Rig*, *Sāma*, *Yajur*, and *Atharva*—composed prior to 1000 B.C..

Viśiṣṭādvaita Vedānta The qualified non-dualistic school of Vedanta represented by Rāmānuja.

voidness an alternate translation of *śūnyatā* or emptiness.

Vyāsa Fourth century commentator on Patañjali's *Yoga Sūtra.*

Wang Yang-ming (1472-1529) Key thinker of the Lu-Wang school of Neo-Confucianism, which stressed the identity of knowledge and action.

yajña The celebrative ritual based on the Vedas that constitutes the core of Vedic religious life.

Yajur Veda The Veda that is chanted at Vedic ritual performances. Includes many Rig Vedic verses.

yang Fundamental polarity of change.

Yen-tzu Student of Confucius, famous for his dedication to learning the way of becoming a Sage.

yin One of the fundamental polarities of change

Yin-Yang Chinese school emphasizing the polarity of *yin* and *yang* and the five agencies of change.

Yoga Hindu philosophical system concerned with self-understanding and self-control.

Yoga Sūtra The aphorisms of Pantañjali constituting the basic teachings of the Yoga tradition.

Yogācāra School of Mahāyāna Buddhism that emphasizes the way of meditative insight into true reality.

Zen A form of Mahāyāna Buddhism that flourished in Japan. Emphasizes direct meditative insight.

Zenki Shibayama Zen master of Nanzenji monastery in Kyoto (1948-1967), commentator on the *Mumonkan.*

INDEX

Abe, Masao, 346
Abhidharma, 190, 283, 306, 307
Ācārāṅga Sūtra, 133, 134, 135
Action, 171, 281, 544; as cause of bondage, 93, 94, 95, 96, 101, 113; in the *Gītā*, 37-42, 45; path of, 33, 36-43
Activity, 522, 546-547, 563
Aditi, 9, 10
Advaita, 92
Affirmation, 136-140
Agency, 105
Aggregates (*see also* Five aggregates), 309, 315, 328
Ahaṁkāra ("I-maker"), 55, 56
Ahiṁsā, 129, 130, 132, 161-164
Aitareya Upaniṣad, 5
All-Maker, 10, 11
Allinson, Robert E., 445
Altruism (*shu*), 434
Anacker, Stefan, 307, 323
Analects (Lun-Yü), 405, 407-421, 424
Analogy, 53, 73, 78
Anambhaṭṭa, 69-70, 80
Anekāntavāda, 2, 129
Anger, 39
Annihilationism, 504-507
Apperception, 281
Apūrva, 90
Āraṇyakas, 5
Arhat (P. *Arahant*), 258, 260, 377
Arjuna, 33-49, 125
Āryadeva, 392
Asaṅga, 277, 306-322
Ashoka, 189
Atharva Veda, 5, 24
Ātman (*see also* Self), 93-115
Atoms, 335-337
Attachment, 37, 38, 40, 42, 50, 57, 99, 115, 189, 221, 231, 233, 234, 235, 236, 237, 238, 263, 285, 325, 341, 370, 506
Attachment groups, 221, 225, 231-232
Aurobindo Ghose, 144, 165-177
Authority, as means of knowledge, 52
Avatamsaka Sūtra, 397

Bādarāyana, 82, 91, 92
Basho, Master, 398
Baso, Master, 352, 353, 354, 356, 357
Batchelor, Stephen, 263, 272
Being, 36, 178, 233, 262, 271, 310
Being time, 354-358
Benevolence (*jen*), 411, 412, 414, 415, 417-422, 426, 429, 478, 480, 481, 485, 486, 497
Benevolent man, the, 462, 463
Bhagavad Gītā, 33-49, 51, 92, 125, 168
Bhakti (*see also* Devotion), 128, 186
Bhatt, Govardhan P., 81
Bhattacharya, Ram Shankar, 51
Bielfeldt, Carl, 345
Birth, 233, 234, 235, 236, 237, 238, 245, 327
Birth-and-death (*samsāra*), 249, 270, 271, 360-361, 509, 510
Bodde, Dirk, 405, 556
Bodhidharma, 502
Bodhisattva, 247, 248-253, 254, 258, 260, 262, 272, 277, 282, 297, 310, 312, 313, 320-322, 393, 404
Body, 93, 94, 96, 97, 99, 100, 101, 102, 104, 106, 107, 113, 114, 117, 122, 123, 126, 127, 170, 173, 205, 243, 251, 253, 312, 325, 328, 334, 514, 548

Body-mind, 349
Bondage, 63, 64, 120, 129, 130, 298
Book of Changes (I-Ching), 523, 529, 552, 555, 564
Book of History (Shu Ching), 407, 482, 490, 492, 531, 553
Book of Poetry (Book of Odes) (Shih Ching), 407, 425, 426, 429, 430, 434-436, 440-443, 466, 467, 480, 489, 531
Bose, Nirmal Kumar, 144
Brahma Sūtra, 92
Brahman, 6, 12, 19-21, 30-32, 92, 93, 94, 95, 98, 99, 100, 101, 104, 104, 116-128, 181
Brāhmaṇas, 5, 116
Bṛhadāraṇyaka Upaniṣad, 5, 6, 12-24
Buddha, 129, 164, 189, 190, 193, 217, 218, 248, 252, 254, 260, 267, 269, 271, 277, 282, 284, 287, 291, 296, 347, 348, 349, 354, 359, 360, 361, 369, 381, 396, 508, 509, 515, 516, 518
Buddha Nature, 362, 365, 371, 502, 509
Buddha Way, 349, 350, 356, 513
Buddhadharma, 509
Buddhadharmas, 310-312, 322
Buddhaghoṣa, 190, 221, 225
Buddhahood, 404, 501
Buddhi (intelligence), 55-57
Buddhism, 2, 51, 189-402, 403; Chinese Buddhism, 501-520, 521, 550

Candrakīrti, 262, 263, 272-297, 298, 299, 386, 392, 393
Carman, John B., 93
Carter, John Ross, 194
Cārvāka, 2, 283, 284
Categories, 70, 124
Causality, 263, 264-265
Cause, 53, 54, 73-74, 100, 105, 126, 268, 272, 274, 291, 292
Central Harmony (Chung-yung) (*see also Doctrine of the Mean*), 405, 407, 408, 433-443
Ch'an, 247, 501, 502, 508-520
Ch'eng brothers, 423, 424, 522, 536, 539
Ch'eng Hao, 522, 527-531, 540-541
Ch'eng I, 522, 531-535, 542-543, 563, 565
Ch'i (*see also* Material force), 476, 523
Chakrabarti, Kisor, 70
Chan, Wing-tsit, 405, 408, 433, 502, 517, 521, 522, 524, 525, 536, 538, 548, 556, 562
Chāndogya Upaniṣad, 5, 6
Chang Carsun, 522
Chang Tsai, 521, 522, 525-527, 528, 563
Chang Tung-sun, 555
Chang, Chung-yuan, 445
Change, 530, 547
Ching, Julia, 537
Chittamātra (mind-only), 277-283, 380, 381
Chou Tun-i, 521, 522-525, 546
Chu Hsi, 404, 405, 407, 408, 422-424, 432, 522, 536, 537, 538-548, 548, 556, 563, 564
Chuang Tzu, 445
Chuang-tzu, the, 444, 445, 450-460
Chün-tzu, 408
Chung-yung, 409
Circuminsessional interpenetration, 397, 398, 401
Cittas (mental states), 324-330, 331, 341
Clear character, 548-554
Cleary, Thomas, 345, 346, 502
Co-ordinate prediction, 123, 124
Cognition, 82, 121, 140, 141, 275, 276, 281
Compassion, 194, 247, 248-250, 379, 480, 481, 514
Concentration, 59-67, 103, 186
Conceptual dualities, 306
Confucianism, 403-443, 461, 476, 501, 555
Confucius, 407-421, 422, 423, 424, 426, 433-443, 444, 459, 461, 484, 527, 533, 538, 540, 544
Conscientiousness (*chung*), 434
Consciousness, 60, 116, 117, 118, 119, 166, 167, 169, 172, 173, 173, 176, 179, 233, 234, 235, 236, 237, 238, 277-283, 289, 307, 330, 333, 338-344, 383, 384, 385, 387, 388, 392, 539; as *skandha* 223-224, 231-232, 240, 242, 327-330; pure consciousness, 97, 98, 99, 108, 109, 110, 111, 112, 113, 120
Contact, 233, 234, 235, 236, 237, 238
Contemplation, 37
Conventional reality, 300, 302-304
Conze, Edward, 190, 247, 263
Cook, Francis H., 346, 502
Cosmic heat (*tapas*), 11
Craving, 38
Creation hymn, 6
Creel, H. G., 408
Cua, A. S., 477

Dalai Lama, 372, 379-393
Datta, D. M., 144
De Bary, Wm. Theodore, 405, 537
Death, 114
Deep sleep state, 99, 100, 110, 111, 114
Delusion, 47, 98, 101, 109, 133, 194, 197, 216, 310, 318, 349, 513
Demonstration-and-proof reason, 309, 316
Dependent origination (*pratītya samutpāda*), 221, 233-238, 262, 268, 285, 379, 385, 392
Desire, 38, 39, 40, 42, 233, 234, 235, 236, 237, 238, 534, 544, 550
Detachment, 39, 61, 62
Deutsch, Eliot, 7, 25, 30, 33, 92
Devotion, 43-50
Dewey, John, 405
Dhammapada, 194, 212-219, 376, 377
Dharma, 33, 57, 82, 85, 86, 89

Dharma, the (Buddha's teaching), 193, 199, 218, 258, 260, 261, 267, 268, 269, 312, 315, 322, 326, 333, 334, 508-516
Dharmakāya, 513-515
Dharmadhātu, 255
Dharmakīrti, 382
Dharmas, 252, 253, 308, 309, 310, 312-317, 501, 505, 513, 515, 518, 547
Diagram of the Great Ultimate, 522-525
Diamond Sūtra, 247, 258-261, 508, 511, 516
Difference, 501, 503-507
Dignāga, 2, 382
Discipline (yoga), 41, 42, 43, 44, 47, 49
Discriminating knowledge, 366, 368
Discursive thought, 309, 318, 320
Disintegration, 501, 503-507
Divine life, 165, 170, 171
Divinity, 168, 171
Doctrine of the Mean (Chung-yung) (see also Central Harmony), 408, 433-443, 542, 544
Dōgen, 345, 346-361
Dream-state, 16-18, 99, 102, 108, 110, 111, 115, 119, 121, 331, 339
Dualism, 1, 51
Dualistic knowledge, 346
Duality, 98, 99, 101, 248, 502
Dukkha (skt. *duḥkha*), 189, 193, 194, 195, 202, 216, 220, 221, 222, 247, 248
Dumoulin, Heinrich, 346, 502
Dutifulness, 480, 481, 485
Duty (*dharma*), 35, 37, 39, 40, 115, 322

Earth (*see also* Heaven and Earth), 549
Eckel, Malcolm David, 263
Edgerton, Franklin, 6, 12
Ego, 146, 147, 154, 155, 156, 172, 174, 175, 236
Eightfold path, 195, 216, 247, 352
Embodied souls, 131
Embree, Ainslie, 3, 129, 130
Emotions, 498
Emptiness (*śūnyatā*), 96, 122, 248, 253-257, 262, 263, 264-271, 270, 299, 304-305, 306, 347, 368, 372, 379-402, 423; in Taoism, 447
Enlightenment, 59, 248, 249, 252, 258, 268, 295, 310, 311, 312, 322, 349, 350, 356, 403, 439, 502, 503, 511
Epistemology, 81
Essential nature (of *dharmas*), 313-322
Eternalism, 504-507
Existence, 220, 225-226, 233, 270, 271
Existent, the, 25, 27-31, 96
Experience, 97, 107, 146, 154, 178, 307
Extension of knowledge, 534, 543, 545, 552-553
External world, 146

Fa-tsang, 501, 503-507
Faith, path of, 33, 43-50
Faithfulness, 527, 531
Fallacies, 76-78
Feelings, 207-208, 323, 524, 531, 538, 542, 543
Fifth Patriarch (Jung-jen), 508-511
Filial piety (*hsiao*), 411, 426, 428, 429, 436, 467
Fingarette, Herbert, 408
Fischer, Louis, 144
Five agents (of change), 523, 540, 547
five aggregates, 209, 254, 255, 256, 257, 283, 286-289, 291, 295, 299, 296, 307, 323-330, 346
Five groups (*see also* Five aggregates), 231-232
Five human relationships, 437, 483
Form (as *skandha*), 222-224, 231-232, 240, 242, 248, 253-257, 282, 289, 316, 347, 393
Foundation consciousness (*ālaya vijñāna*), 276, 277
Four beginnings (of *jen*), 541
Four books (of Confucianism), 405, 408
Four noble truths, 196, 211, 216, 246, 262, 266-270, 309, 376
Fourth state (*turīya*), 100
Friendliness, 248, 259
Fu, Charles Wei-shun, 405
Function, 538
Fung Yu-lan, 405, 555, 556, 562-568

Gandhi, Mohandas K., 144, 156-165, 181, 182
Gaṅgeśa, 69
Gardner, Daniel, 408, 422
Gārgī, 13-14
Gautama Siddhārtha (P. Gotama), 189, 239, 240, 242
Gautama, 69, 80
Gentleman, the, (*chün-tzu*) 412-421, 486-487, 493, 497, 498, 499
Gnosis, 179
Gnostic life, 176
God, 48, 116, 128, 145, 155-158, 175, 180, 181, 184, 185, 186, 446
Golden embryo, 9
Gomez, Luis, 307
Good, 373-379; highest good, 550-552
Goodness (of human nature), 477-487, 492, 494
Graham, A. C., 408, 444, 450, 462
Grasping, 189
Great doubt, 366
Great Learning (Ta Hsüeh), 405, 407, 408, 422-433, 544, 548-554
Great Ultimate (*T'ai-chi*), 403, 521, 522-525, 563-564
Griffiths, Paul J., 220
Gross elements, 55, 66
Guṇas, 53, 54, 55, 58, 61, 62
Gyatso, Tenzin (Dalai Lama), 372, 379-393

Hakuin, Master, 364, 369
Han Fei-tzu, 461, 462, 468-475, 476, 477
Han Yü, 404, 521
Hanchow conference, 555
Hariharānanda Araṇya, Swami, 52, 59
Heart Sūtra, 247, 253-257, 263
Heaven, 403, 404, 409, 410, 414, 420, 422, 423, 433-443, 447, 448, 449, 451, 454, 457, 460, 461, 473, 477, 481, 486, 487-492, 493, 496, 497, 498, 526, 534, 540, 542, 543, 549, 565
Heaven and Earth, 523-528, 529, 530, 533, 438-548
Herman Arthur L., 190
Hindu systems, 5, 6-127
History of Chinese philosophy, 566-568
Hoffman, Frank J., 194, 220
Hotetsu, Master, 351
Hsiung Shih-li, 555
Hsün-tzu, 476, 477, 487-499, 536
Hua-yen, 501-507
Hua-yen Treatise, 502, 503-507
Huang-po, 517-520
Hughes, E. R., 556
Hui-neng, 502, 508-516
Human nature, 433, 477-481, 485, 492-500, 524, 525, 536, 537, 540-543, 552
Humanity (*jen*), 438, 522, 531, 544, 547
Humanness (*jen*), 405
Hume, R. E., 7
Huntington, C. W. Jr., 263
Hurting (*hiṁsā*), *130*

I-Ching school, 403, 521
I-hsuan, 502, 517-520
I-notion, 97, 106, 109
Idealism, 307, 566-568
Identity, 501, 503-507
Ignorance, 57, 63, 94, 95, 102, 173, 189, 201, 202, 221, 233, 234, 235, 236, 237, 238, 284, 285, 325, 385, 514
Illusion, 61, 99, 119, 121, 257, 307
Illusory nature, 306
Immortal, the, 116
Immortality, 7, 9, 13, 19-24, 95, 116, 166
Imperishable, the, 14, 15, 24, 100, 102, 104
Impermanence, 220, 311, 325
Inada, Kenneth K., 191, 262, 263
Indescribable, 137
Indestructible, the, 36
Individual existence, 307
Indus, 6
Inexpressible, 313, 320
Inference, 52, 61, 67, 73, 75-80, 309
Infinite, the, 100
Inherent existence (*svabhāva*), 254, 257, 280, 284, 286, 289, 290, 291, 383, 385, 387, 388, 392, 393
Insight, 311
Integral insight, 178
Integration, 501, 503-507
Intelligence, 167
Interdependent origination (*pratītya samutpāda*), 503-507
Internal organ (*antaḥkaraṇa*), 56-57
Interpenetration (of *dharmas*), 501, 503-507
Intrinsically identifiable existence, 299, 300, 303
Intrinsically identifiable intrinsic reality (*svalakṣaṇasiddhasvabhāvasat*), 298
Intrinsically identifiable reality, 299, 304
Intrinsically identifiable status, 299, 303, 304
Investigation of principle, 535
Iqbal, Mohammed, 143, 145-156
Īśa Upaniṣad, 5
Islam, 150
Isolation (*kaivalya*), 55, 59
Īśvara (God), 63, 64, 117, 123, 124, 125, 181
Īśvarakṛṣṇa, 51-52
Iyer, Raghavan, 144

Jaimini, 81, 81
Jaini, Padmanabh S., 129
Jainism, 2, 129
Janaka, 15-22
Jayatilleke, K. N., 372-379
Jen, 404, 522, 527-531, 528, 531, 536, 538-548, 565, 566
Jha, Ganganatha, 81, 82
Jina, 129
Jīva, 119, 123, 125, 127, 129
Joshu, Master, 346, 361-370
Jung, 151
Jung-jen, 508-511

K'ang Yu-wei, 555
Kaltenberg, Max, 445
Kalupahana, David, 190, 263
Kant, 145, 146, 398
Kao Tzu, 477-479, 540
Kapleau, Philip, 346
Karaṇa (knowing instrument), 56-57
Karma, 18, 60, 93, 115, 116, 118, 125, 127, 131, 132, 181, 186, 233, 234, 235, 236, 237, 238
Kasulis, Thomas P., 346
Kaṭha Upaniṣad, 5
Kauṣītakī Upaniṣad, 5
Kena Upaniṣad, 5
Kim, Hee-Jin, 345, 346
Knower, 98, 100, 102, 104, 112
Knowledge, 40, 41, 45, 52, 57, 61, 67, 89, 95, 98, 99, 102, 105, 114, 115, 127, 165, 171, 267, 306, 318, 544, 552, 556; of reality, 308-322; of *Brahman/Ātman*, 94, 97, 102, 117, 118, 119, 120, 121, 128; path of, 33, 37-43
Kōan, 346, 361-371, 502
Koller, John M., 2, 190, 405
Krishna, 33-49

Kung-tu Tzu, 479-481
Kuppuswami Sastri, 69

LaFleur, William R., 190
Lancaster, Lewis, 307
Lao-tzu, the, 444, 445-450, 492, 564
Larson, Gerald, 51, 52
Lau, D.C., 408, 444, 445, 476
Learning of mind-and-heart, 437
Legalism, 403, 444, 461, 462, 477
Li, (*see also* Rites) 407, 477
Li Ao, 404, 521
Liberation (*mokṣa*), 33, 117, 129, 281, 285, 293, 315, 385
Life-breath (*prāṇa*), 20
Lin-chi (Rinzai), 502
Lipner, Julius, 93
Logic, 69-80, 556
Lopez, Donald S., 190, 247
Lotus Sūtra, 404
Love, 156, 157, 158, 159, 198, 313, 525, 539, 540

Mādhayamaka (see also Middle way philosophy), 2, 190, 262, 263, 285, 345, 380, 381
Madhva, 92
Mādhyamakāvatara, 262, 272-297, 386
Mahat, 55
Mahāvīra, 129, 130, 133, 134, 164
Māhāyana, 189, 194, 248, 315, 345, 380, 381, 404, 501, 515
Mahīśāsaka, 307
Maitreyanatha, 306
Maitreyī, 23-24
Malik, Hafeez, 143
Māluṅkyāputta, 222, 242-246
Man (*puruṣa*), hymn of, 7, 8
Mandate of Heaven, 436, 527, 540-541
Māṇḍukya Upaniṣad, 5
Manifest, the (*vyakta*), 52, 53, 54
Mao Tse-tung, 405, 555, 556-562
Maoist-Marxist thought, 405, 556-562
Marx, Karl, 556
Marxism, 555
Marxist-Leninist thought, 405, 555, 556-562
Material force (*ch'i*), 523, 527, 534, 540, 541, 547, 548, 562, 563
Materialism, 556, 566-568
Materialities (*rūpa*), 323, 329
Matilal, Bimal, 70, 130
Matter, 166, 167
Māyā, 125
Mayeda, Sengaku, 93
McDermott, Robert, 144, 145
Mean, the (*chung*), 523, 531, 532, 542
Measuring square, 429
Meditation, 116, 185, 189, 194, 247, 253, 324, 511-513
Meditational insight, 306, 307
Memory, 66
Mencius, 407, 423, 476, 476-487, 493, 529, 532, 536, 553, 566
Mencius, the, 405, 424, 477-487
Mental modifications, 60-69
Mental objects, 208-212
Mental states, 212
Middle Way, 193, 195, 220, 221, 233, 248, 310, 387
Middle way philosophy, (*see also Mādhyamaka*), 404, 501
Milinda, 221, 222-225
Miller, Barbara Stoler, 33, 34
Mīmāṁsā, 1, 5, 51, 81-91
Mīmāṁsā Sūtra, 81-91
Mind, 55-57, 60, 61, 64, 65, 72, 98, 166, 170, 208, 212, 257, 277-283, 282, 288, 325, 326, 328, 330, 380, 389, 403, 405, 518, 522, 525, 532, 535, 539, 542, 543, 547, 551, 552, 553
Mind-and-heart (*hsin*), 476
Mind-only (*see also Chittamātra*), 282
Mindfulness, 194, 205-212, 312, 326, 359
Minor, Robert, 33, 144
Mo-tzu, 407, 462-468, 476, 492
Mo-tzu, the, 462-468
Modes of *Brahman*, 118, 122, 123, 124, 125, 126
Modes of substance, 135-141
Mohism, 403, 444, 461
Mokṣa, (liberation), 271
Mondo, 363, 365, 366
Moore, Charles A., 129, 135
Moral character, 527, 542
Moral knowledge, 537
Moral principles, 523, 531, 545
Moral qualities, 538-548
Morality, 189
Motivating dispositions (*saṁskāras*), 307, 324-327
Mu (*kōan*), 346, 361-371
Muhammad, 150
Mukhopadhyaya, Pradyot Kumar, 70
Mūlamādhyamakakārikā, 262, 263, 264-271, 385
Mumōn, Master, 346, 361-371
Mumōnkan, 346, 361-371
Munro, Donald, 476, 537
Music, 414, 422, 441, 485
Mysticism, 145

Nāgārjuna, 262, 263, 264-271, 272, 273, 281, 285, 297, 298, 385, 388-389, 391
Nagasena, 221, 222-225, 228-231, 306
Name and form, 225, 228, 230, 233, 234, 235, 236, 237, 238
Named, the, 445
Nameless, the, 445
Nansen, Master, 362-363
Napper, Elizabeth, 263
Nature, 169, 170, 171, 174, 403, 522, 535
Nature of things, 351-354

Negation, 136-140; of ultimate status, 297-305, 384, 387; of intrinsic identifiability, 297-305
Nietzsche, 147, 149, 153
Neo-Confucianism, 403-405, 521-554, 555
Neo-Taoism, 404, 501
Nescience (*avidyā*), 95, 100, 105, 106, 115, 117, 118, 119, 120, 121, 127, 166
New *Nyāya* (*Nava Nyāya*), 69
New wisdom, 247
Nihilism, 306, 372, 381
Nikāyas, 193
Nirmāṅakāya, 513-515
Nirvāṇa (P. *Nibbana*), 189, 194, 195, 199, 212, 215, 220, 222, 240, 245, 247, 248, 252, 254, 256, 257, 259, 262, 268, 270-271, 285, 313, 314, 316, 325, 356, 360, 361, 375, 377, 378, 380
Nishitani, Keiji, 372, 393-402
No-self, 201, 222, 309
No-thought, 512, 516
Non-abiding, 512
Non-attachment, 33, 37, 57, 134, 221
Non-being, 36, 233, 262, 271, 310
Non-dual, 99, 100, 102, 104, 115, 255
Non-duality, 101, 365
Non-existence, 138-140, 225-226, 270, 271, 306, 384
Non-existent, the, 25, 31
Non-form, 512
Non-ultimate, 563-564, 565
Non-violence (*see also ahiṁsā*), 159, 160-164
Nothingness (*śūnyatā*), 369, 400
Nyāya, 1, 51, 69-80

O'Flaherty, Wendy Doniger, 6
Obscurations of defilement, 308
Obscurations to the knowable, 308, 309
One-pointedness, 324
Original mind, 528
Original nature, 510, 512, 513, 515, 516, 531
Own-being, 331, 343

Palihawadana, Mahinda, 194
Parinirvāṇa, 311, 313, 321
Particularity, 318-321, 501, 503-507
Passive resistance, 161
Patañjali, 51-59
Perception, 52, 61, 73-74, 82, 83, 109, 110, 114, 119, 122, 279, 280, 309, 330, 338, 339, 342
Perception (as *skandha*), 223-224, 231-232, 240, 242, 323
Perception-only, 330
Perfect nature, 306
Perfection of concentration, 251-253, 295
Perfection of giving, 251-253, 258, 295
Perfection of morality, 251-253, 295
Perfection of patience, 251-253, 258, 295
Perfection of vigour, 251-253, 295
Perfection of wisdom, 251-255, 262, 295
Perfections (*pāramitās*), 247, 248-253, 295
Platform Sūtra, 502, 508-516
Potter, Karl, 2, 70
Prajāpati, 9, 18, 19
Prajñā, 509, 511, 515, 516
Prajñāpāramitā, 515
Prakṛti, 1, 51-59, 124, 126
Pramāṇas, 74-80, 107
Prāpti, 326
Prāsaṅgika, 381, 383
Praśastapāda, 69
Praśāstrasena, 248, 255-257
Praśna Upaniṣad, 5
Prebisch, Charles, 190
Predispositions (*saṁskāra skandha*), 223-224, 232-232, 240, 242
Principle (*li*), 405, 522, 525, 527-535, 536, 537, 546-548, 550, 551, 562, 563, 565
Principle of Heaven, 527
Principle of Nature, 530, 538, 540, 543, 544, 550
Propriety, 527, 531, 534, 538-541
Pure consciousness, 93, 102
Pure Land, 501
Puruṣa, 1, 51-59, 60, 125, 126

Qualified nondualism, 92
Qualities, 70-73, 390

Rabten, Geshe, 262, 263, 272
Radhakrishnan, Sarvapalli, 3, 7, 144, 177-187, 129, 135
Raghavachar, S. S., 93, 115
Rahula, Walpola, 193, 220
Rajas, 54, 58, 60
Rāmānuja, 92
Rational knowledge, 306
Reality, 118, 166, 173, 253, 282, 315; true reality 512, 515-516
Reason, 309
Rebirth, 196, 220, 222, 228-230
Rectification of mind, 532
Rectification of names, 417
Relative nature, 306
Relativity, 298, 299, 397
Release, 103, 104
Religion, 145, 149, 150, 153, 177-187, 245
Religious experience, 146, 147, 150, 153
Religious life, 151, 184
Renunciation, 38, 41, 62, 95
Respect, 480-481
Revelation (*śruti*), 94, 95, 96, 98, 117, 120, 122
Rig Veda, 5, 6, 24, 27, 165, 166
Righteousness (*i*), 437, 477-481, 486, 497, 527, 531, 538-541, 543
Rinzai (Zen), 345, 357, 369
Rites (*li*), 410, 411, 414, 415, 422, 436, 441, 480, 485, 493-497
Robinson, Richard S., 263

Rumi, 148
Russell, Bertrand, 405

Śabara, 81, 82
Sacrifice, 86, 87, 88, 91
Sacrifice, creation of, 8, 9
Sage, 404, 442, 446, 457, 472, 482, 483, 488, 493, 496, 498, 499, 523, 529, 530, 532, 541, 565, 566
Sāma Veda, 5, 24, 27
Samādhi, 50, 59-67, 254, 400, 401, 516
Sambhogakāya, 513-515
Sāṁkhya, 1, 55-59, 273, 286
Sāṁkhya Kārikā, 51-59
Sammitīya school, 287, 289
Saṁsāra, 250, 256, 257, 271, 277, 284, 291, 297, 310, 311, 312, 319, 321, 322, 328
Saṁskāras (dispositions), 59
Sangha, 218, 267, 269
Śaṅkara, 2, 92, 93
Śantideva, 383
Sargeant, Winthrop, 33
Sastri, Kuppuswami, 69, 70
Satōri, 367, 368, 369
Sattva, 54, 55, 58, 60
Satyagraha, 161
Sautrāntika, 2, 306, 380, 381
Schilip, Paul, 145
Schwartz, Benjamin, 408, 462
Science, 147, 154
Seer (of *Brahman*), 98, 102, 103
Sekito, Master, 356, 357
Self (*Ātman*), 12-24, 40, 46, 47, 64, 71, 92-115, 116, 117, 124, 125, 126, 170, 173, 203, 222-227, 232, 240, 259, 261, 287-289, 334
Self, embodied, 36, 41, 115, 175, 393
Self, ineffable, 341, 373
Self-cultivation, 404, 543
Self-examination, 486, 534, 542
Self-interest, 461, 476
Self-knowledge, 41
Self-nature (*svabhāva*), 265, 268, 269, 509
Self-realization, 92, 372, 409
Self-surrender, 128
Selfishness, 529, 530
Selflessness, 293, 298-305, 328, 334, 380
Sensation, 233, 234, 235, 236, 237, 238; as *skandha*, 223-224, 226-227, 231-232, 240, 242
Sense fields, 328, 334, 335
Sense organs, 55, 233, 253, 278, 280
Senses, 56, 57, 100, 104, 114, 275
Seriousness (*ching*), 527, 542-543
Shakyamuni (Buddha), 352, 353, 359
Shame, 480-481, 539, 544
Shao Yung, 521, 524-525, 565
Sharma, Arvind, 34
Sharpe, Eric, 34
Sheikh Ahmad, 152
Shen-hsui, 509-510
Shen-hui, 502
Shibayama, Zenkei, 346, 361-371
Shōbōgenzō, 345, 346-361
Simultaneity, 83, 84, 274
Sincerity (*ch'eng*), 409, 439, 440, 525
Six characteristics (of *dharmas*), 501, 503-507
Sixth Patriarch (Hui-neng), 508-516
Skandhas (*see also* Five aggregates), 265, 271
Smart, Ninian, 372
Snellgrove, David, 263
Son of Heaven, 422, 425, 435, 436, 441, 466
Soo, Francis Y. K., 556
Sōtō (Zen), 345
Soul, 126, 136, 243, 259, 261
Speech, 81
Spirit, 168, 169, 170, 173, 174, 180, 185
Spiritual evolution, 168
Spiritual experience, 179, 180
Store consciousness, 307, 327, 328, 342
Substance, 70-71, 123, 124, 135, 136, 138, 287, 538
Subtle body, 56, 57
Subtle elements, 55-57, 66
Suchness, 273, 275, 282, 310, 316, 318, 328, 343, 393, 397
Sudden Doctrine, 515
Sudden enlightenment, 511
Suffering, 52, 189, 248, 250, 254, 262, 265-266, 269, 270, 312, 379
Sufism, 153, 155
Śūnyatā, (*see also* Emptiness), 262-271, 393-402, 501; field of 393, 399, 400
Superimposition, 96, 97, 105, 106, 107, 114, 120
Supermind, 167, 168
Supreme Reality, 116, 126, 128, 177, 178, 179, 180, 181, 186, 313
Sūtrakṛtāṅga, 130, 131, 133
Suzuki, D. T., 241, 308
Svātantrika, 381
Śvetaketu, 25-30
Śvetāśvatara Upaniṣad, 5
Syādavāda, 135-142
Syllogism, 75-76

T'ien Tai, 501
Taittirīya Upaniṣad, 5, 6
Tamas, 54, 55, 58, 60
Tantra, 247
Tao, *the*, 444, 445-450, 513, 564
Taoism, 403-405, 461, 501, 521, 550
Tarkasaṁgraha, 69-80
Tathāgata, 195, 219, 240, 243, 248, 254, 256, 257, 258, 259, 287, 311, 318, 322, 398, 514
Ten thousand things, 486, 492
Tendai, 345
Testimony, 61, 67, 73, 78-80, 309

Theravāda, 189, 190, 193, 194, 372
Thirst, 195
Thousand Teachings, A, 93-115
Three natures, 306
Three vehicles, 312
Thurman, Robert A. F., 263
Time, 262, 266, 395, 396
Tīrthaṅkaras, 129, 133
Tradition (smṛti), 89, 90, 94, 125
Tranquillity, 522, 523, 528, 546-547, 563
Transcendent wisdom, 346, 347-351
Transcendentally changeless, 102, 109, 110, 111, 113, 114, 115
Transmigratory existence (*saṁsāra*), 93, 94, 95, 97, 104, 105, 115, 118, 127
Triṁśikā Kārikā, 307, 341-344
Truth, 117, 156, 157, 158, 159, 160, 165, 166, 178; relative (or conventional), 267, 268, 275, 281, 282, 385-386; ultimate, 267, 268, 275, 281, 282, 315, 363, 371, 385-386
Truths, two, 267, 275, 276, 282, 283, 386
Tseng-tzu, 407, 409, 412, 414, 423, 425-432, 484, 497
Tsong Khapa, 262, 263, 297-305
Tu, Wei-ming, 408, 537
Tung Chung-shu, 403, 476
Tzu-ssu, 407

Uddālaka, 12-13, 25-30
Ultimate status (of existence), 297-305
Understanding, 38, 40, 42, 45, 101, 311, 338
Unity, 539; of knowing and acting, 556
Universal love, 461, 462-468
Universality, 463-468, 501, 503-507
Unmanifest, the (*avyakta*), 52, 53, 54
Upaniṣads, 1, 3, 5, 6, 12-31, 92, 95, 115, 124, 178, 179
Usarbudh Arya, Pandit, 52
Utilitarianism, 462
Utilitarians, 461

Vacchagotta, 221, 239-246
Vahid, S. A., 143
Vaibhāṣika, 2, 336, 380, 381
Vaiśeṣika, 1, 69-80, 286
Van Buitenen, J. A. B., 6, 25, 30, 92
Varadachari, K.C., 93
Varenne, Jean, 52
Vasubandhu, 306, 307, 323-344
Vedānta, 1, 5, 92-128
Vedārthasaṁgraha, 93, 115-128
Vedas, 1, 3, 5, 18, 24, 81, 85, 88, 89, 91, 92, 93, 101, 104, 115, 116, 122, 126
Vedic injunction, 85-90, 94
Verbal designation, 310, 314, 315
Vimalakīrti Sūtra, 513
Viṁśatika Kārikā, 307, 330-341
Violence, 159, 162
Virtue, 424, 425, 430, 435, 436, 441, 476, 477, 486
Voidness (*śūnyatā*), 272, 276, 277, 285, 293-297, 310, 311, 315, 316
Vyāsa, 52-59

Waking state, 99, 108, 110, 111, 114, 115
Wang Yang-ming, 537, 548-554, 568
Wangchen, Geshe Namgyal, 263
Warren, Henry Clarke, 220, 222
Watson, Burton, 462, 477, 487
Way of becoming a sage, 531
Way of Heaven, 407
Way of the ruler, 468-471
Way, the (*tao*), 403, 410, 417, 419, 424, 433-443, 445-450, 471-474, 480, 486, 487, 489, 491, 492, 493, 525, 527, 528, 530, 533, 538, 540, 541, 542, 548
Western Inscription, 521, 525-527
Wheel of truth, 194, 195
Will, 551, 552
Willis, Janice Dean, 307, 308
Wisdom, 179, 189, 221, 245, 247, 248, 249, 272, 290, 346, 359, 440, 480, 485, 511-513, 527, 531, 538-541
Witness (*sākṣin*), 98, 104
Word, 82, 83
Wu, Kuang-ming, 445

yajña, 5
Yājñavalkya, 12-24
Yajur Veda, 5, 24, 27
Yakuzan, Master, 356, 357
Yampolsky, Philip B., 502, 508
Yang, 403, 452
Yang Chu, 444
Yen Tzu, 531-533, 535
Yin, 403, 546
Yin and *Yang*, 488-490, 521, 522-525, 541, 546, 457
Yin-Yang school, 403, 404
Yoga, 1, 51-52, 59-67, 186, 306
Yoga Sūtra, 51, 59-67
Yogācāra, 190, 306-344, 345
Yogācārabhūmi, 307, 308-322
You are that (*tat tvam asi*), 28-30, 117, 123

Zazen, 368
Zen, 247, 345-371, 372